Contemporary Urbanisation in India

About the Editor

Dr. Anuradha Banerjee is an Associate Professor in The Centre for the Study of Regional Development, School of Social Sciences, Jawaharlal Nehru University, New Delhi, India. She offers courses in Geography and Population Studies at MA and M.Phil. Levels. 29 M.Phil. and 7 Ph.D. students have been awarded degrees under her supervision. Her research areas include Urbanisation and Migration, Population and Environment; Maternal and Child Health; Reproductive Health; Sexual Health; HIV/AIDS; Human Ecology; Integrated Coast Zone, Management; Development Studies; Human Settlements and Application of Remote Sensing and GIS in Geographical Analysis. She has authored several articles in journals and chapters in different edited books and has published a book on Environment, Population and Settlements in Sundarban Delta.

She has been associated with various projects sponsored by the Department of Women and Child Development, HRD, GOI; UGC-UNFPA; EU; UNIFEM; IIDS and ICSSR.

She has been an Executive Council Member of NAGI (The National Association of Geographers India); EC Member of INCA (Indian National Cartographic Association) and a member of UGC nominated Planning and Monitoring Board of Chettinad University, Tamil Nadu. Presently, she is Vice President of INCA and the Joint Editor of the Annals of the Association of Indian Geographers.

CONTEMPORARY URBANISATION IN INDIA

ISSUES AND CHALLENGES

Edited by
Anuradha Banerjee

CONCEPT PUBLISHING COMPANY PVT. LTD.,
NEW DELHI-110059

ISBN-13: 978-81-8069-954-2

First Published 2013

Published and Printed by

Concept Since 1974

Concept Publishing Company Pvt. Ltd.
A/15-16, Commercial Block, Mohan Garden
New Delhi-110059 (India)
T: 25351460, 25351794, *F*: 091-11-25357109
E: publishing@conceptpub.com, W: www.conceptpub.com
Editorial Office: H-13, Bali Nagar, New Delhi-110 015, India.

Cataloging in Publication Data--Courtesy: D.K. Agencies (P) Ltd. <docinfo@dkagencies.com>

Contemporary urbanisation in India : issues and challenges in the 21st century / edited by Anuradha Banerjee.

p. cm.
Contributed articles.
Includes bibliographical references and index.
ISBN 9788180699542

1. Urbanization—India. 2. Urbanization—Economic aspects—India. 3. Cities and towns—India—Growth. 4. City planning—Health aspects—India. I. Banerjee, Anuradha, 1961-

DDC 307.760954 23

Foreword

The study of urbanisation, urbanism and urban planning was once a favourite topic for investigation among the geographers. However, such issues got lesser priority in the wake of challenges within the subject and developments happening outside the realm of this discipline. Over and above, the technology induced studies, particularly associated with geographical information system and remote sensing temporarily shifted our goal posts. The human components in geographical researches got a setback. Human expression over the geographic space was reduced to grey level of a pixel or their combination. In such a situation, this book on contemporary urbanisation is a welcome change. It reminds us about the doctrine of our subject, i.e. the study of man and environment. Dr. Anuradha Banerjee and her team of authors must be congratulated for such an initiative.

The study of urbanisation has become extremely important because as per the last census (2011), some of the states are having very close to fifty per cent population residing in urban areas. The statutory towns have increased from 3,799 to 4,041 in the last decade. During the same period, the census towns have multiplied from 1,362 to 3,892 indicating urban growth around the main city or large urban centres. On the other hand, the number of villages has reduced in the states like Punjab, Uttarakhand, Haryana, Uttar Pradesh, Bihar, West Bengal, Jharkhand and the like. Such a trend has also been found in almost all the Union territories. Further, in the rural areas, the population is largely accepting urban way of life. Hence, urbanism is making ripples all over the country. Dr. Abdul Kalam, former President of India, has rightly mooted the idea of PURA, i.e. providing urban amenities in rural areas. This concept is finding wider acceptability now-a-days.

Since there is concentration of population in urban centres, in a democratic setup such areas can no longer be ignored. They have become centres of political power, agents of change and hubs of ideological motivations. These centres can make or break the governments at local, state and even at the centre. They have largest share in GDP. Hence, infrastructure, quality of life, urban transportation, environment, household amenities and services have become important issues and challenges in the urban areas for governments. Several projects under urban renewal mission have been undertaken in most of the urban centres.

I am delighted to note that the above issues have been dealt in this book with greater importance. The issues related to migration, composition of urban population, spatial pattern of urban growth, slums, urban environment and health, lifestyle problems and urban policies have been dealt here. They throw light on the trends and patterns which have been narrated lucidly. The national, state and local level studies do come out with the important issues which have to be viewed in an integrated way. The geographers have an important task in such integration, spatially and conceptually. This volume has met this objective. I am sure it will help in working out policies and strategies for a desirable pattern of urbanisation in India in the twenty first century.

1st August, 2012

Dr. Prithvish Nag
Vice-Chancellor
Mahatma Gandhi Kashi Vidyapeeth

Acknowledgements

Rapid urbanisation in contemporary India has thrown up several challenges that require in-depth investigation. Increasing concentration of population in the leading cities and metropolises in India has brought about complexities in socio-economic formations, service delivery and in several aspects of city management. This book is an effort to highlight some of the problems of urban India that need the attention of social scientists, city planners and research scholars. The aim has been to begin with a macro-perspective framework and gradually focus on the problems with a micro-perspective approach. Based on varied sources of secondary and field generated data, the book presents some of the contemporary realities of Urban India.

At the onset, I would like to place on record my heartfelt thanks and regards to Dr. Prithvish Nag, Vice Chancellor, Kashi Vidyapeeth University, Benaras, ex-director National Atlas and Thematic Mapping Organisation, Department of Science and Technology, Government of India, and ex-Surveyor General, Survey of India for introducing this volume. Besides, I am immensely indebted to his valuable suggestions and help at various stages of this work.

My profession as a teacher and a research supervisor in Geography and Population Studies in the Centre for the Study of Regional Development, School of Social Sciences, Jawaharlal Nehru University, New Delhi, India has benefitted me immensely in nurturing with contemporary aspects of urbanisation in India. I owe my allegiance to my Centre, School and University for being able to complete this task of compiling, writing and editing of this volume.

My appreciation goes to the scholars who had worked under my supervision for their M.Phil and Ph.D. degrees and have contributed the articles from their unpublished research works. Many of them are well placed as faculties and research fellows in reputed institutions in India. This book therefore is an attempt to acknowledge their arduous attempt not only to understand the problems of urban India, but to work on them relentlessly and decipher meaningful results.

The responsibility of editing this volume has been shouldered by Ms. Chandrani Dutta, senior Ph.D. research scholar, CSRD, SSS, JNU, who has also contributed articles for this volume.

Besides, I acknowledge the contribution by Dr. Debjani Roy, Reader in Department of Geography, Nirmala College, Ranchi, Jharkahand; Dr. Amit Kumar Singh, Research Officer at the Indian Institute of Public Administration, I.P. Estate, Ring Road, New Delhi-110002; Dr. Sharmistha Das Research Learning and Impact Officer at the Save the Children, Kolkata; Dr. Naresh Kumar, Assistant Professor at the Central University of Gujarat, Gandhinagar; Dr. Vinod Kumar Mishra and Dr. Chandramallika Biswas, Research Fellows at the Indian Institute of Dalit Studies, New Delhi.

I also acknowledge the contributions made by Ms. Mala Mukherjee, Mr. Mashkoor Ahmad and Mr. Vidyasagar Trigun, senior doctoral research fellows; Ms. Chandreyee Banerjee, Lecturer in Geography in Government College at Alwar, Rajasthan, and direct Ph.D Research Scholar; Mr. Praveen Shukla, Mr. Motilal Sulia, Ms. Sunita Kumari, Ms. Eshita Tripathy, Mr. Gourabmaya Pradhan, Ph.D. research scholars and Ms. Chetna Naskar, M. Phil student in Geography at the Centre for the Study of Regional Development (CSRD), School of Social Sciences (SSS), Jawaharlal Nehru University (JNU), New Delhi.

My effort would not have succeeded without the support of my family members, my husband Mr. Jay Prakash Singh and my daughter Ms. Twisha Singh who had borne my engrossment with this volume often overlooking my day-to-day family chores.

Last but not the least, my sincere thanks to Mr. Ashok Mittal, Director, Concept Publishing Company Pvt. Ltd., New Delhi for readily agreeing to the proposal of publishing this volume and helping me with logistics and support needed for the same.

Content

SECTION I

Contemporary Urbanisation in India: Urban Growth and Characteristics

SECTION V
Urban Policies in India

List of Contributors

Amit Kumar Singh is a Research Officer at the Indian Institute of Public Administration, I.P. Estate, Ring Road, New Delhi-110002. He holds a Ph.D. from the Centre for the Study of Regional Development, School of Social Sciences, Jawaharlal Nehru University, New Delhi.

Chandramallika Biswas is a Research Fellow (January 2012- present) at the Indian Institute of Dalit Studies, New Delhi. She has a Ph.D. from the Centre for the Study of Regional Development, School of Social Sciences, Jawaharlal Nehru University, New Delhi.

Chandrani Dutta is at present a Doctoral Research Fellow at the Centre for the Study of Regional Development (CSRD) in School of Social Sciences (SSS) of Jawaharlal Nehru University (JNU), New Delhi.

Chandreyi Banerjee is a Lecturer in Geography in Government College at Alwar, Rajasthan, and is also a Senior Ph.D. Research Scholar at the Centre for the Study of Regional Development (CSRD) in School of Social Sciences (SSS) of Jawaharlal Nehru University (JNU), New Delhi.

Chetana Naskar is a M.Phil. research student in Geography at the Centre for the Study of Regional Development (CSRD) in School of Social Sciences (SSS) of Jawaharlal Nehru University (JNU), New Delhi.

Debjani Roy is a Reader and Head of Department of Geography, Nirmala College, Ranchi, Jharkhand.

Eshita Tripathy a Doctoral Research scholar at the Centre for the Study of Regional Development (CSRD) in School of Social Sciences (SSS) of Jawaharlal Nehru University (JNU), New Delhi.

Gourabamaya Pradhan is a Doctoral Research Scholar at the Centre for the Study of Regional Development (CSRD) in School of Social Sciences (SSS) of Jawaharlal Nehru University (JNU), New Delhi.

Mala Mukherjee is at present a Doctoral Research Scholar at the Centre for the

Study of Regional Development (CSRD) in School of Social Sciences (SSS) of Jawaharlal Nehru University (JNU), New Delhi.

Mashkoor Ahmad is a Doctoral Research Scholar at the Centre for the Study of Regional Development, School of Social Sciences, Jawaharlal Nehru University (JNU), New Delhi.

Motilal Sulia is a Doctoral Research Scholar at the Centre for the Study of Regional Development (CSRD) in School of Social Sciences (SSS) of Jawaharlal Nehru University (JNU), New Delhi.

Naresh Kumar is an Assistant Professor at the Central University of Gujarat. Gandhinagar. He has a Ph.D. from the Centre for the Study of Regional Development, School of Social Sciences, Jawaharlal Nehru University (JNU), New Delhi.

Pravin Kumar Shukla is a Doctoral Research Scholar at the Centre for the Study of Regional Development (CSRD) in School of Social Sciences (SSS) of Jawaharlal Nehru University (JNU), New Delhi.

Sharmistha Das is currently working as Research Learning and Impact Officer at the Save the Children, Kolkata. She holds a Ph.D. from the Centre for the Study of Regional Development, School of Social Sciences. Jawaharlal Nehru University (JNU), New Delhi.

Sunita Kumari is a Doctoral Research Scholar at the Centre for the Study of Regional Development, School of Social Sciences, Jawaharlal Nehru University, New Delhi.

Vidyasagar Trigun is a Doctoral Research Scholar in the Centre for the Study of Regional Development, Jawaharlal Nehru University (JNU). New Delhi.

Vinod Kumar Mishra is an Associate Fellow at the Indian Institute of Dalit Studies, New Delhi. He has a Ph.D. from the Centre for the Study of Regional Development, School of Social Sciences, Jawaharlal Nehru University. New Delhi.

Introduction

Contemporary urbanisation in India is taking place at an accelerated pace and urban growth has become a marked feature of large cities and metropolises. Such urbanisation has thrown up several issues and challenges like imbalances/unequal distribution of urban population concentration and its variable characteristics, employment, infrastructure, housing and basic amenities, slums, urban environment and health. The nature of problems associated with India's urbanisation varies across regions. For instance, very low level of urbanisation, infrastructure, amenities and facilities may dominate backward regions and states; whereas urbanisation in the developed states are also facing several bottlenecks primarily that of incorporating huge population concentrations in the urban areas, thereby placing considerable challenges for efficient management of urban areas. Though several policies have been put into practice targeting various categories of urban settlements, the city management has to face further complications with the passage of time particularly due to unabated population increase.

This book is an anthology of nineteen articles, primarily being a collaborative effort of M.Phil. and Ph.D. research scholars who have been supervised by me and have been awarded degrees in the broad area of India's urbanisation in the Centre for the Study of Regional Development, School of Social Sciences, Jawaharlal Nehru University, New Delhi. Most of them today are well placed in terms of their career development. Their tireless and relentless efforts in investigating the issues and challenges related to urbanisation processes in India, makes me produce this compilation of their research efforts through this book. Besides, these scholarly articles, the first, eleventh and fourteenth article has been also authored by me. The second article has been prepared by Dr. Debjani Roy,

Reader and Head of Department of Geography in Nirmala College, Ranchi on urbanisation processes in Jharkhand. The book begins with a macro perspective on urbanisation and gradually moves on to focus several specific issues pertaining to urban areas of different regions of India. The articles not only focus the developed states of India, but also portray the problems related to urbanisation in the backward regions. Finally, the concluding article provides an overview of several policies targeting urban areas across the nation.

The articles produced in this book have been carved out from the unpublished Ph.D. theses and papers presented in seminars and conferences by researchers. The methodologies incorporated include both quantitative and qualitative analyses. The articles, apart from the main text also include tabular representations of analysed data as well as visual representation/illustration in the form of graphs and maps. Interesting case studies based on primary field research experiences have strengthened the secondary data sources like the Census of India, Sample Registration System, National Sample Survey and National Family Health Survey. Some of the articles are entirely based on in-depth analysis of field based research work done by scholars that has also acted as a motivation for preparing this volume. This book would, therefore, not only bring to the fore the contemporary issues in urbanisation both at the macro and micro levels having considerable relevance to processes of urbanisation in India, but would also act as a motivation for these budding social scientists through the final output in the form of a published book, that would further enhance their career development. The book has been prepared keeping in mind the interdisciplinary nature of various sister disciplines of social sciences like geography, history, population studies, sociology, urban studies among others.

The book has been designed in five sections, viz.

SECTION-I : Contemporary Urbanisation in India: Urban Growth and Characteristics
SECTION-II : Urban Employment and Infrastructure
SECTION-III : Urban Housing, Slums and Basic Amenities
SECTION-IV : Urban Environment and Health
SECTION-V : Urban Policies in India

The First Section of the book on Contemporary Urbanisation in India: Urban Growth and Characteristics consists of seven articles.

The first article has been contributed by Chetna Naskar, Pravin Kumar

Shukla and myself and is entitled as "Contemporary Urbanisation in India: Characteristics, Trends and Patterns". The article provides an overview of urbanisation in India since historical times to the present Census (2011). Though the history of urbanisation can be traced back to the advent of early civilisation in India, rapid urbanisation is a feature of recent decades only. India is at a transitional level of urbanisation with large scale variations in the trend and pattern of urbanisation over the decades and also across the states. There is an increase in number of towns and cities over the decades though the level of urbanisation is still low compared to the Western standards and even among certain Asian countries. Maximum concentration of urban population is limited to the class I cities, metropolises and mega cities. Thus, India's urbanisation follows top-heavy pattern, or can be said to be lopsided when compared across the various size classes of urban centres.

Urbanisation in India is mainly a product of demographic explosion and poverty driven rural to urban migration dominated by distress. The rural to urban migration is predominantly a result of rural push rather than urban pull; where the rural areas due to their stagnation and in the absence of non-farm employment opportunities result in higher incidence of poverty, compelling population to move towards urban areas and large cities in particular. This leads to higher concentration of population in a few cities and command of a large proportion of population over limited resources thus resulting in a decline in the standards of city life and giving rise to urban poverty, deprivation, unemployment and the multiplication of slum and squatter settlements within the cities.

Many cities experiencing over-urbanisation have reached a saturation level where further influx of population is detrimental. The spilling over of population in large cities has led to urban sprawl, beyond the municipal limits of the city and has fostered sub-urbanisation. Metropolises of Kolkata and Mumbai have already reached their level of saturation and this has resulted in insurmountable problems for the city dwellers. This uneven growth of urban population is mainly due to concentration of economic activities only in a few urban centres. The policy implications of such processes urgently calls for upgrading the overall developmental process in the backward regions and thereby reducing existing regional disparities so as to induce dispersed urban growth and level of urbanisation in the country.

Debjani Roy has contributed the second article on "Spatio-Temporal Characteristics of Urbanisation in Jharkhand", where the author with her long standing research experience in the field of urbanisation and population geography, brings out the processes, patterns and trends of urbanisation in the recently formed State of Jharkhand lying in the mineral rich belt of India and forming part of the erstwhile state of Bihar. The article focuses primarily on urban growth to be an important indicator of development of a region. This phenomenon is more pronounced in Developing World where the growth is three times that of the Developed World often accompanied by high population growth rates and growing in-migration. The trend and pattern of urbanisation in Jharkhand are very different from the model of urban development backed by indigenous industrialisation and modernisation as propagated by neo-classical economists. It began with the setting up of urban centres way back in the nineteenth century to support British administration and trade. The State still has very low level of urbanisation but the trend has been rapid in the last two decades. Urbanisation is top heavy in Jharkhand like in India, with 65 per cent of the population being concentrated in three major towns. Industrialisation, which initiated urban growth in the last century, has now taken a back seat with tertiary activities overshadowing all other activities. Urban growth of Jharkhand has been due to the "push factor" sending poor rural masses into urban centres thereby exposing the state's failure to ensure adequate growth of the rural economy. The entire State of Jharkhand is aflame with vertical construction to house its logarithmic increase in population and plagued by problems like poor infrastructure, poor sanitation and sewerage conditions, insufficient transport and communication facilities, uncontrolled law and order and a high number of urban and white collar crimes. The State now needs to sit up and take notice of the rapidly crumbling infrastructure and implement the schemes offered for urban renewal and development.

"Urbanisation, Urban Growth and Urban Development in Bihar" is the third article in the book authored by Amit Kumar Singh. Studies of urbanisation often focus on developed states and leading cities of India. However, urbanisation in a State like Bihar that portrays low levels of development conveys a completely different picture. Bihar is a state where agricultural and allied activities predominate the overall economy. The state economy is not well-diversified, leaving little opportunities for gainful employment, thereby making it impossible for the state to create additional employment opportunities for the surplus labour in rural areas. It is a state which has been continuously experiencing out-migration of people to other states in the country. On the other hand, there has been a major deficiency in the provision of urban infrastructure and services in the State. The spatial analysis of urban infrastructure and basic amenities based on Census of India, reveals considerable inequality among the different districts of Bihar. Nature of development in Bihar has been skewed in nature, being concentrated mostly in the biggest of the urban centres.

The fourth article in the book has been prepared by Chandreyi Banerjee on "Urbanisation and Characteristics of Urban Settlements in Rajasthan: A Comparative Study of Western and Eastern Plains". The study brings out the nature and characteristics of urban settlements in the ecologically diversified state of Rajasthan in north-western India. Rajasthan is a land of both the Aravallis and the shifting sand dunes of the Great Thar Desert of scorching heat and freezing cold, presenting a great variation in the distribution of its population. The same is true in its urban settlements. Temporally, urbanisation was practically negligible in the erstwhile Rajputana, in the decades of feudal rule due to scarcity of water, uncertainty of rainfall, frequent droughts etc., with their consequent adverse effects on the economy. Urban settlements were largely confined to favourable pockets like along major rivers and their tributaries, around fresh water and salt lakes, caravan route crossings, rocky tops and higher slopes. Fortified urban settlements arose due to security purposes arising out of frequent clashes between different ethnic descendants like Rajputs, Jats, Gujjars, etc. Over the years, urban population in Rajasthan has registered growth with potentialities of mineral occurrence, availability of power resources, irrigation development and development of transport and communication.

Rajasthan is one of the largest States of India covering an area of 3.42 lakh sq. km; but in terms of its percentage share to the total urban population of the country, Rajasthan occupied a bottom rank of 16, according to 2001 Census with only 222 urban centres. Based on similarities in physical landscape, economic parameters and cultural elements, the State may be divided into four geographical regions, namely the Western Sandy Plains, the Eastern Plains, the Aravalli Hill Region and the Hadauti Plateau Region. Of these, both the Western Sandy Plains and the Eastern Plains are plain lands lying on either side of the Aravallis and form distinct geographical regions. The author has tried to unravel whether such distinctness also exists in the urban settlements of these two regions in terms of pattern, growth, size classes of urban settlements, functional specialisation and rank size rule of settlement ordering.

The fifth article on "Declining Urban Child Sex Ratio in India: A Case Study of Selected States" has been contributed by Naresh Kumar. The article brings to the fore that the socio-cultural and religious strands of India are predominantly patriarchal and patrilineal contributing extensively to the subordinate status of women. Infanticide, in addition to foeticide, under-enumeration at birth and a general negligent and irresponsible behaviour of our society towards the girl child have led to the decline in the child sex ratio which further gets reflected largely in the decline in India's general sex ratio. Data has revealed that there has been a downward trend from 1991 to the recent 2011 Census with respect to the child sex ratio (from 945 females per 1000 males in 1991 to 914 in 2011). Child sex ratio paints a bleak picture in the northern and the north-western states of India, exhibiting very low ratios compared to the rest of the country. Moreover, in case of the urban areas, the rate of decline is even more marked, which forms the basis of the present article. States like Haryana, Punjab, Gujarat and Himachal Pradesh have witnessed significant decline while the southern states like Karnataka, Tamil Nadu have the least decline in child sex ratio. Based on the 1991, 2001 and 2011 Census data, the paper has been devised such as to trace the various reasons contributing to this dismal state of male-female balance of the population particularly in the urban areas.

Mashkoor Ahmed has contributed the sixth article entitled "A Geographical Study of Urbanisation and In-Migration in Ghaziabad District, Uttar Pradesh". Urbanisation and internal migration are inter-related socio-economic phenomena affecting the organisation of human population in our country. During the last few decades, in some regions internal migration has been the chief contributor to urban population growth through rural-urban flow and also through population transfers from small and medium sized towns. But urban population growth especially caused by migration, results in unorganised and unplanned spatial growth of cities and towns. Therefore, the study of migration and urbanisation of a region is necessary for policy purposes. In the present article, an attempt has been made to look into the processes of urbanisation and migration in Ghaziabad district of Uttar Pradesh. The State of Uttar Pradesh, in which the district is situated, is however one of the highly out-migrating states of India. Unlike the out-migrating character of Uttar Pradesh, Ghaziabad district has emerged as one of the highly in-migrating districts of the State. The article deals with the processes of urbanisation and migration and has been divided into three sections. The first section incorporates an outline of the process of urbanisation especially the level and rate of growth of urban population in the district during the present century. High inflow of population from different parts of the country has kept the rate of urbanisation very high. The second section focuses on patterns of migration in the district from various parts of the country. Finally, in the third section, an attempt has been made to analyse the characteristics of migrants themselves.

The seventh article has been prepared by Mala Mukherjee on "Urban Growth and Spatial Transformation: A Comparison between Kolkata Urban Agglomeration and Kolkata Municipal Corporation". Kolkata metropolis depicts the typical characteristics of the legacy of a colonial port city with unplanned urban growth, mixed land use pattern along with development of slums almost everywhere within the city. The specific objective of the article is to study not only variations in urban growth across two spatial units; i.e. KMC and KUA, but also to analyse the varying pattern of growth within each of these units. The methodologies followed are—extraction of data on urban growth, density, areal changes from the Census 2001 and 1991; joining operations of spatial and Census data; Query Building ($x > n\%$, where x = indicator/attribute) to find out the localities with haphazard urban growth and high slum population; and finally, thematic mapping using ARC-GIS. The main findings indicate that in case of the main city, wards with high growth are concentrated in the periphery. The city is gradually growing towards the south and the east by encroachment into the surrounding rural areas. Though the growth towards the west has been restricted by the River Hooghly, but the most surprising fact is that Kolkata's growth towards the north is not impressive. In case of the urban agglomeration, linear urban growth is found along the both sides of the river Hooghly, but most of the west bank municipalities show decline in urban growth, while the east bank municipalities close to the core city show an impressive growth (e.g. the spectacular growth of Bidhannagar near Kolkata in the east and decline in urban growth in Hooghly Chinsurah in the west). GIS mapping of slums shows that certain wards have more than ninety per cent of the population living in the slums and are concentrated in the northern and eastern parts of the city. Slums are also found outside the main city and ubiquitously distributed between the west and the east bank municipalities. Though, it is an obvious fact that the Hooghly industrial belt may have slums, but here, maximum slums are found to be concentrated again in the east bank municipalities.

The **Second Section** of the book is on "Urban Employment and Infrastructure" consists of three articles.

The eighth article entitled "Status of Infrastructure Development in the cities and Towns of Odisha: Problems and Constraints" has been contributed by Gourabamaya Pradhan on the level of infrastructural facilities in the urban centres of Odisha. The steady growth of urban population has thrown immense challenge of developing adequate infrastructure in urban centres. The article attempts to examine the existing status of urban infrastructure in Odisha. Townwise analysis of various dimensions of infrastructure such as road connectivity, electricity connections, sewerage, medical and educational facilities and their temporal change during 1971-2001 revealed serious deficiencies in urban Odisha. Using the data published by Census of India, the results have been presented by simple statistical techniques such as rates and ratio. The Z-Score method has been applied to compute the Index of Infrastructure Development across towns and cities. The analysis has revealed that many towns were found to be in the category of low infrastructure facilities from 1990s onwards. Despite aggregate improvement in physical infrastructure in urban Odisha, other aspects like sewerage and medical facilities have been decreasing over the years. The perceived improvement in certain sectors seemed to be far less than desired level of infrastructure facilities.

Eshita Tripathy has contributed the ninth article on "Functional Structure, Specialisation, and Diversification of Class-I Cities of Uttar Pradesh". Presently, the cities are performing more and more services that are essential for the existence of the society. Functions are the driving force that basically influence the growth, structure and morphology of any particular city and are in turn influenced by it. The functions of cities are mostly related to non-primary or non-agricultural activities. Any town is generally not known by a single dominant function it performs, but most of these cities are diversified in nature or poly-functional. The article includes the study of Class-I cities in Uttar Pradesh and has been carried under two sub-heads: Firstly, an overall analysis of urban characteristics across 54 Class-I cities and secondly, regional analysis of urban characteristics across 54 Class-I cities. The main objectives are to examine the functional classification of urban centres on the basis of Nelson's Method and to assess the concentration or diversification in Class-I cities of Uttar Pradesh. The larger cities have been found to be more diversified and multi-functional while the smaller cities are specialised and mono-functional.

Motilal Sulia has prepared the tenth article on "Urban Infrastructure Development in Towns of Goa", a small state that has performed well in urbanisation. It is also the richest state in terms of per capita Gross Domestic Product and one of the most urbanised states of India with about half of the total population residing in urban areas. Since, the initiation of economic reforms in 1991, the State has witnessed a mushrooming of smaller towns in the periphery of the larger towns. In this context, the present article examines the process of urban infrastructure development in Goa in the post reform period particularly in the light of tourism development in the State. Taking recourse to data from Census of India, Principal Component Analysis (PCA Method) has been used to construct index of infrastructure development. Haphazard growth of towns with a heavy concentration of urban population in coastal areas marks the pattern of urbanisation in Goa. However, the overall infrastructure provision, especially medical facilities, road density and recreational infrastructure are relatively lower in the urbanised talukas of coastal areas. This indicates that provision of infrastructure has not kept pace with population concentration in urban areas of the State.

The **Third Section** of the book is on "Urban Housing, Slums and Basic Amenities" and consists of three articles.

The eleventh article entitled "Slums in India Metropolis: Challenges to Urbanisation and Urban Development in the 21st Century" has been authored by Sharmistha Das and Anuradha Banerjee. Rapid and "top heavy" urbanisation of India in the twenty first century is characterised by the mushrooming of slums and associated multiple deprivations, extreme congestion, inadequate basic services, insecurity of tenure, deplorable living environment and health. The article explores to trace the evolution, demographics, basic amenities and living environment of slum population in metropolitan India within a comparative regional framework; utilising statistical methods such as exponential growth rates and principal component analysis. A case study based on primary investigation has been attempted on housing, living environment and tenure characteristics of slum households in Kolkata (Calcutta) Metropolis, based on different slum settlements. The analysis brings to the fore the complex problems associated with metropolitan slums and indicates that the government's policies for slum upgradation have not met with success. The article calls for a necessity of multiple actors working within a holistic framework to ameliorate the problems of India's slum dwellers.

Chandrani Dutta has contributed the twelfth article on "Status of Urban Poor and Poverty Alleviation Programmes in India: A Regional Perspective". Non-availability of basic services like safe drinking water, electricity, sanitation facilities, apart from low consumption expenditure determines the incidence of poverty especially in urban areas in recent times. It is in this backdrop that this article focuses on the status of urban poor in India taking recourse to varied secondary data sources. With the help of diagrammatic representations, the conditions of urban poor in different states and major urban centres of India have been explored in detail. In India, Mumbai, Kolkata, Delhi and the other metropolitan cities having population more than 1 million are burdened with a large size of urban poor households living in slums. The study unfolds that despite various poverty alleviation measures introduced by the Government of India, there remains a strong gap between demand for and supply of basic services in all the cities resulting in proliferation of urban poor in the slum settlements.

The thirteenth article is on "Socio-Economic Characteristics, Access to Basic Amenities and Health Status of Slum Population in India" contributed by Vinod Kumar Mishra. The article points to the alarming increase of slum population in India through rural to urban migration. Rural poverty often gets spilled over to urban areas and it becomes difficult for this particular section of population to afford descent housing in urban areas. The present study portrays the socio-economic condition of the slum population based on Census of India and large scale sample surveys like the NSSO and NFHS. The major objective is to analyse the characteristics of slum population in the states reporting slums in 2001. Composite indices have been calculated to measure the social and economic conditions of the slums in states reporting slums. It has been estimated that at present about one-third of the world's urban population does not have access to adequate housing, safe drinking water and sanitation according to the United Nations in 2003. Findings from NSSO state, although the living condition in slums improved during 2008-09 in comparison to 2002, but the situation did not improve drastically in case of the non-notified slums.

The **Fourth Section** of the book is on "Urban Environment and Health" and comprises five articles.

The fourteenth article is by Anuradha Banerjee and is entitled as "Status of Environment and Infrastructure in Indian Metropolis". Rapid urbanisation marked by population explosion in the Indian cities can be largely attributed to the large scale rural to urban migration. Due to the uncontrolled urbanisation in India, the quality of life is under threat particularly in the big cities. Environmental degradation has been occurring very rapidly and causing excessive air and water pollution, water shortage in water scarce regions, problems of disposal of solid and hazardous wastes, noise pollution, housing shortage and mushrooming of slums in most of the metropolises of India. Today the social environment of the cities is also under threat. On account of peculiar problems like unchecked migration, illegal settlements, diverse socio-cultural disparities, uneven distribution of incomes, the phenomenon of urban poverty etc., the metropolitan cities are facing increased criminal activities. Organised groups, gangsters, professional criminals and even youth and juveniles find crime as a short-cut for a lavish life in these cities. Moreover, unabated population increase has also led to a pressure on the existing physical and social infrastructure of the cities like power supply, supply of potable water, urban transport, educational and health institutions. Today, urbanisation in India is characterized by unplanned and uncontrolled growth leading to urban sprawl. Landuse planning and the pattern of development, relationship between residential areas and industrial areas, commercial and office complexes have a considerable impact on the environment. Most of all, appropriate infrastructure provision has not kept pace with economic growth. Consequently, the environment of urban areas, particularly of larger cities, has been deteriorating rapidly. Urban Local Bodies (ULBs) in India are faced with a plethora of issues that directly impact their capacities to manage municipal service delivery while simultaneously addressing environmental concerns. Where the municipalities are struggling to provide the basic amenities, to citizens, issues of environmental pollution of hazard management are not accorded priority till matters reach the proportions of a crisis.

Vidyasagar Trigun has prepared the fifteenth article on "Fertility and Contraceptive Behaviour in Urban India", where the author attempts to analyse fertility and contraceptive behaviour in urban India. The nature and variations in crude birth rate, age specific fertility rate, and total fertility rate among urban women of India across various states show diverse picture of the pattern of fertility in urban society. Urban India as a whole achieved replacement level fertility, but some states are still lagging behind. Contraceptive use has also been gradually rising particularly modern contraceptive methods and the role of public sector as a source of providing female and male sterilization is prominent. Private centres are the leading providers of pills, IUDs (Intra Uterine Device) and condoms in urban India which are mainly used for spacing of births. The nature of use of contraception is gender insensitive and women seem to be burdened with the responsibilty of family planning. NFHS-III and SRS data have been used for the study to bring out the regional variations in fertility and contraceptive behaviour in urban India.

"Socio-Economic Status and Health Care in Urban Eastern India" is the sixteenth article contributed by Sunita Kumari. There are three conventional models of health inequalities—a racial genetic model, a health behaviour or lifestyle model, and a socio-economic status model. This study focuses on the socio-economic model of health inequalities in urban eastern India that consists of four states of India, namely Bihar, Jharkhand, Odisha and West Bengal. Urban health care services are physically more accessible compared to the rural counterpart, but social and economic inaccessibility is more prominent in urban areas, particularly arising out of the gap between the rich and the poor. There is an accelerated flight to the private sector and declining utilisation of public services. In case of morbidity prevalence and hospitalisation rate, eastern India has very sundry pictures. The morbidity rate is the lowest in Jharkhand and hospitalisation rate is found to be the lowest in Bihar not only for eastern India but also for India in general.

The seventeenth article entitled as "Health and Lifestyle Problems of Urban Youth in India: A Case Study of Kolkata Metropolis" has been contributed by Chandramallika Biswas. The article points out that today urban youth are in the midst of transition. They are faced with opposing challenges of traditionalism and modernisation brought about by globalisation and media. Modern technology, lifestyle and rapid transformation in the way of living have given rise to a host of new problems and vulnerabilities among urban youth, for which they are not well prepared. New avenues of education and employment opportunities have raised the standard of living, aspirations, competition and social networking among the youth. They fail to understand the hidden problems and effects of modern urban lifestyle which makes them vulnerable to many risks. Being young, they are ready to take up challenges and risks, but do not have the maturity to deal with the fallouts or after effects. Hence, it is important to learn about the problems and factors leading to such vulnerabilities and identify ways to arrest such risks.

The eighteenth article has been contributed by Vinod Kumar Mishra on "Living Environment in Million plus Cities of India". Rapid growth of population coupled with dearth of infrastructure has resulted in the deterioration of the living environment in million plus urban agglomerations in India. While analysing the living environment of million plus cities not only the number of dwelling units are important but also equally important is their quality in term of structures, characteristics and amenities. Against this backdrop, the present study provides a perspective on the living environment of the million plus cities. Based on various data sources like Census of India and National Sample Surveys, the indicators for the measurement of living environment reflect considerable variations across the largest cities of India.

The final or the **Fifth Section** of the book is on "Urban Policies in India". The article on "Government Policies and Programmes for Urban India: A Critical Appraisal" has been jointly authored by Chandrani Dutta, Pravin Kumar Shukla and Mala Mukherjee.

Contrary to popular concepts of a predominantly rural India, an increasingly larger percentage of Indian population lives in the urban areas. Today, India's urban population is second largest in the world after China. Over the last fifty years, while the country's population has grown by 2.5 times, in the urban areas it has grown by five times. It is estimated that in 1947, only 60 million people (15 per cent of the total population at that time) lived in urban areas, while it increased up to 285 million (27.78%) in 2001 and to 31.16 per cent in 2011 having the urban population about 377 million. In 2011, the number of metropolitan cities has jumped to 53 from 35 in 2011, which house 160.73 million people, constituting 42.62 per cent of total urban population. The steep growth in number of people is partly due to the skewed development that has led to proliferation of commercial activities and great job opportunities in towns and cities. This has resulted in environmental degradation and exerted a lot of pressure on the facilities like housing, sanitation, health, drinking water, education and on the infrastructure like roadways, telecommunication, airports, railways and ports. Although several policies and programmes of Government are going on to cater to this grim situation but due to lack of effective implementation they are unable to suffice to the needs of people in urban areas. The new vision must include comprehensive planning, a new urban land policy which treats land as a source for creating a social environment which can sustain itself in harmony; a new framework of urban institutions which can fulfil the emerging requirements of growing metropolises; a new cadre of urban administrators who have the training and motivation to meet new challenges; geared towards the betterment of the society by devising holistic framework for sustainable urban systems.

SECTION I

Contemporary Urbanisation in India: Urban Growth and Characteristics

SECTION I

Contemporary Urbanisation in India: Urban Growth and Characteristics

1

Contemporary Urbanisation in India

Characteristics, Trends and Patterns

Anuradha Banerjee, Pravin Kumar Shukla and *Chetna Naskar*

Introduction

The twenty-first century has revealed rapid and unprecedented urbanisation in Asia, particularly for the population giants like China and India, though urbanisation processes have been firmly entrenched globally across most of the regions. This, therefore, has become the major focal area of interdisciplinary work and research among social scientists, urban planners and environmentalists. In general parlance, the process of becoming urban refers to a concentration of a territory's population in towns and cities. Processes of urbanisation however draws strands from several interrelated social sciences like history, geography, demography, economics, sociology, political science and the rest.

Urbanisation is a *historical process* since it evolves over time and a *geographical* one since it involves spatial dimensions whether at the regional level or at the micro level, i.e. within the urban area itself. It is also a *demographic process* as it involves population concentration in towns and cities, mostly occurring through rural to urban migration, though the factor of natural increase cannot be overlooked. *Economic forces* have been predominating migration and urbanisation since early times, though the major spurt in urbanisation resulted from industrial revolution and evolution of capitalism. *Structural urbanisation* includes the transformation of the society into a capitalist economy with cities being the foci of production, distribution and exchange, due to economies of scale. At present the economic forces shaping urbanisation are being guided by contemporary globalisation, particularly being marked by the advent of the 'global cities' performing the *global control functions* and their domination over a chain of other cities in the global *urban hierarchic system*. Again, *urbanism* or the urban way of life entails the *sociological processes* and also involves *behavioural urbanisation*, or societal changes i.e. change in the social values and attitudes of those residing in an urban milieu and birth of new social norms and their diffusion through the entire urban system. *Urban social ecology* also traces urbanisation processes through the significant contribution of many scholars.

Urbanisation in India is an age old process that started with the early advent of civilisation and continues till date though with different intensity. In fact, the Indus Valley civilisation or the Harappan civilisation can be considered as the first phase of urbanisation associated with Harappa urbanism. The cities of Harappan civilisation had a definite planning to which several scholars reflect as being urban or proto-urban. Harappan cities flourished for about 600 years, between 2350 B.C. and 1750 B.C. Two major towns of the Indus civilisation, viz. Harappa and Mohen-jodaro are now in Pakistan. Other important towns of this culture located in India are Lothal, Surkotada, Rangpur and Rojdi (Gujarat), Kalibangan (Rajasthan), Banwali (Haryana) and Ropar (Punjab). This was followed by a prolonged period of about one thousand years in which there was no evidence of urbanisation in India. From around 600 B.C. onwards, towns and cities grew in association with two cultural streams, viz. the Aryan and the Dravidian civilisations. The major cities, that evolved during this period were Mathura, Ayodhya, Kapilavastu, Vaishali, Patliputra, Varanasi and Champa in north India; Ujjain, in central India and Nagarjunakonda, Kancheepuram and Madurai in south India. Cities grew both in number and size during the Mauryan and post-Mauryan periods (from 300 B.C. to A.D. 600) in the north, as well as in the south. However, the northern part of India saw a decline in urban growth during the post-Gupta period from A.D. 600 to about AD. 1000. Later on, the invasion of Turks followed by the Sultanate rule helped in revival of urban development in India to some extent. This phase started around 11th century A.D. and continued with some changes till the fall of the Mughal Empire in the 17th century AD. The cities, that flourished during this period include Ludhiana, Hisar, Bikaner, Jaipur, Jodhpur, Udaipur, Kota, Chittaurgarh, Moradabad, Agra, Jaunpur, Vijaynagar, Hyderabad (Golcunda) and Mysore.

The nature of urbanisation in India changed remarkably under British colonisation and the advent of the British East India Company. The major contribution of the British to the Indian urban scene was the creation of three metropolitan port cities or the colonial cities of Mumbai (Bombay),

Kolkata (Calcutta) and Chennai (Madras); the creation of a chain of hill stations in the Himalayan region and in South India; the modification of the urban landscape of the existing cities with the introduction of civil lines and cantonments; the introduction of railways and modern industry, and finally, the improvements in urban amenities and administration in selected cities. However, urban primacy or the 'gate-way cities' reflected the colonial impositions on India's urban scene.

Some of the towns that came up during the British period were the hill stations of Shimla, Mussoorie, Dehradun, Almora, Nainital, Darjeeling and Shillong in the north and Ooty, Kodaikanal in the south. Secondly, this period also witnessed the growth of the port cities of Mumbai, Panaji, Marmagao, Cannanore, Alleppey, Karaikal, Puduchery, Chennai and Kolkata. The industrial cities that had their rudiments in the colonial rule are Kanpur, Dhanbad, Jamshedpur, Asansol and Bhadravati. Besides, these, the development of transportation laid the foundation of towns like Bhusawal, Jalgaon and Siliguri. Certain other towns like Sriganganagar, Bhilwara and Ranchi also came up during British imperialism in India.

Different phases in Indian history mark urbanisation in India. During 1800, India had about 16 cities with a population of one lakh or more and about 1,500 towns. About 11 per cent of the total population of the country lived in urban areas at that time. At the time of first Imperial Census (non-synchronous) in 1872, the urban population declined to 8.7 per cent. Thus major part of the 19th century was marked by stagnation or decline in urbanisation in India. As a matter of fact, the cities of Kolkata, Mumbai, Delhi and Chennai showed remarkable growth while most of the pre-British cities declined considerably (Bose, 1980).

These developments ultimately got translated into the 'top heavy' nature of urbanisation in independent India, where the maximum population is concentrated in the largest cities portraying an uneven distribution of population across the various size classes. This top heavy urban structure often gets manifested through urban sprawl, mushrooming of slums and decline in living standards in these cities due to lack of proper infrastructure arising out of excess population pressure on limited resources. "Urbanisation in India is dysfunctional, where urban hierarchy reflects an extremely inefficient organisation of space and the top heavy character of urban structure is reflected in more and more of its urban population tending to agglomerate in a disproportionately small number of urban conurbations" (Kundu, A., 1980). Again, the rapid increase in urban population in India in the million plus cities is more due to rural push (often termed as distress migration) rather than the pull generated by largest urban centres. Several terms have been associated with this pattern of urbanisation in India like over-urbanisation; hyper-urbanisation, spurious and pseudo-urbanisation, basically reflecting accentuated urbanisation then that justified by the urban economic base. There was political and structural economic changes following the years after India's independence in 1947, particularly during the Second and the Third Five Year Plan periods and the existing urban hierarchy was restructured, but this could not reduce the top heaviness in India's urban structure. This was due to persistent regional disparities in spite of the increasing role played by the public sector in concentrating efforts in the backward areas of the country (Kundu, 2011).

Urban population growth is an important attribute that influence the level of urbanisation. Though the present level of urbanisation in India is low, there is a rapid increase in the absolute number of urban population over the years. According to 2011 Census, the decadal increase in urban population (91.8 million) for the first time surpassed the increase in the rural population (91.5 million), therefore, indicating the increase in tempo of urbanisation presently, which had become sluggish during the later period of 20th and early 21st century. The number of urban agglomerations/towns increased to 7935 and million plus cities increased considerably from 1 in 1901 to 53 in 2011. This indicates that contemporary India is urbanising rapidly, though there are inequalities across the urban scale and significant disparities in the human dimensions. Presently, the level of urbanisation though low in India compared to other countries, but the pace of urbanisation is higher than the rest of the world.

This study aims to portray urbanisation in India, particularly in recent years, in terms of urban growth, levels of urbanisation and metropolitanisation across the various regions of the country. For analytical purpose, data has been captured from the Census of India.

Defining "Urban"

The Census of India defines urban areas as:

1. *Statutory Towns*: All places with a municipality, corporation, cantonment board or notified town area committee, etc. The statutory towns are notified under law by concerned State/UT Government irrespective of their demographic characteristics.

II. *Census Towns*: All other places that satisfy the following criteria:
   (i) A minimum population of 5,000;
   (ii) At least 75 per cent of male main working population engaged in non-agricultural pursuits; and
   (iii) A density of population of at least 400 persons per sq. km.

Based on certain characteristics, the Census also defines certain urban settlements as:

Urban Agglomeration (UA)

An urban agglomeration is a continuous urban spread constituting a town and its adjoining outgrowths or two or more physical contiguous towns together with or without the outgrowths of such towns. An Urban Agglomeration must consist of at least a statutory town and its total population (i.e. all the constituents put together) should not be less than 20,000 as per the 2001 census.

Urban Out Growth (OG)

An out growth is a variable unit such as a village, a hamlet or an enumeration block which is identifiable in terms of boundaries and location. Out growths of cities and towns are also treated as urban in the Census and in the calculation of the growth rate, both urban agglomeration and individual town/city could be considered.

In the 2011 Census, 475 places with 981 OGs have been identified as Urban Agglomerations as against 384 Urban Agglomeration with 962 Out Growths in 2001 Census.

Urbanisation Trends in India

As stated earlier that the level of urbanisation though low, India has experienced an ever increasing urban growth over the years, since the first synchronous Census conducted in 1881. The composition of urban growth in India consists of the following elements:

1. Rural to urban migration,
2. Natural Increase (Births minus deaths),
3. Reclassification of rural settlements into urban, and
4. Changes in boundaries of existing urban settlements.

The low level of urbanisation in India is attributed to the fact that, though there is an increase in the urban population, the increase in the rural population was also considerable. However, the present Census of 2011 reveals that for the first time the decadal increase in the urban population (2001 to 2011) was more by 91.8 million than that of rural population (91.5 million).

The total urban population in 2011 stands at 377,106,000 as against 43,763,000 in 2001. The per cent decadal growth rate in 2011 is 31.8 as against 17.6 in 2001. The urbanisation rate (level of urbanisation) in 2011 is 31.2 per cent as against 27.8 per cent in 2001. The urban population figures as given by the Census of India before and after 1961 are not strictly comparable since there had been stringent definitional changes adopted by the Census in 1961. Hence, 810 towns of the 1951 Census had been declassified on the eve of the 1961 Census. Therefore, for all purposes of comparison, efforts should be made on identifying the the pattern that has emerged over the decades (Premi and Das, 2011).

Table 1.1: Decadal Variation in Urban and Rural Population, 1901-2011

Year	*No. of towns*	*Urban population (in millions)*	*Rural population (in millions)*	*Difference in rural-urban population growth*	*Per cent urban population to total population*	*Per cent rural population to total population*
1901	1915	25.85	212.55	186.70	10.84	89.16
1911	1864	25.94	226.15	200.21	10.29	89.71
1921	2018	28.09	223.23	195.14	11.18	88.82
1931	2188	33.46	245.52	212.06	11.99	88.01
1941	2392	44.15	274.51	241.06	13.86	86.14
1951	3035	62.44	298.66	236.22	17.29	82.71
1961	2657	78.94	360.15	281.21	17.97	82.03
1971	3081	109.11	489.12	380.01	18.24	81.76
1981	3981	159.46	523.87	364.41	23.34	76.66
1991	4615	217.55	628.84	411.29	25.72	74.28
2001	5161	286.12	742.49	456.37	27.78	72.22
2011	7935	377.11	833.08	455.97	31.16	68.84

Source: Census of India 1901 to 2001, 2011, Series 1, India, *Provisional Population Total,* Paper 2, 2011.

Level of Urbanisation

The level of urbanisation in India has increased from 1901 to 2011 in a

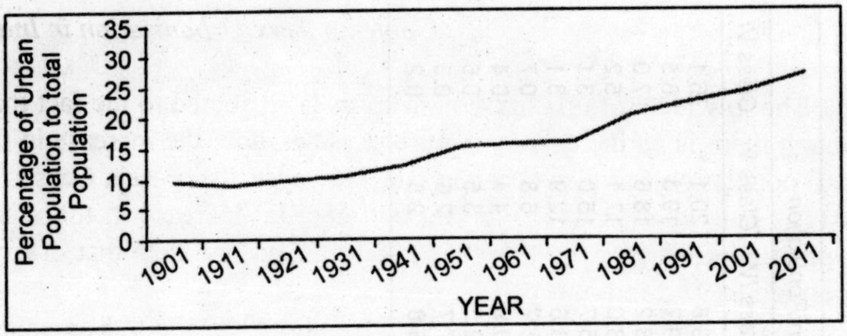

Fig. 1.1: Level of Urbanisation in India 1901 to 2011

gradual speed. In 1901 this was only 10.84 that has increased to 31.15 per cent stating almost a threefold increase in the share of urban population. The share of urban population in total population has also increased from 25.85 million in 1901 to 377.11 million in 2011. It can be thus stated that India now has reached an accelerating rate of urbanisation. However, taking into account the time period, i.e. 110 years, the level of urbanisation has not been very high.

Number of Towns

There has been also a marked increase in the number of towns from 1901 to 2011. In 1901 there were only 1915 towns which increased to 5161 in 2001 and 7935 in 2011. However, the number of town decreased in 1961, which is mainly due to rigorous application of Census criteria for demarcating the towns in the stated Census year, leading to large scale declassification of the so called new towns, defined very loosely in 1951 i.e. the first Census conducted after independence. Nevertheless, there is a marked increase in the number of towns in 2011. This increase in the number of towns can be attributed to increase in the population of many urban out growths or previously suburbanised areas that fit into the criteria of becoming an urban centre given by the Census.

Share of Population in Size-Class Towns

An analysis of the data reveals that though there is an increase in the number of towns in all size classes, maximum concentration of population has taken place in the class I category. Though the number of class I cities has increased from 24 in 1901 to 393 in 2001, the concentration of urban population has almost tripled, from 26 to 68.6 per cent over the decades.

Table 1.2: Number of Towns and Percentage of Urban Population in Different Size Classes, 1901 to 2001

Year	No of Towns						Percentage Urban Population					
	Class I	Class II	Class III	Class IV	Class V	Class VI	Class I	Class II	Class III	Class IV	Class V	Class VI
1901	24	43	130	391	744	479	26.0	11.2	15.6	20.8	20.1	6.1
1911	23	40	135	364	707	485	27.4	10.5	16.4	19.7	19.3	6.5
1921	29	45	145	370	734	571	29.7	10.3	15.9	18.2	18.6	7.0
1931	35	56	183	434	800	509	31.2	11.6	16.8	18.0	17.1	5.2
1941	49	74	242	498	920	407	38.2	11.4	16.3	15.7	15.0	3.1
1951	76	91	327	608	1124	569	44.6	9.9	15.7	13.6	12.9	3.1
1961	102	129	437	719	711	172	51.4	11.2	16.9	12.7	6.8	0.7
1971	148	173	558	827	623	147	57.2	10.9	16.0	10.9	4.4	0.4
1981	218	270	743	1059	758	253	60.3	11.6	14.3	9.5	3.5	0.5
1991	300	345	947	1167	740	197	64.8	10.9	13.1	7.7	2.6	0.3
2001	393	401	1151	1344	888	191	68.6	9.7	12.2	6.8	2.3	0.2

Source: Census of India, 1991-2001.

Census data reveal a continuous increase in the concentration of the urban population in Class I category till 1941, however, the increase in the share of urban population in class I town got triggered from 1951 and there was significant decrease in share of urban population in rest of the classes mainly Class VI towns. Though the proportion of towns in most of the size classes (except VI) has increased the percentage share of population decreased except in Class I town. 393 cities out of 5161 cities in size-class I in 2001 have a share of more than half the urban population of the country. The basic reason for the dominance of class I cities is the graduation of lower order towns to class I category (Kundu, 1994). This feature of urbanisation proves increasing imbalance and inequality in distribution of urban population and a top heavy pattern of urbanisation in India. Thus the concentration of urban population only in a few mega-cities and metropolises exert pressure on urban infrastructure and resources ultimately leading to congestion, overcrowding, decrease in overall standard of living of the population, mushrooming of slums and associated problems, increasing unemployment and poverty among others.

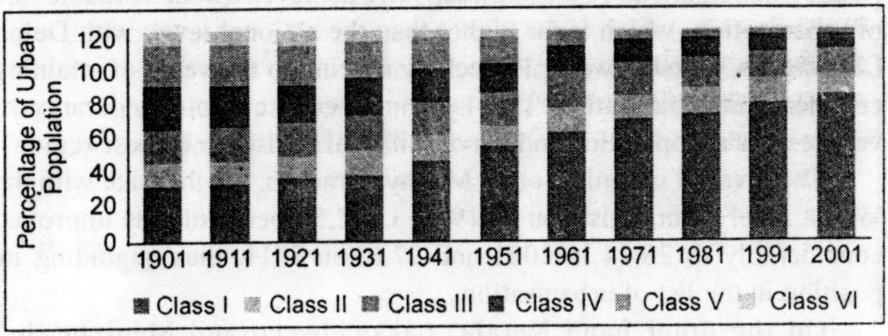

Fig. 1.2: Percentage of Urban Population in Different Size Class, 1991-2001

Trends and Pattern of Urbanisation: A State Level Analysis

There is a large variation in the inter-state pattern and trend of urbanisation due to variations in urban population concentration across the states. Urbanisation is mostly a feature of a few states and almost half of the urban population is concentrated in six states, viz. Maharashtra, Tamil Nadu, Karnataka, Gujarat, Punjab and West Bengal. This pattern is an inheritance from the colonial period and all these states report a percentage of urban population much higher than the national average of 31.1 in

2011. Several studies have shown that higher levels of urbanisation is a feature of States with high per capita income, the opposite being the case in less urbanised States (Sivaramakrishna, Kundu and Singh, 2005).

Levels of Urbanisation

Though there is marked variation in the level of urbanisation across the States and Union Territories (UTs), the rate has increased for all the States/ UTs from 1991 to 2011. However, the pace of urbanisation has fluctuated across the States and the UTs through the decades. 1991 and 2001 have witnessed sluggish rate of urbanisation though the rate has accelerated considerably in 2011. There are many States and UTs where the urbanisation process has almost doubled in 2011. This can be attributed to the increase in share of urban population in the present decade. However, the accelerating rate of urbanisation can be witnessed mostly for already highly urbanised regions whereas the States with low urbanisation rate have improved only marginally.

Delhi, Daman and Diu, Goa, Kerala, Dadra and Nagar Haveli, Tamil Nadu, Chandigarh and Lakshadweep have achieved a commendable rate of urbanisation, which is far higher than the national level; with Delhi, Chandigarh, Lakshadweep, Puduchery nearing to the verge of attaining cent-per cent urbanisation. This is mainly because of preponderance of very less rural population and almost nil rural landscape in these regions.

The level of urbanisation in Madhya Pradesh, i.e. the state with the lowest level of urbanisation in 1991, i.e. 2.53 per cent, has improved considerably to 26.44 in 2001 and 27.63 in 2011, thus upgrading its position in the list of urbanisation.

On the other hand Kerala, Lakshadweep and Manipur that experienced a decrease in the rate of urbanisation in 2001 also improved their position significantly in 2011 with Kerala and Lakshadweep attaining a commendable rate of urbanisation and moving up in the ladder of ranking. On the contrary, states with very low level of urbanisation like Assam, Odisha, Bihar, Himachal Pradesh continues to retain their positions.

Increase in Absolute Number of Towns across States and Union Territories

The state-wise distribution pattern of total number of towns is much diversified in nature. States like Uttar Pradesh, Tamil Nadu, West Bengal

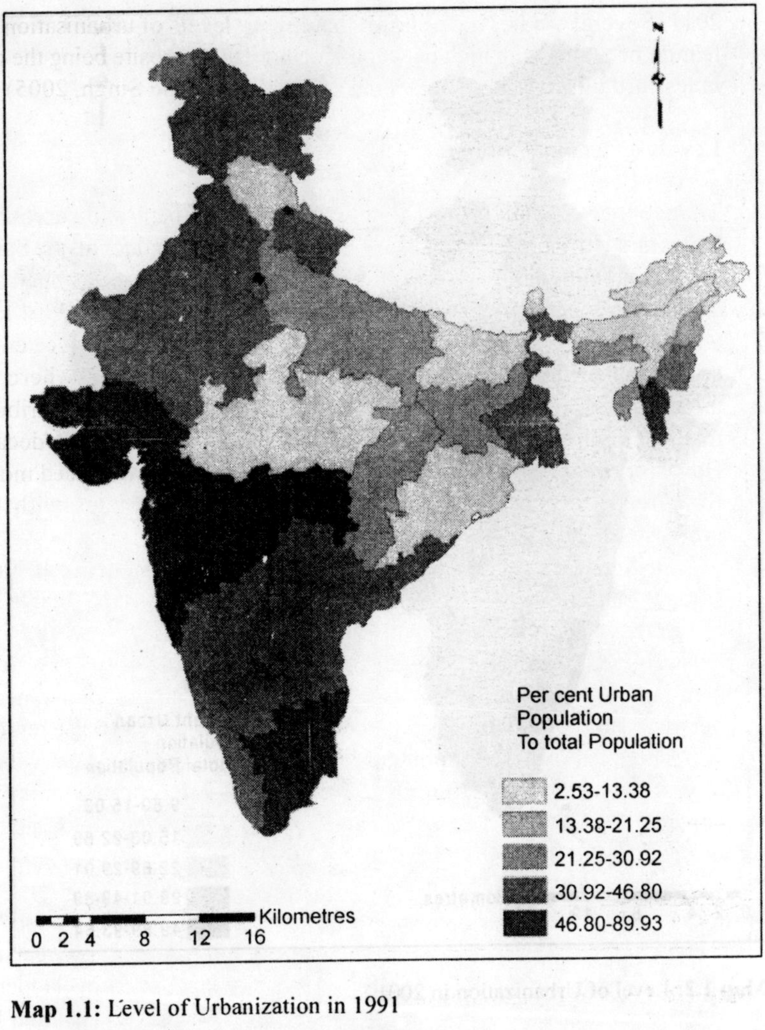

Map 1.1: Level of Urbanization in 1991

and Maharashtra have recorded large number of towns as compared to the north eastern states that have recorded very few number of towns. However, though, for all the 35 States and UTs the number of towns in 2011 has increased than the two earlier Census years. In 2001, Andhra Pradesh, Bihar, Chandigarh, Himachal Pradesh, Karnataka, Kerala, West Bengal and Lakshadweep have experienced a decrease in the count of towns from 1991. This is mainly due to declassification of many urban centres in 2001 that had rural characteristics and were given urban status

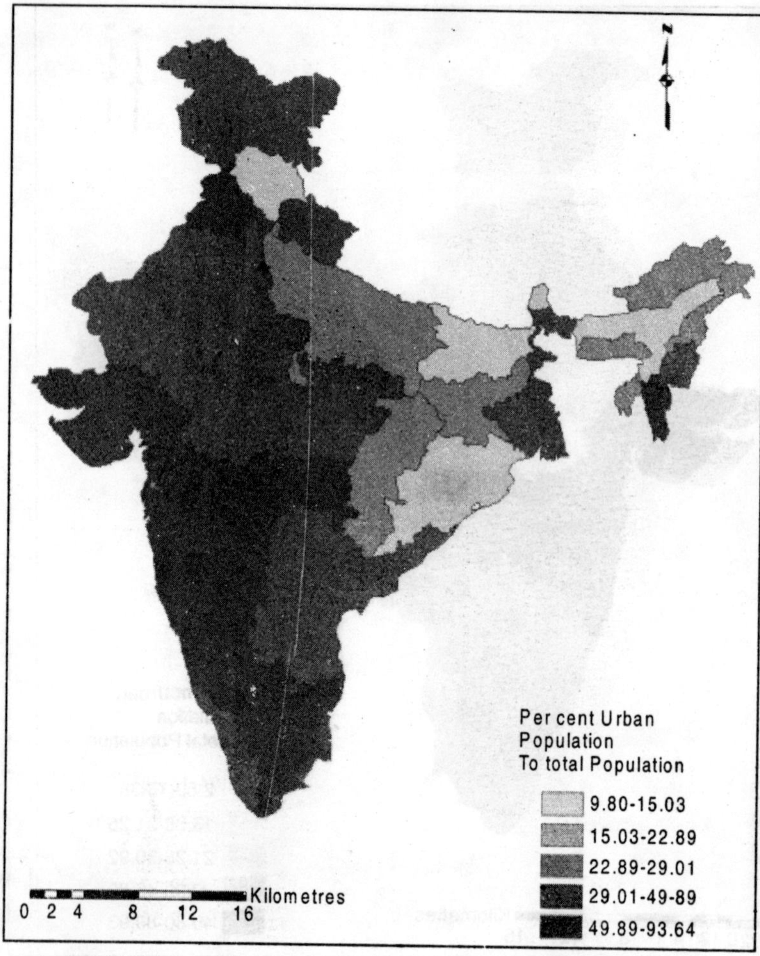

Map 1.2: Level of Urbanization in 2001

in the previous Census years. Nevertheless, all States experienced an increase in cities and towns in 2011 surpassing that of 1991. Very few States have experienced a marginal increase in the number of towns whereas for most of the States and UTs the number of towns has increased considerably in 2011. This is mainly because of declaration of many urban out growths as towns, fulfilling the Census criteria and also due to the increase in the urban growth rate of population which had slowed down during 1971-2001.

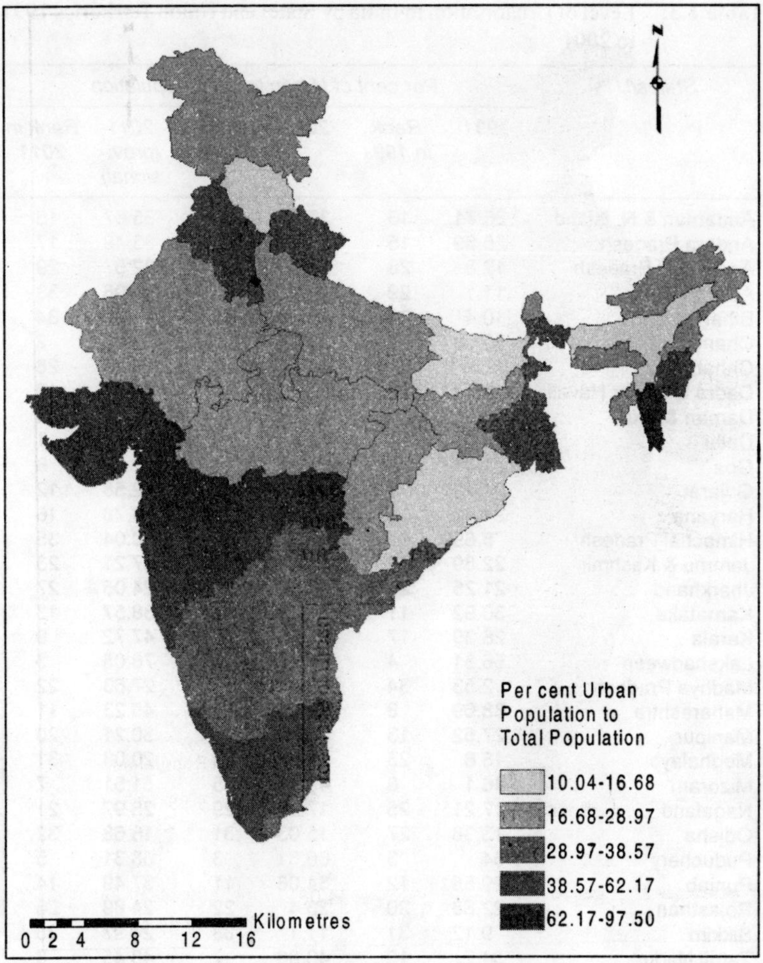

Map 1.3: Level of Urbanization in 2011

In 1991 Uttar Pradesh ranked first in the number of towns followed by Tamil Nadu and West Bengal; but in 2001 Tamil Nadu surpassed Uttar Pradesh in the town count adding about 400 settlements followed by Uttar Pradesh and West Bengal. The position though remains intact in 2011, West Bengal has recorded a remarkable increase in number of towns from 375 to 909, i.e. an increase of 534 towns in the present Census year. The increase in number of towns is also attributed to large size and concentration of urban population in these states.

Table 1.3: Level of Urbanisation in India by States and Union Territories 1991 to 2001

States/UTs	*Per cent cf Urban to Total Population*					
	1991	*Rank in 1991*	*2001*	*Rank in 2001*	*2011 (provi-sional)*	*Rank in 2011*
Andaman & N. Island	26.71	16	32.62	13	35.67	15
Andhra Pradesh	26.89	15	27.48	16	33.49	17
Arunachal Pradesh	12.8	28	20.89	25	22.67	29
Assam	11.1	29	12.91	32	14.08	33
Bihar	10.4	30	10.48	34	11.30	34
Chandigarh	89.69	2	89.74	2	97.25	2
Chhattisgarh	17.4	24	20.13	27	23.24	28
Dadra & Nagar Haveli	8.47	33	22.89	23	46.62	10
Daman & Diu	46.8	5	36.28	10	75.16	4
Delhi	89.93	1	93.64	1	97.5	1
Goa	41.01	7	49.89	4	62.17	6
Gujarat	34.49	9	37.41	9	42.58	12
Haryana	24.63	18	29.01	14	34.79	16
Himachal Pradesh	8.69	32	9.8	35	10.04	35
Jammu & Kashmir	22.89	19	24.99	20	27.21	23
Jharkhand	21.25	21	22.27	24	24.05	27
Karnataka	30.92	11	34.06	12	38.57	13
Kerala	26.39	17	25.97	18	47.72	9
Lakshadweep	56.31	4	44.5	6	78.08	3
Madhya Pradesh	2.53	34	26.44	17	27.63	22
Maharashtra	38.69	8	42.48	8	45.23	11
Manipur	27.52	13	24.11	21	30.21	20
Meghalaya	18.6	23	19.69	28	20.08	31
Mizoram	46.1	6	49.49	5	51.51	7
Nagaland	17.21	25	17.24	29	28.97	21
Odisha	13.38	27	15.03	31	16.68	32
Puduchery	64	3	66.61	3	68.31	5
Punjab	29.55	12	34.08	11	37.49	14
Rajasthan	22.88	20	23.4	22	24.89	26
Sikkim	9.12	31	11.1	33	24.97	25
Tamil Nadu	34.2	10	43.86	7	48.45	8
Tripura	15.26	26	17.02	30	26.18	24
Uttarakhand	–	–	25.59	19	30.55	19
Uttar Pradesh	19.89	22	20.78	26	22.28	30
West Bengal	27.39	14	28.03	15	31.89	18

Across the different size classes, the number of towns in Class I have either remained same or increased marginally from 1991 to 2001. Within the Classes II category, only Delhi has experienced a decrease in towns as most of the towns have moved on to Class I category due to increase in population in 2001. The total number of Class III towns have increased in all the states whereas Tamil Nadu has experienced a higher

Table 1.4: Number of Cities and Towns in India by States and Union Territories, 1991 to 2011

States/UTs	*Total No of Cities/ Towns (1991)*	*Total No of Cities/ Towns (2001)*	*Total No of Cities/ Towns (2011)*
Andaman & Nicobar Island	1	3	5
Andhra Pradesh	264	210	353
Arunachal Pradesh	10	17	27
Assam	93	125	214
Bihar	138	130	199
Chandigarh	5	1	6
Chhattisgarh	95	97	182
Dadra & Nagar Haveli	0	2	6
Daman & Diu	2	2	8
Delhi	32	62	113
Goa	31	44	70
Gujarat	264	242	348
Haryana	94	106	154
Himachal Pradesh	58	57	59
Jammu & Kashmir	0	75	122
Jharkhand	133	152	228
Karnataka	306	270	347
Kerala	197	99	520
Lakshadweep	4	3	6
Madhya Pradesh	370	394	476
Maharashtra	336	378	535
Manipur	31	33	51
Meghalaya	12	16	22
Mizoram	22	22	23
Nagaland	9	9	26
Odisha	124	138	223
Puduchery	5	6	10
Punjab	120	157	217
Rajasthan	222	222	297
Sikkim	8	9	9
Tamil Nadu	469	832	1097
Tripura	18	23	42
Uttar Pradesh	670	704	915
Uttaranchal	83	86	116
West Bengal	382	375	909

Source: Census of India, 1991-2011.

increase from 108 in 1991 to 183 in 2001. The total number of Class IV towns has declined in 14 states in 2001, where the decrease in number is quite large for most of the states. However, Tamil Nadu on the other hand has recorded an exceptionally high increase in this class, i.e. from140 to 340, an increase 200 towns. The marked decrease in the number of towns in Class IV is mainly due to the graduation of towns of this Class to

Classes I, II and III. In case of Class V towns, Gujarat, Madhya Pradesh and Uttar Pradesh have experienced a decrease with Uttar Pradesh recording a loss of about 70 towns. Except very few, almost all states have experienced a decrease in Class VI category of towns.

The percentage share of population in Class I towns have increased in most of the states except in some states like Rajasthan, Delhi, Meghalaya and Tamil Nadu. In Rajasthan the percentage of decrease is very high, i.e. from 73.93 in 1991 to 37.74 in 2001. It is worth mentioning that similar to the nation's picture, the percentage share of population in Class I towns are more than half of the total urban population in certain urbanised states, with Maharashtra topping the list with 77 per cent of its urban population concentrated in Class I cities, followed by Andhra Pradesh, West Bengal and Haryana (2001). The entire urban population of Chandigarh is concentrated in Class I only. In Arunachal Pradesh, Nagaland and in other UTs except Delhi, Chandigarh and Puduchery there is no Class I city even in 2001. However, these States and UTs are very small to have a high population count to fulfil the Class I criteria. In case of Class II towns, the percentage share of urban population has decreased in most of the States and UTs except in Haryana, Delhi, Odisha, Maharashtra, Meghalaya, Assam, Andhra Pradesh and Chhattisgarh. The percentage share of population in Class III towns have increased in almost 14 States/UTs, and in Goa its share has increased drastically from 6.60 in 1991 to 92.30 per cent in 2001. In Daman and Diu and Dadra and Nagar Haveli, the total urban population is concentrated in this class due to the graduation of all the Class IV category towns to this class. In most of the states, the percentage share of population in Class IV category has declined except some North Eastern States, Tamil Nadu and Lakshadweep. In Arunachal Pradesh the percentage share of population in this class has increased from 29.42 in 1991 to 66.95 in 2001. Lakshadweep which did not have any share of population in Class IV category recorded an entry into this category which can be attributed to the graduation of Class V towns. Almost all the states except a few have experienced a decline in population share in Class V and Class VI category in 2001, in contrast to Mizoram that has experienced an increase in population in Class VI category in 2001.

Imbalances in the pattern of distribution of urban population in different size class reinstate the top heavy structure. Again, in most of the urbanised States and UTs of Delhi, Chandigarh and Puduchery, the Class I category supports more than half of the urban population. This is mainly due to the economic base and employment opportunities in large cities, particularly in the informal sectors, if not in the formal sector. The

Table 1.5: India: Urban Population by Size Class, 1991 to 2001

States	Distribution of Urban Population by Size Class											
	1991						2001					
	Class I	Class II	Class III	Class IV	Class V	Class VI	Class I	Class II	Class III	Class IV	Class V	Class VI
Andaman & Nicobar Island	Na	Na	Na	Na	Na	Na	59.69	14.04	6.45	11.35	5.69	2.78
Andhra Pradesh	59.32	15.83	19.31	4.54	0.093	0.07	70.66	16.67	9.51	2.42	0.7	0.04
Arunachal Pradesh	0	0	0	66.95	33.05	0	0	0	36.86	29.42	18.76	1.79
Assam	37.19	11.6	23.32	20.09	6.04	1.75	41.88	12.68	20.12	14.77	9.23	1.31
Bihar	42.84	22.16	25.84	8.33	0.71	0.11	55.90	15.8	24.24	3.61	0.49	0
Chandigarh	88.67	0	6.4	2.78	1.36	0.79	100	0	0	0	0	0
Chhattisgarh	47.88	11.53	16.2	18.85	6	0.41	55.65	12.51	14.36	13.15	4.32	0
Dadra & Nagar Haveli	0	0	0	100.00	0	0	0	0	100.00	0	0	0
Daman & Diu	0	0	100	0	0	0	0	0	100.00	0	0	0
Delhi	89.94	5.26	2.64	1.34	0.67	0.15	87.79	5.38	5.06	1.22	0.48	0.08
Goa	0	42.06	6.6	25.23	22.17	3.94	0	36.63	92.3	34.71	16.6	2.83
Gujarat	59.94	15.49	12.10	9.41	2.82	0.24	68.25	13.00	12.92	4.61	1.00	0.23
Haryana	52.92	18.98	13.14	10.78	3.94	0.23	69.36	6.79	12.98	8.68	2.11	0.07
Himachal Pradesh	22.75	0	19.42	21.73	15.81	20.29	23.94	0	25.86	19.06	19.09	12.06
Jharkhand	36.02	24.67	21.37	11.84	5.34	0.75	41.13	23.05	20.48	9.03	5.62	0.69
Karnataka	53.93	12.37	21.11	9.29	2.68	0.62	64.90	10.05	18.12	5.26	1.49	0.19
Kerala	31.65	15.99	39.93	10.7	1.67	0.06	44.66	19.21	27.78	6.85	1.44	0.06
Madhya Pradesh	48.06	12.45	15.02	17.2	7.10	0.16	53.03	11.86	17.21	13.36	4.3	0.25
Maharashtra	75.13	6.93	11.59	5.01	1.20	0.14	77.73	7.58	10.15	3.58	0.89	0.07
Manipur	39.26	0	18.02	14.85	24.27	3.94	39.66	0	19.22	19.03	18.64	3.16
Meghalaya	39.91	0	37.74	15.48	6.87	0	29.26	12.99	31.46	24.39	1.9	0
Mizoram	48.83	0	17.74	12.84	10.05	10.54	51.76	0	16.69	17.65	8.38	5.51
Nagaland	0	52.16	22.01	17.6	8.24	0	0	51.09	35.50	13.41	0	0

(Contd.)

Table 1.5 (*Contd.*)

States	*Distribution of Urban Population by Size Class*											
	1991						*2001*					
	Class I	*Class II*	*Class III*	*Class IV*	*Class V*	*Class VI*	*Class I*	*Class II*	*Class III*	*Class IV*	*Class V*	*Class VI*
Odisha	41.87	14.65	21.99	17.28	3.94	0.28	45.61	18.03	19.92	12.82	3.16	0.45
Puduchery	69.67	11.95	8.32	6.66	3.39	0	71.19	11.48	17.33	0	0	0
Punjab	54.16	19.91	12.92	10.82	1.72	0.47	58.32	15.91	13.10	9.81	2.58	0.28
Rajasthan	73.93	13.64	21.72	13.01	2.03	0.07	37.74	14.67	20.52	7.16	1.18	0.15
Sikkim	0	0	67.62	0	0	32.38	0	0	49.03	23.98	9.07	17.92
Tamil Nadu	50.43	17	17.30	10.65	3.71	0.92	42.55	14.42	19.3	17.38	6.16	0.18
Tripura	37.31	0	27.54	25.08	7.92	2.15	34.81	0	33.39	8.88	8.88	0
Uttar Pradesh	53.50	11.96	15.05	13.07	6.12	0.29	59.72	10.73	15.56	10.81	3.04	0.14
Uttaranchal	32.03	12.94	27.15	17.27	5.63	4.98	35.02	18.31	23.32	11.71	9.42	2.22
West Bengal	64.13	13.06	10.29	7.35	4.71	0.44	74.1	8.81	7.71	4.79	4.02	0.56

Source: Census of India, 1991-2001.

expansion of the service sectors, a manifestation of the globalisation process also incidentally provide, a vast array of jobs, including the 'low end, low paid' jobs that increase livelihood options in large cities making them destination points for the poor.

Urban Growth and Metropolitan Cities

The Metropolitan cities or metropolises are the million plus cities, usually identified through their urban way of life or urbanism and heterogeneity of population. The urban growth pattern in these million plus cities is of utmost importance as metropolisation has been a remarkable feature of urbanisation in India during the post-independence period, due to rapid growth in number and also per cent share of urban population in these cities. In 1901, India had only one million plus city, i.e. Kolkata (Calcutta) which was also the then capital of India. The number increased to 2 in 1911 due to entry of Mumbai (Bombay) in the list. These two cities continued to dominate the urban scene until 1951 when their number reached 5 with entry of Chennai (Madras), Delhi and Hyderabad. Thereafter, the number of million plus cities continued to increase to 23 in 1991, 35 in 2001 and 53 in 2011. The present Census has witnessed a considerable increase in their numbers due to the graduation of many Class I cities to the present metropolises.

Table 1.6: India: Decadal Growth of Population in Million Plus Cities/ Metropolises, 1991 to 2011

Year	*No of Million Plus Cities*	*Population (Million)*	*Percentage of Urban Population*
1901	1	1.51	5.84
1911	2	2.76	10.65
1921	2	3.13	11.14
1931	2	3.41	10.18
1941	2	5.31	12.23
1951	5	11.75	18.81
1961	7	18.10	22.93
1971	9	27.83	25.51
1981	12	42.12	26.41
1991	23	70.66	32.54
2001	35	107.88	38.60
2011	53	161.06	43.00

Source: Census of India, 1991, 2001, 2011 *(provisional population totals)*.

Along with an increase in the number of these metropolises, the growth rate of urban population of these cities, as well as their share in the total population and total urban population have increased over the decades.

Till 1941 only a small share of urban population was contributed by the million plus cities. However, after India's independence and the first Census of independent India, i.e. from 1951, the percentage share started increasingly rapidly. Presently about 161 million out of 1210.19 million people reside in 53 million plus cities with 43 per cent share of total urban population concentrated in these cities. Out of the 161 million, 73 million people live only in six metropolitan cities of Mumbai, Delhi, Kolkata, Chennai, Bangalore and Hyderabad. Thus these six metropolises account for over half of the population of all the metropolises taken together. The high concentration of population only in few metropolitan cities is mainly due to concentration of economic activities in these regions, mobilisation of resources and increased Foreign Direct Investments, whereas the backward regions remain devoid of all such facilities. This again proves the over-concentration of population in the leading cities of India or a lopsided pattern of urbanisation. This high population growth has adversely affected the metropolises of Mumbai and Kolkata in particular, that had an earlier start. Here, the infrastructural development could not keep pace with urban growth. On the contrary, metropolises like Delhi, Chennai, Bangalore and Hyderabad, due to their late start, and considerable higher developmental activities undertaken by the government and private sectors together with the dominance of the knowledge based economy are rising as strong economic centres in contemporary times.

Urban Growth Rate *Verses* Levels of Urbanisation

Although urban population growth rate is considered as a major attribute of urbanisation, increase in the growth rate does not always lead to high degree of urbanisation. The correlation coefficient between urban growth rate and levels of urbanisation in India though positive (0.6), the years with highest growth rate of population does not exhibit highest rate of urbanisation in India. The level of urbanisation in India has increased over the decades steadily whereas fluctuations in growth rates are experienced across the decades. The decadal growth rate has experienced two dips over the deacades 1901 to 2011. The growth rate of urban population was very insignificant in the early decades which reached its peak in 1951 with a decadal growth rate of 41.42 per cent. This high growth rate can be attributed to large scale migration across the borders due to partition of the country and also very loosely defined urban centres in the first Census conducted after independence; though the rate of urbanisation was very low, i.e. 17.29 per cent. This low level of urbanisation can be explained as the reason behind huge increase in

Table 1.7: List of Million Plus Cities/Urban Agglomerations 1991, 2001, 2011

List of Million Plus Urban Agglomerations	*Population in Million (1991)*	*Population in Million (2001)*	*Population in Million (2011)*
1. Mumbai	12.57	16.43	18.41
2. Delhi	8.38	12.88	16.31
3. Kolkata	10.92	13.22	14.11
4. Chennai	5.36	6.42	8.69
5. Bangalore	4.09	5.69	8.50
6. Hyderabad	4.28	5.53	7.75
7. Ahmedabad	3.30	4.52	6.24
8. Pune	2.49	3.75	5.04
9. Surat	1.52	2.81	4.58
10. Jaipur	1.52	2.32	3.07
11. Kanpur	2.11	2.71	2.92
12. Lucknow	1.64	2.24	2.90
13. Nagpur	1.66	2.12	2.50
14. Ghaziabad	**	**	2.36
15. Patna	1.10	1.35	2.50
16. Indore	1.10	1.50	2.17
17. Coimbatore	1.14	1.46	2.15
18. Kochi	1.14	1.35	2.11
19. Kozhikode	**	**	2.03
20. Bhopal	1.06	1.45	1.88
21. Thrissur	**	**	1.85
22. Vadodara	1.12	1.49	1.81
23. Agra	**	1.33	1.74
24. Visakhapatnam	1.05	1.34	1.73
25. Malappuram	**	**	1.69
26. Thiruvananthapuram	**	**	1.69
27. Kannur	**	**	1.64
28. Ludhiana	1.01	1.39	1.61
29. Nashik	**	1.15	1.56
30. Vijayawada	**	1.03	1.49
31. Madurai	1.09	1.20	1.46
32. Varanasi	1.03	1.21	1.43
33. Meerut	**	1.16	1.42
34. Rajkot	**	1.00	1.39
35. Faridabad	**	1.05	1.40
36. Jamshedpur	**	1.10	1.33
37. Srinagar	**	**	1.27
38. Jabalpur	**	1.09	1.26
39. Asansol	**	1.06	1.24
40. Allahabad	**	1.04	1.21
41. Dhanbad	**	1.06	1.19
42. Vasai-Virar	**	**	1.22
43. Aurangabad	**	**	1.18
44. Amritsar	**	1.00	1.18
45. Jodhpur	**	**	1.14

(*Contd.*)

Table 1.7 (*Contd.*)

List of Million Plus Urban Agglomerations	*Population in Million (1991)*	*Population in Million (2001)*	*Population in Million (2011)*
46. Ranchi	**	**	1.26
47. Raipur	**	**	1.12
48. Kollam	**	**	1.11
49. Gwalior	**	**	1.10
50. Durg-Bhilainagar	**	**	1.06
51. Chandigarh	**	**	1.25
52. Tiruchirappalli	**	**	1.02
53. Kota	**	**	1.00
Total	23 Cities / UA	35 Cities / UA	53 Cities /UAs

Note: ** refers to cities/UAs with population less than a million.

Source: Census of India.

Table 1.8: India: Decadal Growth Rate of Urban Population and Level of Urbanisation, 1991-2001

Year	*Urban Population*	*Decadal Growth Rate*	*Level of Urbanisation*
1901	25851873	—	10.84
1911	25941633	0.35	10.29
1921	28086167	8.27	11.18
1931	33455989	19.12	11.99
1941	44153297	31.97	13.86
1951	62443709	41.42	17.29
1961	78936603	26.41	17.97
1971	109113977	38.23	18.24
1981	159462547	46.14	23.34
1991	217177625	36.19	25.72
2001	285354954	31.39	27.78
2011	377105760	32.15	31.16

Source: Census of India, 1991, 2001, 2011 (*provisional population totals*).

rural population and its increasing share in total population of the country.

After 1951 India experienced a dip in the growth rate of urban population which fell considerably to 26.41 per cent in 1961. This decrease in the growth rate is mainly due to more rigorous use of the Census criteria for classification of towns, which led to a large scale declassification of towns along with their constituent population thus decreasing both the share and rate of decadal growth. In 1981 India experienced the highest growth rate of urban population following which there was again decrease in the growth rate; though the level of urbanisation continued to increase. The increase in the growth rate of urban population in 1981 can be attributed partially due to the introduction of the neo liberal policies in 1971 leading to large scale migration of rural population to the urban counterparts providing better economic opportunities and stagnation of the rural economy. Also the emergence of new urban centres in this decade was the highest since independence. Urban growth has experienced a decline after 1981 to 2001. This decrease is again, the result of declassification of many urban centres that mushroomed during the 1980s as new towns, due to very casual application of the definition of the Census towns by a few states. However, there is marginal increase in growth rate of population in 2011 and the level of urbanisation too has also increased from the previous decade. This can be explained by the fact that the overall increase in urban population in the present Census year surpassed the increase in rural population and also increase in the number of new towns which is the largest since independence.

The regional picture of the pattern of urban growth is significantly different from the level of urbanisation across the states in India. As there is an overall decrease in rate of urban growth at the national level during 1991-2001, it is evident that the urban growth rates of the states also have decreased over this decade. Various literature and the Census data of previous decades point out that the urban growth rate has significantly gone down between 1991 and 2001. "More important than the decline in the growth of urban population, however, is the change in the pattern of urban growth in the 1990s, which makes a significant departure from earlier decades. During the four Census decades after Independence until 1991, urban growth was generally high in relatively backward states. The 1990s, however, make a significant departure from this. Most of the developed states like Tamil Nadu, Punjab, Haryana, Maharashtra and Gujarat have registered urban growth above the national average" (Kundu, 2011). The backward states on the contrary has experienced growth rate either equal to or lower than the national average. However, there are few backward states in this decade recording higher growth rate surpassing the national average. The degree of urbanisation remains inclined towards the developed states and larger cities with the backward states and small areas tending to stagnate. Though there are a few states and UTs with very high growth rate of population, they do not show an increase in level of urbanisation as that of the developed states with high growth rate. The overall rate of urbanisation, however, has improved for most of the States and UTs during 1991-2001.

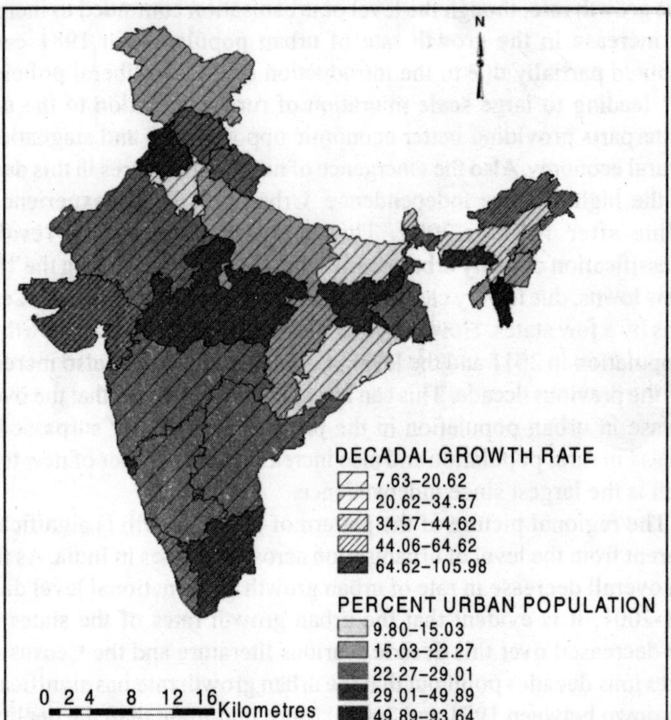

Map 1.4: INDIA: Decadal Urban Growth Rate and Level of Urbanisation 1991-2001

At present, the picture has changed slightly when the decadal growth rate of population is taken into consideration. There is an equal divide among the states and the union territories regarding the increase and decrease in the growth rate of population. Though the growth rate shows a decline in the motion, the growth rates for 16 states and UTs have increased with Lakshadweep, Kerala, and Daman and Diu recording the highest. The decrease in growth rates has been recorded for many of the developed states whose growth rates not only fell below the national average but also below the backward regions, thus once again giving the way for them to chart high growth rates. This decrease in growth rates in developed areas can be a combined result of incapability to accept immigrants and the decrease in the natural increase of population as compared to the backward regions.

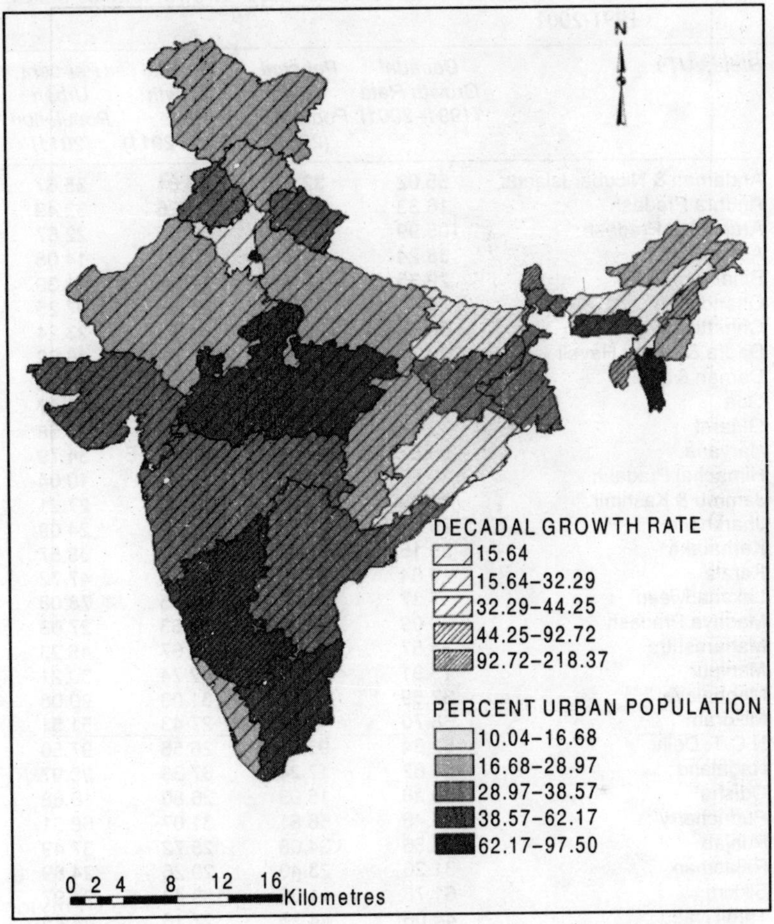

Map 1.5: INDIA: Decadal Urban Growth Rate and Level of Urbanisation 2001-2011

Compared to urban growth rates, the levels of urbanisation for all the States and UTs have increased. The developed areas also have recorded high degree of urbanisation, even though the growth rate has declined for these states. On the other hand, some states and UTs have also recorded increase in the level of urbanisation along with an increase in growth rate of urban population.

Table 1.9: India: Per cent Urban and Decadal Urban Growth Rate by States, 1991-2001

States/UTs	*Decadal Growth Rate (1991–2001)*	*Per cent Urban Population (2001)*	*Decadal Growth Rate (2001–2011)*	*Per cent Urban Population (2011)*
Andaman & Nicobar Islands	55.02	32.62	16.64	35.67
Andhra Pradesh	16.33	27.48	36.26	33.49
Arunachal Pradesh	105.99	20.89	37.55	22.67
Assam	38.24	12.91	27.61	14.08
Bihar	29.35	10.48	35.11	11.30
Chandigarh	40.41	89.74	26.86	97.25
Chhattisgarh	36.58	20.13	41.83	23.24
Dadra & Nagar Haveli	330.39	22.89	216.73	46.62
Daman & Diu	20.62	36.28	218.37	75.16
Goa	39.78	49.89	35.15	62.17
Gujarat	32.88	37.41	35.83	42.58
Haryana	50.82	29.01	44.25	34.79
Himachal Pradesh	32.59	9.80	15.64	10.04
Jammu & Kashmir	40.29	24.99	35.66	27.21
Jharkhand	29.14	22.27	32.29	24.05
Karnataka	29.15	34.06	31.27	38.57
Kerala	7.64	25.97	92.72	47.72
Lakshadweep	-7.37	44.50	86.55	78.08
Madhya Pradesh	30.09	26.44	25.63	27.63
Maharashtra	34.57	42.48	23.67	45.23
Manipur	13.91	24.11	42.74	30.21
Meghalaya	37.59	19.69	31.03	20.08
Mizoram	38.70	49.49	27.43	51.51
N.C.T. Delhi	52.34	93.64	26.56	97.50
Nagaland	64.62	17.24	67.38	28.97
Odisha	30.28	15.03	26.80	16.68
Puducherry	25.46	66.61	31.07	68.31
Punjab	37.86	34.08	25.72	37.49
Rajasthan	31.26	23.40	29.26	24.89
Sikkim	61.78	11.08	153.43	24.97
Tamil Nadu	44.06	44.25	27.16	48.45
Tripura	29.41	17.10	76.08	26.18
Uttar Pradesh	32.99	20.80	28.75	22.28
Uttarakhand	33.35	25.70	41.86	30.55
West Bengal	19.88	27.96	29.90	31.89

Source: Census of India, 1991, 2001, 2011 *(provisional population totals)*

Conclusions

Though the history of urbanisation can be traced back to the advent of early civilisation in India, rapid urbanisation is a feature of the recent decades only. India is at a transitional level of urbanisation with large scale variations in the trend and pattern of urbanisation over the decades and also across the states. There is an increase in number of towns and cities over the decades, though the level of urbanisation is still low compared to the Western standards and even among certain Asian countries. Maximum concentration of urban population is limited to the Class I cities, metropolises and mega cities. Thus, India's urbanisation follows top-heavy pattern, or can be said to be lopsided when compared across the various size classes of urban centres.

Urbanisation in India is mainly a product of demographic explosion and poverty induced rural to urban migration dominated by distress. The rural to urban migration is a result of rural push rather than urban pull where the rural areas due to their stagnation result in higher incidence of poverty, compelling population to move towards urban areas and large cities in particular. This leads to higher concentration of population in a few cities and command of a large proportion of population over limited resources thus resulting in a decline in the standards of city life and giving rise to urban poverty, deprivation, unemployment and the multiplication of slum and squatter settlements within the cities.

Many cities experiencing over-urbanisation have reached a saturation level where further influx of population has a detrimental effect. The spilling over of population in large cities has led to urban sprawl, beyond the municipal limits of the city and has fostered suburbanisation. Metropolises of Kolkata and Mumbai have already reached their level of saturation and this has resulted in insurmountable problems for the city dwellers. This uneven growth of urban population is mainly due to concentration of economic activities only in a few urban centres. The policy implications of such processes urgently calls for upgrading the overall developmental process in the backward regions and thereby reducing existing regional disparities so as to induce if not equal but proper and dispersed urban growth and level of urbanisation in the country.

REFERENCES

Bhagat, R.B. (2004): "Dynamics of Urban Population Growth By Size-Class Of Towns And Cities In India", *Demography India*, Vol. 33 No. 1 (Jan.-June), pp. 47-60.

Bhagat, R.B. (2008): '*Trends and Patterns of India's Urbanisation: A Demographic Assessment*', Annual Meeting of Population Association of America, New Orleans, U.S.A., 16-19 April, 2008.

Breese, G. (1969): *Urbanisation in Newly Developing Countries*, Prentice Hall, New Delhi.

Data, P. (2006): Urbanisation In India, Regional and Sub-Regional Population Dynamics, Population Process in Urban Areas, European Population Conference, 21-24th June, 2006.

Davis Kingsley (1962): "Urbanisation in India—Past and Future", in Turner, R. (ed.) *India's Urbcn Future*, University of California Press, Berkley.

Dutt, A.K., Charles, B. Monroe, Ramesh Vakamudi (1986): 'Rural-Urban Correlates for Indian Urbanisation', *Geographic Review*, Vol. 76, No. 2, Thematic Issue Asian Urbanisation (April, 1986) pp. 173-183.

Kundu, A. (1983): "Theories of City Size Distribution and Indian Urban Structure—A Reappraisal", *Economic and Political Weekly*, 18(3).

Kundu, A. (2001): *Trends and Processes of Urbanisation in India*, IIED and UNFPA 2011.

Mohan, R. (1985): 'Urbanisation in India's Future', *Population and Development Review*, Vol. 11, No. 4 (Dec., 1985), pp. 619-645.

Shaw, A. (1999): Emerging Patterns of Urban Growth in India, *Economic and Political Weekly*, Vol. 34, No. 16/17 (April 17-30, 1999), pp. 969-978.

Sivaramakrishnan, K.C., Amitabh Kundu, B.N.Singh, "*Handbook of Urbanisation in India: An Analysis of Trends and Processes*", Oxford University Press 2005.

Sovani, N.V. (1966): *Urbanisation and Urban India*, Asia Publishing House, Bombay.

2

Spatio-Temporal Characteristics of Urbanisation in Jharkhand

Debjani Roy

Introduction

Urbanisation is the most important socio-economic component of modernity. Today urbanisation is a worldwide phenomenon. Every nation, every city and probably every individual in the world is directly or indirectly involved in the continuing process of urbanisation which is transforming the world rapidly. Urbanisation refers to the process by which a section of people change from the way of agricultural operations in rural living to an urban sub-agricultural life with predominance of secondary and tertiary functions. Thus, urbanisation is a dynamic socio-economic force which involves an urban element that exhibits considerable temporal and spatial variations.

The population figures for Census 2011 show a quantum growth in urban population in India. After 1921 this is the first Census in which the growth of urban population has outstripped the decadal population increase in rural areas. The decadal growth of the urban population was projected at 31.08 per cent, which was much higher than the overall decadal population growth of 17.64 per cent. The increasing rate of urbanisation is also indicated by the unexpected increase in the number of towns from 5161 in 2001 to 7935 in 2011, i.e. a decadal growth of 53.7 per cent. In conventional wisdom, urbanisation has often been equated with economic growth and progress. But such an interpretation of these trends is far from the reality that faces India today.

Jharkhand: The State

Carved out of Bihar, the State of Jharkhand came into existence on 15th November, 2000. It is one of the smaller states of India which is situated in the eastern part of the Indian peninsular plateau. Its population in 2011 has been estimated to be 32.9 million of which 7.9 million are urban. 75 per cent of the population resides in rural areas. On the urban map of India Jharkhand stands among the last ten, considering the number and population of million plus cities and urban agglomerations. Among the 53 major urban agglomerations in India in 2011, only Jamshedpur ranked 33rd with 12,71,441 people, Dhanbad ranked 34th with12, 28,229 people and Ranchi ranked 41st with 10,93,610 people. Jharkhand is one of the poorest and most backward states in the country with low per capita income of INR 30719 only and 54 per cent of the population lives below the poverty line.

Objectives

The chapter endeavours to illuminate on the spatio-temporal growth of urban centres in Jharkhand with emphasis on level and tempo of urbanisation using Indian Census data during the period 1901-2001 and Provisional Census of 2011. The chapter seeks to analyse the trend of urbanisation in the state leading to a near about urban explosion in the capital city. The changing structure of urban population across different size categories of urban centres and a subsequent shift of growth dynamics to first order cities has also been studied and analysed.

Indicators

In order to understand the demographic and geographical dimension of urbanisation in Jharkhand the following indicators have been considered:

1. *Percentage of urban population to total population*—This shows the level of urbanisation in an area.
2. *Decadal growth rate*—This provides the change in urban population in percentage related to the base year.
3. *Percentage of population in Class I cities*—This indicates the dominance of large towns in the process of urbanisation compared to medium and small towns.

History of Urban Growth in Jharkhand

Jharkhand, though relatively a new state has a long urban history sketched over a few centuries. The physical characteristics of this region, however, have always been a hindrance in the way of rapid urbanisation. The rugged terrain full of residual hills with virtually vertical slopes, dense tropical forests have made this region inaccessible in more ways than one. Hence, when great empires were being established in the northern plains of Bihar, Jharkhand, then a part of the above mentioned state remained largely undisturbed. In the medieval period sacred towns of "Pava" and "Deogarh" emerged as places for pilgrims of Jain and Hindu faith. Towns like Garhwa emerged with the advent of the British, the main reason being the nodal location on the convergence of three principal land routes. Another ancient town is Palamu which grew up as a place of strategic importance. Chatra was made the military headquarters by the British in1780 A.D. and later made the administrative headquarters of Hazaribagh district. For a long time however, this town served as an important trading centre but with the construction of railways the direction of trade was diverted and Chatra lost its significance. Hazaribagh owes its existence to the rising of Ramgarh Battalion in 1780 A.D. This town was planned with roads meeting at right angles. Lohardaga developed as the administrative headquarters of Principal Assistant to Agent to the Governor General in1834 and flourished as an administrative town till 1843, when the divisional headquarters were shifted to Ranchi. Daltonganj was established by Colonel Dalton, the Commissioner of Chotanagpur in1862 to serve as headquarters of old division of Palamu. Chaibasa, emerged in 1820 as a place of strategic importance under the British. Chaibasa grew as an administrative town and was declared a town in India's first official Census of 1872. Since, then it has never lost its town status though its growth rate was slow compared to other towns of Singhbhum like Jamshedpur.

It is interesting to note here that all the above mentioned towns dwindled in importance with the passage of town with the exception of Ranchi which became the administrative capital of the State and Jamshedpur remains till date an important industrial city of India.

Trend and Pattern of Urban Growth

Over the years there has been continuous concentration of population in Class I towns. On the contrary concentration of population in medium and small towns either fluctuated or declined (Kundu, 1994).This phenomenon is evident in Jharkhand too. The process of urbanisation began slowly with the setting up of single isolated centres which over the years gained momentum as is evident from the continuous rise of urban population over the past century.

However, the first half of the nineteenth century was the dawn of modern urbanisation. Towns like Chaibasa, Ranchi, Dumka and Lohardaga were established before 1837 mainly due to the initiative of the British. But their urban growth rate was nearly insignificant. Hazaribagh, Chatra and Ranchi were the only towns that got official status of towns in 1872 Census. During this period, Ranchi, Hazaribagh, Chaibasa and Daltonganj were district headquarters and Chatra, Deogarh, Sahibganj and Garhwa were subdivisional headquarters. All these petty urban pockets had bazaars besides serving as administrative headquarters.

The 1891 Census recorded an urban decadal increase of 4.5 per cent over the urban population of 1881 Census. Garhwa recorded a negative growth rate of –7.3 per cent was declassified from the town list. Daltonganj and Chatra also recorded negative population growth as –30.2 per cent and –9.4 per cent respectively. Epidemics and famines were responsible for this as were anomalies in the Census procedure. In 1872 only 1.13 per cent of the population was recorded as urban which rose to 1.89 per cent by 1901. During the period 1891 to 1901 three new towns like Giridih, Madhupur and Bundu were added to the list of towns and Garhwa regained its town status. During this period towns like Sahibganj, Lohardaga, Hazaribagh and Chatra registered a decrease in population while Ranchi and Chaibasa registered a 25 per cent increase. In 1911 Census, Jamshedpur, Dumka and Rajmahal were added to the list of urban centres. Chatra again registered a decline while rate of increase in Sahibganj was the highest at 95.6 per cent.

In 1921, the State recorded an unbelievable increase of 58.62 per cent in urban population mainly due to increase in population of newly born town of Jamshedpur. In 1931, the urban growth rate of towns showed a considerable increase with Chakradharpur, Dhanbad and Jamshedpur recording very high population growth. It was during this period that Jugsalai, in the neighbourhood of Jamshedpur also emerged as a town (Fig. 2.1).

In 1941, several mining towns like Jharia, Bermo, Kargali, Bokaro, Noamundi, Mosabani and Saraikela came up while Garhwa and Lohardaga registered a decline in population. Jamshedpur emerged as a Class I town in 1941with population crossing the one lakh mark. After 1951, urban growth has been particularly significant. Several new towns came up in the areas of coal, iron-ore and mica mines.

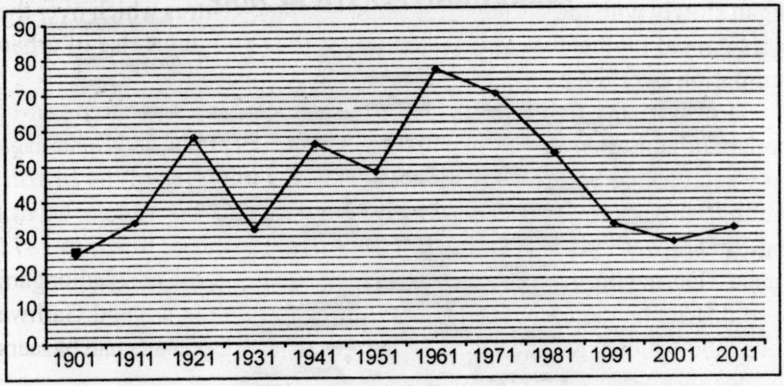

Fig. 2.1: Jharkhand: Decadal Variation of Urban Population

The 1961 Census recorded a decennial increase of 77.8 per cent with the emergence of 30 new towns. Between 1951 and 1961 Sindri recorded an increase of 216.7 per cent due to expansion of fertilizer factory and establishment of thermal power plant. Jhumri Tilaiya also recorded a large growth in urban population due to expansion of mica mining and trade. During the period 1971-81urbanisation became a cumulative product of rural-urban migration, natural increase, emergence of new towns, the extension of territorial jurisdiction of many existing towns and overall development process. The state recorded an increase in urban population to the extent of 70.82 per cent respectively mainly due to the setting up of steel plant at Bokaro in 1973.

But in 1991 urban growth declined from 53 per cent to 33.18 per cent, the lowest being recorded by Jamshedpur and the highest being Bokaro. This was the first Census after bifurcation of the district. Population growth too registered a decline during the decade of 1991-2001. Urban growth had also reached a point of stagnation with places like Khunti registering the lowest growth. The same place recorded very high growth in the very next decade after it was bifurcated from Ranchi district. Thus, it is the elevation of an urban centre to the status of district headquarters which provided impetus for growth. Between 1991 and 2001 Dhanbad topped the districts in the number of urban centres (41Census towns) followed by West Singhbhum with 17 towns. Mining and manufacturing activities were key factors that led to the growth of urban

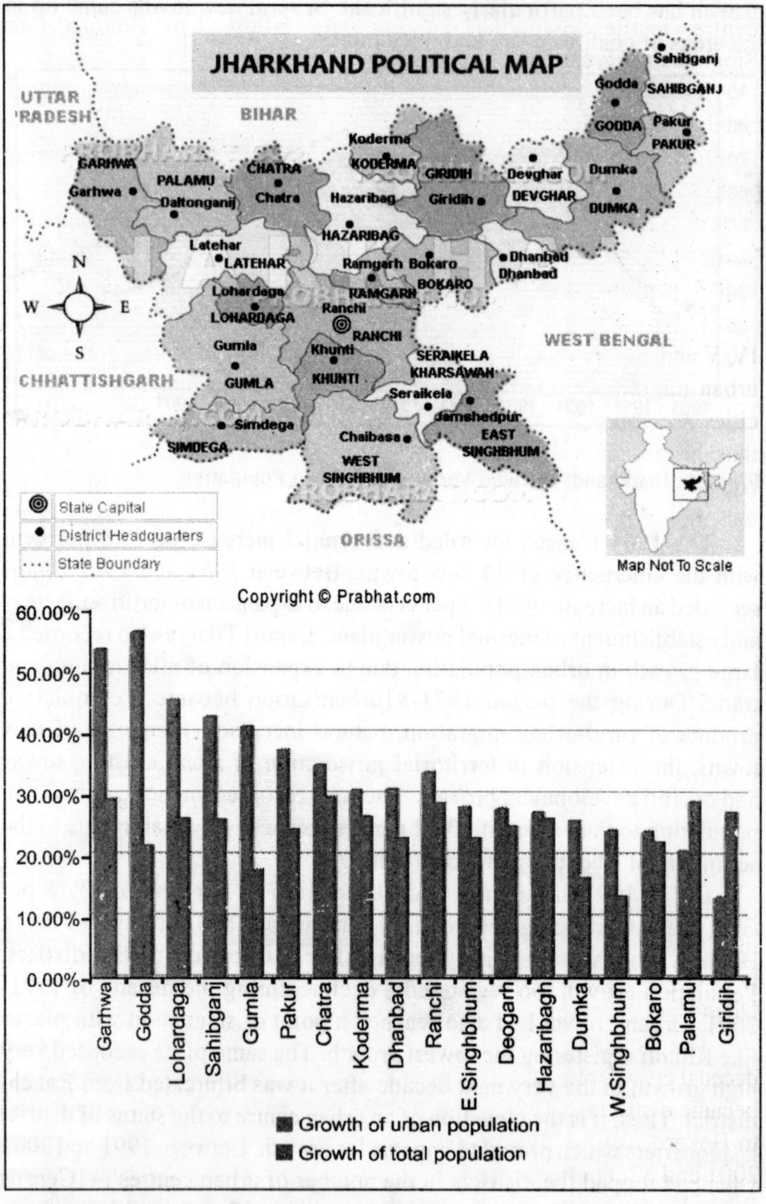

Fig 2.2: Jharkhand: Districtwise Growth 1991-2001

centres in these two districts. This was followed by Bokaro, East Singhbhum, Hazaribagh and Ranchi.

It is indeed interesting to note that urban growth registered a marginal decline in the decade 1991-2001. Districts like Palamu and Giridih recorded very little urban growth (Fig. 2.2).Garhwa, Godda, Sahibganj and Gumla registered high growth of urban population mainly due to inflow of migrants from Bihar. According to 2001 Census, Jharkhand had 152 towns of which 108 were Census towns. The number of towns registered gradual increase from 65 in 1961 to 170 in 2011.

There were only 10 Class I towns and 56 small towns belonging to IV, V and VI Class in 2001. Smaller towns are less attractive for rural to urban migrants so population accretion is high in Class I to Class III cities and towns. Class V and VI towns were not growing rapidly and thus the process was not rooted within the transformation of rural society. Actually, the function of most small towns is essentially that of serving the rural surroundings as market and service centres. The first Class I city that emerged in the urban map of Jharkhand was Jamshedpur followed by Ranchi. Thus it was industrialisation which ushered the growth of large cities and towns. However, cities and towns at present are growing more on the basis of tertiary sector rather than the secondary sector. Of the 18 districts that were formed after the creation of Jharkhand, Dhanbad recorded the highest urban growth followed by East Singhbhum, Ranchi and Bokaro.

The situation changed during 2001-2011 when Jharkhand registered a population growth of 22.34 per cent which was higher than the national average of 17.64 per cent. Khunti which was carved out of Ranchi district registered a growth of 21.9 per cent mainly due to its elevation into a district town and several administrative powers associated with it. As per the Provisional Census of 2011, there are 170 urban centres, the decadal growth for urban centres being 32.29 per cent of which Jamshedpur, Dhanbad, Ranchi and Bokaro top the list.

The situation is slightly different in Koderma which registered a decadal growth rate of 32.5 per cent in 2011. Koderma, Chatra and Bokaro became districts in 1991 and Koderma lost some of its urban population to Bokaro, yet the district registered a growth rate of 30.7 per cent in 2001 and 32.5 per cent in 2011 mainly due to inflow of population from Bihar. Koderma has only two major towns in the district, viz. Koderma and Jhumri Tilaiya which implies that the population is concentrated in these two urban centres (Fig. 2.2).

A comparison of the decadal variation over the last two decades reveals that population growth has been sporadic, bearing a chequered character over space. While the overall growth rate has gone down from 23.4 per cent to 22.3 per cent, the district with highest urban population, i.e Dhanbad, registered the least growth in the decade 2001-2011. It may be due to a lull in industrial activity in this region during the last decade. Ranchi, the capital registered maximum growth (8.9%) in the last decade. This further reiterates the fact that urban growth in the state is largely concentrated in large cities. An interesting observation is the population

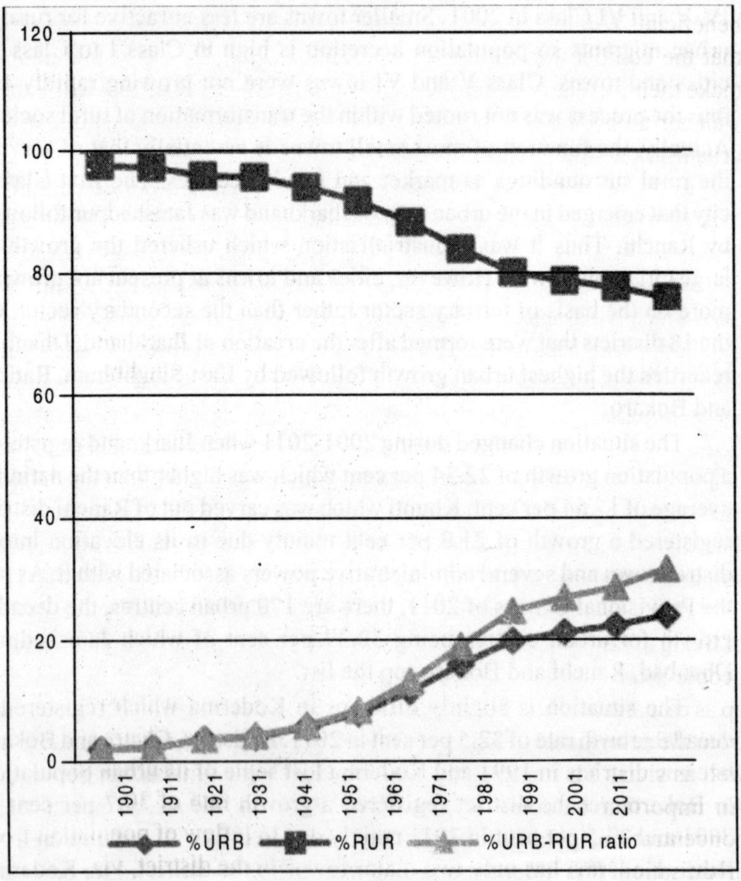

Fig. 2.3: Jharkhand: Degree of Urbanisation

growth in Koderma, erstwhile an important mining hub and presently attracting migrants from the adjoining district of Giridih which is affected by subversive activities and political unrest. It may also be mentioned here that Koderma is an important nodal centre and the intersection point of major roads. The district is also well connected by rail routes with the rest of North India.

Impact of Urbanisation in Jharkhand

Urbanisation brings with it several consequences—both adverse and beneficial. While it is true that opportunities exist in cities, it is also true that the competition for these opportunities is fierce. Very few people make their fortunes, and the rest must still find ways to subsist while they wait for their chance. This leads to one of the most obvious effects of urbanisation—the growth of slums.

In the resource rich State of Jharkhand, where corporate capital is looking to exploit natural resources, the rate of growth of urban population is not as high as that of Maharashtra, Gujarat, Andhra Pradesh or Karnataka. There has been sufficient corporate penetration within the state which is extractive in character. Here dispossession and displacement is taking place because of the exploitation of cheap raw materials and labour. The dispossession is likely to lead to migration and the growth of urban population in other states. Such migration is hardly ever captured in Census but several field studies show how female tribal and *dalit* labour is forced into seasonal migration, especially in industries like brick kilns and in other casual work. Some other routine features of urbanisation in Jharkhand are political violence and antagonism between the sons of the soil and outsiders.

There is an increasing competition for facilities due to high standard of living in urban areas which has triggered several negative effects. Many people including farmers move to cities in search of better life and end up as casual labourers. In Ranchi there is a daily inflow of 20,000 labourers from the nearby area. This has led to the growth of floating population as well as slums for many of the migrants who do not return immediately. An important outcome of urban growth is the degree of population concentration in large cities. This is a manifestation of top heavy urbanisation. It is indeed interesting to note that the three larger cities of the state have recorded a growth of 65 per cent during the period 1951-2001.

Another aspect that requires closer scrutiny is the gendered nature of the urban population growth. Provisional figures of 2011 Census indicate that the decadal increase in the female urban population was 33.73 per cent as compared 30.06 per cent increase in the population of urban males. In Jharkhand too it was as high as 35.32 per cent indicating a high percentage of decadal growth of urban female population. This figure does not reveal much in itself, but makes sense when we see the difference between the urban male and female population growth percentages in Jharkhand that is 14.55 per cent. Such differentials may indicate that women from surrounding regions are coming to urban areas, not merely because of marriage but also for other reasons that are not generally reflected in Census figures. One explanation for this burgeoning growth of female urban population may be simply that the number of females born in the urban areas is more than that of the males. But this explanation does not hold much weight as it comes in the wake of a dipping child sex ratio in the urban areas from 906 to 902 per thousand. In contrast to this the increase in the imbalances sex ratio by residence is an alarming 26 per cent. The growth rate of females in urban centres is 35.32 per cent, i.e. much more than males which is 29.66 per cent. One positive outcome of increasing urban population in Jharkhand was a rise in literacy rate. Urban literacy stood at 83.30 per cent. Sex ratio too improved in the state with rural sex ratio being 960 and urban being 908.The overall sex ratio stood at 947 against a national average of only 940.

Conclusions

The trend and pattern of urbanisation in Jharkhand are very different from the model of urban development backed up by indigenous industrialisation and modernisation as propagated by neo-classical economists. Urbanisation in Jharkhand is slow but significant with 25 per cent urban population in 2011.The cities are bursting at the seams to accommodate a regular influx of people with population increasing one and a half times more than the villages in the last decade. The trend has been more to bigger centres as smaller centres have not turned into cities but have decayed gradually. Thus the trend of urbanisation which began with industrialisation in the previous decade lost its essence exposing the state's failure to ensure adequate growth of the rural economy. Dhanbad and East Singhbhum known for their industry and mining industry continued to register the highest urban growth while Godda bore the brunt of de-urbanisation with a marginal growth of merely 5 per cent urban population. The urban growth of Jharkhand was due to the "push factor" sending rural masses into urban centres. It is an example of unorganised growth of cities which lack basic infrastructural facilities. The dilemma that plagues Jharkhand is that the administration has failed to provide six basic necessities in rural areas, namely food, clothing, housing, electricity, roads and drinking water thereby failing to check rural migration. A notable feature, however, is that tribal population does not seem keen to move to urban areas evident from Simdega, Lohardaga, Khunti and Latehar registering lowest urban growth. Similarly, tribal dominated Giridih and Palamu also had registered a very nominal urban growth.

Urban growth in Jharkhand has been rapid especially after its separation from the State of Bihar but almost all of these centres are plagued by problems like poor infrastructure, poor sanitation and sewerage conditions, insufficient transport and communication facilities, uncontrolled law and order and a high number of urban and white collar crimes. The entire State of Jharkhand is aflame with vertical construction to house its logarithmic increase in population. This has taken its toll on the environment leading to a process of environmental degradation. The State now needs to sit up and take notice of the rapidly crumbling infrastructure and implement the schemes offered for urban renewal and development.

REFERENCES

Bhagat, R.B. (1992): Components of Urban growth in India with reference to Haryana. Findings from Recent Censuses, *Nagarlok*, Vol. 25, No. 3, pp. 10-14.

Breese, G. (1969): *Urbanisation in Newly Developing Countries*, Prentice Hall, New Delhi.

Forbes, D. & Lindfield, M. (1997): *Urbanisation in Asia: Lesson Learned and . Innovative Responses*, Aus Aid, Canberra.

Kingsley, D. (1962): "Urbanisation in India—Past and Future" in Turner, R. (ed.) *India's Urban Future*, University of California Press, Berkley.

Kundu, A. (1983): "Theories of city size distribution and Indian urban structure-A Reappraisal", *Economic and Political Weekly*, 18(3).

Kundu, A. (1994): "Patterns of urbanisation with special reference to small and medium towns in India" in Chadda, G.K. (ed) *Sectoral Issues in Indian Economy*, Har Anand Publication, New Delhi.

Kundu, A. (1997): "Trends and structure of employment in the 1990s: Implication for Urban Growth" *Economic and Political Weekly*, 32(24).

Kundu, A. and Basu, S. (1998): "Informal Manufacturing Sector in Urban Areas—An analysis of recent trends", *Manpower Journal*, 43(1), April-June.

Kundu, A. (2009): Urbanisation and Migration: An analysis of trends patterns and policies in Asia, United Nations Development Programme, *Human Development Reports Research Paper 2009/16*.

Mohan Rakesh & Dasgupta, S. (2005): The 21st Century: Asia becomes urban", *Economic and Political Weekly*, Vol. 15, January.

Nachana, D.M. (ed) (2011): *India Development Report*, Oxford University Press, New Delhi.

Prasad, A., "Provisional Census findings", *People's Democracy*, Vol XXXV No. 4 October 2, 2010.

Registrar General (2001): Census of India, India, New Delhi.

Verma, V.S. (2006): *Urbanisation in Jharkhand: Past and Present*, Indian Geographical Foundation, Kolkata.

3

Urbanisation, Urban Growth and Urban Development in Bihar

Amit Kumar Singh

Introduction

In this age of urbanisation, the State of Bihar is still fundamentally rural. When half of the world's population and three-fourth of the population in developed countries have become urbanised, almost ninety per cent of Bihar's population dwells in rural areas. All other societal changes in the present times, for example, levels of economic development, industrialisation, character of the family and fertility situations, indeed civilisation itself, are contingent on the urban factor (Hall, 1998). Experiences of developed countries prove that urbanisation has close links with the process of economic development especially industrialisation. But the urbanisation process in developing regions, particularly in a State like Bihar conveys a completely different story. It is, therefore, imperative to probe into the exact reasons behind a region's underdevelopment; whether the backward traits of the rural areas or the non-availability of adequate basic infrastructure and amenities in urban areas stand as impediments, responsible for obstructing a state's development prospects. In case of Bihar, one of the underdeveloped states in India, it is an amalgamation of both the factors that have hindered any prospects of urbanisation.

The process of urbanisation, as defined by the various scholars is the movement of rural population to the urban areas. Taylor (1953) has used the term in the same way and stated that 'Urbanisation is a shift of people from village to city'. Ehrlich (1956) has defined urbanisation as a process of population concentration at the place, i.e. urban. Davis and Golden (1954) have also explained urbanisation in an elaborate way.

According to them, "urbanisation represents a revolutionary change in the whole pattern of social life and itself is a product of basic economic and technological developments." Prakasa Rao (1983) has expressed a similar thought about urbanisation and has also stated that urbanisation involves the transformation of rural attributes to urban ones, the concentration of people at a point and also the multiplication of points of concentration, i.e. urban settlements.

In view of these definitions and descriptions, the process of urbanisation in Bihar neither can be defined wholly as the shift of people from rural to urban areas nor is it a resultant of industrialisation and economic development. Actually urban growth taking place in Bihar is primarily out of the natural increase of urban population. According to 2001 Census, the decadal growth of urban population was 29.80 per cent and the share of natural increase of urban population to the total urban population growth was 60 per cent. As far as the contribution of industrialisation and economic development in the process of urbanisation is concerned, these factors definitely have not been able to accelerate the pace of urbanisation in the State. The economic growth rate of the State during the 1990s was lowest in India. During 1990s, in the non-agricultural sector, the growth rate of Bihar was only 3.19, while for India it was 7.25 per cent. This gets reflected in the per capita income as well. The per capita income of Bihar grew only 0.12 per cent as against 4.08 per cent in India during the same period.

Bihar is an agricultural State where agricultural and allied activities predominates the overall economy. The data for the sectoral distribution of workers (across primary, secondary and tertiary sectors) clearly indicates that until the present about 75 per cent of total workforce of the state is engaged in agriculture and allied activities as compared to 59.28 per cent for India. Likewise, the share of secondary sector is merely 8 per cent to the total workforce of Bihar. The services sector also is not well-developed in Bihar, as it generates only 17 per cent of employment. However, in 2005, the largest share of non-agricultural employment has been generated by the government sector. Overall, the State economy is not well-diversified, leaving little opportunities to the people for gainful employment. Therefore, it is impossible for the state to create additional employment opportunities for the surplus labour of rural areas.

While in many parts of the world, urbanisation is being accelerated by a new global economy, Bihar is struggling to get into this contemporary developmental race. While most of the cities from other states have been benefited by this global economic integration, cities and towns of Bihar remained isolated and depended on the leftovers from the rural economy. Bihar is a State that has been continuously experiencing out-migration of people to other states. People from small towns have been leaving the state to escape poverty and to secure any sort of employment in states like Delhi, Maharashtra, Gujarat and the like. In the long run, this large scale out-migration from the state will have an immeasurable socio-economic repercussion on the rural economy as it would create immense shortage of labour force.

Another primary reason for the low level of urbanisation in the State is the lack of investment in infrastructure and basic services, particularly in the urban areas. In general, piped water supply, telecommunications, sanitation and sewerage, solid waste management, piped gas, urban transport (road, railway, waterway and airport), power supply, health services, banks, post offices form the basic infrastructure and services for efficient functioning of a city (World Development Report, 1994). However, they are in poor condition in the State. Several other contributing factors, for instance, weak financial condition of Urban Local Bodies (ULBs), low access to credit, shortage of skilled urban planners, poor law and order, etc. are also adding to the problems that hinder the path of smooth urban development. If the towns and cities of Bihar do not enter the mainstream of national economic growth and prosperity, the state level performance and disparities will continue to widen significantly.

In the light of the above discussions and facts, the present study delineates the trends in the patterns and processes of urbanisation in Bihar. The analysis has been done by taking into consideration the changing economic development of the State. The first part of the study focus on the spatio-temporal context of urbanisation in Bihar. In the next part the factors influencing the urbanisation process of the state have been considered. Finally, an attempt has been made to place forward a perspective for infrastructural development that can bring about a balanced regional development in the State. The main objectives of the present study are to trace the temporal changes and the growth pattern of the urban centres, processes of urbanisation; to delineate the factors contributing to the industrial work force and migration and finally to analyse the status of physical and social infi astructure and basic amenities in the urban centres of the State.

Evolution and Growth of Urban Centres in Bihar

The State, particularly the central region of Bihar is one of the oldest cradle of Indian civilisation and contains many of the oldest towns of the country. This region has a long and rich tradition of urbanism. Therefore, a study of evolution and growth of urban centres of Bihar possibly raises several issues on urbanisation and urban development of India. A perusal of the progress in urbanisation is necessary to understand the nature and magnitude of the urban forces and processes operating in the region and also to discern the pattern of urban growth itself. Such a study might also be helpful in visualising the future prospects of urbanisation. The history of urbanisation in Bihar dates back to the post-Vedic period and the emergence of '*Janapadas*' and '*Mahajanpadas*' and their multiplication during the 'Mauryan' period which boosted the growth of urban centres. The ancient towns grew as seats of administration, centres of religion and as trading centres along the river banks or ancient highways. Patliputra, Champa (Bhagalpur), Vaishali and Rajgriha (Rajgir) have historical origins while Gaya and Deoghar rose into eminence because of their religious significance.

During the medieval period, most of the large urban centres of ancient period dwindled into insignificance either with the fall of a dynasty or with the shifting of the capital. However, the process of urbanisation was accelerated during the medieval period. During this period, few of the established towns grew in size while some large number of towns were added by local administrators and vassals. Urbanisation during this period was associated with three important facts. Firstly, the advent of Muslim rule gave great impetus to the establishment of a number of well-fortified regional headquarters of the Delhi Sultanate dynasties or the seats of ruling dynasties. Important among them were Buxar, Hajipur, Patna, Monghyr, Tughlaqpur (Darbhanga), Samsuddinipur (Samastipur), Bhagalpur, Teliagarh, Purnia, Rajmahal and so on. Secondly, most of the towns grew and developed as a result of increasing trade and exchange between the states and towns.

The process of urbanisation was again accelerated during British period and large number of towns developed for administrative purpose. Some of them were Chapra, Manihari, Naugachhia, Lalganj, Rosera, Khagaria, Arrah, Sasaram, etc. During this period establishment of rail transport and improvement in roads had considerably enhanced the urbanisation process in the state. Several towns were developed in this period, like Katihar, Barauni, Maharajganj, Mirganj, Siwan, Chanpatia, Tighra, Narkatiaganj, and Forbesganj. In 1901 Census, 44 settlements were counted as towns in Bihar.

Figure 3.1 indicates the growth pattern in the number of towns of Bihar since 1901. Bihar has witnessed four types of growth pattern.

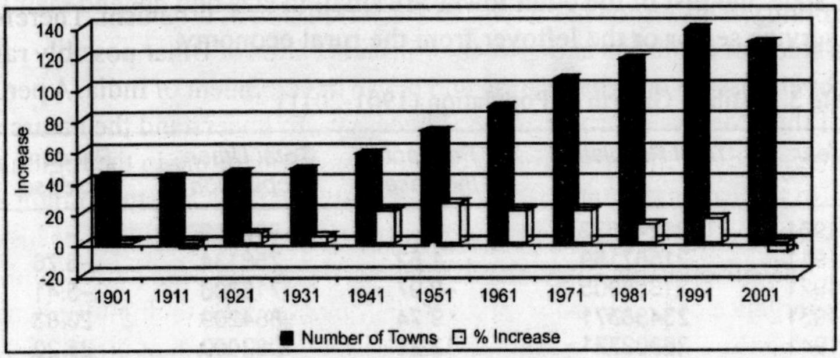

Fig. 3.1: Bihar: Progress in Number of Towns (1901-2001)
Source: Census of India, General Population Tables, Bihar, 1991 and 2001.

(1) During 1901-1911 the number of towns decreased from 44 to 43. During this period Patna was the main administrative and commercial centre of the State and it was the only Class I city of Bihar till 1931. (2) In the next two decades, the number of towns remained almost constant. There were 43 towns in 1911 Census which increased only to 48 in 1931 Census. (3) During 1931-91, the number of towns increased rapidly. For instance in the year 1931 there were 48 towns in Bihar which rose to 73 in 1952, 106 in 1971 and 138 in 1991. In 1941, Gaya became the second Class I city of the State. After that the number of Class I cities continuously increased in each Census period and it increased to 11 in the 2001 Census. (4) Post 1991, there was a decline in the number of towns in Bihar and the number reduced to 130 in 2001, but the number of Class I cities rose to 20.

Population Growth and the Processes of Urbanisation

Bihar is the third largest populated State of India. It comprises a total population of over 103.81 million in the recently declared 2011 Census. Though it has many important urban centres that have flourished from time to time since 6th century B.C., it is still predominantly a rural state even in this 21st century. Interestingly, when Jharkhand was a part of the Bihar State, many of the industrial centres were established in different parts of the State, such as Dhanbad, Jamshedpur, Ranchi, Bokaro, etc. In 1991, the level of urbanisation of combined Bihar and Jharkhand was 13.8 per cent. But after the bifurcation of the State in 2000, the level of urbanisation has gone down to 10 per cent. Furthermore, in 2011 Census, it has been only 10.45 per cent. At present, Patna is the only major city of the State and rest of the other towns are small in size and depend mainly on service sector or the leftover from the rural economy.

Table 3.1: Bihar: Growth in Population (1901-2011)

Year	*Total Population*	*Per cent Increase*	*Total Urban Population*	*Per cent Increase*
1901	21243632	–	802308	–
1911	21567159	1.52	756134	–5.76
1921	21358905	–0.97	715206	–5.41
1931	23438371	9.74	864209	20.83
1941	26302771	12.22	1082000	25.20
1951	29085017	10.58	1454168	34.40
1961	34840968	19.79	1995595	37.23
1971	42126236	20.91	3346240	67.68
1981	52302665	24.16	5151100	53.94
1991	64530554	23.38	6688718	29.85
2001	82998509	28.62	8681800	29.80
2011	103804637	25.07	11729609	35.11

Source: Census of India, General Population Tables, Bihar, 1991 and 2001.

Urban population of Bihar has increased from 0.8 million in 1901 to 1.2 million in 1951 and to 10.4 million in 2011, thereby exhibiting more than fourteen fold increase in the total urban population. On the other hand, the total population of the state has increased five fold from 21.24 million to 103.8 million during 1901-2011. If a comparison is made between the total population growth rate of Bihar and India it can be observed that except few decades, the rate of population growth of India was always higher than Bihar. Fig. 3.2 shows that except 1911-21 and 1991-2001 in all other decades the total population growth rate of India was always higher than Bihar. But after 1991, the total population of Bihar increased sharply and the rate of population growth reached to 28.62 per cent in 2001. It was one of the highest rates among all the major States of India.

However, there are considerable differences between the urban population growth of Bihar with that of India's average urban growth. The urban population growth in Bihar has commenced in a haphazard manner. In the beginning of the 20th century, the population of urban Bihar was 0.8 million which reduced to 0.75 million in 1911 and further declined to 0.71 million in 1921 Census. Therefore, Bihar experienced negative growth rate in terms of its urban population during the first two consecutive decades; i.e. -5.76 per cent during 1901-1911 and -5.41 per cent during 1911-1921 (Fig. 3.2). Up to 1951, the urban growth rate of Bihar has always been lower than that of urban India. After that, there has been a sharp increase in Bihar's urban population and during 1951-61, for the first time Bihar recorded a higher urban growth rate than urban India which was 67.38 per cent during 1961-71; while during the same period India's urban population growth rate was only 38.23 per cent. Since then, there was significant decline in urban population growth rate in Bihar during 1981-91 and 1991-2001 to 28.58 and 28.80 per cent respectively.

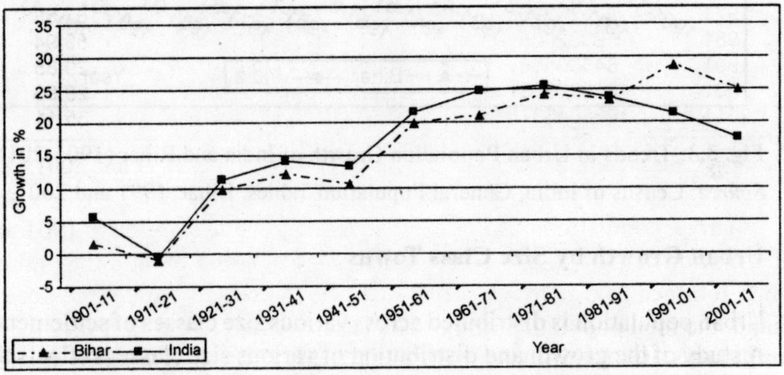

Fig. 3.2: Growth of Population: India and Bihar (1901-2011)

Source: Census of India, General Population Tables, Bihar, 1991 and 2001.

This was the period when Bihar witnessed very low levels of economic development compared to most of the states in India. Since, 1991-92, after the adoption of new economic policy, while the overall industrial sector in the country saw a surge in industrial sector outputs and productivity, Bihar was not benefited precisely on account of its weak infrastructure and dysfunctional support institutions. Therefore, most of the towns/cities as well as their hinterlands failed to attain accelerated urbanisation in Bihar. Nevertheless, since last five to seven years, the economy of Bihar has shown considerable growth in three sectors, viz. construction, communications and trade, hotels and restaurants. Hence, the growth of GSDP in Bihar during 2004-05 to 2008-09 recorded 11.35 per cent which was much higher than what it was during the preceding five years. This has been one of the important reasons behind Bihar recording a much faster growth in the urban population during the last decade.

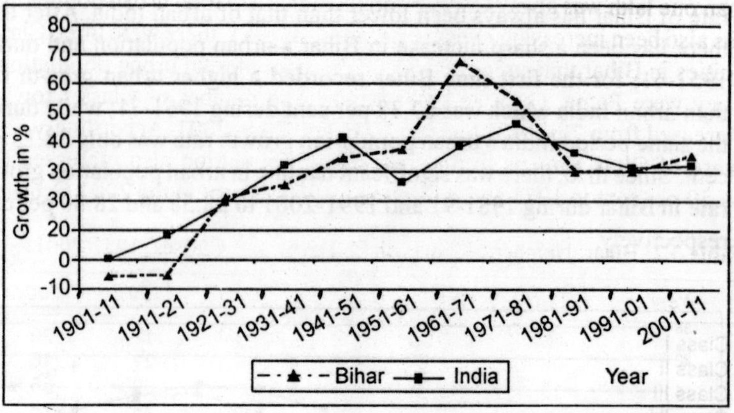

Fig. 3.3: Trends in Urban Population Growth of India and Bihar (1901-2011)
Source: Census of India, General Population Tables, Bihar, 1991 and 2001.

Urban Growth by Size Class Towns

Urban population is distributed across various size classes of settlements. A study of the growth and distribution of various size classes reflects the changing socio-economic setting of the region and also that of the towns and cities. For instance, higher concentration of population in a town and city reflects the growing importance of that particular town or city in that particular region, either through creating better employment and economic opportunities for the migrant population or through the provision of different basic services and infrastructural facilities.

In Bihar, the number of urban centres has been small compared to other neighbouring states. In 1901, there were only 44 towns in Bihar. In the 1951 Census, the number of towns increased to 68. This indicates, in the first 50 years of twentieth century, only 24 new towns have been able to evolve in Bihar. The number of towns grew from 86 in 1971 to 138 in 2001. But, in 2001 Census this number declined to 130. The distribution and growth of different size towns is given in Table 3.2.

In the Indian Census, the urban centres have been classified into six categories—Class-I to Class-VI based on the size of the towns. Table 3.2 and Table 3.3 indicate the number and percentage of population living in different size class towns/cities of Bihar. In general, across the world, people tend to live in large agglomerations. Bihar is no exception in that respect. Since 1951, the share of large towns having population more than one lakh was always higher and their share to total urban population has also been increasing over the decades. In 1951, there were three Class I cities in Bihar that supported 31.02 per cent of total urban population. They were Patna, Gaya and Bhagalpur. The number of Class I towns increased from 7 in 1971 to 11 in 1981 and 20 in 2001. Accordingly, the share of Class I towns to the total urban population also increased to 45.59 per cent in 1971 and it became 59.20 per cent in the 2001 Census.

Table 3.2: Bihar: Number of Towns in Different Size Classes (1951-2001)

Year	*1951*	*1961*	*1971*	*1981*	*1991*	*2001*
Class I	3	5	7	11	11	20
Class II	6	6	7	11	21	16
Class III	13	23	18	45	59	66
Class IV	28	32	39	39	38	25
Class V	17	18	14	8	6	3
Class VI	1	1	1	0	3	0
Total	68	85	86	114	138	130

Source: Census of India, General Population Tables, Bihar, 1991 and 2001.

The population of Class II towns showed a fluctuating trend, there were 6 Class II towns in 1951 which had 22.92 per cent of the total urban population. Though, the number increased to 7 in 1971 and 21 in 1991, the share of Class II towns to the total urban population had reduced considerably over these decades. In 1971 only 10.67 per cent of State's urban population was residing in Class II towns. However, there were some increase in their share to the total urban population in 1991 (21.12%), but it decreased again in 2001 (14.25%). On the other hand the number and population of Class III towns had shown an increasing trend during 1951-1991. In 1951 there was only 13 Class III towns that comprised 17.21 per cent of urban population of the State. In 1971, the number of Class III towns increased to 39 and in 1991 this became 38. Since then, the number of Class III towns decreased to 25 but their share in the total urban population remained constant (23.09%). Again, in the case of Class IV and Class V towns, the percentage share to total urban population decreased in each Census. For example, in 1951, there were 19.65 per cent of urban population of the state living in Class IV towns, but it came down to 15.30 per cent in 1971, 6.18 per cent in 1991 and 3.23 per cent in 2001. In the same way the share of Class V towns reduced from 8.25 per cent in 1951 to 4.46 per cent in 1971 and 0.23 per cent in 2001, out of the total urban population in the State.

Table 3.3: Bihar: Percentage of Population in Different Size Class Town (1971-2001)

Classes	1951	1961	1971	1981	1991	2001
Class I	31.02	37.30	45.59	49.68	50.88	59.20
Class II	22.92	17.44	10.67	14.78	21.12	14.25
Class III	17.21	21.27	23.53	23.02	26.53	23.09
Class IV	19.65	18.32	15.30	11.30	6.18	3.23
Class V	8.25	5.37	4.76	1.19	0.81	0.23
Class VI	0.96	0.29	0.15	0.02	0.44	0.00
All Classes	100.00	100.00	100.00	100.00	105.95	100.00

Source: Census of India, General Population Table, Bihar, 1991 and 2001.

So it can be said that the pattern of urbanisation has been completely governed by Class-I cities, and hence most of the population of the State prefer to live in relatively bigger urban centres. This is also the reason behind the higher growth rate of Class I cities as compared to the smaller towns of the Bihar. It can be also pointed out that Class-I cities have been growing at the cost of other size classes of towns, and their growth has been much faster than other cities and towns in the State. Also, the development activities whatsoever have been taking place, have been concentrated in the larger cities and towns of Bihar, a prime example being Patna.

Degree of Urbanisation

Degree of urbanisation or the level of urbanisation is the proportion of the population living in urban areas. Geographers consider urbanisation in relation to urban spaces and see proportion and growth of urban population in different spatial contexts (Basyal, 2001). It is one of the most important characteristics of urbanisation. In case of Bihar as well as India, the change in the level of urbanisation is quite distinctive.

The decadal change in the level of urbanisation in Bihar and India is shown in Fig. 3.4. In 1901, the level of urbanisation in Bihar was only 3.8 per cent, which slightly increased to 5 per cent in 1951. On the other hand, during the same period, for overall India, this value had increased from 10.8 per cent to 17.3 per cent. The situation did change to some extent during 1951-1981 when Bihar's level of urbanisation increased from 5 per cent to 9.8 per cent. Since, then very less increment has taken place in the following three decades. In 2011, it has only reached to 11.3 per cent whereas it galloped to 31.2 per cent in case of India. It is

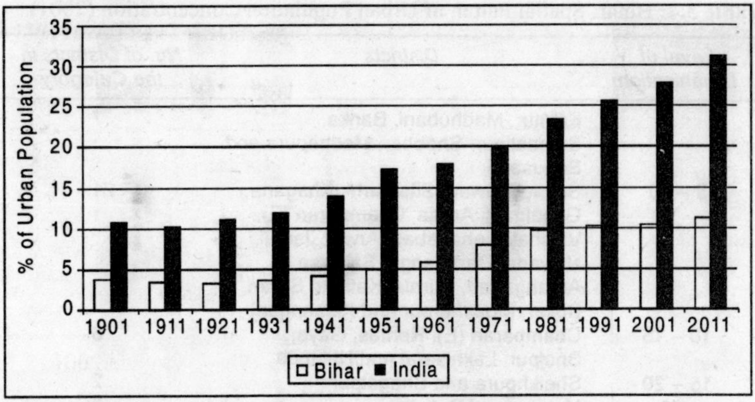

Fig. 3.4: Level of Urbanisation: Bihar and India (1901-2011)

Source: Census of India, General Population Table, Bihar, 1991 and 2001.

unfortunate that Bihar surpassed 10.5 per cent level of urbanisation in 2001 which India did in the year 1901, thus highlighting the fact that Bihar is a century behind in terms of levels of urbanisation when compared to the national average.

Spatial Pattern of Concentration of Urban Population

As mentioned earlier, the concentration of population in cities and towns depends greatly on the economic structure, functional characteristics, employment opportunities and availability of infrastructure and services. However, in many cases the ecological setting of the settlement and their relationship with the hinterland cannot be undermined. In fact, the spatial pattern of urbanisation is the mirror of development across the geographical space. In case of Bihar, though the level of urbanisation is very low in most of the districts, still, there are few districts which have comparatively higher level of urbanisation than the State average. Therefore, to get a better picture of distributional pattern of urban population, all the districts of Bihar have been divided into five categories on the basis of their level of urbanisation. The spatial dimension of such variations across the State can be seen in Table 3.4.

Very High Concentration (Above 20%)

Even in 2001, Bihar was one of the least developed and urbanised states

Table 3.4: Bihar: Spatial Patten of Urban Population Concentration (2001)

Level of Urbanisation	*Districts*	*No. of Districts in the Category*
< 5	Kaimur, Madhubani, Banka, Samastipur, Sheohar, Madhepura and Begusarai	7
5 – 10	Supaul, Siwan, Sitamarhi, Khagaria, Gopalganj, Araria, Champaran (E), Vaishali, Jehanabad, Arwal, Jamui, Nawada, Darbhanga, Saharsa, Aurangabad, Purnia, Katihar, Saran, Buxar, Muzaffarpur and Kishanganj	21
10 – 15	Champaran (E), Rohtas, Gaya, Bhojpur, Lakhisarai and Nalanda	6
15 – 20	Sheikhpura and Bhagalpur	2
>20	Munger and Patna	2
	Total	38

Source: Census of India, General Population Tables, Bihar, 1991 and 2001.

of India, so there were only two districts in Bihar where the level of urbanisation was more than 20 per cent. Patna tops the list with nearly 42 per cent urban to total population; followed by Munger with 28 per cent. Patna, a historical city, is the capital of Bihar. It supports about one-fourth of the State's urban population. Many of the agro-based industries including food, beverages and tobacco along with cotton, jute, leather, etc. are established here. Patna is a major educational centre of Bihar and most of the health facilities of State are located in the city. As far as Munger is concerned, before carving out Begusarai, Munger was the major industrial centre of Bihar. Indian Oil Corporation's Barauni Refinery, one of the country's oldest oil refineries, is situated here. Indian Railways Institute of Mechanical and Electrical Engineering (IRIMEE) and India Tobacco Factory are also established at Munger. Barauni also has thermal power, fertiliser, petro-chemicals, dairy products and several other industries.

Higher Concentration (15-20%)

There are two districts in this category. Bhagalpur with 18.67 per cent urban population is the leading district in this category followed by Sheikhpura (15.47%). Bhagalpur has five towns. Bhagalpur city is also known as 'silk city' as it is famous worldwide for its sericulture and manufacture of silk yarn. The silk industry in this city is 200 years old. Seikhpura district is situated in the Munger region. It is a small district of

Bihar and has two towns as per 2001 Census. Stone crushing has been the main industry.

Moderate Concentration (10-15%)

Moderate concentration of urban population in Bihar is found in Nalanda, Lakhisarai, Bhojpur, Gaya, Rohtas and Champaran (E). Nalanda district has six towns and has a distinct historical background. Except Rohtas, all the other districts in this category have agriculture as the main economic activity. Only Rohtas has a few industries. Dalmianagar has been the main industrial centre of Rohtas, though many of its big industries (cement and paper industry) have been shut down. The plateau region of Kaimur hills is situated here and therefore, stone crushing has become the main industry of the district. Gaya has six towns and it has two important religious centres of India. Gaya is known for Vishnu Pad Temple and is the major religious place for Hindus. Bodh Gaya is an important abode for the Buddhists.

Low Concentration (5-10%)

More than half of the number of districts in Bihar have a level of urbanisation between 5-10 per cent. There are 21 districts, namely Kishanganj, Muzaffarpur, Buxar, Katihar, Purnia, Aurangabad, Saharsa, Darbhanga, Nawada, Jamui, Arwal, Saran, Jehanabad, Vaishali, Champaran (E), Araria, Gopalganj, Khagaria, Sitamarhi, Siwan and Supaul in this category. Except Buxar and Aurangabad, all the other districts of this category get heavily affected by regular occurrence of flood. Flood has now become a perennial feature, hampering the development prospects of this region. Few agro-based industries are located in these districts. Katihar and Purnia have a few jute based industries as jute is abundantly grown here as well as in the hinterland of these two districts. Few sugar industries have also been set up in some districts of this region. These agro-based industries have been small in size and are, therefore, unable to have any impact on the pace of urbanisation in this region.

Very Low Concentration (Below 5%)

Interestingly, till now there are at least seven districts in Bihar where less than 5 per cent of total population are living in urban areas. Kaimur ranks the lowest in this category and has only 3.24 per cent level of urbanisation. Other districts in this category are Madhubani (3.48%), Banka (3.51%), Samastipur (3.64%), Sheohar (4.12%), Madhepura (4.45%) and Begusarai (4.58%). Again, except Kaimur all the other districts of this category are flood prone and entirely characterised by agricultural activities. Therefore, the process of urbanisation in these districts has been very slow. Kaimur and Sheohar have only one urban centre each that functions as district administration centre. Samastipur and Madhubani have four towns each but their small population size lack the qualities to attract migrants looking for better opportunities. Therefore, all the districts falling in this category have the lowest levels of urbanisation not only in Bihar but in the entire country as well.

Housing and Household Amenities in the Urban Areas of Bihar

In this section, the existing infrastructure and amenities available in the urban areas of Bihar have been investigated. The adequacy of infrastructure and basic amenities not only indicates the quality of life of urban population but also determine the level of development of any region. Byoung (2006) emphasised that infrastructure is indispensable to achieve the main development targets in developing countries. In fact, the urbanisation prospect of any region depends strongly on the extent of diversification of its economic activities and superior infrastructure. These not only attract investment from various sectors but also help in raising productivity by lowering costs directly through the economies of scale. If Bihar has to develop fast, there should be rapid action taken so that the urban areas can promptly meet the demand in infrastructure and basic amenities.

In general, piped water supply, telecommunications, sanitation and sewerage, solid waste management, piped gas, urban transport (road, rail, water and air), power supply, health services, banks, post offices comprise the basic infrastructure and services for the efficient functioning of a city (World Development Report, 1994). However, this study covers only six indicators, such as availability of safe drinking water, electricity, good housing condition, sanitation and sewerage and use of LPG for cooking in order to arrive at the overall picture of urban development in the districts of Bihar.

Availability of Safe Drinking Water

Access to safe drinking water is a fundamental human need and therefore, a basic right. From the health perspective, access to safe water and sanitation services is a preventive intervention to reduce the prevalence of water borne diseases and reduction in the number of deaths. However, in States like Bihar, poor access to safe water resources within the household premises and inadequate sanitation are the major causes of higher incidences of diseases and morbidity. According to the Census of India, water supplied through pipe, hand pump, tube-well and covered well comes under the safe sources of drinking water. In many parts of Bihar people are still using open well, ponds, rivers, canals, streams and other water bodies as sources of drinking water. Table 3.5 portrays a detailed picture of district-wise variance (among households) in the availability of safe drinking water. As per Table 3.5, 91.23 per cent of urban households are using safe drinking water. At the district level, there are at least three districts in Bihar where less than 70 per cent of urban population are using safe source for drinking purpose; they are Bhojpur (52.85%), Purnia (63.81%) and Siwan (64.74%). In case of Bhagalpur (99.12%) and Vaishali (99.03%) almost all the urban households are using safe drinking water.

Using improved sources of drinking water is essential but the availability of safe drinking water within premises is another important aspect to determine the level of urban development. In India, women are given responsibility to fetch water. Therefore, if the source of water is located far from the household, women have to employ hard labour to fetch the water for the entire family. Table 3.5 indicates a difficult situation in this regard because about 31.97 per cent of the people of urban Bihar do not have access to safe source of drinking water within their household premises.

Use of Electricity for Household Lighting

Electricity is a crucial factor for the development of any region. Economic growth depends on a commercially viable power sector as it helps to attract fresh investments in the region. Electrification of households in urban areas is not only essential to improve the quality of life but also to initiate the development activities at the local level. As of now, the electricity sector in Bihar is characterised by chronic power shortages and low voltage supplies. The total installed capacity of electricity generation of Bihar was only 584 MW in 2001, whereas Maharashtra had 7571 MW and Uttar Pradesh had 6085 MW electricity generation capacity (Government of Bihar, 2001).

Table 3.5: Availability of Safe Drinking Water in the Urban Areas

Sr. No.	*District*	*From Anywhere*	*Within Premises*	*Sr. No.*	*District*	*From Anywhere*	*Within Premises*
1.	Araria	74.26	45.42	20.	Munger	98.45	70.09
2.	Aurangabad	97.64	65.23	21.	Muzaffarpur	82.92	51.53
3.	Banka	97.65	77.01	22.	Nalanda	96.08	64.10
4.	Begusarai	97.77	62.43	23.	Nawada	94.61	63.88
5.	Bhagalpur	99.12	42.51	24.	Pash.Champaran	92.27	69.47
6.	Bhojpur	52.85	39.65	25.	Patna	99.4	76.23
7.	Buxar	85.29	59.09	26.	Purba Champaran	92.9	63.96
8.	Darbhanga	91.36	67.09	27.	Purnia	63.81	44.66
9.	Gaya	97.91	73.08	28.	Rohtas	97.71	71.21
10.	Gopalganj	95.76	77.06	29.	Saharsa	94.82	73.91
11.	Jamui	98.96	76.74	30.	Samastipur	98.64	63.19
12.	Jehanabad	97.9	66.58	31.	Saran	91.4	63.08
13.	Kaimur (Bhabua)	91.71	77.11	32.	Sheikhpura	96.04	76.15
14.	Katihar	98.21	70.38	33.	Sheohar	90.83	61.99
15.	Khagaria	86.92	67.64	34.	Sitamarhi	94.78	75.82
16.	Kishanganj	74.27	52.94	35.	Siwan	64.74	39.55
17.	Lakhisarai	98.01	70.39	36.	Supaul	94.25	74.68
18.	Madhepura	74.55	56.37	37.	Vaishali	99.03	78.54
19.	Madhubani	98.87	49.04		Bihar	91.23	68.03

Source: Census of Bihar, Housing and Household Amenities, 2001.

It can be categorically observed from Table 3.6 that even after 60 years of independence only 59.28 per cent urban households of Bihar are able to use electricity for lighting. In rural Bihar, condition is more pathetic, only a negligible per cent of households (5.13%) have electricity connection which shows a great disparity in the provision of an essential amenity in the State. The district-wise figures almost present the same picture. It can be seen from the table that the district with highest household connectivity is Patna where 84.92 per cent households are using electricity for lighting purpose. It is quite surprising that in 2001 Census there were 20 districts in Bihar where more than half of the urban households did not have electricity. The lowest electricity connectivity is found in Sheohar District (18.95%), followed by Supaul (31.41%), Kishanganj (31.55%), Gopalganj (31.75%), Banka (35.99%), W. Champaran (36.62%) and Seikhpura (38.74%).

Table 3.6: Urban Bihar: Use of Electricity for Household Consumption

Sl. No.	*District*	*Use of Electricity for Household Consumption*	*Sl. No.*	*District*	*Use of Electricity for Household Consumption*
1.	Araria	42.19	20.	Munger	59.58
2.	Aurangabad	50.31	21.	Muzaffarpur	70.30
3.	Banka	35.99	22.	Nalanda	53.71
4.	Begusarai	74.53	23.	Nawada	55.75
5.	Bhagalpur	60.94	24.	W. Champaran	36.62
6.	Bhojpur	54.80	25.	Patna	84.92
7.	Buxar	60.00	26.	E. Champaran	48.90
8.	Darbhanga	58.07	27.	Purnia	51.55
9	Gaya	68.26	28.	Rohtas	59.39
10.	Gopalganj	31.75	29.	Saharsa	48.60
11.	Jamui	45.09	30.	Samastipur	52.68
12.	Jehanabad	46.28	31.	Saran	43.53
13.	Kaimur (Bhabua)	76.62	32.	Sheikhpura	38.74
14.	Katihar	52.23	33.	Sheohar	18.95
15.	Khagaria	47.78	34.	Sitamarhi	41.07
16.	Kishanganj	31.55	35.	Siwan	45.35
17.	Lakhisarai	45.08	36.	Supaul	31.41
18.	Madhepura	39.44	37.	Vaishali	42.09
19.	Madhubani	42.07		Bihar	59.28

Source: Census of Bihar, Housing and Household Amenities, 2001.

Distribution of Households Connected to Drainage

A proper drainage system at household level is not only important for the purpose of hygiene but also for the removal of flood water from the area or settlement and particularly for a State like Bihar which is one of the worst flood hit states in the country. Table 3.7 depicts that those districts where no proper drainage system is developed, incidentally also have high intensity of flooding. For example, the districts of Madhepura, Purnia, Araria, Darbhanga, Kishanganj, Supaul and others are flood prone areas of Bihar and have underdeveloped drainage system. Several studies have suggested that the chronic poverty of Bihar is also related to flood episodes, therefore, it is important to analyse the per cent of households connected by waste water outlet.

Table 3.7: Urban Bihar: Distribution of Households by Drainage Connectivity for Waste Water Outlet

Sl. No.	*District*	*Percentage of Households connected with Drainage*	*Sl. No.*	*District*	*Percentage of Households connected with Drainage*
1.	Araria	38.47	20.	Munger	77.45
2.	Aurangabad	81.31	21.	Muzaffarpur	65.29
3.	Banka	50.08	22.	Nalanda	86.52
4.	Begusarai	70.09	23.	Nawada	82.78
5.	Bhagalpur	75.51	24.	W. Champaran	51.27
6.	Bhojpur	82.37	25.	Patna	84.48
7.	Buxar	82.74	26.	E. Champaran	54.04
8.	Darbhanga	70.28	27.	Purnia	32.93
9.	Gaya	84.13	28.	Rohtas	87.10
10.	Gopalganj	47.79	29.	Saharsa	36.65
11.	Jamui	53.27	30.	Samastipur	59.89
12.	Jehanabad	73.82	31.	Saran	71.91
13.	Kaimur (Bhabua)	77.59	32.	Sheikhpura	75.82
14.	Katihar	51.74	33.	Sheohar	42.16
15.	Khagaria	44.44	34.	Sitamarhi	43.10
16.	Kishanganj	25.92	35.	Siwan	73.82
17.	Lakhisarai	70.32	36.	Supaul	36.96
18.	Madhepura	26.71	37.	Vaishali	39.22
19.	Madhubani	36.78		Bihar	68.61

Source: Census of Bihar, Housing and Household Amenities, 2001.

Overall, 68.61 per cent of the urban households are connected with drainage for waste water outlet. However, at district level, Table 3.7

indicates a great variation in the household connectivity to the drainage system. The district with lowest percentage of households having drainage connectivity is found in Kishanganj (25.92%) whereas in Rohtas 87.1 per cent households are connected to drainage outlet for waste water. The other districts where less than 40 per cent households having adequate drainage facility are Madhepura (26.71%), Purnia (32.93%), Saharsa (36.65%), Madhubani (36.78%), Araria (38.47%) and Vaishali (39.22%). At the same time, districts with more than 80 per cent households connected to the drainage system are, Nalanda (86.52%). Patna (84.48%) Gaya (84.13%), Buxar (82.74%), Bhojpur (82.37%) and Aurangabad (81.31%).

Availability of Toilet Facility

The absence of toilet facilitates promotes the transmission of oral-fecal diseases, including diarrhoea and a range of intestinal worm infections such as hookworm and roundworm. According to the Asian Development Bank (2009), India is losing billions of dollars each year because of poor sanitation. Illnesses are costly to families, and to the economy as a whole in terms of productivity losses and expenditures on medicines, health care, and funerals.

Table 3.8 shows that only 69.69 per cent of urban households of Bihar have toilet facility and rest of the households have to go to the open. It is important to note that the availability of public toilet is limited in the urban areas, therefore, the urban people who do not have toilets in their house, are forced to go outside for hygiene practices. As far as district-wise availability is concerned, the situation is rather dismal. At present there are at 5 districts in Bihar where more than 50 per cent urban households do not have toilets. The situation is particularly serious in Sheohar where 70 per cent urban households do not have toilet facility. Other districts where the percentage of households with functioning latrines is less than 50 per cent are Banka (43.18%), Gopalganj (43.9%), Kishanganj (46.15%) and Supaul (46.85%). Among the districts that performed much better in this indicator, Patna topped the list with 96.73 per cent of the urban households having toilet facility, followed by Begusarai (79.96%), Muzaffarpur (79.93%), Gaya (77.08%), Darbhanga (76.45%) and Bhagalpur (75.41%).

Table 3.8: Distribution of Households by Availability of Latrine within the House

Sl. No.	District	Percentage of Households connected with Drainage	Sl. No.	District	Percentage of Households connected with Drainage
1.	Araria	53.84	20.	Munger	72.30
2.	Aurangabad	62.33	21.	Muzaffarpur	79.93
3.	Banka	43.18	22.	Nalanda	73.27
4.	Begusarai	79.96	23.	Nawada	73.15
5.	Bhagalpur	75.41	24.	W. Champaran	51.44
6.	Bhojpur	66.29	25.	Patna	86.73
7.	Buxar	63.02	26.	E. Champaran	56.23
8.	Darbhanga	76.45	27.	Purnia	63.43
9.	Gaya	77.08	28.	Rohtas	70.52
10.	Gopalganj	43.90	29.	Saharsa	67.27
11.	Jamui	51.59	30.	Samastipur	68.81
12.	Jehanabad	60.64	31.	Saran	55.99
13.	Kaimur (Bhabua)	69.53	32.	Sheikhpura	53.89
14.	Katihar	66.89	33.	Sheohar	30.05
15.	Khagaria	61.40	34.	Sitamarhi	54.61
16.	Kishanganj	46.15	35.	Siwan	68.04
17.	Lakhisarai	53.13	36.	Supaul	46.85
18.	Madhepura	55.69	37.	Vaishali	58.64
19.	Madhubani	54.43		BIHAR	69.69

Source: Census of Bihar, Housing and Household Amenities, 2001.

Conclusions

In Bihar, the pattern and processes of urbanisation have been very much governed by Class-I cities. Data analysis has clearly revealed that over the decades an unbalanced pattern of urban development has taken place in Bihar. Class-I cities alone account for about two-third of the total urban population of the State. Thus, Class-I cities are growing at the cost of other small towns, and their growth is much faster than other cities and towns in the State. It has been also found that the distribution of towns is quite uneven in Bihar; most of the towns being located only in few districts.

The preceding sections also indicate that there has been a major deficiency in the provision of urban basic amenities in the state. The spatial analysis of urban infrastructure and basic amenities also revealed considerable inequality among the different districts of Bihar, indicating that the nature of urban development in Bihar is highly skewed in nature, being concentrated in the biggest urban centres. It is an established fact that urban centres play a key role in both the process of modernisation and in economic development. Adequate provision of infrastructure and basic services help cities to become engines of development. On that note, the State Government must play an active role in providing these services uniformly across the districts so that a balanced urban development can be attained in future.

REFERENCES

Asian Development Bank (2009): *India's Sanitation for All: How to Make it Happen*, Asian Development Bank, Manila, Philippines, http://www.adb.org/documents/books/water_for_all_series/Indian-sanitation/Indian -sanitation.pdf

Davis, K. and Golden, H. (1954): "Urbanisation and the Development of Pre-Industrial Areas", *Economic Development and Cultural Change*, October, p. 8.

Ehrilich, H.T. (1956): "The Process of Urbanisation", in J.J. Spangler and O.P. Duncan (eds.), *Demographic Analysis*, Glencoe, Ill: Free Press (1956), p. 338.

Government of Bihar (2001): *States Installed Capacity (MW)*, Energy Department, Government of Bihar, http://energy.bih.nic.in/Indicators.htm

Gugler, J. (1988). "Over-Urbanisation Reconsidered." in J. In Gugler (ed.) *The Urbanisation of the Third World*. Oxford: Oxford University Press.

Hall, P. (1998). *Cities in Civilisation.* London: Weidenfeld and Nicolson.

Kundu, Amitabh. (2006). "Urbanisation and Urban Governance: Search for a Perspective Beyond Neo-Liberalism." In A. Shaw (ed). *Indian Cities in Transition*. Hyderabad: Orient Longman.

Prakasa Rao, V.L.S. (1983): *Urbanism in India: Spatial Dimension*, Concept Publishing Company Pvt. Ltd., New Delhi, pp. 13-18.

Singh, A.K. (2010): *Patterns and Process of Urban Development*, Abhijeet Publications, New Delhi.

Taylor, G. (1953): *Geography in the Twentieth Century*, Mitheun & Co. Ltd. London, pp. 524-527.

Thakur, B. (1979): *Urban Settlements in Eastern India*, Concept Publishing Company Pvt. Ltd., New Delhi.

World Development Report (2006): *Equity and Development*, A Co-publication of the World Bank and Oxford University Press, New York.

4

Urbanisation and Characteristics of Urban Settlements in Rajasthan

A Comparative Study of Western and Eastern Plains

Chandreyi Banerjee

Introduction

Urban settlements and the process involved that is, the process of urbanisation is fair indices of socio-economic development. Urbanisation is the process of becoming urban and urban relates to towns and cities. In other words, urbanisation means the concentration of population in towns and cities. Urban settlements may be of different sizes and range from small towns, sometimes even smaller than a large village to sprawling cities of the scale of a megalopolis. Though the definition of urban settlement is a difficult one and varies from country to country, economic activities are largely the criteria for distinguishing urban from rural.

Area-wise Rajasthan is one of the largest states of India covering an area of 3.42 lakh sq. km but in terms of its percentage share to the total urban population of the country, Rajasthan occupied a bottom rank of 16, according to 2001 Census with 222 urban centres.

Temporally, urbanisation was practically negligible in the erstwhile Rajputana, in the decades of feudal rule. Scarcity of water, uncertainty of rainfall, frequent droughts, etc., with their consequent adverse effects on the economy greatly hindered the process of urbanisation. Urban settlements were largely confined to favourable pockets like along major rivers and their tributaries, around fresh water and salt lakes, caravan route crossings, rocky tops and on higher slopes. Fortified urban settlements in Rajasthan owe their origin in security purposes due to frequent clashes between different ethnic descendants like Rajputs, Jats, Gujjars and so on. However, archaeological evidences do find traces of many flourishing urban centres like Ahar, Kali Banga, Pili Banga, etc., in the historical past. Over the years, urban population in Rajasthan has grown due to potentialities of mineral occurrence, availability of power resources, irrigation development and development of transport and communication. But the most important reason for variable growth of urban settlements in Rajasthan may be arising out of the great diversity in its physical landscape.

Geographical Background

"Physiographically, it is difficult to find a region more varied and diverse than Rajasthan with the present relief being ultimately the product of past fluvial cycles of erosion and recent aeolian cycle of erosion" (Bhalla, 1996). With the desert forming a dominant part of the physical landscape, it is the Aravallis which stretches like a midrib across the state in a south-west to north-east alignment and divides Rajasthan almost into two equal parts.

Based on similarities in physical landscape, economic parameters and cultural elements (Fig. 4.1), the State of Rajasthan may be divided into four geographical regions, namely,

- The Western Sandy Plains,
- The Eastern Plains,
- The Aravalli Hill Region, and
- The Hadauti Plateau Region in the south-east.

The first two regions, that is, the Western Sandy Plains and the Eastern Plains, both are flat lands but, they lie on either side of the Aravallis and form two distinct geographical regions. Hence, the focus of the present study is to probe whether the different ecological zones also shape the urban settlements of these two different regions.

Conforming to administrative boundaries, the Western Sandy Plains comprises 12 districts of Barmer, Bikaner, Churu, Hanumangarh, Jaisalmer, Jalore, Jhunjhunu, Jodhpur, Nagaur, Pali, Sikar and Sriganganagar. It is a vast expansion of wind-blown sand with rocky outcrops in between. The general elevation of the region is 300m in the north and 150m in the south. The average annual rainfall ranges from 10-20 cm with great extremes of temperature.

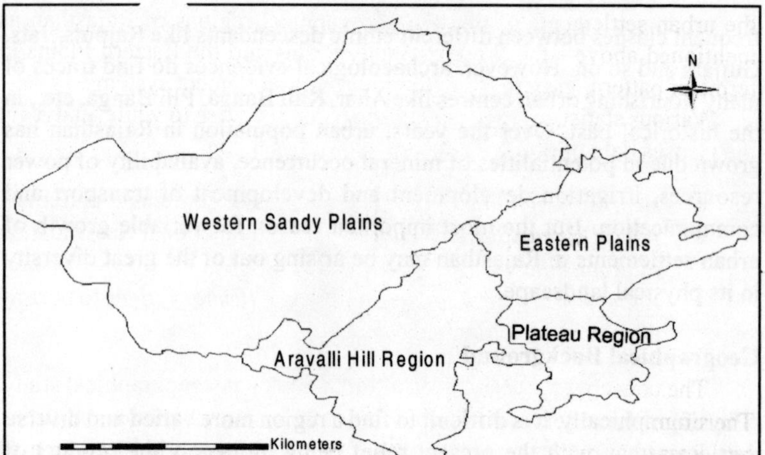

Fig. 4.1: Geographical Regions of Rajasthan

The Eastern Plains comprises the 8 districts of Alwar, Bharatpur, Dausa, Dhaulpur, Jaipur, Karauli, Sawai Madhopur and Tonk. It presents an amalgam of lowland and upland topography which are products of both geological history and exogenetic forces like peneplanation, warping, intrusion and so on. The average elevation of the region is 300 m. The climate is comparatively favourable with average annual rainfall ranging from 40-80 cm.

As per 2001 Census, the Western Sandy Plains had the maximum number of urban settlements, i.e. 88 of total 222 urban units in the State whereas the Eastern Plains had only 51 urban centres. However, in terms of the percentage share to the total urban population of Rajasthan, there was not much difference between the two regions. The Western Sandy Plains covering the largest portion of the State (61 per cent of the total area) had around 37 per cent of the total urban population of Rajasthan. On the other hand, the Eastern Plains comprising 14.1 per cent of the total area of Rajasthan hosted about 33 per cent of the total urban population in 2001.

Objectives, Database and Methodologies

The broad objective of this study is to undertake a comparative study of the urban settlements of the two geographical regions of Rajasthan as mentioned above—the Western Sandy Plains and the Eastern Plains in terms of pattern, growth, size, functions and settlement systems.

Various statistical tools have been taken recourse to while analysing the Census data of 2001. These are as follows:

- *Nearest Neighbour Analysis* to determine settlement patterns.
- Ashok Mitra's *Ternary Diagram* for the functional classification of urban centres.
- *Rank-Size Rule* of Zipf and Jefferson's *Primacy Index* to portray the nature of settlement systems.

The concept of *'space'* is a central theme in any geographical study. Therefore, for a geographer, spatial pattern of any phenomenon, urban settlements in this case, becomes a vital issue especially in an area so diversified as Rajasthan.

In theory, three different spatial patterns of settlements may be found to exist, viz.,

- *Uniform* spatial pattern where the settlements are spaced regularly at equal intervals apart.
- *Random* spatial pattern which is a state of total disorganisation in which the settlements are randomly distributed over space.
- *Clustered* spatial pattern which is a state of equilibrium in the settlement system. In this, some settlements are located close to each other while others may be located far apart.

Using *Nearest Neighbour Index*, the spatial pattern of urban settlements in both the regions may be identified. A map of scale 1: 50,00,000 showing the urban centres of these regions has been used for the purpose. Nearest Neighbour index denoted by R is the ratio of the actual mean nearest neighbour distance in a given region (D_o) and the expected mean nearest neighbour distance of all the urban settlements (D_r).

Hence, $R = D_o/D_r$

D_r may be worked out using the formula,

$D_r = 0.5/D$

where,

D = N/A or density of settlements in a given region,

N being the number of settlements in the region, and,
A, the area of the region.

The value of R ranges between 0 through 1 to 2.15. If it is 1 then it is a random distribution; if between 0 and 1 then it may be said to approach a clustered settlement pattern while if between 1 and 2.15, then a uniform pattern exists.

The *standard error* of D_r may be worked out as:

$$S.E\ (D_r) = 0.26126/(N/A)$$

The *standard normal variate* (the limit of which at 1 per cent and 5 per cent levels of significance are 2.58 and 1.96 respectively) Z is used to test the significance of the difference between D_r and D_o where,

$$Z = (D_o - D_r)/S.E\ (D_r)$$

Table 4.1 depicts that while the Western Sandy Plains exhibit a random distribution of its urban units, those in the Eastern Plains on the other hand, shows a pattern that is approaching uniformity.

Table 4.1: Settlement Pattern Based on Nearest Neighbour Indices

Regions	*Value of R*	*D_o (in kms)*	*D_r (in kms)*	*S.E (D_r)*	*Value of Z*	*Settlement Pattern*
Western Sandy Plains	0.93	22.64	24.34	1.356	–1.254 (not significant even at 5% level of significance; rather negative)	Random
Eastern Plains	1.279	19.68	15.38	1.125	3.82 (significant at 1% level of significance)	Approaching uniform pattern

Source: Computed from Topographical Sheets, Survey of India, Government of India.

Equally important as the concept of space is the concept of time as part of the *'space-time framework'*; time here being expressed in terms of *'growth'* of urban settlements, which may either be positive or negative. The factors leading to the growth of urban settlements have changed from time to time. Earlier, urban centres grew due to surplus agricultural production and the concentration of political power and organised commerce. Today, growth of urban units may be said to be a function of socio-economic changes taking place through time.

From the first Census in 1961, after the State of Rajasthan came into being in 1956 till 2001 Census, the number of urban centres has increased over the decades with the maximum increase being recorded in between 1971and 1981. The same trend is observed in the two mentioned regions as well, with the number of urban units growing, again with the maximum growth recorded from 1971to 1981. The percentage growth of urban centres over the Census years is higher in the Eastern Plains as compared to the Western Plains. In fact, growth of urban settlements in the Eastern Plains was even more than the state-level figure up to 1991. While the State registered no growth in the number of urban units between 1991 and 2001, both the regions experienced slight decrease in the number, from 1981 onwards in the Western Plains and from 1991 in the Eastern Plains.

Table 4.2: Number of Urban Settlements (1961-2001)

Census Year	*Rajasthan*	*Western Sandy Plains*	*Eastern Plains*
1961	141	68	32
1971	153 (+8.4)	72 (+5.9)	36 (+12.5)
1981	201 (+31.3)	91 (+26.4)	48 (+33.3)
1991	222 (+10.4)	90 (-1.1)	54 (+12.5)
2001	222 (0.0)	88 (-2.2)	51 (-5.6)

Note: Figures in the parentheses shows the percentage change in the number of urban settlements over the preceding Census year.

Source: Census of India, Rajasthan Final Population Totals, 2006.

The percentage of urban population in the specified time period in the state as well as the two selected regions is given in Table 4.3.

A similar trend may be observed in the percentage of urban population as in the number of urban settlements. The percentage of urban population has increased over time in the state as well as in the two regions. The maximum increase is recorded in the decade 1971-81. Till 1981 in fact, the two regions had greater percentages of urban population than the state as a whole. In 1961, the Western Sandy Plains showed greater percentage compared to the other spatial units. From 1971 onwards, this was replaced by the Eastern Plains. From 1981, though the percentage of urban population has increased in the State as well as in the two regions, but the units of change show a decreasing trend everywhere with the figure becoming even negative in the Western Plains from 1991 to 2001.

Table 4.3: Percentage of Urban Population (1961-2001)

Census Year	*Rajasthan*	*Western Sandy Plains*	*Eastern Plains*
1961	16.28	17.76	16.37
1971	17.63 (+1.35)	18.42 (+0.66)	18.50 (+2.13)
1981	21.05 (+3.42)	21.39 (+2.97)	22.55 (+4.03)
1991	22.88 (+1.83)	22.29 (+0.9)	25.23 (+2.68)
2001	23.38 (+0.5)	19.79 (-2.5)	27.12 (+1.89)

(*Note:* Figures in the parentheses show the units of change in the percentage of urban population over the preceding Census year).

Source: Census of India, Rajasthan Final Population Totals, 2006.

Urban settlements are not uniform in size; size being coterminous with population. The Indian Census provides for six size classes of urban settlements based on their population, namely,

Table 4.4: Size Class of Urban Centres

Size Class	*Population*
I (cities)	1,00,000 and above
II (medium towns)	50,000 – 99,999
III (medium towns)	20,000 – 49,999
IV (small towns)	10,000 – 19,999
V (small towns)	5,000 – 9,999
VI (mini towns)	less than 5,000

It can be inferred from Table 4.5 that, there exists not much difference between the two regions. In both the regions maximum urban settlements are medium towns (Class III) followed by small (Class IV) towns. The proportion of cities is almost the same in both the regions and even less than 10 per cent of the total number. This scenario closely matches with that of the State as a whole. However, compared to the state-level figure or with the Western Plains, the percentage share of Class I cities are slightly more in the Eastern Plains. The Western Plains have the highest percentage of Class II category towns. Individually, the Eastern Plains have the greatest proportion of Class III towns while the state shows the lowest figure. Small towns (Class IV and V) are proportionally more in the State than the other two spatial units. Mini towns are least compared to the other categories in Rajasthan as well as in the Western Plains, while this

Table 4.5: Rajasthan: Number of Urban Settlements According to Size Classes in 2001

Size Classes of Urban Centres	*Rajasthan*	*Western Sandy Plains*	*Eastern Plains*
I	20 (9.0)	8 (9.1)	5 (9.8)
II	26 (11.7)	14 (15.9)	7 (13.7)
III	86 (38.7)	40 (45.5)	25 (49.1)
IV	63 (28.4)	23 (26.1)	10 (19.6)
V	22 (9.9)	2 (2.3)	4 (7.8)
VI	5 (2.3)	1 (1.1)	–
Total	222 (100.0)	88 (100.0)	51 (100.0)

Note: Figures in the parentheses shows the percentage share of each size classes to the total number of urban settlements.

Source: Census of India, Rajasthan Final Population Tables, 2006.

is absolutely absent in the Eastern Plains. The percentage share of the total urban population of these regions in each size classes is given in Table 4.6.

Table 4.6: Rajasthan: Percentage Share of the Total Urban Population in Each Size Class in 2001

Size Classes of Urban Centres	*Rajasthan*	*Western Sandy Plains*	*Eastern Plains*
I	56.3	47.0	69.1
II	14.7	19.6	11.6
III	20.8	25.6	15.6
IV	7.0	7.3	3.4
V	1.1	0.4	0.3
VI	0.1	0.1	0.0
Total	**100.0**	**100.0**	**100.0**

Source: Computed from Census data, 2001.

When the percentage share of the total urban population in each size class of urban units are considered, the scenario is slightly different. Surprisingly, in both the regions, the major share of the total urban population is not in the Class III category towns as in case of the number of urban settlements but, in the cities, specially so in the Eastern Plains whereas the Western Plains have a lower share in this category. The Class III towns are next to follow the Class I and Class II cities, in which the Western Plains shows the greatest percentage and the Eastern Plains differ significantly as in case of the number of urban centres in this category having the lowest figure. In fact, in all the three size Classes of II, III and IV, the Western Plains have the maximum proportion of urban population and the Eastern Plains lags behind consistently. There is a little change in the Class V category with the state-level figure replacing the Western Plains in terms of highest percentage. As in case of the number of urban settlements in each size category, here too, the figures for the mini towns are the same.

Urban Settlements not only vary with space and time but may be different from each other also in terms of other parameters. An urban settlement may be said to have evolved on a specific *physical landscape*, have a particular *demographic feature* and many also have a distinct *functional or economic background.* These may broadly be called the characteristics of urban settlements all of which provide basis for their classification. In fact, "the classification of urban places, as such, is a fundamental first step in scientific enquiry into the character of urban places" (Ramachandran, 1989).

Regarding the physical setting it can be said that since both the selected regions are by and large plain lands, so the urban settlements here are also low land towns. However, those in the ***Western Sandy Plains*** may be categorised as ***dry plain towns*** and those in the ***Eastern Plains*** with a comparatively higher amount of rainfall as can be termed as ***humid or 'wet' plain towns***.

The Indian Census classifies urban units into different size classes on the basis of population size. If *population density* (i.e. the number of persons per square unit of area) be also treated as an expression of demographic feature, then the urban settlements in these regions may be classified as shown in Table 4.7.

Table 4.7 depicts that most of the urban settlements in the Western and Eastern Plains have low to medium population densities. The extremes of very low and very high population density towns are almost equal everywhere. There is a slight difference in the sense that while in Rajasthan and the Western Plains maximum towns have medium population density, in the Eastern Plains low population density towns dominate. In each individual category of population density, interestingly, the Western Plains have the maximum proportion in both extremes of very low and very high density towns compared to the other region.

Every urban unit perform some function or have some dominant economic activity generally of the tertiary or secondary type which

Table 4.7: Rajasthan: Urban Settlements and Population Densities

Population Densities (persons/sq. km)	*Category*	*Eastern Plains (Number and Percentage of Urban Settlements)*	*Western Sandy Plains (Number and Percentage of Urban Settlements)*	*Rajasthan (Number and Percentage of Urban Settlements)*
Less than 500	Very low	2 (3.9)	6 (6.8)	12 (5.4)
500-1,999	Low	21 (41.2)	25 (28.4)	80 (36.0)
2,000-4,999	Medium	20 (39.2)	35 (39.8)	90 (40.5)
5,000-9,999	High	6 (11.8)	15 (17.0)	29 (13.1)
10,000 and above	Very High	2 (3.9)	7 (8.0)	11 (5.0)
		51 (100.0)	88 (100.0)	222 (100.0)

Note: Figures in the parentheses show the percentage of urban settlements in each category of population density.

Source: Census of India, Rajasthan Town Directory, Series-18, 2001.

essentially distinguish it from a rural unit engaged in primary activities. The classification of urban units based on their economic activities or dominant functions may be considered as the most meaningful form of classification. Several methods of functional classification of urban places have been put forward by various scholars from time-to-time. In the Indian context, a most comprehensive classification system based on the dominant function of the town was given by the then Registrar General of India, Ashok Mitra in 1961.

Seven Census categories of workers were grouped into three broad non-agricultural categories to obtain three major functional types as:

- ***Industrial towns*** in which the percentage of workers in the industrial categories of III, IV, V and VI put together were greater than either the workers in the industrial categories of VII and VIII put together or in category IX.
- ***Trade and transport towns*** where the percentage of workers in the industrial categories VII and VIII put together were greater than either the workers in the industrial categories III, IV, V and VI put together or in the category IX.
- ***Service towns*** in which the percentage of workers in the industrial category IX was greater than either the workers in the industrial categories III, IV, V and VI put together or in the categories VII and VIII put together.

Categories I and II, i.e. of agricultural labourers and cultivators were excluded for they involved in primary activities. A *ternary diagram,* i.e. an equilateral triangle was used, the sides of which formed three scales graduated from 0 to 100 such that each apex formed 0 on two scales and 100 per cent on the third. The three variables were converted into percentages adding up to 100 and the position of a town in the triangle was taken as the main determinant of its functions. The in-centre of this triangle represented a town in which there was no functional specialisation as the percentage of workers in each of the three groups was exactly same and 33.3 per cent. Towns further from the in-centre showed increasing tendency towards specialisation. So, three circles with centre at the in-centre of the triangle were drawn with radii $6^2/_3$, $11^2/_3$ and $16^2/_3$ intersecting the axes at 40 per cent, 45 per cent and 50 per cent respectively to show the degree of specialisation as given in Table 4.8.

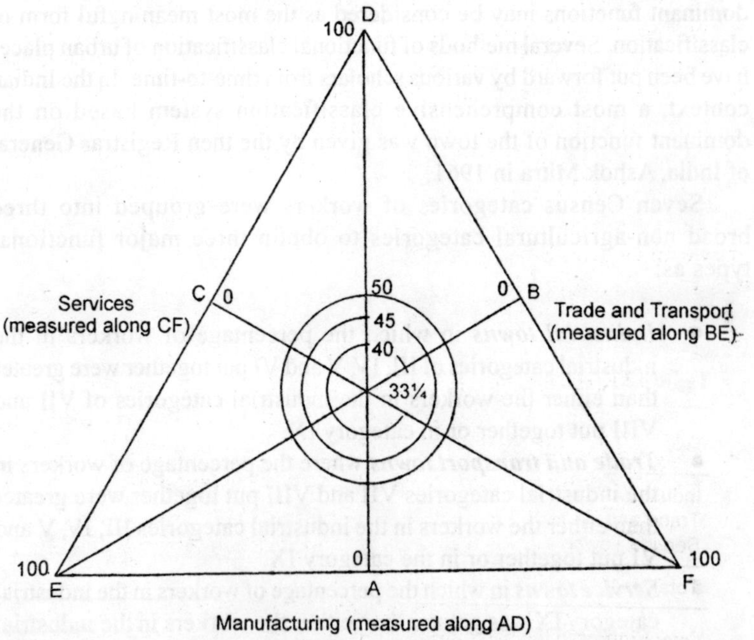

Fig. 4.3: Ashok Mitra's Triangular Method for Measurement of Degree of Specialisation of Functions

Table 4.8: Degrees of Specialisation (After Ashok Mitra)

Degree of Specialisation	*Code*	*Position*	*Total Workforce in Percentage*
Functions highly diversified	FHD	Within 1st circle	No group has more than 40 per cent
Functions moderately diversified	FMD	Between 1st and 2nd Circle	One group has 40-45 per cent
Predominant function accentuated	PFA	Between 2nd and 3rd Circle	One group has 45-50 per cent
Predominant function highly accentuated	PFHA	Outside 3rd circle	Dominant function has over 50 per cent

Using this method a classification of urban settlements in the two selected regions may be attempted. Since the 2001 Census do not provide data for percentage of workers in the industrial categories for all size classes of towns, as an exception the 1991 data was used for the purpose, assuming things may not have changed drastically and especially in Rajasthan where the number of urban settlements almost had remained the same over the decade.

Table 4.9 shows that in the State as well as its two regions, the service towns are least, speaking of the low development of the tertiary sector. This sector, however, is comparatively more developed in the Eastern Plains. Trade and transport towns dominate everywhere followed by industrial towns. In the Eastern Plains these two functional types form in equal proportion.

The degree of specialisation in these towns has been calculated to be as follows:

Table 4.9: Rajasthan: Urban Settlements with Functional Classification

Functional Types	*Rajasthan*	*Western Sandy Plains*	*Eastern Plains*
Industrial Towns	87 (39.2)	40 (44.4)	19 (35.2)
Trade and Transport Towns	91 (41.0)	42 (46.7)	19 (35.2)
Service Towns	44 (19.8)	8 (8.9)	16 (29.6)
Total	222 (100.0)	90 (100.0)	54 (100.0)

Note: Figures in the parentheses show the percentage of towns in each functional type.

Source: Computed from Census data, 1991.

Table 4.10: Rajasthan: Urban Settlements with Degree of Specialisation

Degree of Specialisation	*Rajasthan*	*Western Sandy Plains*	*Eastern Plains*
FHD	89 (40.1)	30 (33.3)	21 (38.9)
FMD	90 (40.5)	43 (47.8)	21 (38.9)
PFA	9 (4.1)	6 (6.7)	2 (3.7)
PFHA	34 (15.3)	11 (12.2)	10 (18.5)
Total	222 (100.0)	90 (100.0)	54 (100.0)

Note: Figures in the parentheses show the percentage of urban settlements in each degree of specialisation.

Source: Computed from Census Data, 1991.

As can be inferred from Table 4.10, most of the urban units in Rajasthan as well as in its two chosen regions have diversified functions. The percentage of FHD towns and FMD towns are equal in the state and its Eastern Plains while FMD towns are predominant in the Western Plains. The PFA category forms the minimum proportion everywhere, whether at the state-level or at the regional level. The Eastern Plains have the highest percentage of towns where the *predominant functions are highly accentuated.*

Urban settlements, no matter how much different they are from each other, cannot exist in isolation and are part of a unified whole or a *'settlement system.'* A settlement system in an ideal state is conceived as a balanced system of settlements with a stepped hierarchy and uniform distribution over space. Several models have been used to demonstrate this balanced system. The most popular among these are:

The ***Rank-Size Rule*** formulated by G.K. Zipf (1940) which can be expressed in the following mathematical form—

$$P_r = P_1/r^q$$

where,

P_r = population of the r ranking city;
P_1 = population of the first ranking city; and
q = an exponent which can take any value but not negative.

When the value of *'q'* ranges between 0 and 1, decline in population with rank is gradual, while a value greater than unity suggests rapid decline. Assuming the value of *'q'* to be unity, the rule suggests that the second ranking settlement would have half the population of the first ranking settlement and the third ranking settlement one-third and so on.

The concept of a '*primate city*' given by *Mark Jefferson* (1939) which is a direct contrast to above and conceives of a first city several times larger than the second; dominating the cultural, political and economic scenario of the entire region. Primacy can be measured using the *'primacy index'* which can be a—

(i) two-city index whereby, Primacy Index (PI)= P_1/P_2 where,
   P_1 = population of the first ranking city; and
   P_2 = population of the second ranking city.

(ii) four-city index whereby, Primacy Index (PI) = $P_1/P_2 + P_3 + P_4$ where,
   P_1 and P_2 are same as above.
   P_3 = population of the third ranking city; and
   P_4 = population of the fourth ranking city.

"Rank size relationships appear to hold good in three states in India: Rajasthan, Haryana and Uttar Pradesh. Among these Rajasthan alone has a near ideal fit to the rank size rule" (Ramachandran, 1989).

Statistically, rank-size rule may be examined by using the formula,

$$P = KR^{-b}$$

where,
P is the population of the town whose rank is R, and
K and b are constants.

Thereafter, the relationship may be transformed into a linear relationship by taking the logarithmic values of both the sides. Then the regression equation of log P on log R may be obtained where log P and log R are the dependent (Y) and independent variables (X) respectively. The regression coefficient 'b' reflects the degree of primacy in the cntire urban system.

Table 4.11 depicts that in Rajasthan, though there are 146 surplus centres out of 222 (65.7%), but they mostly constitute the medium category towns rather than cities. This accounts for the state having an actual population much lesser than the expected population as per rank-size rule. At the regional level, in the Western Sandy Plains the actual

Table 4.11: Rajasthan: Rank-Size Rule

Regions	*Expected Population*	*Actual Population*	*Difference*	*Percen-tage of Difference*	*No. of Surplus Centres*	*No. of Deficit Centres*
Rajasthan	1,37,77,009	1,32,32,485	+5,44,524	+4.12%	146	76
Western Sandy Plains	20,06,882	21,00,971	-94,089	-4.48%	62	26
Eastern Plains	40,89,595	44,03,983	-3,14,388	-7.14%	1	50

Source: Computed from Census Data, Year1991.

population is slightly more than the expected population. There are 62 surplus centres out of 88 urban units in the region but again they are mainly the medium and small towns except the first two cities of the region, i.e. Jodhpur and Bikaner. In the Eastern Plains also, the actual population is more than the expected population, but the excess is contributed by only one urban centre, that is, Jaipur. Jaipur is the capital and the only million-plus city in the State and its population overshadows all other urban centres of the region. Hence, a distinct primacy pattern may be observed in the Eastern Plains where Jaipur is the primate city. Jaipur has an actual population of 23,22,575 in 1991 whereas its expected population is 6,67,424 an excess of 16,55,151 (247.9%). In a two-city primacy index, Jaipur is almost 9 (8.7) times larger than the 2nd ranking city of the region, Alwar. Even in case of four-city primacy index, Jaipur was found to be almost 4 (3.8) times larger than the total population of Alwar, Bharatpur and Tonk. Therefore, rank-size rule is not applicable in this region. The rule however is applicable when we consider the State as a whole. Conforming to the rule, the population of the first ranking city Jaipur was found to be a little more than twice (2.6) the population of the second ranking city, i.e. Jodhpur and thrice (3.3) the population of the third ranking city, i.e. Kota, four times (4.4) that of the fourth ranking city Bikaner and so on. The Western Plains also exhibit a system close to rank-size rule where the first ranking city of the region, Jodhpur had almost double the population (1.6) than that of Bikaner, 3.8 times the population of Ganganagar and so on. This region, however, is in, between the two sides of the scale, that is, the Eastern Plains on one hand with distinct primacy pattern and the state as a whole on the other conforming to rank-size rule. This is supported by the fact that the *regression coefficient'b'* which reflects the degree of primacy in the urban system, is least for Rajasthan as a whole (-1.000645007) and highest for the Eastern Plains (-0.834219667).

Thus, if the urban settlements in the Western Sandy Plains and the Eastern Plains of Rajasthan are compared, the following points emerge:

1. While the Western Sandy Plains exhibit a random distribution of its urban units, those in the Eastern Plains on the other hand, shows a pattern that is approaching uniformity.
2. The percentage growth of urban centres over the Census years is more in the Eastern Plains as compared to the Western Plains. Both the regions experienced slight decrease in the number of urban settlements from 1981 onwards in the Western Plains and from 1991 in the Eastern Plains.
3. In 1961, the first Census year after Rajasthan came into existence, the Western Sandy Plains showed greater percentage of urban population compared to the Eastern Plains. From 1971 onwards, this was replaced by the Eastern Plains.
4. In both the regions maximum urban settlements are medium towns (Class III) followed by small (Class IV) towns. The proportion of cities, however, compared to the Western Plains, is slightly more in the Eastern Plains. The Western Plains have a greater percentage of Class II and Class IV category towns while the Eastern Plains have a greater proportion of Class III and Class V towns. Mini towns are least compared to the other categories in the Western Plains, while it is absolutely absent in the Eastern Plains.
5. When the percentage share of the total urban population in each size classes of urban units are considered, the scenario is slightly different. Surprisingly, in both the regions, the major share of the total urban population is not in the Class III category towns as in case of the number of urban settlements but, in the cities, specially so in the Eastern Plains. In all the four size Classes of II, III, IV and V, the Western Plains have a greater proportion of urban population than the Eastern Plains. As in case of the number of urban settlements in each size category, here too, the figures for the mini towns are the same.
6. Both the selected regions are plain lands, so the urban settlements here are also low point settlements. However, those in the Western Sandy Plains may be categorised as dry plain towns

and those in the Eastern Plains with a comparatively higher amount of rainfall as humid or wet point towns.

7. Most of the urban settlements in both the geographical regions have low to medium population densities. However, while in the Western Plains maximum towns have medium population densities, in the Eastern Plains low population density towns dominate.
8. In the two regions, the service towns are least, speaking of the low development of the tertiary sector. This sector, however, is comparatively more developed in the Eastern Plains. In general, trade and transport towns dominate followed by industrial towns. In the Eastern Plains these two functional types form equal proportion.
9. The degree of specialisation in the towns reflects that most of the urban units in the two chosen regions have diversified functions. The percentage of FHD towns and FMD towns are equal in the Eastern Plains while FMD towns are predominant in the Western Plains. The PFA category forms the minimum proportion in both the regions. The Eastern Plains have a higher percentage of towns in which the predominant functions are highly accentuated.
10. A distinct primacy pattern may be observed in the Eastern Plains where Jaipur is the primate city. The Western Plains exhibit a system close to rank-size rule.

Conclusions

Rajasthan is a land of diversity which finds expression in its physical and cultural landscape. In this study of urban settlements and urbanisation based on two regions of the state—the Western Sandy Plains and the Eastern Plains— this diversity gets essentially reflected. Both the regions are plain land, yet they form two distinct geographical regions and the urban settlements of the two regions greatly varies from each other thus, enabling a comparative study.

REFERENCES

Bhalla, L.R. (1996), "*Geography of Rajasthan*", Kuldeep Publications, Ajmer.

Census of India (2001), "*Town Directory of Rajasthan*", Series-18, Ministry of Home Affairs, Government of India, India.

Mahmood, Aslam (1977), *Statistical Methods in Geographical Studies*, Rajesh Publications, New Delhi.

Mitra, Asok (1964), *A Functional Classification of Indian Towns*, Institute of Economic Growth, New Delhi.

Ramachandran, R. (1989), *Urbanisation and Urban Systems in India*, OUP, New Delhi.

State Gazetteer of Rajasthan (1986), *Land and People*, Volume I, Jaipur.

—

5

Declining Urban Child Sex Ratio in India

A Case Study of Selected States

Naresh Kumar

Introduction

The decline in child sex ratio has been one of the most important concerns in India's demography in contemporary times. Census 2001 has revealed the fact that the sex ratio of the population of one to six years has declined during 1991 to 2001 from 945 to 927 per thousand. According to the 2011 Census data, in the last decade alone, the child sex ratio has dipped from 927 to 914 per 1000, the lowest since Independence. The worst affected regions according to the Census of India are western Maharashtra, western Uttar Pradesh and Rajasthan. Despite several policies to protect the girl child, their number below six years of age has fallen sharply. Patri-linearity, patri-locality and patriarchal attitudes have resulted in women and girls having subordinate position in the family. Denial of property rights and low paid or under paid jobs has further degraded their position in the society. The immediate cause for the decline in child sex ratio in India is the practice of female foeticide and in general a negligence of the girl child. Daughters are perceived as an economic and social burden to the family due to several factors such as dowry, the danger to her chastity and worry about getting her married. In such a scenario, the easy accessibility to technology that detects the sex of the unborn child allows families to abort female foetus or a negligent behaviour the manifestation of which results in an adverse child sex ratio.

Earlier Works on Child Sex Ratio

In a seminal article in 1990, Amartya Sen has opined that worldwide, particularly in Asia, millions of women are missing from the population totals of several countries. He has also noted the alarming fact that the child sex ratio in China, India and South Korea is actually deteriorating while the overall sex ratio in these countries has marginally improved. Ansley Coale (1991) has drawn attention to unusually high sex ratios at birth but high female mortality rates relative to males, especially in the years of early childhood. Croll (2002) raises the controversial question as to why millions of girls do not appear to be surviving to adulthood in contemporary Asia. Subsequent studies have proved the fact that it is excessive female mortality before birth, after birth, in infancy and in childhood, which mainly account for the imbalance in child sex ratios and results in an absence of a large number of girls in Asia. High masculine sex ratio of Indian population has been a matter of concern for many decades. Considerable attention has been paid to different dimensions of female deficits in India and existing regional variations (Agnihotri, 2000; Dasgupta and Bhatt, 1995; Miller, 1981 and 1989; Natarajan, 1972). The results of 2001 Census have set off a further debate on the issue and narrowed down the focus on the changes in the juvenile sex ratio. A combination of factors namely, son preference, small family norm, access to pre-natal sex determination test and abortion has worsened the situation for the girl child (Bose, 2002; Mallik, 2003 and Dasgupta, 2005). The concept of new household economy is emerging which characterises fewer children with at least one boy who will carry the family name and will look after old parents in future (Dyson, 2001; Lal, 2006). The usually known explanations like sex differentials in mortality, under-enumeration, biologically determined sex ratio at birth and sex selective migration have negligible impact in the present day imbalance in child sex ratio in Indian population (Arnold *et al.*, 2002; Bora and Tyagi, 2007; Bhat, 2002 and Dyson, 2001). Both in rural and urban India especially in the north western states, if the first born child is a girl, the sex ratio at the second birth largely worsen against girls. If the first birth is a male child, the sex ratio of second birth for the entire north western states is in favour of females (Retherford and Roy, 2003). Acceptance of small family norm has further worsened the situation. The aim of population policy is to achieve fertility decline but in north western states the common consensus is to achieve at least one son and for achieving at least one male heir, sex selective abortion has jeopardised the survival of girls. As the Total Fertility Rate (TFR) falls, the parity specific discrimination against girls becomes more pronounced (Dasgupta and Mari Bhat, 1997). This problem becomes more acute in urban India where couples can access different technologies to detect the sex of the unborn child. Slightly educated mothers and well to do families practice more sophisticated technologies to eradicate girls even before their births for avoiding the burden of dowry. Therefore, education alone cannot change the situation. Lack of social security for aged, women and girls, system of arranged marriages within castes, hypergamy and systematic subordination of women by other family members have further endangered the situation.

Regional Disparity in the Decline of Child Sex Ratio Rates in India

Although overall sex ratio in India has shown an improvement since 1991 but decline in child sex ratio has been unabated since 1961. The child sex ratio has been consistently declining since 1961 when it stood at 967 females per 1000 males. According to the provisional results of 2011 Census it is 914. The 2011 Census figures show that in 27 States/Union Territories, the child sex ratio has shown a decline over Census 2001. The only positive aspect here is that Punjab and Haryana, that continue to have the lowest child sex ratios at 846 and 830 respectively, have improved from 798 and 819 during Census 2001. Himachal Pradesh, Gujarat, Tamil Nadu, Mizoram and the Andaman and Nicobar Islands are the only other States/UTs that have shown an increase in the child sex ratio in 2011. In 2011 some other states and UTs *v.i.z.* Uttar Pradesh (899, down from 916), Maharashtra (883, down from 913), Chandigarh (867, down from 845) and Jammu and Kashmir (859) have the most worrisome figures though the southern states, Kerala (959), Andhra Pradesh (943), Karnataka (943), and Tamil Nadu (946), all have higher sex ratios when compared to the national average of 914, they have worsened in 2011 Census when compared to 2001.

However, the decline in child sex ratio (2001 to 2011) is less steep from that of the previous decade (1991 to 2001). In 1991, it was 945 and declined to 927 in 2001, a fall of 18 points (1.9%). In 2011 Census, this has fallen to 914, a fall of 13 points (1.4%).

Under natural circumstances slightly more boys than girls are born in each year but in India this ratio has been declining sharply over the second half of the twentieth century (Fig. 5.1).

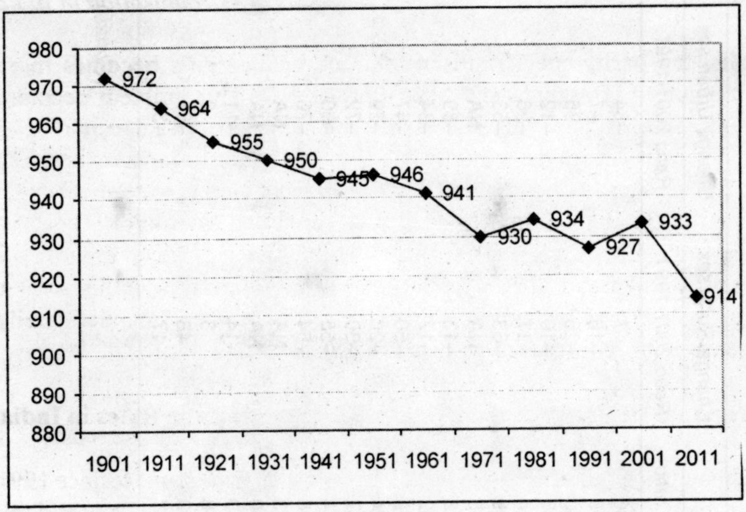

Fig. 5.1: Sex Ratio in India 1901-1911

Map 5.1 portrays the changes in child sex ratio during the last decade (1991 and 2001) in various districts of India. During 1991, only one district of Tamil Nadu has accounted for child sex ratio below 850, on the other hand 68 districts of Punjab, Haryana, Western Rajasthan, Eastern Gujarat, Western Uttar Pradesh, northern Madhya Pradesh and few districts of Tamil Nadu have recorded child sex ratio below the national average (945 in 1991).

In 2001, when the child sex ratio had dropped to 927 from 945, many new districts had entered into the range of 'below national average'. Fourteen districts of Punjab and Haryana had depicted a gloomy picture of very low child sex ratio (below 800), 33 districts of Punjab, Haryana, Rajasthan, Gujarat, Madhya Pradesh, western Uttar Pradesh, Tamil Nadu, Maharashtra and Delhi recorded a very low range of child sex ratio varying between 800 to 849. A total of about 118 districts in these above mentioned States recorded a child sex ratio below the national average (927). On the other hand, districts of Kerala, Karnataka, Chhattisgarh, Odisha, West Bengal, Sikkim, North Eastern states and Jammu and Kashmir recorded child sex ratio much above the national average.

Map 5.2 depicts the decline in child sex ratio by districts during the decade of 1991 and 2001. A total of sixty districts of India located in various states like Delhi, Punjab, Haryana, Himachal Pradesh, Uttar

Table 5.1: Rural Urban Change in Child Sex Ratio in India 1991-2001

States	*1991(0-6)*		*2001(0-6)*		*Change Rural sex*	*Change Urban sex*
	R sex ratio	*U sex ratio*	*R sex ratio*	*U sex ratio*	*Ratio 2001-1991*	*Ratio 2001-1991*
1. A. & N. Islands	973	970	966	936	–7	–34
2. Andhra Pradesh	979	962	963	955	–16	–7
3. Arunachal Pradesh	986	946	960	980	–26	35
4. Assam	977	955	967	943	–10	–12
5. Bihar	961	950	944	924	–17	–26
6. Chandigrah	910	897	847	845	–63	–53
7. Chhattisgrah	NA	NA	982	938	NA	NA
8. D. & N. Haveli	1015	977	1003	888	–13	–89
9. Daman & Diu	933	996	916	962	–17	–34
10. Delhi	900	917	850	870	–50	–47
11. Goa	972	953	952	924	–20	–29
12. Gujarat	936	909	906	837	–30	–72
13. Himachal Pradesh	955	904	900	844	–55	–60
14. Haryana	877	884	823	808	–54	–76
15. Jammu & Kashmir	NA	NA	957	873	NA	NA
16. Jharkhand	NA	NA	973	930	NA	NA
17. Karnataka	963	951	949	940	–14	–11
18. Kerala	958	958	961	958	3	0
19. Lakshadweep	951	963	999	900	48	–63
20. Madhya Pradesh	956	937	939	907	–17	–30

(Contd.)

Table 5.1 (*Contd.*)

States	1991(0-6)		2001(0-6)		Change Rural sex	Change Urban sex
	R sex ratio	U sex ratio	R sex ratio	U sex ratio	Ratio 2001-1991	Ratio 2001-1991
21. Maharashtra	953	934	934	908	–19	–26
22. Manipur	975	972	956	961	–19	–11
23. Meghalaya	989	968	973	969	–16	1
24. Mizoram	973	965	965	963	–7	–2
25. Nagaland	1001	959	969	939	–32	–21
26. Odisha	969	949	955	933	–14	–16
27. Puduchery	963	962	967	967	4	5
28. Punjab	878	866	799	796	–79	–70
29. Rajasthan	919	909	914	887	–4	–21
30. Sikkim	967	936	966	922	–1	–15
31. Tamil Nadu	945	955	933	955	–12	0
32. Tripura	968	959	968	948	0	–11
33. Uttar Pradesh	928	929	919	890	–9	–38
34. Uttarakhand	NA	NA	918	872	0	0
35. West Bengal	969	955	963	948	–7	–7
INDIA	**948**	**935**	**934**	**906**	**–15**	**–29**

Sources: Derived from Census of India 1991, 2001.

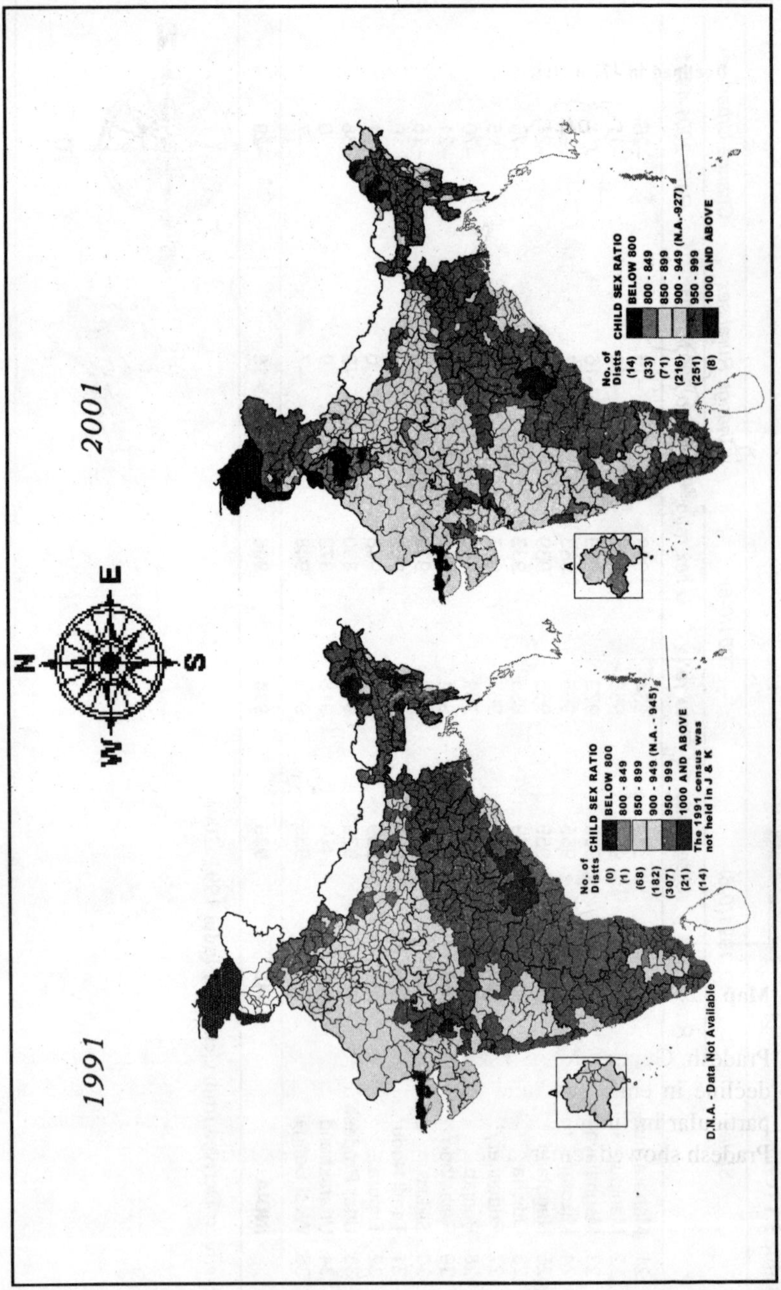

Map 5.1: India: Child Sex Ratio in Age Group 0-6 (Districts)

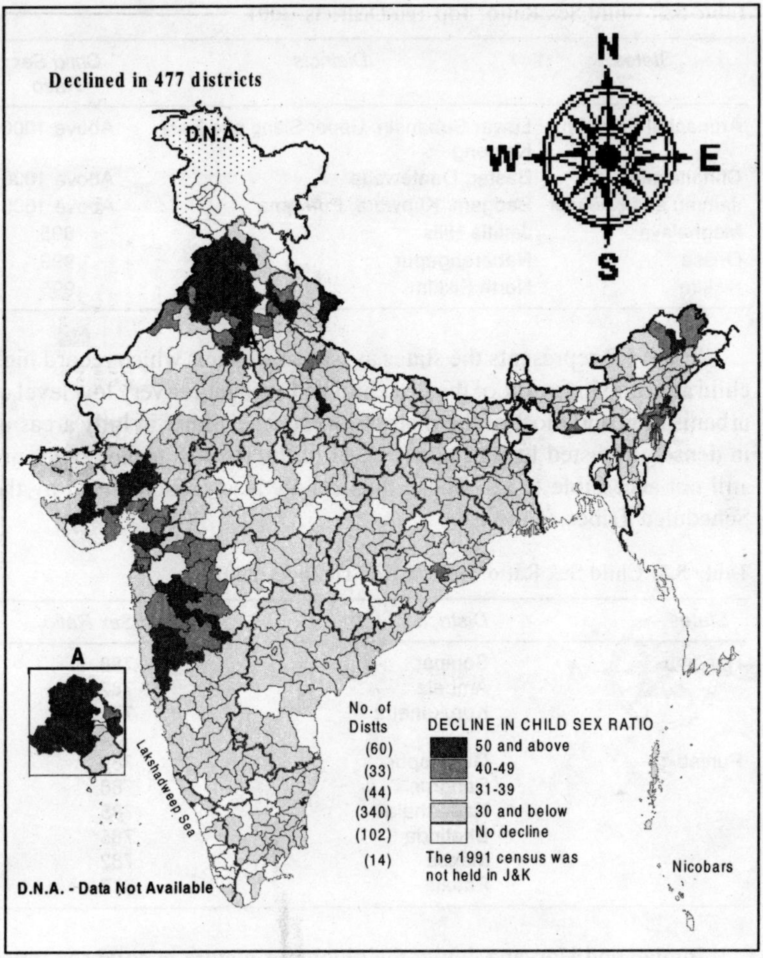

Map 5.2: India: Decline in Child Sex Ratio During 1991-2001 (Districts)

Pradesh, Gujarat, Maharashtra and Arunachal Pradesh recorded highest decline in child sex ratio (more than 50). The north Indian states in particular including Delhi, western states and some parts of Arunachal Pradesh showed remarkable decline in child sex ratio.

Table 5.2: Child Sex Ratio: Top Ten Districts, 2001

States	*Districts*	*Child Sex Ratio*
Arunachal Pradesh	Lower Subansiri, Upper Siang and East Kameng	Above 1000
Chhattisgarh	Bastar, Dantewada	Above 1000
Jammu and Kashmir	Badgam, Kupwara, Pulwama	Above 1000
Meghalaya	Jaintia Hills	995
Orissa	Nabarangapur	999
Sikkim	North Sikkim	995

Table 5.2 represents the states as well as districts which record high child sex ratio in favour of the girl child and account for very low level of urbanisation and most of the districts are located either in hilly areas or in densely forested locales where most of the modern technologies are still not accessible to all. These districts are also predominated by the Scheduled Tribes of India.

Table 5.3: Child Sex Ratio: Bottom Ten Districts, 2001

States	*Districts*	*Child Sex Ratio*
Haryana	Sonipat	788
	Ambala	782
	Kurukshetra	771
Punjab	Gurdaspur	789
	Sangrur	786
	Kapurthala	785
	Bhatinda	785
	Mansa	782
	Patiala	777

Punjab and Haryana depict the gloomiest picture in child sex ratio. These two states record high level of urbanisation and are also agriculturally developed. In these ten districts child sex ratio is lower than 800 (far below the national average).

Decline in Child Sex Ratio: State Level Disparity

According to the 2001 Census, the child sex ratio in urban India was 906 girls per thousand males as compared to 935 in the 1991 Census and hence the decline of child sex ratio in urban India was by 29 points

(Table 5.1). The range of decline in child sex ratio across the various states of India can be categorised into the following groups.

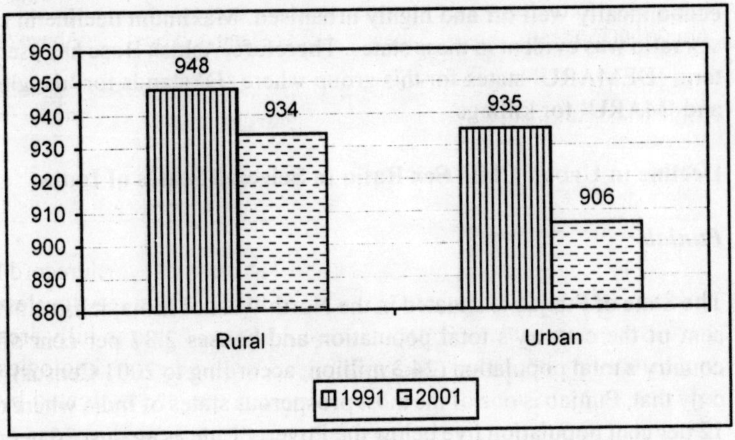

Fig. 5.2: Child sex Ratio, 1991 and 2001
Source: Census of India 1991, 2001.

(A) *Highest decline* (Above 50 points): Highest decline in the child sex ratio is recorded in four major states, i.e. Haryana (-76 points), Gujarat (-72 points), Punjab (-70 points) and Himachal Pradesh (-60 points) and in two Union Territories, i.e. Dadra and Nagar Haveli (-89), Chandigarh (-53).

(B) *Moderate decline* (15-50): The major states that come under this category are Uttar Pradesh (-38 points), followed by Madhya Pradesh (-30 points), Maharashtra (-26 points), Rajasthan (-21 points), Odisha (-16 points) and the smaller States and Union Territories like Delhi (-47), Daman and Diu (-34 points), Andaman and Nicobar Islands (-34 points).

(C) *Lowest decline* (Below15 points): Lowest decline in child sex ratio is recorded in Karnataka (-11 points), Andhra Pradesh (-7 points), Assam (-12 points), Manipur (-11 points), Sikkim (-15 points), Tripura (-11 points) and Nagaland (-11 points).

The decline of child sex ratio is so widespread that of the 35 States and Union Territories only 4 states, namely Kerala, Tripura, Mizoram, Sikkim and one UT, Lakshadweep (+33) seem to be free from this imbalance. The States and Union Territories that had accounted for a sharp decline in child sex ratio were Punjab, Haryana, Himachal Pradesh, Chandigarh, Gujarat and Delhi, though these States and UTs are economically well off and highly urbanised. Maximum decline in child sex ratio was evident in these states. Therefore, Ashish Bose has used the term 'DEMARU' states for this group where 'D' stands for 'daughters' and 'MARU' for killings.

Decline in Urban Child Sex Ratio in Selected States of India

Punjab

The State of Punjab is situated in the North West of India; it has 1.57 per cent of the country's total population and houses 2.37 per cent of the country's total population (24.3 million, according to 2001 Census). Not only that, Punjab is one of the most prosperous states of India where only 12 per cent population live below the Poverty Line as against 36 per cent for India in general. The state has a very high per capita income and has played a very crucial role in the success of the Green Revolution. Unfortunately, the state records the lowest child sex ratio, i.e. 876 females per thousand males among all Indian states. In 2001, the child sex ratio is 793, i.e. incidentally also the lowest in the entire world. In 2001, out of the ten bottom most districts in India, Punjab had the distinction of being the most critical as seven out of these ten were in Punjab.

Also, there has been a fall in overall sex ratio by 8 points from 882 in 1991 to 875 in 2001. What is more alarming is the sharp fall in the child sex ratio, i.e. the sex ratio of children in the age group of 0-6 years. According to Census 2001, the child sex ratio in Punjab was 793 girls per 1000 boys. The child sex ratio in 2001 showed a decline of 82 points compared to the child sex ratio of 1981 Census (908) and child sex ratio in 1991 showed a decline of 33 points from the earlier decade. While in the previous three decades (1961-1981) child sex ratio showed a marginal decline or remained constant.

The sharp decline in child sex ratio during the decade 1991-2001 is not only at the State level but also in almost all the districts. Out of 17 districts, 16 districts have shown a decline of more than 50 points. Four districts have shown a decline of more than 100 points. These districts are Fatehgarh Sahib (-120), Kapurthala (-104), Gurdaspur (-103) and Patiala (-101). Fatehgarh Sahib District of Punjab has earned the dubious

Table 5.4: Rural Urban Change Child Sex Ratio in Punjab 1991-2001

Sl. No.	*State/District*	*CSR*		*Change*	*CSR (Rural)*		*CSR (Urban)*		*Change (R)*	*Change (U)*
		1991	*2001*	*2001-1991*	*2001*	*1991*	*2001*	*1991*	*2001-1991*	*2001-1991*
	PUNJAB	875	793	–82	799	878	796	866	–79	–70
1.	Nawanshar	900	810	–90	809	NA	804	NA	NA	NA
2.	Muktsar	858	807	–51	814	NA	804	NA	NA	NA
3.	Moga	868	819	–49	822	NA	802	NA	NA	NA
4.	Mansa	873	779	–94	783	NA	778	NA	NA	NA
5.	Fatehgarh Sahib	874	754	–120	757	NA	791	NA	NA	NA
6.	Faridkot	865	805	–60	820	866	797	855	–46	–58
7.	Firozpur	887	819	–68	825	892	813	863	–67	–50
8.	Amritsar	861	783	–78	793	864	784	856	–71	NA
9.	Ludhiana	877	814	–63	815	887	819	869	–72	–50
10.	Jalandhar	886	797	–89	817	891	793	882	–74	NA
11.	Hoshiarpur	884	NA	NA	815	890	800	873	–75	–73
12.	Bathinda	860	779	–81	795	873	762	836	–78	NA
13.	Gurdaspur	878	775	–103	797	881	762	868	–84	–106
14.	Rupnagar	884	791	–93	793	884	799	886	–91	–87
15.	Kapurthala	879	775	–104	782	875	792	891	–93	NA
16.	Sangrur	873	784	–89	779	876	803	863	–97	–60
17.	Patiala	871	770	–101	769	868	794	874	–99	–80

NA = Not available

Sources: Derived from Census of India 1991, 2001.

distinction of being the bottom most district in the country with CSR of 766 females per thousand males.

1.1 Rural-Urban Change in Child Sex Ratio in Punjab

According to Census 2001, the urban child sex ratio in Punjab is 796 girls per 1000 boys. Compared to the child sex ratio of 1991 Census (866), the urban child sex ratio in 2001 showed a decline of 70 points (Table 5.4).

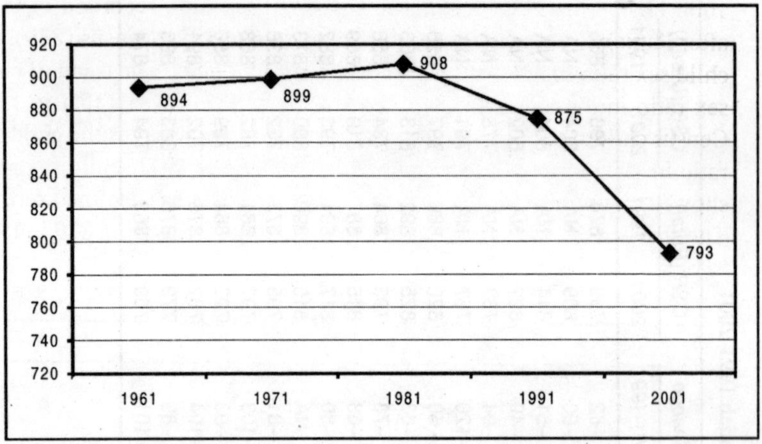

Fig. 5.3: Trend of Child Sex Ration in Punjab 1961-2001

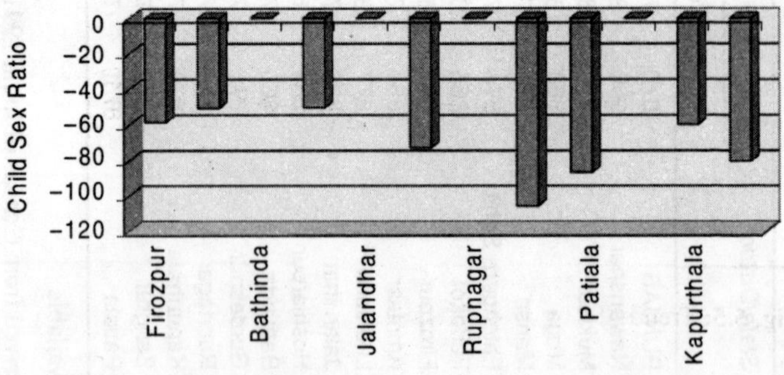

Fig. 5.4: Change in Urban Child Sex Ratio in Punjab 1991-2001

The decline in urban child sex ratio is observed in all the districts of Punjab, and the decline is higher than the decline in rural child sex ratio. The districts having the highest decline include Gurdaspur (-106 points), followed by Kapurthala (-99 points) and Jalandhar (-89 points). The district with the least decline was Ludhiana (-50 points) and Firozpur (-50 points) (Fig. 5.4).

Haryana

According to Census 2001, child sex ratio in Haryana is 820 girls per 1000 boys. This is the second lowest child sex ratio recorded in India after Punjab. Compared to the child sex ratio of 1991 Census (879), the child sex ratio in 2001 showed a decline of 59 points. The trend of child sex ratio in the last three decades (1961 to 1981) reveals that in 1961 Census child sex ratio was 910 per thousand males whereas the child sex ratio in 1971 showed a decline of 12 points. After 1971, child sex ratio showed an improvement, but from 1981 onwards it has declined further. The sharpest decline has been recorded in 2001 Census from 879 in 1991 to 820 in 2001 (Table 5.5).

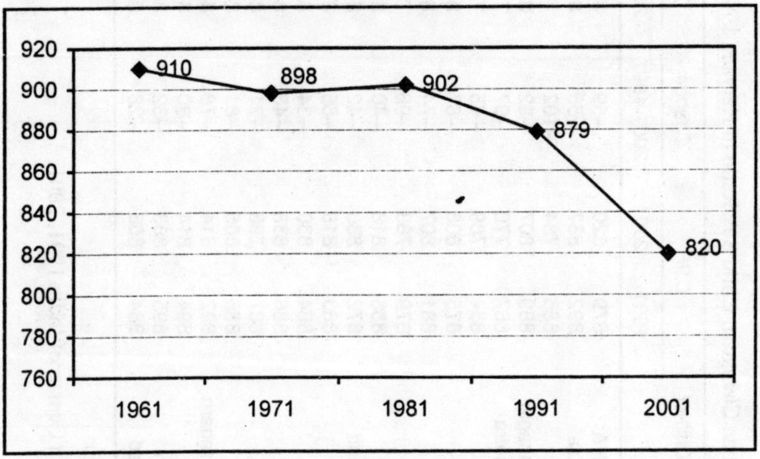

Fig. 5.5: Trend of Child Sex Ratio in Haryana 1961-2001

According to Census 2001, the overall sex ratio in Haryana was 861 females per 1000 males as compared to 933 females per 1000 males for India. This is the lowest sex ratio since independence and lowest among the major states of India. Sex ratio in all the districts of Haryana is below

Table 5.5: Rural Urban Change in Child Sex Ratio in Haryana 1991-2001

Sl. No.	State/District	CSR		Change	CSR (Rural)		CSR (Urban)		Change (R)	Change (U)
		1991	2001	2001-1991	2001	1991	2001	1991	2001-1991	2001-1991
	HARYANA	879	820	–59	824	877	809	884	–53	–75
1.	Panchkula	892	837	–55	839	NA	813	NA	NA	NA
2.	Ambala	886	784	–102	770	888	808	888	–118	–80
3.	Yamunanagar	889	807	–82	814	890	789	886	–76	–97
4.	Kurukshetra	867	770	–97	773	867	766	865	–94	–99
5.	Kaithal	854	789	–65	796	854	769	857	–58	–88
6.	Karnal	875	808	–67	813	876	792	872	–63	–80
7.	Panipat	881	807	–74	810	874	807	905	–64	–98
8.	Sonipat	879	783	–96	792	876	775	892	–84	–117
9.	Jind	858	818	–40	828	855	775	875	–27	–100
10.	Fatehabad	872	830	–42	834	NA	798	NA	NA	NA
11.	Sirsa	883	818	–65	823	885	801	874	–62	–73
12.	Hisar	864	830	–34	839	868	806	867	–29	–61
13.	Biwani	886	838	–48	844	885	827	891	–41	–64
14.	Rohtak	867	796	–71	807	875	781	879	–68	–98
15.	Jhajjar	886	805	–81	800	NA	804	NA	NA	NA
16.	Mahendragarh	892	814	–78	821	891	795	896	–70	–101
17.	Rewari	894	814	–80	810	891	816	911	–81	–95
18.	Gurgaon	895	863	–32	866	896	816	889	–30	–73
19.	Faridabad	884	856	–28	851	875	848	895	–24	–47

NA = Not available

Source: Derived from Census of India 1991, 2001.

the national average (933). In fact there has been a fall in sex ratio by 4 points from 865 in 1991 to 861 in 2001. What is more alarming is the sharp decline in the child sex ratio, i.e. the sex ratio of children in the age group of 0-6 years (Table 5.5).

In Haryana none of the districts has recorded child sex ratio favouring girls. Out of 19 districts 17 had recorded a child sex ratio of below 850 girls to 1000 boys. Districts like Ambala, Kurukshetra, Kaithal, Sonipat and Rohtak are critical with less than 800 girls to 1000 boys. The lowest child sex ratio was observed in Kurukshetra district (770). The sharp decline in child sex ratio during the decade 1991-2001 is not only at the state level but also across all the districts. Out of 19 districts, 13 districts have shown decline of more than 50 points. These districts are: Ambala (-102), Kurukshetra (-97), Sonipat (-96), Yamuna Nagar (-82), Jhajjar (-81), Rewari (-79), Mahendragarh (-77), Panipat (-74), Rohtak (-71), Karnal (-67), Kaithal (-66), Sirsa (-64) and Panchkula (-55).

2.1 Rural Urban Change in Child Sex Ratio in Haryana

In the 2001 Census, urban child sex ratio in Haryana was 809 females per 1000 males as compared to 884 females per 1000 males in 1991 Census. The urban child sex ratio in 2001 showed a sharp decline of 75 points. According to the Census 2001, all the total 19 districts observed decline in urban child sex ratio in Haryana. Decline in Urban child sex ratio in fact was higher than the rural counterpart. Almost all districts showed a decline in urban child sex ratio higher than in the rural areas,

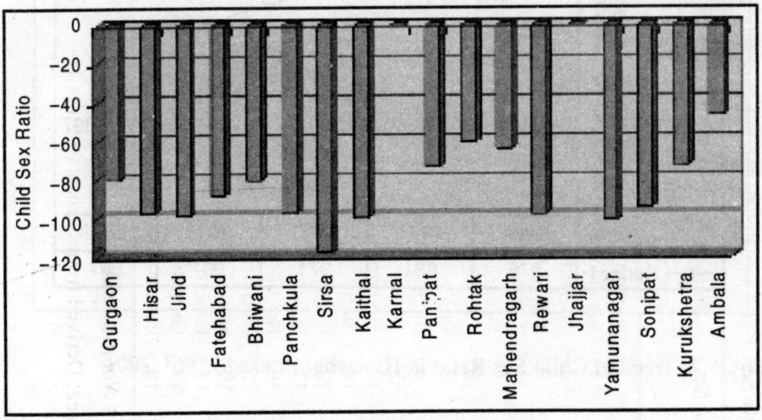

Fig. 5.6: Changes in Urban Child Sex Ratio in Haryana, 1991-2001

except some of the new district for which data was not available. The districts with the highest decline were Sonipat (-117 points), followed by Mahendragarh (-101), Jind (-100 points), Kurukshetra (-99 points), Rohtak (-98 points), Panipat (-98 points) and Rewari (-95 points). The districts with the least decline was Faridabad (-47 points). It is also the same district, which had least decline in rural child sex ratio, followed by Hissar (-61 points), Gurgaon (-73 points), Ambala (-80 points) and Karnal (-80 points).

Himachal Pradesh

Masculinity in child sex ratio has been observed in Himachal Pradesh since its statehood with male-female imbalance continuously widening since 1971 when the data is available. However, the scenario seems to have worsened drastically after 1981, with the femininity level in child population dropping to 897 females per 1000 males for Himachal Pradesh in 2001. Census based sex ratio points out substantial rise in already masculine child population and female child deficit between 1981 and 2001. The origin of the current imbalance seems to have been in the late eighties and early nineties with deficit at its maximum level in 2001 (Fig. 5.7).

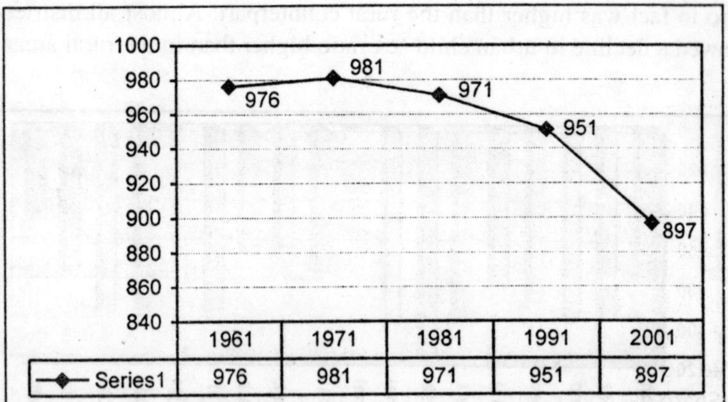

Fig. 5.7: Trend of Child Sex Ratio in Himachal Pradesh, 1961-2001

Table 5.6: Rural Urban Change in Child Sex Ratio in Himachal Pradesh 1991-2001

Sl. No.	*State / District*	*CSR*		*Change*	*CSR (Rural)*		*CSR (Urban)*		*Change (R)*	*Change (U)*
		1991	*2001*	*2001-1991*	*2001*	*1991*	*2001*	*1991*	*2001-1991*	*2001-1991*
	Himachal Pradesh	951	897	–54	900	955	844	904	–55	–60
1.	Chamba	965	962	–3	961	970	853	887	–9	–34
2.	Kangra	939	836	–103	853	942	852	885	–89	–33
3.	Lahul Spiti	951	986	35	961	951	0	NA	10	NA
4.	Kullu	966	960	–6	967	967	855	939	0	–84
5.	Mandi	968	916	–52	922	969	840	943	–47	–103
6.	Hamirpur	938	864	–74	851	940	842	907	–89	–65
7.	Una	923	839	–84	839	926	820	885	–87	–65
8.	Bilaspur	923	884	–39	884	925	837	877	–41	–40
9.	Solan	951	900	–51	905	952	876	939	–47	–63
10.	Sirmaur	973	940	–33	944	984	834	857	–40	–23
11.	Shimla	958	930	–28	953	968	832	909	–15	–77
12.	Kinnaur	958	Na	NA	979	958	0	NA	21	NA

NA = Not available

Sources: Derived from Census of India 1991, 2001.

District Level Variation in Child Sex Ratio in Himachal Pradesh (1991-2001)

According to the Census 2001, child sex ratio in Himachal Pradesh is 897 girls per 1000 boys. This is the third lowest child sex ratio in India after Punjab and Haryana. Child sex ratio showed a decline of 54 points from 1991 Census to 2001 Census. In Himachal Pradesh none of the districts had recorded child sex ratio favouring girls except Lahul and Spiti and Kinnaur. Out of the 12 districts, three districts have recorded child sex ratio of 950 and above while four districts can be placed under the category 900-949. These districts were Shimla, Sirmaur, Mandi and Solan. While the other districts showed child sex ratios to be below the state average. These were Hamirpur, Bilaspur, Kangra, Una etc. (Table 5.6).

Sharp decline in child sex ratio during the last decade was recorded in Kangra (-103), Una (-84), Hamirpur (-74), Solan (-51), Mandi (-52) that points out that, out of a total of 12 districts, 3 districts had 75 points decline in child sex ratio, and 3 districts showed a decline in the order of 50-75 points in child sex ratio. The rest of the districts portrayed a decline less than 50 points.

According to the Census 2001, the urban child sex ratio in Himachal Pradesh was 844 girls per 1000 boys. Compared to the child sex ratio of 1991 Census (904), the urban child sex ratio in 2001 showed a decline of 60 points, which was more than the rural child sex ratio. Again according to the Census 2001, 10 out of a total of 12 districts had recorded a decline in urban child sex ratio. Some of the districts that had shown large decline in urban child sex ratio were Mandi (-103 points), Kullu (-84 points), Shimla (-77 points), Una (-65 points) and Hamirpur (-65 points).

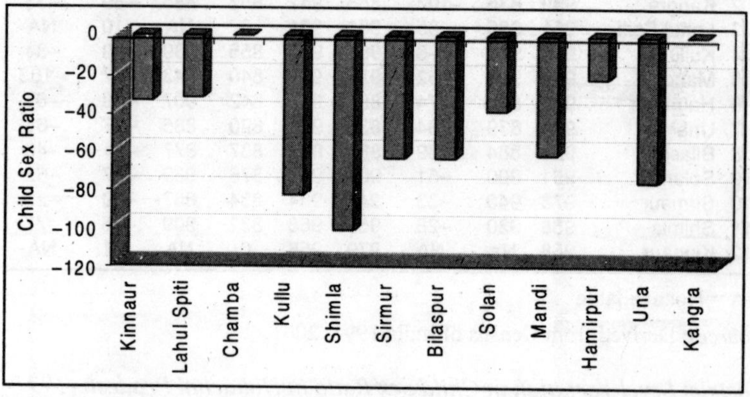

Fig. 5.8: Changes in Urban Child Sex Ration in Himachal Pradesh 1991-2001

Lahul and Spiti and Kinnaur districts had shown a absence urban population due to rough terrain and climatic conditions. In Kullu, Mandi, Shimla and Chamba districts urban child sex ratio declined sharply than the rural child sex ratio, while Kangra, Hamirpur and Una districts showed a higher decline in rural child sex ratio than the urban counterpart.

Delhi

According to the Census 2001, the child sex ratio in Delhi was 868 girls per 1000 boys. Among all the states and union territories, this is the fifth lowest child sex ratio in India after Punjab, Haryana, Himachal Pradesh and Chandigarh. Compared to the child sex ratio of 1991 Census (915), the child sex ratio in 2001showed a decline of 47 points. In 1981 Census the child sex ratio was somewhat better at 926 females per thousand males.

1981 onwards a decreasing trend in child sex ratio has been noticed in Delhi till 2001 Census. In 1961 Census the child sex ratio was 923 while in 1971 it declined by 14 points to 909. Some improvement was observed in 1981 when the child sex ratio rose to 926. However, since 1981 there has been a consistent decline to reach 865 in 2001.

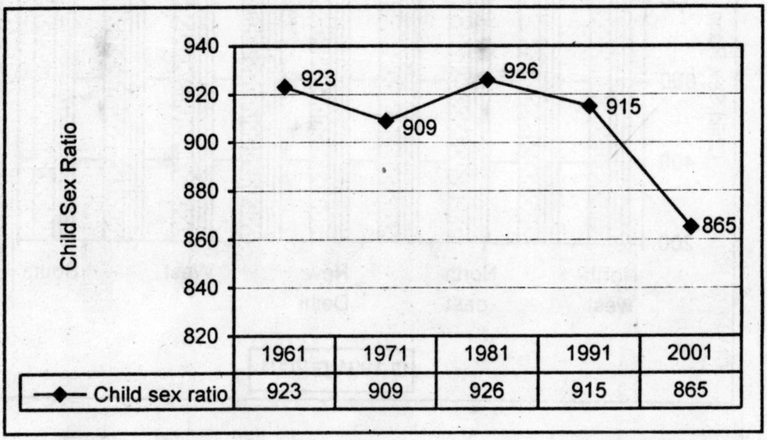

Fig 5.9: Trend in Child Sex Ratio in Delhi 1961-2001

According to the Census 2001, the urban child sex ratio in Delhi was 870 girls per 1000 boys. Compared to the child sex ratio of 1991 Census (917), the urban child sex ratio in 2001 showed a decline of 47 points. In 2001 Census, the district level urban child sex ratio was found to be the lowest in South West district (852), followed by West (859), North-West (859), and the highest urban child sex ratio was recorded in Central District (903), New Delhi (898), and in the South District (889) (Fig. 5.10).

In 1991, Delhi was a Union Territory and did not have any districts. While in 2001, Delhi was divided into 9 districts and hence the rural urban child sex ratio had not been computed.

Gujarat

Gujarat is another State which recorded child sex ratio much below the national average. Urbanised districts like Ahmedabad, Gandhinagar, Mehsana and Rajkot recorded the lowest juvenile sex ratios. Mehsana had the lowest child sex ratio in 2001 (only 797), followed by Ahmedabad (814) and Gandhinagar (816); all three are economically well developed and urbanised districts of Gujarat. Recently, Government of Gujarat has

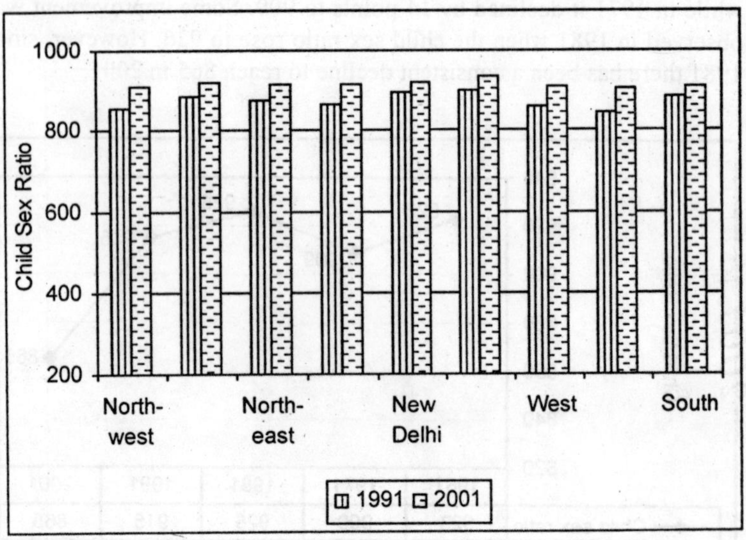

Fig. 5.10: Rural Urban Child Sex Ratio in Delhi 1991-2001

Table 5.7: Rural Urban Change in Child Sex Ratio in Delhi 1991-2001

Sl. No.	*State/ District*	*CSR*		*Change*	*CSR (Rural)*		*CSR (Urban)*		*Change (R)*	*Change (U)*
		1991	*2001*	*2001-1991*	*2001*	*1991*	*2001*	*1991*	*2001-1991*	*2001-1991*
	Delhi	915	868	–47	850	900	870	917	–50	–47
1.	North-west	913	857	–56	833	NA	859	NA	NA	NA
2.	North	920	886	–34	875	NA	887	NA	NA	NA
3.	North-east	917	875	–42	895	NA	874	NA	NA	NA
4.	East	918	865	–53	934	NA	864	NA	NA	NA
5.	New Delhi	919	898	–21	NA	NA	898	NA	NA	NA
6.	Central	937	903	–34	NA	NA	903	NA	NA	NA
7.	West	913	859	–54	865	NA	859	NA	NA	NA
8.	South West	904	846	–58	805	NA	852	NA	NA	NA
9.	South	912	888	–24	870	NA	889	NA	NA	NA

NA = Not available

Source: Derived from Census of India 1991, 2001.

taken strict action against sex selective abortions and has launched '*Beti Bachao Andolan*' to save the infant girls. The 2011 Census reveals that Gujarat has managed to halt the speedy decline in child sex ratio, but still

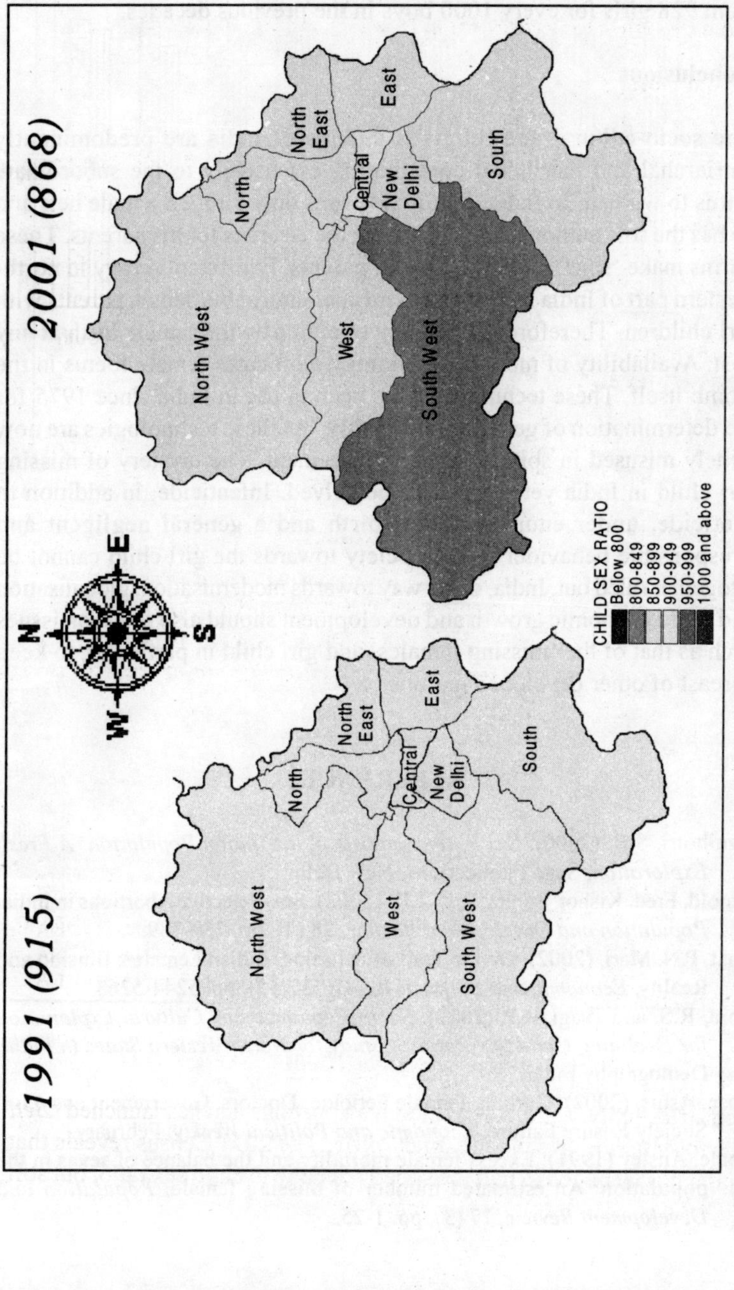

Map 5.3: Delhi: Child Sex Ratio in Age Group 0-6 (Districts)

the state has a long way to go as the current sex ratio is far below the national average. In the nineties the child sex ratio had slipped to 883 from 928 girls for every 1000 boys in the previous decades.

Conclusions

The socio-cultural and religious strands of India are predominantly patriarchal and patrilineal contributing extensively to the subordinate status to women. In India, family line runs only through a male heir and he has the sole authority of performing the last rites for his parents. These norms make 'sons' most valuable to parents. Exorbitant dowry in north-western part of India has placed extra economical burden on parents with girl children. Therefore, parents try to eliminate the female birth at any cost. Availability of modern technology eliminates female foetus in the womb itself. These techniques have been in use in India since 1975 for the determination of genetic abnormality, but these technologies are now widely misused in spite of legal enforcement. The mystery of missing girl child in India yet remains to be solved. Infanticide, in addition to foeticide, under enumeration at birth and a general negligent and irresponsible behaviour of our society towards the girl child cannot be altogether ruled out. India, on its way towards modernisation, globalisation and rapid economic growth and development should also focus on issues such as that of the 'missing females' and girl child in particular, to keep abreast of other developed nations.

REFERENCES

Agnihotri, S.B. (2000): *Sex Ratio Patterns in the Indian Population: A Fresh Exploration*, Sage Publications, New Delhi.

Arnold, Fred; Kishor, Sunita; Roy, T.K. (2002): Sex-Selective Abortions in India. *Population and Development Review*, 28 (4), pp. 759-789.

Bhat, P.N. Mari, (2002): On the Trail of 'Missing' Indian Females: Illusion and Reality, *Economic and Political Weekly*, 37(52), pp. 5244-5263.

Bora, R.S. and Tyagi, R.P. (2007): *Socio-Economic and Cultural Explanation for Declining Child Sex Ratio: A Study for North-Western States in India*, Demography India.

Bose, Ashis, (2002): Curbing Female Feticide: Doctors, Government and Civil Society Ensure Failure, *Economic and Political Weekly*, February.

Coale, Ansley (1991): Excess female mortality and the balance of sexes in the population: An estimated number of missing female, *Population and Development Review*, 17 (3), pp. 1-25.

Croll, Elisabeth (2002): *Endangered Daughters: Discrimination and Development in Asia*, Routledge, New York.

Dasgupta, M. and P.N. Mari, Bhatt (1995): Fertility Decline and Increased Manifestation of Sex Bias in India, *Population Studies*, 31 (3): pp. 529-535.

Dasgupta, M. (2005): Explaining Asia's Missing Women: A New Look at the Data, *Population and Development Review*, 31 (3), pp. 529-535.

Dyson, T. (2001): The Preliminary Demography of the 2001 Census of India, *Population and Development Review* 27(2), 341-356.

Lal, Deepak. (2006): India's Population Change and its Consequence, *Population and Development*, a supplement to volume 32, 2006, pp. 145-182.

Mallik, Rupsa. (2003): *Negative Choice: Sex Determination and Sex Selective Abortion in India*, Centre for Enquiry into Health and Allied Themes (CEHAT).

Miller, B.D. (1981): *The Endangered Sex*, Cornell University Press, Ithaca, New York.

Miller, B.D. (1989): Changing Patterns of Juvenile Sex Ratios in India: 1961 to 1971, *Economic and Political Weekly*, 24 (22), pp. 1229-35.

Natarajan, D. (1972): Changes in Sex Ratio, *Census Centenary Monograph*, No. 6, New Delhi, Office of the Registrar General, India.

Retherford, R.D. and Roy, T.K. (2003): Factors Affecting Sex-Selective Abortion in India and 17 Major States, *National Family Health Survey Reports*, No. 21, Mumbai, IIPS and Hawaii, East-West Centre.

Sen, Amartya (1990): More than 100 Million Women Are Missing: *New York Review of Books*, 20 December, pp. 61-66.

6

A Geographical Study of Urbanisation and In-Migration in Ghaziabad District, Uttar Pradesh

Mashkoor Ahmed

Urbanisation and Internal Migration: An Overview

Urbanisation has been a remarkable socio-economic phenomenon in the world that has transformed the spatial and social configurations of human society (Shen, 2000). Internal migration is also a significant process of socio-economic transformation, reflecting demographic and political dynamics of various regions in a country. However, the consequences of migration may be favourable for the area of provenance and unfavourable for the area of destination and *vice versa*. Therefore, keeping in view the pivotal importance of urbanisation and migration for human society, academicians and researchers place special attention to address these processes. Voluminous work has been done both on urbanisation and migration at the global level as well as in India and there exists a vast body of literature dealing with urbanisation and migration especially since independence when the country saw a huge shift of population between rural and urban areas both in and across the national borders. Many scholars have attempted to show the consequences of migration on urbanisation and *vice versa*. A brief discussion of such studies has been presented here to understand the inter-relationships between urbanisation and migration. Oberai and Singh (1983) have tried to show that migrants may contribute to the growth of urban economy through increased supply of unskilled and semi-skilled labour that may result in greater labour productivity, higher incomes and diversification of industry and services. On the other hand, they may simply burden the economy through increased under employment and unemployment levels, lower levels of productivity and a greater demand for urban services. The net economic impact of in-migration on urban areas will largely depend on the type of migrants involved, and on their characteristics. Singh (2007) has showed that how migration has significantly changed the demographic profile of Mumbai and contributed to its population growth. Migration has played a major role in the expansion of the urban economy, by increasing the labour supply as well as has resulted in increased labour force participation rate among urban population (Dupont, 1992). However, whether migration is a strong or a weak force in the urbanisation process depends upon the nature and pattern of migration (Bhagat *et al.*, 2009). Reisinger (2003) has accepted that major movement of population have been associated with significant economic changes. In most cases migrants feel economic satisfaction at the place of their destination and economic conditions of migrants are favourably comparable with that of the host population. The movement of population within a country indirectly reflects the level of development and imbalances in economic opportunities (Singh, 2005). Industrial development provides the impetus for urbanisation and the evolution of urban structure in a region, and this process is always accompanied by migration. Migration is both the outcome and the concomitant process of regional industrial development, and migration in turn has complex influence on regional development. It is an important indicator of regional competitiveness (Ren, 2006). Truly speaking in a country, like India, internal migration occurs as a result of regional disparities in economic and social conditions of the area and the people concerned of those regions. However, spatial movement of people has to be seen in context of the socio-economic conditions of regions, the place at which the conditions are changing and the consequences arising from such changing patterns (Smita and Chandna, 1991). The migration flows are considered to have important effects on the development process such as employment or regional development, so an increased understanding of migration can aid the formulation of development policies (Falaris, 1979).

STUDY AREA: GHAZIABAD DISTRICT

Location

Ghaziabad district is situated in the western part of Uttar Pradesh between 28°25′ to 28°55′ north parallels of latitude and longitude 77°12′ to 78°15′.

It is bounded on the east by Jyotiba Phule Nagar district and on the south-west by Delhi and is separated by the rivers Ganga and Yamuna in the east and west respectively. In the north lies the district of Meerut and in the south Gautam Budh Nagar and Bulandshahr districts. The length of the district from east to west is nearly 88 km and maximum breadth from north to south is nearly 51km. The geographical area of the district is 1148 sq.km. As the district's boundary is adjacent to Delhi, it acts as the main entrance of Uttar Pradesh and, therefore, it is also called the 'Gateway to Uttar Pradesh'. Ganga, Yamuna and Hindon are the prominent rivers flowing through the district and they are filled with water throughout the year. Apart from these, there are some small rain fed rivers, important among them is the Kali river. Besides these rivers, the Ganga Canal flows through the district and irrigation is carried out through different branches of this Canal. The Ganga Canal also fulfils the drinking water needs of the people of Ghaziabad district. For administrative and development purposes the district has been divided into four tehsils and eight Community Development Blocks. The district has 560 villages, out of which 522 are inhabited and 38 uninhabited. There are 17 towns in the district.

Socio-Economic and Demographic Profile

According to Census of India 2001, the total population of Ghaziabad district is 3,290,586 comprising 53.76 per cent males and 46.24 per cent females resulting in a sex ratio of 860 (number of females per 1000 males). 55.2 per cent of its total population resides in urban areas and 44.8 per cent are housed in the rural part of the district. The population density in the district is 2866 persons per sq. km. which is much higher than the state average of 690 persons per sq. km. The district with a literacy rate of 69.5 per cent ranks third in Uttar Pradesh. Ghaziabad district is one of the most industrialised districts of Uttar Pradesh. The district has made a tremendous headway in industrial development. One of the important factors that has given rise to its pivotal position in industry is its proximity to Delhi. Apart from industrial development, being situated in the fertile tract of Ganga-Yamuna *doab* Ghaziabad district is also agriculturally developed. Land surface of the district is made up of fertile soil brought by the rivers Ganga and Yamuna for over thousands of years and hence extensive cultivation is done. Availability of extensive irrigation facilities also helps in agricultural activities in the districts.

Data and Methodology

The present study is entirely based on secondary sources such as Census of India especially A- and D-series, District Census Handbook of Ghaziabad district, and Town Directory of Uttar Pradesh. The patterns of migration have been analysed on the basis of Place of Birth (POB) data. By using these data, patterns of in-migration, out-migration and net-migration have been explored. Besides Place of Last Residence (POLR) data have been employed to identify various types of in-migration streams in the district. The level of urbanisation has been represented as the share of a region's (district, state or country) total population that live in urban areas. Simple statistical methods have been applied for the analysis of data and the presentation of data have been done through diagrams.

Levels and Trends of Urbanisation

Urbanisation is a finite process experienced by all nations in their transition from an agrarian to an industrial society; thus, different levels of urbanisation reflect differing degrees of economic development (Ledent, 1982). Urbanisation and migration are the two most significant phenomena in various parts of our country and both are mutually interdependent. According to 2001 Census of India 27.81 per cent of the total population in India was urban. However, the process of urbanisation has slowed down in India. In 1901 urban population of India was only 25.85 million which constituted 10.84 per cent of the country's total population and in 2001 the urban population of the country became 286.11 million. Not all regions have the same level of urbanisation and thus among different States and Union Territories of India there are conspicuous variations in the levels of urbanisation. At one extreme are the states with low levels of urbanisation such as Himachal Pradesh (9.8%), Bihar (10.46%) and Uttar Pradesh (20.78%) and on the other extreme are the states and union territories with very high level of urbanisation, for example, Maharashtra (42.43%), Mizoram (49.43%), Goa (49.76%), Chandigarh (89.77%) and Delhi (93.18%).

Though, Uttar Pradesh is the most populous state with 166.1 million population and supports one of the largest urban systems in the country (704 cities and towns), yet it ranks 18th in the level of urbanisation. In 2001 urban population of Uttar Pradesh was 34.5 million which constituted 20.78 per cent of the state's total population. There are conspicuous variations in the population growth and size class of different cities and towns. Class-I cities and metropolitan urban areas are growing at very high rates due to which the urban system is becoming 'top heavy'. About 28 per cent of the total urban population of the State is confined in 6 metropolitan cities and nearly 60 per cent of the state's urban population is concentrated in 54 Class-I cities (including 6 metropolitan cities). The remaining 40 per cent of the urban population is distributed among a large number of other class towns ranging from Class-II to Class-VI. Due to out-migration most of these towns have shown either declining or fluctuating population growth rate, and many small towns have also registered a negative population growth rate during the past decades.

Urbanisation is intimately related to internal migration in a country. Generally, internal migration is accepted as a prominent component in the process of urbanisation. Internal migration through its rural-urban flow has become increasingly one of the major components of urban population growth. However, it does not seem to increase the population of all the cities in a state or country at an equal rate. It highly favours the growth of big cities or the towns and urban centres surrounding them. The recent high population growth of many cities, for example in Uttar Pradesh, may be attributed to migration from rural areas and small and medium size cities. An examination of the population growth of Class-I cities of Uttar Pradesh, reveals that for the past few decades the population of the cities in the western part of the state especially those in the vicinity of Delhi for example Ghaziabad, Modinagar, Loni, Noida, Meerut, Muzaffarnagar, Moradabad and Hapur have experienced an unprecedented increase in their population. For example, Ghaziabad city in 1951 had a population of only 38217 which increased to 968256 in 2001. Likewise, the population of Meerut during the same period rose from 167315 to 1068772. But the cities of the eastern part of the state like Shahjahanpur, Mirzapur, Varanasi, Allahabad, etc., recorded very slow increase in their population. This is reflected by the fact that in 1951 the population of Shahjahanpur was 98949 which rose to only 301393 during the same period. The population of Mirzapur rose from 85228 to 205053 and that of Varanasi increased from 345253 to 1103952. This pattern of the growth of Class-I cities of Uttar Pradesh thereby indicates that high population growth has taken place in the cities situated in the western part of the state particularly those near Delhi. This may be attributed to high in-migration in these cities while the slow population growth of the cities in the eastern part reflects low levels of in-migration.

Ghaziabad district is one of the three highly urbanised districts of Uttar Pradesh which has more than half of its population living in urban areas and ranks third in the level of urbanisation of the State. This can be seen in the light of the fact that the State of Uttar Pradesh, in which the district is situated, is predominantly rural one with 79.22 per cent of its population living in rural areas and only 20.78 per cent of its population is urban. During the last few decades, the district has experienced spectacular population growth rates. Many towns and cities in Ghaziabad district have witnessed higher population growth rate as compared to other cities and towns of other districts of Uttar Pradesh.

Table 6.1 illustrates that at the beginning of twentieth century (1901) the urban population of Ghaziabad district was only 15.09 per cent and with slight fluctuations it remained almost static up to 1941. During this period the district experienced population growth rates of -8.0 per cent and -9.6 per cent during the decade 1901-1911 and 1911-1921 respectively. After 1941 especially since independence the district reflects high population growth rates. During 1941-1951 the urban population growth rate was as high as 46.7 per cent and it decreased to 35.5 per cent between 1951and1961. However, since 1961 when the level of urbanisation was 21.71 per cent, the district witnessed very rapid growth in urban population and consequently more than half (55.20%) of the population became urbanised in 2001. High population growth of cities and towns of the district may be attributed to a combination of many factors such as strategic locations on many major rail and road routes connecting with Delhi and other parts of the country, proximity to Delhi, establishment of planned industrial estate, discouragement to the establishment of the large scale industries in Delhi, availability of cheap and skilled labour from neighbouring densely populated areas for setting up new industries, productivity of land and presence of educational institutions. During the last few years, the tertiary sector has also flourished in many towns of Ghaziabad district. Since 1921 the decadal growth rate of urban population has been higher than the rural counterpart and this difference became more conspicuous since 1971.

Table 6.2 portrays the population growth rates in the cities and towns of Ghaziabad district. During the last two decades, Loni city of the district has grown at the fastest rate in the tune of +256.38 per cent and +230.80 per cent during 1981-91 and 1991-2001 respectively. Ghaziabad city, the headquarters of the district has grown rapidly after the country became independent. In 1901, it started as a small town with a population of only 11,275 and up to 1951, when it had a population of 38,271. But since 1951 the city recorded a spurt in its population growth and consequently with 9.6 lakh population in 2001 it emerged as one of the big cities in

Table 6.1: Decadal Population Growth and Level of Urbanisation in Ghaziabad District (1901-2001)

Decadal Year	*Decadal Population*			*Decadal Population Growth Rate in Percentage*			*Level of Urbanisation in percentage*
	Urban	*Rural*	*Total*	*Urban*	*Rural*	*Total*	
1901	73,726	414,718	488,444	–	–	–	15.09*
1911	67,802	414,110	481,912	–8	–0.2	–1.3	14.07
1921	61,271	415,741	477,012	–9.6	0.4	–1	12.84
1931	74,084	435,600	509,684	20.9	4.8	6.9	14.54
1941	95,186	506,408	601,594	28.5	16.3	18.0	15.82
1951	139,672	578,513	718,185	46.7	14.2	19.4	19.45
1961	189,232	682,315	871,547	35.5	17.9	21.4	21.71
1971	317,199	818,578	1,135,777	67.6	20.0	30.3	27.93
1981	609,353	968,224	1,577,577	92.1	18.3	38.9	38.63
1991	1,061,550	1,174,125	2,235,675	74.2	21.3	41.7	47.48
2001	1,816,415	1,474,171	3,290,586	71.1	25.6	47.2	55.20

Source: District Census Handbook, Ghaziabad District, 2001.

Table 6.2: Decadal Population Growth in Cities and Towns of Ghaziabad District (1951-2001)

Name of City/Town	*Size Class of Urban Centres*	*1951–61*	*1961–71*	*1971–81*	*1981–91*	*1991–2001*
Patala	V	—	—	—	17	6.01
Niwari	V	—	—	—	24.91	12.22
Bisokhar	IV	—	—	—	—	29.17
Muradnagar	II	33.32	69.35	86.25	70.44	67.03
Ordinance Factory Muradnagar	IV	—	—	45.66	–2.70	–15.92
Begumabad Budhana	IV	—	—	—	43.38	20.18
Modinagar	I	97.22	79.14	79.99	29.93	11.37
Faridnagar	IV	4.67	20.08	20.89	20.01	3.03
Ghaziabad	I	65.35	88.06	132.1	64.66	113.2
Dasna	III	—	—	—	—	44.04
Loni	I	Declassified	Declassified	—	256.38	230.8
Behta Hajipur	II	—	—	—	—	210.6
Pilakhuwa	II	39.46	49.4	58.24	32.41	33.38
Hapur	I	12.14	28.99	44.3	42.23	44.93
Babugarh	V	Declassified	Declassified	—	49.9	65.85
Garhmukteshwar	III	32.98	25.47	63.79	40.9	34.1

Source: Town Directory of Uttar Pradesh, 2001.

Uttar Pradesh. Based on 2011 Census, the population of Ghaziabad city has been projected to be as high as 15 lakh. Ghaziabad city is situated only about 22 km. from Delhi. New developments, well-planned infrastructure, industrialisation, strategic location, cheaper urban infrastructure and housing make this city the most preferred destination for residential and business activities within the NCR (National Capital Region). The cities and towns of Ghaziabad district, apart from fulfilling their own demands also supply a variety of manufactured products to Delhi and other parts of the country. These include rail coaches, diesel engines, electroplating materials, bicycles, tapestries, glassware, pottery, paints and varnishes, automobile parts, flour mills, iron and steel products, ceramics, pipes, vegetable oils, picture tubes, medicines, beverages and so on. These industries have attracted migrants from other districts of Uttar Pradesh and also from other states of India. Very high inflow of people in the cities and towns of the district have contributed to rapid urban population growth. With the increase of population, the size and appearance of the towns and cities have changed both horizontally and vertically. But social and infrastructural development could not keep pace with increasing urban population. Therefore, urban areas of the district are subjected to the problems such as congestions, unplanned industrialisation, unauthorised colonies, poor solid waste management and tremendous pressure on other physical and social infrastructural facilities. A report of the Ministry of Urban Development (2009) has pointed out that massive urban growth has led to complex problems of inadequacy of basic urban services. About 21 per cent of the urban population is living in squatter settlements where access to the basic services is very poor or non-existent. About 80 per cent of the population living in urban areas though has access to safe drinking water but there are severe deficiencies with regard to equitable distribution of water in terms of duration and frequency of supply.

PATTERNS OF MIGRATION IN GHAZIABAD DISTRICT

In-Migration Across Different Spatial Scales

During the last few decades, Ghaziabad district has witnessed very remarkable population growth among 70 districts of Uttar Pradesh. This exceptionally high population growth especially in cities and towns of Ghaziabad district is the result of heavy inflow of population from the rural and urban areas of other districts of Uttar Pradesh as well as other states of India. In 1901 the district had a total population of 4.88 lakh which reduced to only 4.87 lakh in 1911 and further to 4.77 lakh in 1921. But since 1931 when its total population was 5.09 lakh, the district has been registering continuous increase in growth rates and, therefore, reported a population of 32.9 lakh in 2001. This high population growth of the district in absolute terms is due to high in-migration.

Indian Census records place of birth of each and every person with rural and urban distinction which directly helps to identify migrants. According to place of birth data, migrants are those who are enumerated at a village/town at the time of Census other than their place of birth. Using Place of Birth (POB) data of 2001 Census, all the migrants in Ghaziabad district have been classified into three categories based on administrative boundaries. These include intra-district migrants (born elsewhere in Ghaziabad district), inter-district migrants (born in another district of Uttar Pradesh) and inter-state migrants (born in another state in India outside Uttar Pradesh). The last two categories of migrants have significantly affected the size and composition of population in Ghaziabad district. Fig. 6.1 demonstrates the percentage distribution of migrants by place of birth. The analysis of place of birth data has unveiled that there were 1.22 million migrants in Ghaziabad district, which represented 37.27 per cent of the district's total population. It is interesting to note that the percentage of migrants to the total population in Ghaziabad district was highest among all districts of Uttar Pradesh and was followed by Gautam Budh Nagar (35.77%) and Sonbhadra (29.75%).

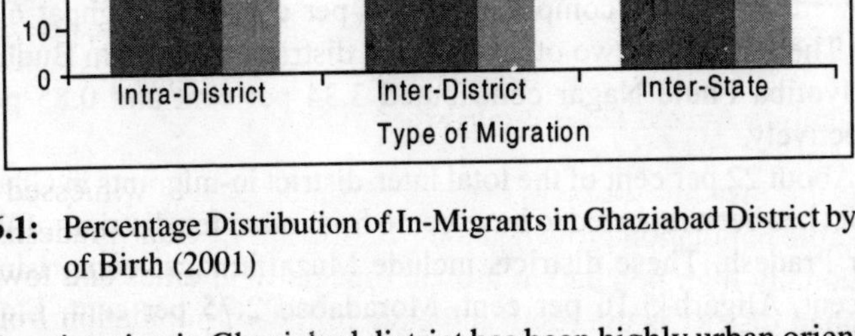

Fig. 6.1: Percentage Distribution of In-Migrants in Ghaziabad District by Place of Birth (2001)

In-migration in Ghaziabad district has been highly urban oriented as 64.06 per cent migrants have been reported in urban areas compared to

35.94 per cent in rural areas. More than half of the in-migrants (53.03%) were inter-district migrants, majority of them being from neighbouring districts. Intra-district migrants constituted slightly less than one-fourth of total in-migrants followed by inter-state migrants which contributed 22.81 per cent of the total migrants by place of birth in Ghaziabad district. Approximately half (51.14%) of the total male migrants in Ghaziabad district have moved from other districts of Uttar Pradesh followed by inter-state male migrants who constituted 27.40 per cent. Only 21.46 per cent of the total males have migrated within district boundaries especially from rural to urban areas particularly for economic motives. However, unlike male migrants, major portion of the female in-migrants (54.50%) have been involved in inter-district migration. Whereas one-fourth females moved within district boundary, 19.87 per cent had migrated from other states.

Inter-District In- and Out-Migration

Table 6.3 depicts the distribution of inter-district in-migration, out-migration and net-migration in Ghaziabad district from other districts of Uttar Pradesh by place of birth data, 2001. The data portray that in Ghaziabad district about 0.65 million people have been identified as those in-migrants who were born in other districts of Uttar Pradesh. Majority of these inter-district in-migrants were from neighbouring districts. Most of the districts of Uttar Pradesh are agrarian and lack employment opportunities. This creates rural push resulting in-migration towards urban and industrialised district of Ghaziabad. The five adjacent districts of Ghaziabad district collectively contributed 56.02 per cent (0.36 million persons) to the total volume of inter-district in-migrants. These adjacent districts include Bulandshahr which contributed about 22.97 per cent (149887 persons) to the total inter-district in-migrants and was closely followed by Meerut comprising 22.68 per cent and Baghpat 6.17 per cent. The remaining two other adjacent districts of Gautam Budh Nagar and Jyotiba Phule Nagar contributed 3.34 per cent and 0.85 per cent respectively.

About 22 per cent of the total inter-district in-migrants in Ghaziabad district has been reported to have come from other ten districts of Western Uttar Pradesh. These districts include Muzaffarnagar comprising 5.48 per cent, Aligarh 5.16 per cent, Moradabad 2.75 per cent, Etah 1.84 per cent, Badaun 1.42 per cent, Agra 1.23 per cent, Saharanpur 1.21 per cent, Etawah 1.05 per cent and Mathura 0.99 per cent of the total

Table 6.3: Inter-District Migration in Ghaziabad District by Place of Birth (2001)

Name of District	*In-Migrants to Ghaziabad District*		*Out-Migrants from Ghaziabad District*		*Net-Migrants of Ghaziabad District*
	In Numbers	*In per cent*	*In Numbers*	*In per cent*	*In Numbers*
Saharanpur	7,900	1.21	2,838	1.31	+5,062
Muzaffarnagar	35,761	5.48	11,410	5.26	+24,351
Bijnor	9,254	1.42	1,464	0.67	+7,790
Moradabad	17,956	2.75	2,051	0.94	+15,905
Jyotiba Phule Nagar	5,551	0.85	5,388	2.48	+163
Meerut	147,943	22.68	94,753	43.66	+53,190
Baghpat	40,256	6.17	23,006	10.6	+17,250
Gautam Budh Nagar	21,799	3.34	27,063	12.47	–5,264
Bulandshahr	149,887	22.98	34,967	16.11	+114,920
Aligarh	33,677	5.16	2,129	0.98	+31,548
Mathura	6,458	0.99	725	0.33	+5,733
Agra	8,046	1.23	585	0.27	+7,461
Etah	12,006	1.84	331	0.15	+11,675
Budaun	9,625	1.48	463	0.21	+9,162
Bareilly	6,327	0.97	597	0.28	+5,730
Farrukhabad	5,141	0.79	106	0.05	+5,035
Etawah	6,846	1.05	121	0.06	+6,725
Kanpur Nagar	8,508	1.3	807	0.37	+7,701
Allahabad	6,067	0.93	354	0.16	+5,713
Gorakhpur	6,010	0.92	122	0.06	+5,888
Azamgarh	5,741	0.88	298	0.14	+5,443
Other Districts	101,623	15.58	7,461	3.44	+94,162
Total	652,382	100.00	217,039	100.00	+435,343

Source: Calculation based on Census of India 2001, D-Series, Table D-1.

inter-district in-migrants in the district. The share of all other districts of Uttar Pradesh separately (except Kanpur Nagar with 1.3%) was less than 1 per cent of the total in-migrants in Ghaziabad district. Ghaziabad district as has been already stated is one of the highly industrialised, urbanised and socio-economically developed districts in Uttar Pradesh and hence it is one of the most preferred destination for people from other districts of the State, which are predominantly agrarian. Also, middle income groups who are unable to afford high rent values in Delhi, can easily purchase land in Ghaziabad district keeping in mind its proximity and good communication and transportation facilities.

As far as the distributional pattern of out-migrants is concerned Table 6.3 brings to the fore that only 0.21 million out-migrants from

Ghaziabad district moved to other districts of Uttar Pradesh. However, their number has been quite low in comparison to the inter-district in-migrants (0.36 million persons). Data unveil that distributional pattern of out-migrants from Ghaziabad district to other districts of Uttar Pradesh has been very uneven. About 85 per cent of the population of Ghaziabad district had migrated to five adjacent districts. About 43.66 per cent of the total out-migrants from Ghaziabad district were found alone in Meerut district which was followed by Bulandshahr (16.11%) and Gautam Budh Nagar district (12.47%). Among the five adjacent districts Baghpat and Jyotiba Phule Nagar attracted 10.48 per cent and 2.48 per cent respectively of the total inter-district out-migrants from Ghaziabad district. While Muzaffarnagar and Saharanpur received 5.26 per cent and 1.31 per cent respectively of the total out-migrants who had migrated from Ghaziabad to other districts during the same reference period.

Table 6.3 also portrays the distribution of net-migrants of Ghaziabad district and its district level break-up of total migrants. The district recorded inter-district positive net-migration of 435343 persons. Ghaziabad district showed positive net-migration with all the districts of Uttar Pradesh with the exception of three districts that had shown negative net-migration. These three districts were Gautam Budh Nagar, Sonbhadra and Kaushambhi. There was more out-migration from Ghaziabad to these three districts over in-migration. Ghaziabad district exhibited highest net-migration with respect to Bulandshahr district (+114920 migrants) followed by Meerut, Muzaffarnagar and Aligarh districts.

Inter-State In-Migration

Table 6.4 depicts the percentage distribution of in-migrants from various states of India (excluding U.P.) by Place of Birth (POB) in Ghaziabad district. During 2001 there were 2.79 lakh inter-state in-migrants in the district which constituted 8.50 per cent of the total population and about 23 per cent of the total migrants by place of birth in the district. The inter-state migrants were highly urban oriented as 88 per cent of them were recorded in urban areas and only 22 per cent were registered in rural parts of the district. About 36 per cent inter-state migrants found in the district were having their place of birth in Delhi. Again about 30 per cent of the total male and 40 per cent of the total female in-migrants by place of birth belonged to Delhi. Very high migration from Delhi to Ghaziabad district may be due to its proximity and low cost of living. Many towns of Ghaziabad district are very close to Delhi and are connected by good rail and road routes. Besides, during the recent years many industries as well as MNCs and hi-tec industries have been located in Delhi to Ghaziabad district that induces in-migration. This is manifested by the fact that during last decade (1991-2001) about half (49.80%) of the total inter-state in-migrants by place of last residence were from Delhi alone (Census of India, 2001, D-series, Table D-2). The second most contributor of in-migrants in Ghaziabad district was Bihar (17.23%) followed by Uttarakhand (14.44%). About 8 per cent of the migrants in the district were having their place of birth in Haryana and 4.64 per cent in Punjab, followed by West Bengal (3.55%), Rajasthan (3.38%), Madhya Pradesh (2.93%), and Jharkhand (2.43%) while the remaining states and union territories collectively constituted only about 8 per cent of the total inter-state in-migrants in Ghaziabad district thereby exhibiting a strong distant-decay in in-migration. The sex ratio of inter-state in-migrants in the district was in favour of females (53%) than males (47%) and this was due to very high female in-migration from Delhi to Ghaziabad district. Of the total in-migration from Delhi 60 per cent were females.

Thus, it is clear that Ghaziabad district has also received a large number of migrants from various States of India. Cities and towns of the district are developing at a very high rate especially Ghaziabad city that has emerged as one of highly developed and planned cities of Northern India. Many educational institutions, hospitals, parks, malls have come

Table 6.4: Percentage Distribution of Inter-State In-Migrants in Ghaziabad District (2001)

Name of the State of Origin	*In-Migrants in Number*			*In-Migrants in Per Cent*		
	Persons	*Males*	*Females*	*Persons*	*Males*	*Females*
Punjab	12,978	6,294	6,684	4.64	4.79	4.50
Uttarakhand	40,410	21,065	19,345	14.44	16.03	13.04
Haryana	21,784	6,686	15,098	7.79	5.09	10.17
Delhi	99,569	39,530	60,039	35.59	30.08	40.46
Rajasthan	9,444	4,739	4,705	3.38	3.61	3.17
Bihar	48,199	28,806	19,393	17.23	21.92	13.07
West Bengal	9,927	5,035	4,892	3.55	3.83	3.30
Jharkhand	6,796	3,783	3,013	2.43	2.88	2.03
Madhya Pradesh	8,195	4,237	3,958	2.93	3.22	2.67
Other States	22,496	11,234	11,262	8.04	8.55	7.59
Total	279,798	131,409	148,389	100.0	100.0	100.0

Source: Calculation based on Census of India 2001, D-Series Table D-1.

up in Ghaziabad. Many cities and towns are highly industrialised and being situated near Delhi. These have good infrastructural facilities and amenities and therefore attract migrants from other states of India.

IN-MIGRATION STREAMS

A migration stream is defined as a group of migrants who depart from a common area of origin and arrive at a common area of destination during a specified migration interval (Bogue, 1959). Considering the area of origin and destination as rural/urban four types of migration streams, namely, rural-rural, rural-urban, urban-urban and urban-rural operate at different spatial scales. These are responsible for redistribution of population between rural and urban areas of a country and thus, to a large extent, determine the ratio of rural/urban population. The above mentioned four types of migration steams have been separately analysed for inter-district and inter-state in-migration in Ghaziabad district.

Inter-District In-Migration Streams

During the previous decade (1991-2001) 0.22 million migrants (incorporating 42.78 per cent males and 57.22 per cent females) involving in various types of migration streams, have moved to Ghaziabad district from other districts of Uttar Pradesh. At inter-district level, rural-urban in-migration stream was the most dominating as it alone attracted 43.86 per cent in-migrants to the urban areas of Ghaziabad district. These migrants hailed from the rural areas of other districts of Uttar Pradesh. The rural to urban stream constituted slightly more than half (51.45%) of the total males and 38.19 per cent of the total females. Rural to urban migration stream was followed by rural-rural migration stream that constituted of 29.56 per cent of the total inter-district in-migrants. About one-fifth (20.93%) of the males and 36.01 per cent of the females moved to the rural areas of Ghaziabad district from the rural areas of other districts. Urban to urban migration stream constituted of 22.90 per cent migrants from other districts of Uttar Pradesh. The break-up of this stream revealed that one-fourth (24.11%) of the total male migrants and 22 per cent of the total female migrants were from other districts of Uttar Pradesh. At inter-district level, urban-rural migration stream was the least dominating as only 3.68 per cent migrants moved into rural areas of Ghaziabad district from the urban areas of other districts of Uttar Pradesh.

Table 6.5: Inter-District in Migration Streams in Ghaziabad District during (1991-2001)

Migration Stream	*In–Migrants in Per Cent*			*Sex Ratio in Per Cent*	
	Persons	*Males*	*Females*	*Males*	*Females*
Rural–Rural	29.56	20.93	36.01	30.29	69.71
Rural–Urban	43.86	51.45	38.19	50.18	49.82
Urban–Rural	3.68	3.51	3.80	40.85	59.15
Urban–Urban	22.90	24.11	22.00	45.04	54.96
Total	100.00	100.00	100.00	42.78	57.22

Source: Calculation based on Census of India 2001, D-Series, Table D-2.

Table 6.5 shows the sex ratio of migrants involved in inter-district in-migration streams in Ghaziabad district. Rural to rural in-migration stream was disproportionately dominated by females where they constituted about 70 per cent compared to 30 per cent males. However, in rural to urban migration stream the ratio male to female, was approximately equal. Both in urban to rural and urban to urban migration steams the ratio of females was higher and was as recorded 59.15 per cent and 54.96 per cent respectively as compared to 40.85 per cent males in urban to rural and 45.04 per cent males in urban to urban in-migration stream.

Inter-State In-Migration Streams

During 1991-2001, considerable in-migration took place from various states (excluding Uttar Pradesh) of India to Ghaziabad district. Urban to urban migration stream attracted the lion's share of inter-state in-migrants in Ghaziabad district as 55.88 per cent of the total inter-state in-migrants were involved in this type of streams. Many people from urban areas of various states migrated into the urban areas of Ghaziabad district and majority of them were from Delhi. Urban to urban stream incorporated 52.22 per cent males and 58.44 per cent females of the total inter-state male and female migrants respectively. Rural to urban migration stream was the second most dominating stream which constituted slightly less than one-fourth (23.37%) of the total inter-state in-migrants. Here the percentage of male and female migrants to total male and female migrants was 26.14 per cent and 20.51 per cent respectively. Rural to rural migration stream contributed 11.42 per cent followed by urban-rural migration stream which constituted 9.94 per cent of the total inter-state in-migrants.

It is worth mentioning here that the overall ratio of males and females in inter-state migration streams was almost equal. In fact, in all the four migration streams there was differentials in sex-ratio as compared to the inter-district migration streams.

Table 6.6: Inter-State In-Migration Streams in Ghaziabad District during 1991-2001

Migration Stream	*In-Migrants in Per Cent*			*Sex Ratio in Per Cent*	
	Persons	*Males*	*Females*	*Males*	*Females*
Rural– Rural	11.42	11.81	11.01	52.51	47.49
Rural–Urban	23.37	26.14	20.51	56.77	43.23
Urban–Rural	9.94	9.84	10.04	50.23	49.77
Urban–Urban	55.28	52.22	58.44	47.94	52.06
Total	100.00	100.00	100.00	50.75	49.25

Source: Calculation based on Census of India 2001, D-Series, Table D-2.

Duration of Residence

Migration is a spatio-temporal phenomenon. On the basis of duration of residence all migrants in Ghaziabad district can be classified into six categories, namely less than one year, 1-4 years, 5-9 years, 10-19 years, 20+ years and duration not stated. Table 6.7 depicts that only 2.12 per cent of the total migrants in Ghaziabad district were reported having their duration of residence less than one year. This category involved 2.61 per cent males and 1.81 per cent females respectively to the total male and female migrants. The next category of migrants with duration of residence 1-4 years constituted 18.87 per cent and the proportion of males and females was 21.72 per cent and 17.04 per cent respectively. 16.73 per cent migrants had their duration of residence between 5-9 years. In this group the proportion of males and females to total male and female migrants was 17.88 per cent and 15.98 per cent respectively. Thus about 38 per cent in-migrants in the district came during last decade (1991-2001). The highest percentage (23.05%) of migrants has been found with duration of residence between 10-19 years. In this group about one-fifth (21.93%) were males and about one-fourth were females. 21.68 per cent migrants reported their duration of residence more than 20 years. In this category male and female migrants represented 12.76 per cent and 27.44 per cent of the total male and female migrants respectively. 17.54 per cent migrants were unaccounted for as their duration of residence was unknown. The proportion of male migrants in this category was 23.06 per cent while that of females was 13.98 per cent.

Table 6.7: Duration of Residences of Migrants in Ghaziabad District (2001)

Duration of Residence	*Migrants in Per Cent*		
	Persons	*Males*	*Females*
Less than 1 year	2.12	2.61	1.81
1–4 years	18.87	21.72	17.04
5–9 years	16.73	17.88	15.98
10–19 years	23.05	21.97	23.75
20+ years	21.68	12.76	27.44
Duration not stated	17.54	23.06	13.98
Total	100	100	100.00

Source: Calculation based on Census of India 2001, D-Series, Table D-2.

Characteristics of In-Migrants

Migrants tend to differ from the rest of the population both at origin and the destination in certain socio-economic, demographic and personal aspects such as age, sex, marital status, education, occupation and decision-making. Thus migration of population involves a choice and hence may alter the social-economic, demographic characteristics of regions concerned.

Age Sex Structure of Migrants

Age is one of the most important demographic components of population. In or out migration of people of a particular sex and age group in substantial number significantly changes the age and sex composition of population. Therefore, it is imperative to study such characteristics of migrants. Fig. 6.2 shows the percentage distribution of migrants among different age groups. It is evident that majority of the in-migrants (37.07%) were having their ages between 20-29 years. It is important to note that about half (48.60%) of the female migrants and 22.34 per cent of the male migrants have moved between 20-29 years. The movement of males in this age group may partly be due to employment and partly because of education. While in case of females, migration may be due to a combination of marriage, moved with households and education and to a small extent for employment also. The next dominating age group was 30-39 years which constituted 18.38 per cent migrants. In this category the proportion of males to females was 22.43 per cent and 15.22 per cent respectively to total male and female migrants. This was followed by 10-19 years age group that comprised 16.18 per cent of the total migrants. This age group involved 18.84 per cent males and 14.11 per cent females of the total male and female migrants. 0-9 years of age group involved 13.75 per cent of the total migrants. 16.69 per cent of males and 11.45 per cent of females were having their age between 0-9 years. About 7 per cent of the in-migrants moved between 40-49 years of age and about one tenth of the total males moved during this age group while the proportion of females in this age group was one-twentieth. 3.44 per cent in-migrants moved between the ages of 50-59 years. However, only 3.35 per cent of the migrants were above 60 years of age. An insignificant proportion of migrants, i.e. 0.30 per cent did not report their age.

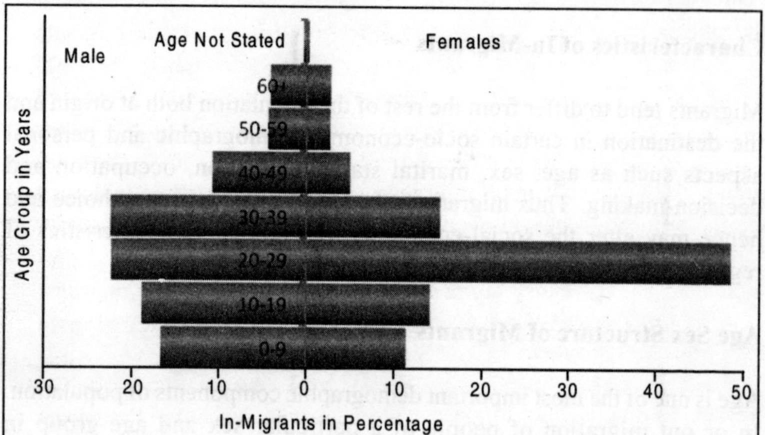

Fig. 6.2: Age Sex Composition of In-Migrants in Ghaziabad District (1991-2001)

Marital Status of Migrants

Marital status is a measureable demographic characteristics which is relevant to the manner in which migration affects population change. Since marriage is associated with family ties, it inevitably affects the propensity to migrate. In a situation where a volume of youthful migration is fairly high, the marital status of the migrants can significantly affect the *marital composition* of the population (Hollmann, 1977). Marital status of migrants can also affect many other components of the population a region. For example if the migrants entering a region are recently married couples they can have an effect on the fertility of that region and thereby a rapid population growth. On the other hand if majority of them are unmarried the sex ratio the region may remarkably be distorted in favour of males. On the basis of marital status all the in-migrants in Ghaziabad district can be divided into four categories, namely; (1) never married, (2) currently married, (3) widowed, (4) divorced and separated. The following analysis demonstrates differences in the marital status of migrants by sex.

Table 6.8 exhibits the distribution of migrants in Ghaziabad district by marital status. It is evident that 32.73 per cent migrants in Ghaziabad district were reported as unmarried. The proportion of male migrants in the category was 45.22 per cent while that of females was 22.95 per cent to the total male and female migrants respectively. Majority of the migrants were currently married and accounted for 65.16 per cent of the total migrants. About 75 per cent female migrants also were currently married while the proportion of male migrants in this category was 53.36 per cent. Widowed migrants contributed only about 2 per cent to the total migrants. 1.34 per cent male migrants were also reported as widowed while the proportion of widowed female migrants was 2.56 per cent. A very negligible proportion (0.09%) of migrants was divorced and separated. In this category the proportion of male and female migrants was only 0.08 per cent and 0.10 per cent respectively to the total male and female migrants.

Table 6.8: Distribution of In-Migrants by Marital Status and Sex in Percentage 1991-2001

Marital Status of In-Migrants	*In-Migrants in Per Cent*			*Sex Ratio in Per Cent*	
	Persons	*Males*	*Females*	*Males*	*Females*
Never married	32.73	45.22	22.95	60.66	39.34
Currently married	65.16	53.36	74.39	35.94	64.06
Widowed	2.02	1.34	2.56	29.12	70.88
Divorced and separated	0.09	0.08	0.10	37.44	62.56
Total	100.00	100.00	100.00	43.89	56.11

Source: Calculation based on Census of India 2001, D-Series, Table D-10.

Conclusions

It can be noted that though Uttar Pradesh is one of the highly out-migrating states of India, the preceding discussion reveals that Ghaziabad district has emerged as a highly in-migrating district and the proportion of migrants to total population is highest here, among all the other districts in Uttar Pradesh. High level of in-migration has significantly contributed to the urban growth in the district making it one of the three districts in Uttar Pradesh where more than half of the total population reside in urban areas. The location of the district on major road and rail routes in the vicinity of Delhi along with other factors such as high level of indistrialisation, good connectivity with Delhi, relatively low man-land pressure and house rent, easy availability of good quality of fresh water, presence of institutions of professional and higher education, social facilities and amenities as well as good infrastructural base are some of the major pull factors for high level of in-migration and urban growth in the district. In-migration is expected to increase further in future leading to a very high level of urban growth in the district. Therefore, it is suggested that infrastructural base of the district should be strengthened and urban development should take place in a sustainable and planned manner so that the quality of life in urban areas in Ghaziabad should not deteriorate in future.

REFERENCES

Bhagat, R.B. and Mohanty, S., (2009), Emerging Pattern of Urbanisation and the Contribution of Migration in Urban Growth in India, *Asian Population Studies*, 5(1): 5-20.

Bogue, D.J., (1959), "Internal Migration". In P.M. Hauser and O.D. Duncan (eds.), *The Study of Population: An Inventory and Appraisal*, The Chicago University Press, Chicago, pp. 486-509.

District Census Handbook, (2001), of Ghaziabad District, Series-10, Part XII-A & B, Directorate of Census Operation Uttar Pradesh, Lucknow.

Dupont, V., (1992), Impact of In-Migration on Industrial Development: Case Study of Tejpur in Gujarat, *Economic and Political Weekly*, 27 (45): 2423-29+2431-36.

Falaris, E.M., (1979), The Determinants of Internal Migration in Peru: An Economic Analysis, *Economic Development and Cultural Change*, 27(2): 327-341.

Hollmann, F.W., (1977), The Demographic Effect of Migration on Urban Population: Migration to and from West Berlin, 1952-1971. In A.A. Brown and E. Neuberger (eds.) *Internal Migration: A Comparative Perspective*, Academic Press, New York, pp. 349-378.

Ledent, J., (1982), "Rural-Urban Migration, Urbanisation, and Economic Development," *Economic Development and Cultural Change*, 30(3), Third World Migration and Urbanisation: A Symposium, pp. 507-538.

Ministry of Urban Development (2009), Government of India, Urban Infrastructure Development Scheme for Small & Medium towns (UIDSSMT): Overview and salient features.

Oberai, A.S. and Singh, H.K.M., (1983), *Causes and Consequences of Internal Migration—A Case Study in the Indian Punjab*, Oxford University Press, Bombay.

Ren, Y., (2006), Forms of Internal Migration and Combined Effects on Regional Urban Structure in the Yangtze River Delta Area in China, Working Paper Series, *Centre for Urban and Regional Studies*, Vol. 2006-28, Fudan University, pp. 1-33.

Shen, J., (2000), Chinese Urbanisation and Urban Policy. In: C.M. Lau and J. Shen (eds), *China Review*, Chinese University Press, Hong Kong, pp. 455-480.

Singh, D.P., (2005), Migration in India: Evidence Based on National Sample Survey Data, *Demography India*, 34(2): 271-298.

Singh, D.P., (2007), Migration in Mumbai: Trends in Fifty Years, *Demography India*, 36(2): 315-327.

Smita and Chandna, R.C., (1991), Migration Patterns in India, *Population Geography*, 13(1 & 2): 31-52.

7

Urban Growth and Spatial Transformation

A Comparison between Kolkata Urban Agglomeration and Kolkata Municipal Corporation

Mala Mukherjee

Introduction

It is undoubtedly true that some of the modern Indian metro cities of today have their origin in the pre-independence era and present day Indian urbanisation is an extension of the two hundred years long colonial legacy. Even in 2001, the level of urbanisation in India was 27.78 per cent, that is much lower than other developing countries of Asia, Latin America and Africa. The definition of an urban area varies from one country to another and the Indian Census follows a rigorous definition of 'urban' area which includes civic status as well as demographic criteria. Therefore, many settlements that may be treated as urban in an African or a Latin American country, may be defined as 'rural' in India. This practice of designating urban yields a much lower rate of urbanisation for India than that of the other countries. Apart from this fact, Indian urbanisation is characterised by 'metropolitan dominance' or urban growth in a few enclaves. In 2001, the country had thirty-five million plus cities or metropolises which literally means 'primate city' or a large city. These thirty-five million plus cities together support 107.9 million population or nearly 39 per cent urban population of India. It is interesting to note that Kolkata formerly known as Calcutta was the only million plus city at the beginning of twentieth century and within one century India has produced another 34 'million plus cities'. Erstwhile colonial port cities like Mumbai, Kolkata and Chennai have experienced population explosion after the Independence and each of these cities faces unique challenges quite different from other cities and, therefore, Indian Urban Geographers as well as planners have to address problems related to metro-cities separately.

Literature Review

The study of 'urban growth' has always enjoyed special attention of Population Geographers and Demographers who are interested about 'migration' and 'natural increase' statistics, but the study of 'urban space and its transformation' has received popularity only after the Second World War, when war-ravaged European as well as American cities required reconstruction and remodelling. Thus Harold M. Mayor (1967) has opined that to understand a city and its influence on surrounding settlements or hinterland, a student of Urban Geography must emphasise on the physical and cultural conditions that have been involved in the origin of the settlement, phase by phase, as well as the functional, morphological transformation, life and organisation of the contemporary city. The study of 'morphological transformation' of cities has received new direction under the scholarship of Burgess, Hoyt, Harris and Ullman. E.M. Burgess has identified functional zones around the Central Business District of a city and his theory gained popularity in the name of 'Concentric Zone Model'. Burgess has treated urban growth in terms of its physical expansion and spatial differentiation. Homer Hoyt in 1939 has tried to modify this theory and has analysed that urban growth usually occurs around major transport lines towards the outskirts of the city. Therefore, a city is divided into a number of sectors and each sector reflects a segregation of population groups according to income and social status. C.D. Harris and Ulman in 1945 have further modified the theory by introducing more than one nuclei or Central Business Districts for a city, but none of these western theories and models can successfully describe the urban growth and spatial transformation of Indian cities, because the cities of the Orient have different socio-political set-up. Brush (1974) has identified two characteristics of Indian cities. These are, extremely high densities occur in inland cities and erstwhile colonial port cities, but the former British port cities show a sharp difference in the density of population between central wards or older parts characterised by congestion and old obsolete buildings and the peripheries characterised by low density cantonments, civil lines and notified areas. D.S. Rao and Reddy (1988) have reflected that in case of big cities, peripheries grow faster than the city core, but Kolkata resembles a semi-colonial structure.

Chittaranjan Pathak (2000) has opined that the urban agglomeration of Kolkata instead of exerting a generative force plays a parasitic role in the rural economy. Sanjay Chakraborty (2001) has identified three phases of spatial transformation of Kolkata. The CBD of Kolkata has shifted several times after the Independence. After the Battle of Plassey (1757) Gobindapur became the CBD and development of jute mills along the Hooghly River had created an elongated CBD. After Independence Burrabazar-BBD Bagh became the CBD of Kolkata. Recently, the CBD is shifting towards Bidhan Nagar or Salt Lake Area. Therefore, remarkable spatial transformation is occurring in the immediate neighbourhood of Salt Lake. Urban growth also remarkably varies between urban agglomeration and city core. Bonani Ghosh's (1970) research has identified that the number of congested wards has increased from 54 to 80 in Kolkata from 1961 to 1971. Researches conducted by National Atlas and Thematic Mapping Organisation (NATMO) and Calcutta Municipal Development Agency (CMDA) show that depopulation is taking place in the inner city and the peripheries are growing rapidly. The city is expanding towards the south and the east.

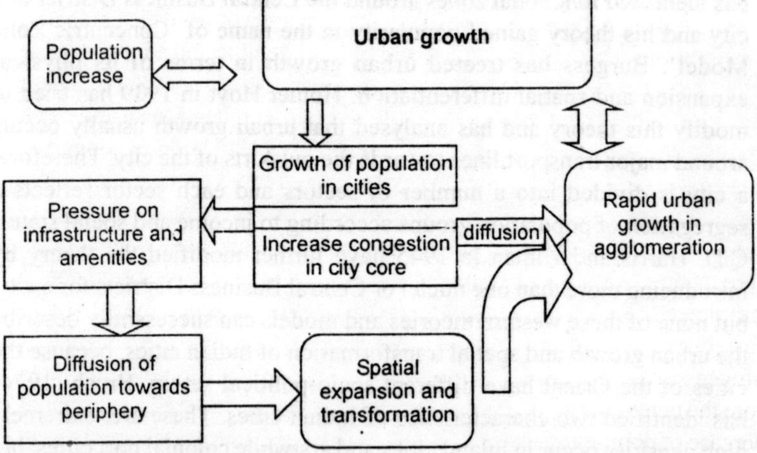

Fig. 7.1: Conceptual Framework

Origin and Development of Kolkata

Kolkata previously known as Calcutta is the second largest metropolis of

India in terms of population and had once enjoyed the status of the capital of British India. In 1912, the British-Indian Government shifted the administrative capital from Calcutta to Delhi, but the city continued to be the major trade centre and port city of India. Before Independence, it was the hub of Indian renaissance as well as one of the main centres of the National Movement. Since independence Kolkata has been the capital of the State of West Bengal. Though this settlement existed long before the advent of the English East India Company in Bengal, but it started its historical life span in 1690, when Job Charnock, an officer of the East India Company laid the city's foundation at Hatkhola in Sutanuty village. Three villages, namely Sutanuty (cotton mart), Gobindopore and Kalikata occupied the present site of modern Kolkata. It is believed that, initially, Kolkata grew with small business houses which gradually grew in number as well as in size. These houses had their administrative head offices in the city. The East India Company expressed their stronghold by fortification of the strategic point in the city, started business offices and series of large business godowns along the river Hooghly. They succeeded in exercising political and administrative control over the local counterpart as well over other foreign traders at that time. After the Battle of Plassey (1757) the city started flourishing economically as well as culturally. Under British rule it witnessed remarkable urban growth as well as spatial transformation, because it was the hub of all economic and administrative activities. The city was racially segregated in two distinct parts. These were the 'White Town' with palatial buildings, monuments, neat and clean boardwalks, well planned drainage, sewerage system and the congested 'Native Town' with an admixture of palatial buildings of the Indian elites and the hutments of the poor. Colonial Kolkata truly depicted 'poverty and pride' side by side. During the Nationalist Movement, some efforts were made to abolish the racial structure of the city, but this could not be completed until India gained her freedom in 1947. Since then, the city started experiencing remarkable transformation. With the influx of refugees after independence from the then East Pakistan and migrants from the neighbouring states and districts, Kolkata witnessed a substantial increase of population in and around the city particularly in the peripheral areas. A group of municipal towns (39 in number) which have encircled the city over time have actually converted the erstwhile isolated town of Kolkata, to a large urban agglomeration (Fig. 7.2). Spatial expansion may be attributed to pull forces which gradually transformed the surrounding rural settlements to new town areas and resulted in the emergence of Kolkata Metropolitan Area (KMA). Pattern of growth of

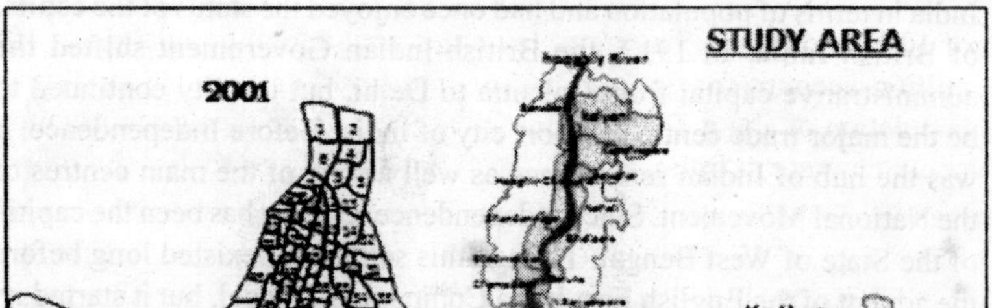

Map 7.1: Kolkata Metropolitan Standard Urban Area (Kolkata Urban Agglomeration)

KMA over the years has direct bearing on the development of infrastructure, density of population and intra city variation in urban growth.

Urban Growth in India and Selected Metropolis

Modern phase of urbanisation in India has begun during the colonial perioc' and still today it is characterised by high urban growth in three colonial port cities and very low rate of urbanisation in the rest of the country. The Census count of 2001 reveals that about 28 per cent of the population in India is urban. It was 25.72 per cent in 1991, 23.73 per cent in 1981 and 20.22 per cent in 1971. In absolute terms, total urban population of 285 million is more than the total population of several countries. There are 35 cities or urban agglomerations with a population of 10 lakh or more. These million cities with a total population of 108 million account for 38 per cent of India's urban population. With a population of about 81 million in 2001, West Bengal is the fourth most populous state in India. It accounts for about 2.7 per cent of the India's area but contains 7.8 per cent of the nation's population. The situation regarding rural-urban composition of population in India and West Bengal is comparable. In 2001 about 22.43 million population comprising 28 per cent of total population has been classified as urban in West Bengal. However, growth of urban population in India is higher than that of West Bengal. However, the concentration of urban population in West Bengal is more in Kolkata. About three-fifths of the total urban population of West Bengal State is still confined to Kolkata itself.

Table 7.1: Population of India, West Bengal (Urban) and Kolkata UA: 1961-2001

(*Million*)

No (a)	*Years (b)*	*Urban (c)*		*Kolkata (UA) (d)*
		India (c 1)	*West Bengal (c 2)*	
1.	1961	78.16	8.54 (10.93)	5.98 (70.02)
2.	1971	107.82	10.97 (10.17)	7.42 (67.64)
3.	1981	159.46	14.45 (9.06)	9.19 (63.60)
4.	1991	217.61	18.71 (8.60)	11.03 (58.95)
5.	2001	285.36	22.43 (7.86)	13.21 (58.89)

Note: 1. Figures in Column c 2 relates to percentage to total for urban India.
2. Figures in parantheses mentioned in Kolkata UA (column d) presents percentage to total urban population of West Bengal.

Source: 1. Census of India, Various Issues.
2. Urban Statistics, TCPO, September 2005.

In 2001 Kolkata UA stood at the second position among the mega cities in India as indicated in Table 7.2.

It may be inferred from Table 7.2 that within the area of large metropolitan cities in India mainly Greater Mumbai, Kolkata, Delhi and Chennai have recorded a fast growth in the periphery than in the core areas. In the beginning of the last century, Kolkata had more than one million population and was the only city in India having the status of a metro city. The population of Kolkata UA increased from 1510008 in

Table 7.2: Total Population and Growth of Mega Cities in India

Sl. No.	*Cities*	*Population (lakh)*			*Annual Exponential Growth Rate*	
		1981	*1991*	*2001*	*1981-91*	*1991-01*
1.	Greater Mumbai	82.43	125.96	163.68	4.22	2.62
2.	Kolkata	91.94	110.22	132.17	1.72	1.82
3.	Delhi	57.29	84.19	127.91	3.80	4.18
4.	Chennai	42.89	54.21	64.25	2.23	1.70
5.	Bangalore	29.22	41.30	56.86	3.36	3.20
6.	Hyderabad	25.46	43.44	55.33	5.20	2.42
7.	Ahmedabad	25.48	33.12	45.19	2.58	3.11

Source: *Handbook of Urbanization in India* by K.C Sivaramakrishna, Amitabh Kundu and B.N. Singh, 2005.

Table 7.3: Nature of Growth in the Mega Cities of India (1981-2001)

Sl. No.	*Cities*	*1981-91*		*1991-2001*	
		Core	*Periphery*	*Core*	*Periphery*
1.	Greater Mumbai	1.86	4.22	1.82	2.62
2.	Kolkata	0.64	1.72	0.40	1.82
3.	Delhi	3.59	3.80	3.09	4.18
4.	Chennai	1.59	2.23	0.93	1.70
5.	Bangalore	0.71	3.36	4.79	3.20
6.	Hyderabad	3.31	5.20	1.58	2.42

Source: *Handbook of Urbanization in India* by K.C Sivaramakrishna, Amitabh Kundu and B.N. Singh, 2005.

1901 to 13205697 in 2001. The annual growth rate of population in Kolkata UA during the last century works out to 7.75 per cent. The highest decadal growth of population in Kolkata UA was observed during 1941-51 at 69.34 per cent and the lowest was in 1911-21 at 8 per cent. After 1961 the growth rate of population in Kolkata has been declining (Fig. 7.2). Growth of population was not accompanied by proportionate increase in area that has resulted in increase of density of population in selected locations.

In case of Kolkata, urban growth is not equally distributed across all municipalities. In fact, urban growth is fairly high in some wards of the Kolkata Municipal Corporation. Variations in urban growth also affect the spatial transformation of the city.

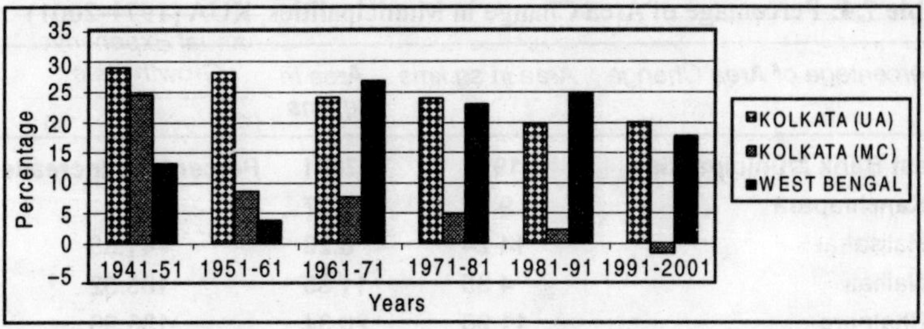

Fig. 7.2: Variation in Population Growth in Kolkata and Kolkata (UA)

Variation in Urban Growth and Spatial Transformation in Kolkata Urban Agglomeration

Kolkata Urban Agglomeration or Kolkata Standard Urban Area has been delineated as a planning region by Kolkata Metropolitan District Development Authority in 1971. Currently, it covers an area of 1785 sq. km with three municipal corporations and 38 municipalities and many non-municipal towns as well as villages in its fringe. All these towns have a separate history of origin and growth. Most of them have started their history as colonial ports and business centres, but gradually lost their glory before Calcutta's supremacy. These towns together form the Hooghly Industrial Belt and have received attention of the town planner only after 1970s. This planning region has undergone several spatial changes and boundary adjustments over time.

There is a marked differentiation between east bank municipalities of the River Hooghly and west bank municipalities in terms of population growth and spatial expansion. Municipalities of the eastern bank of the River Hooghly account higher rate of urban growth and noticeable spatial expansion during the last three decades. On the other hand, west bank municipalities do not show impressive urban growth. Proximity of Kolkata has a direct impact on the growth of east bank municipalities.

(A) Spatial Expansion of Municipalities

In KUA, New Barrackpore records highest increase of area followed by Barasat, Rajpur, Naihati, Bhatpara, Garulia and North Dum Dum (Sonarpore was added to Rajpur). On the other hand, among the west bank municipalities, Uttarpara recorded impressive spatial increase, because Kotrung got merged with it. Rishrah and Hooghly-Chinsurah

Table 7.4: Percentage of Area Change in Municipalities, KUA (1971-2001)

Percentage of Area Change	*Area in sq.kms*	*Area in sq.kms*	
East Bank Municipalities	**1971**	**2001**	**Percentage Increase**
Kanchrapara	9.07	9.07	0
Halisahar	14.24	8.28	–41.85
Naihati	4.35	11.55	165.52
Bhatpara	11.96	28.34	136.96
Garulia	3.88	6.48	67.01
North Barrack Pore	8.42	8.42	0
Barrack Pore	11.65	11.65	0
Titagarh	3.24	3.24	0
Khardah	3.88	6.87	77.06
Panihati	19.43	19.43	0
Kamarhati	10.96	10.96	0
Baranagar	7.12	7.12	0
Barasat	7.50	32.83	337.73
New Barrack Pore	2.90	17.17	492.07
North Dum Dum	15.60	25.32	62.31
Dum Dum	2.90	3.11	7.24
Rajpur	20.90	57.90	177.03
Baruipore	9.07	9.07	0
Calcutta	104.00	185.00	77.88
West Bank Municipalities			
Bansberia	9.7	9.7	0
Hooghly-Chinsurah	15.54	21.52	38.48
Bhadreswar	6.47	6.47	0
Chapdani	6.47	6.47	0
Baidyabati	9.06	9.06	0
Serampore	5.88	5.88	0
Rishra	3.24	6.48	100
Konnagar	4.33	4.33	0
Uttarpara-Kotrung	7.25	18.15	150.34

also recorded impressive spatial expansion in the last twenty years. Kalyani, Gayeshpore, Bidhannagar, Pujali, Maheshtala, Madhyamgram became separate municipalities after 1990. Though KMDA's (Kolkata Metropolitan Development Agency) current regionalisation scheme has many shortcomings and it also overlaps with various administrative units, but currently it is in operation. KMDA has already proposed the concept of 'Kolkata Metropolitan Region' on the basis of daily communication and flow of essential goods, but this concept is still in a stage of infancy and is highly theoretical in nature. In 2001, Kolkata (UA) had three municipal corporations, one cantonment, sixteen outgrowths, 38 municipalities, 99 urban units and 58 Census towns, housing about 13.21 million people.

(B) Variation in Urban Growth across Municipalities

Kolkata (MC) as a whole recorded 3.93 per cent growth rate, which was much lower than Chandannagar (MC) (15.59%) and Howrah (MC) 6.01 per cent.

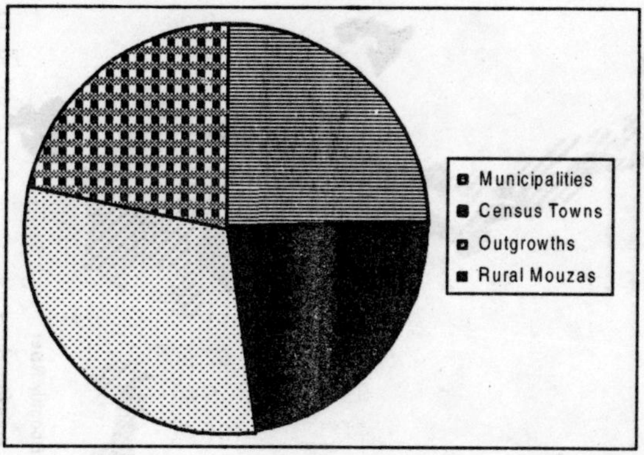

Fig. 7.3: Components-wise Variation of Urban Growth in Kolkata S.U.A.

Sixteen outgrowths together accounted for 32.69 per cent population growth, which is highest among all other components. Rural units also recorded impressive population growth, slightly lower than the municipalities and Census towns.

During 1991 to 1981 the highest growth rate was recorded in Bidhannagar, followed by Khardah. Kalyani, Panihati, Baranagar, Barasat, Garulia, Rajpur, Barrackpore and North Dum Dum. Konnagar was the only west bank municipality having very high growth rate. Other municipalities of the west bank (of the river Hooghly) had moderate to low growth rate. Barrackpore cantonment had the lowest grcwth rate. During 1991-2001, Dum Dum recorded highest growth rate followed by Howrah, Uluberia, Garulia, Khardah, Baranagar and Hooghly-Chinsurah

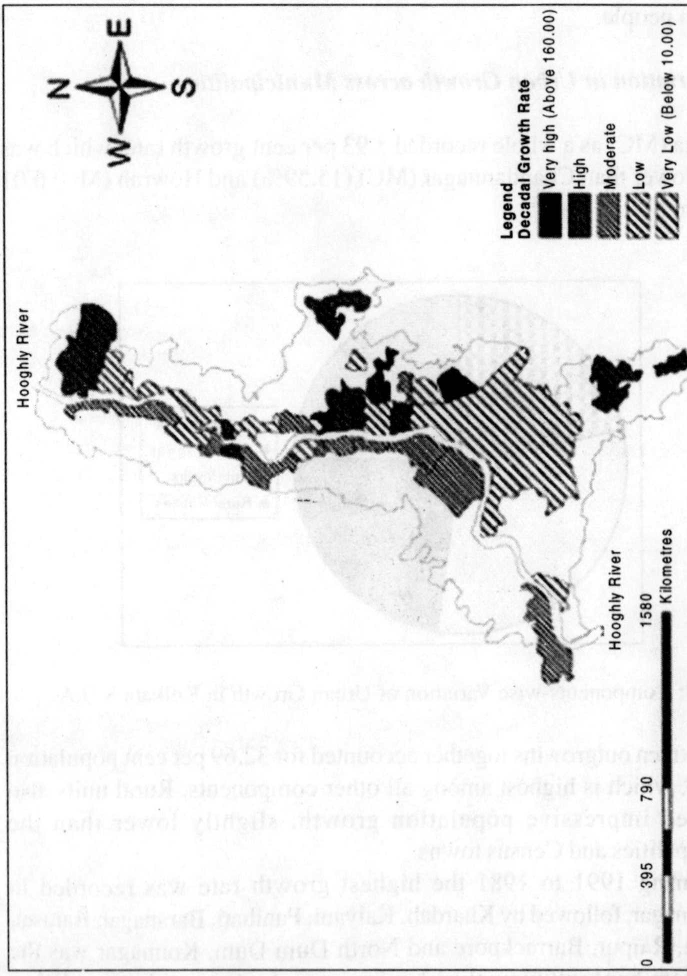

Map 7.2: Decadal Growth Rate (1991-2001) (Kolkata Urban Agglomeration)

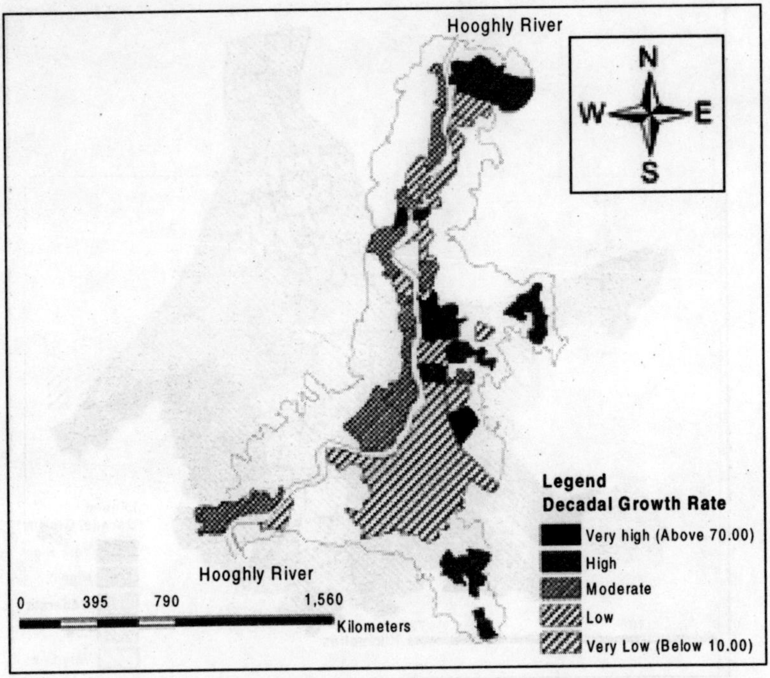

Map 7.3: Decadal Growth Rate (1931-1991) (Kolkata Urban Agglomeration)

municipalities. It is interesting to note that population growth had rapidly declined in South Dum Dum, Panihati and other municipalities, that earlier recorded very high growth rate (see Maps 7.2 and 7.3).

Variation in Urban Growth and Spatial Transformation in Kolkata Municipal Corporation

Urban growth is also not uniform across the 141 wards of Kolkata Municipal Corporation, the city has recorded very high population growth in southern and south-eastern part of the municipality (Garden Reach, Jadavpur and Eastern Bypass areas), while ward number 108 has accounted for highest growth rate (Maps 7.4 and 7.5). However, in terms of population density the core city has high figures that decline towards the periphery. Wards with high population densities record low rate of urban growth and are hence situated mostly in the core areas.

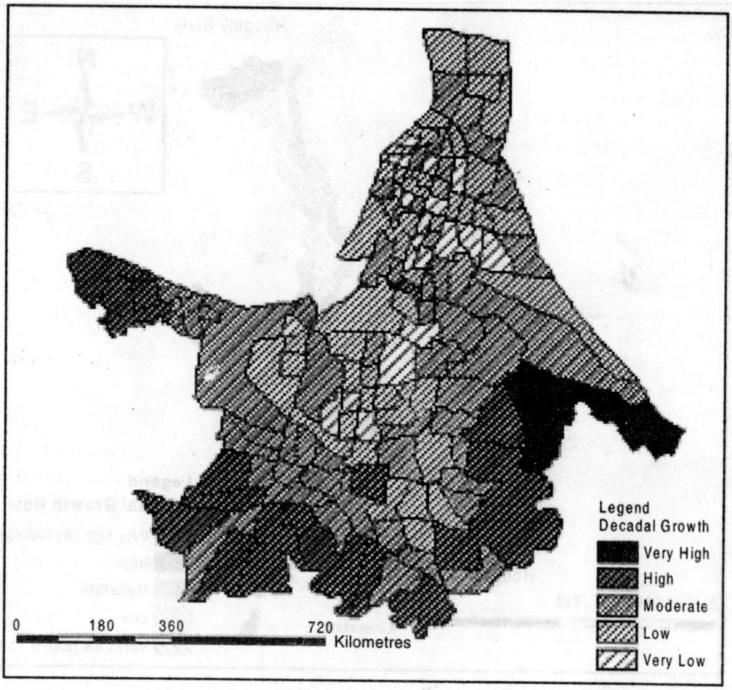

Map 7.4: Population Growth of Kolkata Municipality (1921-2001)

Kolkata Municipal Corporation itself has undergone several phases of spatial expansion since the Independence. In between 1981 and 1991 the city has been extended towards the south and the south east incorporating the areas adjoining to Eastern Bypass, Jadavpur and Garden Reach. Spatial expansion has also influenced spatial transformation and therefore, land use pattern of the city has changed remarkably.

During the last forty years, the percentage of vacant land has declined sharply, while the percentage of residential land use has increased. Percentage of land under industrial use has increased slightly, while land under transportation, recreation and commercial do not show any remarkable change. Their proportion is very much negligible. Therefore, there is a clear indication of high demand for urban housing in Kolkata and residential land use gets the highest priority among all other uses.

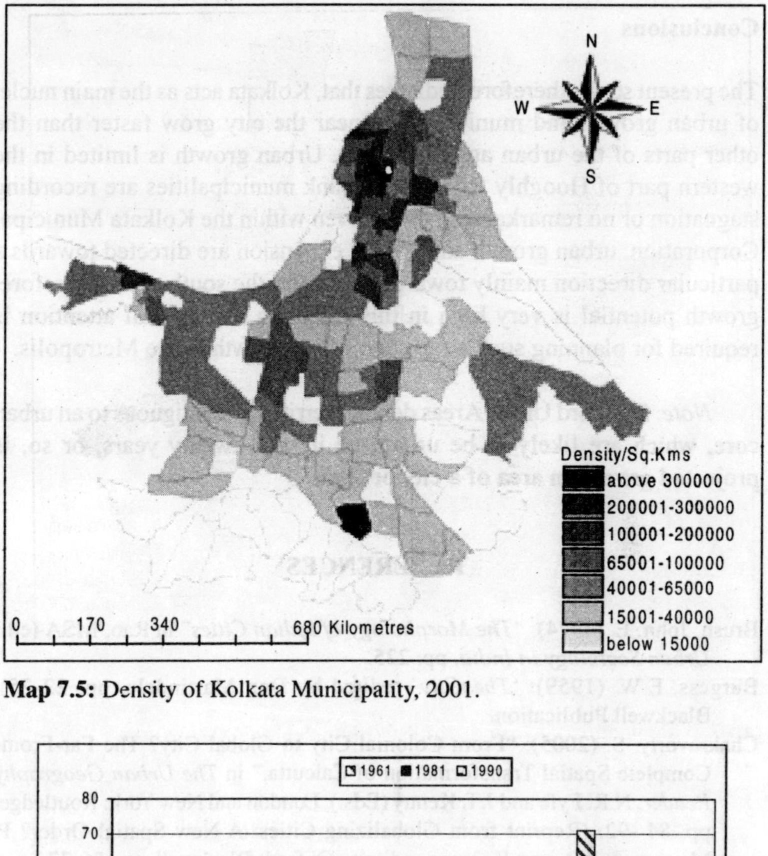

Map 7.5: Density of Kolkata Municipality, 2001.

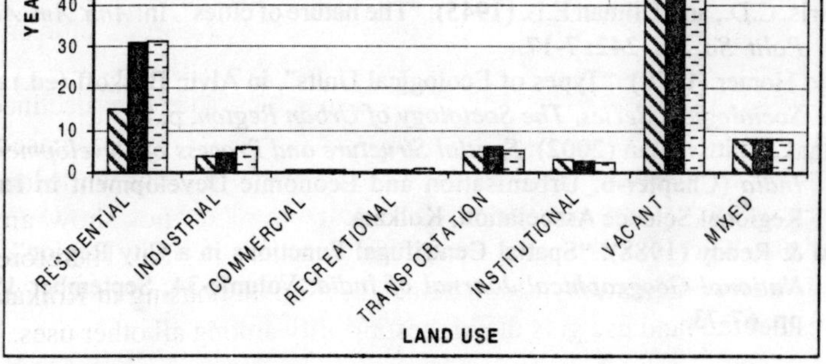

Fig. 7.4 : Land use Changes of Kolkata Metropolis (1961-1990)

Conclusions

The present study, therefore, indicates that, Kolkata acts as the main nuclei of urban growth and municipalities near the city grow faster than the other parts of the urban agglomeration. Urban growth is limited in the western part of Hooghly River. West bank municipalities are recording stagnation or no remarkable growth. Even within the Kolkata Municipal Corporation, urban growth and spatial expansion are directed towards a particular direction mainly towards south and the south east. Therefore, growth potential is very high in this direction and special attention is required for planning such an uneven urban growth in the Metropolis.

Note: Standard Urban Areas denotes territories contiguous to an urban core, which are likely to be urbanised in next twenty years, or so, is projected growth in area of a city or town.

REFERENCES

Brush, John. E. (1974): "*The Morphology of Indian Cities*" in Rao, MSA (ed.) *Urban Sociology in India*, pp. 225.

Burgess, E.W. (1959): '*The City*' (edited by Don Martindele, pp. 22-25), Blackwell Publication.

Chakravorty, S. (2005): "From Colonial City to Global City? The Far-From-Complete Spatial Transformation of Calcutta," in *The Urban Geography Reader*, N.R. Fyfe and J.T. Kenny (Eds.), London and New York: Routledge. pp. 84 -92. (Reprint from Globalizing Cities: A New Spatial Order? P. Marcuse and R. van Kempen, editors, Oxford: Blackwell. pp. 56-77.)

Harold, M. Mayor and C.F. Kohn (edited), (1967): *Readings in Urban Geography*, Chicago, 1967.

Harris, C.D., and Ullman E.L. (1945): "The nature of cities". In: *Ann. Am. Acad. Polit. So. Sci.* 242: 7-17.

Hoyt Homer (1970): "Types of Ecological Units", in Alvin Boskoff (ed.) Acc. *Sociological Series, The Sociology of Urban Region*, p. 83.

Pathak, Chittaranjan (2002): *Spatial Structure and Process of Development in India* (Chapter-6: Urbanisation and Economic Development in India) Regional Science Association, Kolkata.

Rao & Reddy (1988): "Spatial Centrifugal Functions in a City Region", *The National Geographical Journal of India*, Volume-34, September 1988, pp. 67-73.

Official Documents

'Administrative Reports of the Commissioners of the Town of Calcutta, 1866-1940', Municipality Administrative reports of Calcutta.

Basic Development Plan For the CMD (1966-1986), CMPO Government of West Bengal.

Calcutta At A Glance: first edition 1987, second edition 1997 (Calcutta Corporation)

Master Plan for Water Supply within KMA (2001-2025), Final Draft.

SECTION II

Urban Employment and Infrastructure

8

Status of Infrastructure Development in Cities and Towns of Odisha

Problems and Constraints

Gourabamaya Pradhan

Introduction

The overwhelming importance of infrastructure in the progress of any region is well understood. With steady population growth, infrastructure facilities need to be expanded in accordance to the former. However, numerous studies have indicated that absence of commensurate infrastructure development with population growth to be one of the characteristic features of development in urban India. Recognising the critical importance of infrastructure, World Bank stated that 'the adequacy of infrastructure helps to determine one country's success and another's failure—in diversifying production, expanding trade, coping with population growth, reducing poverty, or improving environmental conditions'. (WDR, 1994:2). The issues of urban infrastructure provision and service delivery mechanism are key factors in the process of urban development. The increasing role of towns and cities in the development of a region further emphasises the need of adequate infrastructure in urban centres. In addition to this, in the present competitive free market economy, infrastructure development provides the key to direct the investment flows to the city. As towns and cities are the chief production centres of economy, the development of infrastructure is nothing less than the immediate requirement and policy formulations seek to bridge the gap between demand and supply of urban infrastructure.

As rapid growth of urban population acquires serious proportions, the study of infrastructure development is attracting more and more attention from researchers, planners, and the governments concerned. The present study aims to examine the infrastructure availability in towns and cities of Odisha. The total population in Odisha increased less than three times in 2001 from that of 1951, whereas the urban population increased more than nine times during the same period. Moreover, with a growth rate of 69 per cent, the urban population increased at a rate of four times higher than the rural population which recorded 16 per cent growth during 1971-81. Urban growth is still more than double of its rural counterpart in subsequent decades. This continuous and high growth of urban population in recent past has caused great strain on the existing urban infrastructure such as road network facility, source of water supply and capacity of water storage, medical facilities, educational facilities and so on. Urban growth caused by both natural increase and accelerated flow of in-migration has resulted in inadequacy of such basic facilities when viewed from the angle of per capita availability and in general, the quality of life in urban areas has suffered. Cities and towns of India are visibly deficient in the quality of services they provide, even to the existing population (Report on Indian Urban Infrastructure and Services, 2011). Problems like over-congestion, inadequacy of safe drinking water, poor sanitation and sewerage facilities, decreasing educational and medical availability has hindered the economic progress and has resulted in environmental degradation and pollution in urban areas. A study by the Ministry of Urban Development, Government of India (2009) reveals that 23 million children below the age of 14 in urban India are at risk of poor sanitation and about 8 million children in urban areas are at risk of poor water supply. Furthermore, out of the 5161 cities and towns in India in 2001, 4861 do not have even a partial sewerage network (Census of India, 2001). The poor state of urban basic services act as obstacles in exploiting the growth potential of available resources therein. It can be argued that towns and cities can act as the engines of growth only when they have adequate infrastructure facilities which foster optimal productivity of functions performed by them.

Present Study

At the backdrop of high urban population growth, the present study endeavours to examine the availability of infrastructure facilities in towns and cities of Odisha. The status of physical infrastructure like road network, electricity connection, water supply, sewerage, fire fighting services; social infrastructure such as medical and educational facilities, recreational facilities and economic infrastructure like number of banks have been analysed across the towns of Odisha. The town-wise analysis of above mentioned dimensions of infrastructure for the time period 1971-2001 has been carried out in this study. The first section deals with analysis of various elements of infrastructure availability during 1971-2001 at state level followed by the estimation of *Index of Infrastructure Development* in all towns during the same period. The temporal trend and pattern of infrastructure development has been attempted and on that basis the towns of Odisha have been categorised in the later part of this chapter.

Database and Methodology

This study is based on the secondary data published by the Census of India. The data published in the Odisha, Town Directory, 1971-2001 has been used for the analysis. Certain adjustments had to be made in few occasions to present a comparative analysis of infrastructure in different time periods. To estimate the percentage of towns having tap as major source of water only those towns were taken where tap was the important source, since several sources of water has been included in the Town Directory of the Census of India. The same procedure was followed in case of sewerage. To compute the composite index of infrastructure development, Z-Score (Z) method has been applied. As the indicators taken are presented in different units, they have been made scale free by the following formula:

$$\text{Standardised Score (Z)} = \frac{\text{Actual Value} - \text{mean}}{\text{Standard Deviation}}$$

The summation of Z-scores of all indicators divided by the number of indicators of a town is considered as the infrastructure index of that town. The infrastructure development of towns has been calculated separately for 1971, 1981, 1991 and 2001 and the temporal change has been analysed. The relative variation of the index values of the towns has been the basis of categorising them into different classes such as very high, high, medium, low and very low.

Discussion

The existing status of various infrastructure facilities such as road connectivity, source of water supply, sewerage system, electricity, medical and educational services have been analysed. The temporal change in such facilities in towns of Odisha has therefore been examined under the following heads.

Road Density

The urban centres are the focal points in the process of economic development and this is facilitated by a well connected transport network. The inadequacy of rail network facility in Odisha further emphasises the importance of roads as the major means of transportation for enhancing the productivity and efficiency of economic activities. To show the level of road network facility, the road density measured in terms total road length in kilometres (both *pucca* and *kutcha* road) per area of one square kilometre has been taken here. The road density in urban Odisha was 1.88 km per sq.km. and it increased to 2.79 km. per sq.km.in 1981. Continuing this improving trend, road density further went up to 3.82 km. per sq.km in 1991. The progress has been more significant in the next decade as road density was recorded to be 5.53 km per sq.km in 2001. If taken in terms of road length per thousand population, then continuous increase is discernible in each reference period from 1971 to 2001 though the rate of improvement in terms of road density is faster. Thus, in general, an improvement in road infrastructure in urban areas has been noticed in urban Odisha.

Source of Water Supply

The source of water supply is another important basic amenity of urban centres. The accessibility to clean and safe source of water supply is a critical indicator of health and well-being. In Odisha, the provision of protected water supply appears dismal. Less than three-fourth of the total towns in 1971 had tap as their major source of water supply. Tube-well was the major source of water supply in seven per cent of the towns. However, the share of towns having tap as their major source of water has been increasing in Odisha with marginal decline in 1981-91. Tap water is considered to be safe and 74 per cent of towns in Odisha had this facility as a major source of water in 1971 and the percentage of towns served by tap water in 1981 went up to 79 per cent. Tube-wells were the second most important source of water in towns of Odisha and in 1981 it served as the major source in 16 per cent of towns—all of them are small towns except Jatni (a medium town). However, it is disheartening to note that the tap water facility decreased in 1991 as 77 per cent (from 79 per cent in 1981) of towns had received their water from taps. This decrease in the percentage of towns served by tap water in 1991 is explained by fact that most of the Census towns newly added in 1991 had received water from sources other than taps. However, in the next decade tap water facility improved as 86 per cent of total towns in 2001 reported taps to be their major source of water supply.

Apart from taps and tube-wells the third important source of water supply is wells. The share of towns depending on wells for their water requirements was 2 per cent in 1971 and it increased to 5 per cent in 1981, 7 per cent in 1991 and 2001. Understandably, the towns having wells as major source of water supply are not only small but are located in the interior, towns located away from the large and medium towns. This generalisation is violated by the observation that district headquarters like Sonepur depended on wells till 1981, and Jajpur in 1991. Even at present, wells and tube wells serve as the major sources of water supply in 14 per cent of towns in 2001 whereas this was 11 per cent in 1991.

System of Sewerage

The mechanism of waste water disposal and the system of sewerage in urban centres holds great significance so far as environmental and health risks are concerned. The picture of sewerage system in towns of Odisha is grossly dismal. Majority of them are served by the open surface drains that have the potential of polluting environment and can cause unhygienic conditions. The extremely sad state of affairs is very much apparent from the fact that in 1971, major system of sewerage was Open Surface Drains (OSD) in 93 per cent of the towns. Out of a total of 81 towns, only five towns, namely Bhubaneswar, Cuttack, Puri, Rourkela Steel Township and Sunabeda reported sewers to be their main drainage and waste water disposal method. In 1981, the situation had improved slightly as the proportion of towns having sewer facility increased from 6 per cent of the towns in 1971 to 10 per cent in 1981. Open surface drains was the important system of sewerage in 71 per cent of towns in 1931 and BSD (Box Surface Drain), and pits are found to be important types only in 19 per cent of towns.

Table 8.1: Levels of Infrastructure in Urban Odisha

Infrastructure facilities	*Means of Measurement*	*1971*	*1981*	*1991*	*2001*
Road	Length in km. per sq.km	1.88	4.53	3.82	5.53
	Length in km. per 1000 persons	1.65	2.09	2.24	2.8
Electricity	Domestic connections per 100 households	25	33	41	47
	Road Light Points per sq.km.	18	26	36	51
Percentage of Towns having Water Supply# from:	Tap	74	79	77	86
	Tube-well	7	16	4	7
	Well	2	5	7	7
	Others*	16	1	12	0
Fire Fighting Service	Percentage of Towns having within own premises	28	46	55	62
System of Sewerage	Percentage of towns having Sewer facility	6	10	8	2

As major *Source*.

* Others included tanks and towns for which data is not available.

Source: Census of India, Town Directory Odisha, 1971 (series 16), 1981 (Series 16), 1991 (Series 19), 2001 (Series 21).

The marginal improvement of sewerage facilities has been again offset in the next decade. The percentage of towns where system of sewerage is open surface drain increased from 71 per cent in 1981 to 83 per cent in 1991 thereby highlighting the very poor condition of sewerage in the towns of Odisha. Sewer, which is considered to be best form of drainage system, is found in very few selected towns. In 2001, out of a total of 138 towns only three towns, namely Fertilizer Corporation of India Township, Talcher Thermal Power Station Township and NALCO (National Aluminium Company Limited), i.e. all three industrial towns had sewer as their important drainage system. Apart from these, in few large cities like Bhubaneswar, Raurkela Industrial Township and Raurkela, sewers were the second most important after open surface drains. In 1991, few small towns like Balimela, Barbil, Chitrakonda, and Sunabeda had partial sewer facilities. However, it is surprising to observe that in the capital city of Bhubaneswar, open surface drains are important means of waste water disposal, followed by sewers. While it is always desirable to have sewer facilities for waste water disposal, towns like Paradip, Balimela, Barbil and Sunabeda had shed their partial existing sewer facilities in

1990s and in 2001 they are completely covered by open surface drains. Thus, it can be stated that open surface drains still serve as the chief mode of disposal of sewerage in majority of towns including the large towns/cities of Odisha.

Electricity

The power sector is another important element of the modern economy especially in urban centres. The status of electrification in towns of Odisha has been analysed by taking the number of electricity connections as given by the Census of India. In 1971, the number of domestic electric connections per 100 households in urban Odisha was found to be as low as 25. It can further be noted that only 14 out 81 towns had reported to have more number of connections than the State's average figure. Cuttack, one of the largest and oldest cities in the state did not possess a significantly better situation as it reported 28 domestic connections per 100 households. Berhampur, another big city (Class I) was again found to be in the lower side having the corresponding figure at 29 and the remaining two Class I cities, namely Bhubaneswar and Raurkela Steel Township recorded more than fifty domestic electric connections per 100 households.

The next decade experienced improvement in electricity supply and number of domestic electric connections per 100 households increased to 33 in 1981. This trend continued and the corresponding figure was found to be 41 in 1991 and 47 in 2001. The latest data (2001 Census) showed Angul town had 410 domestic connections per 100 households and this is explained by the fact that it is situated in one of the power surplus districts of Odisha (i.e. Angul District). In fact this happens to be the one of the focal areas of power production in India. The hydroelectricity plant in Rengali and National Thermal Power Corporation (NTPC) in the district has resulted in surplus power. O.C.L. Industrial Township, Bolangir, Fertiliser Corporation of India Township and Bhanjanagar are other towns which had more than hundred domestic connections per 100 households.

Street lights or road light points are also vital components of a city's infrastructure. There should not be a major distance between two street light points as proper street lighting is considered as a safety measure in road transport. It also leads to a sense of security to commuters and avoids crime, theft, etc. The number of road light points per one sq. km area can well indicate the availability of street lights. Census data has pointed out that there were 18 road light points per one square km. area. Dhenkanal and Paralakhemundi are the two towns which had more than 100 road light points per sq.km area and all Class I towns had 50 or more road light points per sq.km area except Bhubaneswar which recorded 40 light points per sq.km area. On the other hand, the corresponding figure was found to be less than 10 in as many as 38 out of 81 towns. Nevertheless, improvement in street lighting has been noticed. In 1981, the number of road lighting points increased to 26 per sq. km and further went up to 36 in 1991. Odisha being the first State in India to undertake reforms in power sector, recorded rapid improvement in last two decades or so. During mid 1990s, the State experienced progress in generating and distributing power through promoting privatisation and setting up of many institutions. This is evident from the rapid improvement observed in 2001 when the number of road light points per sq.km was found to be 47, from its corresponding figure of 36 in 1991. NALCO recorded the highest number of road light points (3043 per sq.km area) and this is probably due to its very small area and the fact that it is principally an industrial town having the largest aluminium factory. The industrial and large towns showed sharp improvement in this front in 1990s. The number of road light points per sq. km. in Cuttack doubled in 2001 from what it was in 1991. Similarly, in the state capital, the corresponding figure tripled during 1971 to 2001. Thus, it can be argued that the electricity connections—both domestic and road light points, are increasing in the towns of Odisha and much faster improvement was noticed during 1990s that is attributable to the power sector reforms in the State.

Fire Fighting Services

This service is very much lacking in urban Odisha. Many towns in the Odisha are devoid of this emergency service. In 1971, only 28 per cent of towns had the facility of fire fighting service within their own premises. In the next decade, substantial improvement was recorded as fire stations were available in 46 per cent of towns. Unlike rural areas, towns are expected to have this kind of higher order infrastructural facilities as they need this service more often than their counterparts. Fire fighting service was existent in 55 per cent of towns in 1991 and 62 per cent of towns in 2001. In most of the small towns (Class IV, V, VI town), this service was not available and they had to depend on the nearest big cities. The poor status of this facility is further highlighted by the observation that few Class II towns like Brajrajnagar, Barbil, Sunabeda and other medium towns such as Hirakud, Rajgangpur, Biramitrapur etc. did not have any fire fighting service and the nearest service centre was their respective district headquarters.

Medical Facilities

Health is an integral part of human well-being. However, urban Odisha represents poor health facilities. In many small and medium towns the medical facilities are practically absent. 19 out of 81 towns did not have any hospital in 1971, most of them being served only by dispensaries. In 12 per cent of towns, none of the medical facilities such as hospitals, health centres or dispensaries are found. Except few big cities, most of the towns are served by only one hospital irrespective of their population size. Surprisingly, there was no hospital found in as many as 56 out of total 138 towns in 2001 and maximum of them are served either by a dispensary or a health centre. Six medium towns, namely Brajrajnagar, Pattamundai, Kantabaji, Basudebpur, Soro and Remuna come under this category. Furthermore, another 61 towns including one Class I town (Sambalpur) and nine Class II towns are served by only one hospital. In 2001, eight hospitals were found in Bhubaneswar (the highest) followed by Cuttack and Brahmapur both having six each, Baripada (five), and Jharsuguda (four). However, given their large population base, this status seems to be inadequate. If, these medical facilities are analysed from the population point of view, the decline in medical status is clearly discernible.

However, beds per thousand populations provide better insights for studying population pressure on medical facilities.

Table 8.2: Medical and Educational Facilities in Urban Odisha

Year	*No. of Towns*	*Urban Population*	*Medical Beds / 1000 pop.**	*Primary and Middle Schools/1000 pop.*
1971	81	1814147	3.65	0.68
1981	108	3110287	2.93	0.66
1991	124	4234983	2.76	0.63
2001	138	5517238	2.51	0.67

* It included all medical institutions hospitals, health centres, dispensaries, family welfare centres, TB Clinics, Nurshing Homes, and other medical institutions.

Source: Census of India, Town Directory Odisha, 1971 (series 16), 1981 (Series 16), 1991 (Series 19), 2001 (Series 21).

The number of beds per 1000 population in all medical institutions (that include hospitals, dispensaries, health centres, family welfare centres, nursing homes, and other medical institutions) has decreased over the years in urban Odisha. There were 3.65 number of beds per thousand urban population in 1971, and this sharply decreased to 2.93 in 1981. Further decline in beds per thousand population was noticed as the corresponding figures were 2.76 and 2.51 in1991 and 2001 respectively. It clearly indicates that the development of medical facilities has not been commensurate to population growth. Rather this facility shows a declining trend if considered from the perspective of availability per thousand population. The mere presence of one hospital or health centre with gross inadequacy of beds highlights the deplorable condition of medical facilities in the towns and cities of the State.

Educational Facilities

Basic educational facilities in terms of primary and middle schools per thousand population have also been found to be low in urban Odisha and not much change has taken place during 1971 to 2001. The number of primary and middle schools per thousand population marginally decreased from 0.68 in 1971 to 0.66 in 1981 and further declined to 0.63 in 1991. However, there has been a departure from this in 2001, when the corresponding figure stood at 0.67. Out of a total of 138 towns, 54 towns have recorded less than the State's average in number of primary and middle schools per thousand population. Interestingly, all the Class I cities and nine out of total fifteen Class II towns came in this category.

The number of colleges increased four times from 61 in 1971 to 243 in 2001 in urban Odisha. The number of colleges included all colleges including Arts College, Arts and Science College, Arts, Science and Commerce College and Science College. In the field of higher education, Bhubaneswar and Cuttack, also known as the 'twin cities' have excelled and have been way ahead as main educational centres of the State. In 2001, 24 out of total 138 towns did not have any college whereas the highest number of colleges were found in Bhubaneswar (eighteen) followed by Cuttack (fifteen) and Brahmapur and Rourkela having seven each. It is interesting to note that the medium towns located in interior region had more number of colleges than coastal towns. This is probably due to the fact that coastal medium towns located in coastal areas like Choudwar and Jatni are situated near to bigger cities and hence they depend on them for higher education.

Index of Infrastructure Development

In this section an attempt has been made to estimate the overall infrastructure development in the towns of Odisha and to trace the temporal change in the status of infrastructure facilities. In order to gauge the infrastructure development of a town, one needs to consider various units of infrastructure like road density, electricity connections, medical facility, educational facility as well as cultural or recreation centres. Also, since towns perform more of economic functions, credit facilities like banks should be considered. The level of different infrastructure facilities and other basic amenities varies among the towns. In other words, a town having better road connectivity may not have adequate number of hospitals or proper educational facilities. Thus, a measure based on the incorporation of all such indicators can only reflect the level of infrastructure development in a town. Therefore, a composite index calculated by taking most representative and best possible indicators can serve this. Considering various factors like data availability, the nature of towns and the variations in the levels of infrastructure units, following indicators have been chosen to construct the '*Index of Infrastructure Development*'.

Physical Infrastructure

(a) Weighted Road Length per square kilometre *

(b) Electricity
- Number of Domestic Connections per 100 households
- Number of Road Lighting Points per square kilometre

Social Infrastructure

(a) *Medical Facilities*
- Number of Hospitals per 5000 population
- Number of Dispensaries and health centres per 5000 population
- Number of Beds in all Medical Institutions per 1000 population**

* *Pucca* Road was given a weight of '3' and *kutcha* road was given '1'

** It included number of beds in Hospitals, Health Centres, Dispensaries, TB clinics, Family Health Centres, Nurshing Homes, other medical institutions.

(b) *Educational facilities*

- Number of Primary and Middle Schools per 5000 population
- Number of Secondary and Senior Secondary Schools per 5000 population
- Number of Colleges[#]

(c) *Recreational Facilities*

- Number of Cinema Halls
- Number of Auditoriums
- Number of Public Libraries and Reading Rooms

Economic Infrastructure

(A) Number of Banks

The number of colleges and banks in towns is generally very few irrespective of the size of the town. This is the reason that did not necessitate these indicators of being standardised.

Based on the values of the infrastructure index five groups have been identified such as very high, high, medium, low and very low (Table 8.3). It has been found that infrastructure development in towns of Odisha has taken place from 1971 to 1981, but has declined subsequently. The number of towns placed under highly developed category has increased from just one in 1971 to four in 1981. Moreover, the percentage of towns in the medium development category has increased substantially from 7 to 24 per cent, i.e. more than three times. Many of the towns with very low infrastructure facilities have moved one step up to the 'low' category.

There has been a deceleration in infrastructure development in towns in 1991 as more number of towns came under the 'low' category and further decline was observed in 2001. As high as 62 per cent of towns possessed 'very low' infrastructure facility in 2001 and another 28 per cent of towns came under the 'low' development category. In the next section, an analysis of the category wise infrastructure development has been done in order to identify the towns experiencing improvement in infrastructure *vis-à-vis* those placed at the other end of the spectrum.

\# It included Arts College, Science Colleges, Commerce Colleges, Arts and Science Colleges, Arts and Commerce Colleges and Arts, Science & Commerce Colleges.

Table 8.3: Categories of Infrastructure Development in Towns in Odisha, 1971-2001

Category	*Values*	*No. of Towns*	*Percentage of Towns*	*Category*	*Values*	*No. of Towns*	*Percentage of Towns*
	1971				**1981**		
Very High	more than 1.763	1	1.23	Very High	more than 0.705	4	3.70
High	1.736 - 1.111	2	2.47	High	0.705 - 0.405	3	2.78
Medium	1.110 - 0.485	6	7.41	Medium	0.404 - 0.103	73	24.07
Low	0.484 - (-0.141)	27	33.33	Low	0.102 - (-0.199)	47	43.52
Very Low	less than (-0.142)	45	55.56	Very Low	less than (-0.200)	28	25.93
Total Towns		**81**	**100.00**	**Total Towns**		**108**	**100.00**
	1991				**2001**		
Very High	more than 1.352		0.81	Very High	more than 1.663	1	0.72
High	1.352 - 0.774	1	2.42	High	1.663 - 1.102	2	1.45
Medium	0.773 - 0.195	3	18.55	Medium	1.101 - 0.540	11	7.97
Low	0.194 - (-0.384)	23	65.32	Low	0.539 - (-0.022)	39	28.26
Very Low	less than (-0.385)	81	12.90	Very Low	less than (-0.223)	85	61.59
Total Towns		**124**	**100.00**	**Total Towns**		**138**	**100.00**

Source: Computed from Census of India 1971, 1981, 1991 2001, Government of India.

I. Very High Level

Cuttack was the only town in 1971 which had very high level of infrastructure facilities. This was because Cuttack has been the single most important centre of business, education and other services in the State since historical times. In almost all the sectors, Cuttack is well ahead of other towns and cities with an estimated index value of 2.4 compared to the second most developed city of Bhubaneswar (an index value of 1.4). In 1981, Fertiliser Corporation of India Township and Talcher Thermal Power Station Township were the towns with very high development which could be attributed to the fact that with their low population base, these industrial towns had better physical infrastructure facilities in terms of road density, electricity connections, and street light points. Unexpectedly, Gopalpur and G. Udaygiri are the other two towns in this category as the physical infrastructure is well developed in the former and schooling facilities are markedly high in the later along with reasonable facilities with regard to infrastructure elements. Again, Cuttack and Bhubaneswar are only towns to be classified under this category in 1991 and 2001 respectively. In 2001, the state capital was the only town to be classified as highly developed in almost all aspects of infrastructure facilities. Well developed educational facilities with better roads and reasonably adequate medical facilities have earned it the status of being very highly developed with respect to infrastructure. It may be noted that it is also the second most planned city in India after Chandigarh.

II. High Level

The holy city of Puri and Brahmapur, were the towns having high infrastructure development. Baleswar and other two small towns—Khariar and Kantilo also have been included in this category. These small towns with lesser population and smaller area reported to have higher values in road density, street lights per sq. km. and other medical and educational facilities taken in terms of five thousand population. Brahmapur moved from low category in 1981 to high development category in 1991 and remained in this category in 2001 as well. NALCO (an industrial town) also improved its infrastructure base and hence qualified to be classified under this category.

In 2001, the top rank was replaced by Bhubaneswar and Cuttack slipped to the 'high' development category from very high development category in 1991.

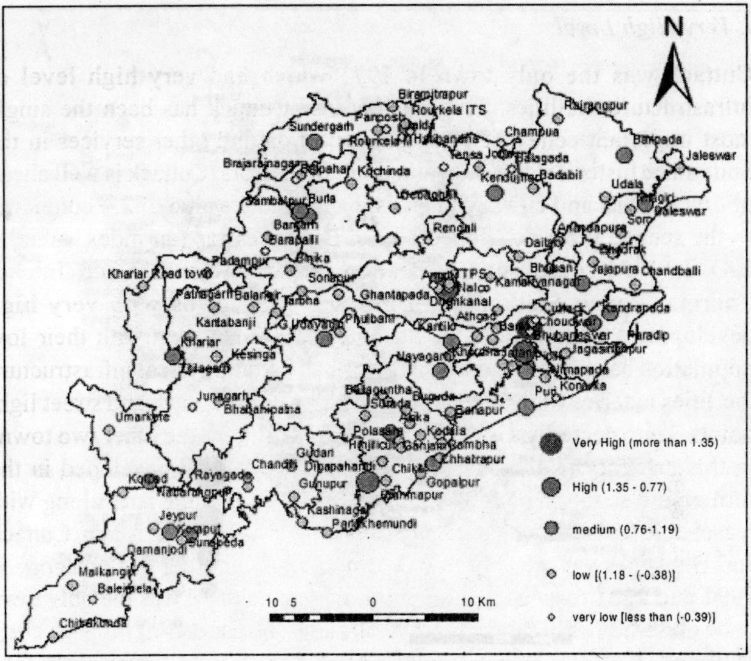

Fig. 8.1: Odisha: Level of Infrastructure Development across all Size Class Towns, 1991

III. Medium Level

The towns having medium level of infrastructure facilities dominate the urban scene in Odisha. The share of moderately developed towns has increased till 1991 but most of them were pushed to the low development category in 2001. Barring few big cities, most of the district headquarters were found to have a medium level of infrastructure development. In 1971, Bhubaneswar, Sambalpur, Baleswar, Baripada, Paralakhemundi were the towns with medium level of infrastructure development. In 1981, many medium and small towns were placed in this category. Raurkela Steel Township, Puri, Nayagarh, Keonjhar, Cuttack, Chowdwar, Jajpur, Koraput, and Talcher had modest infrastructure development. The index values of 1991 showed that majority of them again reported moderate level of infrastructure development. In 2001, out of total nine Class I towns, three were in the category of medium infrastructure development. Except big towns like Sambalpur, Raurkela, Puri and few other medium

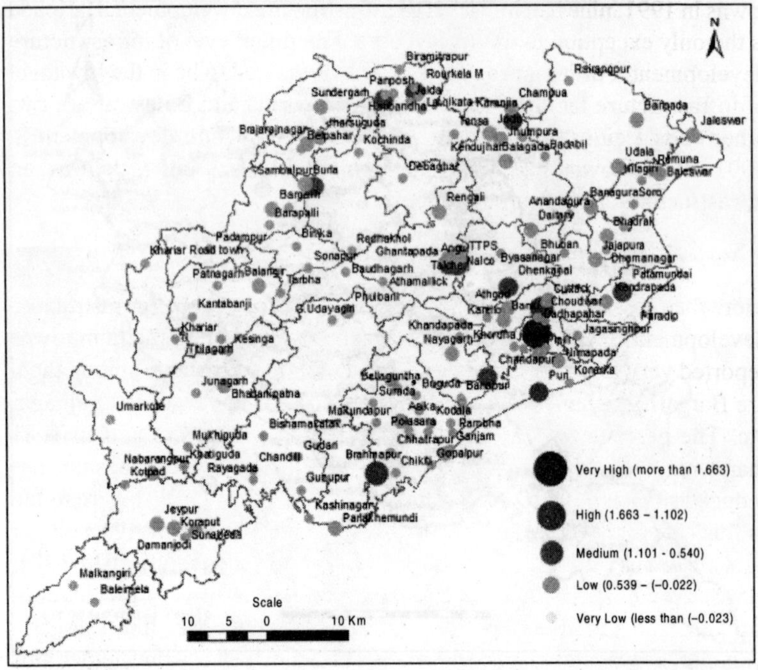

Fig. 8.2: Odisha: Level of Infrastucture Development across all Size Class Town-2001

towns, most of the towns having fair level of urban infrastructure slipped to low category. Again, Sambalpur, Keonjhar, Pattamundai and all towns having medium level of infrastructure level in 1991 acquired low development level due to their inability to meet to the requirement of adequate infrastructure. The percentage of towns in the medium category reduced from 19 per cent in 1991 to almost half in 2001 (Table 8.3).

IV. Low Level

Along with small towns, many of the large and medium towns were also found to have low level of infrastructure facilities. Rourkela Steel Township, Anugul, Keonjhar, Jharsuguda in 1971; Sundergarh, Bhubaneswar, Bhawanipatna, Bargarh in 1981; Bhadrak, Jharsuguda, Bolangir in 1991 and Baleswar, Brajrajnagar in 2001 were reported to have low infrastructure development. In 1991, 68 per cent of the towns had low infrastructure facilities. It is discernible that out of total 10 Class II towns in 1991, nine had low level of infrastructure development. Baripada is the only exception to this as it reported medium level of infrastructure development. Furthermore, eight of them remained to be in the low level of infrastructure facilities also in 2001. Baripada and Baleswar are two other class I cities that had low level of infrastructure development in 2001. These towns had significant population size but lacked urban infrastructure or other urban functions.

V. Very Low Level

More than half of the towns have recorded very low level of infrastructure development in 1971. As many as 10 out of a total of 22 medium towns reported very low ranks in the infrastructure index. Notable among them are Bargarh, Rayagada, Bhadrak, Rajgangpur, Chowdwar, Brajrajnagar etc. The percentage of towns in this category reduced to half in 1981 than what it was in the previous decade. In the next two decades this has reduced substantially as only 13 per cent of the towns in 1991 were found in this category. This trend was reversed in 2001 and as many as 62 per cent of towns had very low level of infrastructure facilities. In 1981, major towns like Bolangir Baripada, Jharsuguda had very low level of infrastructure. In 2001, few of the district headquarters like Deogarh, Sonepur, Rayagada, Jagatsinghpur, and Baudh also came under this category. Surprisingly, Raurkela Industrial Township, a Class I city was found to have very low level of infrastructure indicating that it served mainly as an industrial town. A very low index value of this town was probably because of the poor educational and medical facilities. The majority of population here depends on Raurkela Civil Township when such needs arise.

Conclusions

The above analysis reveals that infrastructure development has not been commensurate with required demand in urban Odisha, particularly after 1991. This means that though the infrastructure increased in absolute terms but the per capita availability has decreased especially in the case medical facilities. Many of the infrastructural facilities like hospitals, colleges or other recreational facilities are completely non-existent in most of the small towns and the population of such towns depend on the nearest bigger urban centres. The most important physical infrastructure like water supply, system of sewerage etc. are also found to be in a very critical condition. The observation that open surface drains served as important system of sewerage in more than 80 per cent of towns in 2001 highlights the serious deficiency of infrastructure facilities. It is surprising to note that the important system of sewerage in the State Capital (Bhuvaneswar) was open surface drain in 2001. However, physical infrastructure like road length per square kilometre and number electric road light points per square kilometre has increased substantially from 1971 to 2001. Facilities of higher education like senior secondary schools and number of colleges have increased manifold, but that is restricted to few large cities like Bhubaneswar, Cuttack, Raurkela, Brahmapur and other medium towns. The capital city of Bhubaneswar as well as Cuttack, Brahmapur, Puri had by and large maintained fairly good level of infrastructure and other big cities like Sambalpur, Baleshwar remained in the medium category. Few industrial towns like Fertiliser Corporation of India Township, Talcher Thermal Power Station Township, and NALCO also possessed high or very high index value of infrastructure development.

From the viewpoint of temporal changes in infrastructural development, Bhubaneswar has witnessed significant improvement after 1981. This can be attributed to the fact that being the state capital, it received high attention of policy makers and investors thereby enabling better finance management in urban service delivery mechanism. In that process, the other towns have been seemingly marginalised and the post 1991 period many towns having medium and low infrastructure have been pushed to the category of very low level of infrastructure development. Based on the analysis of infrastructure development in urban Odisha, one can argue that a maximum of small and medium towns served as regional market centres without the existence of significant infrastructure facilities. Even at present, many of the small and few medium towns do not have hospitals and other basic amenities within their premises, despite having sizable population. In recent years, there has been growing realisation of the necessity of upgradation of infrastructure and basic amenities and more importantly the service delivery mechanism in urban areas. Since infrastructure development and urban productivity are reciprocally interlinked, it is highly felt that the maintenance and upgradation of existing infrastructure must be considered seriously. Given the high resource potential, a State like Odisha should be provided with fast and time bound infrastructure building projects facilitated by better funding and capital generation processes, if it is sought to harness the optimal productivity which can certainly help in poverty reduction.

REFERENCES

Bhandari, L. (2006), 'Social Infrastructure: Urban Health and Mission', in 3iNetwork (ed.), *India Infrastructure Report 2006: Urban Infrastructure*, Oxford University Press, New Delhi.

Brockerhoff, M. and Brennam, E. (1998), 'The Poverty of Cities In Developing Regions', *Populations and Development Review*, Vol. 24, No. 1, pp. 75-114.

Das, J. and Mukhopadhaya, S.C. (1999), 'Water Supply and Drainage Status in S. Dum Dum Municipal of Calcutta' in R.R.M. Rao and S. Shimadri (eds), *Indian Cities: Towards Next Millennium*, Rawat Publication, Jaipur.

Government of India. (2009b). 'National Urban Sanitation Policy: A Perspective', Ministry of Urban Development, Government of India.

Government of India. (2011), 'Report on Indian Urban Infrastructure and Services', March 2011, The High Powered Expert Committee (HPEC) for Estimating the Investment Requirements for Urban Infrastructure Services, Ministry of Urban Development, Government of India.

Kewalramani, G (1997), 'The Role of Medium Towns in the Spatial Diffusion of Development: The Case Study of Konkan Region' in Dedee, J. (ed), *Indian Medium Towns: An Appraisal of their Role as Growth Centres*, Rawat Publication, Jaipur.

Kundu, A., S. Bagchi, and D. Kundu (1999), 'Regional Distribution of Infrastructure and Basic Amenities in Urban India', *Economic and Political Weekly*, 34(28): 1893-1906.

Kundu, A., S. Maitra and D. Kundu (1996), 'Housing and Basic Amenities in Urban India: An Analysis of Regional Pattern and Accessibility in the Context of Changing Perspective of Governance', Planning Commission, New Delhi.

Pethe, A. and M. Ghedke (2002), 'Funding Urban Infrastructure: From Government to Markets', *Economic and Political Weekly*, June 22, 2002.

Savage, D. and S. Dasgupta (2006), 'Governance Framework for Delivery of Urban Services', in 3iNetwork (ed.), *India Infrastructure Report 2006: Urban Infrastructure*, Oxford University Press, New Delhi.

Shaw, A. (1999), 'Emerging Patterns of Urban Growth in India', *Economic and Political Weekly*, Vol. 34, No. 16/17 (April 17-30, 1999), pp. 969-978.

Sridhar, K.S. and A.V. Reddy (2010), *State of Urban Services in Indian Cities: Spending and Financing*, Oxford University Press, 2010.

World Bank (1994), *World Development Report 1994: Infrastructure for Development*, Oxford University Press, New York, 1994.

9

Functional Structure, Specialisation and Diversification of Class-I Cities of Uttar Pradesh

Eshita Tripathy

Introduction

Towns and cities can be categorised on the basis of various characteristics such as age, population, geographical location, area etc., but most important aspect for classifying cities is based on the functions that it performs. Contemporary urban places or cities are performing a multitude of services that are essential for existence of the societies. The functions are the driving force that influence the growth, structure, characteristic and morphology of any urban place. The functions performed by urban places are mostly related to non-primary or non-agricultural activities and includes manufacturing, administration, transport, communication, trade and commerce etc., that in turn may be categorised under secondary, tertiary and quaternary activities. Furthermore, there are other services such as socio-cultural, public utility services, public administration, recreational, professional, etc., that are provided by urban centres. Hence, a town or a city is generally not known by a single dominant function that it performs, but most of these cities are diversified in nature or poly-functional, i.e. they perform more than one function simultaneously. Broadly, urban functions may be clubbed under two broad categories, i.e. basic or city-forming and non-basic or city serving.

Part of the employed population of an urban unit is engaged either in the production of goods or in the performance of services for areas and people outside the city itself. Actually, these are the workers who are engaged in export and other activities, whose efforts result in money flowing into the city. Collectively, they constitute the 'basic sector' of the city's total economic structure. The other section, i.e. of 'non-basic sector' comprises workers who support themselves by producing goods and services for residents of the urban unit itself. Their efforts are necessary for the successful functioning of the urban settlement. Cities and towns have their own individuality, some are sometimes highly industrialised, some are well known as pilgrim or tourist centres, while others may be well known for trade and commerce.

Study Area

Uttar Pradesh lies between 23°52′N and 31°28′N latitudes and 77°3′E and 84°39′E longitudes. This northern State is surrounded by Bihar in the east; Madhya Pradesh in the south; Rajasthan, Delhi, Himachal Pradesh and Haryana in the west; Uttaranchal and Nepal in the north (Map 9.1). The State has a population of 166.1 million as per 2001 Census and occupies a total geographical area of 2.41 lakh sq. km. It is also the fourth largest state in area, covering 9.0 per cent of the country's geographical area, while its share in country's population is 16.2 per cent. The erstwhile composite State of Uttar Pradesh was bifurcated by transferring 13 districts to carve out the new state of Uttaranchal (now Uttarakhand) in November, 2000. Administratively, in 2001 Census the state consist of 70 districts, 300 tahsils and 704 towns including 638 Statutory Towns and 66 Census Towns. The area of present research work includes the Class-I cities in Uttar Pradesh and has been carried under two sub-heads:

1. Overall analysis of urban characteristics across 54 Class-I cities.
2. Region-wise analysis of urban characteristics across 54 Class-I cities.

One of the prime reason cited for selection of the study area is that the Class-I cities are the centres where economic growth and development are not ubiquitous while these house the major chunk of population. Furthermore, these cities present striking differences when compared to smaller towns and cities in terms of population size and scale of activities.

Literature Review

The concept of functional classification of towns and cities was initiated

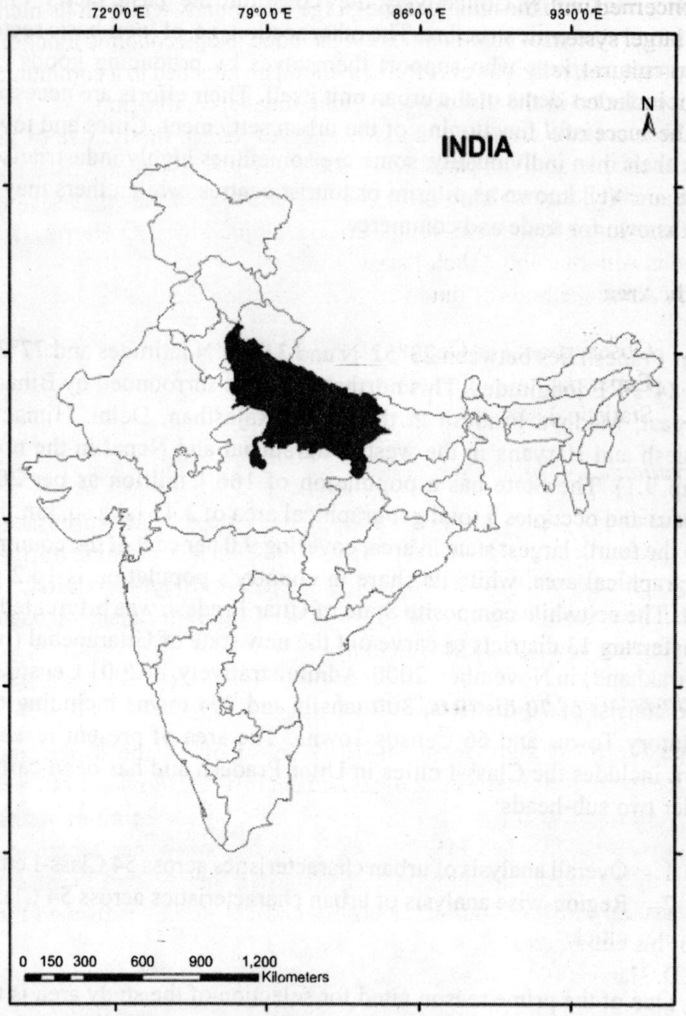

Map 9.1: India: Study Area: Uttar Pradesh
Source: Census of India, 2001.

in the early eighteenth century and today this has undergone tremendous change both by as its definition and also in relation to urban planning.

Roy Kass (1973) highlights that the term "function" is used to refer to economic activities and economic organisation. Thus all activities that are concerned with the maintenance of the community and with its niche in the larger system of communities are included. Non-economic functions such as cultural, religious or historic symbolism attached to a community are not included in the discussion of functional specialisation.

There are two criteria of classification of towns, firstly, size of the towns or the hierarchical classification as used by Christaller, Losch and Zipf. Secondly, that which is based on the functions of the cities such as manufacturing, educational, retail, etc. as adopted by C.D Harris, H.J. Nelson in America and Ashok Mitra in India.

The three methods of functional classification include:

1. Observational or Qualitative Method
2. Experimental or Quantitative Method
3. Statistical Method.

Observational or Qualitative Method

First of all the best known classification was advanced by M. Aurousseau (1921) who classified towns into six categories, viz. administrative, defence, culture, production towns, communication and recreation. In this classification he tried to distinguish between the primary or basic and secondary and non-basic functions.

Experimental or Quantitative Method

Perhaps the most significant and influential of all the functional classification of the cities was that worked out by C.D Harris in 1943. He was the first geographer who classified 605 American cities using quantitative method based on Census data. He developed specific criteria for classifying cities functionally and suggested quantitative limits for each class. Employment figures and occupational structures formed the basis of his classification.

C.D. Harris (1943) used employment figures as the major criterion for his classification, but occupational data were also utilised and they formed the basis for distinguishing two of the functional types, i.e. transportation centres and mining towns. In order to simplify comparisons, Harris reduced all figures to percentages: occupations to percentages of all gainful workers and employment to percentages of workers in manufacturing, wholesale and retail combined. For two classes, i.e. university as well as resort and retirement towns he depended upon other sources of data. The functional classification given by Harris has been criticised on following grounds.

Firstly, his selection of cut offs in the form of percentages of certain functions is subjective. Secondly, he conceived that the city is specialised only in a single function which is not true as any city performs a number of diversified functions simultaneously. A more advanced classification appears in a chapter by Victor Jones (1953) in the Municipal Year Book of 1953. It is based on the data from 1948 Census of Manufacturing and Census of Business of that same year. Jones method is patterned after Harris', although his percentages are somewhat different.

Statistical Methods

Howard J. Nelson (1955) made an attempt in 1955 to overcome the shortcomings and weaknesses which were inherent in the classification of Harris. His own classification was based on statistical techniques, quantitative methods and subjective considerations. He divided 897 cities of U.S.A into ten functional types—manufacturing, retail, finance, wholesale, transport, personal services, public administration, professional services, mining and diversified; for which he took employment structure into consideration. He classified only 897 cities because the data was not available for the rest of the cities.

According to Nelson the two major problems in the previous classifications were judicious selection of the cities and reliance on the author's judgement only due to limited data availability.

Nelson claimed that the proportion of the labour force of a city engaged in performing a service is the best means of measuring that activity. Thus, he decided to base his classification entirely upon industrial groups as listed in the 1950 Census for Standard Metropolitan areas, urbanised areas and the urban places of 10,000 or more population in the US.

His new methodology yielded several results such as classification of 897 urban concentrations, city-wise service classification for the entire group of cities, production of a series of maps showing the distribution of each of the different service classes and finally, provision of explanation for the distributional pattern of each class.

However, there has been some drawbacks of his method like—problems arising out of the data, and his usage of substantial mathematical calculations. Nonetheless, his classification is comparatively more logical and scientific as compared to other methods of functional classification.

Bert F. Hoselitz (1959) expresses that the thesis of Amrit Lal emphasise spatial relations, though his work also concentrates on functional distinctions. He used the Location Quotient method in order to determine the functional type of 67 Class I cities in India. According to his findings, with the exception of four mono-functional cities, all the Indian cities are multi-functional in nature. Among the twelve bi-functional cities, the most commonly occurring functions are manufacturing, transport and public administration. On the other hand, specialisation in wholesale trade, FIR services, education, professional services and retail trade are commonly associated with cities that specialise in three or more functions. According to the intensity of specialisation, retail trade has the largest number of cities with a normal specialisation that is followed by manufacturing, transport, other professions, education, wholesale trade and public administration. The small number of cities with normal specialisation in public administration and wholesale trade may represent the sporadic character of their distribution in contrast to retail trade and other functions which are more ubiquitous.

Quazi Ahmad (1965) used 62 variables to classify 102 Indian cities on the basis of their functions. The factor analysis revealed that 10 dimensions were required to account for over 70 per cent of the correlations among variables.

Ashok Mitra (1973) used seven categories of workers as variables grouped into three major functional types, viz. manufacturing, trade and transport and services. Thus out of the 2528 towns and cities appearing in the 1961 and 1971 Censuses, 655 were classified as manufacturing, 708 as trade and transport towns and 429 specialising in services. In his modified classification of 1981, Mitra grouped 219 Class-I cities of the country into seven broad categories. These include manufacturing (80), trade (78), services (41), transport (9), artisan (8), mining and plantation (1). It has been inferred that the cities that are involved in manufacturing are well distributed throughout the country except in the case of states like Kerala and Assam. According to him, some of the cities such as Jamshedpur, Ulhasnagar, Ludhiana, Salem, Ahmedabad, and Surat exhibit high degree of specialisation in this field. The cities associated with trading as a function generally have low level of specialisation and are more or less ubiquitous. The cities which are highly specialised under this category are Vijaywada, Siliguri and Katihar. The cities specialising in services are also uniformly distributed like Chandigarh, Shillong, Bhubaneshwar and Agartala. Cities exhibiting high degree of specialisation in the field of transport and artisans are Dhanbad, Asansol, Andal and railway towns like Bhusawal and Kharagpur. Kolar and Bermo are the two mining towns while only one town is found to specialise in plantations, i.e. Valparai in Tamil Nadu.

The classification of towns of Mysore State by V.L.S. Prakasha Rao (1964) was on the basis of regression analysis. In this method he tried to correlate population size with the percentage of people in a particular function. According to Rao, a higher degree of specialisation resulted in a decrease in the percentage of industrial workers of a town or a city. In other words, he tried to correlate population size with the percentage of population in a particular function. According to him, Nelson's Standard Deviation method is useful only in case of homogeneous population. But in a state like Karnataka exhibiting a high degree of specialisation the standard deviation method becomes meaningless.

Another Indian geographer who classified Indian cities on the basis of functions is Kashi Nath. He classified the cities in the state of Uttar Pradesh on the basis of the Standard Deviation method.

Objectives

The salient aim of this study is to examine the functional diversification of the Class-I cities as well as to assess the concentration or diversification of Class-I cities in Uttar Pradesh.

This study is based on the secondary data from the Census of India, 1991 and 2001. Decadal computation for functional diversification is carried out for fifty-four Class I cities of Uttar Pradesh in 2001 and thirty-eight Class I, fourteen Class II, one Class III and one Class V city in 1991, to maintain comparability between 1991 and 2001. The cities and towns considered for 1991 had graduated to Class I in 2001. For functional diversification in urban areas, data is obtained from Census 2001, B-Series, and B19-for Main Workers as well as Primary Census Abstract.

Urbanisation is a multi-dimensional phenomenon and various methodologies are required for its analysis like quantitative, qualitative, cartographic and statistical methods. The present study incorporates.

Quantitative methods like Functional Classification using Nelson's Method and Diversification Index (based on Herfindahl Index).

Functional Classification

Number of persons employed in different activities mainly highlights the functional base of that particular region. Census of India divides the workers into nine industrial categories that are mentioned in Table 9.1.

For computing functional classification of the cities in Uttar Pradesh, the first two categories that of Cultivation and Agricultural Labour are not taken into consideration because these are under the domain of primary sector which do not come under urban functions.

Table 9.1: Industrial Category of Workers

Industrial Category	*Workers*
I	Cultivation
II	Agricultural Labour
III	Forestry, Plantations, Horticulture, Floriculture, Livestock, Fishing, Silviculture and Apiculture
IV	Mining and Quarrying
V(a)	Manufacturing, processing, Servicing and repairs in household industry
V(b)	Manufacturing, processing, Servicing and repairs in non-household industry
VI	Construction
VII	Trade and Commerce
VIII	Transport, Storage and Communication
IX	Other Services

Using Nelson's method the following steps have been undertaken:

1. After the categories have been decided upon, the percentages of the total labour force in different activity group for each of the 54 Class I urban centres are calculated.
2. However, since individual percentages are almost pointless without some point of reference, the arithmetic averages for each activity group have been computed.
3. Next, Standard Deviations from the mean are calculated for each of the seven activity groups. Three degrees of variation from the average are recognised, and the cities grouped in their appropriate categories. Cities that are over + 1 SD from the average in manufacturing are given a rating of Manufacturing 1 (or Mf 1) if, over 2 SD's then a rating of Mf 2 and MF3 if over 3 or more SDs.
4. This has been followed by the selection of the degrees of specialisation, i.e.

   If the value lies in between Mean to Mean + 1 S.D then the urban centre if diversified;

   If the value lies in between Mean +1 S.D. to Mean + 2 S.D then it is less diversified; and

   If the value lies in between Mean +2 S.D. to Mean + 3 S.D—then the urban centre is moderately specialised and finally if the value is more than Mean +3 S.D. then it is highly specialised.

Perhaps the most useful device for our purposes is the Standard Deviation. In the first place (regardless of the theoretical criticisms that may be levelled against it) the SD is the simplest and most widely understood of all statistical measures of variation. Secondly, the degree of variation can be compared by the use of the SD even if in some cases one deals with large percentages or with small numbers (as in skewed distribution). This would seem to be an advantage over the simple percentage deviation used by Pownall (1953).[1]

Herfindahl Index

In order to measure the specialisation and diversification of the cities Herfindahl Index (HI) has been adopted. For computing this index the first two categories that of Cultivation and Agricultural Labourers are not taken into consideration. From the remaining seven categories Herfindahl Index is computed by taking the proportion of workers of particular category to that of total workers in all the categories and raising them to the power of two.

The index is computed as follows—

$$HI = \Sigma P_i^2$$

Where,

N = the total number of industrial categories (here seven)

P_i = represents proportion of workers under ith category to total workers in the seven categories.

The Herfindahl index is also known as Herfindahl-Hirschman Index or HHI. The index was first used to measure the regional concentration of industries (Theil, 1967)[2]. The value of HI varies between 0 to1. If the value is nearer to 0 then the N becomes larger, i.e. total number of industrial categories becomes more and if the value is near 1 then only one category exists which refers that specialisation is taking place.

It is to be pointed that the main weakness of this index is that it cannot take the theoretical minimum value of zero when there is equal distribution of workers in all the categories. But, since this condition was not observed anywhere in the data available, therefore, the method suits the best in this situation. If the value is near unity then there is concentration and if the value is away from unity then diversification takes place. The value of Transformed Herfindahl Index (i.e. 1-HI) presented here increases with the diversification and assumes zero value when there is perfect concentration, i.e. when all the workers are employed only in a single category.

However, this index provides the value, which shows the extent of specialisation and diversification of activities in the city. In order to complement this index, a different method is used which shows exactly the type of activity in which the city is categorised. This method was put forward by H.J. Nelson (Nelson, 1955)[3] in "service classification of American cities" to label the cities with a function or group of functions. Here also the "population and labour force of a town engaged in any service is regarded as the best means of measuring the distribution of that particular activity".

Based on the average of the mean and the standard deviation of the distribution showing the extent of variation above the average, categorisation has been done (from the mean) as given below—

Table 9.2: Mean of the distributors and standard deviation categories

Range	*Category*	*Example*
X+1 O to X+2 O	Specialised	M2
X+2 O to X+3 O	High Specialisation	M3
Above X+3 O	Very High Specialisation	M4

Further, the city may fall in one or more of the above true category and can accordingly be classified as mono-functional, bi-functional or diversified. If the city does not fall in any of these three then it is regarded that it has no distinct function.

Functional Categorisation of Workers

The activities or jobs followed by workers cover a wide range. Due to this wide range of activities among workers and to have a fairly good idea of the nature of distribution of workers these activities have been grouped into the nine industrial categories by the Census of India which is listed as below along with their codes.

In this section, functional comparison of cities of Uttar Pradesh between 1991 and 2001 has been provided. After the categories had been decided the percentages of the total labour force in each activity group for each of the fifty-four Class-I cities has been calculated. Furthermore, in order to categorise the cities functionally the "Nelson Method" of town classification has been used. It is to be noted that while classifying the cities functionally, first two industrial categories pertaining to the primary activities are omitted and are not part of this study because these are considered as rural functions.

Table 9.3: Classification of Workers in Functional Categories

Industrial Category	*Workers*	*Codes (as mentioned in the Appendix)*
I	Cultivation	Omitted
II	Agricultural Labour	Omitted
III	Forestry,Plantations,Horticulture,Floriculture,Live stock,Fishing,Silviculture and Apiculture	L
IV	Mining and Quarrying	Mq
V(a)	Manufacturing, processing, Servicing and repairs in household industry	Mh
V(b)	Manufacturing, processing, Servicing and repairs in non-household industry	M
VI	Construction	C
VII	Trade and Commerce	Tr
VIII	Transport, Storage and Communication	Tt
IX	Other Services	O

Labelling of Class-I Cities

The categorisation of the cities in different functional classes exhibits that a town is regarded as shifting towards specialisation if the proportion of the workers exceeds the mean employment by at least one Standard Deviation (SD). For deciding the degree of specialisation the decisive factor is the distance of the mean from the Standard Deviation, e.g. if any city specialises in Trade and Commerce and its value is between Mean to Mean + 1 Standard Deviation and Mean to Mean + 2 Standard Deviation, then it is assigned the status of Tr2. Thus, three degree specialisation is ascertained for every activity and the cities are classified accordingly. Each town is assigned letter and number of codes depending on the degree of specialisation. In other words, standard deviations from the mean are, therefore, calculated for each of the seven activity groups.

The degree of specialisation is determined primarily by the proportion of workers in that category in relation to the value of Mean and Standard Deviation of that category. Thus, the Mean and S.D. together make four classes. Codes are assigned (according to these classes) to the values that are above mean. Thus, the unusually high proportion in any service (in relation to other cities) will place that city in the "specialised" category.

Nelson's categories are not mutually exclusive. In other words, a city can "specialise" in two or more activities as it can have values more than Mean + S.D. in more than one service.

For instance, if the city of Sultanpur is assigned the code of Mq_3Tt_2 then it has more than two Standard Deviations above the mean in Mining and Quarrying and more than one Standard Deviation in Transport, Storage and Communication (Census, 2001). By following the standard of quantitative classification of the towns of Uttar Pradesh, some subjective analysis is made to observe the ground reality.

Furthermore, the cities are grouped on the basis of their functional specialisation into following groups: (I) Mono-functional (II) Bi functional (III) Diversified, and (IV) Cities with No Distinct Function.

I. *Mono-functional towns* and cities reveal functional specialization in a single parameter like mining and quarrying for instance and represent the initial stage of urban development.

II. *Bi-functional* urban forms resemble functional specialisation in two parameters revealing a higher order settlement.

III. *Diversified* towns and cities have many functional types (7 types) and do not specialize in one or two parameters. They resemble complexities in functional organization.

IV. *Lostly* there are urban forms that do not have a single distinct function and are poorly developed.

Functional Categories of Cities

Table 9.4 presents the overall proportion of Class-I cities in different functional categories thereby depicting that the highest share of towns both of 1991 and 2001 are Mono-functional. This is followed by Diversified and Bi-functional categories respectively. The per cent share in these 3 above mentioned categories are 59.26 per cent, 25.93 per cent and 14.81 per cent respectively in 1991. The per cent share of cities in Mono-functional category reduced to 38.89 per cent, while the share of Diversified increased from 25.93 per cent in 1991 to 35.19 per cent in 2001. Even Bi-functional showed augmentation from 14.81 per cent in 1991 to 25.93 per cent in 2001. Therefore, increase in the per cent share of cities in Bi-functional and Diversified towns reveals the fact that the cities are performing more functions than even before and are also heading towards diversification.

A regional analysis reveals that the highest share of Mono-functional towns are present in the Eastern Region (71.43%) which is followed by

Table 9.4: Overall Proportion of Class-I Cities of Different Functional Categories in Uttar Pradesh, 1991 and 2001

Functional Category	*Total*			
	1991		*2001*	
	No. of Towns	*Per cent*	*No. of Towns*	*Per cent*
Mono	32	59.26	21	38.89
Bi	8	14.81	14	25.93
Div	14	25.93	19	35.19
No	0	0	0	0
Total	**54**	**100**	**54**	**100**

Note: Mono-Mono-functional, Bi—Bi-functional, Div--Diversified, No—No Distinct Function

Source: Census of India, 1991 and 2001.

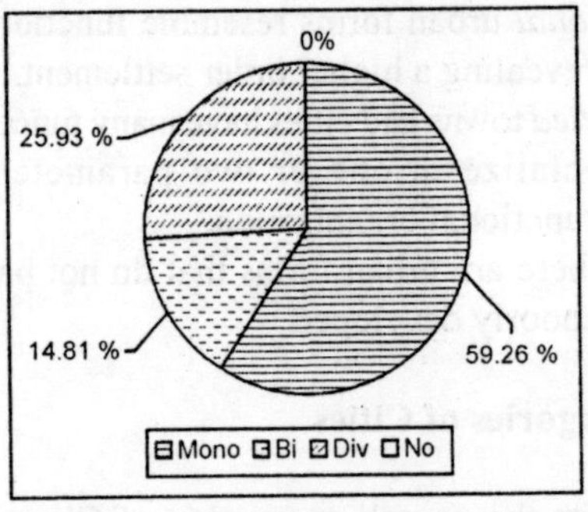

Fig. 9.1: Distribution of Class I Cities by Functional Categories, U.P. 1991

Central (63.64%), Western (53.85%) and Southern Region (33.33%) of Uttar Pradesh respectively. However, in 2001, the share of Mono-functional towns show remarkable reduction with the highest share being recorded in the central part (54.55%) followed by Western and Eastern with their share of 38.46 per cent and 35.71 per cent respectively, while in the Southern Region, mono-functional cities are altogether absent. Among the Bi-functional towns, the highest share is contributed by the Southern Region with 33.33 per cent followed by Western, Eastern and Central Regions with values of 15.38, 14.29, and 9.09 per cent respectively. In 2001, the per cent of Bi-functional cities increased in the Southern (66.67%), Eastern (42.86%) and Western Regions (23.08%) while in the Central Region this category was absent altogether.

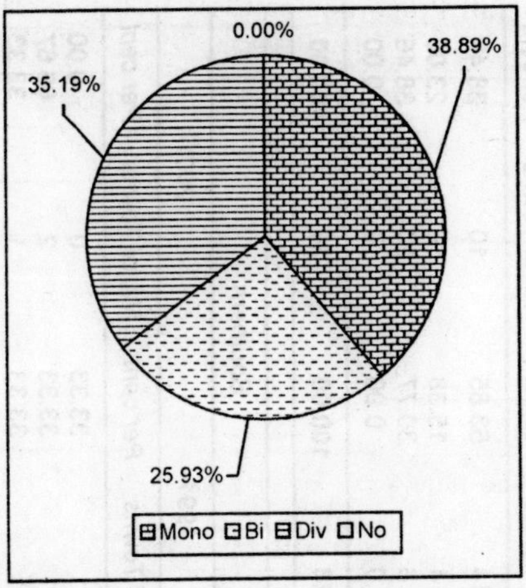

Fig. 9.2: Distribution of Class I Cities by Functional Categories, U.P. 2001

In case of Diversified category the per cent share of cities have increased in all the four regions. In 1991, the highest share of towns in this category was recorded in the Southern Region (33.33%) is followed by Western (30.77%), Central (27.77%) and Eastern regions (14.29%). In 2001, the Central Region occupies the topmost place with 45.45 per cent in this category followed by the Western (38.46%), Southern (33.33%) and Eastern Regions (21.43%). To sum up, over time period, the proportionate share of urban centres had progressively shifted from Mono-functional to Bi-functional and Diversified categories. This may be due to the fact that urban centres are becoming dynamic in nature in the performance of several functions. Thus in the evolutional history, diversification has become the order of the day.

Functional Classification of Cities (1991)

A Service Classification of the Towns and Cities of Uttar Pradesh Reveal the Following Categories in 1991:

1. Forestry, Plantations, Horticulture, Floriculture, Livestock, Fishing, Silviculture and Apiculture (L): Towns engaged in this category are Banda, Chandausi, Deoria, Pilibhit, Rae Bareli, Sultanpur and Unnao. The eastern fringe of the Awadh plain

Table 9.5: Region-wise Proportion of Class-I Cites of Different Categories in Uttar Pradesh 1991 and 2001

Functional Category	Central				Western			
	1991		2001		1991		2001	
	No. of Towns	Per cent	No. of Towns	Per cent	No. of Towns	Per cent	No. of Towns	Per cent
Mono	7	63.64	6	54.55	14	53.85	10	38.46
Bi	1	9.09	0	0.00	4	15.38	6	23.08
Div	3	27.27	5	45.45	8	30.77	10	38.46
No	0	0.00	0	0.00	0	0.00	0	0.00
Total	**11**	**100.00**	**11**	**100.00**	**26**	**100.00**	**26**	**100.00**

Functional Category	Eastern				Southern			
	1991		2001		1991		2001	
	No. of Towns	Per cent	No. of Towns	Per cent	No. of Towns	Per cent	No. of Towns	Per cent
Mono	10	71.43	5	35.71	1	33.33	0	0.00
Bi	2	14.29	6	42.86	1	33.33	2	66.67
Div	2	14.29	3	21.43	1	33.33	1	33.33
No	0	0.00	0	0.00	0	0.00	0	0.00
Total	**14**	**100.00**	**14**	**100.00**	**3**	**100.00**	**3**	**100.00**

Note: Mono—Mono-Functional, Bi—Bi-Functional, Div—Diversified, No—No Distinct Function

Source: Census of India, 1991 and 2001.

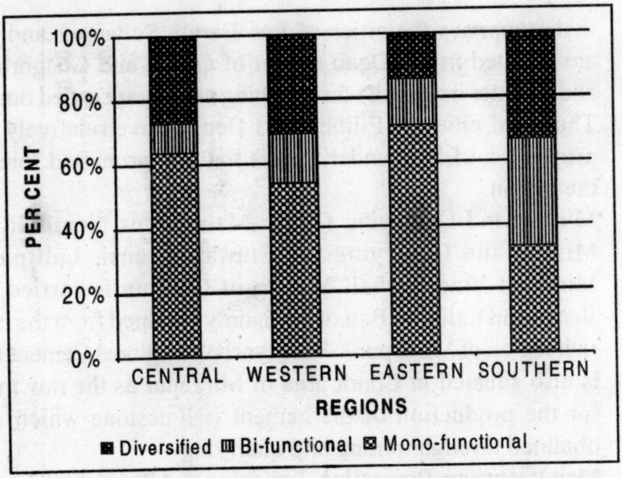

Fig. 9.3: Distribution of Towns by Functional Categories: Region-wise Uttar Pradesh, 1991 .

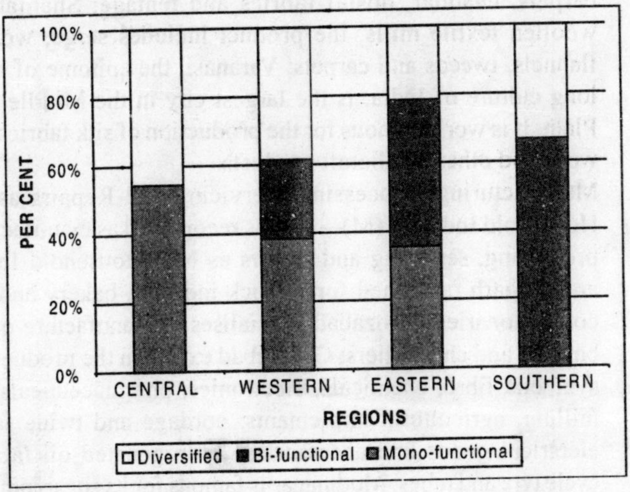

Fig. 9.4: Distribution of Towns by Functional Categories: Region-wise Uttar Pradesh, 2001

that comprises the cities of Rae Bareli, Sultanpur and Unnao are situated in the Doab region of Ganga and Ghaghra rivers and is better irrigated, where fishing activity is carried out easily. The Terai cities of Pilibhit and Deoria have relatively higher proportion of land under forests that has promoted forestry in the region.

2. Mining and Quarrying (MQ): Main towns identified under Mining and Quarrying are Etawah, Jhansi, Lalitpur, and Mirzapur-Vindhyachal. Mining of Gypsum is carried out in Jhansi and Lalitpur. Bauxite is mainly obtained from the mineral rich region of Mirzapur—Vindhyachal. Regional Cement factory is also situated in Churk area of Mirzapur as the raw material for the production of the cement is limestone which can be obtained through mining and quarrying.
3. Manufacturing, Processing, Servicing and Repairs as Household Industry (Mh)—Towns and Cities included in this functional category include Maunath Bhanjan which is known for its cotton mills and its manufactures include yarn, coloured fabrics, hosiery, carpets, chaddar, dosuti fabrics and tentage; Shahjahanpur woollen textile mills, the product includes serge, worsteds, flannels, tweeds and carpets; Varanasi, the epitome of the age long culture of India, is the largest city in the Middle Ganga Plain. It is world famous for the production of silk fabrics, brass work and other handicraft products.
4. Manufacturing, Processing, Servicing and Repairs as Non-Household Industry (M)—Towns recognised as manufacturing, processing, servicing and repairs as Non-Household Industry are: Aligarh renowned for its lock industry, bakery and sugar confectionaries; Firozabad specialises in manufacture of glass bangles and chandeliers; Ghaziabad excels in the production of synthetic fibre, chemicals, electronics, pharmaceuticals, flour milling, agricultural implements, cordage and twine factory, electrical goods and accessories, hydrogenated oil factories, cycle tyre and tubes; Modinagar is famous for its sugar industries, paperboard units and paper mills, cigarettes industry; Moradabad and Rae Bareli for Indian Telephone Industry (ITI), Rampur for beer manufacturing units, textile, knives manufacturing; Saharanpur is well known for sugar industries, paperboard units and paper mills, cigarettes industry, bakery and sugar confectionary.

5. Construction (C)—The cities included in this category include Amroha, Loni, NOIDA, Orai and Rae Bareli. The principle objective behind setting up of NOIDA is to create a new planned industrial town which would attract industry from non-conforming areas in Delhi (decentralisation) as well as the incorporation of small scale industries to reduce in-migration to Delhi and to provide additional areas for meeting the residential needs of the population of Delhi.
6. Trade and Commerce (Tr)—Ballia, Basti, Chandausi, Deoria, Etah, Ghazipur, Gonda, Gorakhpur, Hathras, Jaunpur, Lakhimpur and Sultanpur are the cities that are engaged in trade and commerce. The city of Deoria is developed as a centre along the junction of the overland routes of local distributive and collective trade and has acquired importance due to the presence of roads and railways.
7. Transport, Storage and Communication (Tt)—Towns recognised for transportation, storage and communication are— Chandausi, Jhansi, Lucknow and Sambhal. Lucknow is predominantly an administrative and cultural centre of the state and has few large scale industries. Because of administrative functions, it is well connected with various means of transportation. Jhansi is railway junction and it serves the North-western and Central-western region of India.
8. Others (O): Budaun, Faizabad, Farrukhabad-Fatehgarh, Fatehpur, Hardoi, Kanpur CB, Lakhimpur, Mainpuri and Sitapur are placed in this category. These cities perform the rest of the functions other than the above existing industrial functions.

   Faizabad is important for sugar production; Sitapur has sugar producing centres and plywood units; Mainpuri has rice mills; Farrukhabad-Fatehgarh has tannery centres, calico printing units, brass and copper ware industries and Fatehpur is important for tannery centres, iron and steel goods and utensils.

   Kanpur was originally a military cantonment at the border line dividing the then British Frontier from the province of Oudh and the territory of the Mughal kings of Delhi. It grew as one of the most important industrial hub of the nation. After 1857, many industrial units were established at Kanpur. The city had already become famous for tanning and leather processing and production of leather goods, especially of boots and saddlery for military. The city witnessed development of great industrial establishments, i.e. the Government Harness and Saddler Factory, Cooper Allen Co., North-West Tanneries Ltd., and several cotton mills like Elgin, Muir, Victoria, Kanpur Woollen Mills and Army Cloth Manufacturing Co. Ltd, etc. Furthermore, with the expansion of the railway yard, it became advantageous for the factories and small mills to occupy a site in the southern periphery. This led to the establishment of chain of ginning presses and mills in the southern part of the city. It has also become an important centre of advanced education including technical, and the IIT has added a new township to the city.

Functional Classification of the Cities 2001

1. Forestry, Plantations, Horticulture, Floriculture, Livestock, Fishing, Silviculture and Apiculture (L): The towns recognised to have these functions are Bahraich, Chandausi, Fatehpur, Gonda and Rae Bareli. Fresh water aqua culture is mainly carried in Gonda, Fatehpur and Rae Bareli because these cities lie in the Doab region of Ganga and Ghaghra rivers. Chandausi is located in the Western Region of Uttar Pradesh where domestication of livestock is an important activity of people. The Terai cities of Bahraich and Gonda have relatively higher proportion of land under forests that promotes forest based industries.
2. Mining and Quarrying (Mq): Allahabad, Lalitpur, Modinagar, Orai and Sultanpur are the cities where mining and quarrying activities are carried on. Main source of silica sand is obtained from the Vindhyan sandstones from Lohagra, Bargarh and Shankargarh areas that provide raw material for Glass Industry. Naini in Allahabad produces glass sheets. Lalitpur and Orai both lie in mineral rich region from where bauxite and gypsum are obtained.
3. Manufacturing, Processing, Servicing and Repairs in Household Industry (Mh): Towns recognised as manufacturing, processing, servicing and repairs as Household Industry include Amroha for calico printing; Maunath Bhanjan has cotton mills and manufactures include yarn, coloured fabrics, hosiery, carpets, chaddar, dosuti fabrics and tentage; Rampur is famous for production of cotton and Hookah tobacco, calico printing,

knives; Varanasi is well known for zari work on the banarsi sarees, brass work and other handicraft products.

4. Manufacturing, Processing, Servicing and Repairs as Non-Household Industry (M): The cities falling under this category are Aligarh where lock industry, insulated wires and cables, dal mills, edible oil industry, bakery and sugar confectionary factories are centred; Firozabad is an important glass and glass products centre and the industry has established itself successfully in the face of competition with Japan and Czechoslovakia; Modinagar has paper mills, polyester and nylon filament yarn units, cotton units, and Vanaspati manufacturing units. Modipuram in Modinagar is well known for automobile tyres, sugar, textile, soap and engineering industry; Moradabad is famous for brassware and copper-ware industry, glass factories in Bahjoi is located near Moradabad; whereas Saharanpur has sugar industries, paperboard units, paper mills, and cigarette industries.
5. Construction (C): The cities included in this functional category are Banda, Hapur, Loni, Meerut, Orai and Shahjahanpur.
6. Trade and Commerce (Tr): Under Trade and Commerce category cities that are included are Bahraich, Ballia, Basti, Chandausi, Deoria, Ghazipur, Hathras, Mainpuri and Muzaffarnagar.
7. Transport, Storage and Communication (Tt): Chandausi, Gonda, Gorakhpur, Hapur, Jhansi and Sambhal fall in this category. Gorakhpur is headquarter of North East Railway Zone. In Jhansi and Gorakhpur railway workshops are located.
8. Others (O): Allahabad, Basti, Etah, Hardoi, Kanpur CB, Lakhimpur, Mainpuri and NOIDA are included in 'Others' category. The city of Allahabad possess industries pertaining to glass, engineering, sports goods, match box, cigarette production units, nitrogenous and phosphatic fertilizer units at Phulpur (IIFCO), Indian Telephone Industry (ITI) and paper board units at Naini. Structurals include steel plant structure for railway bridges, penstocks and hydraulic gates, etc., of these the Triveni Structurals Limited in Naini is a joint venture of the Government of India and M/s Voest of Austria, set-up in 1965. It manufactures complex steel structures such as building structurals, power transmission towers, pressure vessels and crane ropeways. A plant for heavy compressors and pumps (BPCL) required for setting up fertilizer, chemical, petro-chemical and steel plants is

also situated in Naini. The city is an important educational, professional and administrative centre. Etah (at Neoli has sugar industry, iron and steel goods and utensils), Basti (sugar factory), Mainpuri (rice mills), Hardoi (iron and steel goods and utensils) are other industrial centres; NOIDA is emerging as a great industrial complex and the formation of National Capital Region has boosted up the industrial development in this area; Kanpur CB enjoys the premier position in having factories of all categories such as jute industry, cotton mills, leather industry, rayon units, woollen industry, edible oil industry, aircraft industry (builds HS-748 aircrafts), Indian Explosives Limited and New Central Jute Mill Limited.

Functional Shifts in Class-I Cities of Uttar Pradesh, 1991-2001

Table 9.6 reveals that 20.37 per cent of the total cities in Uttar Pradesh have retained their functions between 1991 and 2001. However, 14.81 per cent of the cities have specialised in their functions with respect to their earlier functions over the last decade. Furthermore, 12.96 per cent of the cities have diversified with respect to their earlier functions, while 3.7 per cent of the cities have registered a change of which maximum shift is mainly observed in the Diversified-Retained (25.93%) followed

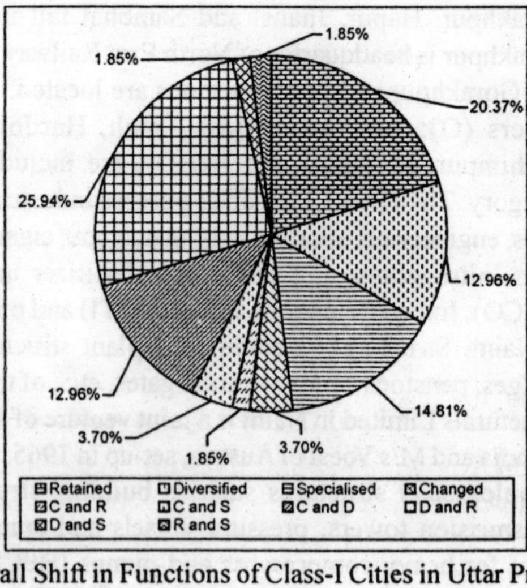

Fig. 9.5: Overall Shift in Functions of Class-I Cities in Uttar Pradesh between 1991 and 2001

Table 9.6: Shift in Functions of Class-I Cities in Uttar Pradesh, 1991 and 2001

Functions	*Total*		*Western*		*Eastern*		*Central*		*Southern*	
	No. of Towns	*Per cent*	*No. of Towns*	*Per cent*	*No. of Towns*	*Per cent*	*No. of Towns*	*Per cent*	*No. of Towns*	*Per cent*
Retained	11	20.37	5	19.23	2	18.18	3	21.43	1	33.33
Diversified	7	12.96	2	7.69	2	18.18	3	21.43	0	0.00
Specialised	8	14.81	4	15.38	1	9.09	3	21.43	0	0.00
Changed	2	3.70	1	3.85	0	0.00	1	7.14	0	0.00
C and R	1	1.85	0	0.00	0	0.00	1	7.14	0	0.00
C and S	2	3.70	1	3.85	0	0.00	1	7.14	0	0.00
C and D	7	12.96	5	19.23	1	9.09	1	7.14	0	0.00
D and R	14	25.93	7	26.92	5	45.45	0	0.00	2	66.67
D and S	1	1.85	0	0.00	0	0.00	1	7.14	0	0.00
R and S	1	1.85	1	3.85	0	0.00	0	0.00	0	0.00
Total	**54**	**100.00**	**26**	**100.00**	**11**	**100.00**	**14**	**100.00**	**3**	**100.00**

Note: C–Changed, R–Retained, D–Diversified and S–Specialised.

Source: Derived from Census of India, 1991 and 2001.

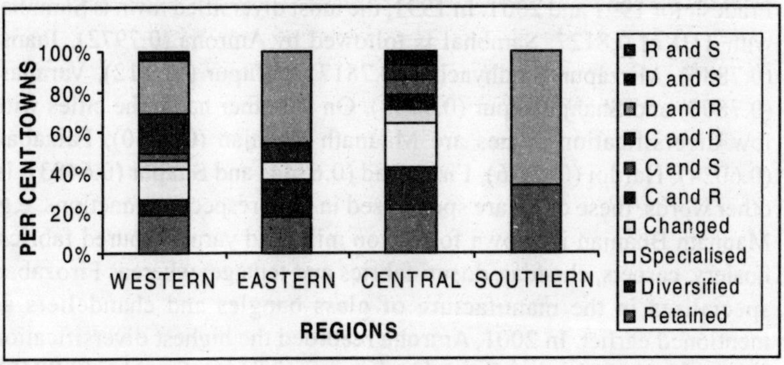

Fig. 9.6: Shift in Functions of Class-I Cities in Uttar Pradesh, 1991 and 2001

by Changed-Diversified (12.96%) and Changed-Specialised (3.7%). Diversified towns are those where existing seven functions are prevailing.

While taking regional divisions into consideration, it is observed that the Southern Region accounts for 33.33 per cent, where most of the functions are retained and this is accompanied by Central (21.43%),

Western (19.23%) and lastly the Eastern Regions (18.18%). Maximum shift in Diversified functions is observed in the Central Region (21.43%) which is accompanied by Eastern (18.18%) and Western Regions (7.69%). In the category of specialised functions, shift is observed in Central Region (21.43%), Western (15.38%) and Eastern Regions (9.09%) respectively. Most of the functions have changed in the Central Region (7.14%) followed by the Western Region (3.85%) respectively. On the other hand, no change or shift in functions is seen in the Eastern and Southern Regions.

Extent of Diversification across Cities

Tables 9.7 and 9.8 depict the extent of diversification across the towns and regions. Both the tables give the value of Transformed Herfindahl Index (THI) for 54 cities and towns during the Census years, 1991 and 2001. The value of THI varies between 0 and 1; if it nears 1 then the city is diversified and if the value is approaching 0, then it is specialised.

Overall Extent of Diversification

Table 9.7 presents a comparative study of the overall values of the Transformed Herfindahl Index of diversification for Class-I cities of Uttar Pradesh for 1991 and 2001. In 1991, the most diversified town is Sambhal with THI of 0.8127. Sambhal is followed by Amroha (0.7972), Jhansi (0.7886), Mirzapur-Vindhyachal (0.7817), Lalitpur (0.7812), Varanasi (0.7808) and Shahjahanpur (0.7783). On the other hand, the cities with low diversification values are Maunath Bhanjan (0.5850), Faizabad (0.6024), Hardoi (0.6336), Firozabad (0.6344) and Sitapur (0.6483). In other words, these cities are specialised in their respective functions, e.g. Maunath Bhanjan is known for cotton mills and yarn, coloured fabrics, hosiery, carpets, chaddar, dosuti fabrics and tentage; whereas Firozabad specialises in the manufacture of glass bangles and chandeliers as mentioned earlier. In 2001, Amroha recorded the highest diversification value of 0.8161, that is followed by Rampur (0.8146), Sambhal (0.8045), Farrukhabad-Fatehpur (0.8020) and Mirzapur-Vindhyachal (0.8005). The cities that exhibited specialisation are Maunath Bhanjan (0.5567), Firozabad (0.66463), Deoria (0.6672), Mainpuri (0.6733) and Basti (0.6858). Mainpuri, Basti and Deoria specialize in trade and commerce; whereas Firozabad for glass work and Maunath Bhanjan for cotton manufacturing as stated above.

Table 9.7: Overall Transformed Herfindahl Index in Cities of U.P. 1991 and 2001

Cities	*THI*	*Ranks_ THI_91*	*THI*	*Ranks_ THI_01*
1. Agra	0.7601	15	0.7705	23
2. Aligarh	0.7588	17	0.7787	16
3. Allahabad	0.7092	37	0.7112	44
4. Amroha	0.7972	2	0.8161	1
5. Bahraich	0.7545	20	0.7579	36
6. Ballia	0.6894	43	0.7018	46
7. Banda	0.7497	23	0.7512	37
8. Bareilly	0.7382	29	0.7905	12
9. Basti	0.6892	44	0.6858	50
10. Budaun	0.7005	39	0.7594	32
11. Bulandshahr	0.7385	28	0.7469	39
12. Chandausi	0.7649	12	0.7797	15
13. Deoria	0.6791	45	0.6672	52
14. Etah	0.7202	36	0.6950	48
15. Etawah	0.7519	21	0.7780	17
16. Faizabad	0.6024	53	0.7599	31
17. Farrukhabad-Fatehgarh	0.6983	41	0.8020	4
18. Fatehpur	0.6766	46	0.7916	10
19. Firozabad	0.6344	51	0.6463	53
20. Ghaziabad	0.7575	18	0.7712	21
21. Ghazipur	0.7001	40	0.7001	47
22. Gonda	0.7316	31	0.7672	28
23. Gorakhpur	0.7629	13	0.7700	25
24. Hapur	0.7499	22	0.7929	9
25. Hardoi	0.6336	52	0.7134	43
26. Hathras	0.7599	16	0.7727	18
27. Jaunpur	0.7255	35	0.7707	22
28. Jhansi	0.7886	3	0.7809	14
29. Kanpur CB	0.6898	42	0.7253	42
30. Kanpur MC	0.7269	34	0.7642	29
31. Lakhimpur	0.6707	48	0.7026	45
32. Lalitpur	0.7812	5	0.7974	6
33. Loni	0.7655	11	0.7906	11
34. Lucknow	0.7286	33	0.7583	34
35. Mainpuri	0.6733	47	0.6733	51
36. Mathura	0.7461	25	0.7831	13
37. Maunath Bhanjan	0.5850	54	0.5567	54
38. Meerut	0.7736	8	0.7934	8
39. Mirzapur-Vindhyachal	0.7817	4	0.8005	5
40. Modinagar	0.6556	49	0.7641	30
41. Moradabad	0.7380	30	0.7582	35

(*Contd.*)

Table 9.7 (*Contd.*)

Cities	*THI*	*Ranks_ THI91*	*THI*	*Ranks_ THI_01*
42. Muzaffarnagar	0.7546	19	0.7684	27
43. Noida	0.7400	27	0.6941	49
44. Orai	0.7306	32	0.7509	38
45. Pilibhit	0.7675	10	0.7702	24
46. Rae Bareli	0.7623	14	0.7713	20
47. Rampur	0.7735	9	0.8146	2
48. Saharanpur	0.7481	24	0.7687	26
49. Sambhal	0.8127	1	0.8045	3
50. Shahjahanpur	0.7783	7	0.7941	7
51. Sitapur	0.6483	50	0.7386	40
52. Sultanpur	0.7088	38	0.7331	41
53. Unnao	0.7421	26	0.7584	33
54. Varanasi	0.7808	6	0.7727	19

Note: Transformed Herfindahl Index is calculated for 54 Class I cities in 2001 and 38 Class I, 14 Class II, 1 Class III and 1 Class V Cities in 1991.

Source: Census, UP, 1991 and 2001.

Extent of Diversification Across Regions

Table 9.8 presents the values of Transformed Herfindahl Index in the cities of Uttar Pradesh across various regions. In 1991, the highly diversified city in the Western Region is Sambhal which is followed by Amroha, Shahjahanpur, Meerut and Rampur. In 2001, Amroha shifted to first position in terms of diversification which is followed by Rampur, Sambhal and Farrukhabad. The most specialised cities of this region are Firozabad, Mainpuri and NOIDA, and Modinagar. Fatehpur in the Central Region is the most diversified city and is followed by Varanasi, Rae Bareli and Kanpur MC (2001). On the other hand, Etah is the most specialised city accompanied by Lakhimpur, Hardoi and Kanpur CB. In 1991, the most diversified city is Varanasi followed by Rae Bareli and Unnao while the most specialised city of the region is Hardoi, accompanied by Sitapur and Lakimpur. In the Eastern Region, both in 1991 and 2001 the most diversified city is Mirzapur-Vindhyachal while the most specialised city is Maunath Bhanjan. In 2001, Mirzapur is accompanied by Jaunpur and Gorakhpur in terms of diversification, while Deoria and Basti followed Maunath Bhanjan in terms of specialisation. In 1991, Gorakhpur and Bahraich show high diversification followed by Mirzapur-Vindhyachal.

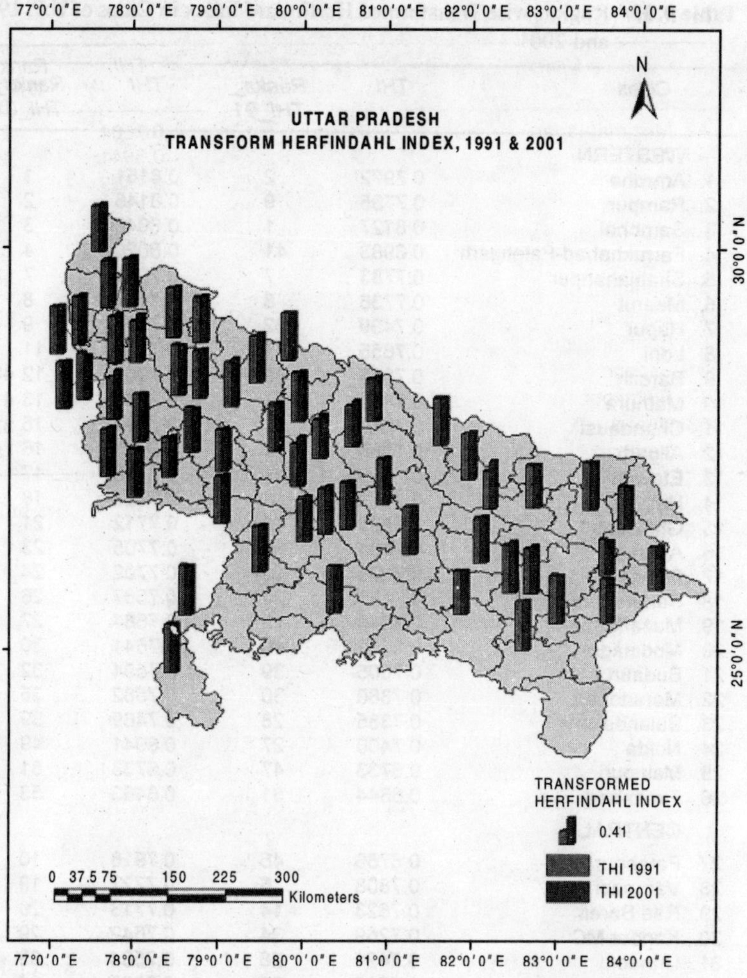

Map 9.2: Uttar Pradesh: Transform Herfindahl Index, 1991 and 2001

On the other hand, in terms of specialisation, Maunath Bhanjan is followed by Faizabad and Deoria.

In the Southern Region, in 1991 the most diversified city is Jhansi which is followed by Lalitpur and Orai. In 2001 also, Lalitpur is most diversified city followed by Jhansi and Orai. The city of Orai specialises in construction related activities.

Table 9.8: Region-wise Transformed Herfindahl Index in Cities of U.P. 1991 and 2001

Cities	*THI*	*Ranks_ THI_91*	*THI*	*Ranks_ THI_01*
WESTERN				
1. Amroha	0.7972	2	0.8161	1
2. Rampur	0.7735	9	0.8146	2
3. Sambhal	0.8127	1	0.8045	3
4. Farrukhabad-Fatehgarh	0.6983	41	0.8020	4
5. Shahjahanpur	0.7783	7	0.7941	7
6. Meerut	0.7736	8	0.7934	8
7. Hapur	0.7499	22	0.7929	9
8. Loni	0.7655	11	0.7906	11
9. Bareilly	0.7382	29	0.7905	12
10. Mathura	0.7461	25	0.7831	13
11. Chandausi	0.7649	12	0.7797	15
12. Aligarh	0.7588	17	0.7787	16
13. Etawah	0.7519	21	0.7780	17
14. Hathras	0.7599	16	0.7727	18
15. Ghaziabad	0.7575	18	0.7712	21
16. Agra	0.7601	15	0.7705	23
17. Pilibhit	0.7675	10	0.7702	24
18. Saharanpur	0.7481	24	0.7687	26
19. Muzaffarnagar	0.7546	19	0.7684	27
20. Modinagar	0.6556	49	0.7641	30
21. Budaun	0.7005	39	0.7594	32
22. Moradabad	0.7380	30	0.7582	35
23. Bulandshahr	0.7385	28	0.7469	39
24. Noida	0.7400	27	0.6941	49
25. Mainpuri	0.6733	47	0.6733	51
26. Firozabad	0.6344	51	0.6463	53
CENTRAL				
27. Fatehpur	0.6766	46	0.7916	10
28. Varanasi	0.7808	6	0.7727	19
29. Rae Bareli	0.7623	14	0.7713	20
30. Kanpur MC	0.7269	34	0.7642	29
31. Unnao	0.7421	26	0.7584	33
32. Lucknow	0.7286	33	0.7583	34
33. Sitapur	0.6483	50	0.7386	40
34. Kanpur CB	0.6898	42	0.7253	42
35. Hardoi	0.6336	52	0.7134	43
36. Lakhimpur	0.6707	48	0.7026	45
37. Etah	0.7202	36	0.6950	48
EASTERN				
38. Mirzapur-Vindhyachal	0.7817	4	0.8005	5
39. Jaunpur	0.7255	35	0.7707	22
40. Gorakhpur	0.7629	13	0.7700	25
41. Gonda	0.7316	31	0.7672	28

(Contd.)

Table 9.8 (*Contd.*)

Cities	*THI*	*RANKS_ THI_91*	*THI*	*RANKS_ THI_01*
42. Faizabad	0.6024	53	0.7599	31
43. Bahraich	0.7545	20	0.7579	36
44. Banda	0.7497	23	0.7512	37
45. Sultanpur	0.7088	38	0.7331	41
46. Allahabad	0.7092	37	0.7112	44
47. Ballia	0.6894	43	0.7018	46
48. Ghazipur	0.7001	40	0.7001	47
49. Basti	0.6892	44	0.6858	50
50. Deoria	0.6791	45	0.6672	52
51. Maunath Bhanjan	0.5850	54	0.5567	54
SOUTHERN				
52. Lalitpur	0.7812	5	0.7974	6
53. Jhansi	0.7886	3	0.7809	14
54. Orai	0.7306	32	0.7509	38

Note: Transformed Herfindahl Index is calculated for 54 Class I cities in 2001 and 38 Class I, 14 Class, II, 1 Class III and 1 Class V Cities in 1991.

Source: Census, U.P, 1991 and 2001.

Conclusions

Cities and towns are not separate entities, they are linked to each other in an urban system; each provides services and products for its surrounding region or the hinterland. These linkages reflect complementarities and the processes of spatial interactions that are rooted in different units within an urban system. However, all the activities carried on within the cities do not intend to connect them with the outside world while some are necessary to support the city itself. Together, these two levels of activities make the economic base of any urban settlement in the world.

The study brings to the fore certain salient facts like the maximum growth rate of urban population is recorded in Shahjahanpur while the minimum per cent change of urban population is found in Kanpur CB. Again, the overall proportion of Class-I cities in different functional categories highlights that in both the Census years highest per cent share is observed in Mono-functional cities which is followed by Diversified and Bi-functional cities and towns. It is to be noted that the per cent share of cities in Mono-functional category has reduced while in case of Bi-functional and Diversified the per cent share of cities has increased from 1991. This implies the fact that the cities are heading towards diversification with the passage of time.

The overall shift in the functions of Class-I cities in the State between 1991 and 2001, reflect that 20.37 per cent of cites have retained their functions which refers that most of the workers are carrying out the very same functions that existed in 1991. On the other hand, 14.81 per cent cities are specialised in nature which is followed by 12.96 per cent in the diversified category.

The overall extent of diversification, exhibits that in 1991, Sambhal holds the topmost position followed by Amroha. On the other hand, Maunath Bhanjan is the most specialised city both in 1991 and in 2001.

In the activities and services scale the most diversified function is that of mining and quarrying followed by livestock, forestry and fishing; manufacturing, processing, servicing and repairs as household industry and construction respectively. On the other hand, 'other services' accounts for the most specialised function followed by trade and commerce and manufacturing, processing, servicing and repairs in non-household industry respectively. Functions that dominated in 1991 are at the same position even in 2001 with slight or no change in per cent which indicates that hardly any development has taken place in the last one decade. This reflects that state government has not accomplished any achievement in terms of adaptation of new policies for changing the existing scenario.

To sum up, though the cities of Uttar Pradesh are heading towards diversification yet the functional categories retain almost the same percentages over the decade 1991 to 2001. Urban functions that are predominating remains unchangeable reflecting that economic development has staggered in the state.

NOTES

1. Pownall, L.L. (1953). "Functions of New Zealand Town," *Annual Association American Geographers*, Vol. 43, pp. 332-50.
2. Theil, H. (1967). *Economics and Information Theory*, North Holland Publishing Company, Amsterdam.
3. Nelson, H.J.: (1955). "A Service Classification of American Cities" *Economic Geography,* Vol. 31, No. 3, pp. 189-210.

REFERENCES

Ahmad, Qazi: "Indian Cities: Characteristics and Correlate", Research Paper No. 102, University of Chicago: Department of Geography, pp. 114.

Aurousseau, M. (1924). "Recent Contributions to Urban Geography", *Geographical Review,* Vol. XIV, pp. 444-45.

Harris, C.D. (1943). "Functional Classification of Cities in the U.S.A", *Geographical Review*, Vol. 33, pp. 86-99.

Hoselitz, Bert F. (1959). "The Cities of India and Their Problems", *Association of American Geographers*, Vol. 49, pp. 223-231.

Jones, V. (1953). "*Economic Classification of Cities and Metropolitan Areas*", The Municipal Year Book, pp. 49-54 and 69.

Kass, Roy (1973). "A Functional Classification of Metropolitan Communities", *Demography*, Vol. 10, No. 3, pp. 427-445.

Pownall, L.L. (1953). "Functions of New Zealand Towns," *Annals Association American Geographers*, Vol. 43, pp. 332-350.

Mitra, A. (1973). "A Functional Classification of India's Towns", An All India Seminar on Population, 12-14 March, Institute of Economic Growth, at Registrar General of India's Office.

Nelson, H.J. (1955). "A Service Classification of American Cities", *Economic Geography,* Vol. 31, No. 3, pp. 189-210.

Rao, V.L.S.P. (1964). *Towns of Mysore State*, Indian Statistical Institute, Calcutta.

10

Urban Infrastructure Development in Towns of Goa

Motilal Sulia

Introduction

India is among the many developing countries depicting low level of urbanisation with only 28.57 per cent population living in urban areas according to 2001 Census. The process of urbanisation in India is characterised by dualism with decelerating urban growth at macro level in contrast to the accelerating population growth in Class-I cities (cities with 100000 and above population). While India's urbanisation is characterised by heterogeneity, Goa is an exception with a decentralised pattern of urban development. Located along Arabian Sea in western part of India and smallest in terms of area, Goa is the richest state in terms of per capita GDP and one of the most urbanised states of India with about half of the total population residing in urban areas.

Since, the initiation of economic reforms in 1991, the State has witnessed a mushrooming of smaller towns in the periphery of the larger towns. In this context, the present study examines the process of urban infrastructure development in Goa in the post reform period particularly in the light of tourism development in the State. In order to sustain its population, the level of infrastructure development should be parallel to the pace of urbanisation. It is found that large cities are facing a shortage of adequate infrastructure. The uncontrolled population growth makes it almost impossible for the metropolitan region to expand and update its stock of urban amenities. Most of them are unable to provide water, sewerage and drainage to a large of portion of the urban population (Mishra *et al.*,1998). Urban infrastructure is not ubiquitous in different size class towns and cities. Some are rich and some are poor (Kundu *et al.*, 1999). Hence, an investigation of the level of infrastructure development is necessary for the purpose of future policy implications. Urban infrastructure plays dominant role in the development of any region. These are the key factors that attract people and encourage urban development.

The process of urbanisation in Goa has taken place at a much faster rate than in any other state in India. Goa has a population of about 13.44 lakhs covering an area of about 3702 square kilometres. About half (49.8%) of the population live in urban areas. The level of urbanisation was about 14.8 per cent during the time of its liberation. It consists of two districts, North Goa and South Goa, comprising 11 talukas. The distribution of population in the State is highly uneven. Most of the population of the state is concentrated in the coastal region. Density of population is also higher in the coastal areas. The total numbers of towns have increased from 5 in 1950 to 44 in 2001. More than one-third of the population is residing in the three largest towns, i.e. Panaji, Margao and Mormugao.

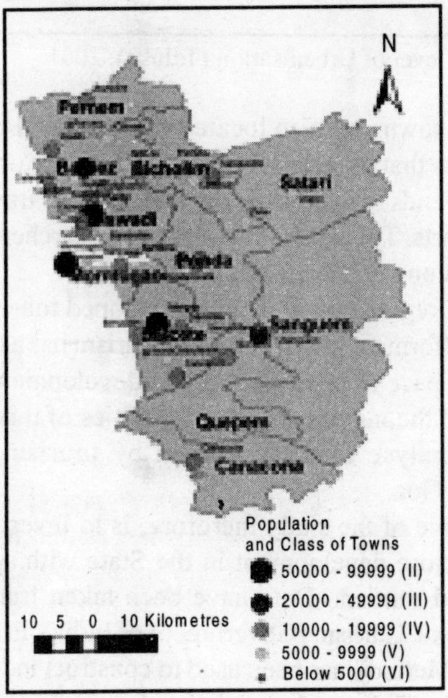

Map 10.1: Goa: Distribution of Size Class Towns, 2001

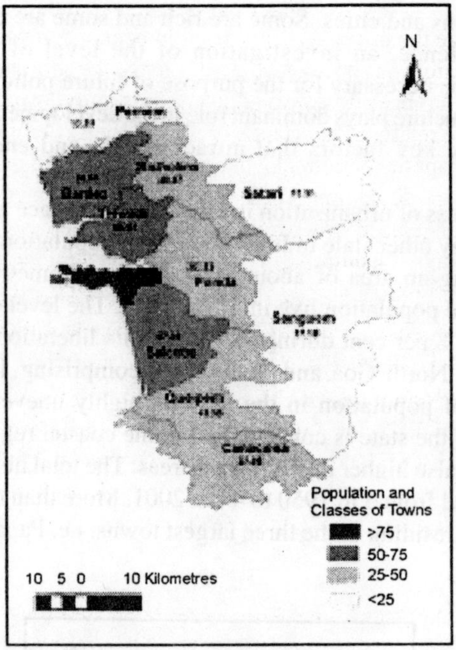

Map 10.2: Goa: Level of Urbanisation (Taluka), 2001

Most of the towns are also located in the coastal region (Map 10.1). Map 10.2 depicts that the coastal talukas are highly urbanised. The level of urbanisation tends to decrease drastically as one travels from the coast to the interior parts. This factor encourages researchers to investigate the multiple dimensions of urbanisation.

The coastal regions of Goa have developed tourism industry due to picturesque landform and environment. Tourism has a tremendous impact accelerating the pace of urbanisation and development of infrastructure, since it is one of the major economic activities of this State. Hence, it is important to analyse the role played by tourism in infrastructure development in Goa.

The objective of the study therefore, is to investigate the nature of urban infrastructure development in the State with special reference to urbanisation and tourism. Data have been taken from Census of India and Department of Tourism (Government of India). Principal Component Analysis (PCA Method) has been used to construct index of infrastructure development. Coefficient of correlation has been computed to find out the nature of relation between urbanisation, infrastructure development and tourism.

To analyze the infrastructural development, a composite index of the selected indicators has been calculated. Firstly, the sub-unit of each unit of infrastructure has been given weightage. These units have been particularly decided by the relative importance of the sub-units (Table 10.1).

The Principal Component Analysis has been used to construct index of infrastructure development. It requires an orthogonal transformation of a set of inter-related structural variables into a new set of independent variables. Principal Component Analysis (PCA) has been done by eigen value, which is obtained by decomposition of a correlation matrix. Using the eigen value as weight, conversion of original values into standard scores is done. These values so obtained are the scores of the first principal component.

Civic Amenities and Urban Infrastructure

Road Density

Road density has been measured in terms of kilometre of roads per thousand population. Road density has improved in urban Goa since 1971 (Fig. 10.1 and Table 10.2). In 1971, the road density was measured as 0.55 kilometre per thousand population and it improved to 0.86 kilometre with an improvement of 57 per cent in 1981. In 1991, a larger number of less populated towns were added in the state and hence, the road density rose to 1.37 kilometre with an improvement of 58 per cent. It showed an improvement again in 2001 to 1.58 kilometre with an increase of 14.83 per cent. Table 10.2 gives the total centrality scores of the different infrastructural provisions of the size class towns of Goa. Majority of the towns with higher road densities were the newly added smaller towns. The larger towns had relatively lower road densities due to population pressure. During 1991-2001, the Class-VI towns have shown maximum growth of 77 per cent in road density. This was followed by Class-III towns with 63.92 per cent, Class-IV towns with 43 per cent and Class-V towns with 14.74 per cent growth.

Water Storage Capacity

The per capita water storage capacity of urban Goa is 102 litres. The overall water storage capacity has fluctuated over time. The 1981 Census reported a decline in water storage capacities in all the towns of Goa. In 1991, 17 towns recorded per capita water storage capacity above 100 litres (Fig. 10.1 and Table 10.2).

Table 10.1: List of Indicators with their Weightages

Sl. No.	*Infrastructural Units*	*Infrastructural Sub-Units*	*Weight-ages*
1.	Electricity Connections	Domestic	2
		Industrial	4
		Commercial	3
		Others	1
2.	Medical Facilities	Hospital	4
		Dispensary	2
		Health Centres	3
		Family Planning Centres	4
		TB Hospitals	5
		Others	1
3.	Educational facilities	Primary Schools	1
		Mid/Secondary Schools	2
		Higher Secondary Schools	3
		Arts College	4
		Science College	5
		Commerce College	5
		Arts and Science College	6
		Arts and Commerce College	7
		Arts, Science and Commerce College	7
		Medical College	8
		Engineering College	8
		Polytechnic College	7
4.	Recreational Facilities	Stadia	4
		Cinema	2
		Auditorium	3
		Public Library	1
		Reading Room	1
5.	Credit facilities	Banks	3
		Agricultural Credit	2
		Non-Agricultural Credit	1

The overall water storage capacity has improved by 50.86 per cent during 1991-2001. Class-VI towns have shown maximum improvement with 140 per cent, followed by Class-III towns with 120 per cent. The three largest towns have shown an improvement of 84.5 per cent. The Class-IV towns have not shown any remarkable change during this period.

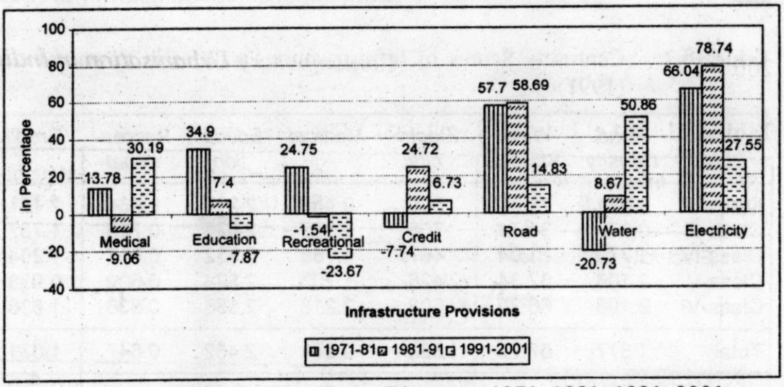

Source: Census of India, Goa, Town Directory, 1971, 1981, 1991, 2001.

Fig. 10.1: Percentage Change in Infrastructure Provision in Towns of Goa

Electricity

The improvement of power situation in Goa is quite phenomenal. During the last three decades the provision of electricity has improved in the state. During 1971-81, 1981-91 and 1991-2001 availability of electricity has increased by 66 per cent, 78 per cent and 27.55 per cent respectively. Class-V towns have registered a high growth rate of 50 per cent. This has been followed by Class-IV and II towns with 35 per cent and 26 per cent respectively. Class-III towns have shown a declining trend during this period.

Medical Facilities

Medical facilities in urban Goa has improved after 1971. During 1971-81, a growth of 13 per cent in this category has been observed. But in the next decade, it had declined by 9 per cent. Canacona has the highest medical facilities, followed by Margao and Valpoi. It has been observed that the three largest towns Panaji, Margao and Mormugao had the highest medical infrastructure but in 1991 and 2001, the newly added towns took over the three largest towns of Goa.

During 1991-2001, the overall improvement of medical facilities in the towns of Goa was 30 per cent. During this time, thirteen towns have shown declining trends. The growth in the Class-VI towns was negative. Highest growth of medical facilities was found in Class-III towns with 83 per cent. This was followed by Class-II and V towns with 65 per cent and 56 per cent respectively.

Table 10.2: Centrality Scores of Infrastructure Facilities in Towns of Goa (1991)

Size Class	Road Density	Water Storage	Electricity	Medical	Education	Recreational	Credit
Class-II	0.981	71.37	560	0.486	2.210	0.634	2.151
Class-III	0.976	34.74	705	0.537	2.526	0.726	1.737
Class-IV	1.370	71.04	467	0.768	2.632	0.637	1.264
Class-V	2.106	67.34	426	1.203	2.524	0.609	0.938
Class-VI	2.198	66.20	608	2.218	2.856	0.838	1.636
Total	1.377	67.77	522	0.871	2.452	0.647	1.631

Centrality scores of infrastructure facilities in towns of Goa (2001)

Town	Road Density	Water Storage	Electricity	Medical	Education	Recreational	Credit
Class-II	0.656	131.71	706	0.761	2.064	0.529	2.317
Class-III	1.600	76.74	697	0.986	2.084	0.582	2.294
Class-IV	1.963	71.74	632	1.100	2.114	0.442	1.207
Class-V	2.417	105.49	639	1.986	3.145	0.557	1.465
Class-VI	3.893	158.87	631	1.841	1.946	0.000	0.631
Total	1.581	102.24	666	1.133	2.259	0.494	1.740

Change in centrality scores of infrastructure facilities in towns of Goa 1991-2001

Town	Road Density	Water Storage	Electricity	Medical	Education	Recreational	Credit
Class-II	–33.20	84.55	26.09	56.75	–6.61	–16.57	7.70
Class-III	63.92	120.93	–1.12	83.59	–17.50	–19.92	32.09
Class-IV	43.30	0.99	35.23	43.22	–19.68	–30.51	–4.51
Class-V	14.76	56.65	50.03	65.08	24.59	–8.49	56.12
Class-VI	77.13	140.00	3.86	–16.99	–31.84	—	–61.42
TOTAL	14.83	50.86	27.55	30.19	–7.87	–23.67	6.73

Source: Census of India, Goa, Town Directory, 1991, 2001.

Educational Facilities

Educational facilities and its adequacy have been quite significant up to the year 1991. During 1971-1981, it had improved by 34.9 per cent. A little improvement of 7.4 per cent was observed in the next Census. In 1981, the largest three towns (Class-II) Panaji, Margao and Mormugao were having highest educational facilities. The overall growth between 1991 and 2001 however was reduced by 7.87 per cent. During this time

27 towns have recorded a decline in educational infrastructure. The highest decline has been observed in Class-VI towns (-31.84%), followed by Class-IV, III and II towns with -19 per cent, -17 per cent and -6 per cent respectively. In spite of this decline, it has been observed that in 2001, educational facilities were more or less equally distributed in all the towns of Goa.

Recreational Facilities

Recreational infrastructure is also one of the important indicators of quality of life. This has shown a decreasing trend in the towns of Goa, due to high population pressure. During 1971-81, the State of stadiums, cinemas, auditoria and public libraries have shown an improvement of 24 per cent. But it started to decline later. Till 1981, recreational facilities in the larger towns were not comensurate to the population size. However, Panaji improved much during 1991-2001. Between 1991and 2001, the overall provision of recreational facilities have declined by 23.67 per cent. During this time, 19 towns have shown a decline in their recreational facilities.

Credit Facilities

Overall credit facilities have declined by 7.74 per cent between 1971 and 1981. However, this had improved by 24 per cent in 1991 and 6.73 per cent in 2001. In 1991, the capital town had the largest credit facilities and also retained the same position in 2001. During 1991-2001, the Class-V towns have shown maximum growth rate with 56 per cent. This was followed by Class-III and II towns with 32 per cent and 7.7 per cent respectively. The Class-VI and IV towns had shown reductions during the same period. Six towns had recorded a decline in credit facilities. It has been observed that the economic transactions in larger towns were much higher than the smaller towns in Goa.

Infrastructure Development

The overall infrastructure development should match with urbanisation in any state, without which additional population would result in a burden on the existing facilities. Therefore, an index of infrastructural development has been calculated using the principle component analysis. This also can be correlated with the urban population growth rate and also can be categorised to find out the levels of development.

There were 11 towns in Goa in 1971, 15 in 1981 and 44 in 1991 and 2001. First, a inter town comparison has been attempted among the 11 towns which were present in the 1971 Census (Table 10.3). Since, these 11 towns are comparable all through the Census periods.

Table 10.3: Principal Component Index (Index of Infrastructure Development) in the Towns of Goa, 1971-2001

Sl. No.	*Towns*	*1971*	*Rank*	*1981*	*Rank*	*1991*	*Rank*	*2001*	*Rank*
1.	Panaji	–0.631	11	0.725	3	–0.160	6	–0.047	5
2.	Margao	–0.451	9	1.119	2	–0.803	8	–0.968	10
3.	Mormugao	–0.629	10	2.052	1	–1.163	11	–1.461	11
4.	Mapusa	–0.388	7	–0.525	8	–1.085	10	–0.476	8
5.	Bicholim	–0.439	8	0.269	4	–0.828	9	–0.458	7
6.	Ponda	–0.260	5	–0.337	7	–0.761	7	–0.382	6
7.	Sanguem	–0.269	6	–0.188	6	1.438	1	0.873	2
8.	Pernem	0.462	2	–1.280	11	1.218	2	2.109	1
9.	Quepem	–0.134	3	–0.649	9	0.239	5	–0.510	9
10.	Valpoi	–0.137	4	–1.207	10	0.713	4	0.630	4
11.	Canacona	2.876	1	0.021	5	1.191	3	0.691	3

Source: Compiled from Census of India, Goa, Town Directory, 1971, 1981, 1991, 2001.

Table 10.3 gives the infrastructure development index for 1971, 1981, 1991 and 2001. Comparatively smaller towns have been relatively better in infrastructure provision than the larger towns in 1971. In 1971, Canacona topped the list of infrastructure development, whereas Panaji had the last rank. The development index of Canacona town was extremely high and due to this factor, all the remaining towns were below average. Hence, it can be concluded that the infrastructure facilities were highly localised. In 1981, certain changes were observed in the infrastructure development process. The larger towns had shown an acceleration. Mormugao topped in infrastructure development and this was followed by Margao and Panaji. In 1991, the smaller towns had not only shown faster development but had also retained their similar status in 2001.

Secondly, a comparison of all 44 towns between 1991 and 2001 has been attempted, because the towns in 1991 remained in 2001 and no additional towns have been added in 2001. These towns have been grouped into five categories (Table 10.4).

In 1991, Sanvordem, a Class-VI town held the highest position in infrastructure development in Goa. Vacra was second in infrastructure development followed by Sanquelim, Saligoa, Socorro and Aquem. It has been found that the comparatively less populated towns had better

Table 10.4: Principal Component Scores and Categories of Infrastructure Development in Towns of Goa (1991-2001)

Categories	*Principal Component Score*	*1991*		*2001*	
		No. of towns	*Share*	*No. of towns*	*Share*
Very high	Above 1.8414	3	6.82	3	6.82
High	0.979 to 1.841	6	13.64	5	11.36
Medium	0.118 to 0.980	8	18.18	10	22.73
Low	–0.730 to 0.118	14	31.82	17	38.64
Very low	Below –1.605	13	29.55	9	20.45
Total	—	44	100	44	100.00

Source: Compiled from Census of India, Goa, Town Directory, 1991, 2001.

infrastructure provision and *vice versa*. A significant negative correlation between total population and index of infrastructure development for all towns of Goa, i.e. –0.33 was found, which is significant at 5 per cent level of significance.

In 2001, no significant correlation has been found between these two variables. During 1991, the largest town Mormugao stayed in the last position in infrastructure development. It was preceded by Curti, Bicholim, Pele Churchurem and Calangute. These towns remained at the bottom of infrastructure development (Map 10.3).

In 2001, there was little change in infrastructure development in the towns of Goa. Pernem a Class-IV town was ranked first in the index of

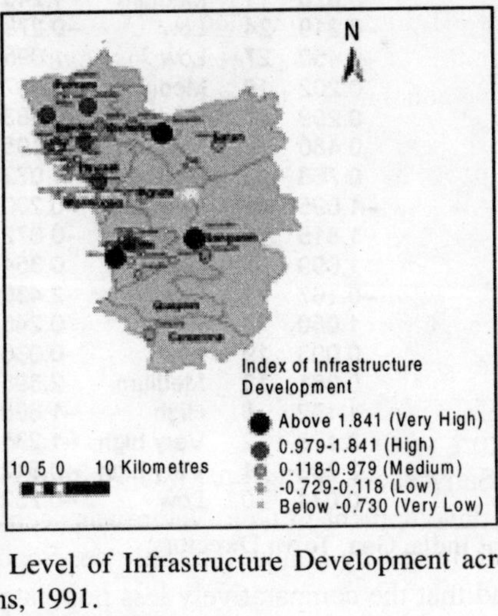

Map 10.3: Goa: Level of Infrastructure Development across all size Class Towns, 1991.

Table 10.5: Index of Infrastructure Development, 1991-2001

Sl. No.	Towns	1991	RANK	Level	2001	RANKK	Level
1.	Mormugao	–1.385	44	Very low	–0.653	33	Low
2.	Margao	–0.432	26	Low	–0.544	30	Low
3.	Panaji	–0.215	23	Low	1.067	8	High
4.	Mapusa	–0.800	33	Very low	0.083	19	Low
5.	Churchorem-Cacora	–1.056	40	Very low	0.061	20	Low
6.	Ponda	0.083	18	Low	0.279	13	Medium
7.	Cuncolim	–0.651	30	Low	0.177	16	Medium
8.	Calangute	–1.031	39	Very low	–0.471	28	Low
9.	Sancoale	–0.852	34	Very low	–1.035	38	Very low
10.	Penha De Franca	–0.853	35	Very low	0.142	18	Medium
11.	Bicholim	–1.175	42	Very low	0.160	17	Medium
12.	Curti	–1.245	43	Very low	–0.983	36	Very low
13.	Quepem	–0.709	31	Low	–0.058	23	Low
14.	Bandora	–0.917	37	Very low	–0.098	24	Low
15.	Chimbel	–0.760	32	Very low	–1.287	42	Very low
16.	Canacona	0.140	17	Medium	1.512	4	High
17.	Calapor	–1.024	38	Very low	–1.106	40	Very low
18.	Sanquelim	2.000	3	Very high	0.575	10	Medium
19.	Navelim	–0.532	28	Low	–0.611	32	Low
20.	Davorlim	–0.234	25	Low	–1.574	43	Very low
21.	Siolim	1.009	9	High	0.537	11	Medium
22.	Socorro (Serula)	1.303	5	High	–0.997	37	Very low
23.	Benaulim	–0.538	29	Low	–0.728	35	Low
24.	Reis Magos	–0.917	36	Very low	–0.005	21	Low
25.	Candolim	–0.196	22	Low	–0.552	31	Low
26.	Sao Jose De Areal	0.311	14	Medium	–1.069	39	Very low
27.	Valpoi	0.526	11	Medium	1.240	5	High
28.	Chialim	–0.219	24	Low	–0.273	26	Low
29.	Chinchinim	–0.450	27	Low	1.095	6	High
30.	Aldona	0.202	16	Medium	0.867	9	Medium
31.	Guirim	0.299	15	Medium	–0.463	27	Low
32.	Sanguem	0.480	12	Medium	2.105	3	Very high
33.	Bambolim	0.768	10	Medium	1.072	7	High
34.	Pele	–1.095	41	Very low	0.200	15	Medium
35.	Saligao	1.815	4	High	–0.672	34	Low
36.	Colvale	1.099	7	High	0.354	12	Medium
37.	Queula	–0.167	21	Low	2.430	2	Very high
38.	Goa Velha	1.050	8	High	0.245	14	Medium
39.	Carapur	0.003	19	Low	–0.036	22	Low
40.	Pernem	0.361	13	Medium	2.595	1	Very high
41.	Aquem	1.192	6	High	–1.605	44	Very low
42.	Varca	2.178	2	Very high	–1.235	41	Very low
43.	Sanvordem	2.703	1	Very high	–0.512	29	Low
44.	Parcem	–0.071	20	Low	–0.232	25	Low

Source: Census of India, Goa, Town Directory.

infrastructure. It was followed by Quela, Sanguem, Canacona and Valpoi. Panaji ranked twenty-third in 1991and improved to eighth rank in 2001. Mormugao which was last in 1991 moved to thirty-third rank in 2001. Aquem, which was ranked sixth in 1991 moved down to the last rank in 2001. According to the index of infrastructure development, it is found that 25 out of 44 towns in 1991 had lower level of development than the average. However, the number decreased slightly to 24 in 2001 (Map 10.4). The details of the five categories of infrastructure development of the towns of Goa are given below.

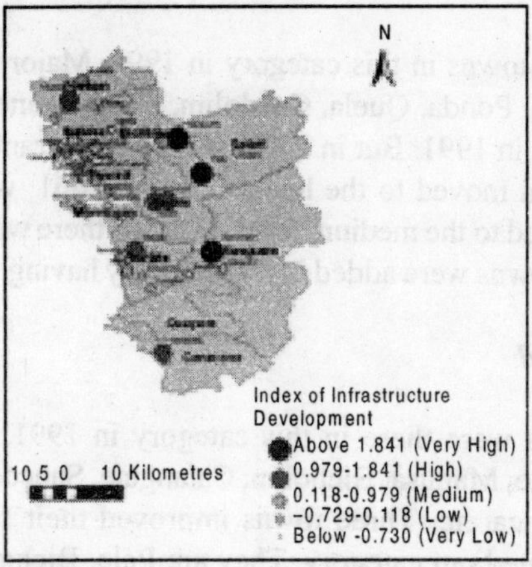

Map 10.4: Goa: Level of Infrastructure Development across all size Class Towns, 2001.

Very High Level

In 1991, only three out of the fourty-four towns had very high level of infrastructural facilities. These towns were Sanvordem, Vacra and Sanquelim. These towns constituted only 6.82 per cent of the total number of towns in Goa. These towns lost their status in 2001 and were replaced by Sanguem, Pernem and Quela.

High Level

There were six towns in this category in 1991, which constituted about 13 per cent of the total urban centres. They were Saligoa, Socorro, Aquem, Colvale, Goa Velha and Siolim. All these towns had lost their status and moved down in scale in 2001. Five new towns were added in this category in 2001. They were Bambolim, Canacona, Panaji, Chinchinim and Valpoi in decreasing order.

Medium Level

There were eight towns in this category in 1991. Out of them five towns moved to higher levels in 2001. They are Bambolim, Valpoi, Sanguem, Pernem, and Canacona.

Low Level

There were 14 towns in this category in 1991. Major towns of Goa like Panaji, Margao, Ponda, Quela, Candolim, Quepem and Chinchinim were in this category in 1991. But in 2001, some of their ranks changed. Panaji and Chinchinim moved to the higher level in 2001, whereas Ponda and Cuncolim moved to the medium level. In 2001, there were 17 towns in this category. Six towns were added in this category having low status in 1991.

Very Low Level

Thirteen towns were there in this category in 1991. The major towns were Mormugao, Mapusa, Bicholim, Calangute, Sancoale, Chimbel, Pele, Pehna De Franca etc. Three towns improved their status in 2001 and moved to the medium category. They are Pele, Bicholim and Pehna De Franca. Four towns remained in the same category. However, the total numbers of towns in this category came down to nine in 2001.

It has been observed that the many of the coastal towns had higher level of infrastructure development in 1991 (in comparison to the towns located in the interior region), but the level of infrastructure also increased in the interior regions in 2001 (Map 10.3 and Map 10.4). In 2001, many of the towns situated inland had relatively higher levels of infrastructure development in the State. This is mainly due to the high growth of population in the towns located in the coastal region and therefore, the per capita availability of infrastructure became inadequate.

Taluka Level Infrastructure Facilities

It is clear from Table 10.6 and Map 10.2 that the distribution of urban infrastructure facilities in different talukas was variable. Urbanised talukas had relatively lower level of infrastructure development. Hence,

Table 10.6: Index of Infrastructure Development in Goa, 2001

Region	*Taluka*	*Road Density*	*Latrine*	*Electricity*	*Medical*	*Educational*	*Recreational*	*Credit*	*Infrastructure Development Index*	*Rank*
Coastal	Mormugao	0.55	290	386	0.31	1.52	0.19	1.21	–1.90	11
	Bardez	2.57	424	737	1.22	2.05	0.46	1.72	0.08	5
	Tiswadi	0.89	419	735	0.77	2.19	0.51	2.82	–0.34	7
	Salcete	1.70	418	816	0.79	1.83	0.38	1.48	–0.73	9
	Pernem	2.91	212	552	2.50	3.85	0.73	2.18	1.21	2
Plateau	Quepem	1.27	414	452	0.88	2.32	0.32	1.12	–0.88	10
	Bicholim	1.91	296	867	2.00	2.08	0.65	1.81	0.02	6
	Ponda	2.02	366	728	0.64	2.32	0.56	1.71	–0.41	8
	Canacona	1.76	297	463	1.18	3.95	1.09	2.02	0.52	4
Mountainous	Sanguem	2.45	480	223	2.63	3.18	0.64	2.00	1.40	1
	Sattari	2.53	331	756	1.64	5.18	0.51	2.40	1.04	3

Source: Census of India, Goa, Town Directory, 2001 (Series-31).

Mormugao, Tiswadi and Salcete, had lower infrastructure development than the average level of urban Goa, probably due to their large population size. The coastal talukas had lower level of infrastructure development because of high population base. In contrast to these, talukas situated in the plateau and hilly regions had a better level of infrastructure development owing to their smaller population size.

Table 10.7 shows the tourism density as well as intensity by Talukas. It is clear that urbanised talukas have relatively high level of tourism density and intensity. However, both density and intensity of tourism decrease towards the hinterland. This is due to the fact that coastal tourism is predominating in Goa over any other type.

Relationship between Population Growth, Infrastructural Facilities and Tourism

The relationship between population growth and infrastructural development in the towns of Goa have been analysed in this section. Percentage change in population between 1971 and 1991 has been correlated with percentage change in sub-infrastructure development. These were again done for 1991-2001. Correlation between infrastructure sub-units, tourism density and intensity and the level of urbanisation have been used to find out the relationship status.

Table 10.7: Tourist Density and Tourism Intensity in Talukas of Goa, 2001

Regions	*Talukas*	*Tourists Density*	*Tourism Intensity*	*Urbanisation*
Coastal	Mormugao	1499.0	109.6	83.04
	Tiswadi	2184.3	271.2	65.63
	Bardez	2211.3	151	58.61
	Salcete	1281.5	147.9	57.85
	Pernem	30.7	10.2	13.35
Plateau	Quepem	N.A.	N.A.	45.90
	Bicholim	32.1	8.3	40.87
	Ponda	158.7	30.5	32.53
	Canacona	17.1	14.1	27.05
Mountain	Sanguem	5.3	7.3	17.18
	Sattari	N.A.	N.A.	13.51
Goa	Total	372.9	102	49.76

Source: Tourist Statistics, Department of Tourism, Government of Goa.

The highly urbanised talukas have high level of tourism density and intensity. Tourist density is the number of tourist inflow per square kilometre of area. A strong correlation of 0.833 is found between the tourist density and the level of urbanisation in the nine talukas of Goa during 2001. Higher tourism intensity is also found in the highly urbanised talukas. A strong correlation of 0.754 exists between tourism intensity and the level of urbanisation, which is significant at 5 per cent level of significance.

Principal component index calculated for infrastructure development in the talukas of the State has been correlated with level of urbanisation for the same year. The correlation coefficient is -0.890, which is significant at 1 per cent level of significance. About 79.1 per cent of the total variation in the infrastructure development is explained by the level of urbanisation. The standard error is 0.48. This suggests that a lower level of infrastructure prevails in the highly urbanised talukas. Hence, the talukas located in the coastal region had lower per capita infrastructure provision than the talukas located in the interior parts.

Further, it is found that the tourists tend to get located in the highly urbanised talukas of the state. A high positive correlation of 0.754 found between the level of urbanisation and tourism intensity. Thus, tourism in Goa can be termed as a coastal tourism because tourism is concentrated mostly along the beautiful and highly diversified coastline.

A high negative correlation exists between tourism intensity and the index of infrastructure development. The correlation coefficient is -0.548. This suggests that the lower level of infrastructure development prevails in the talukas of higher level of tourism intensity and *vice versa.* The talukas of coastal regions are highly urbanised with developed tourism industry but have inadequate infrastructure facilities to support them. In contrast to this, the talukas of western plateaus and hilly regions have lower level of urbanisation as well as tourism industry but have adequate infrastructure facilities. Therefore, it can be said that the infrastructure facilities are inadequate in the locations where tourism is concentrated, thereby reflecting a lopsided development pattern.

Tourism intensity is negatively correlated with road density, medical, educational and credit facilities. However, the coefficients of correlations are not significant, but can predict the trend of distribution of infrastructure in the tourist areas. The talukas that are developed in tourism suffer for want of roads, medical, educational and recreational facilities. However, here infrastructure provision is better in terms of sanitation, electricity connections and credit facilities. These infrastructures constitute the basic needs of any tourist destination and have developed accordingly in the tourism concentrated locations.

During 1971-91, a significant negative correlation existed between population growth and growth in per capita water storage. The correlation coefficient is -0.763, which is significant at 5 per cent level of freedom. Growth of recreational, electricity and medical facilities are also negatively correlated with population growth. However, growth in road density, educational infrastructure and credit facilities have positive correlation with population growth.

Another significant negative correlation of 0.359 has been found between growth in medical facilities and total population during 1991-2001. It is significant at 5 per cent level of freedom. Besides this, all sub-infrastructural units have negative correlation with population growth. However, growth in credit facilities is an exceptional case.

A negative significant correlation exists between the level of infrastructure development and the level of urbanisation in the talukas of Goa. The coefficient of correlation is -0.890, which is significant at 1 per cent degrees of freedom. About 79.1 per cent of the total variation in the index of infrastructure is explained by the level of urbanisation. Besides latrine and electricity facilities, all others infrastructure exhibit negatively correlations with the level of urbanisation.

Conclusions

There is an uneven distribution of population in the State of Goa. More than half of the total population of the State is residing in the urban areas. Most of the towns are located in the coastal regions. Besides this, four talukas, namely Mormugao, Salcete, Bardez and Tiswadi are the homeland of about two thirds of the total population and three quarters of the total urban population of the State. Rest of the urban population is distributed sparsely over the remaining seven talukas of Goa.

The civic amenities and infrastructure facilities in urban areas of Goa have shown continuous improvement particularly in electricity and road density during 1971-1991. Other facilities have fluctuated over the years. During 1971-81, significant improvement occurred in medical, educational and recreational facilities; road density and electricity. The credit facilities and water storage facilities have declined by 7.74 per cent and 20.73 per cent respectively. During 1981-91, besides medical and recreational facilities, all others infrastructure provisions have shown improvement. During 1991-2001, the provision of road density has improved by 14.83 per cent, electricity by 27.55 per cent, water storage by 50.86 per cent, credit facilities by 6.73 per cent, and medical facilities by 30.19 per cent. But educational and recreational facilities have declined by 7.87 per cent and 23.67 per cent respectively during the same time period.

Relatively small and medium towns in Goa have registered very high growth rate in infrastructure during 1991 and 2001. About half of the towns of Goa have low levels of infrastructural development. During 1991, relatively smaller towns had higher levels of infrastructure development and *vice versa*. However, the extent of correlation reduced in 2001.

In all towns of the State during 1971-1991, educational facilities, road density and credit facilities have also shown positive correlations with population growth. Medical facilities have been negatively affected by population growth. Hence, the nature of growth in medical facilities of the towns of Goa is not satisfactory.

Haphazard growth of towns and population with a heavy concentration in coastal areas marks the pattern of urbanisation in Goa. The overall infrastructure provision, especially medical facilities, road density and recreational infrastructure are relatively lower in the higher urbanised talukas of coastal areas. The state government thereby should formulate policies for providing adequate infrastructure to coastal talukas and urban areas since a large part of Goa's economy revolves round tourism and tourist related industries.

REFERENCES

Bagchi, S., and A. Kundu., (2003), "Development of Municipal Bond Market in India: Issues concerning Financing of Urban Infrastructure", *Economic and Political Weekly*, Vol. 38, No. 8, pp. 789-798.

De Souza, T.R., (1990), *Goa Through the Ages,* New Delhi : Concept Publishing Company (India).

Fonseca, Da, and Jose Nicolau, (2001), *An historical and archaeological sketch of the city of Goa*, New Delhi, Asian Educational Services Publications Pvt. Ltd, 4th edition.

Gomes, O.J.F., (2004), *Goa,* New Delhi, India, National Book Trust.

Harding, Paul, and Bryn Thoma, (2003), *Goa: Where the beach meets the bazaar,* Hong Kong, China, Lonely Planet Publication Pvt. Ltd., 3rd edition.

Henn, Alexander., (2008), "Crossroads of Religions: Shrines, Mobility and Urban Space in Goa", *International Journal of Urban and Regional Research*, Volume 32, pp. 658-670.

Kundu. Amitabh., (2001), "Institutional Innovations for Urban Infrastructural Development: The Indian Scenario", *Development in Practice*, Vol. 11, No. 2/3, pp. 174-189.

Kundu, Amitabh, (2006), "Trends and Patterns of Urbanisation and their Economic Implications" in *India Infrastructure Report*, 2006. pp. 27-41.

Kundu, Amitabh, Soumen Bagchi and Debolina Kundu, (1999), "Regional Distribution of Infrastructure and Basic Amenities in Urban India: Issues concerning Empowerment of Local Bodies", *Economic and Political Weekly*, Vol. 34, No. 28, pp. 1893-1906.

Mahmood, A., (1977), *Statistical Methods in Geographical Studies,* New Delhi, India, Rajesh Publications.

Misra and Nguyen Tri Dung, (1998), "Large cities of the world: Changing Pattern, Function and structures", in R.P. Misra and K. Misra (edt.), *Million Cities of India: Growth Dynamics, International Structure, Quality of Life and Planning,* New Delhi, India, Sustainable Development Foundation, Vol. I & II.

Newman, Robert S., (1984), "Goa: The Transformation of an Indian Region", *Pacific Affairs*, Vol. 57, No. 3, pp. 429-449.

Noronha, Ligia, Alito Siqueira, S. Sreekesh, Lubina Qureshy and Saltanat Kazi, (2002), "Goa: Tourism, Migrations, and Ecosystem Transformations", *Ambio,* Vol. 31, No. 4, Population, Consumption, Environment, pp. 295-302.

Noronha, Frederick, (1997), "Goa: Fighting the Bane of Tourism", *Economic and Political Weekly*, Vol. 32, No. 51 (Dec. 20-26, 1997), pp. 3253-3256.

Raghvan, V.P., (2006), "Economy of Ecotourism in Kerala: A Perspective", *Kurukshetra,* Vol. 55, No. 2, Pages-52, December 2006, pp. 23-24.

Revi, R., S Prakash, R. Mehrotra, G.K. Bhat, K. Gupta and R. Gore, (2006), "Goa 2100: the transition to a sustainable urban design", *Environment & Urbanisation*, Vol. 18, No. 1, pp. 51-65.

Routledge, Paul, (2000), "Consuming Goa: Tourist Site as Dispensable Space", *Economic and Political Weekly*, Vol. 35, No. 30, pp. 2647-265.

Sawkar, K., Ligia Noronha, Antonio Mascarenhas and O.S. Chauhan, (1998), *Tourism and the Environment Case Studies on Goa, India, and the Maldives*, Washington D.C., U.S.A,. The International Bank for reconstruction and Development, The World Bank.

Wilson, David., (1997), "Paradoxes of tourism in Goa", *Annals of Tourism Research*, Vol. 24, No. 1, pp. 52-75.

Government Documents and Reports

Annual Report, Ministry of Tourism, 2008-09.

Government of Goa, Eleventh Five Year Plan 2007-12 and Annual Five Year Plan 2007-08, Directorate of Planning, Statistics and Evaluation, Panaji.

Government of Goa, Economy Figures, 2007, Directorate of Planning, Statistics and Evaluation, Panaji.

SECTION III

Urban Housing Slums and Basic Amenities

11

Slums in Indian Metropolis

Challenges to Urbanisation and Urban Development in the 21st Century

Anuradha Banerjee and *Sharmistha Das*

Context

India is the second largest population giant in the world with current population of 1.03 billion and 1.21 billion in 2011 (Census of India, 2001, 2011). Of this, about 377.11 million people or 31.2 per cent of the total population reside in the urban areas (2011). India in 2001 had 10.02 per cent of the world's urban population and 21.10 per cent of Asia's urban population. In fact, India's urban population is larger than the total population of small countries like France and Germany and larger that of the big countries like Brazil and USA. In 2001, India had as many as 5161 towns and cities which increased to 7935 in 2011 Census. The level of urbanisation in terms of the proportion of urban population to total population is low in India, but the urban population in absolute terms is very high (Table 11.1).

Moreover, most of the urban population is concentrated in the Class I cities accounting for 65 per cent of the total urban population and these cities are expanding at a faster rate than average population growth. A more disaggregated level of analysis reveals that the million plus cities or the metropolitan cities of India are growing very rapidly and their numbers have constantly increased from 12 in 1981 to 23 in 1991, 35 in 2001 and 53 in 2011. The total population of these metros accounts for nearly one-third of the total population; 10.5 per cent of India's total population and 40 per cent of the total urban population of India (Table 11.2). Again, over 50 per cent of the population of these metros live in

Table 11.1: Pattern and Trend of Urbanisation in India, 1901 to 2001

Census Years	*Number of Towns*	*Urban Population (millions)*	*Per cent Urban*	*Annual Exponential Growth Rate*	*Decadal Growth Rate of Urbanisation*
1901	1916	25.9	10.8	—	—
1911	1908	25.9	10.3	0.0	0.35
1921	2048	28.1	11.2	0.8	8.27
1931	2220	33.5	12.0	1.7	19.12
1941	2422	44.2	13.8	2.8	31.97
1951	3060	62.4	17.3	3.5	41.42
1961	2700	78.9	18.0	2.3	26.41
1971	3126	109.1	19.9	3.2	28.23
1981	4029	159.5	23.3	3.8	46.14
1991	4689	217.6	25.7	3.1	37.52
2001	5161	284.5	27.8	2.7	31.52
2011	7935	377.1	31.5	2.6	31.80

Source: Adapted from Census of India, Government of India, 1991, 2001.

the five giant conglomerates—Mumbai (16.3 million), Kolkata (13.2 million), Delhi (12.7 million), Chennai (6.4 million), and Bangalore (5.7 million), 2001.

The population in these cities grew by 52 per cent higher than the growth of urban population in India. Rapid urbanisation marked by population explosion in the Indian cities can be largely attributed to the large scale rural to urban migration. The post-independence period has

Table 11.2: Population Growth of Million Plus Cities in India, 1901-2001

Census Years	*Number of Million Plus Cities*	*Population in Million*	*Per cent Increase*	*Population of Million Cities*	
				Per cent to Total Population	*Per cent to Urban Population*
1901	1	1.51	—	0.6	5.8
1911	2	2.76	82.8	1.1	10.7
1921	2	3.13	13.4	1.3	11.1
1931	2	3.41	8.95	1.2	10.2
1941	2	5.31	5.71	1.7	12.0
1951	5	11.75	21.3	3.3	18.8
1961	7	18.10	54.0	4.1	22.9
1971	9	27.83	53.8	5.1	25.5
1981	12	42.12	51.3	5.2	26.4
1991	23	70.67	67.8	8.4	32.5
2001	35	107.88	52.8	10.5	37.8

Source: Computed from Census of India, GOI.

witnessed massive urban growth with a large number of in-migrants in towns in search of better living condition and income opportunities. Due to uncontrolled urbanisation, cities in India have become "cities for the poor, of the poor and by the poor". Urban growth, especially in the metropolitan areas, has been exploitative and chaotic, resulting in rising unemployment and low productivity work-sharing in the informal sector, squatting in teeming slums, congestion, encroachment on public space, water, noise and air pollution and deteriorating infrastructure and services. The inequality of distribution of resources especially income has led to the deterioration of the living standards of a section of urban people, contributing to the origin of slums in cities.

Definitional Issues in India

A comprehensive definition of the word "slum" is difficult because of different settlement types with varying social and economic conditions are found in this category. Generally, three common points emerge from various attempts of several scholars in defining a slum. First, slum refers to an area or a situation and does not constitute an isolated building. Secondly, it can be identified by a combination of physical attributes and not with reference to any single attribute. Thirdly, there is considerable range of variation in regard to the manifestations of each one of the physical attributes of a slum area, which are: substandard houses, high density and congestion, overcrowding, unhygienic sanitary condition, absence of basic amenities like water supply, drainage, sewerage and clearance of garbage. While these attributes of physical conditions are universal when identifying a slum area, social problems such as crime, delinquency, gambling, prostitution, ownership rights of houses and legality of the area are not the essential attributes in identifying a slum area. These social attributes either constitute to the slumming conditions or appear as likely consequences. This internal variation of characteristics within the slums is also noticeable if the common way of designating a slum in different cities of our country is observed. For example, several local terms are associated to designate slums in India, such as '*Katras*', Galis and *Juggi-Jhopadi* in Delhi; '*Chawls*' in Mumbai; '*Ahatas*' in Kanpur; '*Bustees*' in Kolkata (Calcutta); '*Cheris*' in Chennai; '*Keris*' in Bangalore and '*Petas*' in Hyderabad. The Government of India Slum Area (Improvement and Clearance) Act of 1954 defines a slum as "any predominantly residential area, in which light or sanitary facilities or any combination of these factors are detrimental to the safety, health or morals". According to the Slum Area (Improvement and Clearance) Act, 1956, enacted by the Union Government, slums have been defined as those areas where buildings are usually unfit for human habitation; or are dilapidated, over-crowded and are marked by faulty arrangements and building design; narrowness or faulty arrangements of streets, lack of ventilation, light or sanitary facilities, or any combination of these factors, that are detrimental to safety, health or morals.

Keeping this definition in view, the Census of India describe slum as a chaotically occupied, unsystematically developed and generally neglected area, which is overcrowded with ill repaired and neglected structures. The area may have insufficient communication, improper sanitary arrangements and inadequate amenities that are necessary for the maintenance of physical and social health of human beings and the community. There may be a general absence of social services and welfare agencies to deal with the major social problems of persons and families.

The Census of India considers a slum in the following light:

(i) All specified areas in a town or city notified as 'Slum' by State/ Local Government and UT Administration under any Act including a 'Slum Act';
(ii) All areas recognised as 'Slum' by State/Local Government and UT Administration, Housing and Slum Boards, which may have not been formally notified as slum under any Act; and
(iii) A compact area of at least 300 population or about 60-70 households of poorly built congested tenements, in unhygienic environment usually with inadequate infrastructure and lacking proper sanitary and drinking water facilities.

According to the NSSO (National Sample Survey Organisation, GOI), "A slum is a compact settlement with a collection of poorly built tenements, mostly of temporary nature, crowded together, in unhygienic conditions, usually with inadequate sanitary and drinking water facilities." Such an area is considered as a Non-Notified Slum if at least 20 households live in that area. Notified Slums are those areas notified as slums by Urban Local Bodies (ULBs) or development authorities. Sometimes, when an area develops into an unauthorised settlement with unauthorised structures put up by "squatters", it is termed as squatter settlement. Squatter settlements are slum like settlements, which do not have the stipulated number of 20 households to be classified as a slum.

Causes of Evolution

Slum is one of the important outreach and outcome of rapid urbanisation characterising India. One of the main causes has been industrialisation of urban areas with the attendant in-migration. It is often characterised by distressed migration of rural poor; migration from small towns to big cities (urban to urban migration) and undocumented cross border migration arising out of regional disparities. The vast majority of the city ward migrants belongs to the working class and often do not get efficiently absorbed in the formal sectors and hence casualisation/informalisation results. This section, therefore, earns their livelihood by providing services to the more privileged classes. "Low paid low end" jobs of the urban poor make it extremely difficult to secure accommodation within their means. Therefore, they squat on every open space available, nearby their work places and construct huts with cheap temporary building materials. A life in the slums of India, generally speaking, is therefore a compulsion and not a passion.

Literature Review

Recently various scholars had presented different views, opinions and ideas about the causes for the development of slums, and consequences affecting the socio-economic structure of the city; and the living condition and quality of life in slums. The increasing concern about the slum dwellers in the light of recent trends in Indian cities are widening inequalities, problem of in-migration and urban poverty. Ram Bilas and B.K.S. Yadav (1998), opined that industrialisation of Ghaziabad (Uttar Pradesh) have contributed greatly to the growth and genesis of slums in the city. Chandan Sengupta (1999) mentioned that the issues of urban community based environmental improvements is linked to poverty and related issues of the powerlessness and lack of entitlement to basic services. A.K. Maitra (1999), is of the view that slums emerge in the metro cities of developing countries as land prices in these cities are exceptionally high. Harini Narayanan (2003) mentions that lack of equity in the distribution of urban land to be the most important cause for the emergence of slums. Thus the root cause of slums is not poverty but unequal distribution of urban wealth. Praveen Nangia, K. Gupta and N.C. Tiwari (1996) are of the view that although living conditions are inhuman in slums yet they provide easy accommodation to the poor migrants who cannot afford better housing.

Existing literature shows that slums are the most deprived neighbourhood in the city structure. The hardship of the slum dwellers is likely to increase further in the context of the 21st century's globalisation. This will increase the already highly varied skyline of the Indian city where multi-storeyed affluence is mostly surrounded by the oceans of poverty. The local city governments in their move to increase the efficiency of services would increasingly involve private players to provide basic amenities. The profit motivated private suppliers will charge huge user cost for their services which would further deprive the slum dwellers as they do not have power or political voice. In addition to this, the indifferent attitude showed by the rich section of the society towards slum dwellers is also disheartening and this apathy would increase under global competitiveness.

Objectives and Methodologies

The main issues with regard to slums in India include the mushrooming of slums and associated multiple deprivations, inadequate basic services, insecurity of tenure and deplorable living environment (physical and social). Based on these, the article explores to trace the changes in slum population as well as to analyse the demographic characteristics in the Metropolitan Cities of India.

Further, the article presents an analysis of the status of infrastructural facilities and basic services of metropolitan slums and their regional differences across India. Finally, a case study based on primary investigation (2007) has been attempted on housing, living environment and tenure characteristics of slum households in Kolkata metropolis, based on selected slum settlements.

The study is based on ten Municipal Corporations (cities with more than one million population) representing the commercial centres of the states which have more number of cities/towns reporting slums. Thus only one city is selected so as to represent the state where more number of cities have reported slums. These are Greater Mumbai, Ahmedabad, Jaipur, Chennai, Bangalore, Hyderabad, Kolkata, Indore, Lucknow and Chandigarh. Chandigarh has been selected as a representation of Union Territory (UT) with the maximum number of slum population among the UTs.

At the meso level, an analysis has been attempted to compare proportion of slum population to total population among the million plus cities and their respective states. Here, only those states that have at least one of the selected million plus Municipal Corporations have been selected. These are Maharashtra, Gujarat, Rajasthan, Tamil Nadu, Karnataka, Andhra Pradesh, West Bengal, Madhya Pradesh, Uttar Pradesh and Chandigarh (Union Territory).

Secondary data analysis consists of calculating the percentage and density of slum population over the decades 1981, 1991 and 2001. Here, data for Jaipur (1991) and Chandigarh (1981 and 1991) are not available for analysis. Hence for all purposes analysis has been based on published data by the Census of India.

Annual Exponential Growth Rate of slum population for 1981-91 and 1991-2001 have been calculated by the formula —

$$r = 1/T \log e * xt/xt^{-1}$$

where, r = Annual Exponential Growth Rate
T = Time Period
xt = Present Year
xt^{-1} = Base Year

For computing the levels of availability of urban amenities for 1981 and 1991 the Municipal Corporations are considered based on the Census data. The levels of availability of urban amenities among the slum population are measured by calculating the Composite Index for each city during 1981 and 1991, based on the following indicators:

- Number of latrines available per 1000 slum population,
- Number of tap connections supplying protected drinking water per 1000 slum population, and
- Number of electricity connections per 1000 slum population.

Modified PCA (Principal Composite Index) has been used to give the weightages. The projection matrix is calculated in the following method:

Let 'A' be the scale free matrix using Division by Mean method.

$$A = [\,]\ m*n$$

where, m = Number of cities
n = Number of indicators

Now, Projection Matrix of A

(P) = A′A/m
where, A′ = Transposed A
m = Number of cities

For getting the weightages for each indicator the Eigen vector associated with the largest Eigen value of P matrix is calculated. Because when this vector for weightage is used it maximises the sum of squared correlation among the Composite Index and other indicators. Secondly, the largest Eigen value has the highest explanatory power among all the Eigen values.

$$PY = \wedge Y$$

where, P = Projection Matrix
$\wedge$ = Eigen value
Y = Eigen vector associated with that Eigen value

Finally, to get the Composite Index, the formula used is:

$$AY = Y^*$$

where, A = Scale free data matrix
Y = Eigen vector associated with largest Eigen value
Y^* = Vector which gives Composite Index for each city

Analysis based on a primary survey (September to December, 2007), includes a case study of four slums and a squatter settlement in various parts of the Kolkata (Calcutta) metropolis (West Bengal), representing the diverse nature of the existing slum types in the city. They include two old slums, one new slum, a refugee colony and a squatter settlement.

Analysis and Main Findings

Distribution of Slum Population

At present, India's demographics show that 42.6 million population live in slums (2001). This constitutes 15 per cent of the total urban population of the country and 22.6 per cent of the urban population of the States/ Union territories living in slums and in sub-standard conditions. 11.2 million of the total slum population of India is in Maharashtra, followed by Andhra Pradesh (5.2 million), Uttar Pradesh (4.4 million) and West Bengal (4.1 million). In 2001, 640 cities/towns in 26 States/UTs have reported slum population. Andhra Pradesh has the largest number of towns (77) reporting slums followed by Uttar Pradesh (69), Tamil Nadu (63) and Maharashtra (61).

The percentage of slum population (1981 and 2001), in the selected cities is considerably higher than their state average respectively, except for Ahmedabad in 1981. This has an important implication. As these are also the largest cities of their respective states, so the trend shows that the slums are also getting concentrated in the largest city of each State. Such cities in India have the capacity to provide a vast array of low wage jobs in the urban informal sector. People working in these informal sectors mostly constitute the slum population, as their meagre income is not supportive of a better living environment.

Fig. 11.3 depicts that the highest percentage of slum population is concentrated in the dynamic cities like Greater Mumbai, Kolkata, Chennai and Hyderabad. The only exception is Bangalore, which had comparatively lesser percentage of slum population during 1981 to 2001. While the second level million plus cities like Ahmedabad, Indore, Jaipur, Lucknow and others had very little slum population in 1981, but with the passage of time, their proportion of slum population has increased steadily with one or two exceptions. This is because even after more than 50 years of independence, the 'trickle down effect' (Hirshman, 1958) of development from the four colonial cities (exhibiting urban primacy) has not occurred.

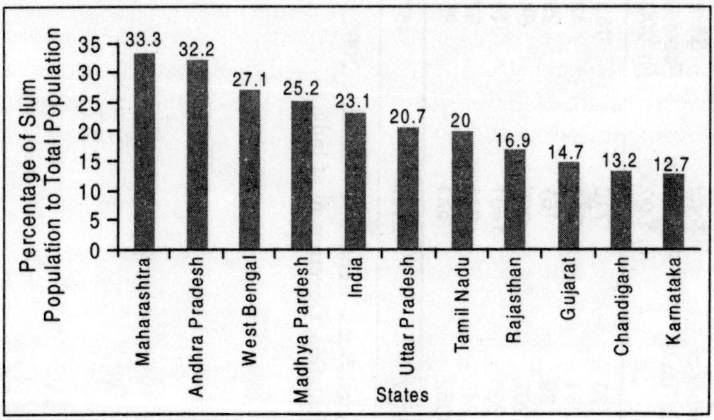

Source: Computed from Census of India, 2001.

Fig. 11.1: Distribution of Slum Population Across Selected States of India 2001

The total slum population in India (Table 11.3), according to size/ class of towns during 1991 showed that 41 per cent of the total slum population was residing in million plus cities, that formed 27 per cent of total urban population. However, cities with population between 0.5-1 million have only 9 per cent of total slum population and 20 per cent of

Table 11.3: Total Slum Population in India According to Size Class of Towns –1991

Size Class/Cities	*Number of Cities/Towns*	*Total Population (in '00000)*	*Slum Population (in '00000)*	*Slum Population as Per cent to Total Population*	*Percentage to Total Slum Population*
More than 1000000	23	710	189	26.6	41.3
500000–1000000	31	215	43	19.8	9.3
300000–499999	39	151	29	18.9	6.3
100000–299999	207	325	54	16.8	11.9
Total Class–I	300	1401	314	22.4	68.8
50000–99999	345	236	47	20.0	10.3
Less than 50000	3052	521	95	18.3	20.9
TOTAL	3697	2158	457	21.2	100.0

Source: Adapted from Selected Socio-Economic Statistics, 2002, Central Statistical Organisation, Ministry of Statistics and Programme Implementation, Government of India.

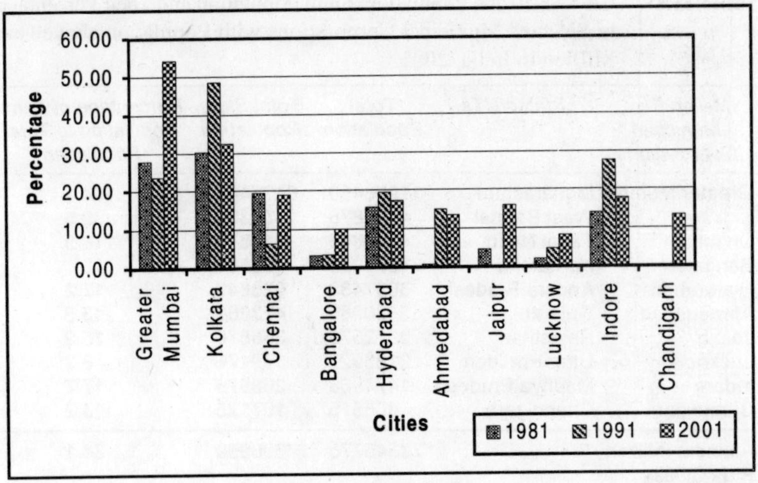

Source: Census of India, Slum Population, 2001.

Fig. 11.2: Percentage of Slum Population to Total Population in Selected Million Plus Cities 1981 to 2001

the total urban population. Further, cities with population between 0.3 to 0.5 million had only 6 per cent of total slum population and 19 per cent of total urban population. This indicates that the opportunity in the medium size cities is less than that offered by the million plus cities. Therefore, the influx of population is more towards the million plus cities that ultimately inflates the slum population. On the other hand, the towns with population less than 50,000 population show slightly higher percentage of slum population (21%) than their share of total urban population (18%). The poor housing quality in the small towns, i.e. of semi-*pucca* and *kutcha* (temporary) houses may have resulted in their inclusion as slums (Table 11.3).

Serious problems are associated with the slum population of the million plus cities of India. A continuous increase has been found in the percentage of slum population over the years in most of the metropolitan cities. In 2001, 17.7 million slum population has been reported in the 27 cities with million plus population. Greater Mumbai Municipal Corporation shows the highest with 6.5 million slum people among all the cities followed by Delhi Municipal Corporation (1.9 million), Kolkata (1.5 million) and Chennai (0.8 million). In the four largest cities, therefore, the concentration of slum population is more in comparison to other metropolitan cities. In Greater Mumbai, more than half of the total

Table 11.4: City-wise Total Population, Slum Population and Their Percentage in Selected Municipal Corporations with Population above One Million in India, 2001

Million Plus Municipal Corporations	*States/UTs*	*Total Population*	*Total Slum Population*	*Percentage of Slum Population to Total Population*
Greater Mumbai	Maharashtra	11978450	6475440	54.1
Kolkata	West Bengal	4572876	1485309	32.5
Chennai	Tamil Nadu	4343645	819873	18.9
Bangalore	Karnataka	4301326	430501	10
Hyderabad	Andhra Pradesh	3637483	626849	17.2
Ahmedabad	Gujarat	3520085	473662	13.5
Jaipur	Rajasthan	2322575	368570	15.9
Lucknow	Uttar Pradesh	2185927	179176	8.2
Indore	Madhya Pradesh	1474968	260975	17.7
Chandigarh	Chandigarh	808515	107125	13.2
All India (Million Plus Cities)		73345775	17696950	24.1

Source: Census of India, Slum Population, 2001.

population (54%) live in slums. For Kolkata, the proportion of slum population is about one-third (33%) of its total population. While in Chennai, a little less than one-fifth of the total population (19%) live in the slums. Out of the total population living in the million plus cities in India, about one-fourth of them (24%) are residents of slums (Table 11.4).

Growth Rate of Slum Population

Population growth in the slums of the million plus cities exhibits considerable change during 1981 to 2001. The proportion of slum population to total population has mostly increased in most of the cities with few exceptions, during the same time period (Table 11.5).

The annual exponential growth rate of the slum population shows that for 1981-1991, Ahmedabad experienced the highest growth rate followed by Lucknow, Indore and Kolkata. The highest growth rate during 1991 to 2001 was experienced in Chennai, Bangalore and Greater Mumbai. Thus, those cities that experienced lower growth rate in the earlier decade experienced higher growth rate in the following decade. Cities like Ahmedabad and Hyderabad experienced negative growth rate during 1991-2001, had earlier experienced higher growth rates. Again, while rest of the cities showed opposite trends in the two decades, Kolkata experienced medium growth rate during 1981-91 but showed a negative

Table 11.5: Exponential Growth Rate and Population Density of Slums in Largest Cities of India, 1981–2001

Million Plus Municipal Corporations	*Percentage of Slum Population to Total Population*			*Exponential Growth Rate 1981–91*	*Exponential Growth Rate 1991–2001*	*Density of Slum Population*	
	1981	*1991*	*2001*			*1981*	*1991*
Greater Mumbai	27.83	23.63	54.06	–1.64	8.28	1074484	5333221
Kolkata	30.26	48.52	32.48	4.72	–4.01	162866	100000
Chennai	19.34	6.23	18.88	–11.33	11.09	NA	3354
Bangalore	3.08	3.26	10.01	0.57	11.22	121835	93840
Hyderabad	15.59	19.41	17.23	2.19	–1.19	93966	16022
Ahmedabad	0.66	14.85	13.46	31.14	–0.98	415	NA
Jaipur	4.45	NA	15.87	0.00	0.00	79	NA
Lucknow	2.03	4.69	8.20	8.37	5.59	NA	10965
Indore	13.92	27.57	17.69	6.83	–4.44	7870	6927
Chandigarh	NA	NA	13.25	0.00	0.00	NA	NA

NA = Not available

Source: Census of India, Town Directory, 1981, 1991, 2001.

growth rate during 1991-2001 (Fig. 11.3). This may be explained by the fact that during the 1990s Kolkata experienced de-industrialisation, capital flight and a general stagnation of the economy. All these factors lead to the decline of employment opportunity in the informal and low-end industrial jobs. As a consequence, the rural migrants who used to come to Kolkata from Bihar, Uttar Pradesh and Odisha declined, which may finally lead to decline in slum population. Another positive factor, that is, the agricultural development experienced by West Bengal from late 1980s may also act as a disincentive for large number of people to migrate from rural Bengal to Kolkata, which may also have its effect on the decline of slum population.

The population density in slums of the million plus cities is alarmingly high. Greater Mumbai had a density as high as 53,33,221 persons/sq. km in 1991, which had increased five folds from the decade 1981. Kolkata (1,00,000 persons/sq. km) also had a very high density of slum population

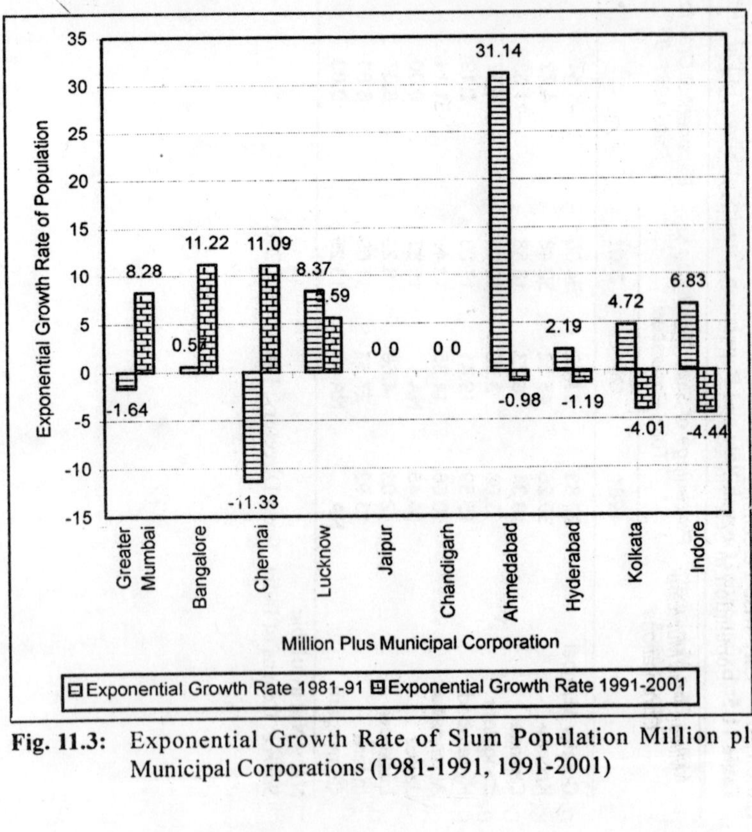

Fig. 11.3: Exponential Growth Rate of Slum Population Million plus Municipal Corporations (1981-1991, 1991-2001)

Table 11.6: City-wise Percentage of Scheduled Caste and Scheduled Tribe Population, Sex Ratio and Literacy Rate of Slum. Population in Selected Million Plus Cities, 2001

Million Plus Municipal Corporations	States/UTs	Percentage of Population in Slums		Sex Ratio of Slum Population	Literacy Rate of Slum Population	
		Scheduled Castes	Scheduled Tribes		Male	Female
Greater Mumbai	Maharashtra	6.0	0.9	770	89.0	75.0
Kolkata	West Bengal	6.2	0.2	805	77.7	67.8
Chennai	Tamil Nadu	32.8	0.2	974	82.9	69.6
Bangalore	Karnataka	32.5	1.6	947	75.3	63.0
Hyderabad	Andhra Pradesh	14.3	1.4	938	77.1	64.5
Ahmedabad	Gujarat	20.2	1.4	850	74.9	53.8
Jaipur	Rajasthan	24.6	5.4	892	73.0	47.0
Lucknow	Uttar Pradesh	13.9	0.1	894	76.0	64.6
Indore	Madhya Pradesh	23.5	1.7	901	87.0	69.7
Chandigarh	Chandigarh	39.1	0.0	868	64.9	39.5
All India (Million Plus Cities)		14.6	1.7	888	82.4	67.6

Source: Census of India, Slum Population, 2001.

but the data reveals that there has been a decrease over the 1981 period. Other million plus cities have also revealed high densities of slum population, which speak of the overcrowding and unhealthy living environment in the slum settlements.

Demographic Characteristics of Slum Population

The percentage distribution of Scheduled Caste (SC) population among the slum dwellers of the million plus cities reveals that Chennai (32.8%) and Bangalore (32.5%) have higher percentages of SC population as against 14.6 per cent, i.e. the all India average comprising of all the million plus cities.

Greater Mumbai (6%) and Kolkata (6.2%) have low SC population among the slum dwellers. Jaipur (5.4%) has a high percentage of Scheduled Tribe (ST) population among the million plus cities, considering the national average of 1.7 per cent among all the million plus cities. Most of the other cities have low concentration of ST among the slum population.

The overall sex ratio of slum dwellers is 888 covering all the million plus cities, which is quite low. Greater Mumbai (770), Kolkata (805) and Ahmedabad (850) have very low sex ratio of slum population. Chennai (974) has a very high sex ratio among slum population followed by Bangalore (947) and Hyderabad (938).

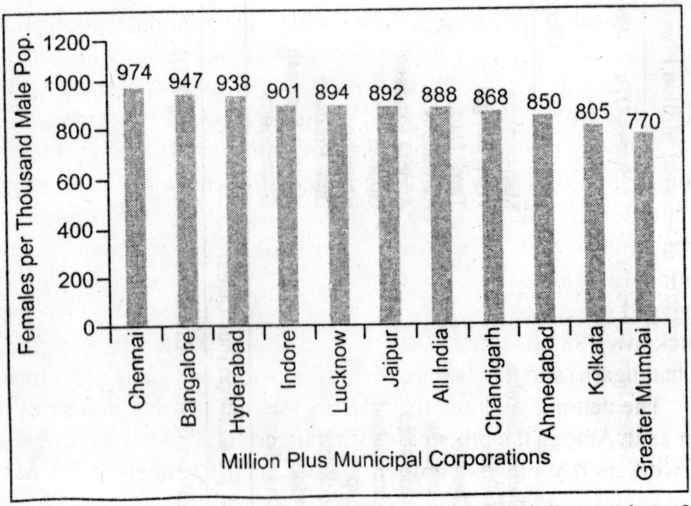

Fig. 11.4: Sex Ratio in Slums of Million plus Municipal Corporations, 2001

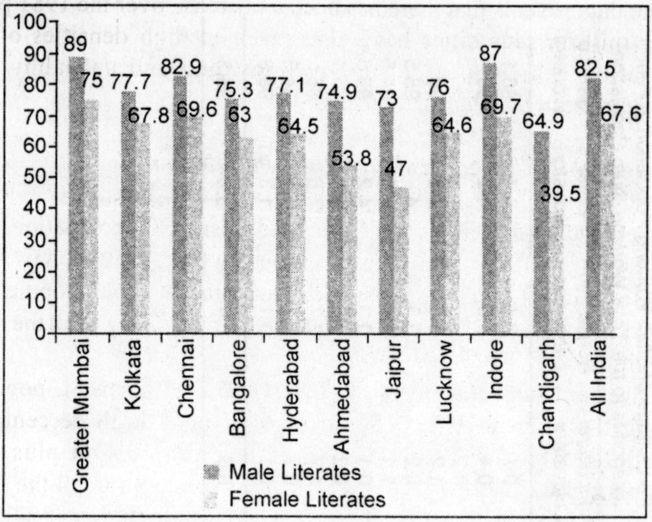

Fig. 11.5: Male and Female Literacy in Slums of Million Plus Cities 2001

The male literacy rate among slum population is highest in Greater Mumbai (89%) followed by Indore (87%) and Chennai (82.9%). The female counterparts of these cities also have high literacy rate, the percentages being 75 per cent, 69.7 per cent and 69.6 per cent respectively. The all India (million plus cities) have male literacy rate of 82.4 per cent and female literacy rate of 67.6 per cent among the slum population.

The male workforce among slum population is 54 per cent and female workforce is 11.4 per cent considering the selected million plus cities of India. Chandigarh (58.3%), Kolkata (56.6%), Greater Mumbai (56.4%) and Bangalore (56.5%) show high male work participation rate among slum population. On the other hand only Bangalore (23.1%) has a proportionally higher female workforce among slum population. Most of the million plus cities have female work participation rate around the national average of 11.4 per cent. Among the total workers, majority are engaged in services (95.3 per cent as the national average). Except for Lucknow (88%), all the other cities range between 98.6 per cent (Chandigarh) and 94.3 per cent (Indore) with hardly any variations.

The national average for workers (slums) in other industries is 3.9 per cent. Among the other cities Chandigarh (1.3%) has its lowest share of workers that ranges between 2.3 per cent (Chennai) to 7.5 per cent (Lucknow), (Table 11.7).

Table 11.7: Percentage of Total Workers and Categories among Working Population in Slums, Selected Million Plus Cities, 2001

Million Plus Municipal Corporations	*States/UTs*	*Percentage of Total Workers to Total Slum Population*		*Percentage of Slum Working Population in Four Categories to the Total Working Slum Population*			
		Male	*Female*	*Agricultural Cultivators*	*Household Labourers*	*Other Industry*	*Service Workers*
Greater Mumbai	Maharashtra	56.4	11.4	0.1	0.1	3.7	96.1
Kolkata	West Bengal	56.6	11.6	0.4	0.5	4.2	95
Chennai	Tamil Nadu	52.4	14.2	1.2	0.5	2.3	96
Bangalore	Karnataka	56.5	23.1	0.2	0.3	4	95.5
Hyderabad	Andhra Pradesh	47.7	11.6	1.1	0.8	3.6	94.5
Ahmedabad	Gujarat	52.0	12.0	0.1	0.3	4.2	95.5
Jaipur	Rajasthan	47.4	9.1	0.2	0.3	4.4	95.1
Lucknow	Uttar Pradesh	46.1	6.6	1.7	2.7	7.5	88
Indore	Madhya Pradesh	50.9	11.7	0.5	0.3	4.8	94.3
Chandigarh	Chandigarh	58.3	13.0	0.1	0.1	1.3	98.6
All India (Million Plus Cities)		54.0	11.4	0.3	0.4	3.9	95.3

Source: Census of India, Slum Population, 2001.

Table 11.8: Selected State–wise Percentage of Notified and Non-notified Slums and Percentage of Households Living in Slums in India (July 2002–December, 2002)

States	*Percentage of Slums Within States/UTs*		*Percentage Distribution of Slums Among States/UTs*	*Percentage of Households Living in*		*Percentage Distribution of Households Living in Slums States/UTs*	*No. of Sample Slums*
	Notified	*Non-notified*		*Notified Slums*	*Non-notified Slums*		
Andhra Pradesh	82.7	17.3	14.9	85.1	14.9	13.7	75
Gujarat	27	73.1	3	38.7	61.3	1.9	43
Karnataka	59.4	40.6	3.8	65.6	34.4	5.9	29
Madhya Pradesh	68.9	31.1	4.3	65.7	34.3	3.7	37
Maharashtra	61.2	38.8	32.2	74.7	25.3	38.7	173
Rajasthan	1.4	98.6	1.7	2.2	97.8	0.7	12
Tamil Nadu	29.4	70.6	6.1	53.5	46.5	7.5	50
Uttar Pradesh	29.3	70.7	5.1	50.6	49.4	2.8	35
West Bengal	35.3	64.7	15.7	52.1	47.9	18.6	94
India	50.6	49.4	100	65.1	34.9	100	692

Source: NSSO, Condition of Urban Slums, NSS Report No. 486, 58th Round (July 2002–December 2002).

According to the NSSO (National Sample Survey Organisation), the State of Maharashtra (32.2%) has the highest percentage of slums among the states, followed by West Bengal (15.7%) and Andhra Pradesh (14.9%). Most of other states have very low percentages of slum population ranging between 1.7 per cent (Rajasthan) and 6.1 per cent (Tamil Nadu). The national average for the percentage of notified slums is 50.6 per cent and that of non-notified slums is 49.4 per cent. In most of the states where the overall proportion of slum population is higher, the percentage of notified slums is also higher. However, the proportion of non-notified slums in general shows higher values.

The percentage distribution of households living in slums across the states reveals somewhat a similar picture with Maharashtra (38.7%) ranking the highest followed by West Bengal (18.6%) and Andhra Pradesh (13.7%). The national average for the percentage distribution of households living in slums is 65.1 per cent for notified slums and 34.9 per cent for non-notified slums (Table 11.8).

Availability of Basic Amenities among Slum Population

The availability of urban amenities has been observed across the selected million plus cities. Basic amenities, i.e. latrines, tap and electricity connections per thousand population usually exhibit pathetic scenario

Table 11.9: Basic Amenities in Slums of Million Plus Cities, 1991-2001

Million Plus Municipal Corporations	*Number of Latrines per 1000 population*		*Number of Tap Connections per 1000 population*		*Number of Electricity Connections per 1000 population*	
	1981	*1991*	*1981*	*1991*	*1981*	*1991*
Greater Mumbai	10.13	23.92	4.88	8.01	0.35	0.12
Kolkata	27.28	21.98	13.64	7.76	0.00	5.06
Chennai	18.23	90.70	4.99	10.89	15.33	88.41
Bangalore	6.88	10.89	1.35	3.82	9.57	21.94
Hyderabad	14.40	0.02	0.22	0.92	9.57	6.55
Ahmedabad	16.74	55.02	6.23	87.13	4.33	60.07
Jaipur	0.00	0.00	0.00	0.00	0.00	0.00
Lucknow	35.27	6.50	0.86	0.00	8.57	0.00
Indore	10.25	7.25	33.90	14.33	24.60	84.02
Chandigarh	NA	NA	NA	NA	NA	NA

NA = Not available

Source: Civic and Other Amenities in the Notified Slums of Class I and II Towns of India, Census of India, 1981 and 1991.

across the slums in most of the cities of India. However, Chennai usually shows higher figures in this respect (Table 11.9). The level of availability of these amenities has been measured by Composite Index for 1981 and 1991. While analysing the rank of each city, it has been contextualised within a macro regional framework.

Regional Perspective

South India

Among the three south Indian cities, viz. Chennai, Hyderabad and Bangalore, Chennai occupies second rank both in 1981 and 1991 indicating that provisioning of basic amenities is relatively better here. However, Bangalore and Hyderabad occupy the bottom half of the ranks; for example, Bangalore was seventh in 1981 and improved to sixth in 1991 due to improvement in electricity facility. On the other hand Hyderabad, which occupied sixth rank in 1981, slipped to the seventh rank in 1991 due to decline in sanitation facilities (Table 11.10). In the macro regional framework, Bangalore and Hyderabad have now become the major engines of the growth of Indian economy (major centres of information technology industries), so large number of in-migration will take place in future in these cities. So it is expected that the percentage of slum population in these cities may increase, making it necessary for local bodies to provide better urban amenities to its slum areas.

Table 11.10: Basic Services of Slum Population: Composite Index and Ranking of Selected Million Plus Cities, 1981, 1991

Municipal Corporations (Million Plus Cities)	*Composite Index*		*Rank*	
	1981	*1991*	*1981*	*1991*
Greater Mumbai	0.755	0.888	8	5
Kolkata	2.013	0.920	3	4
Chennai	2.031	3.963	2	2
Bangalore	0.983	0.788	7	6
Hyderabad	1.053	0.156	6	7
Ahmedabad	1.333	6.292	5	1
Jaipur	0.000	0.000	9	9
Lucknow	1.550	0.138	4	8
Indore	5.369	2.269	1	3
Chandigarh	NA	NA	NA	NA

NA = Not available

West India

The two West Indian cities of Greater Mumbai and Ahmedabad have different levels, but have shown considerable improvements. Greater Mumbai improved its rank from eighth in 1981 to fifth in 1991. This improvement is due to better sanitation facility in 1991. Ahmedabad has shown the significant improvement from fifth rank in 1981 to first in 1991, due to improvement of all the three amenities.

Central India

The central Indian city of Indore occupied first position in 1981 but went down to the third position in 1991 due to deterioration in the provisioning of drinking water.

North India

The north Indian cities of Lucknow and Jaipur are the worst in terms of availability of basic amenities in the slums. In 1981 Jaipur ranked ninth and Lucknow fourth while in 1991 Lucknow ranked eighth (Data of 1991 for Jaipur is not available). In most of the slums of these cities the basic amenities are simply not available. In case of Jaipur in 1981, none of the three amenities was available in any slum in the city. Thus north Indian cities require huge expenditure and political will to provide even the minimum amenities to its slum population.

East India

Kolkata, occupied third position in 1981 and fourth position in 1991. A decline in rank is due to deterioration in drinking water facility. As Kolkata is the only large city in eastern India so it has to take huge amount of in-migration pressure from both within and outside the State. So efforts must be made to provide special assistance to develop the slums of Kolkata.

Case Study of Kolkata (Calcutta) Metropolis

Kolkata is the only major urban centre in eastern India with concentration of industry, financial services and commercial activities in the Calcutta Metropolitan Area (CMA). There are two broad categories of slums: those that are officially authorised are called '*bustees*'; and large number of unauthorised squatter settlements that have grown up by the side of canals, large drains, garbage dumps, railway tracks and roads. The living conditions of the people living in these shanties are the worst. They do not have proper access to basic amenities such as sanitation or water. These squatters not only face tremendous problems regarding eviction and basic facilities but also cause environmental pollution.

The slums of Kolkata can be divided into two groups, the older slums located in the heart of the city, some as old as 150 years (British Period), and the recent slums mostly located in the outskirts of the city. Most of the slums are located in residential areas within the city. Few slums exist on raised land that was previously low-lying wetlands ('*Bheri*' region), along the canals and wetlands and also around the garbage dump in Dhapa.

Notified Slums

1. The slums on the Anando Banerjee Road, Ashutosh Mukherjee Road and Sambhunath Pandit Street, Kasaipara Lane, and Rupnarayan Nandan Lane are the oldest slums in the city, more than 150 years old, bearing the memories of the decades of independence. They are located in the heart of the city's residential area, and are recognised by KMC in terms of service provisioning.
2. The slums in Protapgarh and Manashatola represent the refugee colonies comprising mostly of people immigrating to India from Bangladesh (erstwhile East Pakistan) during the era of partition. They are situated in the southern fringe of the city. After their recognition by the KMC as notified slums they have been provided with some basic amenities.
3. The Jhoro Bustee and Nutan Bustee (new slums), located in the southern part of Kolkata, are about 20 to 25 years old and were recognised by the KMC only in the last 10 years. This recognition resulted in the provisioning of water, tube wells, toilet facilities, electricity connection, paved roads within the slum area and garbage disposal.

Population density in the slums is extremely high averaging around 120 to 150 persons per 1000 metre. There is an acute shortage of space, often with one room being rented to one family and the veranda being rented to another. In most of the slums in Kolkata recognised by the KMC, slum dwellers pay land tax and have secured tenancy or ownership rights. Ownership varies according to the history of slum development. There are three main categories. Population in slums encroached on vacant or government lands have no legal documents (pattas) and have uncertain legal rights to the land they occupy. Some are covered by KMC amenities while others are not. Secondly, small plots of lands bought from a single landowner by the local residents, on which "hutments" are raised, land tax is paid and dwellers have legal ownership and are entitled to amenities such as potable water and electricity. These include mainly the newly developed slums. Thirdly, land owned by large landowners leased out to middlemen who raise "hutments" and collect rents. The middlemen gradually become the direct landowners paying tax to the KMC by collecting house rent. These pockets have been covered under the Thika Tenancy Act (1981) of the Government of West Bengal, protecting the residents from eviction. The residents pay land tax and can sublet rooms. These slums mainly have a high proportion of floating and seasonal migrants/tenants.

The population composition of the surveyed slums in Kolkata comprises about 43.11 per cent male 41.39 per cent female and 15.50 per cent children on an average. The family type of these dwellers can be categorised into four types: single family, mess, nuclear and joint family. The majority of them are members of nuclear families followed by joint families. They are predominantly Bengali speaking (85.18%) and the rest mostly speak Hindi (14.82%). However, in the surveyed area the proportion of Urdu speaking people is negligible, though their presence is high in the older slums of Kolkata (created after partition) and in the refugee colonies. The balance of population comes from almost all the major linguistic regions of India or the neighbouring countries. Religion-wise the dwellers mainly are of Hindu religion followed by the dominance of Muslim religion. It has been found that more than 40 per cent of households have been living in Kolkata's slums for two generations or more. This is followed by those who have originated from adjoining states (25%) while about 14 per cent of them have come here from different states of India. About 18 per cent of households in the slums have migrated from Bangladesh. The process of settlement in these slums started long ago and has proliferated over time. Also, most of them are settled on a permanent basis and they are most likely to continue to live here.

The sex ratio of the slum population is around 900 on an average in the surveyed slums with one of the slums showing an impressive figure of 1515. However, in the 2001 Census, the male-female ratio is 55:45. The ratio for the two largest language groups, the Bengali speaking population is 52:48 and the Urdu speaking population is 54:46, but their ratios indicate that they stay in these slums with their families. For other language groups, most people have come to the city for jobs; hence their tendency is to maintain a minimum family, saving more, so that they can send remittances to their native place. The primary survey reveals that on an average the percentage of households having 3, 4 or 5 members have gone up with the average size of household being 4.41 persons.

Generally, the education levels of females are lower than the males across all levels of education. Any purposeful literacy programme in slum

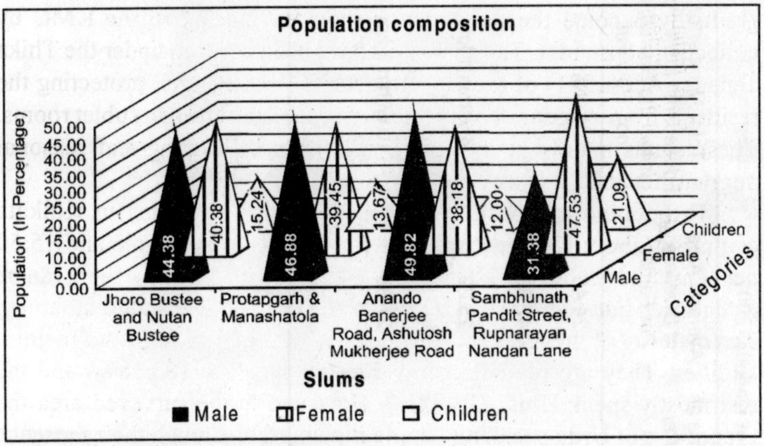

Source: Primary Field Survey, 2007.

Fig. 11.6: Population Composition of Slums in Kolkata, 2007

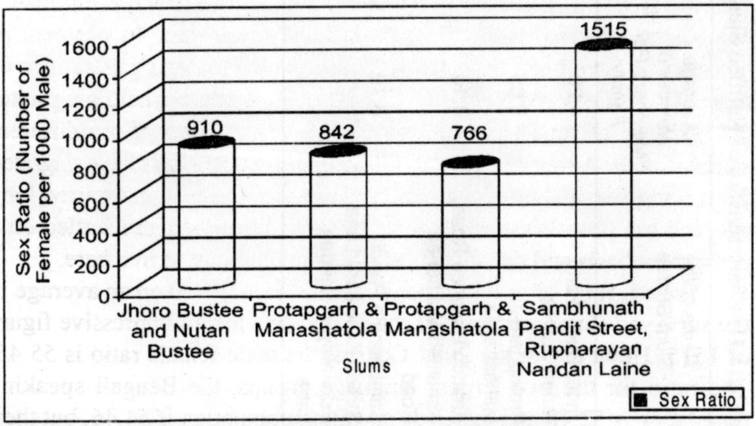

Fig. 11.7: Sex Ratio of Notified Slums in Kolkata, 2007

Table 11.11: Characteristics of Notified Slums / Bustees in Kolkata, 2007

Name of the Slum/Bustee	*Average Number of Members Per Family*	*Average Area of Dwellers Per Premises*	*Average Area of Dwellers Per Family*	*Total Number of Educational Institutions within the Bustee, if not, How Far*	*Total Number of Medical Institutions within the Bustee, if not, How Far*
Jhoro Bustee and Nutan Bustee	4.20	166.35	24.46	Nil	1 within 2 km
Protapgarh & Manashatola	5.65	369.75	342.56	1	Nil
Anando Banerjee Road, Ashutosh Mukherjee Road	4.10	137.5	25.29	4 within 1 km	1 within less than 1 km
Sambhunath Pandit Street, Kasaipara Lane, Rupnarayan Nandan Lane	3.70	108.35	27.88	10 within 5 km	1 within 2 km

areas in Kolkata should consider completely illiterate people and people with below primary level of education as its target group. Another striking feature perceived during the survey is that the illiteracy rates are higher for higher age groups. This denotes a healthy trend suggesting a positive change of attitude of slum dwellers towards education and increased coverage of slum dwellers in education/literacy activities over time. The education level of Bengali speaking population is higher than that of Hindi or Urdu speaking population living in the Kolkata slums. The literacy among the children is showing an improvement in these areas, though the school dropout rates are high in the Government schools.

The people of the slums work in a wide range of occupations: servicing the urban middle-classes, working in small business, production units, government jobs and in organised and unorganised sectors. Some small production units are also located within the slums themselves. The self-employed informal workers have meagre income with manual and construction labourers being among the lowest paid. The relatively higher income groups tend to be factory workers whose wages are low but whose income is regular and secure. The female population mainly engage themselves as maid servants and some as skilled nurses or female attendants. In some slums a good number of families are dependent on begging and aid from charitable organisations for their livelihood.

More than 40 per cent of households have lived in slums for more than 30 years. More than 65 per cent of the households have lived there for more than 15 years. The newcomers to slums with duration of stay up

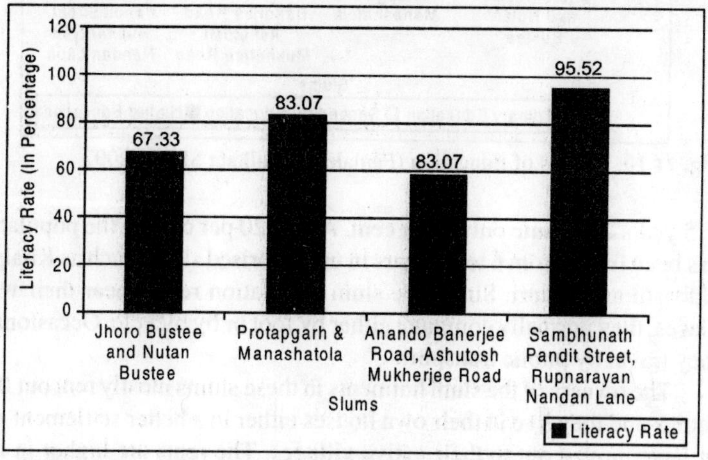

Fig. 11.8: Literacy Rate of Slums in Kolkata, 2007

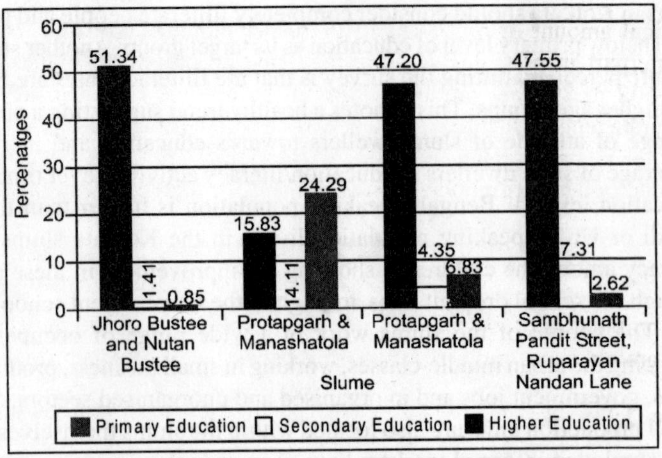

Fig. 11.9: Levels of Education (Male) in Kolkata Slums, 2007

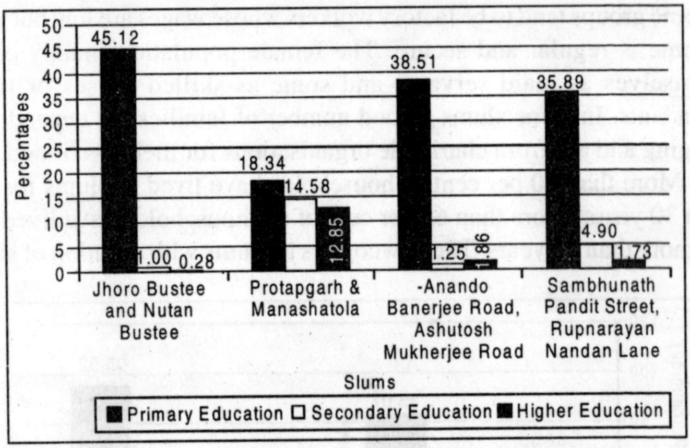

Fig. 11.10: Levels of Education (Female) in Kolkata Slums, 2007

to 5 years constitute only 5 per cent. About 20 per cent of the population has been living from 6 to 15 years in unauthorised slums such as Khalpar, Udbastu and Jhupri. Since, the slum population reside near their work places, they normally commute either by foot or by bicycle. Occasionally they travel by public transport.

The owners of the slum hutments in these slums mostly rent out their rooms and they live in their own houses either in a better settlement area or have moved out to their native villages. The rents are higher in new slums as compared to older slums. The dwellers of the old slums pay nominal amount of rent (Rs. 20 to 30 per month) compared to their counterpart in new slums where they have to pay much higher rents (Rs. 600 to 800 per month), while in the refugee colonies they pay moderate rents (Rs. 200 to 300). The owners of the new slums often evict their tenants at a regular interval so that they can rent them out to new tenants for a higher amount. So for the tenants, there is always a fear of eviction looming large.

Problems

The problems faced by the slum dwellers are of typical nature, whether they are old slums, refugee colonies or new slums. The water pipeline is

Table 11.12: Work Participation, Occupation and Income of Slum Dwellers in Kolkata, 2007

Name of the Bustee	*Work Participation Rate*	*Average Monthly Income Per Family*	*Occupation Details*
Jhoro Bustee and Nutan Bustee	32.86	2000	Service, Drivers, Shop Worker, Maid Servant, Labourer, Small scale Business
Protapgarh & Manashatola	20.96	4000	Service, Small Business, Temporary Service, Driver, Advocate, Labourer, Ironer
Anando Banerjee Road, Ashutosh Mukherjee Road	32.73	2216	Service, Car Driver, Vegetable Shop, Maid Servent, Painter, Female Attendant, TV Shop, Tea Shop, Fish Shop, Fruit Shop, Ironing, Rickshaw Driver, Car Mechanic
Sambhunath Pandit Street, Kasaipara Lane, Rupnarayan Nandan Lane	34.54	8595	Car Driver, Private Service, Government Service, Labourer, Painter, Shop Worker, Motor works, Servant, Grocery Shop, Fruit Shop, Tea Stall, Fish Shop, Paper Seller, Milkman, Hawker, Pan Shop, Construction Worker (Rajmistry), Auto Drtiver, Photographer

Source: Primary Field Survey, 2007.

there in every notified slum but the service is not regular and they demand for more number of pipelines as the existing numbers are not adequate for the increasing population pressure in these areas. Another problem faced by them is the dearth of adequate number of toilets and service latrine facilities in the slums. There is also no facility available for regular garbage disposal for which, they mostly dump them in the surrounding areas making the environment more unhygienic. Due to lack of proper drainage facilities the slums get waterlogged whenever there is heavy downpour.

The slums present the worst forms of health conditions. Their deplorable environmental and economic conditions result in malnutrition among children. Infant as well as maternal mortality rates are higher in the slums. Due to poor hygiene and ventilation conditions, the incidence of infectious as well as respiratory diseases are high in the slums. As the slums have no open spaces and playgrounds, children in the slums often develop mental complexes and physical imbalances. The health facility providers in the slums are mainly the government organisations and recently some NGOs are also providing certain facilities to improve the health conditions of the slum population.

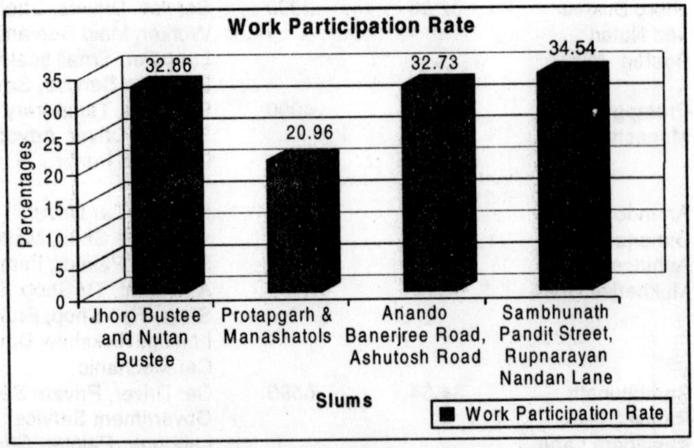

Fig. 11.11: Work Participation Rate in Kolkata Slums, 2007

The inhabitants avail health facilities from the government medical institutions. They complain of poor quality of services in these public institutions, where there is scarcity of beds as well as other infrastructure. They would prefer to go for a private facility but the economic conditions compel them to go for public set up. Often they cannot afford the medicines for which they have to depend upon the free subscriptions; but sometimes

Table 11.13: Drainage System in Slums of Kolkata 2007

Name of the Bustee	*Existing Drainage System of the Bustee Pocket*						*Number of Khatal*
	Sewered Type		*Unsewered Type Pucca*			*Surface Drain Kuchha*	
	Diameter in m	*Length in m*	*Length*	*Width*	*Depth*	*Length*	
Jhoro Bustee and Nutan Bustee	152.40	479.00	Nil	Nil	Nil	Nil	Nil
Protapgarh & Manashatola	228.60	218.00	60	0.1	Nil	Nil	Nil
	304.80	205.00					
	457.20	462.00	60	0.2	Nil		
	609.60	370.00					
Anando Banerjee Road, Ashutosh Mukherjee Road	300	133.5	Nil	Nil	Nil	Nil	Nil
Sambhunath Pandit Street, Kasaipara Lane, Rupnarayan Nandan Lane	300	445	Nil	Nil	Nil	Nil	Nil

Source: Primary Field Survey, 2007.

the stock of these medicines get over and then they have to buy from medicine shops. In case of maternal and child health care, they go for institutional care in government hospitals.

Development Activities

The slum dwellers have formed committees nominating members among themselves to look after the well-being of the community. The Integrated Child Development Scheme (ICDS) programme of the Government of India, Ministry of Health and Family Welfare, has been providing their services to the targeted population. They have set-up a primary school comprising one room where they give elementary education to the slum children. They also have provisions for the mid-day meal as per the schedule of the Sarva Sikhsha Abhiyan. Under the ICDS programme, they also have a unit of *Anganwadi* workers, who look after the pregnant women and children, conduct regular visits for their medical check-up and also provide food to them as per the ICDS schedule. One striking feature which is prominent in the Jhoro Bustee and Nutan Bustee slum is that the Hindu and Muslim children have put up their ICDS units in the same room but with a partition. On one side only the Hindu children are availing education and mid-day meal and on the other side the Muslim children are having their education and meal under the supervision of Muslim teachers. This is quite amazing to perceive such differentiation in secular state system like India.

In some of the slums there are also some NGOs providing micro-credit facilities to the women to organise them into Self-Help Groups (SHGs) to empower them and to make them economically independent. They impart certain trainings in handicraft work or help in setting up cottage or small scale industries making household items or food products. These have marked a good beginning which has gained appreciation from the government as well as the concerned residents. These initiatives have helped women to gain self-confidence as well as economic independence that have uplifted their status.

Squatter Settlement

The squatter surveyed is situated in South Kolkata, comprising migrant population from peripheral areas in search of employment opportunities. They have encroached upon the lands under the KMC and set-up their own shelters out of '*kutcha*' (temporary) materials. With more number of people encroaching upon the area, they started filling up a part of the nearby pond and have expanded their coverage area. The squatter is not provided with any kind of amenities. People get their supply of water from the pipeline across the road and also from the ponds in the area. There is also no electricity facility. The area is very congested with almost no space between two consecutive huts and the unmetalled lanes within the settlement are very narrow. During the rainy season the whole settlement gets waterlogged as no proper drainage facilities are available. There is always a fear of eviction by the authorities as the settlement is not recognised/notified by the municipal body. Most of the male population over here are engaged in service works like drivers, labourers, helpers and rickshaw pullers; and female population work as maid servants. They are mostly illiterate and a small number is primary educated, but they try to send their children to municipal schools. They are working in a group and have their own community to look after their welfare, which is trying to get the slum to be recognised by the KMC so that they can also avail some of the amenities. However, a NGO is working for the people of the squatter, imparting education to the children as well as the adults, providing medical care to all, specially to the children and pregnant women under the ICDS scheme, and also giving them vocational training so that they can earn their own livelihood.

Policy Issues

The policy interventions undertaken so far in Kolkata have focused mostly on slum clearance and removal in the light of urban development. Under the Environment Improvement Scheme (EIS) in the Fourth Five Year Plan a shift was noticed in the strategy, which now aims at the improvement of slum conditions rather than the earlier eradication. The ingredients of the action programme include conversion of service latrines, providing potable water supply connections, surface drainage facilities, construction of paved roads and pathways, arranging street lights and providing garbage vats and dustbins in adequate numbers in the slum areas. Over the years, various slum improvement programmes have been initiated in India. Of these some are for providing better employment opportunities, while others aim at slum area improvement and better housing facilities. But till date the slum dwellers have not seen the bright light of these policy interventions.

In one way the Kolkata Slum Improvement Project (KSIP) is unique in comparison to other cities because the slum problem is seen in totality, i.e. improvement of living environment keeping in mind employment generation. The ongoing Kolkata Environment Improvement Programme (KEIP) funded by various agencies, is looking after the improvement of the slum conditions in a holistic manner. Recently, the Home Ministry has directed the states and local bodies to earmark at least 20 to 25 per cent of developed land in all housing projects (by both public and private agencies) for people belonging to Economically Weaker Section (EWS) and Low Income Groups (LIG). This will help in catering to the housing needs of poor service providers and also prevent mushrooming of slums in cities.

Conclusions

The analysis brings to the fore that the levels of urban amenities available in the slums of million plus cities in India are deplorable. In this respect the various slum improvement activities taken by our government has failed altogether. Thus to solve this perennial problem attempt should be taken to develop the rural areas so that rural peasants are not forced to migrate. Only if the disparity in development can be checked, the problem of the slums can be solved in a more permanent way.

In addition to this, in this era of globalisation where more and more local bodies of these large cities are opting for private services providers, efforts must be made to ensure that our slums are not bypassed in service provisioning. In this regard policy regulations must be framed by the government to ensure that the slum population can have access to basic amenities at a very cheap rate, if not possible to provide them free of cost. In addition to this, education and awareness programmes must be undertaken in the slums to improve the concern about environment of these people. Other measures like providing adequate employment to the slum population at a reasonable wage will help to increase their income. Increase in income will help to increase their bargaining power with the local authorities, which may help to improve their condition.

In the concluding remarks it can be highlighted that the general condition of the slums of India is very vulnerable from the health perspective of the population. The living environment is totally unsuitable for the health and hygiene of the inhabitants of slums. Though, over the years some initiatives have been taken by the government and the NGOs for improvement of basic amenities and infrastructural facilities; a lot still remains to be done. Various private agencies are also giving their hands in bringing about slum development. However, significant efforts are required within a holistic framework to ameliorate the problems of India's slum dwellers.

REFERENCES

Ali, Sabir (2003). *Environmental Situation of Slums in India*, New Delhi; Uppal Publishing House.

Ara, Shabeen (1994). *Old Age among Slum Dwellers*, New Delhi; South Asian Publishers.

Bhatt, Manju (2000). *Slums and Metropolis*, New Delhi; Rajat Publications.

Bilas, R. and B.K.S. Yadav (1998). Socio-economic condition of slum dwellers in Ghaziabad city. *National Geographical Journal of India*, Vol. 44, No. 1-4, pp. 162-173.

Bir, T. and A. Banerjee (Co-investigator), (1994). *Study of Health Behaviour of People Dwelling in the Urban Slums of Gwalior* (M.P.), Under district health system research, Gwalior, New Delhi; Department of Social Sciences, NIHFW.

Bir, Thaneswar (2001). *Dynamics of Health Culture: Urban Slum Community and Behaviour*, New Delhi; Rajat Publications.

Calcutta Metropolitan Development Authority (1997). Participatory impact assessment: Calcutta slum improvement project main findings report by Kamal Kar *et al.*, New Delhi; CMDA, DFID.

Census of India (1981). Negative aspects of urbanisation—A study on the civic and other amenities available in notified slums of class I and class II cities, New Delhi; Census of India.

Census of India (1991). Civic and other amenities in the notified slums of class I and class II towns of India, New Delhi; Census of India.

Chugh, Sunita (2004). *Why Children Drop Out? Case Study of Metropolitan Slum*, New Delhi; Bookwell Publications.

Dewit, M. and H. Schenk (1989). *Shelter for the Poor in India*, New Delhi; Manohar Publication.

Haider, S. (1998). Delhi slums in the season of fresh promise. *Mainstream*, 14th February 1998, pp. 27-29.

Indian Institute of Public Administration (1997). *Slums and Squatter Settlements: In an Indian Million Policies, Programmes and Perspectives*, New Delhi; IIPA.

KMC Survey Report (2002). Report of detailed survey of bustee pockets, Survey report of Civic and socio-economic status of bustees (slums) under KMC, Kolkata; KMC.

Maitra, A.K. (1999). Urban slums: A challenge for 21st century cities. *Spatio-economic Development Record*, Vol. 6, pp. 41-45.

Nangia, P., K. Gupta and N.C. Tewari (1996). Emergence of slums: A case study of Thane urban agglomeration. *The Indian Journal of Social Work*, Vol. 57, Issue 4, pp. 545-562.

Nangia, Sudesh and Sukhdeo Thorat (2000). *Slum in Metropolis: The Living Environment*, Delhi; Shipra Publications.

Narayanan, H. (2003). At the bottom of the food chain: The planned slumming of the metropolitan India. *Himal*, Vol. 16, No. 5, pp. 62-65.

Prasad, D. Ravindra and A. Malla Reddy (1994). *Environmental Improvement of Urban Slums: The Indian Experience (An evaluation of Environmental Improvement of Urban Slums Programme in South Indian States)*, Hyderabad; Booklinks Corporation.

Rao, P. Manohar (1991). *Environment and Upliftment of Slums in India*, Allahabad; Vohra Publishing and Distributors.

Rao, V.L.S. Prakash and U.K. Tewari (1979). *The Structure of an Indian Metropolis*, Bangalore; Allied Publishers Pvt. Ltd.

Schenk, Hans (ed). (2001). *Living in India's slums: A Case Study of Bangalore*, New Delhi; Manohar Publishers and Distributors.

Sengupta, C. (1999). Dynamics of community environmental management in Howrah slums. *Economic and Political Weekly*, 22nd May, 1999, pp. 1292-1296.

Sharma, R.N. and K. Sita (2000). Cities, Slums and Government. *Economic and Political Weekly*, 14th October 2000, pp. 3733-3735.

Sharma, R.N. and K. Sita (ed.) (2001). *Issues in Urban Development*, Jaipur; Rawat Publication.

Shegal, R.L. (1998). *Slum Upgradation: Emerging Issue and Policy Implications*, New Delhi; Bookwell Publications.

Town and Country Planning Organisation (1996). *A compendium of Indian Slums*, Social Infrastructure Planning Division, TCPO, Ministry of Urban Affairs and Employment, Government of India.

University of Calcutta (1992). Thika tenancy in bustees of Calcutta: A study, *Discussion paper No. 6* by Swati Ghosh, Calcutta; CU.

12

Status of the Urban Poor and Poverty Alleviation Programmes in India

A Regional Perspective

Chandrani Dutta

Introduction

Poverty is said to exist in a society when individuals/households are unable to attain a level of material well-being considered to constitute a reasonable minimum by the standards of that society. The Human Poverty Index (HPI) according to United Nations Development Programme comprises three basic parameters of civil existence, firstly, health, secondly, literacy or availability of educational facilities and thirdly inability to have a decent human habitat which includes population without safe drinking water and underweight children with respect to their age (Compendium on Urban Poverty and Urban Slums, 2006). Hence, the spectrum of poverty spans issues like minimum nutritional requirements of individuals to deplorable housing conditions without basic amenities. Different countries have different ways of defining poverty. Urban poverty in the present century has taken precedence over all the major problems associated with development along with the rapid urbanisation in the developing countries. With rapid doubling of the urban population in the developing countries, it is predicted that cities in Asia and Africa would add 1.7 billion new urban dwellers between 2000 and 2030, where most of them, irrespective of being native or migrant would be poor (State of World's Population, 2007).

'Over the past 50 years, the pace of urbanisation and city growth in developing countries has surpassed the ability of municipal actors to keep up with the provision of adequate urban housing and services, with the result that today over 924 million people in developing countries live in slums (UN-HABITAT, 2003, p. 2)' (Grigorivich, 2008). This is quite an obvious observation by the United Nations to describe the status of cities in the developing countries in the present century. Urban poor consisting of the slum and squatter population as well as the homeless in the cities have been the product of failed practices of the municipal bodies in the area of urban management. The inadequate provision of infrastructure and basic amenities to all the sections of the city population over the years has created deprivation in the name of urban poor in the cities of the developing world. Many scholars and organisations have tried to define what urban poor is. In one of such attempt, Urban Poor has been defined as 'people living in overcrowded and dilapidated slums or in squatters built on pavements, along railway tracks, besides pipelines, under bridges, on ill-drained marshlands and on any vacant land available to them, in urban areas. Human living conditions in the absence of basic civic amenities such as safe adequate water supply, sewerage, sanitation and toilets, have been detrimental to the health, safety and comfort in such communities (Hardoy *et al.* 1997)' (Kara, Shikura, Harada, 2003).

The reasons behind the evolution of the slum settlements in the cities of the developing countries can be traced back to the lack of entitlements among the poor migrants coming to the city and a manifestation of exploitative relationships within the capitalist production systems. They are the outcome of the unbalanced urban growth observed in the form of over-concentration of resources in few strategic cities like Mumbai, Kolkata, Delhi and Chennai of India (Sharma and Sita, 2000). With globalisation, the big cities in the developing countries like the mega-cities in India have transformed themselves as the leading cities of their regions pulling towards them huge private investments thereby negating the growth of small and medium urban centres. The firms under the private investors generally run on the concept of agglomeration economies where concentration of multiple activities in the form of trade, manufacturing and services prove to be more profitable than setting up industries in distant areas where even commuting is impossible due to lack of transport facilities (Kundu, 1997). Due to this reason there has been continuous flow of in-migrants, who would rather work as petty traders or in any casual work in the big cities than sit idle in their small towns or rural areas.

In India, due to problems of housing and social infrastructure, there has been a huge section of vulnerable population who live in most unhygienic conditions in the crowded dilapidated settlements generally known as slums. States that have witnessed urbanisation and industrialisation since independence have experienced simultaneous growth of slum population. Slum population generally constitutes the disadvantaged section of the society or the rural poor population who migrate to urban areas in search of employment or better opportunities and ends up living in squatter settlements or in unhygienic housing clusters in cities (Compendium on Urban Poverty and Urban Slums, 2006).

To study the status of urban poor in India and consequently make a note on the various Poverty Alleviation Programmes the following objectives have been incorporated:

- To make an elaborate account of the urban poverty situation in India and in the states and cities of India.
- To study the demographic profile of the slum dwellers in the major urban areas of the country.
- To depict the status of urban poor with respect to household amenities in Indian states and its cities.
- To discuss the various interventions and urban Poverty Alleviation Programmes under the Government of India.

Data from different sources have been incorporated to study the above mentioned objectives which include, Slum Census of India, 2001, National Sample Survey Organisation, 58th Round, Compendium on Urban Poverty and Urban Slums, 2006, City Development Plans under Jawaharlal Nehru National Urban Renewal Mission, among many others. The central methodology in this study is qualitative as well as quantitative representation of data from the mentioned sources to focus on the status of urban poor in different parts of India. Slum population has been considered as the appropriate indicator to study urban poor. The demographic profile of the slum dwellers has been analysed through percentage distribution of slum population across the metropolitan cities of India for selected demographic indicators.

Urban Poverty in India

Indian Labour Conference in 1957 had been the first to introduce the idea of poverty line. Way back in 1962, poverty line was constituted in terms of minimum requirement of an individual in terms of food and non-food items. In value terms, the minimum requirement was of Rs. 20 as per capita expenditure per month at 1960-61 prices for rural areas and

Rs. 25 for urban areas in India. According to the Taskforce on Projection of Minimum Needs and Effective Consumption Demand in 1979, an average of per capita consumer expenditure of Rs. 49.09 in rural areas would correspond to the minimum nutritional requirement of 2400 kilocalories and per capita consumer expenditure of Rs. 56.64 in urban areas, meeting the minimum requirements of 2100 kilocalories. Incidence of poverty has been defined as the Head Count Ratio and is measured by the state specific percentage of people living below the poverty line (Compendium on Urban Poverty and Urban Slums, 2006).

The states have been arranged in descending order in terms of their urban poor population during the period 1999 to 2000. Odisha, Madhya Pradesh and Bihar have been the leading states in India with the highest percentage of urban population living below the poverty line, based on consumption expenditure with a 30-day recall period. Figure 12.1 highlights the incidence of urban poverty in the different states of India, while Fig. 12.2 shows the increase in the average per capita expenditure of urban population from 1993 to 1999.

In spite of a general increase in the consumption expenditure among urban population, urban poverty in the recent decades has manifested itself in the apparent growth of slums with inhospitable conditions. Secured tenure with the availability of basic amenities has been the main concern of slum dwellers with the pressure of population intensifying in the urban areas of the country. Slums in India have been recognised by the Office of the Registrar General and Census Commissioner in 2001 as:

(a) All specified areas in a town or city notified by State, UT Administration or Local Government under any Act including a 'Slum Act'.
(b) All areas recognised by State, UT Administration or Local Government, Housing and Slum Boards, which may have not been formally notified as slum under any Act.
(c) A compact area of at least 300 population or about 60 to 70 households of poorly built congested tenements, in unhygienic environment usually with inadequate infrastructure and lacking in proper sanitary and drinking water facilities.

On the other hand the National Sample Survey Organisation in 1976 and 1977 has defined slums as both declared and undeclared. The declared slums were areas which have been formally declared as 'slum' by the respective municipalities, corporations, local bodies or development

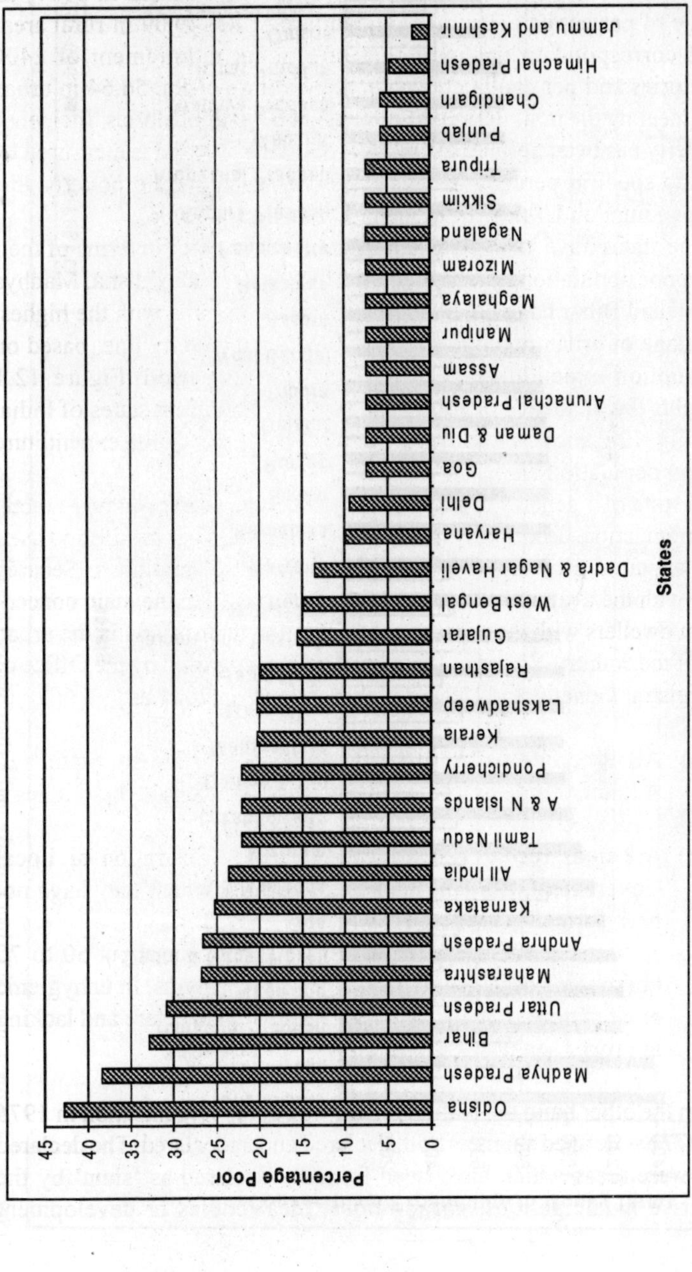

Source: Compendium on Urban Poverty and Urban Slums, December, 2006.

Fig. 12.1: Population below Poverty Line, Urban India, 1999-2000

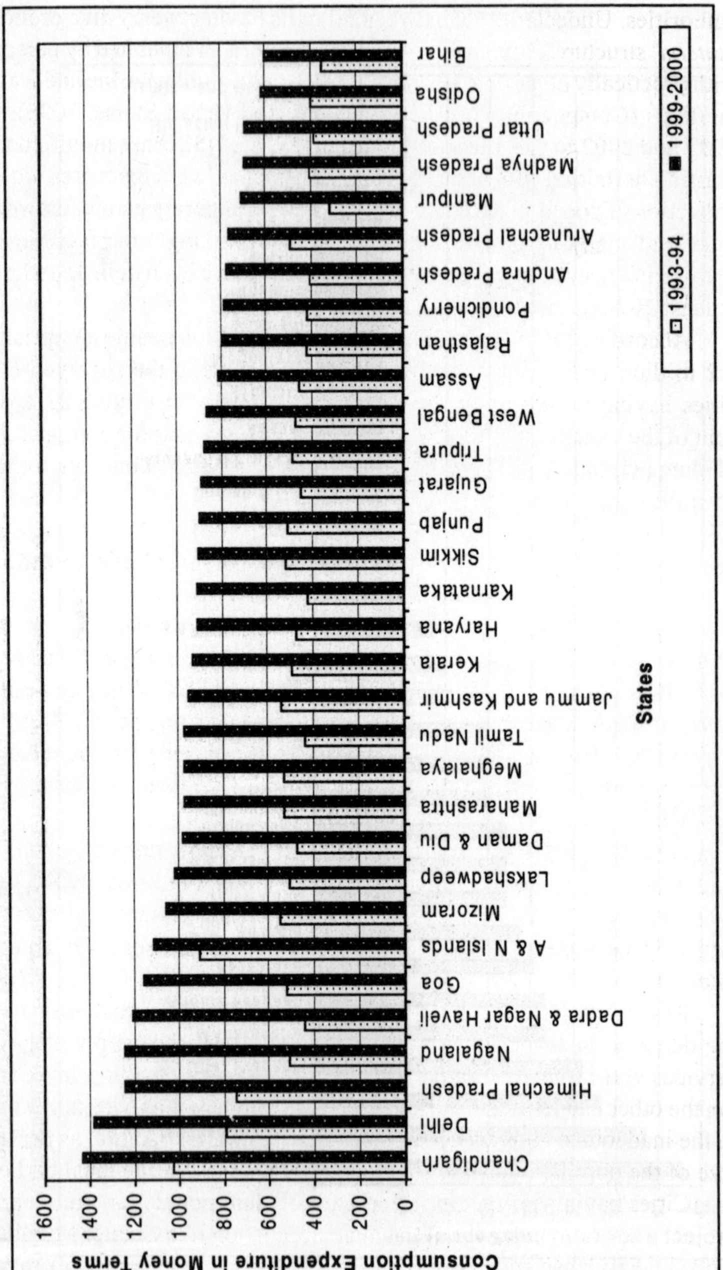

Source: Compendium on Urban Poverty and Urban Slums, December, 2006.

Fig. 12.2: Changes in Monthly Average Per Capita Consumption Expenditure, Urban India

authorities. Undeclared slums are areal units having twenty-five or more '*kutcha*' structures, primarily temporary in nature, or inhabited by persons with practically no private latrine and inadequate public latrine and water facilities (Compendium on Urban Poverty and Urban Slums, 2006). In 1993 and 2002 for the purpose of the survey, the NSSO has modified the existing definition with declared slums defined as 'a compact area with a collection of poorly built tenements, mostly of temporary nature, crowded together usually with inadequate sanitary and drinking water facilities in unhygienic conditions.' The undeclared slums have been defined to have at least 20 households living in that area.

According to Census of India, 2001, 42.6 million people comprising 8.2 million households have been living in slums in the surveyed 607 cities having population more than 50 thousand, constituting 23.1 per cent of the total population of these cities. The demographic composition of slum population has been obtained from the Census Slum data for the 35 million plus cities of India.

Distribution, Density and Composition of Slum Population in Indian Cities

In India, slum population is mostly concentrated in the larger urban centres with cities like Greater Mumbai having 54.06 per cent of the population living in slums. Faridabad has the second highest slum population (46.5%). Among the other mega-cities, Kolkata has 32.48 per cent of the population living in slums, followed by Chennai with 18.88 per cent and Delhi with 18.74 per cent.

Greater Mumbai has the highest population density of slum population, i.e. 10,739 persons per square kilometre, followed by Kolkata with 8029 persons per square kilometre. Surat (Gujarat), another important city has the highest population density of 4529 persons per square kilometre.

Rapid population growth in the large cities leads to situations where the demand for hygienic living conditions exceeds the supply of basic services and infrastructure by the municipal bodies resulting in slums. On the other hand, in small cities, the growth of slums has been attributed to the inadequate delivery of basic services and infrastructure, as per the size of the population owing to poor economic base of the local bodies.

Cities having very high percentages of slum population are seen to project a sex ratio in favour of the male population like Greater Mumbai, Kolkata, Faridabad and Meerut. The southern cities have higher sex ratios

Table 12.1: Demographic Composition of Slum Population in the Selected Cities of India, 2001

Sl. No.	*Cities/ M.C.*	*Per Slum pop.*	*Population Density*	*Sex Ratio*	*Per. Total Workers*
1.	Greater Mumbai	54.06	10739	770	36.83
2.	Faridabad	46.50	2470	795	30.40
3.	Meerut	44.12	3324	875	25.43
4.	Asansol	33.30	1238	898	27.07
5.	Kolkata	32.48	8029	805	36.53
6.	Vijayawada	30.94	NA	984	33.81
7.	Jabalpur	29.56	2047	908	31.05
8.	Madurai	23.83	4269	982	34.78
9.	Amritsar	23.75	1688	858	31.70
10.	Ludhiana	22.52	1976	759	35.61
11.	Surat	20.89	4529	701	42.05
12.	Pune	19.39	1145	928	34.84
13.	Chennai	18.88	4712	974	33.57
14.	Delhi	18.74	3341	780	35.08
15.	Indore	17.69	2005	901	32.32
16.	Visakhapatnam	17.32	1526	974	30.96
17.	Hyderabad	17.23	NA	938	30.22
18.	Rajkot	17.16	1583	890	32.79
19.	Jaipur	15.87	761	892	29.36
20.	Kanpur	14.42	1380	857	27.84
21.	Vadodara	14.24	1718	880	33.83
22.	Ahmedabad	13.46	2482	850	33.60
23.	Allahabad	12.98	1998	722	24.14
24.	Nashik	12.88	536	924	35.04
25.	Varanasi	12.64	1501	884	28.48
26.	Jamshedpur	10.35	763	924	28.15
27.	Bangalore	10.01	2327	947	40.26
28.	Agra	9.55	1010	850	25.26
29.	Coimbatore	6.27	553	966	40.58
30.	Kochi	1.33	83	992	42.99

Source: Computed from Slum Census Report, 2001 (Town Level), India.

more than 950 females per thousand males. One reason for the extremely low slum sex ratio in the cities like Mumbai, Kolkata, and Delhi has been due to the influx of the male migrant population to these cities in search of employment.

The employment situation of urban slum dwellers has been studied with the help of percentage of population engaged in main and marginal activities; to give the idea of the section of the slum population absorbed in the labour-force. Among the selected cities, Kochi has 42.99 per cent of its total slum population designated as workers, followed by Surat with 42.05 per cent. 36.83 per cent of the total slum population in Greater

Mumbai are workers, while Kolkata has 36.53 per cent of the total slum population designated as workers. Bangalore is another city with 40.26 per cent of the total slum population engaged in main or marginal activities, whereas the lowest proportion of workers has been witnessed in Allahabad with 24 per cent.

Slum dwellers, usually being the poor migrant population, have been seeking employment of any form, especially in the informal sector. The probability of slum dwellers getting absorbed in the informal sector is more given the high illiteracy found among them. The section of population, without formal education often being illiterate, finds no job in formal sector. Illiteracy among the slum dwellers force them to take up unskilled or semi-skilled jobs, mostly in the manufacturing activities where education has little role to play (Gupta and Mitra, 2002).

Studies have shown that there have been great differences in literacy between the slum and non-slum population. Higher illiteracy rates found among the slum population indicate their compulsion to work in petty trading activities and menial jobs. This has wider connotation in the area of urban poverty as studies have confirmed the highest incidence of

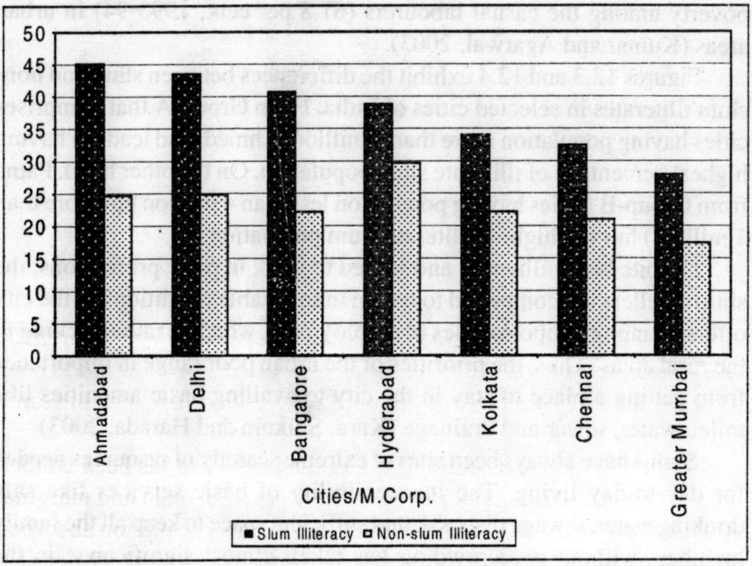

Source: Census of India, 2001.

Fig. 12.3: Slum and Non-Slum Illiteracy in Group: A Cities, 2001

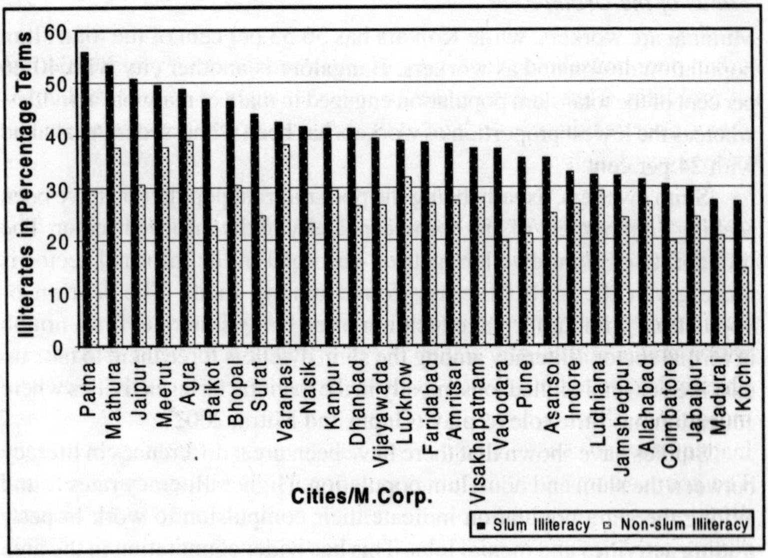

Source: Census of India, 2001.

Fig. 12.4: Slum and Non-Slum Illiteracy in Group-B Cities, 2001

poverty among the casual labourers (61.8 per cent; 1993-94) in urban areas (Kumar and Agarwal, 2003).

Figures 12.3 and 12.4 exhibit the differences between slum and non-slum illiterates in selected cities of India. From Group-A that comprises cities having population more than 4 million, Ahmedabad leads in having highest percentage of illiterate slum population. On the other hand, Patna from Group-B (cities having population less than 4 million but more than 1 million) has the highest illiterate slum population.

Despite being illiterate and forced to work in petty professions, the slum dwellers are compelled to live in inhospitable conditions as the city offers a range of opportunities of employment, which is rather lacking in the rural areas. Thus, the priorities of the urban poor range in importance from getting a place to stay in the city to availing basic amenities like toilet, water, sewer and drainage (Kara, Shikura and Harada, 2003).

Slums have always been sites of extreme scarcity of resources needed for day-to-day living. The inaccessibility of basic services like safe drinking water, sewage disposal, and sufficient space to keep all the family members without overcrowding has taken utmost significance in the policies towards urban management. Despite the lack of interest shown by the municipal administration with regards to provision of basic services, urban poor households continue to increase in the cities amidst all kinds of problems. Thus, a need arises to make an account of the problems of urban poor residing in Indian slums and squatters in terms of service delivery and their accessibility to basic amenities.

Status of Urban Poor with Reference to Household Amenities in India and its Cities

Settlements of the Urban poor in general exhibit very similar attributes which could be categorised into both physical and social. Among the physical aspects, heaps of garbage, un-cleaned drains, plenty of mosquitoes, flies and worms, overflowing gutters, lack of proper latrines, inadequate water supply and poor street lighting have been most evident. The common traits which have been social in nature are open sale and drinking of liquor, local goons, and indifferent attitude to community environment, unemployment and government apathy (Sengupta, 1999). Such has been the interface of urban poverty and environmental degradation. Lack of infrastructure and provision of basic services has eventually led to the scenario described above. Every city in India has a considerable section of urban poor population sharing similar dilemmas. This has been predicted as the price of progress in the great cities confirmed by the UN General Assembly in one of its resolutions "that the lack of adequate housing constitutes one of the most serious deficiencies in the standard of living of large sections of the populations of the world" (Bauer, 1956).

Amenities as demanded by the urban poor have a nature of hierarchy with the availability of toilet facilities as one very important necessity. 'Toilet is one of the most serious and common problems among all urban poor. A large portion of the population practice open defecation in nearby open spaces and drains. Some urban poor's expression of the toilet, especially of women as perceived during the study, simply meant a nightmare' (Kara, Shikura and Harada, 2003).

A quick perusal of the coverage of amenities across the urban households reveals the following figures. According to the 2001 Census estimates, 90 per cent of the households had access to safe water supply, 74 per cent had a latrine within the house, 77 per cent had drainage connectivity and 87 per cent had electricity. The households not covered are the deprived and the underserved settlements. Many explanations given for the incomplete coverage of the services include not just the demand-supply gap due to rapid growth of urban population and the scarce

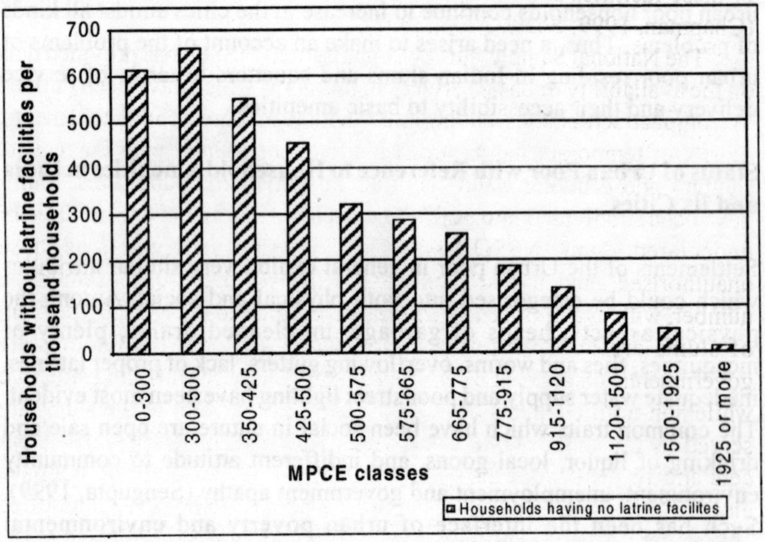

Source: Compendium on Urban Poverty and Urban Slums, December, 2006.

Fig. 12.5: Status of Slum and Squatter Households without Latrine Facilities, Urban India, 2006

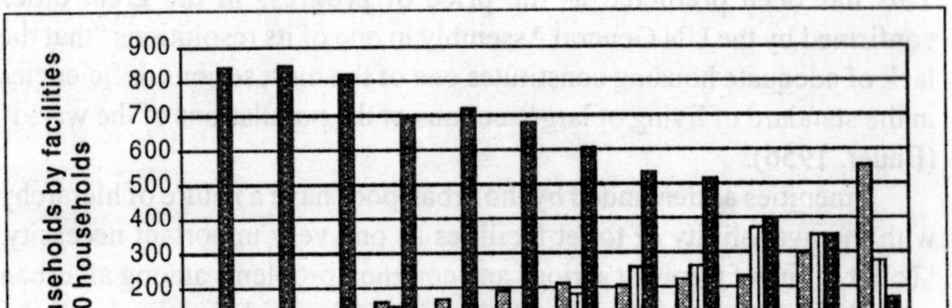

Source: Compendium on Urban Poverty and Urban Slums, December, 2006.

Fig. 12.6: Status of Slum and Squatter Households by Facility of Drinking Water, Urban India, 2006

finances of the urban local bodies but also "political choices in prioritizing of these facilities and institutional problems in their effective delivery" (Chapman, 1999; Shaw, 2003, 2007).

The National Sample Survey Organisation (NSSO) has provided data on the availability of basic services in the slums which have been defined as compact settlements having a collection of poorly built tenements, mostly of temporary nature, crowded together usually with inadequate sanitary and drinking water facilities in unhygienic conditions. Slums have been subdivided into notified or declared slums and non-notified or undeclared slums. NSSO has defined squatter settlements as those unauthorised slum like settlements having less than 20 households in number, with unauthorised structures. According to the NSS, 65 per cent of slums are built on public land owned by local bodies or state governments. 65 per cent of notified slums have pucca dwelling structure while non-notified slums have 35 per cent. 93 per cent of the slums are served by tap or tube-well as the major source of drinking water. 1 per cent and 16 per cent of the notified and non-notified slums do not have electricity respectively. Septic tanks are available in 66 per cent notified and 35 per cent non-notified slums, while underground sewerage exists in 30 per cent notified and 15 per cent non-notified slums. It has been also found that with the rise in monthly per capita consumption expenditures among the slum households, there is a decline in the number of households without latrine facilities, while the number of households availing drinking water from community sources decreases with the rise in their monthly per capita expenditure. The households with no latrine facility and using community drinking water facilities belong to the low Monthly Per Capita Expenditure (MPCE) classes who are not prepared to reduce their expenditure on food to pay for housing and basic amenities, as they are already deficient in nutrition (Kundu, 1988).

The NSS has provided data on the condition of urban slums for Indian States, which has been graphically represented in Figures 12.7, 12.8, 12.9, and 12.10. Conditions of slums and urban poor households with inadequate basic services have also been studied from the data provided by City Development Plans under JNNURM for selected cities. The salient findings arising out of this study on the different slums and squatter settlements in India reveal the following facts.

Firstly, a huge section of the non-notified slum houses have semi-pucca structures. The economically backward States of Bihar, Odisha and Chhattisgarh in India have a higher distribution of semi-pucca structures in the notified slums than in the non-notified slums. Apart from semi-pucca structures, in cities like Kolkata, 90 per cent of the slum dwellers have one room per family. Thus housing has always been one of the scarce basic services accessed by the urban poor. Housing schemes for the poor have been the prerogative of the Central Government, with the implementation of several schemes under the various Five Year Plans, by public housing agencies. There have been 6 types of public sector systems with the help of which an individual could obtain a house. The schemes have been rental housing, hire purchase, self-financing, housing loan, savings linked loans and house rent allowance. Despite all these measures, the Task Force on Urban Development has acknowledged that even the cheapest houses built by public agencies have been much beyond the means of the Economically Weaker Sections and Low Income Groups, therefore, revealing the incapability of the slum dwellers to forego their other important expenditures, to have proper housing (Kundu, 1988).

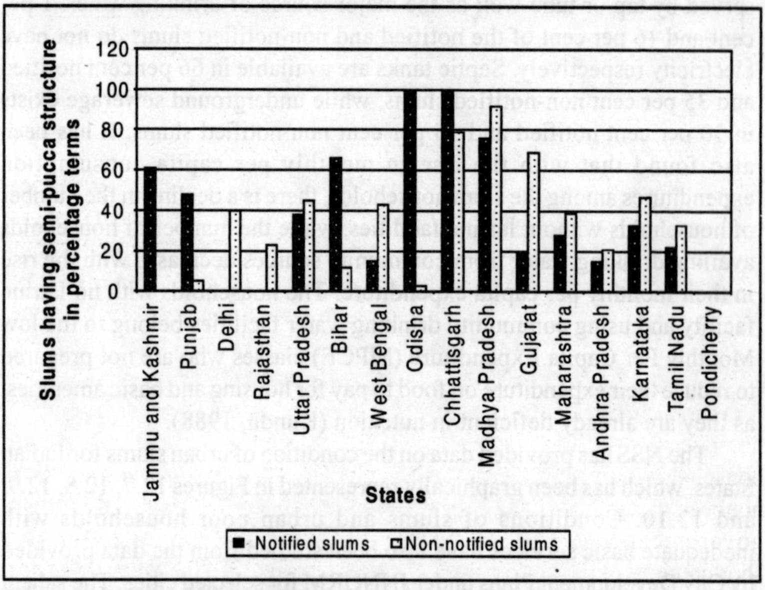

Source: NSS 58th Round, 2002, Conditions of Urban Slums.

Fig. 12.7: Distribution of Semi-Pucca Houses in Notified and Non-Notified Slums of India, 2002

Secondly, the provision of basic services to the urban poor has also been highly insufficient, as the probability of not having latrine facilities is higher with the lower income groups among the slum and squatter

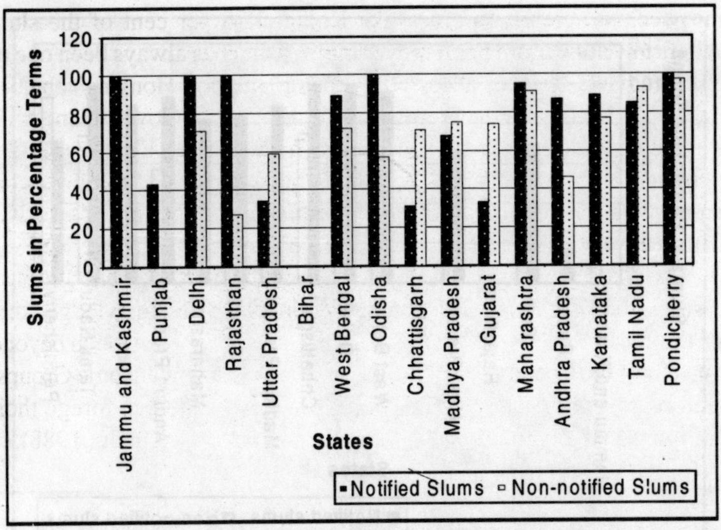

Source: NSS 58th Round, 2002, Conditions of Urban Slums.

Fig. 12.8: Availability of Tap as the Source of Drinking Water in Notified and Non-Notified slums, 2002

households. The percentage of non-notified slums without latrine facilities is relatively higher than the notified slums in most of the states in India as shown in Fig. 12.10. The problem of adequacy of various provisions (services) has been further taken over by the miserable conditions of services available in the cities. The provision of community blocks in the cities of Chennai has shown 1086 persons sharing a single toilet seat and 2871 persons sharing one urinal. 25 per cent of the slum households in Kanpur openly defecate and 45 per cent use community toilets. Sanitation has been identified as the most serious problem of the poor urban households in most of the cities of India. Services like water supply have not been that good either. Tap water is subsidised by the respective state governments, so non-availability of piped supply indicates the shortcomings of the governing bodies. The non-notified slums in the states of Odisha, West Bengal, Delhi, and Rajasthan have lesser coverage than notified slums in terms of tap water supply. Conditions at the city level also give a bleak picture with only 22 per cent of the slum population having access to individual water supply like in the city of Jabalpur in Madhya Pradesh. 215 persons have to take water from one public stand post and hand pump in cities like Faridabad, having the second highest

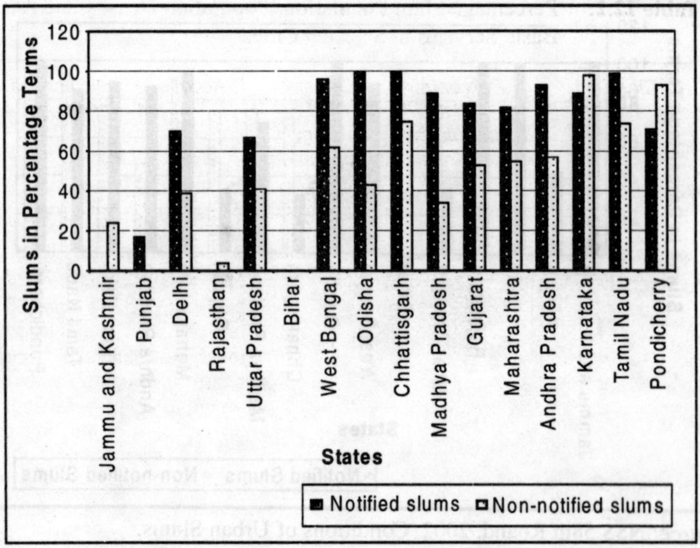

Source: NSS 58th Round, 2002, Conditions of Urban Slums.

Fig. 12.9: Availability of Electricity in Notified and Non-Notified Slums of India, 2002

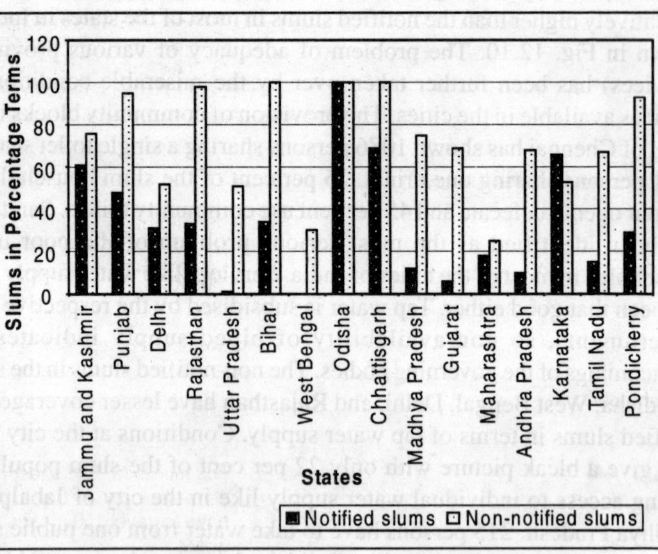

Source: NSS 58th Round, 2002, Conditions of Urban Slums.

Fig. 12.10: Distribution of Slums with No Latrine Facilities in India, 2002

Table 12.2: Percentage Slum Population, Population Density and Access to Basic Services in Selected Cities

City	*Percentage of slum population (Census 2001)*	*Density of slum population*	*Access to basic services for the urban poor*
(1)	(2)	(3)	(4)
Chennai	18.88	4712	620 persons share a tap, 30 per cent get less than 50 litres per day, 1086 persons share a toilet seat and 2871 persons share a urinal, 22.5 per cent resort to open defecation and 68 per cent of the houses are without sewer connection.
Kolkata	32.48	8029	90 per cent of the slum dwellers have one room per family, 85.4 per cent do not have proper drainage facility, open drainage is for 6.9 per cent and covered for 7.7 per cent of the households.
Kanpur	14.42	1380	51 per cent live in Kutcha houses, 55 per cent get water from public stand post, 19 per cent have individual taps, 40 per cent only have electricity, 25 per cent of the slum households openly defecate, and 45 per cent uses community toilets.
Jaipur	15.87	761	30 per cent of urban poor depend on kerosene for light, 16 per cent do not have definite source of water. 74 per cent of the slum households are located in environmentally sensitive areas prone to floods or on main roads and forests.
Jabalpur	29.56	2047	Only 22 per cent and 15 per cent of the slum population has access to individual water supply and individual toilets respectively, slum dwellers in the hilly areas have to travel 150 metres to fetch water.

(Contd.)

Table 12.2 (*Contd.*)

City	*Percentage of slum population (Census 2001)*	*Density of slum population*	*Access to basic services for the urban poor*
(1)	(2)	(3)	(4)
Surat	20.89	4529	72 per cent have private water taps and 35 per cent of the slum households have private latrines, 45 per cent have separate electric connection, 136 persons per public toilet.
Faridabad	46.5	2470	For water 215 persons per public stand post and hand pump, 359 persons per public convenience with reference to sanitation.
Vadodara	14.24	1718	88 per cent have access to water, 46 per cent have access to drainage, 42 per cent to toilet facilities.
Rajkot	17.16	1583	10 per cent slum population with no access to water, and 6 per cent households defecate in the open.
Visakhapatnam	17.32	1526	60 per cent of the slum households have access to safe drinking water, 25 per cent is covered by sewerage system.
Vijayawada	30.94	N.A.	Water supply is covered for 20 per cent of the households, sewerage facility is for 2 per cent of the slum households and 75 per cent have access to community toilets.

Source: City Development Plans, JNNURM, Case of Kolkata, and Census of India, Slum Census, Town level, 2001.

percentage of slum population. The smaller cities due to their paucity of funds have been neglected even more. The depressing picture demonstrated by the status of basic services across the urban areas of the country has been attributed to the rapid growth of urban population, areal expansion of towns and cities (through merging of towns and villages) and low investments in urban development (Kundu, 2006).

Table 12.3: Status of Coverage of Water Supply in Slums in Selected Cities

	Water Supply Coverage in Slums							
	unit	Bangalore	Ahmedabad	Surat	Lucknow	Nagpur	Indore	Chandigarh
Piped Supply	%	10	40	81	20	70	15	25
Non-piped Supply	%	90	60	19	80	30	85	0

Source: City Monitor, 2002.

Economic development in States like Maharashtra, Gujarat, Punjab have always made the cities of these states, better serviced than the economically backward states of Odisha, Madhya Pradesh and Bihar. But a review of the conditions of the slums in the big cities has revealed the plight of the cities like Kolkata, Chennai, Bangaluru and the like in terms of services available and the demands exerted on the limited resources by the growing population. The growth of slum population in the cities only raises the problem of inequality between the slum and non-slum population in availing the basic amenities.

It is not that the government has not taken any initiative to bring about effective distribution of services across the urban centres. Every new plan period have witnessed new policies and programmes catering to the problems of poverty and the different ways to reduce or alleviate poverty from both the urban as well as rural areas. Thus it becomes necessary to look at the different policies and schemes undertaken by the public agencies in the field of housing, basic services and employment generation as probable measures to alleviate poverty.

Government Interventions and Urban Poverty Alleviation Programmes

The Government of India has been instrumental in implementing plans and programmes to eradicate poverty since the inception of the First Five Year Plan. The Five Year Plans have been constituted for overall development of all sections of society and their welfare, focusing on social and economic empowerment of the disadvantaged sections of the Indian society.

The Fifth Five Year Plan (1974 to 1979) has been the first to officially document the problem of poverty in India and aimed for 'removal of poverty' and 'attainment of self-reliance' in the country with the implementation of many poverty alleviation programmes since then. India has witnessed the execution of such programmes even before the Fifth Five year Plan. During the 1950s, poverty alleviation was seen as an indirect measure brought about through the Community Development Programme. However, there have been major efforts by the Government of India in its various policies and programmes in the field of housing and urban basic services following the Fifth Five Year Plan.

Table 12.4: Programmes, Projects under the Housing Sector

Schemes	*Targets and Work Accomplished*
Subsidised Industrial Housing Scheme (1952)	Constructed 282,389 dwelling units at a cost of Rs. 1701.29 crores. 50 per cent of the housing cost was subsidised. Employers providing housing facilities for their workers were given financial assistance up to 75 per cent.
Economic Weaker Section Housing (1952)	11 lakh plots were distributed since 1980. 65352 shelter units were constructed during Sixth Five Year Plan.
Low income Group Housing (1954)	HUDCO allowed construction loans of Rs. 55,000 and repair loans of Rs. 37,500. 1/3rd of the LIGHS houses were to be reserved for EWS.
National Building Organisation (1954)	Instituted to collect, process, disseminate information, related to housing and innovative construction modes.
Slum Areas Improvement and Clearance (SAIC) Programme in 1956	Kolkata, Delhi, Madras, Bombay, Kanpur, and Ahmedabad were prioritised along with towns with a population over 100,000 to upgrade and provide housing, and separate washing platforms by giving subsidies. Under this scheme, Land Acquisition was incorporated.
Minimum Needs Programme	Provide basic minimum services, slum up-gradation like health facilities, water supply, electrification, road connectivity, housing, elementary education and nutrition.
National Housing Policy (1988)	Low cost housing, technology, appropriate materials, information and skills upgradation to artisans and footpath dwellers.
Night Shelter Scheme (1988)	Targeted 2 lakh footpath dwellers in 12 metro cities, set up 56 schemes to provide 19366 beds, 5288 pay and use toilets, 64 baths and 145 urinals.

Source: Sen and Kumar (2006), '*Urban Poverty Alleviation Initiatives and the JNNURM: A Critical Assessment*', NIUA 2006.

Table 12.5: Programmes, Projects to Provide Basic Services and Urban Infrastructure

Programmes, Projects to Provide Basic Services and Urban Infrastructure to Reduce Poverty

Schemes	*Targets and Work Accomplished*
Urban Community Development Programme (1958)	To strengthen local voluntary organisations and establish Basti level Agencies, Self-Help Groups and community organisations, pre-school classes, immunisation schemes, crèches, mid-day meal centres, and medical checkup schemes were launched.
Urban Water Supply and Sanitation (1961)	To provide good sewerage or improve the existing sewerage system. Storm water drains, feeder mains were constructed and clear water reservoirs were rehabilitated.
Mid-Day Meal Programme (1962)	It was started to provide food supplements of 300 calories and 10 grams of protein per child, 600 calories and 20 grams to severely malnourished children and 500 calories and 15-20 grams of protein to pregnant/nursing women
EIUS (1972) in convergence with BSUP since 1993 and National Slum Development Policy since 1996	To provide sanitary latrines, drainage, portable water supply, road connectivity and street lighting. It was a Centrally sponsored scheme till 1974, after which it became the responsibility of the state government.
Integrated Child Development Services	To provide non-formal pre-school education, early stimulation and learning, supplementary nutrition and immunisation for children.
Integrated Development of Small and Medium Towns (1979)	To set-up infrastructure and facilities for towns to serve as service centres for their surrounding rural areas. Each town was given a Central grant of Rs. 52 lakh with Rs. 6 lakh to be used for Low Cost Sanitation.
National Health Policy (1982)	To recognise health infrastructure and improve medical and paramedical training, integrate health plans with health related sectors like water supply, sanitation, food production. It recognised for the first time the roles of voluntary organisations like Rotary Club and Lions Club.
Urban Basic Services Programme; subsumed under Urban Basic Services for the Poor in 1990	To strengthen income generating, skill training for women, early childhood learning facilities, more community taps were installed. Basti Development Plans were formed. To integrate social services, under Urban Basic Services and physical amenities under EIUS.

(*Contd.*)

Table 12.5 (*Contd.*)

Schemes	*Targets and Work Accomplished*
Accelerated Urban Water Supply Programme	It targeted 215 eligible small towns with a population of less than 20,000 (1991 Census) in Class IV, V and VI categories by improving the quality of life of poor by reducing water scarcity, improving the resource base of the urban local bodies and improving their involvement.
National Slum Development Policy (1996)	It looked at the up gradation in infrastructural facilities, community centres, education, housing, credit societies, water and sanitation, primary education, adult literacy, solid waste management, garbage disposal.
Targeted Public Distribution System (1997)	10 kg of food grains especially rice and wheat every month to each BPL family at 40 per cent of the cost.
Valmiki Ambedkar Malin Basti Awas Yojana (VAMBAY 2001)	To identify and meet the shelter needs of the urban poor. 25 per cent of the funds were earmarked for water supply and sanitation. This scheme was under DUEPA, MoUD, HUDCO and poverty alleviation and NGOs.

Source: Sen and Kumar (2006), '*Urban Poverty Alleviation Initiatives and The JNNURM: A Critical Assessment*', NIUA 2006.

Tables 12.4 and 12.5 provides a glimpse of the various policies and programmes implemented by the National Government of India to provide better housing facilities and urban basic services especially for the poor in the urban areas.

Apart from the programmes under Housing and Urban Basic Services and Infrastructure, there have also been employment generation schemes undertaken by the Government of India in the form of:

(i) National Food for Work Programme,
(ii) Scheme of Liberation and Rehabilitation of Scavengers in 1993 as an attempt to provide scavengers especially the SCs and STs with alternative employment.
(iii) Swarna Jayanti Shahari Rojgar Yojana in 1997.
(iv) Swarna Jayanti Shahari Rojgar Yojana Urban Self-Employment Programme targeting the urban poor BPL in all towns, underemployed and unemployed, 30 per cent out of which should be women and 3 per cent disabled.

Each and every programme undertaken by the government has seen limited success owing to a high degree of inflexibility in the schemes. Another reason cited for the lack of success has been paucity of funds with the Central Government and barriers in transferring its financial responsibility gradually to the state and local governments. Programmes like EIUS had started with a central grant of 100 per cent which later had to be financed completely by the state. The issues of transfer of financial accountability and the maintenance of the projects have been responsible for the slow progress and inefficient implementation further leading to non-availability of services, especially for the urban poor (Kundu, 1988). In this situation, the effective role should be played by NGOs, CBOs and private sector in helping to cover the expenses met by the state and the local government in the delivery of basic services and infrastructure.

JNNURM or the Jawaharlal Nehru National Urban Renewal Mission, launched in the year 2006, by the Prime Minister of India, provides a ray of hope as it aims to provide housing and infrastructure for the vulnerable sections of society specially the poor from SC/ST and other oppressed classes focusing on decentralisation of urban governance and the public-private partnership.

Conclusions

The conditions of the urban poor is reflected largely by slum population. National as well as the international organisations have both taken slums as the segment of the urban population who have been denied of the basic services like safe drinking water, electricity, sanitation facilities and so on. The slum settlements are generally overcrowded with unhygienic housing conditions. They have been mostly seen as continuous arrays of houses having deplorable conditions. Thus every city administration along with the management of the slum settlements face the added problem of the squatters and the houseless.

The study of slum population across the cities has revealed the differences existing between the slum and the non-slum population. There has been a positive relationship existing between the size of city and the percentage of slum population. This has been the result of the effect of agglomeration where every new job has been created in the vicinity of the big cities. The poor from the underdeveloped regions have been forced to migrate with the aim to have a better life in the cities. Globalisation has been responsible in creating many world cities where cities like Mumbai have been competing with Shanghai but saddled with a burden of urban poor comprising almost half of the urban population of the city. This has been the price paid by the cities of the developing world in the wake of globalisation. Cities like Mumbai, Delhi, and Kolkata have now been given the status of mega-cities according to the world standard of having more than 10 million population. But this strength of human resource also takes into account the large size of slum population, Mumbai having 54 per cent, Kolkata having 32 per cent and Delhi having 18 per cent of the total urban population.

Apart from the size of the slum dwellers in the cities, the social and economic conditions ascribed to this particular section has been even more appalling. High rates of illiteracy, and percentage of workers less than 40 in most of the cities, only increases the burden on the slum dwellers to avail every basic service along with their high expenditure on food.

With the growing slum population, the urban poor in the cities have been pushed even farther from availing the basic amenities. Ninty per cent of the slum dwellers in cities like Kolkata have only one room for staying and 22.5 per cent of the urban poor in Chennai have to resort to open defecation exposing themselves to a host of communicable diseases.

Urban growth reinforced with rising migration has been held responsible for the growth of urban poor in the cities. Creating employment opportunities for the slum dwellers within the cities and also in the areas from where they have originally come from is the need of the hour. The Integrated Development of Small and Medium Towns has been one such policy which was launched in 1979 to reduce the pressure of growing migrant population on large cities by developing the small and medium towns. Policies like these have not come to any help, thus shifting the focus back again to redevelop and upgrade the slum areas in the large cities as an alternative. Along with these, urban policies have proposed for decentralisation in the urban governance and public-private participation. This is where policies like JNNURM would come to use, where the main focus is on urban renewal, with a decentralised setup coupled with public-private participation intending to bring about effective delivery of basic services and urban infrastructure for the urban poor.

REFERENCES

Anon. (2006), Workshop of JNNURM: Issues and Opportunities held on 22.09.2006 organised by SUSTAIN-PERT-UN-HABITAT-SICCI-CUPA-TUFIDCO, http://www.un_habitat.org/downloads/docs/4152_56990_

Workshop Proceedings of JNNURM-Final Version_R.S.Murali_.pdf, as viewed on Wednesday, September 10, 2008.

Anon. (2006), Compendium on Urban Poverty and urban Slums, Government of India, Ministry of Housing and Urban Poverty Alleviation, National Building Organisation, New Delhi, 98p.

Anon. (2007), State of World Population 2007: Unleashing the Potential of Urban Growth, United Nations Population Fund, http://mirror.undp.org/Mongolian/unfpa/SWOP_2007_ENG.pdf, as viewed on Monday, 21st January, 2008, 99 pgs.

Anon.(2008),2-YearsofJNNURM, 2008, http://www.indiaurbanportal.in/JNNURM/2yrs_JNNURM.pdf, as viewed on Wednesday, September10, 2008.

Banerjee-Guha, S. (1994), Review: Urban Growth and Access to Basic Services, *Economic and Political Weekly*, Vol. 29, No. 48, November, 1994, pp. 3032-3033.

Bauer, C. (1956), 'The Pattern of Urban and Economic Development: Social Implications', *The Annals of the American Academy of Political and Social Science*, 305; 60.

Berner, E. (2000), 'Poverty Alleviation and the Eviction of the Poorest: Towards Urban Land Reforms in the Philippines', *International Journal of Urban and Regional Research*, Vol. 24.3, September, 2000, pp. 554-566.

Benjamin, S. (2000), 'Governance, Economic Settings and Poverty in Bangalore', *Environment and Urbanisation*, 2000:12:35.

Grigorivich, J. (2008), 'Informality and Autonomy in the Slums of the Developing World', *Under Current*, Vol. V, Issue III, Fall/Winter Issue 2008, pp. 20-29.

Gupta, I. and Mitra, A. (2002), 'Rural Migrants and Labour Segmentation: Micro-Level Evidence from Delhi Slums', *Economic and Political Weekly*, Vol. 37, No. 2, January 12-18, 2002, pp. 163-168.

Kapadia-Kundu, N. and Kanitkar, T. (2002), 'Primary Healthcare in Urban Slums', *Economic and Political Weekly*, Vol. 37, No. 51, December 2002, pp. 5086-5089.

Kara, S.K., Shikura, S. and Harada, H. (2003), 'Living Environment and Health of Urban Poor: A study in Mumbai', *Economic and Political Weekly*, Vol. 38, No. 34, August 23-29, 2003, pp. 3575-3586.

Kumar, N. and Aggarwal, S.C. (2003), 'Patterns of Consumption and Poverty in Delhi Slums', *Economic and Political Weekly*, Vol. 38, No. 50, December 13-19, 2003, pp. 5294-5300.

Kundu, A. (2006), 'Changing Perspectives on Urban Governance and Financing of Basic Amenities in Indian Mega Cities', *Seminar on New Forms of Urban Governance in Indian Mega Cities: Under Indo-Dutch Programmeme on Alternatives in Development*, Jawaharlal Nehru University, New Delhi.

Kundu, A. (1993), '*In the Name of Urban Poor: Access to Basic Amenities*', Sage Publications, New Delhi, 299 pgs.

Kundu, A. (1997), 'Trends and Structure of Employment in the 1990s: Implications for Urban Growth', *Economic and Political Weekly*, Vol. 32, No. 24, 14-20 June, 1997, pp. 1394-1405.

Kundu, A. (2000), 'Globalising Gujarat: Urbanisation, Employment, and Poverty', *Economic and Political Weekly*, Vol. 35, No. 35-36, 26 August-8 September, 2000, pp. 3172-3182.

Kundu, A. (2006), 'Trends and Patterns of Urbanisation and their Economic Implications', India Infrastructure Report 2006, http://www.iitk.ac.in/3inetwork/html/reports/IIR2006/Trends&Patt.pdf, as viewed on Thursday, June 4th, 2009, pp. 27-41.

Kundu, A., Bagchi, S. and Kundu, D. (1999), 'Regional Distribution of Infrastructure and Basic Amenities in Urban India: Issues concerning Empowerment of Local Bodies', *Economic and Political Weekly*, Vol. 34, No. 28, July 10-16, 1999, pp. 1893-1906.

Kundu, D. (2006), 'Decentralised Governance in Metro Cities—The Issue of Elite Capture with special reference to Delhi', *Seminar on New Forms of Urban Governance in Indian Mega Cities: Under Indo-Dutch Programmeme on Alternatives in Development*, Jawaharlal Nehru University, New Delhi.

Mitra, A. (1993), 'Status of Basic Services in Indian Cities', in *Urbanisation in Developing Countries*, Institute of Social Sciences, Concept Publishing Company, pp. 174-193.

Paul, S. (1994), '*Public Services for Urban Poor: Report Card on Three Indian Cities*', Vol. 29, No. 50, December 10, 1994, pp. 3131-3134.

Rani, P. (2004), 'Impact of Migration on Urban Poverty', pp. 52-65, in ed. Gaur, K.D., Bakshi, R. and Agarwal, M., *Economics of Urbanisation*, Sunrise Publications, New Delhi, 2004.

Sen, R. and Kumar, N. (2006), 'Urban Poverty Alleviation Initiatives and The JNNURM: A Critical Assessment', NIUA 2006, http://www.niua.org/Publications/.../abstract_urban%20Poverty_Nakul.pdf, as viewed on Monday, February 2, 2009, 43 pp.

Sengupta, C. (1999), 'Dynamics of Community Environmental Management in Howrah Slums', *Economic and Political Weekly*, Vol. 34, No. 21, May 1999, pp. 1292-1296.

Sharma, R.N. and K. Sita (2000), 'Cities, Slums and Government', *Economical and Political Weekly*, Vol. 35, No. 42, October 14 to 20, pp. 3733-3735.

Shaw, A. (1996), 'Urban Policy in Post-Independent India: An Appraisal', *Economic and Political Weekly*, Vol. 31, No. 4, January 1996, pp. 224-228.

Shaw, A. (2007), 'Basic Amenities in Urban India: Analysis at State and Town Level', Working Paper Series, WPS No. 616/December 2007, Indian Institute of Management, Calcutta. http://www.iimcal.ac.in/res/upd/WPS616.pdf, as viewed on Saturday, March 14th, 2009, pp. 1-34.

13

Socio-Economic Characteristics, Access to Basic Amenities and Health Status of Slum Population in India

Vinod Kumar Mishra

Introduction

The countries of the developing world are witnessing rapid urbanisation. However, these countries have very little capacity to support the rising number of urban population and provide them with housing and basic amenities. Moreover, with the growth of population in urban areas, the number of people living below poverty line is also increasing. All these have resulted in the proliferation of slums in urban areas. Large scale rural to urban migration is taking place particularly in large urban centres. Through rural to urban migration, the rural poverty is getting spilled over to urban areas. Rural to urban migrants are generally semi-skilled or unskilled. So, they get employment only in the informal sector that fetches them low income. Hence, it becomes difficult for them to afford decent housing in urban areas. Thus, it can be said that urban poverty is expressed through slum population. It has been estimated that at present about one-third of the world's urban population does not have access to adequate housing, safe drinking water and sanitation (United Nations, 2003). Slums are generally overcrowded and often situated on marginal and environmentally fragile land. The major objective of present study is to analyse the characteristics of slum population in the states reporting slums in 2001. Composite indices have been calculated to measure the social and economic conditions of the slums in states reporting slums. An analysis of the characteristics of slum population as per NSSO 65th round, 2008-09 and the health condition of the slum population living in the eight million plus cities as per NFHS-3, 2005-06, has also been provided here.

Slum Population in the States Reporting Slums

According to the Census of India 2001, slum dwellers in the country constitute about one-seventh of the total population of the States and Union Territories reporting slum population and 23.1 per cent of population of the 640 cities and towns reporting slums. Table 13.1 shows the distribution of slum population in the States of India. The states have been grouped into different regions on the basis of their location in order to analyse the regional variations of the characteristics of slum population. Moreover, only those states that had million plus cities in 2001 have been selected for the analysis. The proportion of slum population to total urban population reveals that, Maharashtra, located in the western region, has the highest percentage of slum population (27.3%). It is closely followed by the southern state of Andhra Pradesh (24.9%). Haryana, located in the northern region, has 23.2 per cent slum population to total urban population. Kerala has the lowest percentage of slum population (0.8%).

Again, the regional variations in the distribution of slum population portrays that Rajasthan in the northern region has the lowest proportion (9.8%) of slum population. Among the northern States, Rajasthan is one of the least urbanised states. Moreover, the state receives low level of rural to urban migrants. These two factors have lead to the low percentage of slum population in the state. In the central region, the proportion of slum population in Uttar Pradesh is lesser than that of Madhya Pradesh. In the eastern region, West Bengal has the highest proportion of slum population, while Jharkhand has the lowest proportion. The million plus city of Kolkata has contributed to a larger proportion of slum population in West Bengal. Bihar has one of the lowest proportions of slum population in India. In the western region, more than half of the population of Mumbai (in Maharashtra) lives in slums. Besides, other million plus cities of Maharashtra too have high proportion of slum population. This contributes to the highest proportion of slum population in the state.

There is high intra-regional difference in the slum population in the western region. Gujarat has less than 10 per cent slum population which is nearly one-third of the proportion of the slum population of other western states. Among the southern States, Kerala has the lowest proportion of slum population while Andhra Pradesh has the highest.

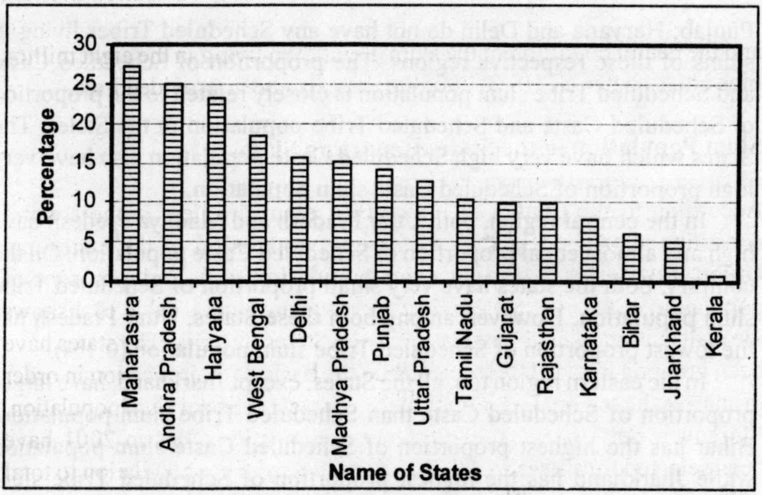

Source: Tables on Slum Population, Census of India, 2001.

Fig. 13.1: Proportion of Slum Population to Total Urban Population in India, 2001

Karnataka has 7.8 per cent, while Tamil Nadu has about 10 per cent slum population. Thus, it is clear that among the southern states too, there is intra-regional variation in the proportion of slum population.

Scheduled Caste and Scheduled Tribe Population of Slums

The study of overall distribution of Scheduled Caste and Scheduled Tribe slum population in the states reveals that the percentage of the Scheduled Caste slum population is comparatively higher than that of the Scheduled Tribe slum population in all the states. If we study the region-wise distribution of Scheduled Caste population, it is evident that western, southern and northern regions have comparatively higher proportion of Scheduled Caste population. In the northern region, Punjab has the highest proportion of Scheduled Caste slum population while Haryana has the lowest proportion of Scheduled Caste slum population. In fact, all the northern states have high proportion of Scheduled Caste slum population. Thus, it is clear that large scale rural to urban migration takes place among the Scheduled Caste population. On the contrary, there is very low proportion of Scheduled Tribe slum population in the northern region. While Rajasthan has 4.1 per cent Scheduled Tribe slum population;

Punjab, Haryana and Delhi do not have any Scheduled Tribes living in slums of these respective regions. The proportion of Scheduled Caste and Scheduled Tribe slum population is closely related to the proportion of Scheduled Caste and Scheduled Tribe population in the States. The States which have very high Scheduled Caste population also have very high proportion of Scheduled Caste slum population.

In the central region, both Uttar Pradesh and Madhya Pradesh have high and almost equal proportion of Scheduled Caste population. On the contrary, both the states have very small proportion of Scheduled Tribe slum population. However, among both these States, Uttar Pradesh has the lowest proportion of Scheduled Tribe slum population (0.1%).

In the eastern region too, all the States, except Jharkhand, have larger proportion of Scheduled Caste than Scheduled Tribe slum population. Bihar has the highest proportion of Scheduled Caste slum population while Jharkhand has the highest proportion of Scheduled Tribe slum population. In the western region, both Gujarat and Maharashtra have higher proportion of Scheduled Caste slum population as compared to the Scheduled Tribes.

Among the southern states, Tamil Nadu has the highest proportion while Kerala has the lowest proportion of Scheduled Caste slum population. However, both Kerala and Tamil Nadu have less than one per cent of Scheduled Tribe slum population. Among the southern states, Karnataka has the second highest proportion of Scheduled Caste slum population (24.2%) and the highest proportion of Scheduled Tribe slum population (4.6%). Thus, it is evident that Karnataka has higher proportion of both Scheduled Caste and Scheduled Tribe slum population among all the southern States. From Table 13.1, it is, therefore, clear that there exists inter-regional and intra-regional variations in the distribution of Scheduled Caste and Scheduled Tribe slum population among all the States. While the northern States have very low proportion of Scheduled Tribe, Scheduled Caste slum population is well distributed among all regions.

Literacy of Slum Population in the States Reporting Slums

Literacy is one of the important social indicators. There exists high level of difference in the level of literacy among the different states reporting slum population. From Table 13.2 it is evident that inter-regional variation exists in the level of literacy among slum population. Male-female gap in literacy is also high among all states except, Kerala and Punjab. In

Table 13.1: Percentage of Slum Population, Scheduled Castes and Scheduled Tribes, 2001

Regions	*Name of the state*	*Total urban population*	*Population living in slums*	*Percentage of slum population to total urban population*	*Percentage of SC population*	*Percentage of ST population*
North	Punjab	8262511	5660268	14.0	28.6	0.0
	Haryana	6115304	4296670	23.2	18.9	0.0
	Delhi	12905780	11277586	15.7	27.2	0.0
	Rajasthan	13214375	7668508	9.8	27.0	4.1
Central	Uttar Pradesh	34539582	21256870	12.7	20.4	0.1
	Madhya Pradesh	15967145	9599007	15.1	21.1	3.8
Eastern	Bihar	8681800	4814512	6.1	17.8	1.5
	West Bengal	22427251	15184596	18.4	13.8	1.2
	Jharkhand	5993741	2422943	5.0	8.7	16.7
Western	Gujarat	18930250	12697360	9.9	13.9	4.5
	Maharashtra	41100980	43635219	27.3	11.5	2.5
Southern	Andhra Pradesh	20808940	16090585	24.9	14.8	2.5
	Karnataka	17961529	11023376	7.8	24.2	4.6
	Kerala	8266925	3196622	0.8	7.5	0.2
	Tamil Nadu	27483998	14337225	10.4	26.0	0.5

Source: Tables on Slum Population, Census of India, 2001.

different regions also the literacy rate of male population is higher than the female population.

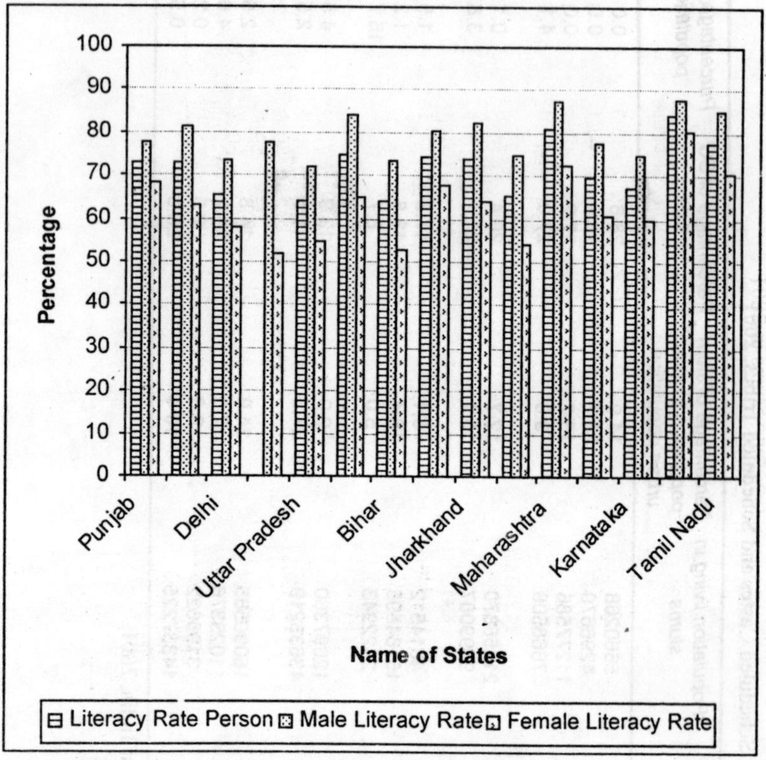

Source: Tables on Slum Population, Census of India, 2001.

Fig. 13.2: Literacy Rate of Slum Population States Reporting Slums, 2001

In the northern region, the literacy rate among slum population is the highest in Punjab and Haryana (73.1%), and the lowest in Delhi (65.6%). In the eastern region, Bihar has the lowest literacy rate (63.8%). The variation in literacy rate among other eastern states is quite less. In the western region, the differences among male and female literacy rate is high. The literacy rate of slum population in Maharashtra is 80.7 per cent, next only to Kerala (83.9%). Among the southern states, literacy rate is poor in Andhra Pradesh and Karnataka. Karnataka infact, has the lowest literacy rate (67.5%) among the southern states.

Table 13.2: Literacy Rate of Slum Population by Gender in States Reporting Slums in 2001

Regions	*Names of States*	*Total urban population*	*Population living in slum*	*Literacy rate of slum population*	*Literacy rate of slum Male*	*Literacy rate of slum Female*	*Gender differentials*
Northern	Punjab	8262511	5660268	73.1	77.4	68.0	9.4
	Haryana	6115304	4296670	73.1	81.3	63.1	18.1
	Delhi	12905780	11277586	65.6	73.2	58.0	15.0
	Rajasthan	13214375	7668508	–	77.8	51.9	25.9
Central	Uttar Pradesh	34539582	21256870	63.9	71.8	54.9	16.8
	Madhya Pradesh	15967145	9599007	74.9	83.9	64.9	19.0
Eastern	Bihar	8681800	4814512	63.8	73.2	52.9	20.3
	West Bengal	22427251	15184596	74.4	80.2	67.6	12.6
	Jharkhand	5993741	2422943	73.6	82.3	63.9	18.5
Western	Gujarat	18930250	12697360	65.5	74.9	54.0	20.9
	Maharashtra	41100980	43635219	80.7	87.6	72.3	15.3
Southern	Andhra Pradesh	20808940	16090585	69.4	77.7	60.9	16.7
	Karnataka	17961529	11023376	67.5	75	59.7	15.3
	Kerala	8266925	3196622	83.9	87.8	80.2	7.6
	Tamil Nadu	27483998	14337225	77.8	85.1	70.4	14.7

Source: Tables on Slum Population, Census of India, 2001.

Table 13.3: Work Participation Rate and Male-female Gap among Slum Population in States Reporting Slums in 2001

Regions	*Name of states*	*Total urban population*	*Population reporting slum*	*Total WPR*	*Male WPR*	*Female WPR*	*Male-Female Gap*
Northern	Punjab	8262511	5660268	33.0	52.6	9.7	43.0
	Haryana	6115304	4296670	30.9	48.8	9.1	39.7
	Delhi	12905780	11277586	30.8	54.5	9.6	44.9
	Rajasthan	13214375	7668508	28.8	46.6	8.9	37.7
Central	Uttar Pradesh	34539582	21256870	26.3	43.8	6.1	37.7
	Madhya Pradesh	15967145	9599007	29.6	46.5	10.9	35.5
Eastern	Bihar	8681800	4814512	25.8	42.0	7.3	34.7
	West Bengal	22427251	15184596	34.2	53.7	11.4	42.4
	Jharkhand	5993741	2422943	27.6	44.0	9.5	34.5
Western	Gujarat	18930250	12697360	35.5	55.4	11.5	43.9
	Maharashtra	41100980	43635219	34.9	53.7	12.0	41.8
Southern	Andhra Pradesh	20808940	16090585	33.7	51.7	15.4	36.3
	Karnataka	17961529	11023376	36.9	53.8	19.4	34.4
	Kerala	8266925	3196622	33.2	53.4	13.7	39.7
	Tamil Nadu	27483998	14337225	35.5	54.3	16.5	37.7

Source: Tables on Slum Population, Census of India, 2001.

Male-Female gap in literacy rate exists in all states reporting slums, though it varies from one region to another. It is highest in Rajasthan (25.9%), Gujarat (20.9%) and Bihar (20.3%) having almost the same male-female gap in literacy rate. In the central region, this gap is higher in Madhya Pradesh than in Uttar Pradesh. In the eastern states, this gap varies from 12.6 per cent in West Bengal to 20.3 per cent in Bihar.

In the western region, male-female gap is higher in Gujarat than in Maharashtra. It is also quite high in all the southern states, except Kerala. In Kerala, both male and female literacy rate is more than 80 per cent.

Work Participation Rate of Slum Population

Work participation rate in slums is one of the important indicators taken for the assessment of economic condition of the slum population. As per the Census of India 2001, nearly one-third of the slum population was recorded as workers which is about 32.3 per cent to the urban work participation rate. The sex-wise work participation rate shows that there are 50 per cent male workers in slums as compared to only 11.9 per cent female workers. This shows acute male-female gap in work participation. Among the States reporting slum population, Karnataka has the highest work participation rate and Bihar the lowest. Among the different regions, the southern region has the highest work participation rate. Western states too have a high work participation rate. In the northern region, Punjab has the highest work participation rate while Rajasthan has the lowest. However, both the states in the central region and the states in the eastern region have somewhat low work participation rate compared to other regions, except West Bengal (34.2%).

There is not much variation in work participation rate among slum population in western and southern states. Among these states, work participation rate varies between 33 and 36 per cent.

There also exists high male-female gap in work participation among different states reporting slum population. This is the highest in Delhi (44.9%) and lowest in Karnataka (34.4%). Among different regions, male-female gap in work participation rate is highest in the western states. In both the states of the western region, the gap is more than 40 per cent. It can be noted that all states have more than 34 per cent male-female gap in work participation rate. Thus, we can conclude that the urban labour market is less conducive to female workers living in slums. The proportion of main workers is very high for slum population in all states which is similar to urban areas.

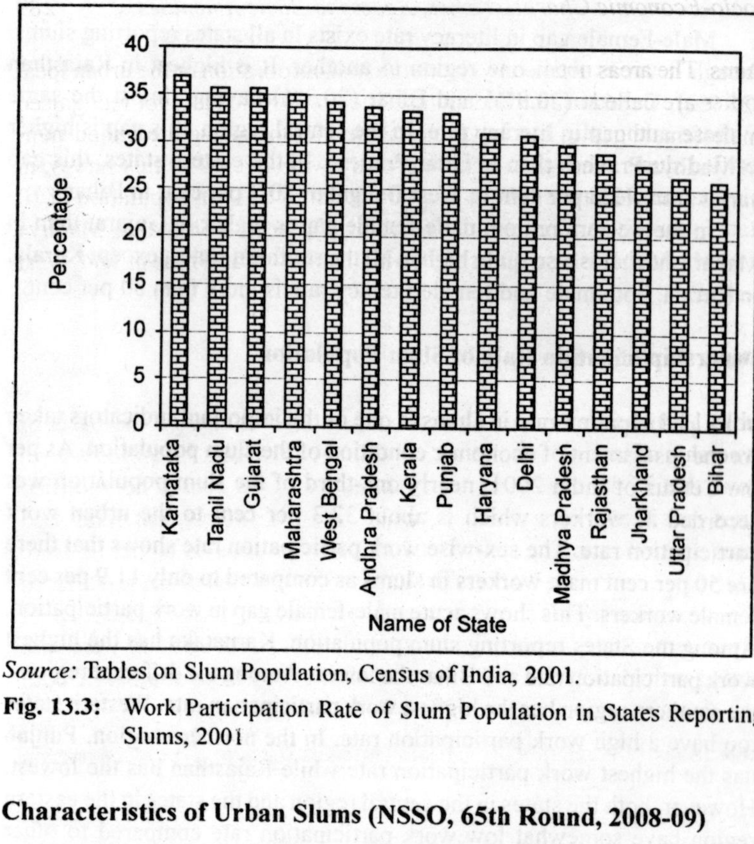

Source: Tables on Slum Population, Census of India, 2001.

Fig. 13.3: Work Participation Rate of Slum Population in States Reporting Slums, 2001

Characteristics of Urban Slums (NSSO, 65th Round, 2008-09)

The National Sample Survey Organisation (NSSO) in its 65th round gathered information regarding the conditions of both notified and non-notified slums. The survey conducted in 2008-09 covers the availability of some basic amenities in the slums of urban areas. The amenities and facilities covered in this round are: ownership of the land on which slums are established, roads within the slum and approach road to the slum, and availability of electricity, drinking water, toilets, drainage, sewerage and garbage disposal.

The NSSO 65th round 2008-09 defines slum as 'compact settlement with poorly built structure, mainly temporary in nature. The slums generally have inadequate sanitary and drinking water facilities and unhygienic condition'. Thus, areas which have at least 20 households and above combined with the above mentioned characteristics are called slums. The areas notified by the municipal corporation or the urban local bodies are called as notified slums. The areas which are not recognised by these authorities but have characteristics of slums are called non-notified slums. Though the entire country was covered by this survey, in this chapter we have studied the characteristics of slum population of 10 States, namely Andhra Pradesh, Delhi, Gujarat, Karnataka, Madhya Pradesh, Maharashtra, Odisha, Tamil Nadu, Uttar Pradesh and West Bengal.

Ownership of Land

Table 13.4 shows the state-wise distribution of slums on the basis of ownership of land on which they are situated. The data for all India level shows that 37 per cent of notified slums and 42 per cent of non-notified slums are situated on private land while as high as 60 per cent of notified slums and 54 per cent of non-notified slums are located on public land. In Karnataka and Odisha, nearly 100 per cent notified slums are located on government-owned land. On the other hand, in Uttar Pradesh, about 73 per cent of notified slums and 81 per cent of non-notified slums are located on private land. This implies that about three-fourths of both

Table 13.4: Distribution of Slums in Different States by Type of Ownership of Land, 2008-09

(In Percentage)

State/UT	Notified slum			Non-notified slum		
	Private	Public	Not known	Private	Public	Not known
Andhra Pradesh	41	59	0	53	46	1
Delhi	12	66	23	29	67	5
Gujarat	50	50	0	20	74	7
Karnataka	2	98	0	47	47	7
Madhya Pradesh	32	68	0	34	66	0
Maharashtra	33	67	1	43	50	7
Odisha	0	100	0	28	71	1
Tamil Nadu	18	80	2	35	66	0
Uttar Pradesh	73	16	11	81	19	0
West Bengal	69	23	7	62	28	10
All India-2008-09	37	60	3	42	54	5
All India 2002	36	64	1	35	63	2

Source: NSSO, 65th round, report no. 534: Some Characteristics of Urban Slums, 2008-09.

notified and non-notified slums in Uttar Pradesh are situated on private land. This is the largest among all states reporting slums. In Gujarat and Odisha, 74 per cent and 71 per cent of non-notified slums are situated on public land respectively, while more than 80 per cent notified slums are located on private land. In Maharashtra, which has one of the largest proportion of slum population in India, about two-thirds of the notified slums and half of the non-notified slums are located on public land. In Delhi, Madhya Pradesh and Tamil Nadu too more than two-thirds of the notified and non-notified slums are located on public land.

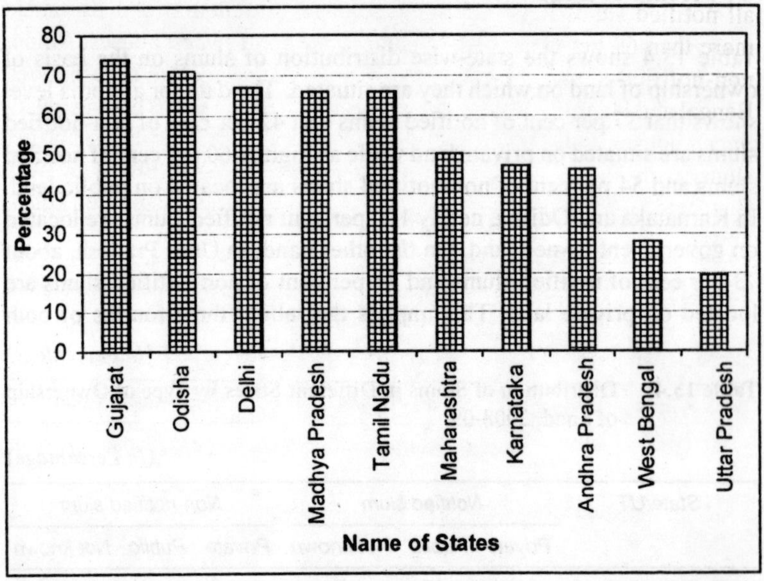

Source: NSSO, 65th round, Report No. 534: Some Characteristics of Urban Slums, 2008-09.

Fig. 13.4: Percentage of Non-Notified Slums Located on Public Land, 2008-09

In West Bengal, 69 per cent of the notified slums are on private land. Among the slums built on public land, quite a high proportion of them are located on the land owned by local bodies. The report points out that about half (44%) of the slums are located on marginal lands that are environmentally fragile. These factors make slum dwellers more vulnerable to poor living conditions.

Structure of Houses

NSSO classifies the type of house into three categories: *pucca*, semi-*pucca* and *katcha*. According to the NSSO 65th round, in 64 per cent of the notified slums and half of the non-notified slums in 2008-09 majority of households were living in *pucca* houses (Table 13.5). The study of the state level variations show that Uttar Pradesh (89%) and Andhra Pradesh (88%) have very high proportion of notified slums that have majority of *pucca* houses. However, none of the notified and non-notified slums of Odisha have majority of the households with *pucca* houses. Here, nearly all notified slums have semi-*pucca* houses. In Gujarat and Karnataka more than 60 per cent notified slums have semi-*pucca* houses. Among non-notified slums, Maharashtra, Karnataka, Andhra Pradesh, West Bengal and Uttar Pradesh have more than half of the slums having mostly *pucca* houses. Odisha has the highest proportion (63%) of non-notified slums with *katcha* houses while Maharashtra (1%) followed by West Bengal (4%) have the lowest proportion of non-notified slums with *katcha* houses.

Table 13.5: Distribution of Slums in Different States by Type of Structure of Majority of Houses, 2008-09

(*In Percentage*)

State/UT	*Notified slum*			*Non-notified slum*		
	Pucca	*Semi-Pucca*	*Kutcha*	*Pucca*	*Semi-Pucca*	*Kutcha*
Andhra Pradesh	88	9	3	63	1	36
Delhi	77	14	9	49	23	28
Gujarat	14	66	20	29	38	33
Karnataka	26	63	12	67	21	11
Madhya Pradesh	19	54	28	35	21	45
Maharashtra	72	26	2	68	31	1
Odisha	0	99	1	0	37	63
Tamil Nadu	43	42	14	32	27	40
Uttar Pradesh	89	1	11	57	5	38
West Bengal	74	16	10	60	36	4
All India-2008-09	64	30	7	50	29	21
All India 2002	65	30	6	30	40	30

Source: NSSO, 65th round, Report No. 534: Some Characteristics of Urban Slums, 2008-09.

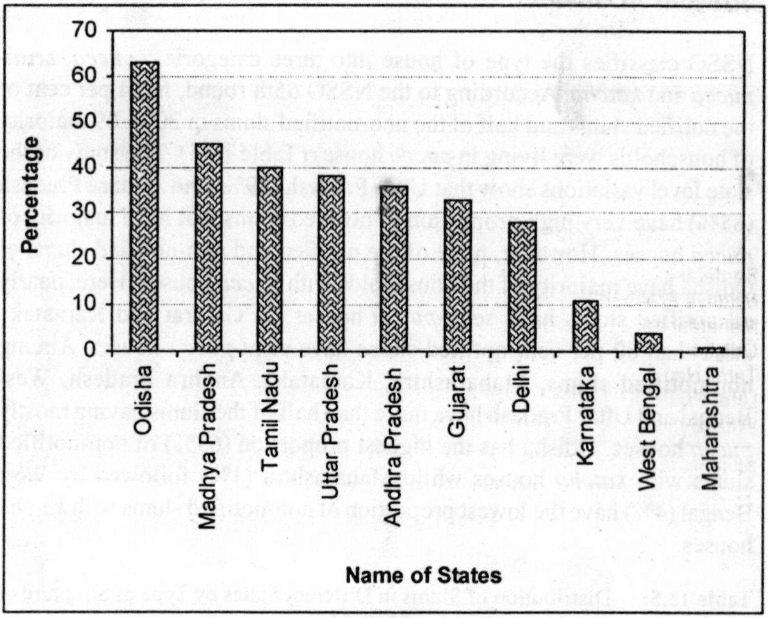

Source: NSSO, 65th round, Report No. 534: Some Characteristics of Urban Slums, 2008-09.

Fig. 13.5: Percentage of Non-Notified Slums Having Majority of Katcha Houses, 2008-09

Source of Drinking Water

The state level variations in the source of drinking water, both in notified and non-notified slums are given in Table 13.6. It is evident that a majority of the slums in all states, except Uttar Pradesh and Odisha, use tap as the main source of drinking water. In Uttar Pradesh, more than 75 per cent of notified and non-notified slums use tube well as the major source of drinking water and less than one-fourth of notified and non-notified slums use tap as a source of drinking water. Uttar Pradesh is closely followed by Odisha where 65 per cent of the notified slums use tube wells instead of tap as the main source of drinking water. Again in Madhya Pradesh 20 per cent of notified slums and 13 per cent of non-notified slums use wells as the source of drinking water. Among non-notified slums, Odisha has the highest proportion (19%) using wells for drinking water.

Table 13.6: Distribution of Slums in Different States by Major Source of Drinking Water, 2008-09

(In Percentage)

State/UT	*Notified slum*				*Non-notified slum*			
	Tap	*Tube-well*	*Well*	*Others*	*Tap*	*Tube-well*	*Well*	*Others*
Andhra Pradesh	80	12	1	9	68	32	0	0
Delhi	95	4	0	2	68	27	0	5
Gujarat	85	15	0	0	84	13	0	2.
Karnataka	88	12	0	0	89	1	0	10
Madhya Pradesh	79	1	20	0	73	4	13	10
Maharashtra	94	5	1	0	90	6	0	3
Odisha	35	65	0	0	56	25	19	0
Tamil Nadu	67	21	2	10	81	11	4	4
Uttar Pradesh	22	79	0	0	24	76	0	0
West Bengal	77	17	3	4	82	12	3	4
All India-2008-09	79	17	1	3	77	17	2	3
All India 2002	84	10	2	4	71	22	2	5

Source: NSSO, 65th round, Report No. 534: Some Characteristics of Urban Slums, 2008-2009.

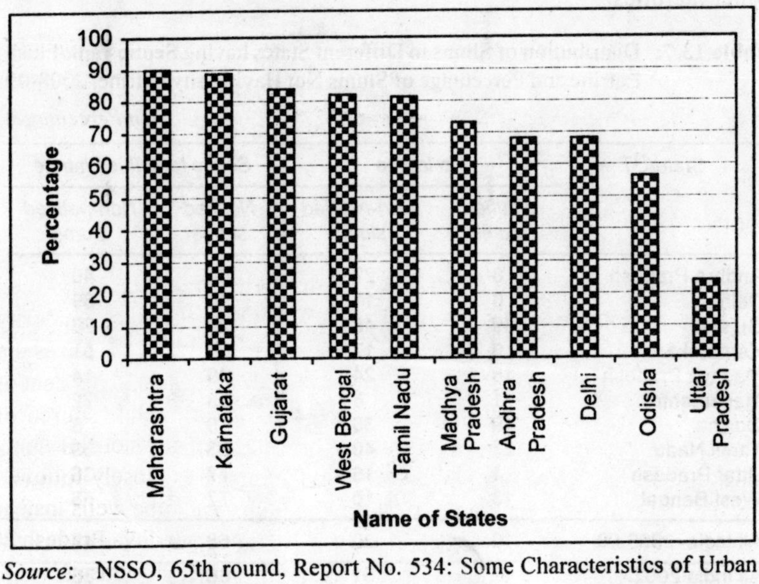

Source: NSSO, 65th round, Report No. 534: Some Characteristics of Urban Slums, 2008-09.

Fig. 13.6: Percentage of Slums Using Tap as Source of Drinking Water in Non-Notified Slum, 2008-09

Availability of Toilet Facility

The availability of toilet facility in slums is one of the most important indicators to assess the prevailing level of sanitation. The NSSO report points out that at all India level, the percentage of notified slums which do not have any toilet facility has decreased from 17 per cent in 2002 to 10 per cent in 2008-09 (Table 13.7). The non-notified slums have shown improvement in this regard where slums without any toilet facility rapidly declined from 51 per cent in 2002 to 20 per cent in 2008-09. However, there exists state level variations in the availability of toilet facilities in both notified and non-notified slums. Odisha has high percentage of notified and non-notified slums which do not have any toilet facility in 2008-09. It is 49 per cent and 36 per cent in notified and non-notified slums respectively. Odisha is followed by Gujarat where 39 per cent of notified slums and 48 per cent of non-notified slums do not have toilet facilities. In all the States the proportion of slums without toilet facilities is higher in case of non-notified slums than notified slums, except in Odisha and West Bengal. In case of Delhi and Karnataka (both 100%), Maharashtra and Uttar Pradesh (both 99%), nearly all notified slums have toilet facilities.

Table 13.7: Distribution of Slums in Different States having Septic Tank/Flush Latrine and Percentage of Slums Not Having any Latrine, 2008-09

(In Percentage)

State/UT	*No latrine*		*Septic tank/flush latrine*	
	Notified slums	*Non-notified slums*	*Notified slums*	*Non-notified slums*
Andhra Pradesh	8	27	64	40
Delhi	0	11	96	69
Gujarat	39	48	20	26
Karnataka	0	17	64	51
Madhya Pradesh	18	24	49	14
Maharashtra	1	6	83	72
Odisha	49	36	0	8
Tamil Nadu	27	40	63	39
Uttar Pradesh	1	16	77	38
West Bengal	13	10	77	56
All India–2008-09	10	20	68	47
All India 2002	17	51	66	35

Source: NSSO, 65th round, Report No. 534: Some Characteristics of Urban Slums, 2008-09.

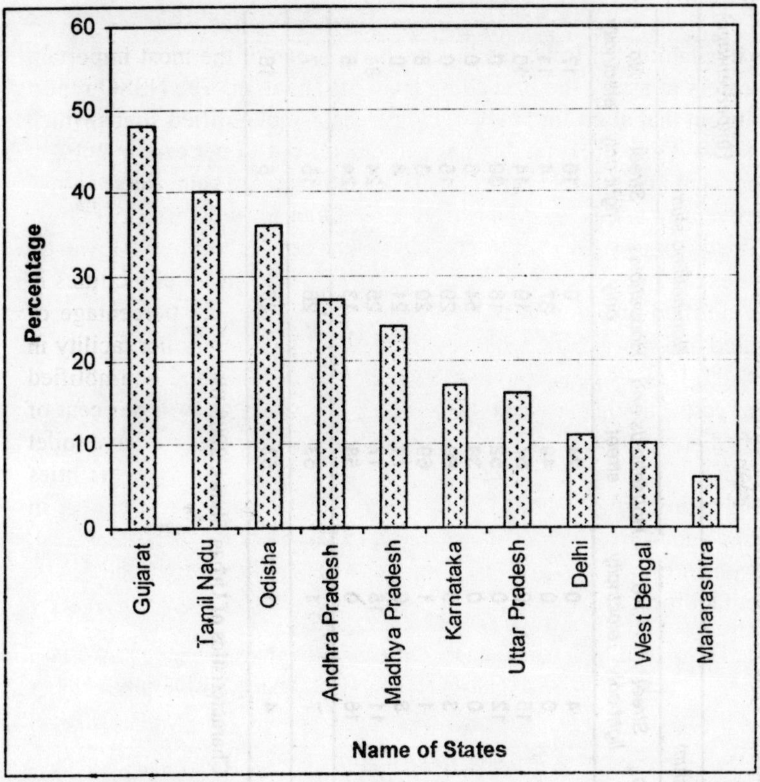

Source: NSSO, 65th round, Report No. 534: Some Characteristics of Urban Slums, 2008-09.

Fig. 13.7: Percentage of Households having no Latrine in Non-Notified Slums, 2008-09

As expected, the condition of non-notified slums is not satisfactory in terms of the availability of toilet facility. The proportion of non-notified slums without toilet facilities is the highest in Gujarat (48%) and the lowest in Maharashtra (6%). In Uttar Pradesh, 16 per cent of non-notified slums do not have toilet facility. In the absence of toilets and resultant open defecation, unhygienic conditions make living environment deplorable in many slums.

Availability of Electricity

NSSO has classified the use of electricity as household use, street light

Table 13.8: Distribution of Slums in Different States by Type of Availability of Electricity Connections, 2008-09

(*in percentage*)

State/UT	*Notified slum*				*Non-notified slum*			
	Households and street	*Households only*	*Street light only*	*No electricity*	*Households and street*	*Households only*	*Street light only*	*No electricity*
Andhra Pradesh	94	3	4	0	74	0	10	17
Delhi	94	6	0	0	49	37	4	11
Gujarat	15	70	15	0	57	19	14	10
Karnataka	89	0	12	0	52	18	30	0
Madhya Pradesh	73	27	0	0	39	54	8	0
Maharashtra	78	19	3	0	56	29	15	0
Odisha	32	66	1	1	69	20	3	8
Tamil Nadu	92	0	8	0	71	21	8	0
Uttar Pradesh	73	1	11	15	17	25	24	34
West Bengal	73	11	16	0	58	13	24	5
All India—2008-09	76	16	7	1	53	26	15	7
All India 2002	84	11	4	1	53	25	6	16

Source: NSSO, 65th round, Report No. 534: Some Characteristics of Urban Slums, 2008-09.

or both. Table 13.8 shows that at all India level only one per cent of notified slums and 7 per cent of non-notified slums do not have any electricity connections. Among all the states, the non-availability of electricity connections is the highest in Uttar Pradesh. It is 15 per cent and 34 per cent for notified and non-notified slums respectively.

Among notified slums, the availability of electricity is higher in Andhra Pradesh, Delhi and Tamil Nadu where more than 90 per cent slums have electricity both in the households as well as street lights. In case of non-notified slums, more than 70 per cent slums in Andhra Pradesh and Tamil Nadu have electricity both in households and as street lights. More than 10 per cent non-notified slums in Andhra Pradesh, Delhi and Gujarat do not have electricity at all.

Availability of Drainage and Sewerage Facilities

Table 13.9 shows the status of slums with reference to sewerage and drainage facilities. None of the notified slums of Uttar Pradesh and none of the non-notified slums of Andhra Pradesh, Odisha and Madhya Pradesh have underground sewerage facilities. However, the condition is much better in notified slums of Delhi where 88 per cent of the slums have underground sewerage facility. Next to Delhi, 60 per cent of notified slums of Karnataka have underground sewerage facility.

In terms of drainage facility, a very high proportion, i.e. 62 per cent of notified slums of Gujarat and nearly half of notified slums of Odisha do not have drainage facilities. In contrast, all notified slums of Delhi, Karnataka, Madhya Pradesh and Maharashtra have either underground or open drainage. In Uttar Pradesh, 90 per cent of notified slums have open drainage while nine per cent have no drainage at all. The condition of drainage is quite poor in case of non-notified slums. The drainage facility is, however, better in Maharashtra, where about 53 per cent of non-notified slums have underground drainage. None of the non-notified slums of Andhra Pradesh, Odisha, Tamil Nadu and Uttar Pradesh have underground drainage facilities. In Karnataka and Madhya Pradesh, more than 80 per cent of non-notified slums have open drainage. Drainage facility is also quite poor in the non-notified slums of Uttar Pradesh and Odisha where 54 and 49 per cent of non-notified slums do not have any drainage facilities respectively. Among all the states, Maharashtra has the highest proportion (91%) of non-notified slums with some type of drainage facility.

Table 13.9: Percentage of Slums in Different States having Underground Sewerage and Percentages of Slums with Different Types of Drainage, 2008-09

State/UT	*Underground sewerage*		*Types of drainage in*					
	Notified	*Non-notified*	*Notified slum*			*Non-notified slum*		
			Underground	Open	No drainage	Underground	Open	No drainage
Andhra Pradesh	24	0	16	77	7	0	63	37
Delhi	88	12	89	11	0	23	65	13
Gujarat	14	18	21	17	62	19	41	40
Karnataka	60	29	45	55	0	3	83	15
Madhya Pradesh	3	0	3	97	0	4	83	13
Maharashtra	41	33	61	39	0	53	38	9
Odisha	1	0	0	51	49	0	51	49
Tamil Nadu	30	8	35	42	24	0	67	33
Uttar Pradesh	0	12	2	90	9	0	46	54
West Bengal	43	29	39	51	9	25	56	20
All India-2008-09	33	19	39	51	10	24	54	23
All India 2002	30	15	25	60	15	13	43	44

Source: NSSO, 65th round, Report No 534: Some Characteristics of Urban Slums, 2008-09.

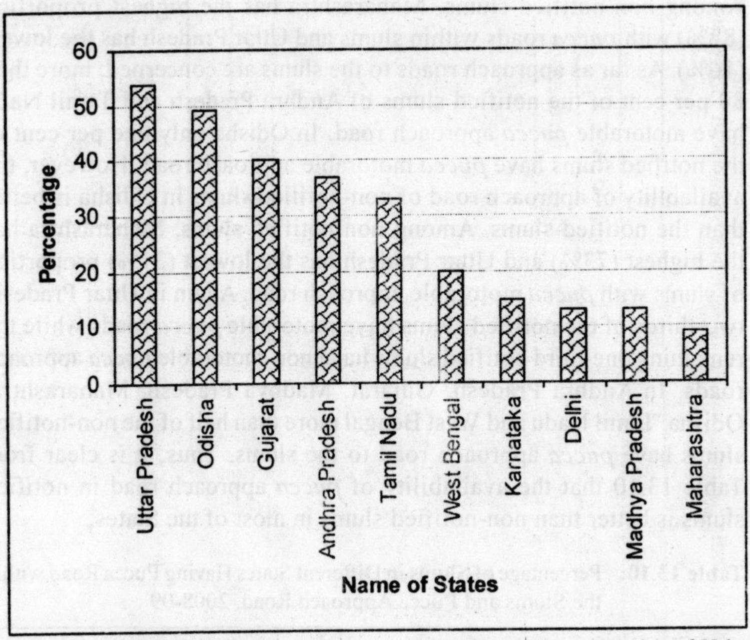

Source: NSSO, 65th round, Report No. 534: Some Characteristics of Urban Slums, 2008-09.

Fig. 13.8: Percentage of Households Having No Drainage in Non-Notified Slums, 2008-09

Availability of Roads within Slums and Approach Road

Type of road within slums and approach road determine the accessibility of different facilities in slums. The households that are situated near motorable road have better access to the amenities and facilities. If roads inside slums and the approach road to slums are not motorable, great difficulty is faced by the residents in availing certain basic amenities. At the all India level, about 92 per cent of notified slums have *pucca* approach road while the corresponding figure for non-notified slums is 76 per cent (Table 13.10). The state level variations in the availability of roads within slums, portray that more than 90 per cent notified slums of Delhi and Maharashtra have *pucca* roads within slums. Andhra Pradesh, Tamil Nadu and West Bengal also have higher proportion (88 per cent each) of notified slums with *pucca* roads, while none of the notified slums in Odisha have *pucca* roads within the slums.

Among non-notified slums, Maharashtra has the highest proportion (82%) with *pucca* roads within slums and Uttar Pradesh has the lowest (16%). As far as approach roads to the slums are concerned, more than 80 per cent of the notified slums of Andhra Pradesh and Tamil Nadu have motorable *pucca* approach road. In Odisha only one per cent of the notified slums have *pucca* motorable approach road. However, the availability of approach road of non-notified slums in Odisha is better than the notified slums. Among non-notified slums, Maharashtra has the highest (73%) and Uttar Pradesh has the lowest (31%) proportion of slums with *pucca* motorable approach road. Again in Uttar Pradesh, two-thirds of the notified slums have motorable *pucca* roads while the remaining one-third notified slums have non-motorable *pucca* approach roads. In Andhra Pradesh, Gujarat, Madhya Pradesh, Maharashtra, Odisha, Tamil Nadu and West Bengal more than half of the non-notified slums have *pucca* approach road to the slums. Thus, it is clear from Table 13.10 that the availability of *pucca* approach road in notified slums is better than non-notified slums in most of the States.

Table 13.10: Percentage of Slums in Different States Having Pucca Road within the Slums and Pucca Approach Road, 2008-09

State/UT	*Pucca road within slum*		*Pucca Approach Road to Slums*			
			Notified		*Non-Notified*	
	Notified slum	*Non-notified slum*	*Motorable*	*Non-motorable*	*Motorable*	*Non-motorable*
Andhra Pradesh	88	46	82	16	61	1
Delhi	91	43	63	37	49	24
Gujarat	19	31	72	2	53	19
Karnataka	40	59	58	23	38	25
Madhya Pradesh	52	62	49	3	55	23
Maharashtra	93	82	78	20	73	20
Odisha	0	52	1	18	57	10
Tamil Nadu	88	43	85	8	56	6
Uttar Pradesh	75	16	66	34	31	3
West Bengal	88	65	71	25	51	33
All India-2008-09	78	57	73	19	58	18
All India 2002	71	37	73	13	55	12

Source: NSSO, 65th round, Report No. 534: Some Characteristics of Urban Slums, 2008-09.

Waterlogging during Monsoons

Slums are generally located in environmentally fragile land. So they face the risk of waterlogging and flood particularly during the monsoon. Hence, during this time, the living environment is greatly affected in the slums. In comparison to 2002, the problem of waterlogging has increased in notified slums in 2008-09. It has increased from 36 per cent in 2002 to 41 per cent in 2008-09 (Table 13.11). However, the situation remained the same in case of non-notified slums where more than half (54%) of the slums continued to face the problem of waterlogging. In Odisha, as high as 99 per cent of the notified slums face the problem of waterlogging during monsoon. In Delhi an insignificant proportion (14%) of the notified slums face the problem of waterlogging during monsoon. However, in States such as Gujarat, Tamil Nadu, Uttar Pradesh and West Bengal more than half of the notified slums face the problem of waterlogging. In case of non-notified slums, Madhya Pradesh has the highest proportion (81%) and Karnataka has the lowest (28%) proportion of slums that face waterlogging during monsoons. In case of Uttar Pradesh, 60 per cent and 66 per cent of notified and non-notified slums face the problem of waterlogging particularly after rains. In comparison to notified slums, the non-notified slums of Andhra Pradesh, Delhi, Madhya Pradesh, Maharashtra and Uttar Pradesh have higher proportion of slums that face waterlogging particularly in the rainy season.

Table 13.11: Percentage Distribution of Slums in Different States Affected by Waterlogging during Monsoon, 2008-09

State/UT	*Notified slum*		*Non-notified slum*	
	Water logged	*Not water logged*	*Water logged*	*Not water logged*
Andhra Pradesh	18	82	43	57
Delhi	14	86	77	23
Gujarat	59	41	53	47
Karnataka	45	55	28	72
Madhya Pradesh	24	76	81	19
Maharashtra	37	63	58	42
Odisha	99	1	38	62
Tamil Nadu	57	43	56	44
Uttar Pradesh	60	40	66	34
West Bengal	52	48	40	60
All India-2008-09	41	59	54	46
All India 2002	36	63	54	46

Source: NSSO, 65th round, Report No. 534: Some Characteristics of Urban Slums, 2008-09.

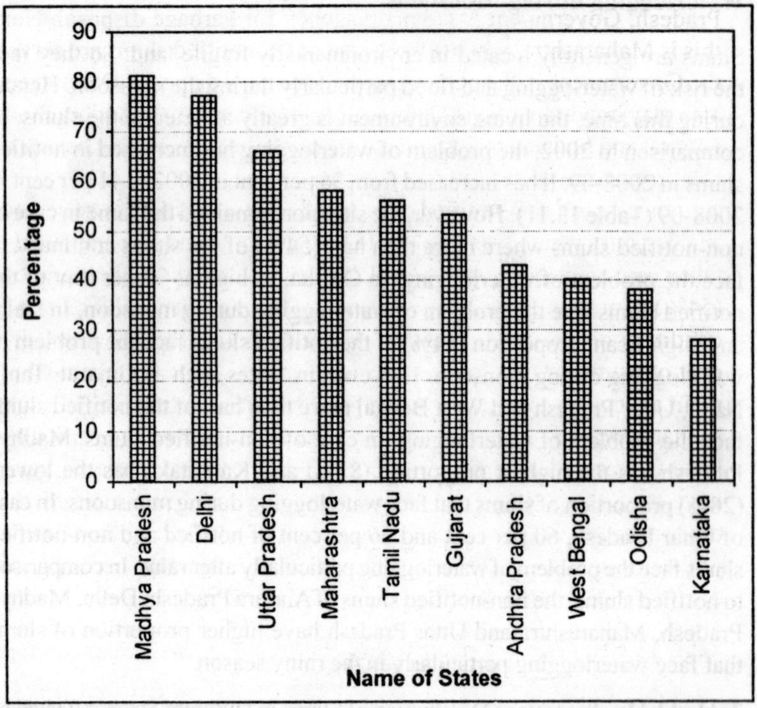

Source: NSSO, 65th round, Report No. 534: Some Characteristics of Urban Slums, 2008-09.

Fig. 13.9: Percentage of Households Facing Waterlogging Problem during Monsoon in Non-Notified Slums, 2008-08.

Garbage Disposal in Slums

Garbage disposal is important to keep the environment clean. If proper mechanism of garbage disposal is not available, the environment becomes dirty and unhygienic and the households living in these areas become vulnerable to various kinds of infectious diseases. Slums face the problem of garbage disposal due to lack of access to civic facilities. Table 13.12 shows the percentage distribution of slums in different states by type of agency disposing garbage. In Delhi and Karnataka, none of the notified slums lack garbage disposal arrangement. However, Gujarat has the highest proportion (62%) of notified slums without any garbage disposal arrangement. Next to Gujarat is Madhya Pradesh. As far as the agency of garbage disposal is concerned, in 94 per cent notified slums of Andhra

Pradesh, Government is the main agency for garbage disposal. Next to this is Maharashtra, where 88 per cent of the notified slums are served by the Government as the main agency for garbage disposal. Other agencies also play important role in Delhi and Madhya Pradesh. In Andhra Pradesh, Gujarat and Maharashtra agencies other than the Government have a small role in garbage collection.

In case of non-notified slums, the best condition is reflected by Maharashtra wherein as much as in 84 per cent slums garbage disposal is taken care of by the Government. Uttar Pradesh has the highest proportion (54%) of non-notified slums without any garbage disposal facilities. The condition of non-notified slums of Odisha is equally bad where 48 per cent of slums have no garbage disposal arrangement. Government is the main agency of garbage disposal in 84 per cent of non-notified slums of Maharashtra. In Uttar Pradesh, only 17 per cent of the non-notified slums have Government as the agency of garbage disposal while 54 per cent have no garbage disposal arrangement. In case of non-notified slums, other agencies play important role in Madhya Pradesh where 58 per cent of the non-notified slums other than the government take care of garbage disposal.

Table 13.12: Percentage Distribution of Slums in Different States by Type of Agency Disposing of Garbage, 2008-09

State/UT	*Percentage of notified slums with agency of garbage disposal*			*Percentage of non-notified slums with agency of garbage disposal*		
	Govt.	*Others*	*No arrange-ment*	*Govt.*	*Others*	*No arrange-ment*
Andhra Pradesh	94	4	3	41	19	40
Delhi	43	57	0	60	21	20
Gujarat	36	2	62	41	26	33
Karnataka	79	21	0	58	28	15
Madhya Pradesh	4	48	48	18	58	24
Maharashtra	88	9	3	84	10	6
Odisha	49	18	33	38	14	48
Tamil Nadu	72	16	12	39	22	39
Uttar Pradesh	46	38	16	17	29	54
West Bengal	79	10	11	57	21	22
All India-2008-09	75	15	10	55	22	23
All India 2002	79	5	16	42	12	46

Source: NSSO, 65th round, Report No. 534: Some Characteristics of Urban Slums, 2008-09.

Availability of Government Primary Schools and Government Hospitals

Education and health are the two basic requirements for human development. Availability and accessibility of schools and hospitals are important for the improvement of quality of life in the slums. The NSSO 65th round collected data on the availability of government schools and hospitals within one km of the slum. From Table 13.13 it is clear that while in West Bengal 100 per cent notified slums have government primary schools within one km of the slums; Andhra Pradesh, Delhi, Gujarat and Karnataka have more than 90 per cent notified slums with primary school within one km of the slums. However, the situation is quite worrisome in Odisha where more than half of the notified slums do not have primary school within one km. Among the non-notified slums, 100 per cent slums of Andhra Pradesh and Madhya Pradesh have government primary school within one km of the slums whereas in Delhi, Tamil Nadu and Uttar Pradesh more than 20 per cent slums do not have such facility. In Uttar Pradesh, 70 per cent of the notified slums and 78 per cent of the non-notified slums have schools within one km of the settlement. Thus, the situation in the non-notified slums of Uttar Pradesh is better than in the notified slums.

Table 13.13: Percentage of Slums in Different States by Distance from Nearest Government Primary School, 2008-09

State/UT	*Distance from nearest government primary school*					
	Notified slum		*Non-notified slum*		*All slums*	
	Within 1 km	*More than 1 km*	*Within 1 km*	*More than 1 km*	*Within 1 km*	*More than 1 km*
Andhra Pradesh	96	4	100	0	97	3
Delhi	96	5	74	26	81	19
Gujarat	96	4	92	8	94	6
Karnataka	94	6	90	10	92	8
Madhya Pradesh	63	37	100	0	87	13
Maharashtra	87	13	85	15	86	14
Odisha	50	51	82	19	71	29
Tamil Nadu	85	15	78	22	82	18
Uttar Pradesh	70	30	78	22	74	26
West Bengal	100	0	89	11	94	6
All India-2008-09	88	12	85	15	87	13

Source NSSO, 65th round, Report No. 534: Some Characteristics of Urban Slums, 2008-09.

In terms of availability of health facility, the situation is also unsatisfactory. In Delhi, 90 per cent of the notified slums have government health facility within one km of the slums (See Table 13.14). On the contrary, only 15 per cent of the notified slums in Madhya Pradesh have health facility within one km of the slums. In Karnataka, Andhra Pradesh, Tamil Nadu, Maharashtra and Uttar Pradesh more than half of the notified slums have government health facility within one km of the slums. In Odisha, more than two-third of the notified slums do not have government health facility within one km of the slums.

Table 13.14: Percentage of Slums in Different States by Distance from Nearest Government Hospitals 2008-09

State/UT	Distance from nearest government hospitals					
	Notified slum		Non-notified slum		All slums	
	Within 1 km	More than 1 km	Within 1 km	More than 1 km	Within 1 km	More than 1 km
Andhra Pradesh	59	41	31	69	52	48
Delhi	90	10	55	46	67	34
Gujarat	48	52	40	60	43	57
Karnataka	81	19	44	56	62	38
Madhya Pradesh	15	85	80	20	58	43
Maharashtra	55	45	53	47	54	46
Odisha	33	67	26	75	28	72
Tamil Nadu	66	34	17	83	42	58
Uttar Pradesh	53	47	14	86	36	64
West Bengal	45	55	29	71	37	63
All India-2008-09	54	46	42	58	48	52
All India 2002	48	52	46	54	47	53

Source: NSSO, 65th round, Report No. 534: Some Characteristics of Urban Slums, 2008-09.

In the non-notified slums of Madhya Pradesh 80 per cent slums have access to government health facility within one km range. Thus, the availability of health facility in the non-notified slums of Madhya Pradesh is far better than in the notified slums. In Delhi and Maharashtra more than half of the non-notified slums have government health facility within one km of the slums. The situation is worst in the non-notified slums of Uttar Pradesh where only 14 per cent slums have government health facility within the stated distance band. In Uttar Pradesh, Tamil Nadu and Odisha more than three-fourths of the non-notified slums do not have government health facility within one km of the slums. The availability of government health facility for all slums, reveal that the situation is the worst in Odisha and the best in Delhi. In Odisha, 72 per cent of all slums do not have this facility whereas in Delhi about 67 per cent of all slums have government health facility within one km of the slums.

Improvement of Facilities in Slums

The 65th round of NSSO also collected information about the improvement of facility in the slums during the last five years (since 2002). The information about the improvement of the facilities was based on the respondent's perceptions. Improvement of the facilities was perceived more by the dwellers in the notified slums than in the non-notified slums in 2008-09.

The improvement of road facility within the slums was perceptible in the notified slums of Delhi and West Bengal (Table 13.15). In the notified slums of Odisha, while there was no improvement in approach road in any of the slums, there was perceptible improvement in case of roads within slums in 32 per cent of the notified slums. In the non-notified slums of Uttar Pradesh, there has been no improvement in the roads within the slums. Again, very low proportion of the non-notified slums in Gujarat (6%) perceived improvement in road facility within slums.

Water supply has improved greatly in 80 per cent of the notified slums in Gujarat. The improvement in the water supply has been also observed in the notified slums of Odisha, Andhra Pradesh, Karnataka, Uttar Pradesh, West Bengal and Tamil Nadu. There has been perceived improvement in water supply in the notified slums of almost all the states. The non-notified slums, however, showed less improvement in water supply. In Tamil Nadu, 61 per cent of the non-notified slums showed improvement in water supply. The improvement in water supply was found to be the least in the non-notified slums of Delhi. In the non-notified slums of Uttar Pradesh, only 24 per cent slums registered improvement in water supply since 2002.

The maximum and minimum improvement in the provision of electricity in the notified slums has been observed in Odisha (81%) and Gujarat (12%) respectively. In the non-notified slums of Uttar Pradesh, a minimum of only 3 per cent of the slums registered improvement in electricity connections while none of the slums perceived improvement in the street lights facility. In the notified slums of Tamil Nadu, Karnataka and West Bengal improvement was perceived in the provision of street

Table 13.15: Percentage of Slums in Different States Reporting Improvement in Specific Facilities During Last 5 Years, 2008-09

	Road		*Water Supply*	*Electricity*	*Street Light*	*Garbage Disposal*	*Education*	*Medical*
	within	*approach*						
Notified Slum								
Andhra Pradesh	49	54	56	29	54	58	13	19
Delhi	73	67	32	33	39	28	52	34
Gujarat	29	12	80	12	26	29	19	1
Karnataka	61	68	57	52	60	64	31	8
Madhya Pradesh	61	24	22	24	24	4	20	21
Maharashtra	53	59	42	31	34	38	27	24
Odisha	32	0	66	81	49	49	49	1
Tamil Nadu	52	49	53	51	60	50	56	45
Uttar Pradesh	55	49	56	50	44	36	10	20
West Bengal	67	65	54	57	46	48	50	25
All India-2008-09	53	52	49	38	43	42	30	22
All India 2002	53	51	48	35	39	41	–	–
Non-notified								
Andhra Pradesh	37	36	32	33	40	19	27	1
Delhi	29	29	14	30	20	16	33	18
Gujarat	6	5	33	37	27	35	16	16
Karnataka	56	58	32	64	71	62	61	23
Madhya Pradesh	45	45	24	47	18	11	24	24
Maharashtra	35	37	25	22	22	33	20	14
Odisha	28	17	48	18	27	18	27	18
Tamil Nadu	23	30	61	32	59	29	21	21
Uttar Pradesh	0	20	24	3	0	1	23	3
West Bengal	36	32	32	25	29	22	25	10
All India 2008-09	30	31	30	29	29	26	25	15
All India 2002	21	40	32	27	23	15	–	–

Source: NSSO, 65th round, Report No. 534: Some Characteristics of Urban Slums, 2008-2009.

lights in more than half of the slums. However, Karnataka perceived the highest (71%) improvement in street light facility in the non-notified slums as compared to notified slums.

There was not much improvement in latrine facilities both in notified and non-notified slums. Among the notified slums, very small proportion of the slums in Madhya Pradesh and Odisha had registered improvement in latrine facility while a large proportion of the slums in Delhi (53%) also had registered improvement in latrine facility. Delhi was closely followed by West Bengal, where 45 per cent of the notified slums showed improvement in latrine facility. Among the non-notified slums, Karnataka registered the highest (46%) improvement while Uttar Pradesh (2%) and Madhya Pradesh (4%) registered the lowest improvement in latrine facility.

Most of the improvement in drainage facility was noticed in the notified slums of Karnataka and Andhra Pradesh, where more than half of the slums had registered improvement over the last five years. However, none of the notified slums of Odisha had registered improvement in drainage facility. Table 13.16 reveals that none of the notified slums of Odisha and the non-notified slums of Uttar Pradesh registered any improvement in drainage and sewerage facilities during the last five years. The improvement in sewerage facility was the highest in Karnataka, where 40 per cent of both notified and non-notified slums registered improvement.

The data on improvement in garbage shows that Karnataka had registered the highest (64%) and Madhya Pradesh had registered the lowest (4%) improvement among the notified slums. Among the non-notified slums, Karnataka again registered the highest (62%) improvement while Uttar Pradesh had registered the lowest improvement (1%).

In terms of educational facilities, Delhi, Tamil Nadu and West Bengal have registered more than 50 per cent improvement among the notified slums while Uttar Pradesh had registered only 10 per cent improvement in this category. In case of non-notified slums, the improvement in educational facility was the highest in Karnataka (61%) and the lowest in Gujarat (16%).

The maximum improvement in medical facility was observed in 45 per cent of the notified slums of Tamil Nadu, while the least improvement was observed in only one per cent of the notified slums each in Odisha and Gujarat during the last five years. During the same time, the non-notified slums showed a very low proportion of improvement in terms of health facility. While 24 per cent of the non-notified slums of Madhya Pradesh had registered improvement in healthcare facility, only one per cent of the non-notified slums of Andhra Pradesh had registered any improvement in healthcare facility. Uttar Pradesh too showed a low proportion (only 3%) improvement in healthcare facilities among the non-notified slums.

Table 13.16: Percentage of Slums in Different States Reporting Improvement in Specific Facilities during Last 5 years, 2008-09

Notified slum	*Latrine*	*Drainage*	*Sewerage*
Andhra Pradesh	34	50	21
Delhi	53	47	35
Gujarat	26	11	11
Karnataka	36	56	40
Madhya Pradesh	4	42	4
Maharashtra	37	39	23
Odisha	1	0	0
Tamil Nadu	35	35	25
Uttar Pradesh	25	36	25
West Bengal	45	43	37
All India-2008-09	34	40	23
All India 2002	50	47	24
Non-notified			
Andhra Pradesh	24	24	15
Delhi	18	16	11
Gujarat	12	25	12
Karnataka	46	50	40
Madhya Pradesh	4	22	0
Maharashtra	36	38	11
Odisha	15	13	8
Tamil Nadu	22	25	9
Uttar Pradesh	2	0	0
West Bengal	30	29	15
All India 2008-09	24	28	11
All India 2002	33	23	6

Source: NSSO, 65th round, Report No. 534: Some Characteristics of Urban Slums, 2008-09.

Health Conditions of Slum Population

Slum population is characterised by poor socio-economic characteristics and deplorable living conditions. They are vulnerable to many health problems due to low nutrition level and unhealthy living conditions. In order to analyse their health conditions, NFHS-3 in 2005-06 collected information on health and living conditions of the slum population. The present section provides the health characteristics of the slum population in eight million plus cities. These cities are Mumbai, Kolkata, Delhi, Chennai, Nagpur, Indore, Hyderabad and Meerut.

Contraceptive Prevalence Rate in Slums

The contraceptive prevalence rate is one of the important indicator of fertility control. It is defined as the percentage of currently married women who use any method of contraceptive. Table 13.17 exhibits that the contraceptive usage rate is higher among the non-slum than the slum population, except Chennai.

Table 13.17: Contraceptive Behaviour of Slum Population in Million Plus Cities, 2005-06

Name of the Million Plus Cities	*Any Contraceptive Method*		*Permanent Contraceptive*		*Not Using any Method*	
	Slum	*Non-Slum*	*Slum*	*Non-Slum*	*Slum*	*Non-Slum*
Delhi	56.6	69.4	28.3	21.6	43.4	30.6
Meerut	58.2	65.1	26.7	22.6	41.8	34.9
Kolkata	71.7	79.5	29.9	22.3	28.3	20.5
Indore	68.8	71.5	47.6	41.5	31.3	28.5
Mumbai	54.4	63.9	38.4	40.5	45.5	36.1
Nagpur	69.8	72.5	57.7	47.0	30.2	27.5
Hyderabad	64.6	66.7	56.8	56.0	35.4	33.3
Chennai	72.3	67.5	64.9	53.8	27.7	32.5

Source: NFHS-3, 2005-06.

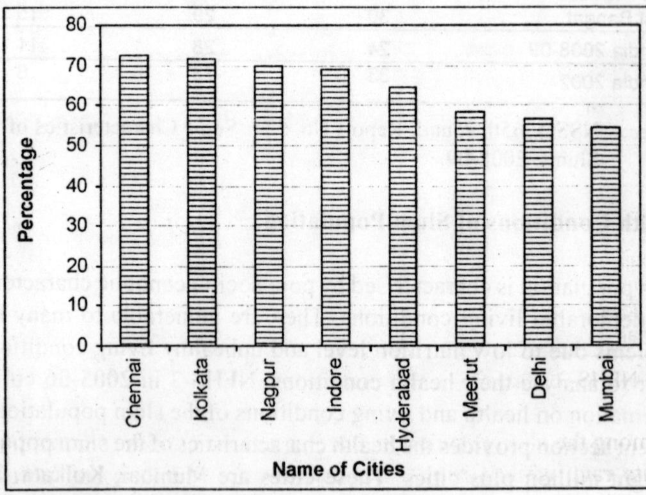

Source: NFHS-3, 2005-06.

Fig. 13.10: Percentage of Currently Married Women Using any Contraceptive in Slums of Million Plus Cities, 2005-06

Among the eight million plus cities, the percentage of married women who use any method of contraceptive is the highest in Chennai (72.3%) followed by Kolkata (71.7%). Mumbai has the lowest (54.4%) contraceptive prevalence rate followed by Meerut (58.2%) and Delhi (56.6%). In Indore and Nagpur, more than two-thirds of the women living in slums use any method of contraception.

Among the different contraceptive methods, the use of permanent method (terminal method) is more popular among the slum dwellers than the non-slum dwellers, except Mumbai. The use of permanent contraceptive method is the highest in Chennai (64.9%) and the lowest in Meerut (26.7%). Among the eight million plus cities, the percentage of currently married women not using any contraceptive method is the highest in Mumbai (45.5%) and the lowest in Chennai (27.7%).

Infant and Child Mortality

The child population living in slums is more vulnerable to various health problems. Table 13.18, exhibits that infant mortality is higher in slums than in non-slum areas. It is also evident that infant mortality in non-slum areas in Kolkata, Mumbai and Hyderabad is higher than in the slums.

Table 13.18: Infant and Child Mortality in Slums of Million Plus Cities in India, 2005-06

Name of the city	*Infant Mortality*		*Child Mortality*	
	Slum	*Non-Slum*	*Slum*	*Non-Slum*
Delhi	54.1	36.1	72.8	40.4
Meerut	71.2	55.0	86.1	69.4
Kolkata	33.4	47.0	44.7	51.6
Indore	56.4	38.4	64.4	48.2
Mumbai	24.9	40.1	32.7	43.6
Nagpur	48.4	39.2	59.5	43.6
Hyderabad	27.9	36.4	33.7	42.3
Chennai	38.0	24.2	46.3	31.5

Source: NFHS-3, 2005-06.

Among the slum population, Meerut has the highest (55.0%) infant mortality rate, while Chennai has the lowest (24.2%) infant mortality rate. Child mortality in the slums is the highest in Meerut (86.1%) and the lowest in Mumbai (32.7%).

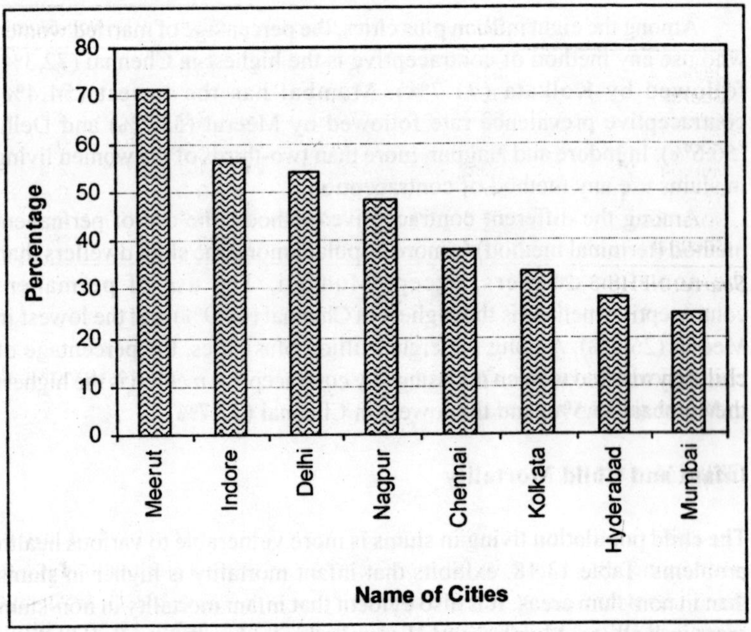

Source: NFHS-3, 2005-06.

Fig. 13.11: Infant Mortality Rate in Slums of Million Plus Cities, 2005-06

Immunisation

Vaccination given to children to protect them against vulnerable diseases is called immunisation. Under Universal Immunisation Programme (UIP), children are given vaccination for six diseases, namely polio, measles, whooping cough, tuberculosis, diphtheria and tetanus. Table 13.19 shows the vaccination status of children living in slums of eight million plus cities. It is evident that, except for Chennai and Mumbai, the vaccination coverage of children in non-slum areas is better than in slums. Among the eight million plus cities, the slums of Chennai have the highest percentage (89.2%) and the slums of Meerut have the lowest percentage (35.1%) of children who have received all basic vaccinations.

It is also evident that the percentage of children who have not received any vaccination is more in the slums than in the non-slum areas. In this case, the slums in Delhi have the highest proportion (13.5%) of children who have not received any vaccination, followed by Kolkata (7.0%). In Meerut and Chennai, all children have received some vaccination which may not be complete for the age. However, in Meerut the proportion of

Table 13.19: Vaccination of Children in Slums of Million Plus Cities, 2005-06

Name of the city	*All Basic Vaccines*		*No Vaccines*	
	Slum	*Non-Slum*	*Slum*	*Non-Slum*
Delhi	51.7	67.0	13.5	8.3
Meerut	35.1	50.0	0	1
Kolkata	63.4	70.8	7.0	4.2
Indore	73.4	76.4	2.5	0
Mumbai	69.8	68.7	1.3	2.5
Nagpur	57.3	62.4	6.7	0
Hyderabad	53.3	62.4	6.7	0
Chennai	89.2	74.1	0	0

Source: NFHS-3, 2005-0.

children who have received all basic vaccinations is the lowest among all the eight million plus cities.

Child Morbidity

The children living in slums are more vulnerable to diseases because of poor living environment. NFHS-3 collected data on the occurrence of three important diseases: Acute Respiratory Infection (ARI), fever and diarrhoea among children under five years of age. Table 13.20 exhibits the prevalence of ARI to be higher among the children living in slums than in non-slum areas, except in Delhi and Mumbai. The prevalence of ARI is highest in Meerut (11%) and the lowest in Hyderabad (1.1%). In Meerut, the difference in the prevalence of ARI among the slum and non-slum children is also very high, i.e. 11 per cent among slum and 5 per cent among non-slum children.

Table 13.20 also shows that among the eight million plus cities, the prevalence of ARI is lower than the prevalence of fever in the preceding two weeks of the survey. The proportion of children who had fever in the preceding two weeks of the survey is the highest in Meerut (23.7%) and the lowest in Hyderabad (7.1%). With the exception of Delhi, fever in the preceding two weeks of the survey is more prevalent among children living in slums than in non-slum areas.

The data on diarrhoea presented in Table 13.20 shows that the prevalence of diarrhoea in the preceding two weeks of the survey is higher than fever in the slums of Indore. However, in all the other six cities, the prevalence of diarrhoea is lower than that of fever. It is also more prevalent

Table 13.20: Prevalence of Disease among Children in Slums of Million Plus Cities, 2005-06

Name of the city	Acute Respiratory Infections (ARI)		Fever		Diarrhoea	
	Slum	Non-slum	Slum	Non-slum	Slum	Non-slum
Delhi	4.9	5.8	8.3	12.5	8.3	7.8
Meerut	11.0	4.6	23.7	17.2	13.3	13.6
Kolkata	7.6	4.8	14.4	11.7	5.6	4.3
Indore	3.8	0.3	11.5	10.3	14.7	11.8
Mumbai	1.6	1.7	9.8	6.0	6.8	4.7
Nagpur	9.1	6.8	19.7	17.6	10.7	6.8
Hyderabad	1.1	0.8	7.1	4.9	4.1	4.3
Chennai	6.8	3.8	15.8	11.1	6.1	3.1

Source: NFHS-3, 2005-06.

among the children living in slum than in non-slum areas. In Meerut, the prevalence of diarrhoea is high both among the children living in slums and in non-slum areas. Among the eight million plus cities, Indore has the highest (14.7%) and Hyderabad has the lowest (4.1%) proportion of children living in slums who suffered from diarrhoea. Indore is followed by Meerut where 13.3 per cent of the children living in slums suffered from diarrhoea.

Prevalence of Anaemia

From Table 13.21 it is evident that the prevalence of anaemia is the highest among children below five years of age compared to females and males. The prevalence of anaemia is higher among the children living in slums than in non-slum areas, except Kolkata. Anaemia is observed among children below five years of age and is the highest in the slums of Chennai (72.2%) and the lowest in Mumbai (50.2%). It is also a matter of serious concern that in the slums of Nagpur and Delhi more than 70 per cent children below five years of age suffer from anaemia. The prevalence of anaemia is also higher among females compared to males. In the slums of Kolkata, Hyderabad and Chennai more than 50 per cent of females suffer from anaemia.

Source of Healthcare

The accessibility of health facility in slums is important for the

Table 13.21: Prevalence of Anaemia among Slum Population in Million Plus Cities, 2005-06

Name of city	*Anaemia (Female)*		*Anaemia (Male)*		*Anaemia (Children)*	
	Slum	*Non-Slum*	*Slum*	*Non-Slum*	*Slum*	*Non-Slum*
Delhi	47.8	43.5	22.1	16.5	71.4	51.6
Meerut	40.1	48.4	12.3	14.3	68.8	66.7
Kolkata	52.3	56.8	17.2	22.0	54.7	55.3
Indore	42.9	39.8	11.7	10.4	59.8	53.4
Mumbai	46.0	47.9	10.9	13.2	50.2	46.9
Nagpur	48.7	51.8	16.6	15.8	71.1	58.4
Hyderabad	54.6	48.9	13.2	12.0	59.0	53.1
Chennai	50.5	51.4	14.7	12.8	72.2	54.9

Source: NFHS-3, 2005-06.

Table 13.22: Source of Healthcare Services in Slums of Million Plus Cities, 2005-06

Name of the city	*Public medical sector*		*Private medical sector*	
	Slum	*Non-slum*	*Slum*	*Non-slum*
Delhi	32.1	27.7	71.2	67.4
Meerut	9.4	8.3	89.6	91.4
Kolkata	28.1	17.4	71.1	82.0
Indore	19.5	13.4	83.4	78.6
Mumbai	25.4	20.9	74.4	77.9
Nagpur	22.1	17.6	77.5	81.5
Hyderabad	20.3	23.9	79.3	75.5
Chennai	47.2	31.1	51.9	68.2

Source: NFHS-3, 2005-06.

improvement of the health of slum population. The source of healthcare determines the affordability and quality of health services. NFHS-3 collected information on the source of healthcare by slum dwellers in eight million plus cities. Table 13.22 shows the distribution of households by sources of healthcare in slums and in non-slum areas. It is evident that in all the eight million plus cities, majority of the households, both in slums and in non-slum areas, visit private rather than public healthcare facility. Chennai and Meerut have the highest (47.2%) and the lowest (9.4%) proportion of slum households who depend upon public healthcare facilities respectively. More than 70 per cent of the slum population in all the eight million plus cities, except Chennai, go to private healthcare facility for treatment. The reasons for not using government healthcare

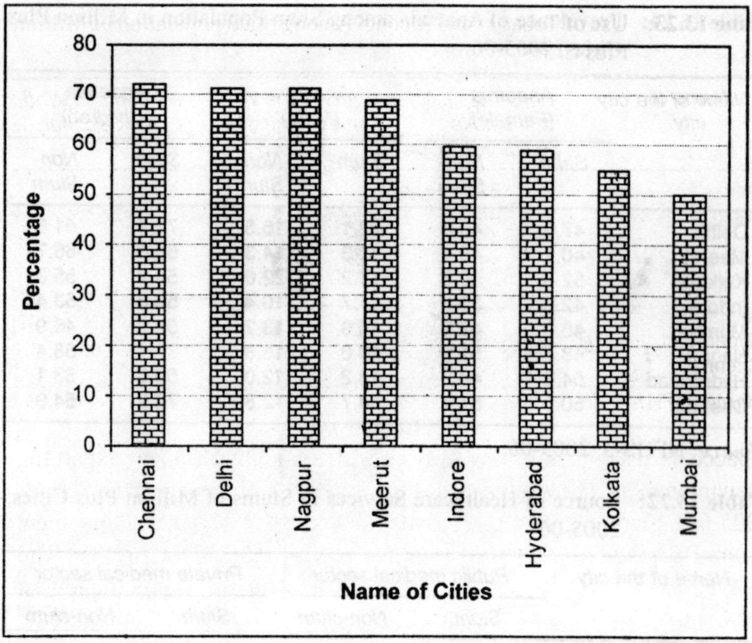

Source: NFHS-3, 2005-06.

Fig. 13.12: Prevalence of Anaemia among Children in Slums of Million Plus Cities, 2005-06

facility include poor quality of care, lack of healthcare facility in the vicinity, and longer waiting time to avail healthcare services. The slum households prefer private healthcare facility because of perceived better and convenient services than that provided by the government.

Tobacco and Alcohol Consumption

Tobacco consumption causes cancer, heart and lung diseases. Tobacco use among women can cause reproductive health problems such as difficulty to conceive. It also increases the risk of infertility and pregnancy complications such as stillbirth and infant death (NFHS-3, 2005-06). Frequent consumption of alcohol causes serious social and psychological problems.

Table 13.23 shows the proportion of slum population who smoke *bidi* or cigarette, use any kind of tobacco and drink alcohol. In India,

Table 13.23: Use of Tobacco and Alcohol Among Slum population of Million Plus Cities

Name of the city	*Percentage Who smoke Bidi or cigarettes*	*Percentage Who use any kind of tobacco*	*Percentage Who Drink alcohol*
Delhi	39.7	60.5	34.7
Meerut	40.0	48.8	27.1
Kolkata	45.5	76.0	33.0
Indore	31.4	65.5	29.0
Mumbai	24.3	54.6	36.7
Nagpur	20.5	72.6	40.0
Hyderabad	26.1	40.4	45.3
Chennai	35.9	47.8	49.7

Source: NFHS-3, 2005-06.

tobacco is used in different ways such as smoking *bidi* or cigarette, chewing *pan masala* or putting tobacco to the teeth or the gum (NFHS-3, 2005-06). Smoking among women is less prevalent than that among men. Among the eight million plus cities, the percentage of slum dwellers who smoke *bidi* or cigarette is the highest in Kolkata (45.5%) and the lowest in Nagpur (20.5%). Use of tobacco, other than smoking *bidi* or cigarette, is the highest in the slums of Kolkata (76%) and the lowest in the slums of Hyderabad (40.4%).

Alcoholism is prevalent in the slums of all eight million plus cities. In Chennai, 49.7 per cent of the slum population consumes alcohol. This is the highest among all the eight million plus cities. Nagpur and Hyderabad too have more than 40 per cent slum population who consume alcohol. Among the eight million plus cities, the consumption of alcohol is the lowest in the slums of Meerut (27.1%).

Conclusions

The present study portrays the socio-economic condition of the slum population based on the data given by the Census of India and large scale sample surveys like the NSSO and NFHS. The proportion of slum population in India is alarming. About a quarter of the total urban population of India lives in slums of which more than half of the population of Greater Mumbai lives in slums and are deprived of the basic amenities and facilities. Chennai and Coimbatore have about one-third Scheduled Caste population living in slums. Nagpur has the largest percentage of Scheduled Tribe population living in slums. These vulnerable groups need special attention through policy interventions so that their living conditions and improved. Kochi has the highest proportion of children living in slums. Child sex ratio exhibits a gross imbalance in all million plus cities in India. Educational attainment of slum population is poor in all the million plus cities. A marked male-female gap is also noticed in case of educational attainment in slums. The work participation rate in slums is high but most of the workforce is engaged in the informal sector. According to NSSO, although the living condition in slums improved in 2008-09 in comparison to 2002, but the situation did not improve drastically in case of the non-notified slums. As per NFHS-3, the health condition of the slum population is deplorable in comparison to the non-slum population, with a significant variation among the slums of the million plus cities.

REFERENCES

Agarwal and Sangar (2005): "Need for Dedicated Focus on Urban Health within National Rural Health Mission", *Indian Journal of Public Health*, Vol. XIX No. 3, July-September 2005.

Agrawal, *et al.* (2007): "Urbanisation, Urban Poverty and Health of the Urban Poor: Status, Challenges and the Way Forward", *Demography India*, Vol. 36, No. 1, (2007), pp. 121-134.

Agrawal, S. and Taneja (2005): "All Slums are not Equal: Child Health Condition among the Urban Poor", *Indian Paediatrics*, Vol. 42, March 17, 2005, 233-243.

Aikara, J. (1996): 'Inequality of Education Opportunities: The Case of Scheduled Caste in India', *Journal of Educational Planning and Administration*, Vol. X, No. 1, January 1996, pp. 1-14.

Ali, Sabir (2005): 'Phenomenon of squatting and the environment in JJ Colonies', *Social Change*, December 2005, Vol. 35, No. 4, 99-01.

Awasthi, S. & Pande (1997): 'Seasonal pattern of morbidities in preschool slum children in Lucknow, North India', *Indian Pediatrics*, Vol. 34, November 1997, pp. 987-993.

Basu, K. (2004): 'Urban poor women: coping with poverty and ill health in slums of Delhi', in M.P. Asthana and Sabir Ali edited '*Urban Poverty in India: Issues and Policies*', Uppal Publishing House, New Delhi, 2004, 202-217.

Chatterjee, Kanak (2003), "Squatter Settlements in Calcutta: A Socio-Economic Profile", *Geographical Review of India,* Vol. 65, No. 3, September 2003, 260-267.

Cox, E. John (1984): "Objective of The UN International year of Shelter for the Homeless (IYSH)-1987", *Ekistics* 307, July/August 1984, 284-288.

Davis, Mike (2004): 'Planet of Slums', *New Left Review*, Vol. 26, March April-2004, pp. 5-33.

Desai, Vandana (1994): 'Migration and Labour Characteristics of slum dwellers in Bombay', *Sociological Bulletin*, Vol. 43. No. 1, March 1994, pp. 51-77.

Dhar, V.K. (2004): 'Equity and access to basic services: Issues and options' in M.P. Asthana and Sabir Ali edited '*Urban Poverty in India: Issues and Policies*', Uppal Publishing, New Delhi, 2004, 268-79.

Dohmen, Thomas J. (2005): "Housing, Mobility and Unemployment", *Regional Science and Economics,* Vol. 35, No. 3, May 2005, 305-25.

Eswaramana *et al.* (2006): 'Socio-Economic characteristics of the slum households in Tirupati town', *Indian Journal of Regional Sciences*, Vol. xxxviii No. 1, 2006, 65-72.

Fernades, W. (1991): 'Urbanisation, Coping Mechanism and Slum Women's Status: A Quarterly Review of Social Trends', *Social Action*, 41(4), 382-98.

Geeta, S. and Swaminathan, Madhura (1996): 'Nutritional Status of Slum Children of Mumbai: A Socio-economic Survey', *Economic and Political Weekly*, April 6, 1996, 896-900.

Gurumukhi, K.T. (2004): 'Approach to Urban Poor Habitat', in M.P. Asthana and Sabir Ali edited '*Urban Poverty in India: Issues and Policies*', Uppal Publishing, New Delhi, 2004, 280-312.

Haider, Saraswati (1998): 'Delhi Slum in the Season of Fresh Promises', *Mainstream*, February 14, 1998, 27-30.

Hossain, N. and Kabeer, N. (2004): 'Achieving Universal Primary Education and Eliminating Gender Disparity', *Economic and Political Weekly,* September 4, 2004, pp. 4093-4099.

Jacobson, Mark (2007): 'All Cities in India are Loud', *National Geographic*, May 2007, 74-95.

Jana, M.M. (2003): "Basic Factors for Deteriorating the Quality of Life in India," *Geographical Review of India,* 65 (4), 2003 (December), 328-43.

Kaur, Ravindra (2004): 'Slum in a Planned City: Some Environmental Concerns (A Case Study of Chandigarh)', '*Man and Development*', June Vol. 26, No. 2, June 2004, pp. 57-74.

Khasnabis, R., and Tara Chatterjee (2007): 'Enrolling and Retaining Slum Children in formal Schools: A Field Survey in Eastern Slums of Kolkata', *Economic and Political Weekly,* Vol.-XIII, No. 22, June 2, 2007, 2091-2098.

Kundu, A. & Sarangi (2007): 'Migration, Employment Status and Poverty: An Analysis Across Urban Centres', *Economic and Political Weekly*, January 27, 2007, Vol.-XIII, No. 4, January 27. 2007, pp. 299-307.

Kundu, A. (1993): *In the Name of Urban Poor*, Sage Publications, New Delhi, 1993.

Kundu, A. (1996): 'Access of Urban Poor to Basic Services the changing policy perspective' in Kulwant Singh and Flarion Steinberg edited *Urban India in Crisis*, New Age International Limited, Publishers, New Delhi, 1996, 191-203.

Kundu, Nandita Kapadia and Kanitkar Tara (2002): 'Primary Health Care in Urban Slums', *Economic and Political Weekly*, December 21, 2002, 5086-5089.

Kundu, (1987): "Shelter and Living Environment in India: Issues, Policies and Perspective," *Man Power Journal*, Vol. 19(4): 57-70.

Kundu, A. *et al.*, (1999): "Regional Distribution of Infrastructure and Basic Amenities," *Economic and Political Weekly*, 34(28), 1999 (10-16 July), 1893-1906.

Maitra, A.K. (1999): 'Urban Slums a Challenge for 21st Century Cities: Environmental Concerns', *Spatio-Economic Development Record*, 6(6), November-December, 41-45.

Malhotra, Neena (2008): 'Environmental Challenges of Urbanisation in India', *Indian Journal of Economics*, 2008.

Mandal, D.B. (1998): "Slum in Socio-Economic and Urban Industrial Perspective," *Journal of Anthropological Survey of India*, Vol. 47, No. 2, June 1998, 43-52.

Mitra, Anup (1993): "Status of Basic Services in India's Cities" in Bidyut Mohanty edited '*Urbanisation in Developing Countries—Basic Services and Community Participation*', Institute of Social Sciences and Concept Publishing Company, New Delhi, 1993.

Mitra, Arup (1994): '*Urbanisation, Slums, Informal Sector Employment and Poverty: An Exploratory Study*', D.K. Publication and Distributor, Delhi.

Mitra, Arup (2010): 'Migration, Livelihood and Well-being: Evidence from Indian City Slum', *Urban Studies*, 47(7), 1371-1390, June 2010.

Mukherjee, S. (2000): 'Urban Decay in India: A Plea for Sustainable Planning', *National Geographical Journal of India*, Vol. 46, (1-4), March-December 2000, 171-182.

Nangia, Sudesh and Thorat Sukhdeo (2000): '*Slum in a Metropolis: The Living Environment*, Shipra Publications, New Delhi, 2000.

Panda, P. *et al.* (1993): 'Health Status of Under-Five in a Ludhiana Slum, Health and Population', *Perspective and Issues*, 16 (3&4), 1993, 133-141.

Patkar and Singh (2007): 'Urban Renewal: At Whose Cost', *Economic and Political Weekly*, XLII (11) 17-23, March 2007, pp. 926-928.

Praveen, Sharma (2004): "Population Growth and Sustainable Development," *Economic and Political Weekly*, 29(7), 2004 (14-20 February), 629-33.

Premi, Mahendra K. (2006): 'India's Urbanisation and its future implications', *Man and Development*: March 2006, 21-38.

Singh, J. (1986): "Population Pollution and the Urban Environment" in H.H. Singh *et al.*, (eds). *Geography and Environment, Issues and Challenges*, Concept Publishing Company, New Delhi, 1986.

Sandhu, Kiran (2007): 'Marginalisation of the Poor in the planning Process' in Sabir Ali edited *Poverty and Deprivation in Urban India*, Book Well Publication, New Delhi, 2007, pp. 71-84.

Sandhu, Kiran (2003): "Social Housing Project: Can they Alleviate Poverty," *Socio-Economic Development Record,* Vol. 10, No. 5, September-October 2003: 24-34.

Shivaramakrishnan, K.C., Kundu A., Singh, B.H. (2005): *Handbook of Urbanisation in India,* Oxford University Press, New Delhi, 2005.

Shivaramakrishnan, K.C. Das Gupta, Biblab and Buch, M.H. (1993): *Urbanisation in India: Basic Services and People's Participation,* Institute of Social Sciences and Concept Publishing Company, New Delhi, 1993.

Smith, Kirk R. (2000): 'National Burden of Disease in India from Indoor Air Pollution', *PNAS,* November 21, 2000, Vol. 97, No. 24, 13286-13293.

Sunder, Ramamani and A. Sharma (2002): 'Morbidity and Utilisation of Health Care Services: A Survey of Urban Poor on Delhi and Chennai', *Economic and Political Weekly,* Vol. 37, No. 47, November 23, 2002.

Tiwari, Piyush and Jyoti, Parikh (1999): "Effective Housing Demand in Mumbai (Bombay) Metropolitan Region," *Urban Studies,* Vol. 36, No. 10, 1999, 1783-1809.

Vijayunni (2000): 'Housing and Amenities in Urban India: An Interstate Analysis' in Amitabh Kundu (edited) *Enequality, Mobility and Urbanisation,* Manak Publications, New Delhi, 2000.

SECTION IV

Urban Environment and Health

14

Status of Environment and Infrastructure in Indian Metropolis

Anuradha Banerjee

Introduction: Impact of Urbanisation on Environmental Quality

Due to increased human activities in the urban centres arising out of industrialisation and commercialisation, there is a copious usage of water, energy and other raw materials, transforming them into goods and services and returning the wastes into the environment in the form of emissions and not usable solid wastes. Therefore, the cities are becoming the major contributors to local, regional and global environmental problems.

The extent of resource use by a city can be captured by its "ecological footprint". The term coined by the Canadian environmentalist William Rees, is concerned with defining the amount of land that is required to supply a city with food and natural resources as well as the area of growing vegetation required to absorb its carbon dioxide output (Rees, 1992). Rees described this as the "carrying capacity" of local and distant ecosystems—an approach that was later adopted by Herbert Girardet who was influential in drawing up the British proposals for Habitat II (Istanbul, Turkey, 1996).

He argued that while cities occupy only 2 per cent of the world's land surface, they consume as much as 75 per cent of the world's resources. In presenting his argument Girardet used London as an example to show how its "footprint" extends over more than 125 times the city's actual area. One should, however, compare the ecological footprint of cities with that of alternatives. Possibly, it is not urbanisation *per se* that stresses the environment, but the level of living and affluence, and if combined with stupendous population growth, then the impact could be disastrous.

It has been observed that the large cities of poorer countries are growing at a much faster rate than similar cities in the developed world, and India forms no exception to it. Such a heavy and uncontrolled growth places a heavy burden on the environment and infrastructure. Resource shortages are intensified by ever increasing demands for services that need to be supplied at a rate which often exceeds the country's economic growth. The current status of environment and infrastructure of the Indian cities raises certain questions in our minds.

- How rapidly are we urbanising?
- What is the impact of rapid urbanisation on environment, infrastructure and society at large?
- What should we do to make our urban system sustainable?

In order to address the first question, we should look into the picture of urbanisation in India.

Pattern and Trend of Urbanisation in India: 1991-2001

The pattern and trend of urban population and the number of towns in India during 1901 to 2001 (Table 14.1), shows that the total urban population has increased more than ten times from 26 million in 1901 to 285 million in 2001; whereas total population has increased less than five times from 238 million to 1027 million during the same period. A continuous increase has been noticed in the percentage of urban population

Table 14.1: Pattern and Trend of Urbanisation in India

Census Years	*Number of Towns*	*Urban Population (millions)*	*Percentage Urban*	*Annual Exponential Growth Rate*	*Rate of Urbanisaton*
1901	1916	25.9	10.8	—	—
1911	1908	25.9	10.3	0.0	–0.46
1921	2048	28.1	11.2	0.8	0.87
1931	2220	33.5	12.0	1.7	0.71
1941	2422	44.2	13.8	2.8	1.50
1951	3060	62.4	17.3	3.5	2.54
1961	2700	78.9	18.0	2.3	0.40
1971	3126	109.1	19.9	3.2	1.06
1981	4029	159.5	23.3	3.8	1.72
1991	4689	217.6	25.7	3.1	1.02
2001	5161	284.5	27.8	2.7	0.82

Source: Census of India, 1991, 2001.

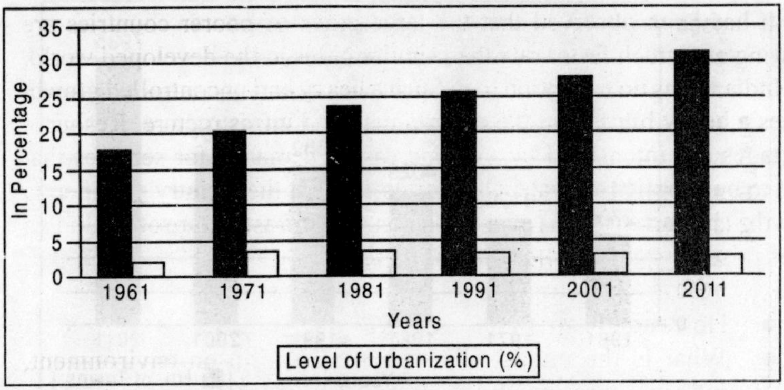

Fig. 14.1: Temporal Pattern of Urbanisation

from 11 per cent in 1901 to 17 per cent in 1951 to further 28 per cent in 2001. In the same fashion, the number of towns has also increased from 1916 in 1901 to 2422 in 1951 and then to 5161 in 2001. This reveals the process of rapid urbanisation in India.

Growth in the Number of Million Plus Cities in India: 1991-2001

Table 14.2 shows that the growth in the number and population of the million plus cities in India during 1991 to 2001. There was only one million plus city (Kolkata), in 1901 in India that had increased to 35 in

Table 14.2: Pattern and Trend of Urbanisation in India

Census Years	*Number of Towns*	*Urban Population (millions)*	*Per cent Urban*	*Annual Exponential Growth Rate*
1901	1916	25.9	10.8	—
1911	1908	25.9	10.3	0
1921	2048	28.1	11.2	0.8
1931	2220	33.5	12.0	1.7
1941	2422	44.2	13.8	2.8
1951	3060	62.4	17.3	3.5
1961	2700	78.9	18.0	2.3
1971	3126	109.1	19.9	3.2
1981	4029	159.5	23.3	3.8
1991	4689	217.6	25.7	3.1
2001	5161	284.5	27.8	2.7
2011	7935	377	31.1	2.7

Source: Census of India, 2001, 2011.

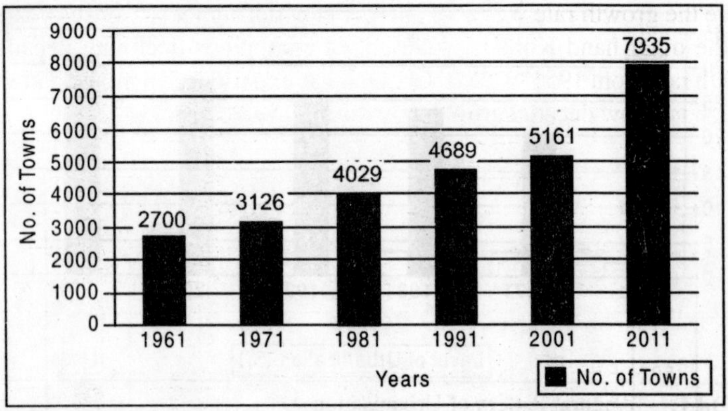

Fig. 14.2: Growth of Towns (1960-2011)

2001. The total population had also increased in the million plus cities from 1.51 million in 1901 to 107.88 million in 2001; showing almost a fifty fold increase. The percentage decadal growth rate in the total population of million plus cities was noticed to be the highest (121%) during 1941 to 1951, which may be attributable to partition of the country. The percentage of total population living in the million plus cities had also shown a considerable increase over the years.

Population Growth Rate in the Four Leading Metropolises in India

More than thirty-fold increase has been noticed in the population of Delhi in 100 years, from 0.41 million in 1901 to 12.8 million in 2001, whereas, there has been twenty-fold increase in Mumbai's population, from 0.8 million to 16.4 million from 1901 to 2001. However, Chennai has experienced more than ten-fold increase (0.59 million to 6.4 million) in its total population during the last 100 years, whereas, Kolkata has experienced the lowest increase (less than nine-fold) in its total population among the metropolitan cities in the last ten decades.

The maximum growth rate has been noticed during 1941 to 1951, highest in Delhi (90%), followed by Mumbai (76%), and Chennai (66%). However, Kolkata has recorded a comparative lower growth rate (29%) during the same period. This was the era of partition in India, when a huge influx of migration has taken place in big cities. After independence, Delhi experienced the highest decadal growth rate (close to 50%), in its total population in all the Censuses (1951to 2001), followed by Mumbai where the growth rate was about 40 per cent during those Census years. On the other hand Kolkata experienced continuous declining decadal growth rate from 1951 to 2001. Chennai has experienced a mixed pattern of high and low decadal growth rate during last 50 years.

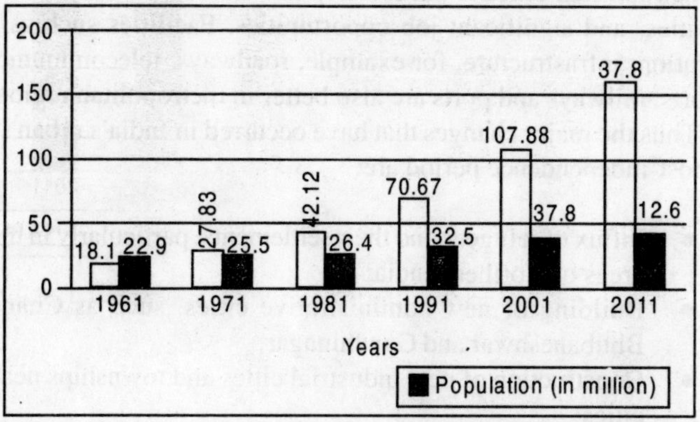

Fig 14.3: Population of Million Plus Cities in India, 1961-2011

Table 14.3: Population Growth of Million Plus Cities: 1901-2001

Census Years	*Number of Million Plus Cities*	*Population in Millon*	*Per cent Increase*	*Population of Million Cities as Per cent of India's*	
				Total population in Million	*Urban Population in Million*
1901	1	1.51	—	0.6	5.8
1911	2	2.76	82.8	1.1	10.7
1921	2	3.13	13.4	1.3	11.1
1931	2	3.41	8.9	1.2	10.2
1941	2	5.31	5.7	1.7	12.0
1951	5	11.75	21.3	3.3	18.8
1961	7	18.10	54.0	4.1	22.9
1971	9	27.83	53.8	5.1	25.5
1981	12	42.12	51.3	5.2	26.4
1991	23	70.67	67.8	8.4	32.5
2001	35	107.88	52.8	10.5	37.8

Source: Computed from Censuses of India.

Initially, Kolkata was the most populous city of India till 1981, but Mumbai surpassed it in 1991 Census. Again, Delhi is expected to cross the population of Kolkata in the next Census of 2011, if both cities will experience same pattern of growth rate. Thus, it is evident from Table 14.4, that Mumbai and Delhi metropoliser are experiencing profuse growth in their population.

Thus the sharp increase in population in urban India, particularly in the metropolitan cities is particularly due to the scope for commercial activities, and significant job opportunities. Facilities such as health, education, infrastructure, for example, roadways, telecommunications, airports, railways and ports are also better in metropolitan regions.

Thus the major changes that have occurred in India's urban scene in the post-independence period are:

- Influx of refugees and their settlements, particularly in the urban areas of Northern India;
- Building of new administrative cities, such as Chandigarh, Bhubaneshwar and Gandhinagar;
- Construction of new industrial cities and townships near major cities;
- Rapid growth of metros;
- Stagnation and in some cases, decline of small towns;
- Massive increase in squatters and proliferation of slums in metro cities and the dramatic changes in the urban-rural fringes.
- Deteriorating urban environment—both physical and social; and finally
- Tremendous pressure on urban infrastructure.

Infact, the positive role of urbanisation in India, has been often overshadowed by the deterioration in the environment and quality of life

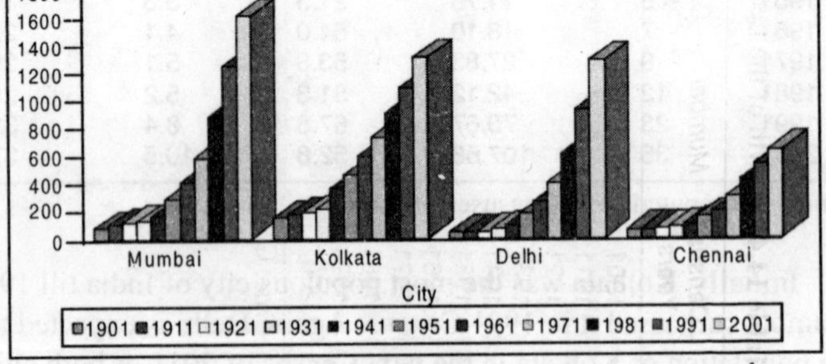

Fig. 14.4: Population Growth of Metropolitan Cities

Table 14.4: Growth of the Leading Metropolitan Cities of India, 1901–2001

Census Years	*Mumbai*	*Growth Rate*	*Kolkata*	*Growth Rate*	*Delhi*	*Growth Rate*	*Chennai*	*Growth Rate*	*India*	*Growth Rate*
1901	81.3	—	151.0	—	40.6	—	59.4	—	2384	—
1911	101.8	25.2	174.5	15.6	41.4	2.0	60.4	1.7	2521	5.7
1921	124.5	22.3	188.5	8.0	48.8	17.9	62.8	4.0	2513	–0.3
1931	126.8	1.8	213.9	13.5	63.6	30.3	77.5	23.4	2786	11.0
1941	168.6	33.0	362.1	69.3	91.8	44.3	92.1	18.8	3187	14.2
1951	296.7	76.0	467.0	29.0	174.4	90.0	153.1	66.2	3611	13.3
1961	415.2	39.9	598.4	28.1	265.9	52.5	192.4	25.7	4392	21.6
1971	597.1	43.8	742.0	24.0	406.6	52.9	305.8	58.9	5482	24.8
1981	891.7	49.3	919.4	23.9	622.0	53.0	428.9	40.3	6833	24.7
1991	1259.6	41.3	1102.2	19.9	942.1	51.5	542.2	26.4	8463	23.8
2001	1636.8	29.9	1321.7	19.9	1297.1	37.7	642.5	18.5	10270	21.4

Source: Computed from Census of India.

in the cities, often caused by the widening gap between demand and supply of services and infrastructure.

Physical Environment

(A) Air Quality

India's urban areas represent complex problems regarding the physical environment. In particular, the quality of the ambient air in these areas have been deteriorating rapidly over the past few decades, due to vehicular, thermal and industrial and domestic emissions. Motor vehicles, which are the main source of vehicular pollution, have been constantly increasing in number particularly since the 1990s (Table 14.4). Within 10 years from 1990 to 2000 there has been almost a three-fold increase in the number of motor vehicles in India. On an average a 10 per cent increase has been found in each year, which is a serious matter regarding air pollution.

Specific case studies reveal that the number of vehicles in Delhi has increased from 1813 thousand in 1991 to 2630 thousand in 1996, a one and half times increase in 6 years followed by Chennai. This is because a lack of suburban trains in Delhi, that also has a huge number of commuting population. On the other hand, increase in the number of vehicles was quite less in Mumbai and Kolkata compared to Delhi and Chennai.

Table 14.5: Growth in the Number of Motor Vehicles in India, 1999-2000

Years	*Number of Vehicles (in thousands)*	*Per cent Increase*
1990	19152	—
1991	21374	11.6
1992	23507	10.0
1993	25505	8.5
1994	27660	8.4
1995	30287	9.5
1996	33850	11.8
1997	37231	10.0
1998	43159	15.9
1999	48240	11.8
2000	53100	10.1

Source: Centre for Pollution Control Board, Ministry of Environment and Forests, Government of India, New Delhi, 2000.

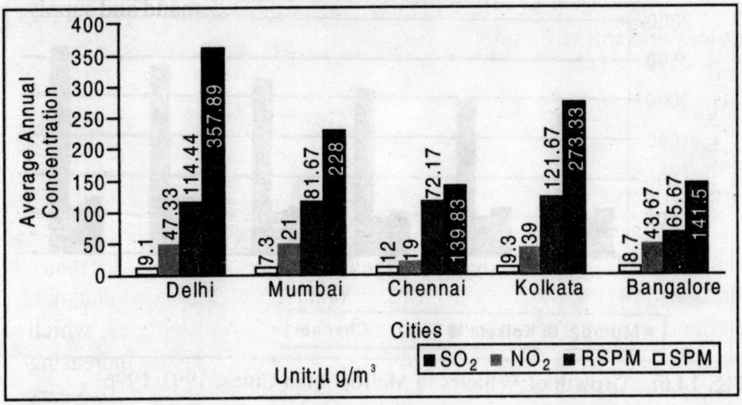

Source: CPCB, 2005.

Fig. 14.5: Air Quality Status, 2005

Moreover, overcongestion tends to degrade roads, decrease fuel efficiency, and exacerbates certain types of air pollution. In the industrial areas, fossil fuels, particularly coal, is one of the major sources of energy and contribute to air pollution in the form of Suspended Particulates. While large industries are willing to control and monitoring air pollution but small industries lack information, technical expertise to check pollution. Trend analysis predicts a considerable rise in pollutant emissions from thermal power as well as industrial sources over the next two decades. The urban households generally use LPG while the households of lower income use coal, kerosene and bio-mass fuels, which are highly polluting and due to poor ventilation it deteriorates indoor air quality and health.

Table 14.6: Growth of Vehicles in Metropolitan Cities: 1991-1996 as on 31st March (In '000s)

Metropolitan Cities	*1991*	*1992*	*1993*	*1994*	*1995*	*1996*
Mumbai	629	647	546	608	667	724
Kolkata	475	497	517	545	561	588
Delhi	1813	1963	2097	2239	2432	2630
Chennai	544	604	641	689	768	812

Source: Transport Research Wing, Motor Transport Statistics of India, 1997, Ministry of Surface Transport, GOI, New Delhi.

Vehicular Pollution

Among all the vehicular emission loads, the amount of carbon monoxide

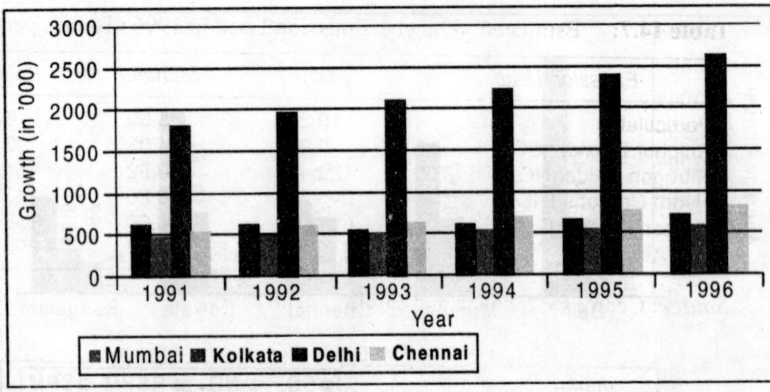

Fig. 14.6: Growth of Vehicles in Metropolitan Cities: 1991-1996

(CO) was found highest, followed by Hydro Carbon and Nitrogen Oxide in all the three metropolitan cities of Delhi, Kolkata and Chennai. The total amount of all types of vehicular emission load was found highest in the atmosphere of Delhi (1046 tonnes per day), followed by Mumbai (660 tonnes per day), and Kolkata (294 tonnes per day). Carbon Monoxide contributed to more than 65 per cent in all the three metro cities, which is 651 tonnes per day in Delhi, followed by Mumbai (497 tonnes per day) and Kolkata (188 tonnes per day). The amount of Suspended Particulate Matter (SPM) in the air is highest in Delhi (10.3 tonnes per day), followed by Mumbai (5.6 tonnes per day), and Kolkata (3.3 tonnes per day). Since, the number of registered vehicles in Delhi is the highest, the vehicular emission load also substantiates it, as all the elements were found highest in Delhi. The components of the vehicular emission load affect the health of the people and deteriorate the quality of life of the residents of metro cities.

State of Ambient Air Quality and Air Pollution in Urban Areas

The most common air pollutants in the urban areas of India are Sulphur Dioxide (SO_2), Nitrogen Dioxides (NO_2) and Suspended Particulate Matter (SPM), (Table 14.7). In general it has been observed that though the presence of certain pollutants like SPM has been declining in most of the cities of India, but there exists wide differences across different cities.

Table 14.7: Estimated Vehicular Emission Load in 1996 (Tonnes per Day)

Emission Load	*Delhi*	*Mumbai*	*Kolkata*
Particulates	10.30	5.59	3.25
Sulphur Dioxide (SO_2)	8.96	4.03	3.65
Nitrogen Oxide (NO_x)	126.46	70.82	54.69
Hydro Carbons (HC)	249.57	108.20	43.88
Carbon Monoxide (CO)	651.01	496.60	188.24
TOTAL	1046.30	659.57	293.71

Source: Centre for Science and Environment 1996.

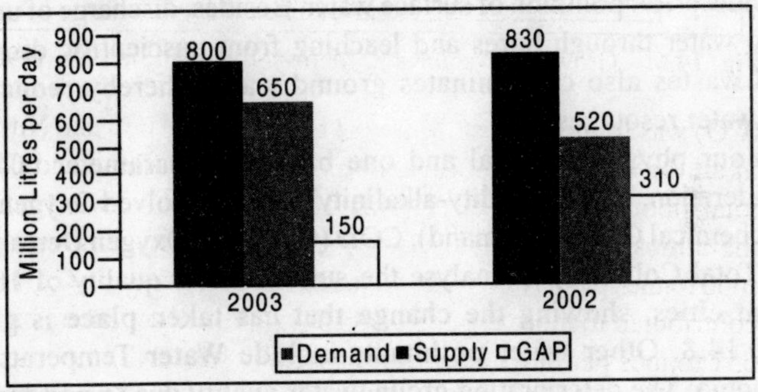

Source: Delhi Jal Board

Fig. 14.7: Demand and Supply Gap in Delhi

In fact, Delhi shows an increasing trend, from 390 mg/cµ.m (milligram/cubic metre), to 410 mg/cu.m from 1991 to 1995. Again the concentration of SO_2 has decreased in Mumbai but it had registered a decline in Kolkata.

(B) Water Quality

Pollution, Collection and Treatment

Like air pollution, water pollution is also one of the major problems in the urban areas of India, resulting out of increased human activities and interference with the natural ecosystems. The major water resources of India including both surface and underground resources are not only diminishing, but are increasingly getting polluted due to human interventions. Wasteful consumption and neglect of conservation of water resources have resulted in the present situation. With rapid urbanisation and industralisation, huge quantities of waste water enter rivers. At the same time, the available per capita water resources have declined due to falling groundwater tables associated with indiscriminate use of water.

In urban areas, water, to a large extent is treated by municipal authorities before supplying to residential areas. However, most Indian rivers today fall short of Central Pollution Control Board standards due to excessive pollution by untreated sewage, and domestic and industrial wastes. Increase in urban population and changing lifestyles have also increased the domestic need for water. Intense competition among users—industry and domestic sectors—is driving the groundwater table lower.

The quality of groundwater is getting severely affected because of the widespread pollution of surface water. Besides, discharge of untreated waste water through bores and leaching from unscientific disposal of solid wastes also contaminates ground water, thereby reducing the freshwater resources.

Four physio-chemical and one biological parameter taken into consideration, i.e. *p*H (acidity-alkalinity), DO (Dissolved Oxygen), BOD (Biochemical Oxygen Demand), COD (Chemical Oxygen Demand), and TC (Total Coliform) to analyse the surface water quality of 16 major Indian cities, showing the change that has taken place is given in Table 14.8. Other water pollutants include Water Temperature and Ammonia. The deteriorating groundwater quality due to pollution from pesticide leaching and toxic metal leaching from the industrial effluents have serious health effects on population.

Table 14.8: Ambient Air Quality in four Metropolises of India: 1991-1995

Metropolitan Cities	*Pollutants (mg/cu.m)*	*1991*	*1992*	*1993*	*1994*	*1995*
Mumbai	SO_2	28	18	22	33	31
	NO_2	29	33	35	34	26
	SPM	244	238	232	231	209
Kolkata	SO_2	63	36	40	48	35
	NO_2	40	27	40	34	29
	SPM	391	307	460	375	354
Delhi	SO_2	20	18	19	25	23
	NO_2	34	30	30	43	47
	SPM	390	364	424	446	410
Chennai	SO_2	14	7	14	16	21
	NO_2	1	3	0	0	0
	SPM	130	74	100	128	127

Source: Anon 1997, Ambient Air Quality Status and Statistics, 1995, NAAQMS/8 1996, Central Pollution Control Board, Delhi.

The volume of domestic waste water generation is highest in the metropolitan city of Mumbai, which is 2228.1 ml/d (million litres/day), followed by Kolkata (1383 ml/d), and Delhi (1270 ml/d) and the lowest is in Chennai only 276 ml/d. The generation of industrial waste water is also highest in Mumbai. Again, looking at the percentage of waste water collection from the four leading metropolitan cities, Chennai and Mumbai performs better than Delhi and Kolkata. Regarding the treatment of the collected waste water in all the metro cities, the water is disposed only after primary and secondary treatment. Again, the collected waste water in Mumbai is mainly disposed in the Arabian Sea, and in Kolkata some amount is disposed in the Hugli river and the rest is used in fish farms. However, in Delhi and Chennai, the waste water is mainly used for agricultural works and the remaining water is disposed in the Yamuna River in Delhi and in the Bay of Bengal in Chennai.

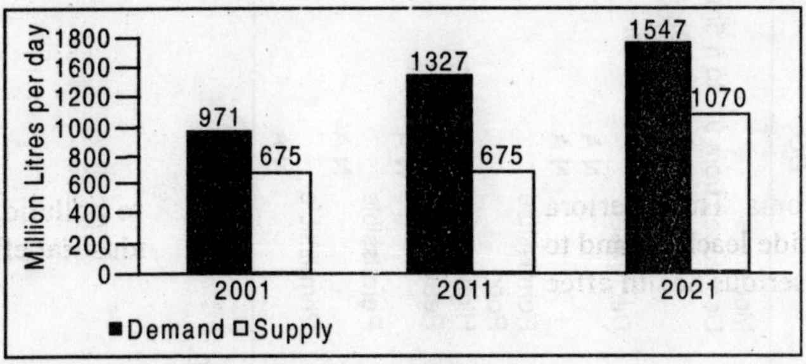

Fig. 14.8: Demand and Supply Status of Chennai

(C) Solid Waste Generation

The problem of municipal solid waste management has acquired alarming dimensions in our country especially over the last decade. Previously, waste management was hardly considered as an issue of concern as the waste could be easily disposed in an environmentally safe manner. However, with time, due to changing lifestyles of people coupled with rapid urbanisation, and industrialisation the waste has not only increased but have become difficult to be managed.

Urban growth, a concomitant of inadequate infrastructural support, is turning India's major cities into waste dumps. The daily per capita generation of MSW (Municipal Solid Waste) in India ranges from about 100g in small towns to 500g in large cities. An estimated 48 million tonnes of Municipal Solid Waste was produced in 1997, e.g. the population of

Table 14.9: Changing Pattern of Water Quality (1990–2000)

Cities	Water Quality	pH	DO	BOD	COD	Total Coliform
1. Kolkata	Moderately good	Moderate	Moderate	Moderate	High	High
2. Delhi	Deteriorated	High	Decreased from 9.1 to 5.5mg/l	High	High	High
3. Hyderabad	Worsened	Worsened	N.A.	Worsened	Worsened	N.A.
4. Ahmedabad	Deteriorated	N.A.	N.A.	Decreased	Decreased	N.A
5. Pune	Moderately good	N.A.	Decreased	High	High	N.A.
6. Kanpur	Improved	N.A.	N.A.	N.A.	N.A.	N.A.
7. Lucknow	Good	N.A.	N.A.	N.A.	N.A.	N.A.
8. Patna	No Variation	Permissible	Permissible	Permissible	Permissible	High
9. Ludhiana	Good	Improved	Poor	Improved	Improved	Improved
10. Agra	Deteriorated	High	High	High	High	permissible
11. Nasik	Good	Permissible	Permissible	High	Permissible	Permissible
12. Jamshedpur	Moderately good	N.A.	N.A.	N.A.	N.A.	N.A.
13. Asansol	Deteriorated	Permissible	Permissible	Permissible	High	High
14. Allahabad	Good	N.A.	N.A.	N.A.	N.A.	N.A.
15. Amritsar	Good	Permissible	Permissible	Permissible	Permissible	Permissible
16. Vijaywada	Very Good	N.A.	N.A.	N.A.	N.A.	N.A.

NA = Not available

Source: Central Pollution Control Board, 1999–2000.

Table 14.10: Waste Water Management in Metropolitan Cities of India 1997

Metropolitan Cities	*Volume of Waste Water Generated (mld)*			*Waste Water Collected*		*Capacity (mld)*	*Treatment*		*Mode of Disposal*
	Domestic	*Industrial*	*Total*	*Volume (mld)*	*Per cent*		*Primary*	*Secondary*	
Mumbai	2228.1	227.9	2456.0	2210.0	90.0	109.0	Yes	Yes	Sea
Kolkata	1383.8	48.4	1432.0	1074.9	75.1	—	—	—	Hugli River Fish Farms
Delhi	1270.0	—	1270.0	1016.0	80.0	981.0	Yes	Yes	Agriculture Yamuna River
Chennai	276.0	—	276.0	257.0	93.1	257.0	Yes	Yes	Agriculture Sea

Source: Control of Urban Pollution Series: Cups/42/1997-98, CPCB, 1997.

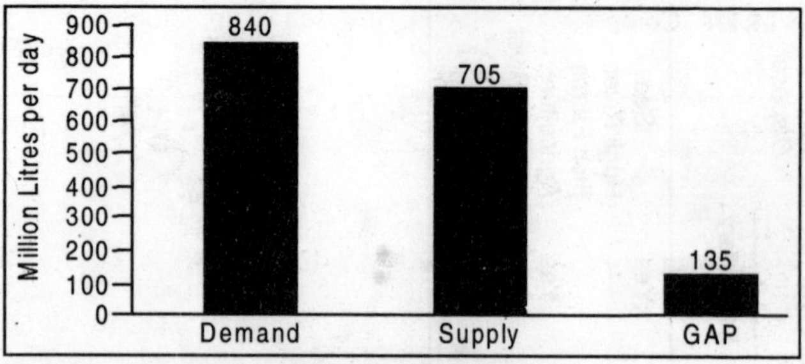

Fig. 14.9: Demand Supply and Gap in Bangalore

Source: Bangalore Water Supply and Sewage Board

Mumbai increased from around 12.3 m in 1991 to 16.3 m in 2001, a growth of about 32.5 per cent while the Municipal waste generation, however, grew from 3200 tonnes per day to 5355 tonnes per day in the same period, a growth of about 67 per cent. This clearly indicates that the growth in Municipal waste generation in the urban centres has outpaced the growth in population in recent years. The reasons for this trend could be the changing life styles, food habits and changes in the standard of living. The per capita waste generation rate has increased from 375g per day to 490 per day during 1971-1997. This increase along with the population increase has tremendously swollen up the figures of total waste generation quantum adding to the problems of local governments responsible for managing it. Analysing the data of MSW generated in 35 metro cities between 1994-95 and from 1999-2000, there has been a 25 per cent increase in this time period and Delhi topping the chart with 50 per cent increase.

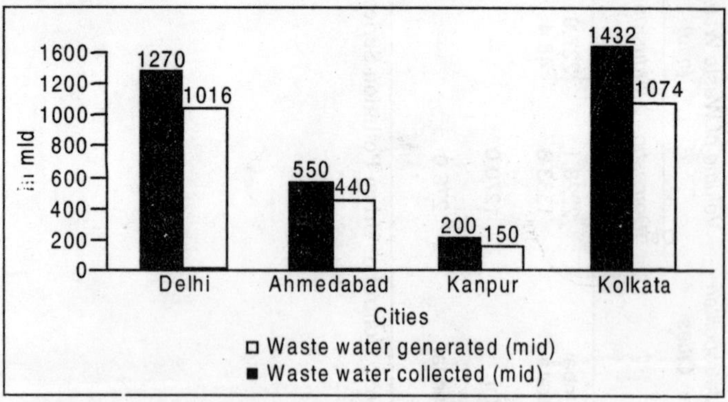

Fig. 14.10: Waste Water Management in Cities, 2000

Table 14.11: Composition of Solid Wastes in Major Cities, 1997

(*In Percentage*)

Cities	*Non–Biodegradable*					*Degradable*
	Paper	*Plastic*	*Metal*	*Glass*	*Ash & Earth*	
Mumbai	10.00	2.00	3.60	0.20	44.20	40.00
Kolkata	3.13	0.65	0.66	0.38	34.00	47.00
Delhi	6.29	0.85	1.21	0.57	36.00	35.00
Bangalore	4.00	2.00	1.50	1.00	13.50	78.00
Nagpur	1.88	1.35	1.33	1.34	41.42	34.81

Source: India Development Report, 1997.

The annual solid waste generated in Indian cities has increased from 6 million tonnes in 1947 to 48 million tonnes in 1997 and is expected to increase to 300 million tonnes per annum by 2047 (CPCB, 2000).

Urban municipal waste is a mix of paper, plastic, metal, glass, and organic matter. Specially worrying is the increase in non-biodegradable plastic waste: discarded plastic bags choke drains, prevent smoother grass growth and exacerbate the damage-potential by preventing the bio-degradation of waste packed in them. The organic matter has remained almost static at 41 per cent in the past three decades; but the recyclables have increased from 9.56 to 17.18 per cent. Amongst various recyclables, plastics have had a quantum jump from 0.69 to 3.9 per cent; more than a five-fold increase within last 20 years. Disposal is the last stage of the waste management cycle. Pace of industrialisation has resulted in

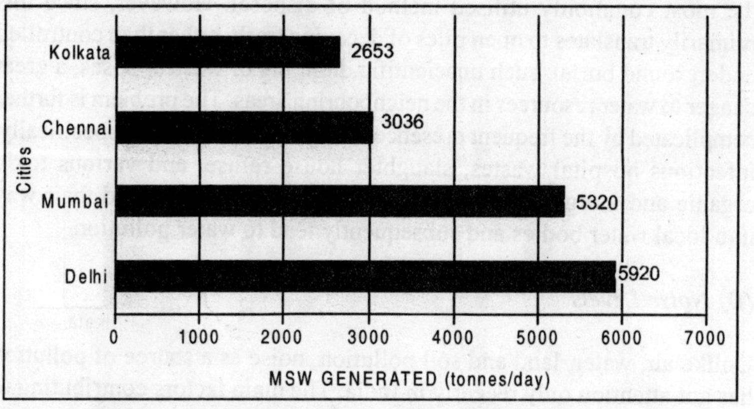

Source: CPCB as cited in state of Environment Report, 2009.

Fig. 14.11: Municipal Solid Waste Generation in Cities (2004-05)

increasing amounts of hazardous wastes every year. In total, at present, around 7.2 million tonnes of hazardous waste is generated in the country of which 1.4 million tonnes is recyclable, 0.1 million tonnes is incinerable and 5.2 m tonnes is destined for disposal of land (Ministry of Environment and Forests, 2001).

The situation here is also grim in collection and transportation of solid wastes. At present most of the MSW in the country is disposed unscientifically. This has adverse impacts not only on the eco-system but also on the human environment. About 90 per cent municipal waste is collected by the civic authorities is dumped in low-lying areas outside the city limits which no provision of leaching. Treatment and landfill gas collection and use are not practiced. Heavy metals find their way to the underground water, rendering it unfit for drinking. The landfill gases too escape into the atmosphere adding to the greenhouse emissions and resulting in the loss of utilising the same alternatively, as thermal fuel or for electricity production. The changes in the average waste collection efficiency of the total generation in Indian cities is around 72 per cent and 70 per cent of Indian cities do not have adequate waste transportation facilities.

In Indian cities, MSW generally remains unmanaged due to various factors, viz. inadequate finances, low political priority, inadequately trained personnel, and the lack of proper disposal sites. As a result, residents are prone to diseases like hepatitis, malaria, dengue fever, elephantiasis, cholera, etc. For the waste that is managed, landfilling is the most commonly utilised method of disposal. However, since this primarily translates to open piles of decaying trash, rather than controlled underground burial, such unscientific dumping of wastes, poses, a great danger to water resources in the neighbouring areas. The problem is further complicated by the frequent presence of other kinds of wastes, specifically, infectious hospital wastes, slaughter house refuse, and various toxic organic and inorganic materials. All these contaminants find their way into local water bodies and subsequently lead to water pollution.

(D) Noise Levels

Unlike air, water, land and soil pollution, noise as a source of pollution has got attention only recently in India. The main factors contributing to noise pollution are vehicular traffic, industrial activities, various electrical appliances, and sources of entertainment such as musical systems, TVs, public addressal systems, etc. It is mostly the people living in metropolitan

Table 14.12: Noise Level in Few Cities of India, 2001

Cities	*Day/Night*	*Industrial Area*	*Commercial Area*	*Residential Area*	*Silence Zone*
Kolkata	Day	78	82	79	79
	Night	67	75	65	65
Mumbai	Day	76	75	70	66
	Night	65	66	62	52
Chennai	Day	71	78	66	63
	Night	66	71	48	49
Bangalore	Day	78	76	67	67
	Night	53	57	50	NA

NA = Not available

Source: Ministry of Environment and Forest (2001).

cities, or other big towns or those working in factories who are victims of noise pollution.

The menace of noise pollution is prevalent in all the major cities of India. Except for noise pollution, during night time, in industrial zone as most of the industries are closed down during this time, the level of noise far exceeds the standard level in all the other zones of the city and the nuisance is more during the day time and is often at a critical level in residential and silence zones. A study has revealed that noise level in residential, commercial and industrial areas and the silence zones in major cities far exceed the standards prescribed by CPCB. The average noise level is in excess of the recommended level of 55dB. Increase in vehicular traffic, industrialisation and overcrowding of cities is generally attributed for the increase in noise levels.

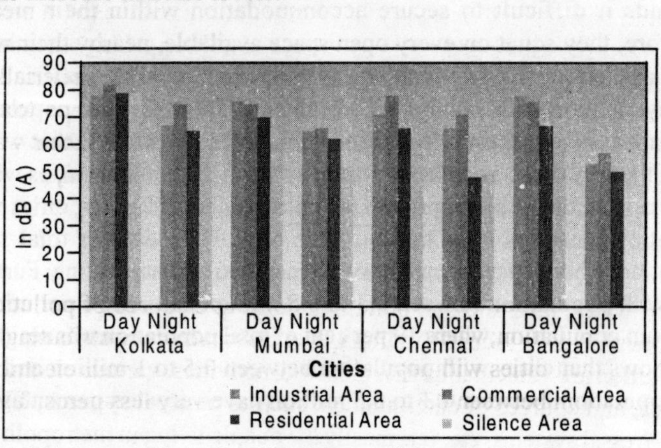

Fig. 14.12: Average Noise Level in Largest Cities of India, 2007

The Environment Protection Act (1986) made a passing reference to noise pollution. Although a notification was further issued in 1989, on Ambient Quality Standards *vice versa* Noise, but it hardly made any impact on controlling noise pollution. Fourteen years later, in February 2000, Ministry of Environment and Forests formulated the Noise Pollution (Regulation and Control) Rules. The salient features of these rules are that the State Governments being the implementation authority, should initiate the process of controlling noise pollution by classifying the areas into residential, commercial, industrial and silence zones. The rules further provide that the governments should ensure that the noise levels do not exceed the permissible limits.

Social Environment

(A) Urbanisation and Slums

The Government of India Slum Area (Improvement and Clearance) Act of 1954 defines a slum as "any predominantly residential area, in which light or sanitary facilities or any combination of these factors are detrimental to the safety, health or morals". According to NSS (National Sample Survey), "a slum is a compact settlement with a collection of poorly built tenements, mostly of temporary nature, crowded together, in unhygienic conditions, usually with inadequate sanitary and drinking water facilities. Such an area is considered as a Non-Notified Slum if at least 20 households live in that area. Notified Slums are those areas notified as Slums by Urban Local Bodies (ULBs) or development authorities. The vast majority of the city ward migrants belongs to the working class and finds it difficult to secure accommodation within their means. Therefore, they squat on every open space available, nearby their work places and construct huts with cheap temporary building materials. In this way, slums grow in number and population. Total and slum population in India according to size/class of towns during 1991 showed that 41 per cent of the total slum population was residing in million plus cities where 27 per cent of the total population of India resided. However, cities with population between 0.5-1 million have only 9 per cent of total slum population, where 20 per cent of the total population was residing. Further, cities with population between 0.3 to 0.5 million had only 6 per cent of total slum population; where 19 per cent of total population was residing. This shows that cities with population between 0.5 to 1 million and city with population between 0.3 to 0.5 million have very less percentage of slum population whereas million plus cities have more percentage of slum population. It reveals that the opportunity in the medium cities is less than that offered by the million cities.

Table 14.13: Total Slum Population in India According to Size Class of Towns-1991

Size Class / Cities	*Number of Cities/ Towns*	*Total Population (in '00000)*	*Per cent to Total Population*	*Slum Population (in '00000)*	*Percentage to total Slum Population*
More than 1000000	23	710	26.6	189	41.3
500000–1000000	31	215	19.8	43	9.3
300000–499999	39	151	18.9	29	6.3
100000–299999	207	325	16.8	54	11.9
50000–99999	345	236	20.0	47	10.3
Less than 50000	3052	521	18.3	95	20.9
TOTAL	3697	2158	21.2	457	100.0

Source: A Compendium of Indian Slums, 1996, Town and Country Planning Organisation.

Therefore, the unskilled population is more attracted towards the million cities and thus joins the slums for their residence. On the other hand, the towns with population less than 50,000 showed little more percentage of total slum population (21%) than their share of total

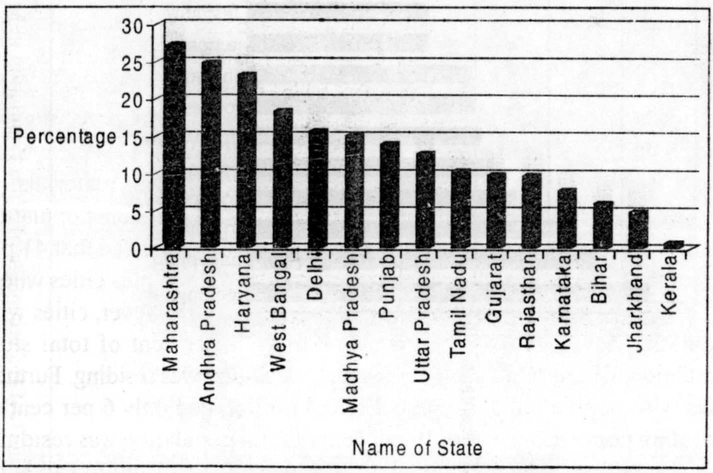

Fig. 14.13: Proportion of Slum Population to Total Urban Population in India, 2001

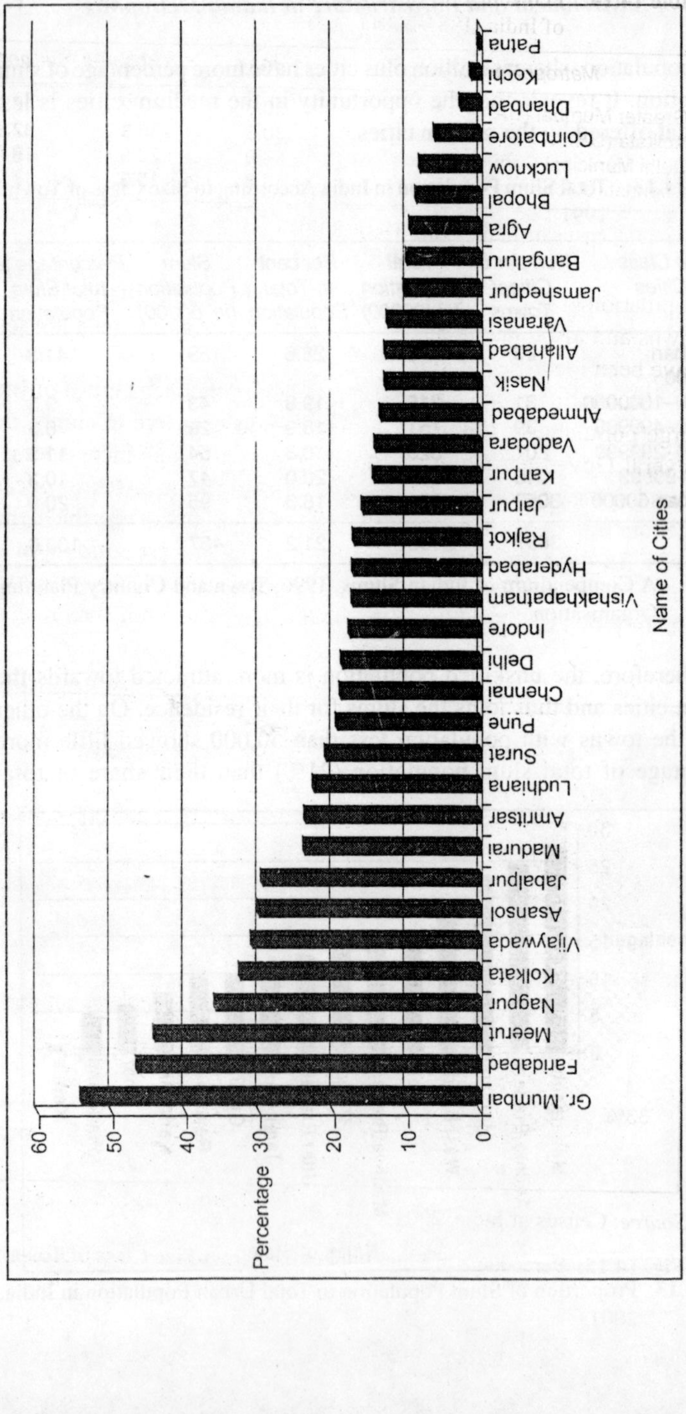

Fig. 14.14: Percentage of Slum Population in Million Plus, 2001

Table 14.14: Percentage of Slum Population in the Four Metropolitan Cities of India (1981-2001)

Metropolitan Cities	*1981*	*1991*	*2001*
Greater Mumbai (UA)	30.8	43.2	48.9
Kolkata (UA)	30.3	36.3	32.6
Delhi Municipal Corp. (UA)	18.0	22.5	18.9
Chennai (U.A.)	13.8	15.3	17.7

Source: Census of India 1981, 1991, 2001.

population (18%). This shows that the poor housing quality in the small towns and also may be because the semi-pucca and kutcha houses may have been identified as slums.

Slum population is a serious problem of the mega cities of India. A large population of Mumbai, Kolkata and Delhi live in slums, despite several Government housing policies. A continuous increase has been found in the percentage of slum population over the last three decades in the four metropolitan cities of India in which Mumbai was the highest. In 1981, 34 per cent of the population of Mumbai were residing in slums, and in 2001, nearly half of Mumbai's population (49%) were living in slums. However, Kolkata, Delhi, and Chennai had not shown as severe

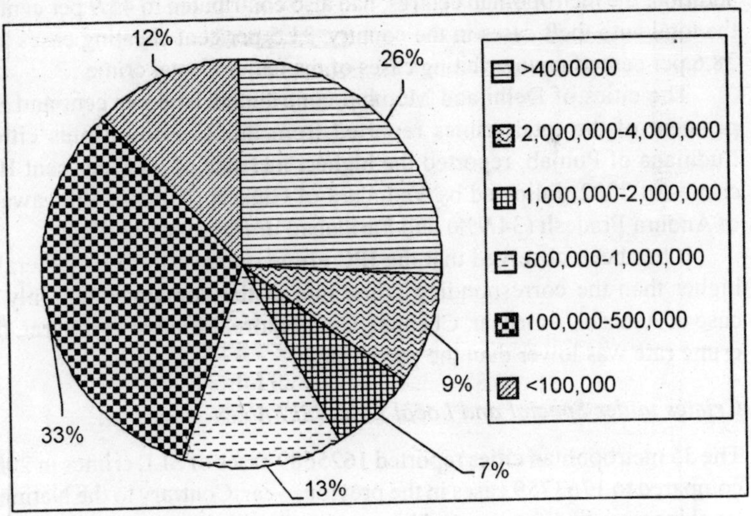

Source: Census of India, 2001.

Fig. 14.15: Percentage of Slum Population across Size Class of Town, 2001

conditions as Mumbai, but Chennai had shown an increase in the slum population over 1991.

Urban slums are marked by deplorable living environment and of often marked by a lack of civic amenities and facilities leading to environmental degradation and higher incidences of morbidity.

(B) Crime in Cities

Indian Penal Code (IPC) Crimes in Cities

Due to the increasing disparities in the urban areas of India, particularly the million plus cities, urban crime has been on the rampant in most of the areas. The common types are theft of property, crime against women, crime against children, crime against the aged and cyber crimes.

A total of 297679 cognizable crimes under the IPC (Indian Penal Code) were reported from the 35 million plus cities in 2002 (National Crime Records Bureau, Ministry of Home Affairs, 2002), as compared to 289775 crimes during 2001, thereby reporting an increase of 2.7 per cent compared to the national scenario on a marginal increase of 0.6 per cent. The Indian metropolises witnessed an increase of murder (5.9%), attempt to commit murder (6.2%), dacoity (37.1), riots (1.3) and dowry deaths (10.1). In addition, the metropolitan centres, had also contributed to 45.9 per cent of the total auto theft cases in the country, 31.5 per cent cheating cases and 28.6 per cent of counterfeiting cases of the nation's total crime.

The cities of Delhi and Mumbai contributed 14.8 per cent and 8.8 per cent of the total crimes reported from the 35 million plus cities. Ludhiana of Punjab, reported the highest increase of 46.8 per cent IPC crimes in 2002, followed by Vadodara of Gujarat (41.0%), Vijayawada of Andhra Pradesh (34.9%) and Faridabad of Haryana (31.5%).

It has been observed that the IPC crime rate in cities was generally higher than the corresponding crime rate of the domain state. Only in case of Asansol, Amritsar, Chennai, Coimbatore, Mumbai and Surat, the crime rate was lower than the parent state.

Crimes under Special and Local Laws (SLL)

The 35 metropolitan cities reported 1625689 cases of SLL crimes in 2002 compared to 1763759 cases in the previous year. Contrary to the National level increase of 4.9 per cent, cities reported a decrease of reported cases of 7.8 per cent over 2001.

Despite this, the 35 million plus cities contributed significantly towards the nation's share for cases under Copyright Act (36.9%), Indecent

Table 14.15: Living Environment of Urban Households Living in Slums, 2002

State	% of Households Living in Slums		Mode of Water Access (%)						% With Underground Sewage		% Without any Drainage		% Without Latrines	
			NS			NNS								
	NS	NNS	% Tap	% Tubewell	% other	% Tap	% Tubewell	% Other	NS	NNS	NS	NNS	NS	NNS
J&K	59.6	40.4	100	0	0	98	2	0	0	0	100	100	61	76
Punjab	75.6	24.4	43	57	0	0	100	0	34	0	0	95	48	95
Delhi	20.5	79.5	100	0	0	71	29	0	0	3	31	24	31	52
Rajasthan	2.2	97.8	100	0	0	27	0	73	0	0	67	98	33	98
UP	50.6	49.4	34	67	0	59	41	0	35	11	1	71	1	51
Bihar	37.8	62.2	0	100	0	0	100	0	0	0	34	75	34	100
West Bengal	52.1	47.9	89	11	0	72	18	10	63	23	0	39	0	30
Odisha	14.2	85.8	100	0	0	57	44	0	0	0	0	90	100	100
Chhattisgarh	46.9	53.1	31	69	0	71	25	4	0	0	0	25	69	100
Madhya Pradesh	65.7	34.3	68	20	12	75	25	0	24	0	31	38	12	75
Gujarat	38.7	61.3	33	2	65	74	26	0	83	7	2	73	6	69
Maharashtra	74.7	25.3	95	3	2	91	3	6	34	27	10	23	18	25
Andhra Pradesh	85.1	14.9	87	2	11	46	55	0	12	0	21	66	10	68
Karnataka	65.6	34.4	89	11	0	77	16	7	23	24	36	24	66	53
Tamil Nadu	53.5	46.5	85	0	15	93	3	4	57	11	16	44	15	68
Pondicherry	29.0	71.0	100	0	0	97	3	0	0	7	0	10	29	93
TOTAL	65.1	34.9	84	10	6	71	22	7	30	15	15	44	17	51

Note: NS– Notified Slum, NNS – Non-Notified Slum.
Source: NSSO (2003a).

Table 14.16: IPC Crime Rate – Metropolitan Cities *versus* Parent State

Sl. No.	*City*	*IPC Crime Rate*	
		City	*Parent State*
1.	Agra	425.2	85.5
2.	Ahmedabad	320.4	206.0
3.	Allahabad	175.0	85.5
4.	Amritsar	106.5	116.2
5.	Asansol	33.3	72.2
6.	Bangalore	512.0	211.8
7.	Bhopal	767.4	309.0
8.	Chennai	132.7	265.2
9.	Coimbatore	223.1	265.2
10.	Delhi	345.2	341.6
11.	Dhanbad	304.7	114.1
12.	Faridabad	408.1	185.5
13.	Hyderabad	260.4	186.7
14.	Indore	712.9	309.0
15.	Jabalpur	603.0	309.0
16.	Jaipur	505.9	260.2
17.	Jamshedpur	218.2	114.1
18.	Kanpur	219.6	75.7
19.	Kochi	481.5	322.9
20.	Kolkata	80.7	72.2
21.	Lucknow	306.7	85.5
22.	Ludhiana	376.0	116.2
23.	Madurai	308.7	265.2
24.	Meerut	200.0	85.5
25.	Mumbai	160.5	167.4
26.	Nagpur	410.8	167.4
27.	Nasik	218.8	167.4
28.	Patna	357.4	110.4
29.	Pune	226.4	167.4
30.	Rajkot	463.5	206.0
31.	Surat	148.4	206.0
32.	Vadodara	476.9	206.0
33.	Varanasi	188.2	85.5
34.	Vijayawada	898.4	186.7
35.	Visakhapatnam	213.5	186.7
	TOTAL	275.9	169.5

Source: Crime in India, 2002, National Crime Records Bureau, Ministry of Home Affairs, GOI.

Representation of Women Prohibition Act (22.4%), Immoral Traffic (P) Act (17.9%) and Arms Act (19.9%). Ludhiana reported the highest percentage of 78.2 per cent, followed by Varanasi 72.3 per cent. In addition, Kolkata and Vijayawada also reported much higher incidences of cases under SLL.

Cyber Crimes

In recent years Cyber Crimes have also increased in the Indian Cities. The Information Technology (IT) Act of 2000, specifies, the criminal acts under the broad head of Cyber Crimes. Of the total 70 cases registered under IT Act, 2000, around 47 per cent cases pertain to obscene publication and transmission in electronic form. 38 persons were taken in custody for such offences during 2002. Other such cases include hacking, signature fraud, breach of confidentiality, etc. The urban centres of Andhra Pradesh, Maharashtra, Karnataka, and Delhi reported the maximum number of these cases.

Environmental Infrastructure

The escalating demand for urban basic services and infrastructure in urban centres is resulting in a serious deterioration of service quality across housing, transport, healthcare, power and water, sanitation and education. Benign neglect of urban sprawls by civic authorities has led cities to be vulnerable to natural disasters and disease. The recent Mumbai floods of July 2005, has pointed out unmistakably that infrastructure of cities in India is crying for help.

In recent years the infrastructure required to meet the requirements of the urban dwellers call for huge investments.

Housing and Housing Amenities and Infrastructure

The urban housing characteristics for entire India and the four leading Metros of Mumbai, Kolkata, Delhi and Chennai reveal the following facts.

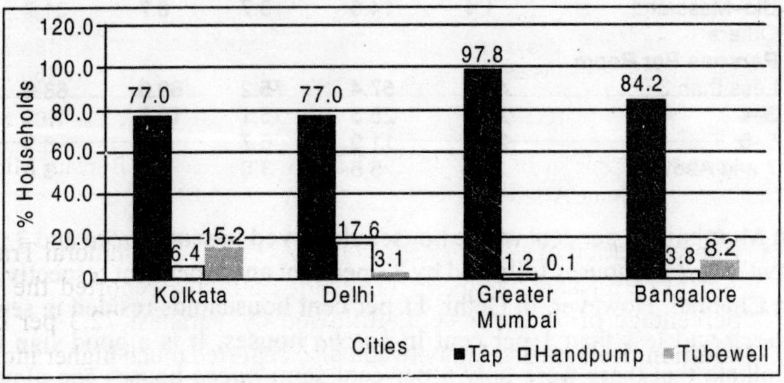

Fig. 14.16: Source of Drinking Water in Major Metro Cities, 2001

Table 14.17: Housing Characteristics of Four Leading Metropolitan Cities and Urban India: 1988–99 *(in percentage)*

Household Characteristics	*Mumbai*	*Kolkata*	*Delhi*	*Chennai*	*All India Urban*
Type of House					
Pucca	62.8	94.1	88.2	57.5	66.0
Semi-Pucca	34.1	5.2	10.7	32.8	24.4
Kutcha	2.8	0.2	0.9	9.2	9.4
Sanitation Facilities					
Flush Toilet	97.4	89.5	85.5	89.1	63.9
Owned Flush Toilet	29.4	—	—	—	—
Shared Flush Toilet	15.2	—	—	—	—
Public Flush Toilet	52.8	—	—	—	—
Pit Toilet	0.1	8.9	8.9	1.6	16.8
No Facility	2.5	1.6	5.6	9.3	19.3
Sources of Drinking Water					
Piped	99.6	64.0	86.7	63.3	74.5
Hand Pump	0.2	34.5	12.0	30.6	18.1
Others	0.2	1.5	1.3	6.1	7.4
Methods of Purifying Drinking Water					
Straining	54.1	1.0	3.9	14.7	25.1
Water Filter	10.2	17.0	18.8	15.1	14.8
Boiling	18.2	5.7	14.4	38.2	13.6
Electronic Purification	2.5	2.7	3.8	3.0	1.2
Other Methods	0.7	1.5	1.0	0.7	2.0
No Purification	27.1	74.2	62.4	42.8	50.4
Electricity					
Yes	99.5	93.8	97.7	89.6	91.3
No	0.5	6.2	2.3	10.4	8.7
Main Type of Fuel used for Cooking					
Kerosene	39.5	50.3	16.3	54.0	21.5
LPG	58.9	39.9	17.0	37.3	46.9
Bio–Mass and Others	1.4	14.6	3.7	8.7	31.7
Persons Per Room					
Less than 3	43.9	57.4	75.2	69.9	68.6
3–4	27.6	25.3	15.1	19.8	19.5
5–6	20.1	11.9	6.7	8.8	8.3
7 and Above	8.3	5.5	3.0	1.1	3.5

In Mumbai, 34 per cent of the households lived in semi-*pucca* and 3 per cent in *kutcha* houses followed by 33 per cent and 9 per cent respectively in Chennai. However, in Delhi, 11 per cent households resided in semi-*pucca* and less than 1 per cent in *kutcha* houses. It is a good sign for Kolkata that there were only 5 per cent semi-*pucca* houses and almost negligible *kutcha* houses. This shows that in Mumbai and Chennai housing situation is poorer than Kolkata and Delhi.

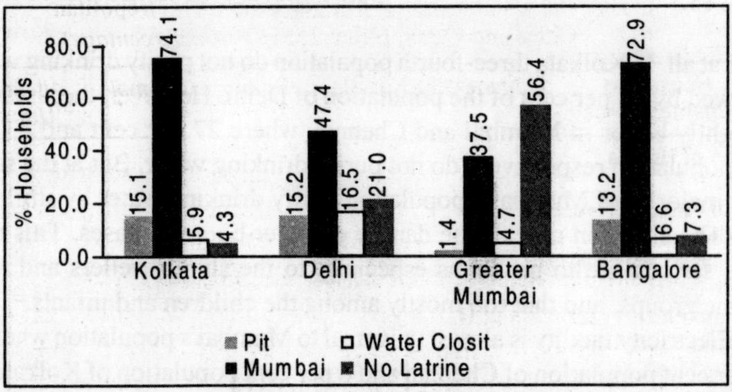

Fig. 14.17: Sanitation Facilities at Households of Major Metros Cities, 2001

On the other hand, the houses in these metros are very much over crowded. More than 3 persons residing in a single room, is the condition of 56 per cent of the population of Mumbai followed by 43 per cent population of Kolkata, 30 per cent population of Chennai and I/4th of the population of Delhi. Further, 5 and more persons residing in a room, such miserable conditions were faced by 28 per cent population of Mumbai, followed by 17 per cent of the population of Kolkata and about 10 per cent population of Delhi and Chennai both.

Looking at the sanitation condition of the metro-cities, it is apparent that almost universal flush toilet facility is available in Mumbai, followed by 90 per cent in Kolkata and 89 per cent in Delhi. However, the matter of fact is that more than half of this facility in Mumbai is available in public place and not within housing premises. Kolkata and Delhi might have the similar situation. Again, it is unfortunate to note that about 9 per cent population of Kolkata and Delhi uses pit toilet. Further, what is worse is that 9 per cent of Chennai's population does not have toilet facility at all, followed by 6 per cent in Delhi. This shows the inadequate planning of Municipal Corporations because of unprecedented population pressure.

As regard to the sources of safe drinking water, the situation is the best in Mumbai, where almost the entire population has access to piped drinking water. However, a substantial population is dependent on hand pump in Kolkata (35%), followed by Chennai (31%) and Delhi (13%). On the other hand, in Chennai 6 per cent of the population is dependent on the sources other than hand pump and tapped/piped water.

Considering the methods of purification of drinking water, it is very strange that half of the urban population in India does not purify drinking water at all. In Kolkata three-fourth population do not purify drinking water followed by 62 per cent of the population of Delhi. However, the situation is slightly better in Mumbai and Chennai, where 27 per cent and 43 per cent population respectively do not purify drinking water. But at the same time, majority of Mumbai's population purify drinking water by straining only. The situation reveals the danger of water-borne diseases. This may cause serious health problems especially to the slum dwellers and low-income groups, and that too mostly among the children and infants.

Electricity facility is almost universal to Mumbai's population whereas 10 per cent population of Chennai and 6 per cent population of Kolkata do not have electricity facility. Main type of fuel used for cooking in urban India is LPG followed by bio-mass fuel and kerosene. However, in Kolkata and Chennai more than 50 per cent population uses kerosene. There is very less percentage (less than 9%) of user of Bio-mass fuel and others in all the four metro-cities, except Kolkata, where 15 per cent population uses it. This enhances the problem of indoor air pollution in the metro-cities.

Energy

The study of energy use in the urban areas is of particular importance in view of the impact of urbanisation on the utilisation of commercial energy resources like coal and oil products. The process of urbanisation leads to the substitution of commercial energy for non-commercial energy in industry, commercial and domestic sectors (the share of consumption of commercial energy carriers by urban areas is about 80 per cent whereas that of urban population is only 32%). Thus one can relate urban development with increased commercial energy use. Urbanites travel *via* energy-intensive transportation modes. Building infrastructure in urban areas to support the high population density requires significant quantity of energy. Also in an urban environment, land use pattern, spatial structures, industrial location etc. affect the levels of energy consumption.

The changes in lifestyle of urban people in recent years have contributed significantly to differences in energy-utilisation levels. In the residential sector fuel wood and charcoal stoves have been replaced with kerosene stoves for the urban poor. The propensity to consume more and more electricity is marked by an increase in the usage of air conditioners, desert coolers, refrigerators micro waves, washing machines, electric geysers, electric kettles and a host of domestic electrical gadgets, including, television, music systems, home theatres etc. Scooters and cars are being frequently used even by the middle-income groups.

Due to the increased availability and affordability, the shares of modern carriers like Liquefied Petroleum Gas (LPG) and electricity are significantly high in the urban areas. Also urban houses utilise larger quantities of superior energy than rural households. Hence, it is important to assess this problem of relative deprivation, both quantitative and qualitative going beyond final to useful energy. Also, since urban areas consume significant quantities of petroleum products, two-third of which are imported, the issue of energy security should be taken into account, while considering urban energy policies.

The increase in urbanisation levels will have a significant impact on energy markets as well as on the global environment. Since, energy production and use is the single most important source of Green House Gas (GHG) emissions, the pattern of energy utilisation and its environmental impact will strongly influence the look towards the environment in the future. The environmental implications are significantly dependent on the type of energy carrier chosen and hence it is important to restrict the use of commercial sources through efficient utilisation.

Transport

Urban transport problems in India are becoming acute mainly because of rapid motorisation. The increasing use of motor vehicles in cities has been rapidly changing the mode-split structure. It has also helped to alter landuse patterns from compact to more dispersed which in turn reinforces the use of personalised motor vehicles. At present motor vehicle ownership in India, including two-wheelers and three-wheelers, is just a little over 40 vehicles per one thousand population. This is low compared to high income countries. During the last decade motor vehicle ownership in India has expanded at roughly 10 per cent a year. But the growth in the metropolitan cities registered over 5 per cent a year during the same period; significantly higher than the National Average. This growth pattern is expected to continue with the growth of per capita income, especially in urban areas. The growth will also be further reinforced by the Central Government policy of relying on a strong domestic auto market for the development of a viable auto industry.

Motorisation has brought a higher level of mobility to the urban economy, and to high income of the urban population. But its adverse impacts are also substantial—the most significant of these impacts being road congestion, air pollution and traffic accidents. The urban transport scene in India, is typically a high mix of noisy traffic comprising two-wheelers, three-wheelers, cars, buses and trucks, all fighting for road space. The streets in most Indian cities are old and narrow, occupying only 6 to 10 per cent of land area. Growing traffic and limited road space have reduced peak hour speeds to 5 to 10 km and are in the central areas of many major cities.

Indian cities face growing risk of traffic accidents, and are considered to be more accident prone in spite of a relatively lower level of vehicular population. In 1997, the number of accidents in the top 15 metropolitan cities were 75,605 with 6242 fatalities. In the same year, the Delhi Metropolitan Region where motor vehicle ownership reached 2.8 million recorded over 11000 traffic accidents, 24 per cent of which were fatal.

Policy Perspectives on Urban Environment Management

The following discussion shows that creating Sustainable Urban Systems have become a necessity under present day urban problems, related to

Table 14.18: Percentage of Urban Households Using Particular Energy Carrier, 2000-01

Energy Carrier	*Low Income*	*Middle Income*	*High Income*	*Total*
Fuel wood	41.64	12.69	2.52	22.21
LPG	12.58	42.35	64.67	35.53
Dung	3.63	1.52	0.56	2.16
Kerosene	26.38	32.63	20.61	27.02
Others	15.76	10.82	11.65	13.09
Total	100.00	100.00	100.00	100.00

Source: CMIE, Reports.

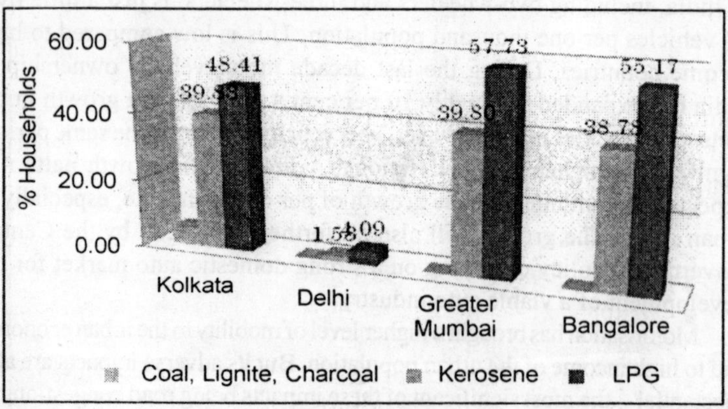

Fig. 14.18: Fuel Used by Households of Major Metro Cities, 2001

Table 14.19: Share of Two-Wheelers and Three-Wheelers, 1997

Cities	*Motor Vehicle Population*	*Share (in percentage)*	
		2– Wheelers	*3– Wheelers*
Ahmedabad	631,019	77	7
Bangalore	972,375	73	6
Kolkata	587,576	44	2
Delhi	2,847,695	66	3
Cochin	226,185	60	13
Mumbai	796,913	41	12
Hyderabad	769,401	87	7
Jaipur	448,625	74	2
Kanpur	246,801	79	2
Lucknow	330753	80	3
Chennai	889,819	73	4
Nagpur	238,576	78	6
Patna	219,513	69	5
Pune	476,372	74	8
Surat	361,838	85	5

Source: CMIE, Infrastructure, 2001.

urban environment and infrastructure. In other words we should not only think about solving the present day urban problems but should make the cities livable for the future generations to come. Let us consider certain critical policy links for Urban Environment Management.

Urban Governance and Urban Environment: Infrastructure and Services Management

In addition to the Urban Local Bodies (WLBs), at the Central level, the Ministry of Urban Development and the Ministry of Urban Employment and Poverty Alleviation (MEPA) form the apex authority of the GOI at the National level to formulate policies, sponsor and support programmes, coordinate the activities of various Central Ministries, State governments and of the nodal authorities and monitor the programmes concerning all issues of urban development and housing.

The key interventions of the GOI are:

- National Urban Transport Policy;
- Guidelines for sector reform and public-private partnership in the urban water and sanitation sector;
- Centrally Sponsored Schemes (CSS), such as integrated development of small and medium towns;

- Mega city schemes;
- Special development plan for National Capital Region;
- Accelerated urban water supply programme;
- Low cost sanitation etc.;
- Administering fiscal concessions such as tax holidays for integrated urban infrastructure development projects;
- Urban environmental infrastructure schemes such as for solid waste management and urban water supply, tax free status for municipal bonds, etc.;
- Training and information: by funding a variety of training programmes; and
- Creating and disseminating manuals such as the Municipal Solid Waste Planning Manual.

The present form of urban local government owes its genesis to the British rule. The first such body called Municipal Corporation was set-up in Madras in 1688, and was followed by the establishment of similar corporations in Bombay and Calcutta in 1762.

Since then, the structure of municipal bodies has remained by and large the same even though the number of urban areas had increased and their problems had become more and more complex. Recent years have witnessed an increasing interest in and growing consciousness of the need and importance of local self-government as a provider of services to the community as well as an instrument of democratic self-government. The 74th CAA, 1992, proposed to form a uniform structure of Municipal Corporations, Municipal Councils and Nagar Panchayats in transitional areas.

Urban local bodies are democratic institutions based on the principle of self-government and should represent people's desires and strengths. ULBs offer

- Enhanced opportunities for people's participation; local government is closest to the citizens and in the best position both to involve them in the decision making process of improving their living conditions and to make use of their knowledge and capabilities in the promotion of all-round development;
- Bottom-up planning; and
- Effective implementation by enhancing coordination and responsiveness to users.

BOX 1: Critical Policy Links for Urban Environment Management

Urban Environment Management Issues	*Underlying Causes*	*Relevant Policy Reforms*
Access to Environmental Infrastructure and Services		
Serviced Land Shelter	Poor functioning of urban land and housing markets: Highly regulated prices, lack of affordable housing for the poor.	Reform property rights; develop mortgage financing; introduce affordable standards and target subsidies to the poor; Reduce unneeded regulations, Governmental regulations and subsidies.
Water supply, sanitation, drainage, solid waste collection and transport	Supply side dominated by government monopoly: prices heavily regulated, heavy subsidies.	Introduce pricing and demand management: reconsider subsidies: move towards decentralisation, privatisation and participation.
Pollution from Urban Wastes and Emissions		
Water Pollution	Uncontrolled municipal and industrial discharges; excessive water use and waste generation: failure to link water quantity and quality issues.	Introduce water pricing and effluent charges; subsidise sewage treatment, strengthen regulations and capacity for monitoring, and enforcement: prepare comprehensive basic plans.
Energy Use and Air Pollution – Ambient air pollution – Indoor air pollution	Increased motorisation and transportation congestion; energy supply side dominated by Government monopoly; heavy energy subsidies, household cottage industry use of low quality fuels.	Introduce energy and fuel pricing, road charges, emission charges; reduce automobiles subsidies, fuel subsidies; integrate transport and landuse planning; promote clean technologies, fuel substitution and vehicle maintenance.
Solid and hazardous waste management	Poor municipal management; Lack of disposal facilities; inadequate regulation and enforcement.	Introduce regulation, licensing and charges; stimulate waste minimization; strengthen operations: privatise disposal operations.
Resource Losses		
Groundwater depletion	Unsustainable extraction link to unclear property rights and treatment as free resource.	Clarify property rights: introduce extraction charges; rain water harvesting and artificial recharge of ground water in water deficit regions.

(Contd.)

Box 1 (*Contd.*)

Urban Environment Management Issues	*Underlying Causes*	*Relevant Policy Reforms*
Land and Ecosystem degradation	Low-income settlements "pushed" onto fragile lands by lack of access to affordable serviced lands;	Coordinate land development; remove artificial shortages of land; develop sustainable uses of sensitive areas: monitor enforce landuse controls.
	Lack of controls over damaging economic activities.	
Loss of agricultural and historic property	Lack of property rights, regulations enforcement, maintenance; failure to reflect social values in land prices.	Introduce tax incentives for preservation; use redevelopment planning, zoning and building codes; develop property rights
Environmental Hazards		
Natural Hazards	Poorly functioning landmarks. Ineffective land policies; poor construction practices.	Enable land markets; provide disincentives to construction practices or occupation of high risk areas, incentives for using disaster-resistant construction techniques; disaster preparation plans.
Man-made Hazards	Inadequate regulation and enforcement; low income settlements alongside hazardous activities.	Introduce and enforce environmental zoning: formulate urban disaster preparedness plans and strengthen response capacity. Disaster mitigation plans.

Source: Economic Survey of Delhi, 2001-02.

The 74th CAA seeks to introduce fundamental changes in urban local bodies. Its salient features are:

- Introduction of 12th Schedule, which lists the functions of ULBs, covering planning, regulation and development aspects;
- Establishment of district and metropolitan planning responsible for election of representatives for the preparation of development plans at district and metropolitan levels;
- Proposed establishment of ward committees in areas having a population over 300000;
- Specification by law of the powers and responsibilities entrusted to municipalities and ward committees;
- Holding of periodic and timely elections;
- Specifying by law the sources of **municipal finance** and their periodic review;
- Restrictions on the power of the state governments to do away with the democratically elected state governments; and
- Reservation of 1/3rd of seats for women and weaker sections for municipal bodies.

In the face of service challenges, there have arisen certain roadblocks undermining the reform initiatives. The ULBs have been confronting several problems and there also seems to be a discontinuity between their revenue collection and service delivery outcomes.

The GOI has also begun to respond to the magnitude of challenges facing urban service provision in India. For the cities of India to realize their full potential and become true engines of growth, it is necessary that focused attention be given to the improvement of infrastructure therein. For achieving this objective a mission mode approach is essential. Accordingly, the Prime Minister of India has launched a mission Jawaharlal Nehru National Urban Renewal Mission (JNNURM) on 3rd December 2005. The mission comprises two submissions: (1) For Basic Services to the Urban Poor (BSUP) and the other for (2) Infrastructure and Governance.

The JNNURM has been implemented in selected 63 cities and the duration of the mission is for seven years beginning with the year 2005-06.

For other cities/towns two schemes, viz. Integrated Housing and Slum Development Programme (IHSDP) and Urban Infrastructure Development for Small and Medium Towns have also been launched along with JNNURM on 3.12.2005. The existing Valmiki Ambedkar Awas

Yojana (VAMBAY) and the discontinued National Slum Development Programme (NSDP) are subsumed in the IHSDP. The IHSDP implemented by the Ministry of Urban Employment Poverty Alleviation (UEPA) has been launched with the objective to strive for holistic slum development healthily and enabling urban environment by providing adequate shelter and basic infrastructure facilities to the slum dwellers of identified urban areas.

Conclusions

On India's onward path to economic development, it is quite inevitable that urbanisation in India would continue for years to come. The unintended cost of increasing urbanisation is deterioration in the environmental quality and a pressure on the existing infrastructure, reinforcing a further degradation of the environment. However, environmental degradation is a manifestation of not only urban population pressure but also the changing lifestyles, which often accompany a rise in income levels of a segment of the population. On the other hand increasing disparities result in impoverishment of the urban poor that also results in deterioration of the urban environment. Today, various interlinked issues are to be addressed on both the environmental and infrastructural front. Features such as neglect of proper disposal of refuse by households, industry and service providers such as hospitals, and water services have resulted in environmental deterioration. Intermittent piped water supply and ineffective treatment of waste water and industrial waste are resulting in a host of problems including contamination of water bodies and land. Increased motorised transport, unavailability of more road space in not only creating air pollution but increasing the number of accidents and other human miseries. Widening disparities among urban social groups have resulted in deterioration of the urban social environment and increase in crime rates particularly in the big cities.

Urban Local Bodies (ULBs), which are entrusted with environmental protection and provision of urban basic services, are often strapped for adequate financial resources as well as knowledge of environmental management. In recent years, however the situation is not as grim as perceived. Supreme Court's intervention in limiting air pollution generated by public transport and government initiatives in using green fuels has improved air quality perceptibly in some cities. Today thoughts are being made to meet the energy requirements in a sustainable fashion, through the Energy Master Plan (EMP) and this should be integrated with the civil master plan so that the problems arising out of the urban sprawl and multiplication of urban activities are minimised. Awareness about sustainable development which includes environmental concerns is gaining grounds and various tools such as ecological foot printing and green accounting are being developed to ensure the quality of environment that we leave for our next generation is better than that we inherited from the past.

REFERENCES

Bansal, Alok, *et al.* (2002), "Urban Transport", Training Programme on Urban Environmental Management, Volume I, December 2-6, 2002; Indira Gandhi Institute of Development Research, Mumbai.

Botkin, Daniel and Edward Keller (1995), *Environmental Science, Earth as a Living Planet*, John Wiley and Sons, Inc. New York.

Buch, M.N. (1993), *Environmental Consciousness and Urban Planning,* Orient Longman, New Delhi.

Kundu, Amitabh (2006), "Trends and Patterns of Urbanization and Their Economic Implications", in *India Infrastructure Report 2006*, Urban Infrastructure, Oxford University Press.

Miller, G. Tyler Jr. (1994), *Sustaining the Earth: An Integrated Approach*, Wadswarth Publishing Company, California.

Pandey, Suneel, Shaheen Singhal, Pragya Jaiswal and Manraj Guliani, (2006), "Urban Environment", in *India Infrastructure Report 2006*, Urban Infrastructure, Oxford University Press.

Parikh and Vibhooti Shukla, (1995), "Urbanisation, Energy Use and Greenhouse Effects in Economic Development", *Global Environmental Change*, Vol. 5, No. 2. pp. 87-103.

Rastogi, Anupam (2006), "The Infrastructure Sector in India", in *India Infrastructure Report 2006*, Urban Infrastructure, Oxford University Press.

Reddy, Sudhakara B. (1998), *Urban Energy Systems*, Concept Publishing Company Pvt. Ltd., New Delhi.

Reddy, Sudhakara B., (2002), "The Urban Challenge", *Training Programme on Urban Environmental Management*, Volume I, December 2-6, 2007; Indira Gandhi Institute of Development Research, Mumbai.

Shukla, Vibhooti and Kirit, S. Parikh (1992), "The Environmental Consequences of Urban Growth", *Urban Geography*, Vol. 5.

Singh, K.P. (ed), (1998), *Infrastructure in India,* National Institute of Management Technology, Ghaziabad.

Toutain, Oliver and S. Gopiprasad (2006), "Planning for Urban Infrastructure" in *India Infrastructure Report 2006*, Urban Infrastructure, Oxford University Press.

Wilderer, Martin Z., *Economic Growth, Environment and Development: The*

Significance of the Eco-industrial Park Concept *in India and Indonesia*, Manak Publications Ltd., New Delhi.

World Resource Institute, (1997), "*World Resources: A Guide to Urban Environment,* Oxford University Press, New York.

Bose. A. (1978), *India's Urbanisation: 1901-2001*, Tata McGraw Hill Publishing Co. Ltd., New Delhi, 1978.

Sivaramakrishnan, K.C., Amitabh Kumd and B.N. Singh (2005), *Handbook of Urbanisation in India: An Analysis of Trends and Processes*, Oxford University Press, New Delhi.

Maitra, A.K., (1993). "Managing Urban Environment in India", *Workshop on Role of Cities*, Vol. II, Times Research Foundation, Kolkata.

Maitra, A.K. (2000), *Urban Environment in Crisis*, New Age International Publishers, Delhi.

Mohan, R. (1996). "Urbanisation in India: Patterns and Emerging Policy Issues" in *The Urban Transformation of the Developing World*; Josef Guglar (ed.), Oxford University Press, Oxford.

Mohan, R., (2001), *State of the Environment: India (Report Number 1999 EE45)*, submitted to the United Nations Environment Programme.

National Institute of Urban Affairs (1998), *Report of the National Commission on Urbanisation*, Vol. 2.

Ministry of Environment and Forests (1992), *Policy Statement for Abatement of Pollution*, GoI, New Delhi.

Ministry of Environment and Forests (1992), *National Conservation Strategy and Policy Document on Environment and Development*, GoI, New Delhi.

Ministry of Environment and Forests (1995), *Annual Report*, GoI, New Delhi, 1994-1995.

Ministry of Environment and Forests (1997). "Minutes of the Consultative Committee of the Members of Parliament Attached to the MOEF", held on August 27, GoI, New Delhi.

Ministry of Environment and Forests (1998), *White Paper on Pollution in Delhi with Action Plan*, GoI, New Delhi.

NEERI (1998), "Introduction of Environmental Economics into Decision Making for Sustainable Development: Air Media", *Project Report submitted to IGIDR under Capacity 21 Project*.

Parikh, Jyoti and Kirit Parikh (1999), *Accounting and Valuation of Environment, Vol. II—Case Studies from the ESCAP Region*, ESCAP publication.

Centre for Science and Environment (1996), Slow Murder: The Deadly Story of Vehicular Pollution of India, New Delhi.

Ministry of Urban Development (1987), *Report of the Study Group of Alternative Systems of. Urban Transport*, GoI, New Delhi.

Opinion Survey (1998), *Pollution in Delhi Threatening to get Out of Hand*, Monthly Public Opinion Survey, March 1998.

15

Fertility and Contraceptive Behaviour in Urban India

Vidyasagar Trigun

Introduction

Human fertility is one of the basic components of population dynamics and is responsible for the biological replacement needed for the maintenance of human society. The process of replacement of a group through fertility is a complicated process. Within the biological limits of human fertility, several social, cultural, psychological, as well as economic, institutional and political factors are found to operate and these are responsible for determining the levels and differentials of fertility in various societies.

Fertility is always referred in demographic parlances to the live births taking place in a society. The term fertility evolves from the Latin etymological derivation, i.e. *ferre,* meaning, to bear, in contrast to the verb, fertilize, which relates to conception. In social science, the capacity to bear children is described as fecundity and the fact of giving birth as fertility.

Fertility has long been identified with fruitfulness and productiveness, not only in terms of human reproduction but also with regard to the availability of yields. Indeed, the perceived relationship of women and fertility has played a major role in religion since Paleolithic times. This old vision of considering woman to be associated with fertility make them instrumental for being worshipped. Again if women produce only sons then her maternity is more praised by family and society. All these are hidden norms in our patriarchal system of the society. The formation and security of patriarchal system maintained by several components such as family, society, religion, politics and culture. These are the stable agents of patriarchy that have prepared the format to direct women. Women in India are still fighting for their space as in terms of gender equality, autonomy and rights which men enjoy themselves. Women should have equal opportunities as men for the development of their own personalities.

However, women in present times are much more aware regarding their autonomy and their rights and this is not only found in urban areas but has also percolated to the rural and remote areas through modern scientific tools and modern communication technology.

The problem, hence, is not only restricted to giving birth of a child but the whole responsibility of taking care of the child is placed on the shoulders of a woman.

Women from the higher social strata often enjoy more freedom regarding reproduction, but women from lower strata of the society are still lacking autonomy and often live under miserable conditions, as they produce more children for the survivorship of kinship and family along with society. Thus there are several ramifications influencing fertility of Indian women.

The common measure of fertility is the Crude Birth Rate (CBR) or the number of live births per year per thousand population. The crude birth rate can prove to be crude, because it does not take into account the differences between reproductive population and non-reproductive population, within a society where immigration or some other social change has distorted the distribution of the population by sex or age. Hence, a more statistically refined measure is required that can relate births only to women of specified age. The General Fertility Rate (GFR) is the ratio of births during a year to the total number of women in 15-49 years of age. Therefore by relating births to women of a specific age, or age range, for a specified period a more meaningful measure, i.e. age specific fertility rate (ASFR) can be computed. This is added for whole reproductive ages result in the Total Fertility Rate (TFR). If only female births are related to mothers of each age, then the cumulative measure is known as the Gross Reproduction Rate (GRR). In various societies the effective measure of reproduction is not live births but surviving children, hence a measure known as the Net Reproduction Rate (NRR) has been introduced. This may be defined as the ratio of female births in the next generation to those in this generation in conditions of constant fertility and mortality. If the society maintains a rate of unity for a considerable period, it will become stationary, while a lower rate will imply eventually a declining population size, and a higher rate would result in a growing population.

The female reproductive span varies among women and between societies (or the same societies at different dates), but approximately spans ages from around 15 years to the late 40s. If fertility were in no way constrained, not even by the institution of marriage or by the practice of breast-feeding which tends to depress fertility, completed family size would be around 15[1] (Bongaarts, 1982 states 15.3 years in his model).

The total marital fertility rate of the Hutterites, a religious community opposed to deliberate birth control, in the western United States in the late 1920s was at least 12.4 [a level employed by Coale (1967) in his model)[2], but this figure was almost certainly rising because of the reduction of the period of breast feeding.

The determinants of fertility have been classified by Davis and Blake in a 1956[3] as:

1. Intercourse variables (age at first entrance to sexual union, the proportion of women never entering a union, the period spent after or between unions, voluntary and involuntary abstinence, and frequency of intercourse).
2. Conception variables (sub-fecundity or infecundity, contraception and sterilisation).
3. Gestation variables (spontaneous or induced abortion).

Bongaarts (1982) has demonstrated that only four factors, i.e. the proportion of the female reproductive period spent in a sexual union (in many societies the period of marriage), the duration of postpartum infecundability (that is, the period without menstruation or ovulation plus any period beyond this of postpartum sexual abstinence), the practice of contraception and its effectiveness, and the extent of induced abortion, provide 96 per cent of the explanation of the variance in fertility levels in nearly all societies.

Objectives and Methodologies

The present study aims to analyse the fertility and contraceptive behaviour of urban women. The main aim is to analyse the levels and trends of fertility in urban India and across states as well as to study the contraceptive behaviour in urban India and across states. Data have been collected from the National Family Health Survey-III, (2005-06), IIPS, Bombay; Sample Registration System, 1981, 1991, and 2001, Office of the Registrar General, India, 2/A, Man Singh Road, New Delhi and also the Sample Registration System, Special Fertility and Mortality Survey, 1998, Office of the Registrar General, India, New Delhi. Quantitative analysis have been done to infer the variations in fertility and contraceptive behaviour of urban women.

Levels and Trends of Fertility in Urban India and Across States (Based on NFHS)

NFHS-1, 2 and 3 provide estimates of Age Specific Fertility Rate (ASFR); Total Fertility Rate (TFR), and Crude Birth Rate (CBR) for the three year preceding the survey.

Table 15.1 presents the trends in ASFR, TFR and CBR from NFHS-1, 2 and 3, based on estimates for the three-year period before the survey. According to NFHS-3, the CBR is 19 births per 1000 population in urban areas which shows a gradually declining trend from NFHS-1 (24.1) to NFHS-2 (20.9) and further (18.8) in NFHS-3.

Table 15.1: Age-Specific and Total Fertility Rates and Crude Birth Rates of Women in Urban India (NFHS-1, 2 and 3)

Age	*NFHS-3*	*NFHS-2*	*NFHS-1*
	Urban	*Urban*	*Urban*
15-19	0.057	0.068	0.075
20-24	0.166	0.179	0.203
25-29	0.123	0.127	0.154
30-34	0.048	0.057	0.071
35-39	0.013	0.018	0.027
40-44	0.004	0.003	0.006
45-49	0.001	0.001	0.004
TFR 15-44	2.060	2.270	2.680
TFR 15-49	2.060	2.270	2.700
CBR	18.800	20.900	24.100

Source: NFHS-III (2005-06).

Total Fertility Rate (TFR) also exhibits in declining trends from NFHS-1 (2.70) to NFHS-2 (2.27) and NFHS-3 (2.06), indicating that, the fertility of urban women in India have almost reached the below replacement level. Though ASFR shows a declining trend from NFHS-1 to NFHS-3, but is revealed that women in the 20-24 and 25-29 age group have higher fertility than the rest of the age groups. The 15-19 age group also exhibits higher birth rates than rest of the other groups thereby indicating teenage pregnancies and deliveries still continuing in India.

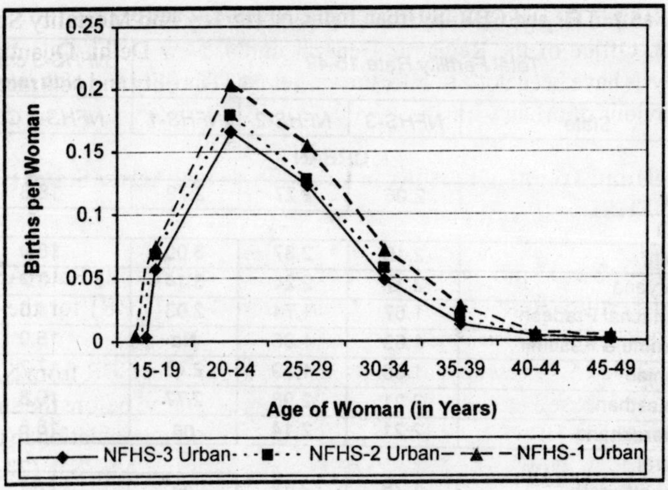

Source: NFHS-III (2005-06).

Fig. 15.1: Trends in Age Specific Fertility Rates NFHS-1, NFHS-2 and NFHS-3 in Urban India

Bearing children in younger ages can be seen in the light of health hazards for both mother and child. Such incidences may result in maternal mortality or infant mortality both being still high in our country.

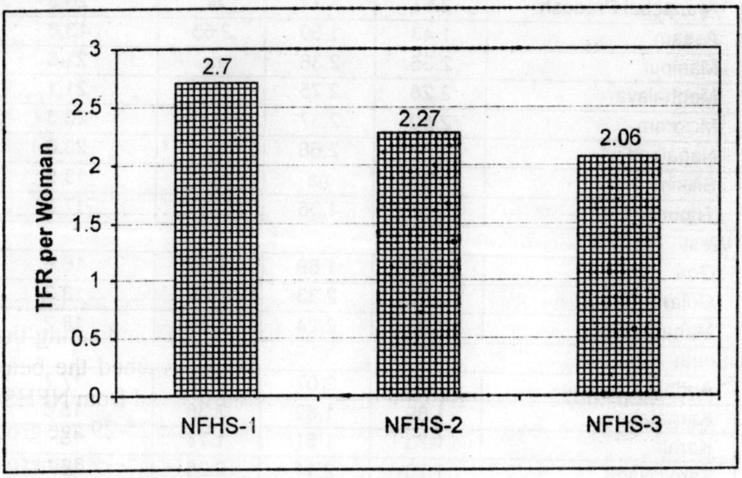

Source: NFHS-III (2005-06).

Fig. 15.2: Trends in Total Fertility Rates in Urban India

Table 15.2: TFR and CBR in Urban India, NFHS-1, 2 and 3

State	Total Fertility Rate 15-49			NFHS-3 crude birth rate
	NFHS-3	NFHS-2	NFHS-1	NFHS-3 CBR
URBAN				
India	2.06	2.27	2.70	18.8
North				
Delhi	2.10	2.37	3.00	18.0
Haryana	2.17	2.24	3.14	18.7
Himachal Pradesh	1.57	1.74	2.03	14.6
Jammu & Kashmir	1.63	1.66	Na	15.0
Punjab	1.88	1.79	2.48	17.7
Rajasthan	2.21	2.98	2.77	19.8
Uttarakhand	2.21	2.14	na	18.5
Central				
Chhattisgarh	1.78	2.12	na	17.1
Madhya Pradesh	2.58	2.68	na	22.1
Uttar Pradesh	2.95	2.91	na	23.5
East				
Bihar	2.87	2.61	na	23.5
Jharkhand	2.32	2.95	na	21.0
Odisha	1.89	2.19	2.53	17.7
West Bengal	1.59	1.69	2.14	14.3
Northeast				
Arunachal Pradesh	2.51	1.77	nc	26.3
Assam	1.43	1.50	2.53	13.6
Manipur	2.35	2.36	nc	21.6
Meghalaya	2.28	2.75	nc	21.1
Mizoram	2.50	2.37	nc	23.3
Nagaland	2.68	2.66	nc	23.8
Sikkim	1.29	na	na	13.5
Tripura	1.66	1.36	nc	17.8
West				
Goa	1.77	1.69	1.80	16.6
Gujarat	1.92	2.33	2.65	18.2
Maharashtra	1.91	2.24	2.54	18.2
South				
Andhra Pradesh	1.73	2.07	2.35	17.7
Karnataka	1.89	1.89	2.38	18.6
Kerala	1.73	1.51	1.78	15.4
Tamil Nadu	1.70	2.11	2.36	16.0

Source: NFHS-III (2005-06).

Fertility in Urban India

There are 29 states which have been grouped into various regions as North, Central, East, Northeast, and West and South in NFHS-III. The northern part consists of Delhi, Haryana, Himachal Pradesh, Jammu and Kashmir, Punjab, Rajasthan and Uttarakhand. The central part has Chhattisgarh, Madhya Pradesh, Uttar Pradesh; eastern part has Bihar, Jharkhand, Odisha, and West Bengal. The northeastern part consists of Arunachal Pradesh, Assam, Manipur, Meghalaya, Mizoram, Nagaland, Sikkim and Tripura. The western region has Goa, Gujarat and Maharashtra and finally, the southern part consists of Andhra Pradesh, Karnataka, Kerala, and Tamil Nadu.

The comparative figure of TFR in NFHS 1, 2 and 3 of urban India reveals that every state portrays a declining trend in total fertility rate in urban areas.

It can be observed that in the North, i.e. Himachal Pradesh, Jammu and Kashmir, and Punjab have already achieved below replacement level fertility, while the TFR of rest of northern states like Delhi (2.10), Haryana (2.17), Rajasthan (2.21), and Uttaranchal (2.21) are very close to replacement level fertility (2.1). In the central region, out of the three states only the urban areas of Chhattisgarh show below replacement level fertility (1.78) and in the two other states, i.e. Madhya Pradesh and Uttar Pradesh above replacement level fertility of 2.58 and 2.95 respectively have been observed.

The eastern region consisting of four states, urban Bihar (2.87) and Jharkhand (2.32) have above the replacement level fertility, that indicates population growth, while Odisha and West Bengal have 1.89 and 1.59 TFR respectively, i.e. below the replacement level.

The northeastern region has eight states and among them urban areas of Arunachal Pradesh (2.51), Manipur (2.35), Meghalaya (2.28), Mizoram (2.50), and Nagaland (2.68) have above replacement level fertility but urban Assam (1.43), Sikkim (1.29) and Tripura (1.66) show below replacement level fertility. In the western region all the three states have achieved below replacement level fertility in the urban areas like Goa (1.77), Gujarat (1.92), and Maharashtra (1.91). Similarly, in the southern states fertility has also gone below replacement level in urban Andhra Pradesh (1.73), Karnataka (1.89), Kerala (1.73) and Tamil Nadu (1.70).

However, in spite of these developments there is also much variation in urban TFR, that may be associated with level of urbanisation and other related factors.

Levels and Trends of Fertility in Urban India

Table 15.3 based on Sample Registration System (SRS) data also reveals the declining trend of CBR from 1981 to 2001 for urban India along with major states. In West Bengal, CBR has gone down to 13.8 in 2001, which is the lowest among other major States, while Uttar Pradesh with 27.0 CBR is on the apex among the major States. Along with Uttar Pradesh, the figures for Bihar (23.4), Madhya Pradesh (23.1), and Rajasthan (24.8) also seem to be very high.

Table 15.3: Crude Birth Rate (CBR) by Urban India, SRS 1981 to 2001

India/States	*1981*	*1991*	*2001*
India	27.0	24.3	20.3
Andhra Pradesh	27.5	24.4	19.7
Assam	23.2	21.3	18.6
Bihar	33.9	25.5	23.4
Gujarat	34.5	25.9	21.5
Haryana	29.6	27.2	22.9
Himachal Pradesh	17.3	18.6	17.1
Karnataka	25.7	24.0	19.0
Kerala	23.5	18.1	16.7
Madhya Pradesh	31.4	29.7	23.1
Maharashtra	24.5	22.9	20.2
Odisha	29.3	21.6	19.7
Punjab	28.5	25.6	18.7
Rajasthan	31.2	30.3	24.8
Tamil Nadu	23.9	20.8	17.8
Uttar Pradesh	31.5	29.0	27.0
West Bengal	20.0	18.5	13.8

Source: Sample Registration System, 1981, 1991 and 2001, Fertility and Mortality indicators. Office of the Registrar General, India, 2/A, Man Singh Road, New Delhi.

Table 15.4 reveals the gradual decline of TFR in urban India from 1981 (3.3) to 1991 (2.7) and further 2.3 in 2001 based on SRS data. The urban areas of major States like Andhra Pradesh, Assam, Himachal Pradesh, Karnataka, Kerala, Odisha, Punjab, Tamil Nadu and West Bengal have achieved replacement level and below replacement level fertility according to the SRS. The major causes of concern are the States like Uttar Pradesh (3.4), Bihar (3.1), Rajasthan (2.8), Haryana (2.5) and Madhya Pradesh (2.5) where more attention should be given to family planning and policy matters to curb fertility of population.

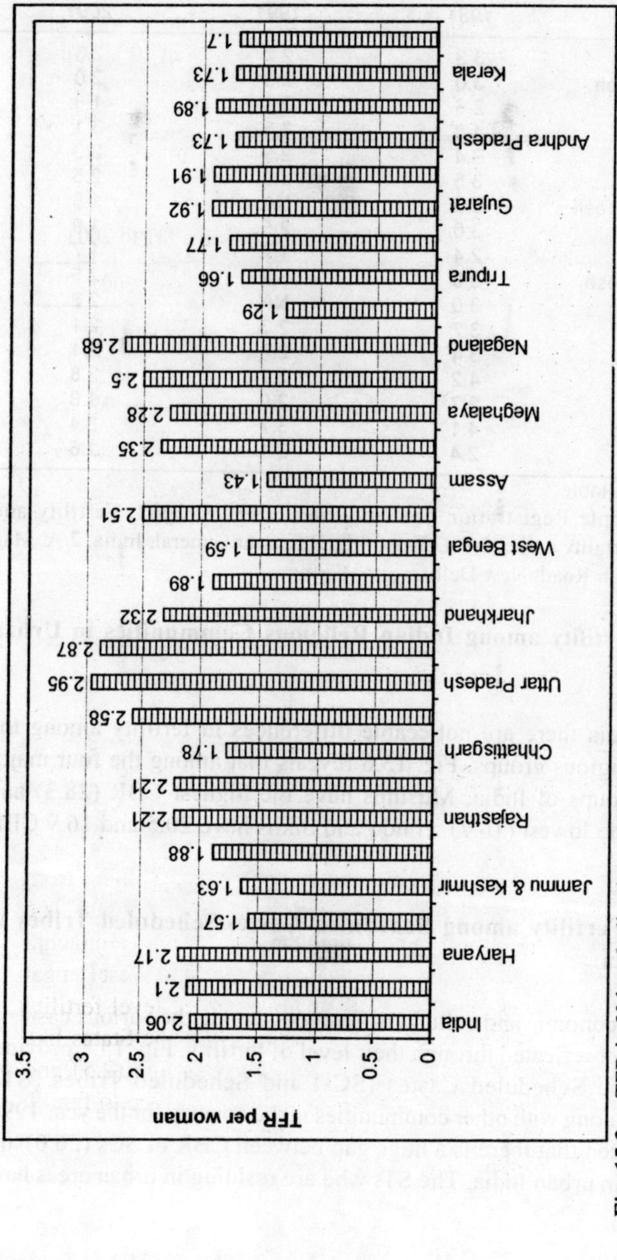

Fig. 15.3: TFR in Urban India along with States, 2005-06

Table 15.4: Total Fertility Rate (TFR) by Urban India, SRS 1981, 1991, and 2001

States	*1981*	*1991*	*2001*
India	3.3	2.7	2.3
Andhra Pradesh	3.0	2.5	2.0
Assam	2.6	2.1	1.8
Bihar	4.8	3.5	3.1
Gujarat	3.4	2.9	2.3
Haryana	3.5	3.0	2.5
Himachal Pradesh	2.0	NA	1.8
Karnataka	3.0	2.5	1.9
Kerala	2.4	1.7	1.7
Madhya Pradesh	3.9	3.4	2.5
Maharashtra	3.0	NA	2.2
Odisha	3.7	2.3	2.1
Punjab	3.4	2.8	2.1
Rajasthan	4.2	3.7	2.8
Tamil Nadu	2.7	2.0	1.8
Uttar Pradesh	4.1	3.7	3.4
West Bengal	2.4	2.1	1.6

NA = Not available

Source: Sample Registration System, 1981. 1991 & 2001. Fertility and Mortality indicators. Office of the Registrar General, India, 2/A, Man Singh Road, New Delhi.

Level of Fertility among Indian Religious Communities in Urban India

In urban India there are noticeable differences in fertility among the different religious groups. Fig. 15.6 reveals that among the four major religious groups of India, Muslims have the highest CBR (28.3) and Christians the lowest (16.7). Hindu and Sikhs have 20.5 and 16.9 CBR respectively.

Levels of Fertility among Scheduled Castes/Scheduled Tribes in Urban India

The socio-economic and cultural differences among the various castes in India also get reflected through their level of fertility. Fig. 15.7 provides CBR for the Scheduled Castes (SCs) and Scheduled Tribes (STs) population along with other communities in the country for the year 1997. It may be seen that there is a huge gap between CBR of SCs (26.0) and STs (20.5) in urban India. The STs who are residing in urban areas have

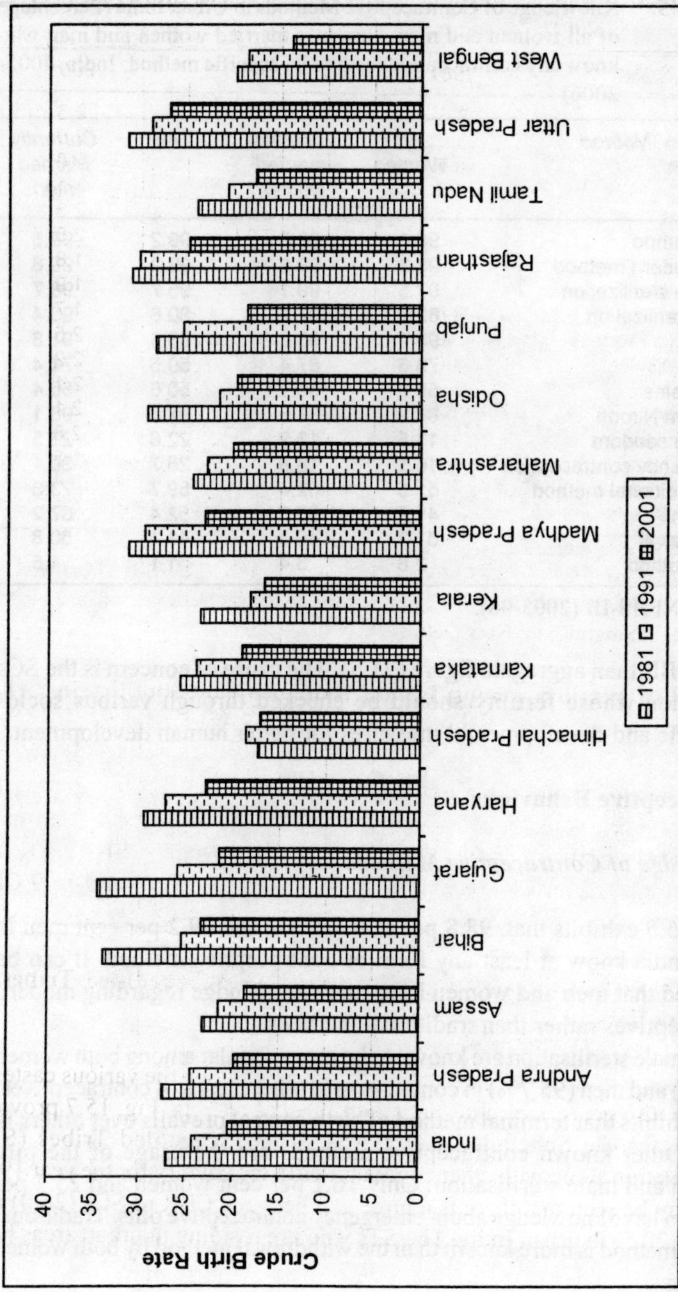

Fig. 15.4: Crude Birth Rate (CBR) by Urban India and Major States, 1981, 1991, and 2001

Table 15.5: Knowledge of Contraceptive Methods in Urban India (Percentage of all women and men, currently married women and men who know any contraceptive method by specific method, India, 2005-2006)

Method	*All Women*	*Currently married women*	*All men*	*Currently Married men*
Any method	98.8	99.6	99.2	99.8
Any modern method	98.8	99.6	99.2	99.8
Female sterilization	97.5	99.1	95.7	98.7
Male sterilization	82.7	87.7	90.6	95.4
Pill	90.7	93.2	88.4	91.6
IUD	79.6	87.4	59.5	71.4
Injectables	55.0	60.1	50.6	56.4
Condom/Nirodh	84.9	87.6	97.6	98.1
Female condom	13.5	13.9	22.6	23.5
Emergency contraception	16.1	18.8	25.7	30.1
Any traditional method	51.5	62.4	59.7	73.6
Rhythm	45.7	55.5	52.4	67.2
Withdrawal	31.3	40.3	41.1	50.8
Folk method	2.8	3.4	1.1	1.5

Source: NFHS-III (2005-06).

lower CBR than aggregate figure (21.5). The cause of concern is the SCs population whose fertility should be checked through various socio-economic and developmental measures for better human development.

Contraceptive Behaviour

Knowledge of Contraceptive Methods

Table 15.5 exhibits that, 98.8 per cent women and 99.2 per cent men in urban India know at least any form of contraceptive method. It can be observed that men and women have more knowledge regarding modern contraceptives rather than traditional methods.

Female sterilisation are known to be more popular among both women (97.5%) and men (95.7%) in comparison to other means of contraceptives. This exhibits that terminal method of birth control prevails over others in India. Other known contraceptive methods are the usage of the pill, condom and male sterilisation. Only 16.1 per cent women and 25.7 per cent men have knowledge about emergency contraceptive pills. Traditional rhythm method is more known than the withdrawal method by both women and men.

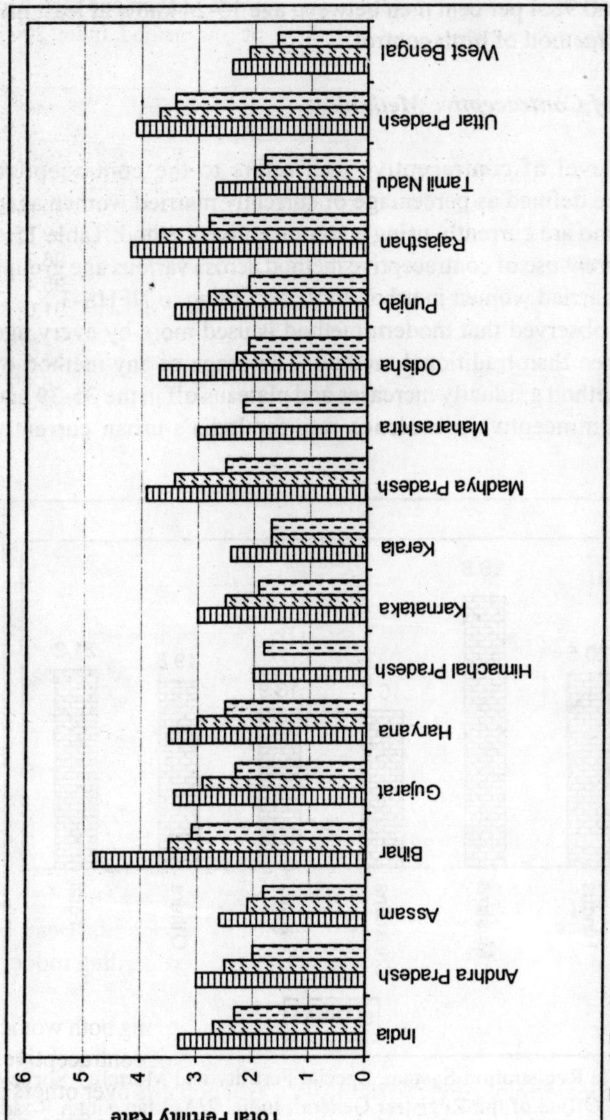

Fig. 15.5: Total Fertility Rate (TFR) Urban India and Major State, 1981, 1991, and 2001

In case of knowledge of contraceptive methods among adolescents (age 15-24) in urban India, NFHS-3 (2005-06) data reveals that 97.3 per cent women and 98.4 per cent men between age 15-24 know at least one contraceptive method of birth control.

Current Use of Contraceptive Methods

The current level of contraceptive use, refers to the contraceptive prevalence rate defined as percentage of currently married women aged 15-49 years who are currently using a contraceptive method. Table 15.6 depicts the current use of contraceptive method across various age groups by currently married women in urban India according to NFHS-3.

It can be observed that modern method is used more by every age group of women than traditional method. The usage of any method or any modern method gradually increases and plateaus off in the 35-39 age group. The contraceptive prevalence rate for India's urban currently

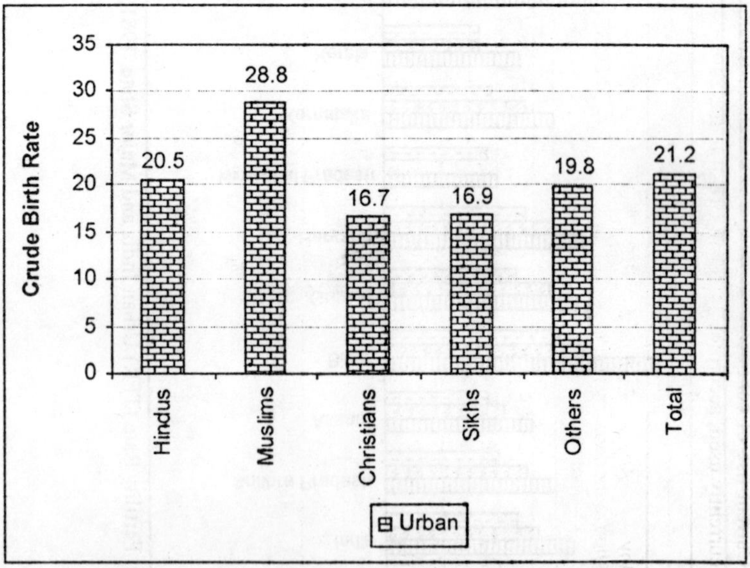

Source: Sample Registration System, Special Fertility and Mortality Survey, 1998, Office of the Registrar General, India, 2/A, Man Singh Road, New Delhi.

Fig. 15.6: Crude Birth Rate by Religion in Urban India-1997

Table 15.6: Current use of contraception by age (Per cent distribution of Currently married women by contraceptive method currently used, according to age in Urban India, 2005-06)

Age		Modern method						Traditional method			
	Any method	Any modern method	Female steriliza-tion	Pill	IUD	Injecta-bles	Condom/ Nirodh	Any tradition-nal method	Rhythm	With-drawal	Folk	Not currently using
15-19	16.0	10.7	1.5	2.5	0.9	0.0	5.8	5.4	3.4	2.0	0.0	84.0
20-24	39.5	32.6	12.1	5.8	3.9	0.2	10.4	6.9	4.2	2.7	0.0	60.5
25-29	62.9	54.3	30.1	6.0	4.4	0.1	13.4	8.7	5.4	3.1	0.1	37.1
30-34	75.3	65.9	43.3	4.3	4.4	0.1	13.2	9.4	5.3	3.8	0.3	24.7
35-39	77.3	68.2	51.3	2.9	3.0	0.1	9.4	9.2	5.7	3.1	0.3	22.7
40-44	72.8	63.6	52.3	1.4	1.9	0.1	5.8	9.2	5.9	2.9	0.4	27.2
45-49	65.7	61.3	53.5	0.6	0.6	0.0	2.5	4.4	2.9	1.4	0.1	34.3
Total	**64.0**	**55.8**	**37.8**	**3.8**	**3.2**	**0.1**	**9.8**	**8.1**	**5.0**	**2.9**	**0.2**	**36.0**

Source: NFHS-3, India, 2005-06.

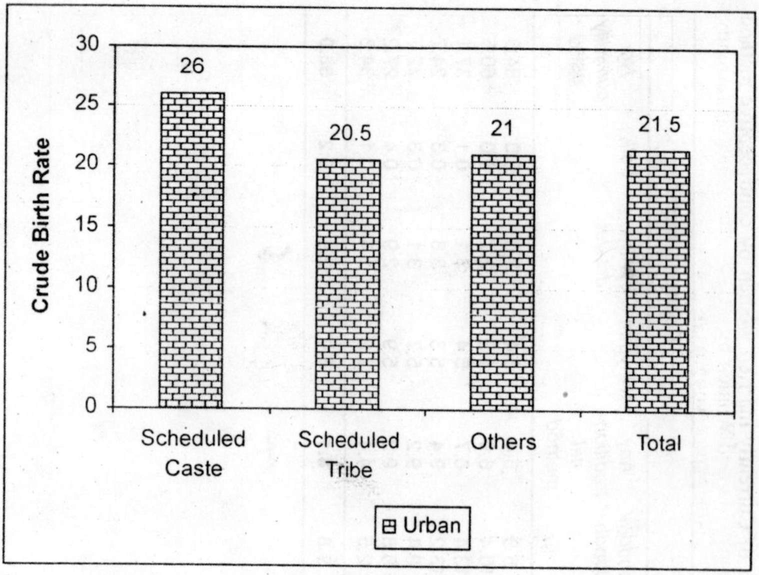

Source: Sample Registration System, Special Fertility & Mortality Survey, 1998. Office of the Registrar General, India, 2/A, Man Singh Road, New Delhi.

Fig. 15.7: Crude Birth Rate by Scheduled Caste/Tribe in Urban India-1997

married women is 65.7 per cent. However, 36 per cent of currently married women are found not using any method to curb their fertility.

Trends in Contraceptive Use

Table 15.7 and Fig. 15.9, exhibit the gradual enhancement in the use of contraception from NFHS-1 (51.1%), NFHS-2 (58.2%) and NFHS-3 (64.0%) in urban India. Use of female sterilisation rises sharply from NFHS-1 to NFHS-2 and then decline in NFHS-3. Use of the Pill, IUD, and condom gradually rises as modern methods, while traditional methods of rhythm and withdrawal also rises from NFHS-1 to NFHS-2 and further to NFHS-3.

Current Use of Contraception by State

Table 15.7 reveals that there are substantial variations among the states regarding the use of contraception. Himachal Pradesh has the highest

Table 15.7: Current use of contraception [Per cent distribution of Currently Married Women by contraceptive method currently used, (Urban) India, NFHS-3 (2005-06), NFHS-2 (1998-99), and NFHS-1(1992-93)]

State	*Modern method*							*Traditional method*				
	Any method	*Any modern method*	*Female sterilization*	*Pill*	*IUD*	*Injectables*	*Condom/ Nirodh*	*Any traditional method*	*Rhythm*	*With-drawal*	*Folk*	*Not currently using*
(1)	(2)	(3)	(4)	(5)	(6)	(7)	(8)	(9)	(10)	(11)	(12)	(13)
NFHS-3	64.0	55.8	37.8	3.8	3.2	0.1	9.8	8.1	5.0	2.9	0.2	36.0
NFHS-2	58.2	51.2	36.0	2.7	3.5	Na	7.2	Na	3.9	2.8	Na	41.8
NFHS-1	51.1	45.3	30.4	1.9	3.9	0.0	5.8	Na	3.5	2.1	Na	48.9
North												
Delhi	67.1	56.5	22.0	4.4	5.0	0.1	23.9	10.6	6.3	4.1	0.2	32.9
Haryana	66.5	59.7	28.2	4.2	5.6	0.0	20.3	6.9	4.2	2.4	0.4	33.5
H.P.	73.7	71.2	32.1	4.6	3.7	0.2	27.2	2.6	1.3	1.3	0.0	26.3
J &K	68.3	55.8	32.8	3.7	2.8	0.4	11.8	12.4	3.3	9.0	0.1	31.7
Punjab	61.7	51.8	21.7	2.8	4.1	0.1	22.1	9.9	4.9	5.0	0.0	38.3
Rajasthan	65.7	62.0	39.6	4.9	2.4	0.2	13.0	3.8	1.8	1.4	0.5	34.3
Uttarakhand	65.3	59.2	20.4	4.7	2.7	0.0	28.3	6.1	2.9	3.2	0.0	34.7
Central												
Chhattisgarh	65.4	58.9	43.9	2.9	2.7	0.0	7.8	6.5	2.6	2.8	1.2	34.6
M.P.	61.1	56.3	36.8	3.6	1.6	0.0	12.6	4.8	2.5	2.1	0.2	38.9
U.P.	56.3	42.4	18.7	3.2	3.2	0.1	16.6	13.9	10.1	3.1	0.6	43.7

(Contd.)

(1)	(2)	(3)	(4)	(5)	(6)	(7)	(8)	(9)	(10)	(11)	(12)	(13)
East												
Bihar	50.6	41.3	31.2	3.1	1.0	0.4	4.7	9.3	6.1	2.7	0.5	49.4
Jharkhand	60.0	49.9	35.0	4.9	1.4	0.0	7.9	10.1	4.1	5.7	0.2	40.0
Odisha	59.4	50.1	30.3	10.2	1.5	0.1	6.7	9.4	3.2	6.0	0.2	40.6
West Bengal	75.5	49.9	28.8	10.7	0.9	0.1	8.7	25.7	15.0	10.6	0.1	24.5
North East												
Arunachal Pradesh	47.3	39.4	19.4	8.7	6.5	0.3	4.5	7.9	2.5	4.8	0.6	52.7
Assam	66.0	37.2	14.1	15.6	1.0	0.0	6.4	28.8	15.9	12.5	0.4	34.0
Manipur	54.5	24.8	8.90	4.7	4.0	0.1	6.4	29.7	9.0	20.4	0.3	45.5
Meghalaya	43.7	36.7	18.9	8.8	3.1	0.7	5.1	7.0	4.6	2.2	0.2	56.3
Mizoram	64.3	64.0	46.0	9.6	6.4	0.0	2.0	0.4	0.0	0.4	0.0	35.7
Nagaland	41.9	31.8	14.8	6.5	4.6	0.2	5.6	10.1	7.6	2.4	0.1	58.1
Sikkim	63.1	51.7	25.0	11.7	2.3	2.7	8.3	11.5	8.1	3.1	0.2	36.9
Tripura	66.8	44.4	16.8	23.0	0.0	0.0	4.3	22.4	11.8	10.6	0.0	33.2
West												
Goa	51.3	38.6	24.5	1.9	2.6	0.2	6.3	12.6	7.7	4.9	0.0	48.7
Gujarat	67.6	57.7	37.5	4.1	6.7	0.1	8.6	9.8	8.1	1.7	0.1	32.4
Maharashtra	66.7	64.0	44.2	3.6	5.3	0.1	9.8	2.7	1.9	0.6	0.1	33.3
South												
Andhra Pradesh	67.7	67.2	61.5	0.6	0.9	0.1	1.1	0.5	0.3	0.2	0.0	32.3
Karnataka	60.8	59.2	49.9	1.2	4.3	0.0	3.5	1.6	1.2	0.4	0.0	39.2
Kerala	68.9	58.5	45.6	0.0	2.4	0.1	8.5	10.4	4.9	5.5	0.0	31.1
Tamil Nadu	60.8	59.2	51.9	0.3	3.0	0.0	3.4	1.6	1.2	0.4	0.0	39.2

Source: NFHS-3, India, 2005-06.

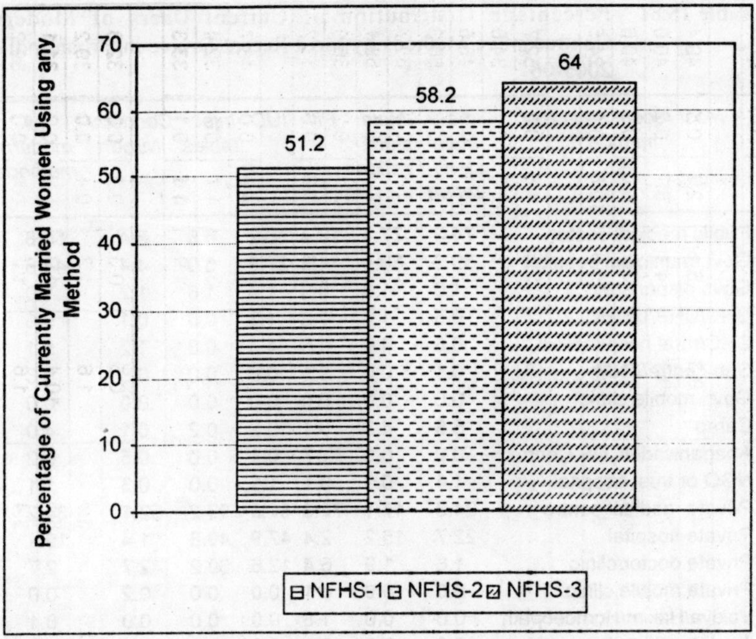

Fig. 15.8: Trends in Current Contraceptive Use in Urban India

contraceptive prevalence rate (73.7%) while Nagaland has the lowest (41.9%). There are several States like Delhi, Haryana, Himachal Pradesh, Jammu and Kashmir, West Bengal, Tripura, Gujarat, Maharashtra, Andhra Pradesh and Kerala whose urban areas have more than two-thirds of contraceptive prevalence rate by any method of contraceptive use. Modern contraceptive methods are more practiced among all states than traditional. Female sterilisation is the highest prevalent terminal method used among the rest.

Contraceptive Pills are more used by currently married women in Odisha, West Bengal, Arunachal Pradesh, Assam, Meghalaya, Mizoram, Nagaland, Sikkim and Tripura. In fact Tripura ranks first (23.0) in the use of Pill. Basically Pill, IUD and condom are used for the spacing of births. Use of Condom is more popular in northern and central states. Again, Delhi, Jammu and Kashmir, Punjab, Uttar Pradesh, Bihar, Jharkhand, Odisha, West Bengal, Assam, Manipur, Nagaland, Sikkim, Tripura, Goa, Gujarat and Kerala are the states where traditional methods are more prevalent than among other states. West Bengal (25.7%), Assam (28.8%) and Manipur (29.7%) are the leading states regarding the use of

Table 15.8: Percentage Distribution of Current Users of Modern Contraceptive Methods by Most Recent Source in Urban India, 2005-06

Most recent source of method	*Female sterilization*	*Male sterilization*	*Pill*	*IUD*	*Injectables*	*Condom/ Nirodh*	*All modern methods*
Public medical sector	74.2	77.4	10.4	36.2	6.8	8.4	56.8
Govt./municipal hospital	59.2	66.0	4.5	27.9	5.0	4.4	44.6
Govt. dispensary	1.0	1.6	0.9	1.3	1.6	1.2	1.0
UHC/UHP/UFWC	0.8	1.0	0.2	1.2	0.0	0.1	0.6
CHC/rural hospital/PHC	6.6	4.0	0.5	4.3	0.0	1.2	5.1
Sub-centre/ANM	0.1	0.0	2.1	0.8	0.0	0.5	0.3
Govt. mobile clinic	0.0	0.0	0.0	0.0	0.0	0.0	0.0
Camp	5.6	4.3	0.1	0.2	0.2	0.1	4.0
Anaganwadi/ICDS Centre	0.0	0.0	1.7	0.1	0.0	0.5	0.2
NGO or trust hospital	1.4	0.9	0.1	1.6	0.0	0.3	1.1
Private medical centre	24.3	17.1	72.9	61.0	93.2	52.1	34.2
Private hospital	22.7	15.2	2.4	47.9	49.8	1.4	19.1
Private doctor/clinic	1.6	1.9	6.4	12.6	30.2	2.7	2.7
Private mobile clinic	0.0	0.0	0.1	0.0	0.0	0.2	0.0
Vaidya/Hakim/Homoeopath	0.0	0.0	1.8	0.0	0.0	0.0	0.1
Traditional healer	0.0	0.0	0.1	0.0	0.0	0.1	0.0
Pharmacy/drugstore	0.0	0.0	60.4	0.4	5.3	45.3	11.6
Other source	0.1	0.0	15.9	0.2	0.0	39.4	7.6
Shop	0.0	0.0	2.4	0.2	0.0	2.7	0.6
Spouse	0.0	0.0	13.1	0.0	0.0	35.6	6.8
Friend relative	0.0	0.0	0.3	0.0	0.0	0.4	0.1
Other	0.1	0.0	0.1	0.1	0.0	0.4	0.1
Don't know	0.0	4.1	0.0	0.0	0.0	0.0	0.1

Source: NFHS-3, India, 2005-06.

traditional contraceptive methods. There are some states like Uttar Pradesh (43.7%), Bihar (49.4%), Jharkhand (40%), Odisha (40.6%), Arunachal Pradesh (52.7%), Manipur (45.5%), Meghalaya (56.3%), Nagaland (58.1%), and Goa (48.7%) where currently married women are not using any contraceptive method.

The major source of family planning services and supplies in urban India are government hospitals and urban family welfare centres. Contraceptives and other family planning services are also provided by private hospitals and clinics and Non-Governmental Organisations (NGOs). Pills and condoms also available in pharmacies and shops for the users. Table 15.8 shows that in urban India, 56.8 per cent users of modern contraceptive methods avail services of the public medical sector

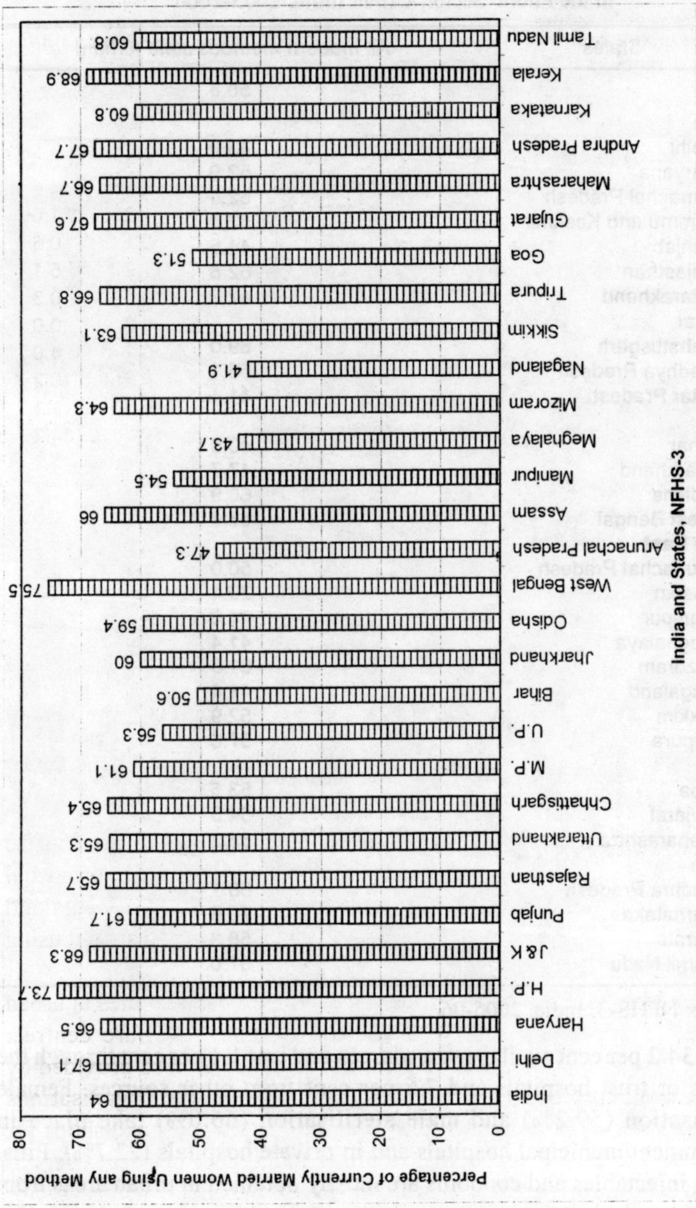

Source: NFHS 3, India 2005-06.

Fig. 15.9: Contraceptive Prevalence Rate in Urban India, 2005-06.

Table 15.9: Percentage of Current Users of Modern Contraceptive Methods in the Public Sector, Urban India, 2005-2006

States	*All modern methods state (urban)*
India	**56.8**
North	
Delhi	43.0
Haryana	52.9
Himachal Pradesh	62.4
Jammu and Kashmir	52.8
Punjab	44.5
Rajasthan	62.8
Uttarakhand	42.2
Central	
Chhattisgarh	69.0
Madhya Pradesh	66.1
Uttar Pradesh	41.1
East	
Bihar	40.6
Jharkhand	47.7
Odisha	60.9
West Bengal	53.1
North East	
Arunachal Pradesh	50.0
Assam	29.1
Manipur	44.6
Meghalaya	41.4
Mizoram	81.3
Nagaland	41.4
Sikkim	52.9
Tripura	37.6
West	
Goa	53.5
Gujarat	54.0
Maharashtra	53.2
South	
Andhra Pradesh	68.1
Karnataka	70.6
Kerala	58.8
Tamil Nadu	67.0

Source: NFHS-3, India, 2005-06.

while 34.2 per cent avail private sources and just 1.1 per cent through the NGOs or trust hospitals and 7.6 per cent from other sources. Female sterilisation (59.2%) and male sterilisation (66.0%) take place in government/municipal hospitals and in private hospitals (22.7%). Pills, IUDs, injectables and condoms are mostly obtained in urban areas from private medical centres in comparison to the public sector. Pills (60.4%)

Table 15.10: Percentage Distribution of Currently Married Women who are not using a Contraceptive Method but who Intend to use in the future by Preferred Method, According to Urban Residence, India, 2005-06

Preferred method	Urban India
Female sterilization	64.3
Male sterilization	0.4
Pill	10.9
IUD	4.3
Injectables	1.6
Implants	0.0
Condom / Nirodh	7.6
Female condom	0.1
Rhythm	2.3
Withdrawal	0.9
Folk method	0.4
Unsure of method	7.2

Source: NFHS-3, India, 2005-06.

and condoms (45.3%) are mostly purchased from pharmacy shops in the private sector.

Public Sector as Providers of Contraceptives

Table 15.9 exhibits 56.8 per cent users of modern contraceptive methods obtain their requirement from the public sector in urban India. Chhattisgarh, Mizoram, Andhra Pradesh, Karnataka and Tamil Nadu have more than two-third of users obtaining modern contraceptives from the public sector. Mizoram (81.3%) is the leading user of the public sector and Assam (29.1%) is the least user.

Preferred Method of Contraception for Future Use

Table 15.10 depicts that 64.3 per cent currently married women express their desire for prefer female sterilisation in the future, while only 0.4 per cent express the need for male sterilisation. 10.9 per cent intend to use the contraceptive pill in future while 7.6 per cent favour condom use. The need for IUD as a future preference is expressed by 4.3 per cent women while 7.2 per cent currently married women are unsure about any method.

Exposure to Family Planning Messages

According to NFHS-3 report, 35.7 per cent, 74.3 per cent, 40 per cent, 41.5 per cent of women heard or saw a family planning message on radio, television, in a newspaper or magazine; or on a wall painting or hoarding respectively in urban India. The same figures for men were 53.4 per cent, 81.4 per cent, 65.2 per cent and 68.1 per cent respectively in urban India. Again, 20.0 per cent women and only 1.9 per cent men replied that they did not get any message of family planning from these media sources.

Conclusions

Fertility has been a frequent cause of concern and debate. For many years it appeared that high fertility would pose a threat to the well-being of societies, regions and even the planet itself.

The study reveals various characteristics of levels and trends of fertility in urban India along with States. Fertility rate in urban India has been declining continuously over the decades. Some of the urban areas of India have already achieved replacement level fertility (NFHS-III). Fertility transition in India came through changes in socio-economic life style of the people and advancement in medical technology that raise the life expectancy of the people and make them more accessible to health facilities. The efforts placed by family planning programmes in India since long had also played an ameliorating role in fertility decline in several states.

The nature of contraceptives and contraceptive behaviour of the people both have been changed over the period of time with the advancemet of modern scientific technology and changing socio-economic and cultural life style of the people. Modern contraceptive methods make people particularly women more liberated and confident over their body and reproductivity since now she can easly check unwanted pregnancy and mental trauma. In urban India, use of modern contraceptive methods has increased and public sector still acts as the major source of contraceptive requirements of the people except spacing methods (pills, IUDs and condoms) that are mostly obtained from private centres.

Finally, it is observed that the nature of use of contraceptives reflect prevalence of female sterilisation still dominates urban India in comparison to male sterilisation.

NOTES

1. Bongaarts, J. (1982), "The fertility-inhabiting effects of the intermediate fertility variables", *Studies in Family Planning*, 13.
2. Coale, A.J. (1967), "Factors associated with the development of low fertility: An historic summary", in *Proceeding of the World Population Conference,* Belgrade, 1965, Vol. II, New York.
3. Davis, K. and Blake, J. (1956), "Social structure and fertility: An analytical framework", *Economic Development and Cultural Change,* 4.

REFERENCES

Bongaarts, J. (1982), "The fertility-inhabiting effects of the intermediate fertility variables", *Studies in Family Planning*, 13.

Coale, A.J. (1967), "Factors associated with the development of low fertility: An historic summary", in *Proceeding of the World Population Conference"* Belgrade, 1965, Vol. II, New York.

Davis, K. and Blake, J. (1956), "Social structure and fertility: An analytical framework", *Economic Development and Cultural Change,* 4.

National Family Health Survey (NFHS-3), 2005-06, *India*, Vol. 1, September 2007.

Sample Registration System, *Special Fertility & Mortality Survey*, 1998, Office of the Registrar General, India, 2/A, Man Singh Road, New Delhi.

Sample Registration System, 1981, 1991 & 2001, *Fertility and Mortality Indicators*. Office of the Registrar General, India, 2/A, Man Singh Road, New Delhi.

16

Socio-Economic Status and Health Care in Urban Eastern India

Sunita Kumari

Introduction

India's urbanisation is often termed as over-urbanisation or pseudo-urbanisation. The big cities attained inordinately large population size leading to a virtual collapse in the urban services and followed by basic problems in the field of housing, slums, water supply, infrastructure, quality of life and so on. All these problems are associated with health. The urban health problems of India are inadequate and inferior health infrastructure, poor public service delivery, lack of quality choices for consumers, and lack of access, especially for the poor. Implementation of policies and schemes are also not up to the mark. Moreover, relatively expensive and privately provided services are more readily available, which are generally not accessible for the poorer segments of the population.

In contemporary times, health is an important component of well-being. There are several conceptions of well-being like "basic needs", "physical quality of life index", "human development index" and many more. Health is common to all these concepts of well-being. Health has come to occupy an important place in development policy, ever since it was realised that income growth alone has not been sufficient for the welfare of the people and attention has to be paid to direct promotion of well-being. This is borne out by the shift from growth-mediated strategies to support-led strategies (Dreze and Sen, 1989). This study explores the association between availability of health infrastructure, socio-economic conditions of individuals and utilisation of health care facilities. This study at the onset focuses on the models related to health inequality and literature survey. Next, an attempt has been made to portray the picture of health care facilities, morbidity and hospitalisation rate in the concerned region and finally the existing socio-economic inequalities in the study region have been analysed.

Models Related to Health Inequalities

There are three models of health inequality considered in this section, viz. racial-genetic model, lifestyle and behaviour model and socio-economic model of health.

The racial-genetic model postulates the group differences in the distribution of some set of genes that gives rise both to phenotypic differences between groups, e.g. skin colour and the propensity to poor health, although precise research has proved that there is no association between diseases and genetic causes. For example, Collins and David (1995), found out that the rate of infant mortality due to known genetic causes does not differ by ethnic groups. Similar case has been found in case of sickle-cell anemia. Therefore, as an explanation for the general phenomena of ethnic health inequalities, a racial-genetic hypothesis is less applicable as a model of health inequality.

The health behaviour/lifestyle hypothesis postulates that health inequalities are functions of unhealthy behaviour, such as smoking, excessive alcohol use, high fat and high sodium diets, lack of physical activity, that are found among different groups. This kind of hypothesis has somewhat more plausibility than a genetic model of health.

In spite of all these facts, lifestyle/behaviour of individuals are controlled by socio-economic conditions of different groups. Therefore, socio-economic model of health is more relevant in context to health inequality. The criticisms of both the racial-genetic and the health behaviour/lifestyle models lead naturally to a consideration of the socio-economic status model. Many have argued that ethnic group/caste membership is confounded with differences in socio-economic status such as income, occupation, and educational attainment; therefore, apparent racial/caste differences in health may simply be a function of this. Similarly, surveys of diet, smoking, alcohol use, and physical activity demonstrate a consistent association of low socio-economic status with detrimental health habits.

According to Dressler (1993), health inequalities that take into account the fact of continuing discrimination against people in colour-conscious societies, (or in the Indian context-caste based societies), a fact that automatically assigns people of a particular colour/caste to a lower position in rank in the social structure. He refers this as "a social structural model."

Literature Review

Data on health outcomes among Scheduled Tribes and Scheduled Castes consistently show that these groups are at a disadvantageous position. Among all backward groups in India, STs tend to have the highest rate of infant mortality (83 per 1000 births) and child mortality, malnutrition and morbidity, followed by the SCs and then by other disadvantaged or backward classes (Nanda, 2004). Morbidity prevalence and hospitalisation rates vary among the different social groups in case of out-patient and in-patient care in India. Across the social groups, utilisation of public health facilities is the highest among ST, followed by SC and the least is among the 'Others' category. The decline in utilisation of public sector health care between the periods 1986-87 and 1995-96 is almost uniform among ST, SC and 'Others'. However, use of public health facilities, between the periods 1995-96 and 2004 is higher among STs followed by SCs and is the least among the 'others'. In other words, not only utilisation of public health care is higher among ST and SC groups but the increament is also greater among these groups when compared to 'Others'. Disparities in utilisation of public health facilities across social groups are relatively sharper in urban areas than in rural areas. In rural areas, where availability of private health care is relatively scarce, more utilisation of public health care takes place. In the case of urban areas with greater availability of private health care, more use of private health care services is found.

Therefore, utilisation of private sector for out-patient care is greatest among the others, especially among 'Other-Hindus' and is less among SC and is the least among ST groups. Further, private sector for ambulatory care is expanding rapidly and public health facility is increasingly being under-utilised. The use of public health care has declined between the periods 1986-87 and 1995-96 whereas between the periods 1986-87 and 2004, it has declined more drastically in the urban areas than in rural areas. In other words, there is still greater dependence on public health services in rural areas than in urban areas.

It can be said that there is a dual relationship between income and health (Smith, 1999). Although there is evidence to show that income is a determinant of health, there is also strong evidence that shows health status of the people to be strongly influenced by their income through their working capacity and productivity. It could also be the case of endogeneity of income in health determination that is, both health and income are determined simultaneously (Ettner, S., 1996).

In a general way, overall income has a casual effect on health; there are two hypotheses about the pathway through which income affects health. One is the "absolute income hypothesis" and another is the "relative income hypothesis. The absolute income hypothesis states that an individual's health depends on his own level of income, irrespective of the income of everybody else in society, (Preston, S.H., 1975; Pritchett, L., 1996; Adler, N.E., 1993). According to this hypothesis, the pathway to health from income is through absolute material deprivation, which affects health directly though lifestyles, access to nutrition, health care etc. According to the "relative income hypothesis", it is the distribution of income in a society that affects the individual's health. It means that it is not only individual's own level of income but his relative position in the income distribution that affects his health. Here one of the ways to health is argued to be through psycho-social stress that leads to erosion of social esteem triggered by relative deprivation of material factors (Wilkinson, R.G., 1996). The other pathway of relative health has been through the pattern of social investment, such as efforts by backward states on education and welfare spending that often accompanies a growing distance between the rich and the poor (Kawachi and Kennedy, 1998). Erosion of social capital has been cited as another mechanism that affects health through relative income (Kennedy, Kawachi and Lochner, 1998).

Objectives of the Study

The objectives of the present study on health care utilisation in urban areas of eastern India are to analyse the spatial distribution of health care facilities in urban areas; to explain social inequalities in utilisation of health care facilities in four eastern states, viz. Bihar, Odisha, Jharkhand and West Bengal and finally, to explore the economic inequalities in utilisation of health care facilities.

Methodologies and Data Sources

The data source of urban health services is the Census of India 1991 and 2001, viz. Town Directory of Bihar, West Bengal, Odisha and Jharkhand. The major health care facilities considered are the number of hospitals, dispensaries, health care centres, nursing homes and other medical institutions with number of beds. Data on health infrastructure is readily available at the city and town level in Town Directory (Census of India 1991 and 2001). The National Sample Survey (NSS) 60th round is the second data source particularly the 2004 one on "Morbidity, Health Care and Condition of the Aged". This gives the data on utilisation of health care facilities and ailments. It also provides data of the household conditions of individuals, their socio-demographic conditions and economic status in society.

The study is based on NSS Unit Level Analysis. Data has been taken from "Schedule 25", levels 2 and 3, where level 2 is household file and level 3 is the individual file, both of the files have been merged together. The purpose of merging the files is to find out data at unit level, i.e. how many individuals (level 3) are availing health care and what are their social and economic conditions (level 2). The sample size of the data has been given in Table 16.1.

Table 16.1: NSS Number of Persons and Households

States/Regions	*Urban HH*	*Urban Persons*	*Total HH*	*Total Persons*
Bihar	638	3792	4174	23851
Jharkhand	598	3400	1996	10954
Orissa	560	2711	2654	13003
West Bengal	1879	8793	5049	24904
Eastern India	3675	18696	13873	72712
India	26566	132563	73868	383338

Source: NSS 60th Round 'Morbidity, Health Care and the Condition of the Aged'.

Provision of Health Care

In 2001 Census, number of hospitals per 1,00,000 population was 2.19, hospital beds per 1,00,000 population were 254.71, and dispensaries for the same population were 6.75 in urban eastern India. Eastern India has more number of dispensaries and total hospital beds compared to the national average, whereas indicators like hospitals per 1,00,000 population exhibit lower values in Eastern India when compared to aggregate figures for India. This may be due to the existing pressure of population in this region. The number of hospital per 1,00,000 is the highest in urban areas of Jharkhand, followed by Odisha and Bihar, whereas West Bengal stands lowest among all. Number of dispensaries per 1,00,000 population is more in Bihar (10.90 per 1,00,000 population), followed by West Bengal

(6.70 per 1,00,000 population). The availability of dispensaries per one lakh population is quite less in Odisha. The availability of total hospital beds per 1,00,000 population is the highest in West Bengal, followed by Odisha and Jharkhand, and it is the least in Bihar (187.45 per 1,00,000 population) (Table 16.2).

Health care centres per 1,00,000 population are more in Jharkhand, when compared to Odisha and West Bengal, both of which stand at the same position (1.81 per 100,000 population), and it is the least in the urban areas of Bihar. Again, eastern India has only 1.78 health care centres per one lakh population, which is slightly more than Bihar. In case of Family Welfare Centres, it is higher in Odisha (2.19 per one lakh population) and low in West Bengal; whereas eastern India has 2.65 family welfare centres per 1,00,000 population, which is more than the aggregate of these four States. The availability of nursing homes is the highest in Bihar, followed by West Bengal, and is the least in Odisha. In case of other medical institutions, the highest availability of the same is found in West Bengal, whereas Jharkhand and Bihar are below the average of the region. Data of other medical institutions are not available for Odisha (Fig. 16.1).

Although the level of urbanisation and urban population is less in Eastern India, it is the lowest in Bihar (only 10.47%). The level of urbanisation has declined further in Bihar during 1991 to 2001, and similar conditions have been observed in Odisha as well. Data for level of urbanisation is not available for Jharkhand in 1991, because earlier, it was a part of Bihar. Though West Bengal has the highest level of urbanisation in this region, but on the whole, the level of urbanisation is low in Eastern India (18.81 per cent, 2001), considering that at the national level, it is 27.7 per cent (Table 16.3).

Table 16.2: Status of Health Infrastructure in Urban Eastern India

States	*Hospitals per 1,00,000 population*	*Dispensaries per 1,00,000 population*	*Total beds per 1,00,000 population*
West Bengal	1.70	6.70	284.54
Bihar	2.42	10.90	187.45
Orissa	2.50	1.41	250.38
Jharkhand	3.39	5.79	245.02
Eastern India	2.19	6.75	254.71
India	3.7	5.5	188.55

Source: Census of India 2001.

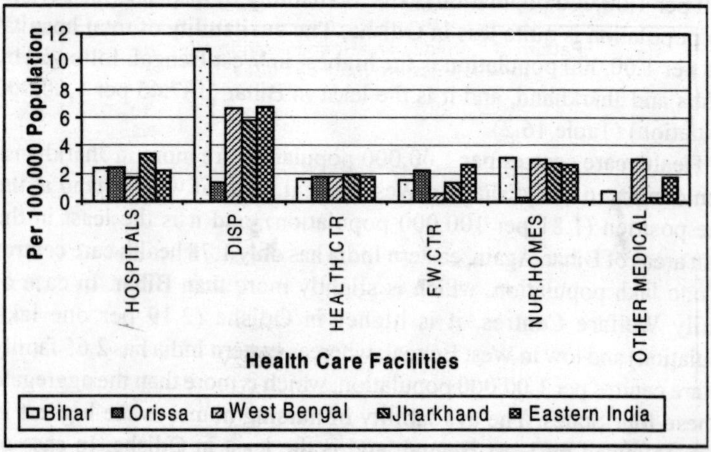

Note: DISP.–Dispensaries, HEALTH.CTR. –Health Centres, F.W.CTR. – Family Welfare Centres, and NUR.HOMES. –Nursing Homes, OTHERS MEDICAL. – Other Medical Institutions.

Source: Census of India 2001.

Fig. 16.1: Health Care Facilities in Urban Eastern India

Table 16.3: Level of Urbanisation and Urban Population in Eastern India

States	*Level of Urbanisation*		*Urban Population*
	1991	*2001*	*2001*
Eastern India	–	18.81	42648696
West Bengal	27.48	28.03	22486481
Bihar	12.47	10.47	8679200
Odisha	13.38	14.97	5496318
Jharkhand	–	22.25	5986697
India	25.71	27.78	285354954

Source: Census of India 1991 and 2001.

Pattern of Morbidity and Hospitalisation

Morbidity prevalence rate in eastern India during the last 15 days of the survey is highest in urban West Bengal, followed by Bihar, and the lowest in Jharkhand (Map 16.1). As a State, Jharkhand has the lowest morbidity prevalence rate not only in urban eastern India, but also in India. Morbidity prevalence rate on the day before the survey is again high in West Bengal, followed by Bihar, and is the lowest in urban areas of Jharkhand. Except West Bengal, other three states have reported lower morbidity prevalence

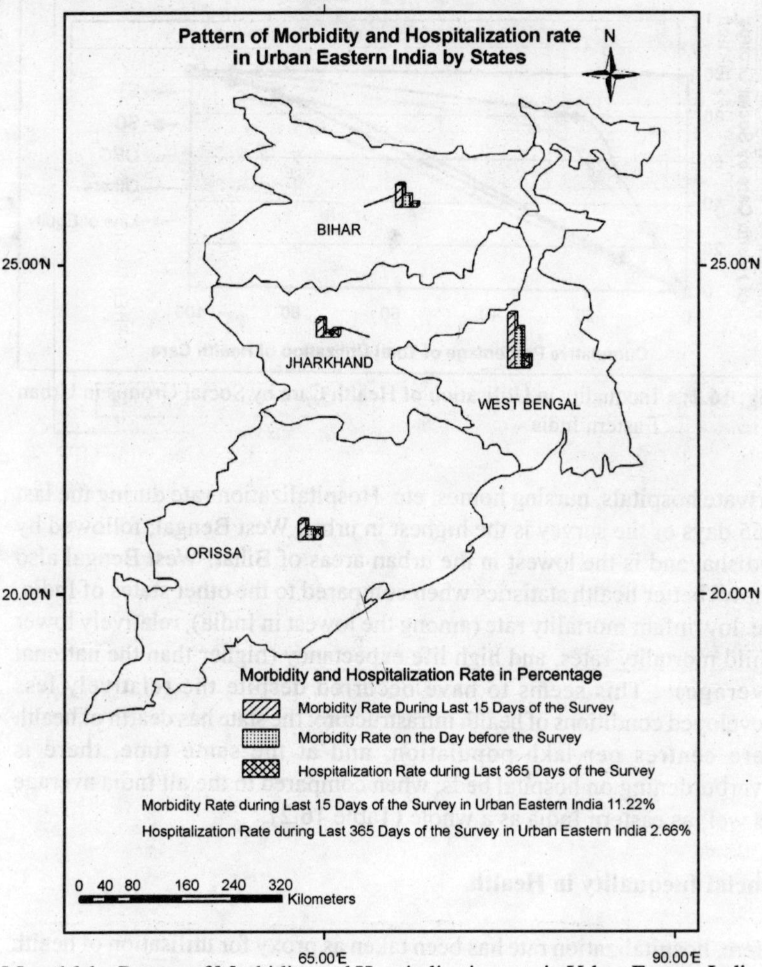

Map 16.1: Pattern of Morbidity and Hospitalisation rate in Urban Eastern India by States

Source: NSS 60th Round, Morbidity Healthcare and conditions of the Aged, 2004.

rates than the average for eastern India. However, this may be due to the incidence of low reporting by these states, a factor of the prevailing conditions of awareness and education levels.

In this study, hospitals covered include public, community health centres and primary health centres (if provided with beds), ESI hospitals,

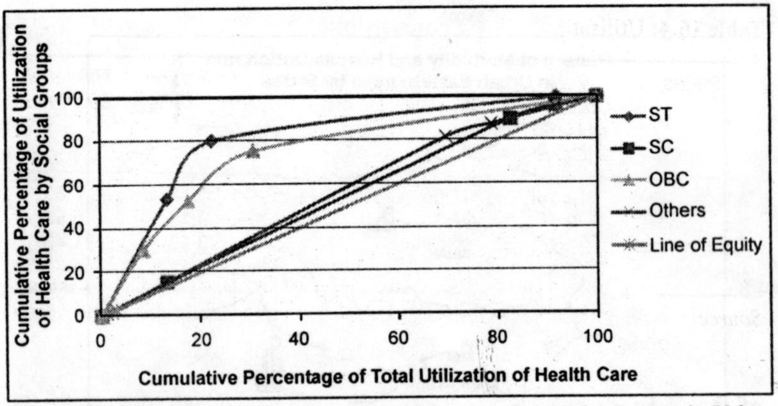

Fig. 16.2: Inequality in Utilisation of Health Care by Social Groups in Urban Eastern India

private hospitals, nursing homes, etc. Hospitalization rate during the last 365 days of the survey is the highest in urban West Bengal, followed by Odisha, and is the lowest in the urban areas of Bihar. West Bengal also shows better health statistics when compared to the other states of India, i.e. low infant mortality rate (among the lowest in India), relatively lower child mortality rates, and high life expectancy (higher than the national average)[1]. This seems to have occurred despite the relatively less developed conditions of health infrastructure: the state has dearth of health care centres per lakh population, and at the same time, there is overburdening on hospital beds, when compared to the all India average as well as eastern India as a whole (Table 16.2).

Social Inequality in Health

Here, hospitalization rate has been taken as proxy for utilisation of health care facilities by social groups. Hospitals include government, private and other hospitals (Table 16.4). According to Fig. 16.2; inequalities in utilisation of healthcare facilities are relatively high among the 'STs' followed by OBCs in the urban eastern India since the Lorenz curve of 'STs' is far away from the line of equality compared to other three social groups; while the Lorenz curve of SC and 'Others' are nearer to the line of equality. Figure 16.3 reveals that about 22.3 cumulative percentage of population of the 'STs' group is utilising 80.35 cumulative percentage of the healthcare facilities whereas remaining 77.7 cumulative percentage

Table 16.4: Utilisation of Healthcare facilities

States	*Total Utilisation of Health Care*	*Utilisation By STs*	*Utilisation By SC*	*Utilisation By OBCs*	*Utilisation By Others*
Orissa	13.15	53.05	15.11	13.15	7.83
Jharkhand	9.15	27.30	6.22	9.15	5.95
West Bengal	69.38	19.64	74.73	69.38	81.46
Bihar	8.32	0	3.94	8.32	4.76

Source: NSS 60th round "Morbidity, Health Care and Conditions of the Aged", 2004.

of the 'STs' population utilise 19.65 cumulative percentage of the healthcare facilities. This shows that most of the healthcare facilities are being utilised by very few people as more than two-thirds of the people use very less health care. 30.62 cumulative per cent of OBCs population is utilising 75.44 cumulative percentage of health care facilities whereas remaining 69.38 cumulative percentage of the SC population use 24.56 cumulative percentage of health care facilities. The Lorenz curve in both cases (STs and OBCs) reflect that inequalities are more prominent than the 'Others'. It can be inferred that the healthcare facilities are being uniformly utilised by the SC group and 'Others'.

Utilisation of Healthcare Facilities by Educational Status

According to educational status, hospitalisation rate is high in the urban areas of West Bengal. It is the least in urban areas of Bihar. Hospitalization rate in the urban areas of West Bengal and Odisha is higher than the average for eastern India. Hospitalization rate is high among the people having diploma followed by the post graduates and above. It is low among the primary educated people in the urban areas of eastern India, thereby reflecting that education plays a key role in awareness and hence has an influence on the rate of hospitalisation (Table 16.5).

Economic Inequality in Healthcare

In urban Bihar the proportion of the poor people availing health services is 28.76 per cent of total number of people hospitalized, whereas for the non-poor, it is 71.24 per cent. The poor, therefore, are found to utilise private health care facilities more compared to the other three states of

Table 16.5: Hospitalisation Rate by Educational Status

States	*Illiterate*	*Below primary & primary*	*Middle*	*Secondary*	*Higher secondary*	*Diploma*	*Graduate*	*Post graduate & above*	*Total*
Bihar	0.85	0.99	1.28	1.28	1.27	7.37	1.15	0.43	1.03
Jharkhand	1.60	2.00	2.68	2.03	3.51	0.00	1.78	1.81	2.12
Orissa	2.59	2.19	3.79	3.54	3.55	4.95	3.04	2.69	2.94
West Bengal	4.22	2.91	3.10	3.28	3.39	8.53	3.45	5.34	3.39
Eastern India	2.70	2.40	2.89	2.66	3.01	6.85	2.63	3.40	2.68

Source: NSS 60th round "Morbidity, Health Care and Conditions of the Aged" 2004.

urban eastern India. West Bengal exhibits the least proportion of poor utilising private health care facilities in urban eastern India. From these facts one may conclude that the quality of the public health services might be better in the urban areas of West Bengal but in case of Bihar they may be not easily accessible or functional, therefore, poor people have no other way than to depend on the private sector. The urban poor in Odisha too use public healthcare facilities less than the other three states of eastern India. On the other hand, the urban poor of Jharkhand use more public health compared to the other three states of eastern India. Overall, the urban poor in eastern India has been found to access more public health care services than private ones. The poor in Odisha are found to be

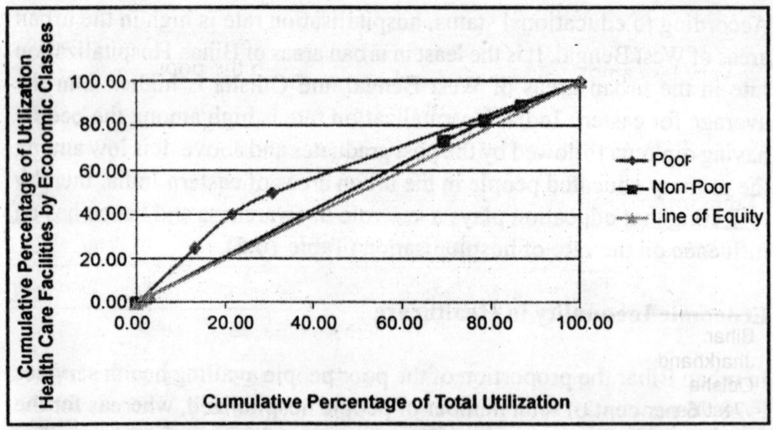

Fig. 16.3: Inequality in Utilization of Health Care by Economic Status in Urban Eastern India

Table 16.6: Utilisation of Health Care by the Urban Poor and Non-Poor

States	*Total Utilisation of Health Care Facilities*	*Utilisation of Health Care Facilities by Poor*	*Utilisation of Health Care Facilities by Non-Poor*
Odisha	13.14	31.86	10.77
Bihar	8.33	31.30	6.89
Jharkhand	9.14	17.83	9.04
West Bengal	69.39	12.17	73.31

Source: NSS 60th round "Morbidity, Health Care and Conditions of the Aged", 2004.

hospitalized more frequently followed by the urban poor in Bihar, West Bengal and Jharkhand in decreasing order (Table 16.7).

Lorenz curve has been computed for measuring economic inequalities in utilisation of healthcare facilities in the urban areas of Eastern India for the poor and non-poor. This reveals that utilisation of healthcare facilities is relatively more concentrated among the poor than the non-poor. A careful inspection of Fig. 16.3 also reveals that 30.61 cumulative percentage of the poor people are using 49.93 cumulative percentage of health care facilities and rest of the population (69.39 cumulative percentage of the poor population) is utilising 50.07 cumulative percentage of public healthcare facilities in the urban areas of eastern India. The curve for the non-poor does not show a high degree of concentration but are found to uniformly utilise healthcare facilities than the poor. The curve for the non-poor is near the line of equality; that points out that inequality is very less among the non-poor as compared to the poor.

Table 16.7: Hospitalization Rate by Poor and Non-Poor

States	*Public Hospital*		*Private Hospital*		*Total*	
	Poor	*Non-Poor*	*Poor*	*Non-poor*	*Poor*	*Non-poor*
Bihar	22.70	77.30	30.85	69.15	28.76	71.24
Jharkhand	30.56	69.44	16.40	83.60	18.36	81.64
Odisha	16.76	83.24	25.75	74.25	29.27	70.73
West Bengal	21.15	78.85	2.91	97.09	11.96	88.04
Eastern India	19.37	80.63	11.16	88.84	16.10	83.90

Source: NSS 60th round "Morbidity, Health Care and Conditions of the Aged", 2004.

Conclusions

The results obtained by using the Lorenz curve in this study enables one to ascertain the findings regarding the socio-economic inequalities in the utilisation of health care facilities in urban eastern India. It has been found that infrastructural, social, economic, and geographical factors as well as infrastructure have significant influence on the utilisation of health care facilities by individuals.

The results provide a better understanding of the availability of health care facilities and this may be helpful for policy-makers. The results reflect that health infrastructure like number of hospitals, dispensaries, health centres, family planning centres, nursing homes and other medical institutions and hospital beds per lakh population is not adequate in urban eastern India, both at the state as well as the district level. It is particularly inadequate in the urban areas of Odisha. This is also reflective of the fact that the health infrastructure in the urban areas of this region is overburdened. People from the rural areas in this region also depend on the healthcare centres of the urban areas for their tertiary health care. One can well imagine that there is extra burden of population on urban health care facilities. Thus, there is a strong need to look into the situation, and the policy makers should make efforts towards bringing about increments in these health care facilities so that people can easily and adequately access health care facilities in the region.

Inequalities in the utilisation of healthcare facilities are also very prominent in the urban areas of eastern India. The differential effect of social groups (ST, SC, OBC and Others), on the hospitalization rate has been observed in this region. According to social groups, inequalities in utilisation are high among the STs. Among the STs, very few people are utilizing most of the healthcare facilities, and this shows a considerable number of STs are deprived from this. Similarly, among the OBCs, healthcare facilities being utilised by few, while the rest remain underprivileged. In such conditions, it is necessary for the policy makers and planners to formulate special plans and schemes for the socially disadvantaged people.

The Monthly Per Capita Expenditures reveal that inequalities are high among the poor of urban eastern India. Therefore, it is important to provide healthcare facilities to the poor people at subsidised rates, particularly in case of private healthcare services. Here, all factors such as poverty and inequality among social groups are very much associated and interlinked with each other. Therefore, there is need for a holistic and multi-pronged approach for the reduction of inequalities in the utilisation of health care facilities in urban eastern India. Such an approach or strategy should entail not only the provisioning of services, but also in providing quality services for various population groups based on equity and equality. Moreover regional differentiations in utilisation reflect that 'area specific approach' should particularly be targeted towards poor regions/states so that the existing disparities are removed.

APPENDICES

Table 16.1: State-Specific Poverty Lines in 2004-05 (Rs. Per capita per month)

Sl. No.	*States*	*Urban*
1.	Bihar	435.00
2.	Jharkhand	451.24
3.	Odisha	528.49
4.	West Bengal	449.32

Source: Planning Commission the Government of India, Poverty estimations 2004-05.

Table 16.2: Cumulative Utilisation of Healthcare Facilities

States	*Total Cumulative %Utilisation of Health Care Facilities*	*Cumulative % of Utilisation By STs*	*Cumulative % of Utilisation By SCs*	*Cumulative % of Utilisation By OBCs*	*Cumulative % of Utilisation By Others*
Odisha	13.15	53.05	15.11	13.15	7.83
Jharkhand	22.30	80.35	21.33	22.30	13.78
West Bengal	91.68	99.99	96.06	91.68	95.24
Bihar	100.00	100.00	100.00	100.00	100.00

Table 16.3: Cumulative Utilisation of Healthcare Facilities

States	*Cumulative % of Total Utilisation of Health Care Facilities*	*Cumulative % of Utilisation of Health Care Facilities by Poor*	*Cumulative % of Utilisation of Health Care Facilities by Non-Poor*
Odisha	10.74	24.81	10.77
Bihar	17.66	40.27	17.66
Jharkhand	26.70	49.93	26.70
West Bengal	100.00	100.00	100.01

NOTE

1. West Bengal, (2004): *West Bengal Human Development Report*, p. 9.

REFERENCES

Adler, E Nancy, Thomas Boyce, Margaret A. Chesney, Sheldon Cohen, Susan Folman, Robert Kahn, and Syme, S. Leonard. (1994). 'Socio-economic Status and Health: The Challenge of the Gradient', *Journal of Health and Social Behaviour*, Vol. 45.

Agarwal, Siddharth *et al.* (2007). 'Urbanisation, Urban Poverty and Health of the Urban Poor: Status, Challenges and the Way Forward', *Demography India*, Vol. 36.

Ateeque and Shamim Kausar. (2004). 'Evaluation of the Health Facilities for Social well-being in Meerut District: A Strategy for Micro-Level Planning', *Indian Journal of Regional Science*, Vol. XXXVI,

Bhandari, Laveesh. (2006). *Social Infrastructure, Urban Health and Education, Urban Infrastructure Report*, Oxford University Press, New Delhi.

CBHI (Central Bureau of Health Intelligence) (various years), Health Information of India, Government of India, New Delhi.

Chakraborty, Achin (2002). 'Issues in Social Indicators, Composite Indices and Inequality', *Economic and Political Weekly*, Vol. 37.

Chakraborty and Mukherjee. (2003). 'Health Care in West Bengal: What is Happening?,' *Economic and Political Weekly*, Vol. 38.

David R. Williams; Chiquita Collins (1995). 'US Socioeconomic and Racial Differences in Health: Patterns and Explanations', *Annual Review of Sociology*, Vol. 21.

Darshinim Mahadevia. (2000). 'Health for All in Gujarat: It Achievable?' *Economic and Political Weekly*, Vol. 35, No. 35/36.

Deaton, Angus. (2003). 'Health, Inequality, and Economic Development', *Journal of Economic Literature*, Vol. 41.

Dev, S. Mahendra and Mooij Jos. (2004). 'Patterns in Social Sector Expenditure Pre and Post Reform Periods', *India Development Report*, IGIDR, Mumbai.

Dressler, William W. (1993). 'Health in the African American Community: Accounting for Health Inequalities', *Medical Anthropology Quarterly, New series*, Vol. 7.

Drèze, J. and Sen, A.K. 1989. *Hunger and Public Action*. Oxford University Press.

Duggal, R., S Nandraj and A. Vadair. (1995). 'Health Expenditure Cross Status: Part I', *Economic and Political Weekly*, Vol. 30.

Duncan, Craig, Kelvyn Jones and Graham Moon. (1993). 'Do Places Matter? A Multi-level Analysis of Regional Variation in Health Related Behaviour in Britain'. *Social Science and Medicine*. Vol. 37.

Duraisamy, P. (1998). 'Morbidity in Tamil Nadu: Levels, Differentials and Determinants', *Economic and Political Weekly*, Vol. 33.

Duraisamy, P. (2001). 'Health Status and Curative Care in Rural India', *Working Paper Series No. 78,* National Council of Applied Economic Research.

East India Human Development Report. (2006). 'National Council of Applied Economic Research', Oxford University Press, New Delhi.

Edelman, Brent and Arup Mitra. (2006). 'Slum Dwellers' Access to Basic Amenities: The Role of Politics Contact, its Determinants and Adverse Effects', *RURDS*, Vol. 18.

Escobedo, Luis G and John P. Peddicord. (1996). 'Smoking Prevalence in U.S. Birth Cohorts: The Influence of Gender and Education', *American Journal of Public Health* Vol. 86.

Ettner, S.L. *et al.* (1997). 'The Impact of Psychiatrics on Labour Market Outcomes', *Industrial Labour Relations Review,* Vol. 51. No. 2.

Fanshel, S. and Bush, J.W. (1970). 'A Health-Status Index and Its Application to Health-Services Outcomes', *Operations Research*, Vol. 18.

Feinstein S. Jonathan (1993). 'The Relationship between Socio-economic Status and Health', *The Milbank Quarterly*, Vol, 71.

Fred C. Pampel and Richard G. Rogers Sources (2004). 'Socio-economic Status, Smoking and Health: A Test of Competing Theories of Cumulative Advantage': *Journal of Health and Social Behaviour*, Vol. 45.

Garg, Renu. (1995). *'Improving the Performance of Reference Health Centre: A case Study Urban Health Centre, Dharavi, Bombay'*, Department of Health Studies, Tata Institute of Social Studies, Mumbai.

Ghosh, Soumitra and Arokisamy, P. (2007). *'Morbidity in India: Trends, Patterns and Determinants'*. IIPS Mumbai.

Glied, Sherry. Adriana Lleras-Muney. (2008).'Technological Innovation and Inequality in Health', *Demography*, Vol. 45.

Graham, Hilary. (1995). 'Cigarette Smoking: A Light on Gender and Class Inequality in Britain', *Journal of Social Policy*, Vol. 24.

Kennedy, B.P. and *et al.* (1998). 'Income distribution, socioeconomic status, and self-rated health in the United States: multilevel analysis', *British Medical Journal.* British Medical Journal. Vol. 370.

Krishnan, T N. (1995), 'Access to Health and Burden of Treatment in India: An Inter-State Comparison' Paper presented at International Workshop on Health Insurance in India, Bangalore, September 20-22.

Kulkarni, K.M. (2006). 'Aspects of Well-Being and Deprivation at Global and National Level,' *Indian Journal of Regional Science*, Vol. XXXVIII.

Kumar, B.G. (1993). 'Low Mortality and High Morbidity Reconsidered', *Population and Development Review*, Vol. 19.

Kundu Amitabh. (1993). *In The Name of the Urban Poor: Access to Basic Amenities*. Sage Publication, New Delhi.

Kundu, Amitabh. (2009). 'Access to Basic Amenities and Urban Security: An Interstate Analysis with a Focus on the Social Sustainability of Cities', Urban Poverty Report, New Delhi, UNDP.

Haynes, R. (1991). 'Inequalities in Health and Health Service Use: Evidence from the General Household Survey', *Social Science and Medicine*. Vol. 33.

Lawlor, Debbie A., Stephen Frankel, Mary Shaw, Shah Ebrahim and George Davey Smith. (2003). 'Smoking and Ill Health: Does Lay Epidemiology Explain the Failure of Smoking Cessation Programmes among Deprived Population?' *American Journal of Public Health*, Vol. 93.

Mahmood Aslam. (1977). *Statistical Methods in Geographical Studies*. Rajesh Publication, New Delhi.

Mirowsky, John and Ross Catherine, E. (2000). 'Socio-economic Status and Subjective Life Expectancy', *Social Psychology Quarterly*, Vol. 63, No. 2.

Mishra, Srijit. (2004). 'Public Health Scenario in India', *India Development Report*, IGIDR. Mumbai.

Nanda, A.R. (2004). 'Obsolescence and Anachronism of Population control: From Demography to Demography' in *Demography India*, Vol. 33, No. 1.

NSSO (National Sample Survey Organisation). (1992). 'Morbidity and Utilisation of Medical Services' (NSS 42nd Round 1986-87), *Sarvekshana*, No. 52, Vol XV, No. 4, April-June.

—— (1998): 'Morbidity and Treatment of Ailments' (Report No. 441) NSS Fifty-Second Round. July 1995–June 1996, Department of Statistics, Government of India, New Delhi.

—— (2004): 'Morbidity, Health Care and the Condition of the Aged' (Report No. 507), NSS 60th Round January-June 2004, Department of Statistics, Government of India, New Delhi.

Nagar, A.L. and R.K. Das. (1976). *Basic Statistics*. Oxford University Press, New York.

Nayak, L.T. and D.S. Narayankar. (2009). 'Identification of Regional Disparities in Levels of Development in Bellary District—Karnataka', *Indian Journal of Regional Science*, Vol. XXXXI.

Pampel, Fred C. (2002). 'Inequality, Diffusion and the Status Gradient in Smoking', *Social Problems,* Vol. 49.

Parikh, S. Kriti. (2006). 'Social Infrastructure as Important as Physical Infrastructure', *India Development Report*, IGIDR. Mumbai.

Preston, Samuel H. and Paul Taubman. ed. (1994). 'Socio-economic differences in Adult Morality and health Status', *Demography of Aging*, edited by Linda Martin and Samuel Preston. National Academy Press, Washington, DC.

Reddy, S. and J. Vandemoortele (1996). 'User Financing of Basic Social Services: A Review of Theoretical Arguments and Empirical Evidence', UNICEF Staff Working Papers, Evaluation, Policy and Planning Series, Number EVL-97-001, UNICEF New York.

Ross, Catharine E. (2000). 'Walking, Exercise and Smoking: Does Neighbourhood Matter?' *Social Science and Medicine*, Vol. 51.

Standing Hilary. (2002). 'An Overview of Changing Agendas in Health Sector Reform', *Reproductive Health Matters*, Vol. 10, No. 20.

Schrijvers, Carola T.M., Karein Stronks, H. Dike van de Mheen and Johan P. Mackenbach. (1999). 'Explaining Educational Differences in Morality: The

Role of Behavioural and Material factors', *American Journal of Public Health* Vol. 89.

Sen, A.K. (1998). 'Mortality as an Indicator of Economic Success and Failure', *The Economic Journal*, Vol. 64.

Sen, Amartya (1997). *On Economic Inequality*. Oxford University Press New York.

Sen, Amartya. (2000). *Development as Freedom*. Oxford University Press, New Delhi.

James, P. Smith (1999). 'Healthy Bodies and Thick Wallets: The Dual Relation between Health and Economic Status,' *Journal of Economic Perspectives*, American Economic Association, Vol. 13(2).

Smith, D.M. (1970). *The Geography of Social Well-Being*. McGraw-Hill Book Company, USA.

Standing, Hilary. (2002). 'An Overview of Changing Agendas in Health Sector Reform', *Reproductive Health Matters*, Vol. 10, No. 20.

Vaidyanathan, A. (1995). 'An Assessment of Nutritional and Health Status', *Discussion Paper No. 3*, UNDP Research Project, CDS.

Visaria, P. and A. Gumber (1994). '*Utilisation of and Expenditure on Health Care in India, 1986-87*', Gujarat Institute of Development Research, Ahmedabad.

Visaria, P. and P. Jacob (1995), 'Illness Levels, Health-care Utilisation and Expenditure in Four States of Andhra Pradesh, Kerala, Madhya Pradesh and Punjab, 1986-87,' Paper Presented at the workshop on *Morbidity Measurement and Health Research*, Thiruvananthapuram.

Williams, David R. (1990). 'Socio-economic Differentials in Health: A Review and Redirection', *Social Psychology Quarterly* Vol. 53.

Wilkinson, R.G. (1996). '*Unhealthy Societies: The Affliction of Inequality*'. London Routledge, 1996.

17

Health and Lifestyle Problems of Urban Youth in India

A Case Study of Kolkata Metropolis

Chandramallika Biswas

Introduction: Urban Youth, Health and Lifestyle

'Youth' is regarded as the period of transition from adolescence to adulthood and this period is supposed to be the healthiest of all periods in human life. During this period, psychological developments take place in the form of a search for identity, search for independence, developing a body image, sex role, a value system, and other positive values of self-reliance.

Human sexuality is the sum total of an individual's biological constitution, life experiences, knowledge, behaviour and attitudes; it is influenced by a number of diverse physical, psychological, interpersonal, and cultural factors. Sexual and reproductive health refers to the physical and emotional well-being of individuals in relation to safe sex, pregnancy and protection from HIV/AIDS and sexually transmitted infections and diseases (STIs and STDs). Although, the need to focus on young people is increasingly being recognised as a means to improve human welfare and reduce the population momentum, relatively little is known about adolescent lives and the factors that determine the successful transition to adulthood.

The concept of 'Lifestyle' tries to focus health behaviour as one element, within a whole range of behavioural patterns, related to demands made by the social, political, economic and cultural situations. This concept of lifestyle thus, creates a close link between the living conditions of an individual, his or her activities and socially formed strategies for coping with life. More than any other age group, young people face profound physical, psychological and social upheavals in their lives, all of which have a bearing on how they live, and what values they imbibe. These also have a great bearing on their health and well-being, both at present and in the future. But youth, generally fail to recognise this, because on the face of it, young people tend to be better endowed with health than any other segment in the population. This is because they have survived the rigours of infancy and early childhood, and have not yet faced the diseases that beset adulthood. In spite of this, today's youth face substantial health problems, largely due to their lifestyle and risk taking behaviour that they are often unaware of.

For the young, risk taking and experimentation is the order of the day, and this includes experimenting not only with drugs, tobacco and alcohol, but also with sex. Heightened sexual urge in young people make them vulnerable to a host of problems, associated with sexuality like molestation and rape, teenage pregnancies, abortion and sexually transmitted diseases.

There is growing evidence to suggest that behavioural problems cluster together. They include alcoholism and drug abuse, cigarette smoking and sexual precocity. Those who smoke cigarettes are more likely to use illicit drugs; drink heavily, and use some other drugs. These result in anti-social behaviour and traffic accidents, which are major causes of death and disability in young persons. The use of tobacco, alcohol and other drugs is associated with poor performance in college, at work and in sports. The use of one drug is more likely to lead to multiple drug use. Substance abuse is primarily a social, rather than a solitary activity among youth. Peer pressure often play significant role in behavioural problems and may be particularly significant for the young person, who comes from a divided family, lives in unrewarding environment and is less successful at college, at sports, or in making friends.

Indian Youth

Youth represent the hope and future of a country. They represent one of the greatest resources of the country. Youth forms a third of the total population of India and constitutes a vibrant resource of our society. They have a vital role to play with regard to fostering and strengthening of social consciousness against communalism and social evils. The existing scenario of the country reflects the problems connected with youth, which often get expressed through many unlawful activities by the misguided youth. The immense resources of youth, if galvanised, can work as a major force of socio-economic change. It is, therefore, imperative to create increasing opportunities for them to develop their personality and their functional capabilities and thus make them economically productive and socially responsible. To channelise their energy into constructive work, a number of programmes and schemes have been implemented by the Government of India, with the aim of inculcating the values of secularism and national integration, training and upgradation of their skills to open up economic opportunities for them and to develop leadership qualities in them.

The National Youth Policy 2003 covers all youth in the country (India) in the age group of 13 to 35 years. It is also acknowledged that all the persons within this age group are unlikely to be one homogenous group, but rather a conglomeration of sub-groups with differing social roles and requirements. The major objectives in the context of knowledge, employment and health were to provide the youth with proper educational and training opportunities and to facilitate access to information in respect of employment opportunities and to other services including entrepreneurial guidance and financial credit. The policy also aims to facilitate access, for all sections of the youth, to health information and services and to promote a social environment which strongly inhibits the use of drugs and other forms of substance abuse, wards off syndromes (like HIV/AIDS), ensures measures for de-addiction and mainstreaming of the affected persons and enhance the availability of sports and recreational facilities as constructive outlets for channelising the abundant energy of the youth.

Table 17.1: Youth Population of India 1971–2016

Year	*Youth Population (In '000)*			*Proportion to Total Population*		
	Male	*Female*	*Total*	*Male*	*Female*	*Total*
1971	85499	82138	167637	30.1	31.1	30.6
1981	113433	107235	220669	32.1	32.5	32.2
1991	146036	138966	285002	33.1	34.0	33.6
1996	161207	153403	314611	33.3	34.1	33.7
2001	184278	171650	355928	35.2	35.1	35.2
2006	209203	192312	401515	37.1	36.4	36.8
2011 (projected)	225842	208166	434009	37.3	36.4	36.7
2016 (projected)	231582	216496	448078	35.7	35.1	35.5

Source: *Census of India*, GOI.

In terms of absolute numbers, the total youth population has been projected to increase from 167.64 million in 1971 to 448.08 million in 2016.

Table 17.2: Average Annual Exponential Growth Rate of Youth Population *vis-à-vis* Total Population in India 1971–2016

	1971–81		*1981–91*		*1991–2001*		*2001–11 (Projected)*		*2011–16 (Projected)*	
	M	*F*	*M*	*F*	*M*	*F*	*M*	*F*	*M*	*F*
All ages	2.18	2.23	2.18	2.10	1.76	1.82	1.47	1.57	1.34	1.43
15–34	2.83	2.67	2.53	2.59	2.32	2.11	2.03	1.93	0.50	0.78

Source: *Census of India*, GOI.

Table 17.1 shows that both youth population and total population experienced a steady decline in growth rate after 1981. However, the growth rate of the youth population remains higher than that of total population except in case of the projected period of 2011-16. The figures up to 2011 indicate change in the age structure of our population.

Young persons constitute a large percentage of the labour force. Of the total population, about 33.7 per cent (2001) were in the age group 15-34, which corresponds to the youth age group in India. Emergence of youth as a powerful social group is one of the most notable features in India in recent times. The role of young persons in education and culture, science, technology and politics has been significant and has directly contributed to the development of India. It has been, therefore, the endeavour of the Government of India to mobilise the potential of youth in different fields and to build up a strong youth movement in India. This has led to the institutionalisation of the young.

The institutionalisation of the young cannot be isolated from the overall development of the people. Hence, an integrated approach has been adopted towards the various faculties that directly provide opportunities to young people to improve themselves.

Characteristics of Indian Youth in Urban Settings

The following are some of the important characteristic features of youth in India:

- A growing proportion of youth are troubled by the irrelevance of the education system to the issues of life which they have to face;

- Conditions of widespread unemployment and underemployment influence the career oriented studies and work attitude of youth;
- A large proportion of educated youth prefer white-collar jobs and they are averse to manual work;
- An increasing proportion of youth are interested to participate in developmental and community efforts and they show concern in social and public problems; and
- Youth in India are becoming more and more conscious of their life's goal. Education facilities have expanded. Social mobility has increased. Opportunities for travel and access to sources of information have widened. Young people are taking advantage of these and have in the process become both agents of change and instruments of development.

Youth in today's world are vulnerable to the changing demands of society. They have grown up in an environment that is different from that of their elders. Youth in contemporary time usually find themselves surrounded by environment that is not only very different but also more challenging and threatening. This may be due to excessive competition and severe scarcity of goods, resources and services like education, employment and housing. Youth today, therefore, have to compete with a much larger and demanding world. Their needs have also changed and so to fulfil these needs, sometimes they take up all kinds of odd jobs or so to make quick money and to make a living out of it.

Urban lifestyles often reflect the changing face of Indian youth. Here young, educated, people are open to considerable risks and vulnerabilities. In different parts of the country, the growing violence and deaths due to dowry where both victims and the abettors are youth including the educated; the incidence of drug addiction amongst students; the rising trend in premarital sex which is often unsafe and risky, makes youth vulnerable to HIV infection. Moreover, there are cases of suicides and attempt to murder that are reflective of the tumultuous time experienced by youth. These incidents are also reflective of the problems faced by youth relating to their inability to cope up with stress and failure in interpersonal relationships, education or career goals; vulnerability to addiction, AIDS and other lifestyle related problems.

The term 'youth' is not a homogenous category, but refers to a heterogeneous group of young people coming from various socio-cultural backgrounds, having different levels of education and skill formation. Educated youth in urban areas are often full of energy, hope, courage, adventure and rigour. They can take up challenges and can aspire to fulfil their dreams. Having greater freedom, they are exposed to new situations, opportunities and problems, having to take decisions on their own. The family may not have the necessary information or experience to guide the youth in the present. At this stage of life, the peer influence is dominant; it need not necessarily be favourable or healthy and hence the youth have chances of falling into bad company. Moreover, media has provided access to several kinds of information about one's aspirations, values and lifestyles. The television (making an audio-visual effect) seems to be the most powerful means of media influence, as compared to print media and radio. Moreover, in urban areas and among contemporary youth, influence of internet, email and mobile services expose them to a much unknown environment, full of new information and for which they may not be adequately equipped to understand whether they should follow blindly or use their analytical skills to choose better options being offered from an immense pool of matter given in them.

Youth as an economic and social concept refers to a separate stage in the lifecycle between childhood and adulthood. This period of transition refers to a complex interplay of personal, institutional and macro-economic changes that most young people have to negotiate in other than wholly traditional societies. The relative importance and intermingling of these factors can vary widely between countries according to their level of economic development. It can also vary within countries according to socio-economic, ethnic and other social groupings.

The changes that young people have to negotiate, revolve around moving from dependence to independence, involving, in most societies, at least four distinct aspects. These are: leaving the parental home and setting up new living arrangements; finishing full-time education; forming close stable personal relationships outside their family of origin, often resulting in marriage and child birth and settling into a more or less stable source of livelihood through employment and/or career choice.

The main anxieties of youth relate to attraction to the opposite sex and to the choice of occupation. Educational institutions have not done much in this respect by giving proper guidance, advice and information on occupational choice. As the opportunity for social contact between the sexes increases in educational institutions, it gives rise to new problems for which our young students are not properly equipped. Students are exposed to the themes of sex and romantic love through literature, films, advertisements and newspapers. Their upbringing does not teach them how to tackle such emotions; neither does their educational structure teach them how to behave in situations where they find themselves in close interaction with the opposite sex. Sexual activities among students have increased over the years but they do not play safe and hence problems of risky sex ends up in unwanted pregnancies, Sexually Transmitted Infections (STIs) and HIV/AIDS.

In urban areas, especially in the metropolitan cities, the composition of youth population is very diverse. Some of them are migrants who have come to avail higher education or for a better job prospect. Living alone for the first time, often result in undertaking wrong decisions for which they have to suffer. The job market where they are engaged is also diverse, rendering complexity to the existing situation.

Lifestyle Related Problems among Youth and Impact of Media and Social Networking

The health and lifestyle practices of an individual are by-products of one's interaction with socialising agents. The key influences are family, friends, mass media and education.

Family

Traditionally, family elders guide and regulate individual choices of lifestyle and behaviour. This control, though positive in many ways, also perpetuates inequalities due to authoritarian modes of family functioning and gender bias. To a certain extent, once these were the demands on the family to perpetuate societal norms, although they are less intense in many contemporary families now.

As individuals experience greater freedom, they are exposed to new situations, opportunities and problems, having to take decisions on their own. The family may not have the information or experience to guide them. At times the clash of values between the adolescents and family elders makes family guidance unacceptable. This erodes the social controls exerted by the family. This is rather undesirable, as in a situation where the environment is harsh or difficult; one expects the family to be a source of support and stability. While it is important to promote the capability and role of the family to adequately perform its functions as a socialising agent, it is equally important to bring about functional changes to strengthen the role of other supplementary socialising agents with whom youth have larger contacts.

In the current reality where the nuclear type of family is on the increase and quite frequently with both parents working, the family responsibilities are to be carried out by the fewer adult members. These developments have not been accompanied by democratisation within the family, with regard to individual roles and responsibilities, thus placing strain on its members. It affects the socialisation of youngsters. Young people do not get adequate time or opportunities for interaction with parents and elders. At the same, family does offer greater opportunity for self-expression and individual autonomy to its members, more than that in the past.

Friends

Friends or peers exert an important influence on adolescents. Adolescence being a stressful period of growth, it is natural that the youth experience a sense of security in being with a group undergoing similar stress and subscribe to the norms of this group. Drug users are more often guided by peer influence in taking drugs. Again, non-users too state that they do not take drugs because their friends do not do so, or because their friends discouraged them. It is not unusual to see students making choices on matters like pursuit of further study, choice of subject, college, extra curricular activities, even matters of personal appearance, food habits, and so on, on the basis of choice(s) made by their peers. While friends are an important influence, they too are products of a family, school and college system that have inadequately provided for their life needs. Though the peer influence is dominant, it need not necessarily be favourable or healthy. Thus, there is tremendous potential in this influence, which remains relatively untapped by change agents.

Mass Media

'*Infotainment*' is a buzz word of present times. Information combined with entertainment flood young minds, and there are few ways to filter this. Violence, sex, social prejudice and offensive language are all products of the mass media these days.

There has been a media invasion in recent years, particularly in urban India. It has provided access to several kinds of information about one's aspirations, values and lifestyles. The television seems to be the most powerful media of influence, as compared to the print media and radio. However, though the access to this media is available to all classes of people, yet, the programmes appear to be geared to the 'haves'. The net result being a disillusionment and increasing discontentment with life amongst the less affluent, as reality places a limit on what they can have as individuals or as a family. Besides, the television is a convenient form of home entertainment, but it has unfavourable impact on outdoor play, reading habits, sitting postures and even eyesight.

Mass Media, IT and Risks

One of the most profound changes in the past decade has been the widespread—although uneven—proliferation of information and communication technology. Social network sites, mobile phone operators and other private actors are implementing savvy methods designed to appeal to the youth in developing countries. These developments are exciting and offer possibilities for transforming learning, civic engagement, innovation, entrepreneurship and much more. But they also pose considerable risks in urban India.

A growing concern for parents, educators and others involved with the welfare and well-being of children and adolescents is related to young people's ability to use these tools safely and effectively. In addition, the explosive growth of ICT also presents challenges to young people's privacy, freedom of expression and physical and psychological well-being and there remains fundamental knowledge gap regarding their impact.

A range of factors—including the setting and means of access, usage patterns, attitudes and skill levels—is important in mapping risks and designing responses. Also, important are factors such as age, gender and socio-economic status, as well as peer behaviour and mediation by parents. Whether a child accesses the internet from home, school or a cyber café, for instance, has significant implication for supervision, just as the speed of access and types of device (i.e. mobile *versus* computers) affect usage and risks. Information fluency and related digital skills to evaluate online materials and perform research are also the basis for identifying predators, avoiding risky situations and safely sharing personal information. These factors do not exist in isolation but interact with the broader technological, economic, institutional, educational and cultural context.

Media and Technology

Young people are keen to take up new content formats, with adolescents in particular having the time to explore and exploit new technologies. Short Message Service (SMS), in turn, is being challenged by mobile

Instant Messaging (IM), which is becoming the platform of choice owing to the increasing number of users, lower costs, popularity in emerging markets and the widespread growth of mobile internet everywhere. Brazil has 18 million mobile IM users representing 23 per cent of the country's mobile youth. In India, 87 million-31 per cent of mobile user youth claim to be mobile IM users.

Problems Faced by Youth in Urban India

Youth in urban areas often have to face certain problems. These problems could be a part of the process of growing-up, personal problems or social problems. But the fact is that problems do exist at every point in life which can also affect ones lifestyle or change and transform one's life. Some problems like depression and attempt to suicide have become public health problems and is not an outcome of personal problems only but may be fallout of the urban lifestyle, stress, loneliness or desertion by a loved one. Some problems like sexual harassment are more gender specific and women are soft targets. Sexual assaults within and outside marriage, incest, rape are just some more examples of problems faced more by women than men and these leave behind scars which are just not physical in nature but psychological and in the long run affect sexual and mental health.

There are two major sources of stress, individual and societal. Individually, adolescents have tremendous uncertainties about their own identity and what the future has in store for them. They need to compete with peers and win social approval. On the one hand the need for parental approval exists; on the other there is this great drive to be independent. Many adolescents are unable to cope with these stresses and react in an unhealthy way and develop neurosis or even psychosis. Societal changes bring their own set of stresses; migration, decline in the traditional family support system and the influence of media place considerable stress on youth.

Urban Youth and Social Networking

Young people in urban areas often develop a sense of self and develop an identity from their surroundings. These surroundings usually offer far greater social, cultural, and ethnic diversity than rural environments. The close proximity and frequent interaction of young people in urban areas facilitates the creation, adaptation, and dissemination of an 'urban youth culture'. The interactions with the urban environment can have an intense impact on the socialisation of young people, exposing them to a multitude of influences as they develop, experiment, question, and assume roles in their societies. The collective identities of urban youth are shaped by and expressed through music, dance, fashion, art, and other cultural forms. Other aspects of youth culture are reflected in certain risk behaviours that are especially prevalent among young men in urban areas, including alcohol, drug consumption and engagement in violence.

Urban Youth and Media

Mass media exposure is an effective instrument to gain knowledge about the outside world. Media exposes the population to important information and increases awareness of health and family welfare issues, in addition to a variety of social issues. To some extent, media exposure can compensate for a lack of education if there is regular exposure to educational media messages. Globalisation has enabled youth culture to become a global phenomenon. Young people are growing up in a world in which goods, capital, technology, information, ideas, and people move swiftly across national borders. With the rapid expansion of fast food restaurants, homogenous shopping malls, and young people who dress alike and listen to the same music, city centres throughout the world increasingly resemble each other. Mass media are especially influential in imparting knowledge to young people and in inculcating certain aspirations, values and attitudes, often in contradiction to the traditional culture. Watching television, listening to the radio, or surfing the internet are important not only for the effects they have on a young person's attitude and behaviour, but also for signifying inclusion and access to knowledge in an increasingly interconnected world. Youth living in cities are far more likely to have access to television, radio, and newspapers than those in rural counterparts. Urban youth are targeted as a new generation of consumers who can be heavily influenced by popular cultural icons and media messages. But media messages are not transmitted and received in a vacuum; young people have many resources that allow them to interpret and reshape these messages without completely abandoning their identities. Superficial similarities in youth culture may obscure the huge differences in family structures, behavioural expectations, and patterns of sexuality, marriage, and reproduction. The fast growth of the internet has ushered in a new digital media culture. Youth are embracing the new technologies much more rapidly than other age groups. The emergence of this new media culture holds both promise and peril for youth. Whether the positive or negative vision of the digital future prevails will be determined, in large part, by decisions being made now and in the next few years in the halls of government and in corporate boardrooms.

Urban Lifestyle Related Problems among Educated Youth

More than any other age group, young people, especially adolescents, face profound physical, psychological and social upheavals in their lives, all of which have a bearing on how they live and what values they imbibe. These have a great bearing on their health and well-being both now, and in the future. But youth generally fail to recognise this.

Drug Use

Drug use is a major concern these days, with increasing number of young people, experimenting with multiple levels of drugs. Drug taking has been associated with the counter culture of the young, who are rebellious against all form of convention. Today, however, the scenario is more frightening with criminal organisations exploiting the young, by providing them, so called securities, in the form of employment, through drug trafficking activities.

Drinking Problem

As in the case of drugs, drinking is also now transcending culture and social class barriers with more and more of the young, increasingly using and abusing alcohol. In the world, over the past thirty to forty years, alcohol consumption among the young has increased, both in quantity and frequency, and the age at which drinking starts has declined.

The more immediate hazards of drinking are manifested as behaviour changes, including aggression, crime, suicidal behaviour, accidents and risky sexual practices. The population at greatest risk are those in areas undergoing rapid socio-cultural and economic changes, where cultural contacts are breaking down and alcohol is becoming increasingly available.

Excessive alcoholic consumption also shortens life span. Heavy drinkers face greater risk of cancers, ulcers, heart disease, malnutrition and liver problems. In a pregnant woman who drinks, the unborn baby is exposed to greater risk of brain damage, growth deficiency and mental retardation.

Tobacco Use

Smoking tobacco is another burning issue. About two decades ago, the average age at which people started to smoke was sixteen, today it is twelve. Smoking is the single biggest preventable enemy of health. Nicotine is a poison. WHO estimates that three million people a year, are killed by the habit of smoking, and unless this is controlled, between two hundred and three hundred million children, now living, will die at an early age—anything from thirty-nine onwards, from diseases caused by the smoking. The sooner the young start smoking, the larger is their loss of life expectancy—eight years if smoking starts at fifteen years, four if at twenty-five. There is also evidence to show, that young people who take to smoking, experience an early onset of cough, phlegm, and shortness of breath on exertion. If tobacco is not taken up in adolescence, it is rarely taken up in later life. The message, therefore, is to start health promotion activities for the young, before they have started the smoking habit. Three factors are strongly associated with tobacco use by young people: peer pressure, examples set by siblings and parents, and employment outside home.

Injuries and Violence

Injuries and violence is another lifestyle problem. Accidents constitute one of the major causes of death in persons between ten and twenty-four years. Many accidents have a behavioural component in their causation, including impulsiveness, risk taking, curiosity, and experimentation with adult ways and in a minority of cases, pathological self-destructive behaviour. But social factors also influence accidents, like access to dangerous substances, advertising which encourages hazardous activities, hazards in the working environment and inadequate safety legislation.

Stress and Mental Health

Adolescents are subject to special stresses, arising from the rapid changes that accompany their transition, from childhood to adulthood and in addition due to other external stresses brought to bear as the result of the transitional state of many societies today. It is estimated that around 20 per cent of the world's adolescents have a mental health or behavioural problem (UNICEF). Depression is the single largest contributor to the global burden of disease for people aged 15-19, and suicide is one of the three leading causes of mortality among people aged 15-35. Globally, an estimated 71,000 adolescents commit suicide annually that can go up to 40 times as many make suicide attempts. About half of lifetime mental disorders begin before the age of 14, and 70 per cent by age 24. The prevalence of mental disorders among adolescents has increased in the past 20-30 years; the increase is attributed to disrupted family structures, growing youth unemployment and unrealistic educational and vocational aspirations of guardians for their children.

Unassisted mental health problems among adolescents are associated with low educational achievement, unemployment, substance use, risk-taking behaviours, crime, poor sexual and reproductive health, self-havoc and inadequate self-care, all of which increase the lifetime risk of morbidity and premature mortality. Mental health problems among adolescents carry high social and economic costs, as they often develop into more disabling conditions later in life. The risk factors for mental health problems are well established and include child abuse; family; school and neighbourhood; violence; poverty; social exclusion and educational disadvantage. Psychiatric illness and substance abuse in parents, as well as marital violence, also place youth at increased risk, as also exposure to social disruption and psychological distress that accompany armed conflict, natural disasters and other humanitarian crisis. The stigma directed towards young people with mental disorders and the human rights violations to which they are subjected amplify the adverse consequences.

Mental health problems in young people thus present a major public health challenge worldwide. Preventive efforts can help forestall the development and progression of mental disorders and intervention can limit their severity. Young people whose mental health are sound, function better socially, perform better in schools and are more likely to develop into well-adjusted and productive adults than those whose needs are unmet. Mental health promotion, prevention and timely treatment also reduce the burden on health care system.

Vulnerabilities of Urban Youth: A Case Study of Kolkata Metropolis

Indicators of Vulnerability among Urban Educated Youth

Vulnerability among urban educated youth may thus arise from faulty lifestyles like taking alcohol, tobacco, smoking, drugs and exposure to adult material. Sometimes family problems like a broken family, family unrest may also lead to psychological depression and further may aggravate to a stage where an individual might take an extreme step such as, attempt to suicide. Some risky behaviour and practices may also make a person vulnerable. The risk of unsafe sex may lead to occurrence of STDs, unwanted pregnancy leading to an abortion; unsafe and unprotected sex may also leave one at risk of acquiring HIV/AIDS. Thus vulnerability is a situation which arises not due to any single causative factor but due to the interplay of various factors taken together. The factors which have been identified for computing vulnerability are as follows:

1. Those who are exposed to smoking are at risk and can be vulnerable since they are prone to respiratory problems in future. The main causes for smoking among youth are due to stress, loneliness and peer influence, group behaviour and social status emblem.
2. Those who are exposed to alcohol or drinking problem are also at risk and may be vulnerable to risky behaviour and sexual health. Alcohol drinking is an important cause of accidents, mental breakdowns and family quarrels. Among youth, too much alcohol can lead to loss of judgment; which in turn can lead to unsafe sex, unwanted pregnancies and increased probability of being involved in rape. In addition, the sex drive is harmed by too much drinking; men produce fewer sex hormones and this results in decreased interest in sex and a reduced ability to make love; sometimes rendering men impotent. Women too, seem to lose interest in sex. Excessive alcohol consumption also shortens life span. Heavy drinkers face greater risk of cancers, ulcers, heart disease, malnutrition and liver problems. In a pregnant woman, who drinks, the unborn baby is exposed to greater risk of brain damage, growth deficiency and mental retardation.
3. Those urban youth who are exposed to pubs and bars may fall prey to a vulnerable and risky lifestyle. They are often swayed away by peer influence and group behaviour. They become addicted to alcohol. The pubs and discs are meeting place of young men and women. They dance and drink till late. This in turn many a times leads to unsafe and unprotected sex and chances of STDs and even HIV/AIDS. These pubs and discs are also joints for flying and high profile sex workers, "escorts". The concept of 'casual sex' and 'one night stand' among youth

all begin from these places. They get drunk, dance and then the passion for sexual desires are ignited and young men and women are unable to control their passion and unsafe sex takes place.

4. Those exposed to taking drugs or IVDU are at a higher risk of contracting HIV/AIDS in case of contaminated syringes and needles that are used when such intravenous drugs are taken. The major causes for taking such drugs are loneliness, excessive mental stress; group or peer influence. Such addictions can cause severe damage to both physical and mental health of the person as these drugs are expensive and to acquire them and to bear the cost, youth take up odd jobs and also petty crimes. It affects them severely and it is very difficult to come out of such addictions.
5. Young people who come from families are also at risk and may become vulnerable in the long run. Such youth, since childhood face mental depression, they lack love and compassion from their parents, may face family violence, which in turn breaks their faith in family bonding. Thus they seek love outside home. This can make them adopt risky behaviour which can later cause harm to their mental and sexual health.
6. Due to globalisation and 'tech savvy urban culture', where internet, mobile (SMS and MMS) and cable TV are easily affordable and easily accessible to urban educated youth, exposure to adult materials, blue films and exposure to materials on indecent depiction of men and women is not a big issue these days. Erotic exposure is positively associated with risk taking. It is the most important factor which affects the sexual behaviour. Obviously, the erotic materials cannot be treated as the right source for acquiring knowledge. Also, an attitude formed on the basis of erotic exposure is not likely to be pertinent particularly from the viewpoint of safe sex. In the Indian context, in the absence of a formal and relevant sex education, erotic materials become the only source of acquiring information about sex and thus a source for attitude formation too.
7. Youth who are exposed to visiting commercial sex workers are open to the risk for STDs or even HIV/AIDS if they indulge in unprotected sex. Urban youth, who are away from home, lonely, exposed to erotic materials and with zeal to experiment sex, under peer influence often end up for paid sex in some brothel or a place where they can buy sex. For the young, risk taking

and experimentation is the order of the day, and this includes experimenting not only with drugs, tobacco and alcohol, but also with sex.

8. Those in urban and metropolitan cities have an opportunity and sometimes without parental restrictions to mix and mingle with the opposite sex. In the present world, socialising with one's partner 'with his/her girl-friend/boy-friend' is the order of the day. Sometimes, this leads to young people having more than one partner or more than one sexual partner. Heightened sexual urge in young people make them vulnerable to a host of problems, associated with sexuality-molestation and rape, teenage pregnancies, abortion and sexually transmitted diseases. Thus mingling is good as long as no sexual behaviour is involved. However, the same under unsafe sex may become a risky behaviour and make youth vulnerable to problems related to sexual health.
9. While pre-marital sexual behaviour among adolescents and youth remain poorly explained topics in India, the available evidence suggests that between 20 and 30 per cent of all males and up to 10 per cent of all females are sexually active during adolescence and before marriage (Jejeebhoy, 2000). Sexual awareness seems to be largely superficial. Sexual activity is frequently risky—casual sex and relations with sex workers are often repeated by young males (NACO, 2001). Moreover, condom use is erratic and sexually active young people are increasingly confronted with unwanted pregnancy, sexually transmitted infection and unwanted sex. Typically, young females have limited decision-making power in their relationships. Thus those exposed to pre-marital sex are also open to the risk and vulnerable to sexual health problems if unsafe sex takes place. Youth treating pre-marital sexual relation as the westernised way of life and covering it up in the envelope of modern way of living and leaving behind the tradition bindings, makes the situation more disastrous—far more than that could ever be thought of. Youngsters, in some cases due to less sexual knowledge and sometimes having full knowledge of sex with the availability of contraception, try to experiment with it in their life. Their excitement is sometimes also heightened by media.
10. The risk of abortion or unmet need of contraception may arise from failure of contraception use or unsafe and unprotected sex.

Thus young and unmarried girls go for abortion. If detected early, medicines help in abortion or else surgical removal of the fetus needs to done. Thus sometimes, young people approach quacks and abortion takes place in unhygienic and unsafe ways which cause sexual health problems for the female and sometimes may even lead to infertility. Hence, those who are exposed to the risk of abortion stand at risk and may be vulnerable to sexual health.

11. Those who have already been exposed to unprotected and unsafe sex stand high chances of getting a sexually transmitted disease. Thus who are suffering from it are highly vulnerable to HIV/AIDS due to negligence and hence are at risk.
12. Substance abuse is primarily a social, rather than a solitary activity in youth. Thus those who are exposed to such substance abuse are at risk and their vulnerability also holds well in this context.
13. Young women are specifically exposed to various kinds of sexual harassment on the roads, at workplace, public places and more so on public transport system. Thus those who face such harassments may be depressed or hurt and a fear may reign in them depending on the act and extent of sexual harassment. Thus such youth exposed to sexual harassment are open to some risk and may be vulnerable too.
14. Youth who are exposed to psychological depression and those who have attempted suicide are at a risk and vulnerable to mental

Table 17.3: Vulnerability Indicators for Youth in Kolkata, 2009-2010

Vulnerability Indicators	*Per cent*
Exposed to Smoking	30.5
Exposed to Alcoholism	36.3
Exposure to Pubs and Bars	32.5
Exposed to Indecent Depiction of Men and Women	52.3
Visit Commercial Sex Workers	3.7
Socialize with Boyfriends/Girlfriends	56.9
Exposed to Drugs	1.5
Exposed to Abortion	3.1
Exposed to Pre-marital Sex	15.2
Attempt to Suicide	10.3
Suffering from Sexually Transmitted Disease	1.5
Exposed to Sexual Harassment	18.0
Exposed to Psychological Depression	27.0
Exposed to Substance Abuse	5.3
Comes from Broken Family	8.1

Source: Computed from Primary Survey 2009-10.

health and unhappiness or stress in personal life. Unassisted mental health problems among youth are associated with low educational achievement, unemployment, substance abuse, risk-taking behaviours, crime, poor sexual and reproductive health, self harm and inadequate self care; all of which increase the lifetime risk of morbidity and also may lead to premature mortality.

Vulnerability Index

To understand the level of vulnerability of the respondents, a vulnerability index was computed based on the indicators of vulnerability (Fig. 17.1). The index was computed based on scoring of each indicator and through additive index. There were 14.1 per cent (64 respondents) who scored zero and hence were considered as 'not vulnerable'. Those who scored between 1 and 14 were grouped into 3 categories as—less vulnerable (46.2%), moderately vulnerable (31.2%) and highly vulnerable (8.6%). For further analysis, the levels of vulnerability were clubbed together as 'vulnerable' and 'not vulnerable' for binary logistic regression and the four levels of vulnerability (i.e. not vulnerable, less vulnerable, moderately vulnerable and highly vulnerable) have been used in Ordinal Regression to study the net impact of background characteristics on vulnerability. To study the gross impact, correlation and cross tabulation with background characteristics was done with the levels of vulnerability.

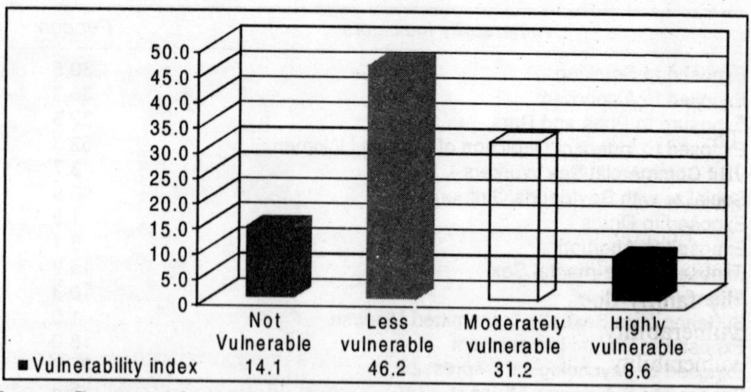

Source: Computed from Primary Survey, 2009-10.

Fig. 17.1: Vulnerability Index among Youth in Kolkata, 2009-2010

Factors Affecting Vulnerability

The demographic characteristics that affect vulnerability are age, sex of the respondents, marital status and status of migration. Age-wise cross-classification of vulnerability shows almost similar pattern without much variation and hence age does not have any significant influence on the levels of vulnerability. More than 75 per cent of the respondents in each category are either less or moderately vulnerable. The sex of the respondent shows significant influence on the levels of vulnerability. Hence, sex of the respondent is statistically significant at less than one per cent level. Males are more vulnerable to risky lifestyle and sexual health than females. This can be due to higher independence, self-efficacy levels, more risk taking and higher stress level for males in the age- group (15-34 years); where they are more influenced by competition, peer influence, social and group behaviour. Unmarried youth are slightly more vulnerable to risky lifestyle than married youth, since they are free, have casual relations, sometimes staying away from family and are often influenced by friends and peers. Married youth are more family oriented, have a sense of responsibility and usually have one steady, faithful sexual partner (their spouse). Migration does not have any significant relation with levels of vulnerability among youth.

Social factors include religion, family type, education and social networking. The levels of education and religion have no significant relation with vulnerability. Though family type does not have a significant relation with levels of vulnerability, but those coming from joint family show a higher proportion in the share of vulnerable groups. Social networking shows a significant relation with the levels of vulnerability. There exists a positive relationship between the two. Thus, vulnerability towards a risky lifestyle increases with an increase in social networking. This explains the influence of peer pressure and group behaviour on the life of the current young generation. The young people are easily swayed away by the actions, attitudes and lifestyles of their friends.

Economic characteristics like occupation, profession and economic status of the family have also been considered. The economic status of the family does not show any significant relation with the levels of vulnerability. However, occupation shows a significant relation with vulnerability. Students are least vulnerable as compared to those in services (more than 45 per cent in the moderate to highly vulnerable group) and those in businesses (more than 53 per cent comprising the moderate to highly vulnerable groups). Those in service and business are exposed to various externalities, stress levels, work pressure, and risky behaviour that make them prone to various levels of vulnerability. Professions have various degrees of vulnerability depending on the type of exposure and activities. Those in education and research are at least risk or least vulnerable. Those in IT/BPO sector, particularly the professionals and those in Media/Hotel/Entertainment are most vulnerable. This could be attributed to the fact that their level of stress, long working hours, proximity to opposite sex and lifestyle make them prone to having a vulnerable lifestyle and risky behaviour.

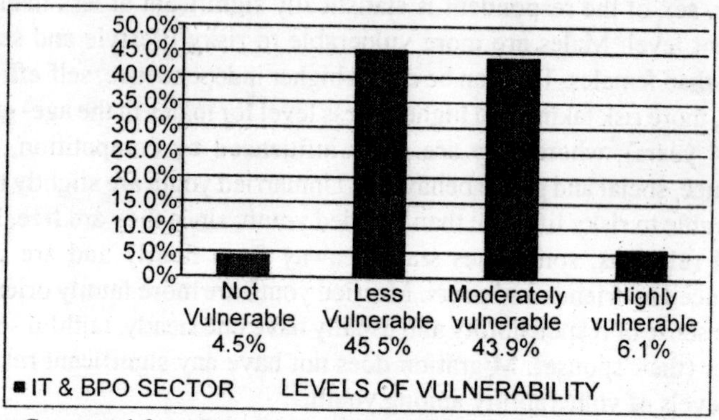

Source: Computed from Primary Survey, 2009-10.

Fig. 17.2: Levels of Vulnerability in the IT and BPO Sector among Youth in Kolkata, 2009-2010

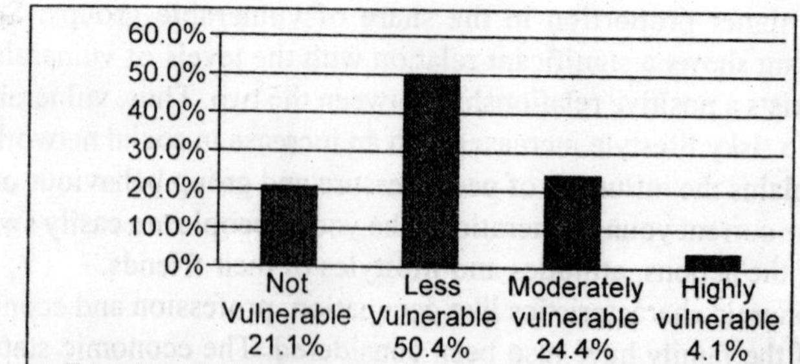

Source: Computed from Primary Survey, 2009-10.

Fig. 17.3: Levels of Vulnerability in Education and Research Sector among Youth in Kolkata, 2009-2010

Table 17.4: Background Characteristics and Vulnerability Index, 2009-10

Background Characteristics		*Vulnerability index*			
		Not Vulner-able	*Less Vulne-rable*	*Modera-tely Vulne-rable*	*Highly Vulner-able*
Demographic Characteristics					
Age	15–24	16.0	44.8	31.6	7.6
	25–34	11.7	47.8	30.7	9.8
Marital Status	Unmarried	13.5	45.1	31.8	9.6
	Married	16.0	50.0	29.0	5.0
Sex*	Females	21.8	53.9	21.4	3.0
	Males	2.7	34.8	45.7	16.8
Migration	Migrant	9.0	48.9	34.6	7.5
	Non-Migrant	16.1	45.0	29.8	9.0
Social characteristics					
Education	Higher Secondary Passed	17.0	44.3	31.1	7.5
	Graduate	12.8	46.0	30.3	10.9
	Post-Graduate and Above	13.8	47.8	32.6	5.8
Religion	Hindu	13.1	45.6	32.2	9.0
	Muslim	28.0	40.0	24.0	8.0
	Christian and Others	14.3	54.8	26.2	4.8
Family Type	Joint family	11.0	47.6	31.7	9.8
	Nuclear Family	15.8	45.4	30.9	7.9
Social Network Index*	Low Networking	23.2	62.3	13.0	1.4
	Moderate Networking	13.2	43.4	32.4	11.0
	High Networking	3.1	29.2	54.1	13.3
Economic Characteristics					
Occupation*	Service	9.1	44.5	34.8	11.6
	Student	18.1	48.8	29.0	4.0
	Business and Others	9.3	37.2	30.2	23.3
Profession*	IT and BPO	4.5	45.5	43.9	6.1
	Education and Research	21.1	50.4	24.4	4.1
	Professionals	4.3	36.2	34.0	25.5
	Media/Hotel/Entertain-ment	11.5	30.8	42.3	15.4
	Other Professions	4.2	52.1	33.3	10.4
Family Wealth Index	Low Middle Class	15.3	47.8	28.7	8.3
	Middle Class	13.0	50.4	30.5	6.1
	High Middle Class	13.8	41.3	34.1	10.8

* Significant at 1 per cent level.

Source: Computed from Field Data.

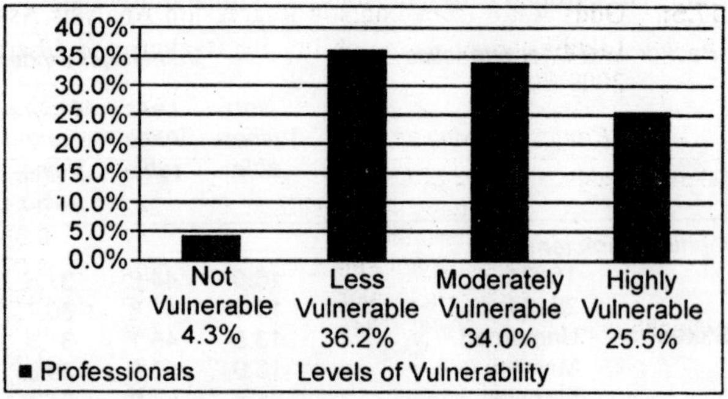

Source: Computed from Primary Survey, 2009-10.

Fig. 17.4: Levels of Vulnerability among Young Professionals in Kolkata, 2009-10

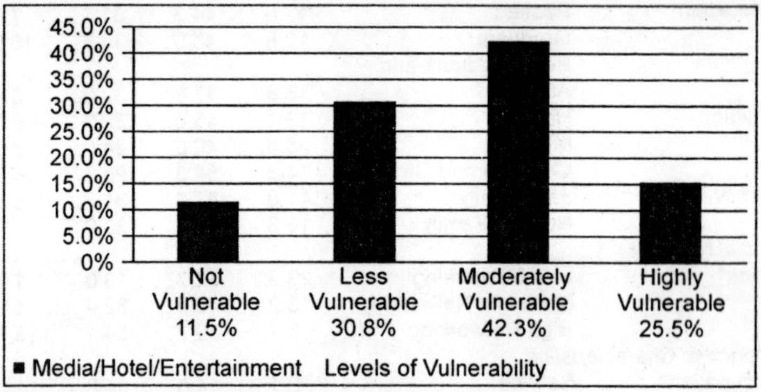

Fig. 17.5: Levels of Vulnerability in the Media/Hotel/Entertainment Sector among Youth in Kolkata, 2009-10

Source: Computed from Primary Survey, 2009-10.

Determinants of Vulnerability

Based on the indicators of vulnerability, an index has been computed for vulnerability. To study the net effect of the background characteristics, a binary logistic regression has been done, controlling all other variables. For the binary logistic regression, the dependent variable used was 'vulnerable' or 'not vulnerable'. The background characteristics are age, marital status, sex, migration, education, religion, social networking, family type, economic status and profession.

The result of the logistic regression reveal that age, marital status, migration, education, religion, economic status, family type, profession

Table 17.5: Odds Ratio from Logistic Regression Analysis Assessing the Likelihood of Vulnerability by Background Characteristics, 2009-2010

Predictor Variables		*Frequency*	*Sig.*	*Exp(B)*
Profession Recoded	IT and BPO (Ref.)	66	0.430	
	Education and Research	242	0.456	0.776
	Professionals	47	0.688	1.304
	Media/Hotel/Entertainment	52	0.071	0.424
	Other Professions	48	0.508	1.533
Family Wealth Index	Low Middle Class (Ref.)	157	0.659	
	Middle Class	131	0.562	1.138
	High Middle Class	167	0.365	0.822
Social Network Index	Low Networking (Ref.)	138	0.008	
	Moderate Networking	219	0.091	0.645
	High Networking	98	0.003	3.627*
Education	Higher Secondary Passed (Ref.)	106	0.888	
	Graduate	211	0.858	0.964
	Post-Graduate and Above	138	0.626	1.129
Religion	Hindu (Ref.)	388	0.198	
	Muslim	25	0.073	0.510
	Christian and Others	42	0.213	1.567
Sex	Females (Ref.)	271		
	Males	184	0.000	2.662*
Family Type Recoded	Joint Family (Ref.)	164		
	Nuclear Family	291	0.624	0.922
Migration	Migrant (Ref.)	133		
	Non-Migrant	322	0.336	0.835
Age Group	15–24 (Ref.)	250		
	25–34	205	0.567	1.123
Marital Status	Unmarried (Ref.)	355		
	Married	100	0.618	0.902
Constant			0.000	16.958

Nagelkerke R Square = 0.242 —2 Log Likelihood= 303.869
Total Sample = 455
* Significant at 1 per cent level
Ref. = Reference Category

Source: Computed from Primary Survey, 2009-10.

do not have any significant impact on vulnerability. However, sex of the respondent and levels of social networking have significant impact. Again, males are more vulnerable (2.662) to a risky lifestyle than females. This is statistically significant at less than one per cent level. Respondents with high social networking are vulnerable (3.627 times more) than those with low social networking. This result is statistically significant at one per cent level. This proves the fact that young people are more influenced

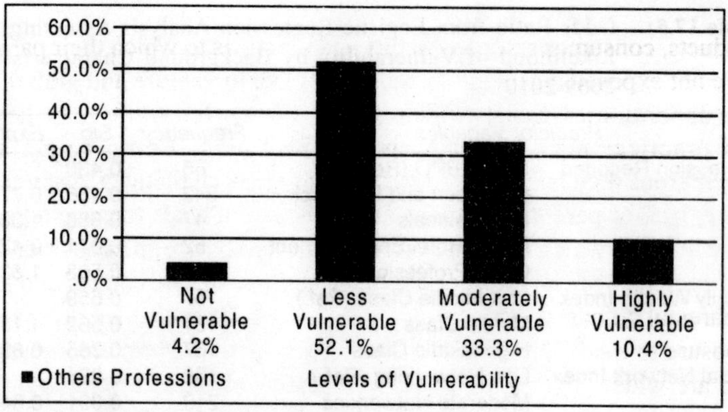

Source: Computed from Primary Survey, 2009-10.

Fig. 17.6: Levels of Vulnerability among Youth in Other Professions in Kolkata, 2009-10

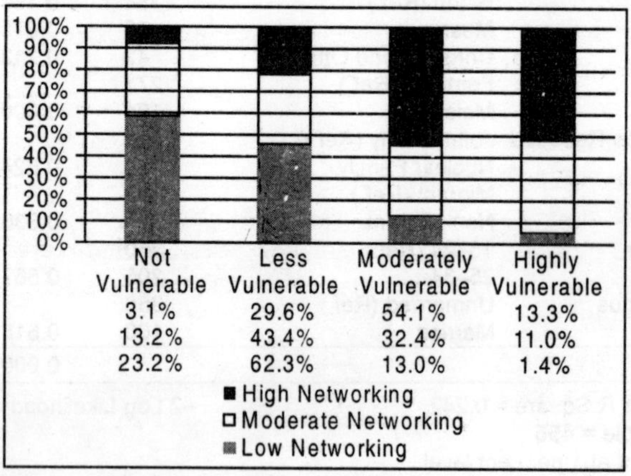

Source: Computed from Primary Survey, 2009-10.

Fig. 17.7: Levels of Vulnerability by Social Networking among Youth in Kolkata, 2009-10

and undertake risky lifestyle under the influence of friends and peers and that males having a stronger peer influence are even more vulnerable.

Conclusions

Urban youth have a greater exposure to new technologies, media, new products, consumerism, risky habits and practices to which their parents were not exposed a generation ago. Youth like to venture and grab these new opportunities. Some of them are for a better life while some habits and practices may hinder their healthy living. Being young and adventurous they leap forward to take these new challenges. Away from home, lack of parental guidance and supervision leads them to adopt a risky lifestyle which are more often aggravated by group behaviour and peer pressure. Social networking, in the absence of self-control and lack of parental guidance has led to risky behaviour. Uncontrolled access and exposure to media have affected the consumerism pattern among youth who are widely opting for smoking and alcoholism as a status symbol ignoring the side effects on health.

Youth in urban areas often have to face certain problems. These problems can be a part of the process of growing-up, personal problems or social problems. But the fact is that problems do exist at every point in life which can also affect ones lifestyle or change and transform one's life. Some problems like depression and attempt to suicide have become a public health problem because these are not outcomes of personal problems only, but may be the fallout of urban lifestyle, stress, loneliness or desertion by a loved one. Some problems like sexual harassment are more gender specific and women are soft targets. Sexual assaults in and outside marriage, incest, rape are just some more examples of the problems faced more by women than men and these leave behind scars which are just not physical in nature but psychological and in the long run affect sexual health.

Some problem behaviour, personal and social issues make youth vulnerable to a risky lifestyle that ultimately affect their sexual health. Thus from the vulnerability index, it is seen that though not all youth were vulnerable, but a large proportion of them are vulnerable. It is found that males and those youth with a high social networking are more vulnerable. Vulnerability has been found to be higher among some professions like those in the media/hotel/entertainment industry and among the professionals. Hence, vulnerability to risky lifestyle and sexual health is mostly affected by peer pressure among friends and colleagues. Thus, professions where considerable free mixing and high networking, coupled with work stress, partying and casual sex and partnerships develop, the chances of being vulnerable gets accentuated.

Keeping these in mind, the Government of India should make laws, and make the working environment such that the burden of workload and stress does not adversely affect the health of the youth. Those who are still in the educational system should be given proper health and sex-education as well as career counselling so that the energy levels and aspirations of the youth are properly channelised to achieve a better qualified and healthy future to make them responsible citizens of the country.

REFERENCES

Birandar, R. (2005): "Structure of employment in ICT Sector in India: Emerging issues and prospects." *The Indian Journal of Labour Economics*, Vol. 48, No. 4, 2005 pp. 837-851.

Chandrakar, Nili (1999): 'Sexual Harassment against Women in an Educational Institution', Unpublished Paper Presented at the University Forum, M.S. University of Baroda, Vadodara.

Gajalakshmi, V. *et al.* (2004): "Tobacco Survey among youth in South India", *Asian Pacific Journal of Cancer Prevention*, Vol. 5, 2004, pp. 273-278.

Goyal, A. (2005): "New Technologies and labour markets: Entrants, outsourcing and matching." *The Indian Journal of Labour Economics*, Vol. 48, No. 4, 2005, pp. 853-868.

Hans, G. (1994): "Life Style Education for Student Youth: Need and Strategy", *Indian Journal of Social Work*, Vol. LV, No. 1, pp. 25-39.

Hans, Gurmeet (1997): "AIDS and Law", *The Indian Journal of Social Work*, Vol. 58, No. 1, pp. 99-110.

Jha, S.S. (1994): "Life style related problems of Youth", *The Indian Journal of Social Work.*, Vol. LV(1) 1994, pp. 3-12.

Khan, M.E. *et al.* (1996): "Sexual Violence within Marriage," *Seminar*, 447, pp. 32-35.

Khatri, A.A. (1972): "The Indian Family: An Empirically Derived Analysis of Shifts in Size and Types," *Journal of Marriage and Family*, Vol. 34(4), pp. 725-734.

Maitra, S.; Schensul, S.L. (2002): "Reflecting Diversity and Complexity in Marital Sexual Relationships in Low Income Community in Mumbai." *Culture, Health & Sexuality*. Vol. 4, No. 2, pp. 133-151.

Pandey, H. and Shukla, K.K. (2010): "The Probability model for risk of vulnerability to STDs/HIV infection among pre-marital female migrants in Urban India". *Journal of Applied Quantitative Methods*, Vol. 5(1), Spring, 2010, pp. 145-151.

Prodhan, M.R. and Ram, U. (2007): "Identifying contexts and vulnerability of the urban youth towards premarital sex: Evidence from Puri, Odisha", *Indian Journal of Youth Affairs*, Vol. 11(2) July-December 2007, pp. 105-114.

Rego, A. and Gandevia, K. (2005): "Sexuality and Substance Use", *The Indian Journal of Social Work*, Vol. 66(4) October 2005, pp. 527-542.

Sankar, S.C. *et al.* (2005): "A study on victims of sexual offences in South Delhi." *The Indian Journal of Family Welfare*, Vol. 51 (1), June 2005, pp. 60-66.

Tjaden, Patricia, G. (1988): "Pornography and sex education", *Journal of Sex Research,* Vol. 24, 1988, pp. 208-12.

18

Living Environment in Million Plus Cities of India

Vinod Kumar Mishra

Introduction

India has witnessed rapid growth of urban population since Independence. This may be primarily attributed to large scale rural to urban migration. Apart from this, due to high population base, natural growth of urban population has also resulted in rapid urbanisation in India. The process of urbanisation in India is not even. Some of the States such as Goa, Tamil Nadu, Maharashtra and Gujarat have larger proportion of their population living in urban area while other States such as Bihar, Rajasthan, Uttar Pradesh etc. have very low proportion of urban population. India also has witnessed a lopsided urbanisation across different size of towns. Around two-third of urban population of India is living in Class-I cities while growth of medium and small towns have been stalled. Within the Class-I cities the growth of million plus cities is quite noticeable. Higher population growth in the Class-I cities is partially due to natural growth and in-migration. Large number of satellite towns have emerged in the vicinity of million plus cities and large number of million plus cities have become urban agglomerations (Sivaramakrishna, Kundu, 2005). It has been observed that the growth of peripheral regions of the cities are higher than the core areas. Rapid growth of population coupled with dearth of infrastructure has resulted in the deterioration of the living environment in million plus urban agglomerations. Unplanned urbanisation has caused many problems. Slum settlements are rapidly increasing in alarming rate in million plus cities. Large scale unemployment due to low rural development causes exodus of rural population to urban areas. Thus rural poverty is carried over to urban areas and proliferation of slums take place. Slums emerge due to the poor's inability to afford the ever increasing high housing prices in urban areas.

Most of the migrants taking shelter in urban areas are semi-skilled or unskilled. They are unable to get well paid jobs in urban labour market. The rural-urban migrants, therefore, have no option left but to get employed in urban informal sector. Thus casualisation of labour takes place in urban areas. Since, income of the urban poor is too low to afford descent housing in urban areas they live in low income localities particularly in the slums. Thus slums are manifestations of urban poverty. Among the factors responsive for the inadequate housing, two inhibiting factors are more responsive, i.e. land and finance (Gupta, 1995). While analysing the living environment of million plus cities not only the number of dwelling units are important but also their quality in term of structures, characteristics, and amenities are important. The housing deficit gets reflected in the growth of slums and congestion in the dwelling units (Bhole, 1988). Thus rapid growth of urbanisation and inflow of migrants have resulted in the expansion of slums (Nangia *et al.,* 2000). The rapid population growth and low investment in urban development have led to inadequate infrastructure and basic amenities in the million plus of India (Kundu *et al.,* 1999). Per capita income and its distribution among households along with the prices of housing define the quality of housing that particular households can afford. Poverty is the main cause for the lack of accessibility basic amenities in urban areas. The condition becomes more serious in large million plus cities. The poor people lack adequate income to afford a dignified standard of living. Thus they cannot improve their living environment and are forced to live in unhealthy living condition.

Against this backdrop, the present study provides a perspective on the living environment of the million plus cities. The indicators taken for the measurement of living environment are percentage of households living in different type, of houses, percentage of households having safe drinking water, percentage of households having toilet facility, and proportion of households using cooking gas as the main fuel used for the cooking. To see the change in the living environment of million plus cities a comparative analysis as per the 1991 and 2001 Census has been done. The cities have been grouped into various categories depending on availability of the particular facility. Finally, the development of living environment index for all million plus cities have been computed. Census of India 1991 and 2001 data has been used here and for the calculation of composite index United Nations method has been used.

The United Nations recognise three broad types of houses on the basis of materials used for the construction of wall, roof and floor. These are permanent, semi-permanent and temporary. When materials are durable like cement, bricks, tiles, metal, the houses have been classified as permanent. When wall and roof are made of non-durable materials such as grasses, thatch, etc. the houses have been classified as temporary. When a mixture of durable and non-durable materials is used the houses have been classified as semi-permanent. Census of India 2001 has also adopted the above mentioned classification.

Quality of Housing in Million Plus Cities 1991

Table 18.1 gives the percentage distribution of households living in permanent, semi-permanent and temporary houses for the Census year of 1991. For clear understanding of the quality of housing stock, each housing type has been classified into five categories.

Distribution of Households Living in Permanent Houses in 1991

The percentage distribution of households living in permanent type of structure made of durable materials in million plus urban agglomerations in 1991 can be grouped into the following five categories to show the status of the quality of housing. The name of the million plus urban agglomerations falling in each category are as follows:

- *Very High Level (more than 90%)*: Greater Mumbai, Jaipur, Ludhiana (highest: 95%), Agra (93%) and Varanasi has the highest percentage of households living in permanent houses.
- *High Level (80 to 90%)*: Kolkata, Delhi, Bangalore, Ahmedabad, Pune, Kanpur, Lucknow, Patna, Kochi, Madurai, Asansol, Faridabad, Allahabad, Amritsar and Rajkot.
- *Medium Level (70 to 80%)*: Chennai, Hyderabad, Surat, Vadodara, Coimbatore, Meerut, Nashik, Jabalpur, Jamshedpur and Dhanbad.
- *Low Level (60 to 70%)*: Indore, Bhopal, Visakhapatnam and Vijayawada.
- *Very Low Level (below 60%)*: Nagpur.

Table 18.1: Households Living in Permanent, Semi-Permanent and Temporary Houses, in Million Plus Urban Agglomerations/Cities in 1991

Name of UA/City	Per cent Perma-nent	Rank	Per cent Semi Perma-nent	Rank	Per cent Tempo-rary	Rank
Greater Mumbai UA	90.57	4	7.42	28	2.02	28
Kolkata UA	83.18	14	14.26	16	2.57	23
Delhi UA	85.48	11	4.47	34	10.05	4
Chennai UA	75.04	25	9.40	24	15.55	3
Bangalore UA	87.77	8	8.39	25	3.84	20
Hyderabad UA	79.61	21	16.52	13	3.87	19
Ahmedabad UA	87.37	10	10.32	20	2.30	26
Pune UA	80.53	18	17.38	12	2.09	27
Surat UA	71.90	29	23.48	6	4.63	13
Kanpur UA	83.81	14	12.55	18	3.64	21
Jaipur	90.25	5	6.63	30	3.12	22
Lucknow UA	87.71	9	6.98	29	5.30	9
Nagpur UA	59.18	35	36.07	1	4.76	12
Patna UA	84.88	13	9.88	23	5.25	10
Indore UA	67.42	32	28.52	2	4.06	15
Vadodara UA	79.02	22	18.57	9	2.41	25
Bhopal UA	68.61	31	22.19	7	9.20	6
Coimbatore UA	77.68	24	18.44	10	3.88	18
Ludhiana	93.42	1	4.62	31	1.96	30
Kochi UA	88.94	6	3.67	35	7.39	8
Visakhapatnam UA	67.38	33	4.57	32	28.06	2
Agra UA*	93.00	2	4.48	33	2.52	24
Varanasi UA	90.81	3	7.81	27	1.38	34
Madurai UA*	80.81	17	11.54	19	7.65	7
Meerut UA*	78.34	23	17.75	11	3.91	16
Nashik UA*	74.05	27	23.94	5	2.01	29
Jabalpur UA*	70.84	30	28.39	3	0.77	35
Jamshedpur UA*	74.88	26	21.02	8	4.11	14
Asansol UA*	80.37	20	15.73	14	3.90	17
Dhanbad UA*	73.65	28	24.87	4	1.48	32
Faridabad*	82.18	16	7.99	26	9.82	5
Allahabad UA*	88.19	7	10.12	22	1.69	31
Amritsar UA*	80.53	19	14.62	15	4.85	11
Vijayawada UA*	61.33	34	10.22	21	28.45	1
Rajkot UA*	85.16	12	13.41	17	1.43	33

UA = Urban Agglomeration

* City was not a million plus city in 1991.

Source: Tables on Houses and Households Amenities, Series-1, Part-VII Census of India, 1991.

Distribution of Households Living in Semi-Permanent Houses in 1991

On the basis of the percentage value of the households living in semi-permanent houses, the million plus urban agglomerations/cities can be grouped into the following five categories:

- *Very High Level (more than 20%)*: Surat, Nagpur, Indore, Bhopal, Nashik, Jamshedpur, and Dhanbad.
- *High Level (15 to 20%)*: Hyderabad, Pune, Vadodara, Coimbatore, Meerut and Asansol.
- *Medium Level (10 to 15%)*: Kolkata, Ahmedabad, Vijayawada, Amritsar and Rajkot.
- *Low Level (5 to 10%)*: Greater Mumbai, Chennai, Bangalore, Jaipur, Lucknow, Patna, Varanasi and Faridabad.
- *Very Low Level (below 5%)*: Delhi, Ludhiana, Kochi, Visakhapatnam, and Agra.

Distribution of Households Living in Temporary Houses in 1991

The percentage of households living in temporary shelter where the houses are predominantly made of non-durable commodities, have been also grouped into the following five categories. Cities with high level of households living in these structures signify low socio-economic situations. Vishakhapatnam, a coastal city of Andhra Pradesh has large number of fishermen living in these temporary hutments; in this case the economic activity is an influencing factor behind the nature of housing.

- *Very High Level (more than 16%)*: Vijayawada and Visakhapatnam.
- *High Level (12 to 16%)*: Chennai.
- *Medium Level (8 to 12%)*: Delhi, Bhopal and Faridabad.
- *Low Level (4 to 8%)*: Surat, Lucknow, Nagpur, Patna, Vadodara, Kochi, Madurai, Jamshedpur and Amritsar.
- *Very Low Level (below 4%)*: Greater Mumbai, Kolkata, Bangalore, Hyderabad, Ahmedabad, Pune, Kanpur, Jaipur, Vadodara, Coimbatore, Ludhiana, Agra, Varanasi, Meerut, Nashik, Jabalpur, Asansol, Dhanbad, Allahabad, and Rajkot.

Quality of Housing Stock in Million Plus Urban Agglomerations/ Cities 2001

Table 18.2 gives the percentage distribution of households living in permanent, semi-permanent and temporary houses in 2001.

Distribution of Households Living in Permanent Houses in 2001

On the basis of data given in Table 18.2, the million plus urban agglomerations/cities have been grouped into the following five categories:

- *Very High Level (more than 90%)*: Greater Mumbai, Delhi, Bangalore, Ahmedabad, Jaipur, Lucknow, Ludhiana, Kochi, Agra, Varanasi, Allahabad, and Rajkot.
- *High Level (85 to 90%)*: Kolkata, Hyderabad, Pune, Kanpur, Patna, Vadodara, Madurai, Faridabad, Amritsar.
- *Medium Level (80 to 85%)*: Chennai, Surat, Indore, Coimbatore, Visakhapatnam and Meerut.
- *Low Level (75 to 80%)*: Bhopal, Nashik, Jamshedpur, Asansol and Vijayawada.
- *Very Low Level (below 75%)*: Nagpur, Jabalpur, and Dhanbad.

Households Living in Semi-Permanent Houses in 2001

Percentage of households living in semi-permanent houses has been grouped into the following categories:

- *Very High (more than 20%)*: Nagpur, Jabalpur and Dhanbad.
- *High Level (15 to 20%)*: Indore, Bhopal, Coimbatore, Nashik, Jamshedpur, and Asansol.
- *Medium Level (10 to 15%)*: Hyderabad, Pune, Surat, Kanpur, Meerut, Amritsar, Vijayawada.
- *Low Level (5 to 10%)*: Greater Mumbai, Chennai, Bangalore, Ahmedabad, Lucknow, Patna, Vadodara, Visakhapatnam, Varanasi, Madurai, Faridabad, Allahabad, and Rajkot.
- *Very Low Level (below 5 to 10%)*: Delhi, Jaipur, Ludhiana, Kochi, and Agra.

Table 18.2: Type of Houses in Million plus UAs/Cities, 2001

Name of UA/City	Per cent Perma-nent	Rank 1	Per cent Semi-Perma-nent	Rank	Per cent Tempo-rary	Rank
Greater Mumbai UA	92.86	6	5.16	29	1.89	18
Kolkata UA	86.18	20	13.06	12	0.72	34
Delhi UA	91.70	10	4.74	31	3.54	9
Chennai UA	84.57	22	8.46	20	6.94	3
Bangalore UA	92.45	7	6.30	26	1.49	22
Hyderabad UA	87.12	18	10.85	15	1.93	17
Ahmedabad UA	93.18	5	5.50	28	1.30	27
Pune UA	87.60	17	10.40	17	1.72	20
Surat UA	84.39	23	14.73	10	0.86	33
Kanpur UA	85.28	21	10.97	14	3.69	6
Jaipur	94.84	3	4.21	32	0.94	31
Lucknow UA	91.27	11	5.11	30	3.61	8
Nagpur UA	71.02	35	26.47	1	2.49	14
Patna UA	87.91	15	8.25	22	3.84	5
Indore UA	80.68	27	17.68	7	1.62	21
Vadodara UA	88.81	13	9.86	18	1.32	26
Bhopal UA	78.07	29	15.13	9	6.80	4
Coimbatore UA	81.05	26	17.60	8	1.33	25
Ludhiana	95.05	1	3.54	35	1.39	24
Kochi UA	94.29	4	3.85	34	1.81	19
Visakhapatnam UA	81.22	25	5.54	27	13.23	1
Agra UA	95.02	2	3.92	33	1.05	29
Varanasi UA	91.95	8	6.56	25	0.99	30
Madurai UA	87.72	16	8.58	19	3.67	7
Meerut UA	83.85	24	14.09	11	2.05	16
Nashik UA	77.92	30	18.60	5	3.13	11
Jabalpur UA	73.49	34	25.31	2	1.20	28
Jamshedpur UA	77.53	31	19.96	4	2.50	13
Asansol UA	78.79	28	18.59	6	2.62	12
Dhanbad UA	74.45	33	25.01	3	0.54	35
Faridabad	88.22	14	8.34	21	3.44	10
Allahabad UA	90.34	12	8.20	23	1.46	23
Amritsar UA	86.54	19	11.28	13	2.15	15
Vijayawada UA	77.27	32	10.42	16	12.30	2
Rajkot UA	91.92	9	7.13	24	0.93	32

UA = Urban Agglormeration

Source: Census of India, 2001 Tables on Houses, Households Amenities and Assets.

Households Living in Temporary Houses in 2001

Table 18.2 shows the percentage distribution of households living in

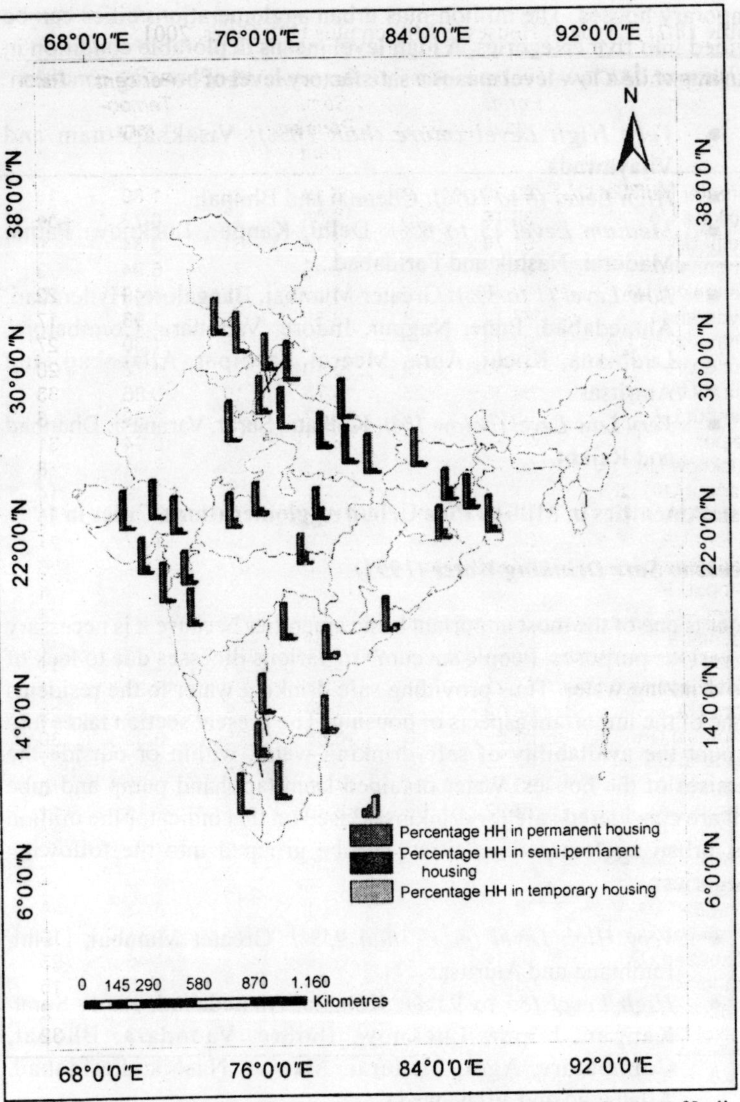

Source: Tables on Houses and Households Amenities, Series-1 Census of India, 2001.

Map 18.1: Type of Housing in Million Plus Cities, 2001

temporary houses. The million plus urban agglomerations/cities can be divided into five categories. A high level means deplorable condition in housing while a low level means a satisfactory level of housing condition.

- *Very High Level (more than 10%)*: Visakhapatnam and Vijayawada.
- *High Level (6 to 10%)*: Chennai and Bhopal.
- *Medium Level (3 to 6%)*: Delhi, Kanpur, Lucknow, Patna, Madurai, Nashik and Faridabad.
- *Low Level (1 to 3%)*: Greater Mumbai, Bangalore, Hyderabad, Ahmedabad, Pune, Nagpur, Indore, Vadodara, Coimbatore, Ludhiana, Kochi, Agra, Meerut, Jabalpur, Allahabad, and Amritsar.
- *Very Low Level (below 1%)*: Kolkata, Surat, Varanasi, Dhanbad and Rajkot.

Basic Amenities in Million Plus Urban Agglomerations/Cities in 1991

Access to Safe Drinking Water (1991)

Water is one of the most important basic amenities because it is necessary for various purposes. People succumb to various illnesses due to lack of safe drinking water. Thus providing safe drinking water to the residents is one of the important aspects of housing. The present section takes into account the availability of safe drinking water, within or outside the premises of the houses. Water obtained from tap, hand pump and tube well are considered safe for drinking. Based on this indicator the million plus urban agglomerations/cities, can be grouped into the following categories:

- *Very High Level (more than 95%)*: Greater Mumbai, Delhi, Ludhiana and Amritsar.
- *High Level (85 to 95%)*: Kolkata, Ahmedabad, Pune, Surat, Kanpur, Jaipur, Lucknow, Indore, Vadodara, Bhopal, Coimbatore, Agra, Madurai, Meerut, Nashik, Faridabad, Allahabad and Vijayawada.
- *Medium Level (75 to 85%)*: Bangalore, Hyderabad, Patna, Varanasi, Jabalpur, Asansol, Dhanbad, Rajkot and Patna.
- *Low Level (65 to 75%)*: Nagpur, Kochi, Jamshedpur, Dhanbad, Visakhapatnam.
- *Very Low Level (below 65%)*: Chennai.

Table 18.3: Access to Basic Amenities in Million Plus Cities in 1991

Name of City/UA	*Per cent Safe drinking water*	*Rank*	*Per cent Toilet*	*Rank*	*Per cent Electri-city*	*Rank*
Greater Mumbai UA	95.68	3	75.45	13	89.77	3
Kolkata UA	92.24	10	89.19	1	77.17	27
Delhi UA	96.27	1	66.81	27	81.34	21
Chennai UA	59.90	35	77.25	12	81.91	18
Bangalore UA	80.89	28	81.54	4	81.82	19
Hyderabad UA	81.73	26	80.70	6	87.88	6
Ahmedabad UA	92.01	11	72.66	18	80.26	23
Pune UA	94.56	5	73.10	16	87.46	7
Surat UA	90.66	13	69.78	22	78.77	25
Kanpur UA	88.74	16	74.14	15	75.49	29
Jaipur	89.72	15	78.46	9	82.73	16
Lucknow UA	88.21	18	73.02	17	76.25	28
Nagpur UA	73.81	31	71.44	19	82.18	17
Patna UA	84.97	23	83.64	3	80.68	22
Indore UA	88.62	17	67.68	25	83.22	15
Vadodara UA	92.56	8	77.60	11	85.52	10
Bhopal UA	93.26	7	71.31	20	85.91	8
Coimbatore UA	89.97	14	58.29	32.	83.93	13
Ludhiana	95.85	2	86.55	2	96.14	1
Kochi UA	73.01	32	81.13	5	75.30	30
Visakhapatnam UA	65.76	34	52.17	34	70.26	33
Agra UA	85.85	22	66.23	28	79.48	24
Varanasi UA	84.53	24	79.66	7	85.66	9
Madurai UA	88.12	19	67.47	26	83.51	14
Meerut UA	92.26	9	78.34	10	84.13	11
Nashik UA	87.83	20	69.42	23	88.38	5
Jabalpur UA	81.93	25	61.53	30	81.79	20
Jamshedpur UA	66.45	33	67.90	24	71.54	32
Asansol UA	80.00	29	59.67	31	63.17	35
Dhanbad UA	78.61	30	47.30	35	66.60	34
Faridabad	94.50	6	57.84	33	78.22	26
Allahabad UA	91.23	12	79.16	8	84.07	12
Amritsar UA	95.37	4	75.41	14	95.72	2
Vijayawada UA	86.60	21	71.01	21	72.07	31
Rajkot UA	81.08	27	64.88	29	88.75	4

UA = Urban Agglormeration

Source: Tables on Houses and Households Amenities, Series-1.Part-VII Census of India, 1991.

Households having Access to Toilet Facility in 1991

Adequate toilet facility ensures the proper disposal of human wastes and minimizes health hazards. Million plus cities can be categorised into the following types based on the percentage of households having access to toilet facility within the house.

- *Very High Level (more than 85%)*: Kolkata and Ludhiana.
- *High Level (75 to 85%)*: Greater Mumbai, Chennai, Jaipur, Vadodara, Patna, Kochi, Varanasi, Meerut, Amritsar, and Allahabad.
- *Medium Level (65 to 75%)*: Delhi, Ahmedabad, Pune, Surat, Kanpur, Lucknow, Nagpur, Indore, Bhopal, Agra, Madurai, Nashik, Jabalpur, Jamshedpur and Vijayawada
- Low Level (55 to 65%): Coimbatore, Jabalpur, Asansol, Faridabad, and Rajkot.
- *Very Low Level (below 55%)*: Visakhapatnam and Dhanbad.

Households Having Access to Electricity in 1991

The availability of electricity is one of the important indicators for assessing the standard of living. Access to electricity is a necessity of urban life-style. The percentage distribution of households having electricity supply in million plus urban agglomerations/cities can be grouped under the following categories:

- *Very High Level (more than 95%)*: Ludhiana and Amritsar.
- *High Level (85 to 95%)*: Greater Mumbai, Hyderabad, Pune, Vadodara, Bhopal, Varanasi, Nashik and Rajkot.
- *Medium Level (75 to 85%)*: Kolkata, Delhi, Chennai, Bangalore, Ahmedabad, Surat, Kanpur, Jaipur, Lucknow, Nagpur, Patna, Indore, Coimbatore, Kochi, Agra, Madurai, Meerut, Jabalpur, Faridabad, and Allahabad.
- *Low Level (65 to 75%)*: Visakhapatnam, Jamshedpur, Dhanbad and Vijayawada.
- *Very Low Level (below 65%)*: Asansol.

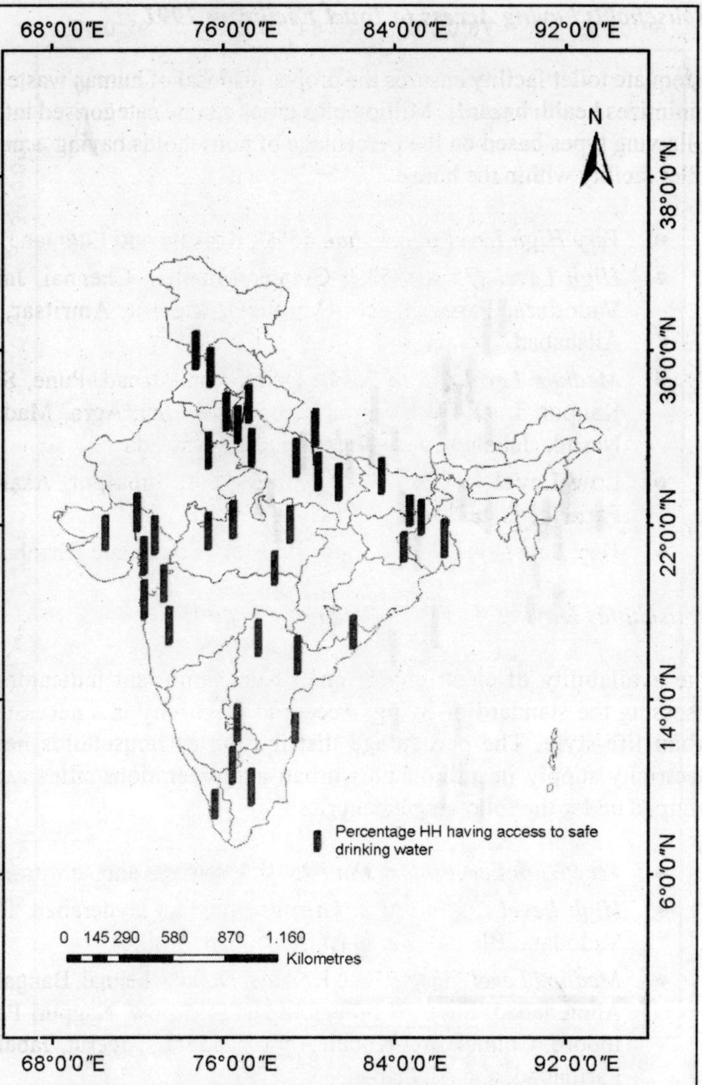

Source: *Tables on Houses and Households Amenities*, Series-1. Census of India, 2001.

Map 18.2: Access to Safe Drinking Water in Million Plus Cities, 2001.

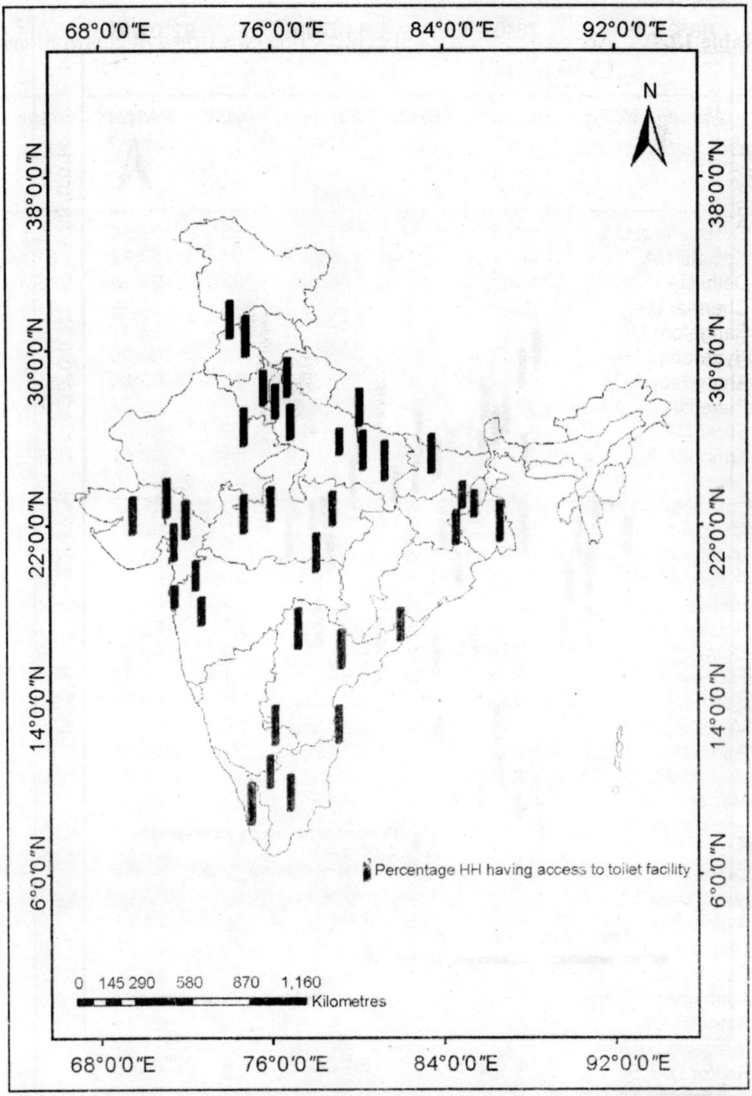

Source: *Tables on Houses and Households Amenities*, Series-1. Census of India, 2001.

Map 18.3: Access to Toilet Facilities in Million Plus Cities, 2001

Table 18.4: Access to Basic Amenities in Million Plus Urban Agglomerations/ Cities in 2001

Name UA/City	*Per cent Safe Drinking water*	*Rank*	*Per cent Toilet*	*Rank*	*Per cent Electri-city*	*Rank*
Gr. Mumbai UA	98.75	5	51.14	35	97.90	2
Kolkata UA	97.53	15	92.36	4	87.82	31
Delhi UA	97.75	12	79.03	23	93.38	16
Chennai UA	75.70	33	87.21	13	94.22	11
Bangalore UA	95.98	19	91.18	5	95.31	9
Hyderabad UA	93.98	24	93.26	3	95.99	7
Ahmedabad UA	98.54	9	87.74	10	93.65	14
Pune UA	97.18	16	65.00	31	96.37	5
Surat UA	97.76	11	84.44	20	94.69	10
Kanpur UA	98.58	8	59.03	34	90.41	26
Jaipur	94.70	23	86.15	17	93.64	15
Lucknow UA	99.19	3	85.27	18	89.62	28
Nagpur UA	86.01	31	86.55	16	92.34	21
Patna UA	93.70	26	89.64	7	89.61	29
Indore UA	95.20	20	86.92	14	97.63	3
Vadodara UA	98.60	6	87.57	12	94.18	12
Bhopal UA	97.55	19	77.69	25	98.58	1
Coimbatore UA	96.36	18	73.32	29	92.94	19
Ludhiana	99.53	1	94.88	1	96.80	4
Kochi UA	73.04	35	94.74	2	89.81	27
Visakhapatnam UA	86.07	30	74.55	28	90.57	25
Agra UA	98.10	10	79.98	22	93.05	18
Varanasi UA	94.95	22	90.11	6	92.65	20
Madurai UA	93.58	27	81.66	21	93.36	17
Meerut UA	99.00	4	87.73	11	89.25	30
Nashik UA	94.96	21	68.15	30	91.12	24
Jabalpur UA	93.71	25	77.21	27	94.05	13
Jamshedpur UA	75.10	34	77.68	26	79.01	34
Asansol UA	88.67	29	60.08	32	77.77	27
Dhanbad UA	79.37	32	59.09	33	84.78	26
Faridabad	97.16	17	78.41	24	86.06	32
Allahabad UA	98.58	7	88.50	9	91.74	35
Amritsar UA	99.34	2	86.82	15	96.16	33
Vijayawada UA	97.61	13	88.67	8	91.51	24
Rajkot UA	88.85	28	84.75	19	95.52	8

UA = Urban Agglormeration

Source: Census of India, 2001 Tables on Houses, Households Amenities and Assets Tables released in compact disc.

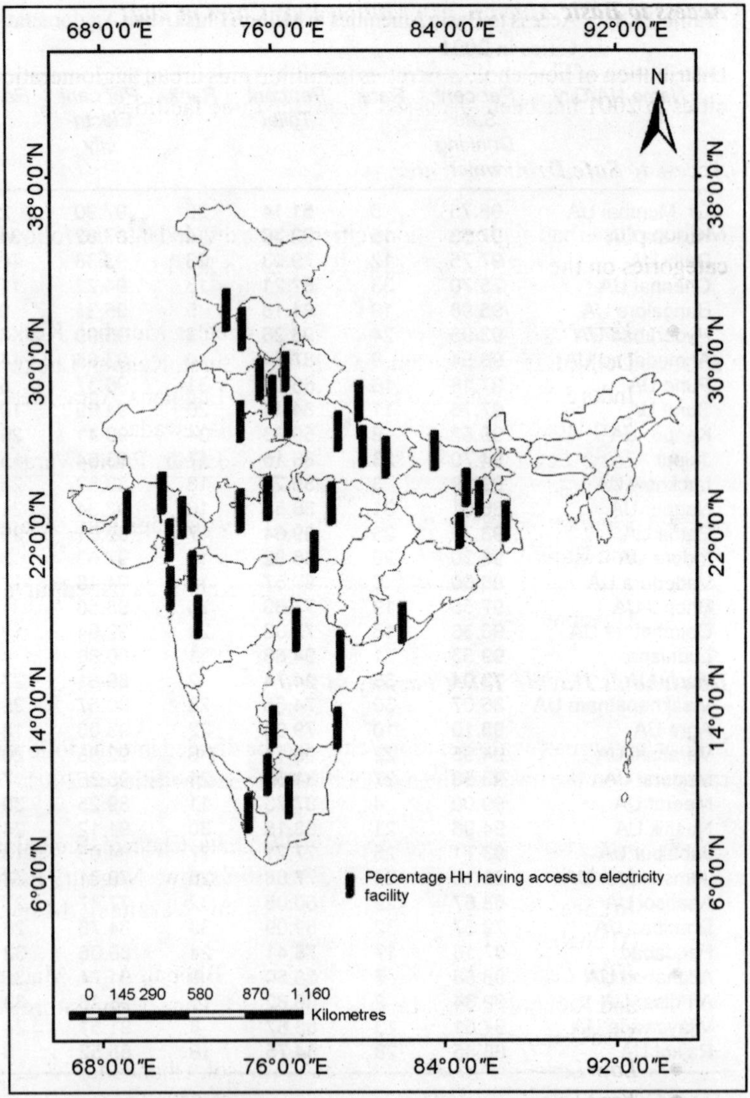

Source: Tables on Houses and Households Amenities, Series-1. Census of India, 2001.

Map 18.4: Access to Electricity Facility in Million Plus Cities, 2001

Access to Basic Amenities in Million Plus Cities in 2001

Distribution of household amenities in million plus urban agglomerations/ cities in 2001 has been discussed for all the three facilities:

Access to Safe Drinking Water

Million plus urban agglomerations/cities can be divided into the following categories on the basis of safe drinking water in 2001.

- *Very High Level (more than 95%)*: Greater Mumbai, Kolkata, Delhi, Bangalore, Ahmedabad, Pune, Surat, Kanpur, Lucknow, Indore, Vadodara, Bhopal, Coimbatore, Ludhiana, Agra, Meerut, Faridabad, Allahabad, Amritsar and Vijayawada.
- *High Level (90 to 95%)*: Hyderabad, Jaipur, Patna, Varanasi, Madurai, Nashik, Jabalpur.
- *Medium Level (85 to 90%)*: Nagpur, Visakhapatnam, Asansol and Rajkot.
- *Low Level (below 85%)*: Chennai, Kochi, Jamshedpur and Dhanbad.

Households Having Toilet Facility in 2001

Million plus urban agglomerations/cities can be divided into the following categories on the basis of the availability of toilet facilities in 2001:

- *Very High Level (more than 85%)*: Kolkata, Chennai, Bangalore, Hyderabad, Ahmedabad, Jaipur, Lucknow, Nagpur, Patna, Indore, Vadodara, Ludhiana, Kochi, Varanasi, Meerut, Allahabad, Amritsar and Vijayawada.
- *High Level (75 to 85%)*: Delhi, Surat, Bhopal, Agra, Madurai and Rajkot Medium Level (65 to 75%): Pune, Coimbatore and Visakhapatnam are included here.
- *Low Level (55 to 65%)*: Kanpur, Asansol, Dhanbad.
- *Very Low Level (less than 65%)*: Greater Mumbai.

Households Having Electricity in 2001

- *Very High Level (more than 95%)*: Greater Mumbai, Bangalore, Hyderabad, Pune, Indore, Bhopal, Ludhiana, Amritsar and Rajkot.

Table 18.5: Households Using Cooking Gas as Fuel in Million plus Urban Agglomerations/Cities in 1991 ánd 2001

Name of City	*Per cent Cooking Gas 1991*	*Rank*	*Per cent Cooking Gas 2001*	*Rank*
Greater Mumbai UA	42.19	11	59.70	17
Kolkata UA	18.88	32	43.03	32
Delhi UA	49.31	2	68.78	5
Chennai UA	32.85	26	57.52	23
Bangalore UA	24.40	29	51.82	28
Hyderabad UA	33.60	25	50.87	29
Ahmedabad UA	48.29	3	64.66	9
Pune UA	44.48	7	66.79	7
Surat UA	37.24	17	53.89	26
Kanpur UA	36.28	13	62.35	12
Jaipur	37.56	16	67.45	6
Lucknow UA	42.24	10	70.35	3
Nagpur UA	46.06	6	63.91	10
Patna UA	33.88	23	58.99	18
Indore UA	48.18	4	73.32	1
Vadodara UA	53.15	1	70.49	2
Bhopal UA	42.91	8	55.00	24
Coimbatore UA	22.02	30	49.91	30
Ludhiana	42.87	9	60.81	14
Kochi UA	26.79	28	53.79	27
Visakhapatnam UA	37.70	15	58.86	19
Agra UA*	33.66	24	65.87	8
Varanasi UA	27.80	27	54.77	25
Madurai UA*	18.86	33	32.69	33
Meerut UA*	38.35	14	58.74	21
Nashik UA*	40.89	12	70.00	4
Jabalpur UA*	35.81	19	58.85	20
Jamshedpur UA*	21.68	31	44.11	31
Asansol UA*	6.00	35	18.03	34
Dhanbad UA*	6.53	34	14.56	35
Faridabad *	35.47	21	59.38	17
Allahabad UA*	35.49	20	63.06	11
Amritsar UA*	47.61	5	60.54	15
Vijayawada UA*	34.49	22	57.85	22
Rajkot UA*	38.99	13	61.94	13

UA = Urban Agglormeration

* City was not a million plus city in 1991.

Source: Tables on Houses and Households Amenities, Series-1, Part-VII Census of India, 1991 and Census of India, 2001 Tables on Houses and Households Amenities & Assets Tables released in compact disc.

- *High Level (90 to 95%)*: Delhi, Chennai, Ahmedabad, Surat, Kanpur, Jaipur, Nagpur, Vadodara, Coimbatore, Visakhapatnam,

Agra, Varanasi, Madurai, Nashik, Jabalpur, Allahabad and Vijayawada.

- *Medium Level (85 to 90%)*: Kolkata, Lucknow, Patna, Kochi, Meerut and Faridabad.
- *Low Level (80 to 85%)*: Dhanbad.
- *Very Low Level (below 80%)*: Asansol and Jamshedpur.

Households Using Cooking Gas as Fuel in 1991

The Census of India 1991 for the first time published data on type of fuel used for cooking. Eight types of fuel, viz. cow dung cake, electricity, coal/coke/lignite, charcoal, cooking gas and wood were identified. The present study considers only cooking gas because it is widely accepted as best fuel used for cooking. The use of cooking gas as fuel can be taken as an indicator of development, because it does not pollute the environment. In 1991 million plus cities can be divided into the following five categories on the basis of the usage of cooking gas as fuel:

- *Very High Level (more than 45%)*: Delhi, Ahmedabad, Nagpur, Indore, Vadodara, and Amritsar. All these cities have good supply of cooking gas through pipelines.
- *High Level (35 to 45%)*: Mumbai, Pune, Lucknow, Bhopal, Ludhiana, Visakhapatnam, Meerut, Nashik, Jabalpur, Faridabad, Allahabad and Rajkot.
- Medium Level (25 to 35%): Chennai, Hyderabad, Patna, Kochi, Agra, Varanasi and Vijayawada.
- *Low Level (15 to 25%)*: Kolkata, Bangalore, Coimbatore, Madurai, Jamshedpur.
- *Very Low Level (below 15%)*: Asansol and Dhanbad.

Households Using Cooking Gas as Fuel in 2001

This can also be divided into the following five categories:

- *Very High Level (more than 70%)*: Lucknow, Indore, Vadodara, Nashik.
- *High Level (60 to 70%)*: Delhi, Ahmedabad, Pune, Kanpur, Jaipur, Nagpur, Ludhiana, Agra, Allahabad, Amritsar and Rajkot.
- *Medium Level (50 to 60%)*: Greater Mumbai, Chennai, Bangalore, Hyderabad, Surat, Patna, Bhopal, Kochi,

Table 18.6: Urban Housing and Basic Amenities Development Index 1991-2001

Sl. No.	Name of UA/City	Index 1991	Rank	Name of UA/City	Index 2001	Rank
1.	Ludhiana	0.942	1	Ludhiana	0.938	1
2.	Greater Mumbai UA	0.830	2	Ahmadabad UA	0.853	2
3.	Amritsar UA*	0.829	3	Jaipur	0.852	3
4.	Vadodara UA	0.776	4	Vadodara UA	0.847	4
5.	Pune UA	0.750	5	Agra UA	0.841	5
6.	Jaipur	0.747	6	Bangalore UA	0.826	6
7.	Ahmedabad UA	0.746	7	Lucknow UA	0.825	7
8.	Allahabad UA*	0.746	8	Amritsar UA	0.824	8
9.	Delhi UA	0.741	9	Allahabad UA	0.823	9
10.	Varanasi UA	0.704	10	Delhi UA	0.819	10
11.	Meerut UA*	0.703	11	Indore UA	0.804	11
12.	Patna UA	0.686	12	Varanasi UA	0.797	12
13.	Lucknow UA	0.679	13	Hyderabad UA	0.783	13
14.	Hyderabad UA	0.666	14	Rajkot UA	0.770	14
15.	Kolkata UA	0.658	15	Surat UA	0.747	15
16.	Bhopal UA	0.648	16	Greater Mumbai UA	0.745	16
17.	Agra UA*	0.648	17	Pune UA	0.740	17
18.	Rajkot UA*	0.648	18	Patna UA	0.737	18
19.	Nashik UA*	0.647	19	Meerut UA	0.732	19
20.	Bangalore UA	0.638	20	Bhopal UA	0.705	20
21.	Kanpur UA	0.634	21	Kolkata UA	0.693	21
22.	Indore UA	0.604	22	Vijayawada UA	0.691	22
23.	Faridabad*	0.592	23	Faridabad	0.681	23
24.	Surat UA	0.578	24	Madurai UA	0.644	24
25.	Kochi UA	0.570	25	Kochi UA	0.637	25
26.	Madurai UA*	0.556	26	Kanpur UA	0.632	26
27.	Coimbatore UA	0.520	27	Coimbatore UA	0.628	27
28.	Jabalpur UA*	0.497	28	Chennai UA	0.620	28
29.	Nagpur UA	0.477	29	Nashik UA	0.619	29
30.	Chennai UA	0.463	30	Jabalpur UA	0.606	30
31.	Vijayawada UA*	0.448	31	Nagpur UA	0.570	31
32.	Jamshedpur UA*	0.344	32	Visakhapatnam UA	0.563	32
33.	Asansol UA*	0.294	33	Jamshedpur UA	0.303	33
34.	Visakhapatnam UA	0.281	34	Asansol UA	0.236	34
35.	Dhanbad UA*	0.211	35	Dhanbad UA	0.181	35

UA = Urban Agglormeration
* The city was not a million plus city in 1991.

Visakhapatnam, Varanasi, Meerut, Jabalpur, Faridabad and Vijayawada.

- *Low Level (40 to 50%)*: Kolkata, Coimbatore and Jamshedpur.
- *Very Low Level (below 40%)*: Dhanbad, Asansol and Madurai.

Urban Housing and Basic Amenities Development in Million Plus Agglomerations/Cities: A Comparative Analysis 1991-2001

For determining the status of housing and basic amenities across the million plus urban agglomerations/cities, a comparative analysis had been done for both the Census periods. Composite index has been worked out for both the Census periods. The following five indicators have been chosen for computing the index:

1. Percentage of households living in permanent houses.
2. Percentage of households having safe drinking water.
3. Percentage of households having electricity.
4. Percentage of households having toilet facility.
5. Percentage distribution of households using cooking gas as fuel.

On the basis of the value of the composite index, five levels of development are considered for finding out the status of urban housing and basic amenities development across all the million plus urban agglomerations/cities for 1991 and 2001. The categories chosen are:

1.	Very high level	(Above 0.80)
2.	High level	(0.70-0.80)
3.	Medium level	(0.60-0.70)
4.	Low level	(0.50-0.60)
5.	Very low level	(below 0.50)

Very High Level (above 0.80): In year 1991 only three urban agglomerations/cities, i.e. Ludhiana, Greater Mumbai and Amritsar were in this level. Ludhiana ranked first in this level because of high rate of development of above five parameters considered in 1991 and 2001. However, the total numbers of urban agglomerations/cities have increased to eleven at this level in the year 2001. It is noteworthy to mention that, Greater Mumbai has lost its position at this level in 2001 due to decrease in the provision of toilet facility (in 2001). Ahmedabad, Jaipur, Vadodara, Agra, Bangalore, Lucknow, Allahabad, Delhi and Indore have also moved to this level in 2001. All these cities have performed better in all five facilities.

High Level (0.7 to 0.8): The composite index value under this category varies from 0.7 to 0.8 in both the Census years. In 1991, Vadodara, Pune, Jaipur, Ahmedabad, Allahabad, Delhi, Varanasi, Meerut were under this category. In 2001 Hyderabad, Rajkot, Surat, Greater

Mumbai, Pune, Patna, Meerut and Bhopal were at this level. Delhi, Jaipur, Ahmedabad and Allahabad have moved from this level to very high level due to improvement in the status of urban housing and basic amenities

Medium Level (0.6 to 0.7): The composite index value under this category varies from 0.6 to 0.7 in both the Census years. In 1991, Patna, Lucknow, Hyderabad, Kolkata, Bhopal, Agra, Rajkot, Nashik, Bangalore, Kanpur, Indore were in this level. In 2001 Kolkata, Vijayawada, Faridabad, Madurai, Kochi, Kanpur, Coimbatore, Chennai, Nashik, Jabalpur and Nagpur had medium level of urban housing and development. These Urban agglomerations/cities did not perform fairly in one or two parameters.

Low Level (0.5 to 0.6): The composite index value under this category varies from 0.5 to 0.6 in both the Census years. In 1991, Faridabad, Surat, Kochi, Madurai, and Coimbatore were at this level. But all these urban agglomerations/cities have performed better in housing and basic amenities development in the last decade and moved to a higher level in 2001. In 2001 only Visakhapatnam ranked in this category.

Very Low Level (below 0.5): The composite index value in this category below 0.5. In 1991 there were eight urban agglomerations/cities at this level and their number has declined to three in 2001. In 1991 Jabalpur, Nagpur, Chennai, Vijayawada, Jamshedpur, Asansol, Visakhapatnam and Dhanbad had very low level of housing and basic amenities. In 2001 all these urban agglomerations/cities have moved to higher level except Asansol and Dhanbad. These urban agglomerations/ cities show very poor level of urban housing and basic amenities development leading to their position at this level.

Conclusions

In the present paper, living environment in million plus cities has been analysed. Housing amenties have been classified in three categories—(a) permanent, (b) semi-permanent, and (c) temporary. Provision of basic amenities in million plus cities for both the Census years of 1991 and 2001 has also been analysed. The percentage distribution of households having safe drinking water, toilet facility, and electricity and cooking gas has been taken for assessing the status of basic amenities in million plus cities in India.

A comparison done between quality of housing in 1991 and 2001 in all million plus cities shows that nearly all million plus cities have recorded increase in percentage of population living in permanent houses. Ludhiana and Kochi recorded very good progress in the housing sector; however, the situation remains worrisome in Nagpur and Bhopal where quite a large percentage of households are still living in houses, which are made of non-durable materials.

The cities which have joined the group of million plus cities for the first times in 2001 have recorded very low increase in percentage of households living in permanent houses. Percentage of households living in permanent houses has even declined in Asansol from 1991 to 2001.This may be attributed to higher growth of population in the city. Percentage of households living in temporary houses has declined in most of the million plus cities except in Kanpur, which has recorded an increase in this category. Visakhapatnam and Vijayawada have very high percentage of households living in temporary houses. Better quality of housing is found in Ludhiana, Agra, Kochi, Greater Mumbai, Delhi, Bangalore and Ahmedabad, while the situation is bad in Nagpur, Bhopal, Nashik, Jabalpur, Jamshedpur, Dhanbad and Vijayawada.

As far as the basic amenities are concerned, most of the million plus cities have shown growth in all the categories. Greater Mumbai, the largest city of India has shown decline in the percentage of households having toilet facility. As far as safe drinking water facility is concerned almost all cities have shown improvement. Most of the million plus cities have more than 90 per cent households enjoying safe water facility within or outside premises. However, Chennai has more than quarter households that do not have access to safe drinking water. In terms of availability of electricity facility most of the cities have more than 90 percentage households having the supply. A composite index calculated for both the Census years shows that Ludhiana has the highest level of development according to all five parameters. The city ranks first among million plus cities in both the Census years while Dhanbad remained at the bottom both in 1991 and 2001.

REFERENCES

Ali, Sabir (2005): "Phenomena of Squatting and Environment," *Social Change*, Vol. 35, No. 4, December 2005, 99-112.

Bansal, Alok *et al.*, (2002): "Urban Transport", *Training Programme on Urban Environmental Management*, Volume I, December 2-6, Indira Gandhi Institute of Development Research, Mumbai.

Bhagat, R.B. (2004): 'Dynamics of Urban Population Growth by Size Class of Towns and Cities in India', *Demography India*, Vol. 33. No. 1: 47-60.

Bhattacharya, Prabir (1998): "The Informal Sector and Rural to Urban Migration: Some Indian Evidence", *Economic and Political Weekly,* Vol. 33 No. 26 May 23: 1255-1261.

Bose, A. (1978): *India's Urbanisation: 1901-2001*, Tata McGraw Hill Publishing Co. Ltd., New Delhi.

Botkin, Daniel and Edward Keller (1995): *Environmental Science, Earth as a Living Planet*, John Wiley and Sons, Inc., New York.

Buch, M.N. (1993): *Environmental Consciousness and Urban Planning*, Orient Longman, New Delhi.

Cedric, Pugh (1990): *Housing and Urbanisation: A Study of India*, Sage Publications, New Delhi, 1990.

Centre for Science and Environment (1996): *Slow Murder: The Deadly Story of Vehicular Pollution of India*, New Delhi, 1996.

Chatterjee, Kanak (2003): "Squatter Settlements in Calcutta: A Socio-Economic Profile", *Geographical Review of India,* Vol. 65, No. 3, September 2003, 260-267.

Chisholm, M. (1992): 'Population Growth and Housing' in W.A. Allen (eds.) '*A Global Strategy for Housing in Third Millennium*', the Royal Society, London.

Desai, Vandana (1994): 'Migration and Labour Characteristics of Slum Dwellers in Bombay', *Sociological Bulletin*, 43(1), March 1994, 51-77.

Devendra, B. Gupta, Sanat Kaul, Rita, Pandey (1993): *Housing and Indian Urban Poor*, Harvard Publication, New Delhi, 1993.

Gilbert, Alan (2000): "Housing in Third World Cities: The Critical Issues", *Geography,* 85 (2) (April), 145-55.

Gilbert, Alan (2000): "Housing in Third World Cities: The Critical Issues", *Geography*, Vol. 85(2), 145-155.

Gupta, R.G. (1995): *Shelter for Poor in the Fourth World*, Vol. I, Shipra Publications, Delhi, 1995.

Kundu, (1987): "Shelter and Living Environment in India: Issues, Policies and Perspective," *Man Power Journal*, Vol. 19(4): 57-70.

Kundu A. (1993): *In the Name of Urban Poor*, Sage Publications, New Delhi.

Kundu, A. *et al*., (1999): "Regional Distribution of Infrastructure and Basic Amenities," *Economic and Political Weekly*, 34(28), (10-16 July), 1893-1906.

Kundu, Amitabh (1990): "Micro-Environment in Urban Planning: Issue Concerning Access to Poor to Basic Amenities," *Demography India,* Vol. 19, No. 1, pp. 79-91.

Kundu, Amitabh (2006): "Trends and Patterns of Urbanisation and Their Economic Implications", in *India Infrastructure Report 2006*, Urban Infrastructure, Oxford University Press.

Maitra, A.K. (1993), "Managing Urban Environment in India"—*Workshop on Role of Cities*, Vol II—Times Research Foundation, Kolkata.

Maitra, A.K. (2000), *Urban Environment in Crisis*, New Age International Publishers, Delhi, 2000.

Miller, G. Tyler Jr. (1994): *Sustaining the Earth: An Integrated Approach*, Wadswarth Publishing Company, California.

Ministry of Environment and Forests (1992): "National Conservation Strategy and Policy Document on Environment and Development", GOI, New Delhi.

Ministry of Environment and Forests (1992): "Policy Statement for Abatement of Pollution", GOI, New Delhi.

Ministry of Environment and Forests (1995): *Annual Report*, GOI, New Delhi, 1994-1995.

Ministry of Environment and Forests (1997): "Minutes of the Consultative Committee of the Members of Parliament Attached to the MOEF", held on August 27, GOI, New Delhi.

Ministry of Environment and Forests (1998): "White Paper on Pollution in Delhi with Action Plan", GOI, New Delhi.

Ministry of Urban Development, (1987): "Report of the Study Group of Alternative Systems of Urban Transport", GOI, New Delhi.

Mitra, Arup (1993): "Status of Basic services in India's cities" in Bidyut Mohanty (ed.): *Urbanisation in Developing countries—Basic Services and Community Participation,* Institute of Social Sciences and Concept Publishing Company, New Delhi.

Mohan, R., (1996): "Urbanisation in India: Patterns and Emerging Policy Issues" in *The Urban Transformation of the Developing World*; Josef Guglar (ed.), Oxford University Press, Oxford.

Mohan, R., (2001): "State of the Environment: India" (Report Number 1999 EE45), submitted to the United Nations Environment Programme.

Mukhija, Amit (2004): The Contradictions in Enabling Private Developers of Affordable Housing: A cautionary case from Ahmadabad, India," *Urban Studies,* Vol. 41, No. 11 October 2004: 2231-2244.

Nangia, Sudesh and Thorat Sukhdeo (2000): *Slum in a Metropolis: The Living Environment,* Shipra Publications, New Delhi.

National Institute of Urban Affairs (1998): *Report of the National Commission on Urbanisation,* Vol. 2.

NEERI, (1998): "Introduction of Environmental Economics into Decision Making for Sustainable Development: Air Media", Project Report submitted to IGIDR under Capacity 21 Project.

Opinion Survey, (1998): "Pollution in Delhi Threatening to get Out of Hand", Monthly Public Opinion Survey, March.

Pandey, Suneel, Shaheen Singhal, Pragya Jaswal and Manraj Guliani (2006): "Urban Environment", in *India Infrastructure Report 2006*, Urban Infrastructure, Oxford University Press.

Parikh and Vibhooti Shukla (1995): "Urbanisation, Energy Use and Greenhouse Effects in Economic Development", *Global Environmental Change*, Vol. 5, No. 2. pp. 87-103.

Parikh, Jyoti and Kirit Parikh, (1999): *Accounting and Valuation of Environment, Vol II—Case Studies from the ESCAP Region*, ESCAP Publication.

Patel, B. Shirish (2005): "Housing Policies for Mumbai," *Economic and Political Weekly,* No. 40(33) (13-19 August): 3669-76.

Praveen, Sharma (2004): "Population Growth and Sustainable Development," *Economic and Political Weekly*, 29(7), (14-20 February), 629-33.

Premi, Mahendra K. (2006): "India's Urbanisation and its Future Implications," *Man and Development*: March: 21-37.

Rastogi, Anupam (2006): "The Infrastructure Sector in India", in *India Infrastructure Report* 2006, Urban Infrastructure, Oxford University Press.

Reddy, Sudhakara B. (1998): *Urban Energy Systems*, Concept Publishing House, New Delhi.

Reddy, Sudhakara B. (2002): *The Urban Challenge, Training Programme on Urban Environmental Management*, Volume I, December 2-6, 2002; Indira Gandhi Institute of Development Research, Mumbai.

Sandhu, Kiran (2003): "Social Housing Project: Can they Alleviate Poverty," *Socio-Economic Development Record,* Vol. 10, No. 5 September-October: 24-34.

Sharma, Utpal and Shriniwas, Swati (2003): "Inspect of Changing Economic Structure on Housing sector in Nashik," *Spatio-Economic Development Record*, 10 (2), (March-April): 9-15.

Shukla, Vibhooti and Kirit S. Parikh (1992): "The Environmental Consequences of Urban Growth", *Urban Geography*, Vol. 5.

Singh, K.P. (ed), (1998): *Infrastructure in India*, National Institute of Management Technology, Ghaziabad.

Singh, S.C. (1986): "Population Pollution and the Urban Environment" in H.H. Singh *et al.*, (eds). *Geography and Environment: Issues and Challenge,* Concept Publishing Company, New Delhi.

Sivaram Krishnan, Lakshmi and Das, Jayati (2001): "Housing programmes in the South Eastern part of Calcutta Metropolitan District," *Geographical Review of India,* No. 1 Vol. 63, March, 24-35.

Sivaram, Krishanan, K.C., Kundu A., Singh B.H. (2005): *Handbook of Urbanisation in India,* Oxford University Press New Delhi.

Sivaram, Krishnan K.C., Das Gupta, Biplab and Buch, M.H. (1993): *Urbanisation in India. Basic Services and People's Participation*, Institute of Social Sciences and Concept Publishing Company, New Delhi.

Sivaramakrishnan, K.C, Amitabh Kumdu and B.N. Singh, (2005): *Handbook of Urbanisation in India: An Analysis of Trends and Processes*, Oxford University Press, New Delhi.

Tiwari, Piyush and Jyoti, Parikh (1999): "Effective Housing Demand in Mumbai (Bombay) Metropolitan Region," *Urban Studies*, Vol. 36, No. 10: 1783-1809.

Tiwari, Piyush and Parikh, Jyoti (1998): "Affordability, Housing Demand and Housing Policy in Urban India," *Urban Studies,* 35(11), November: 2111-29.

Toutain, Oliver and S. Gopiprasad (2006): "Planning for Urban Infrastructure" in *India Infrastructure Report 2006*, Urban Infrastructure, Oxford University Press.

Vijaya Bhole (1988): *Housing and Urban Development in India*, Classical Publishing Company, New Delhi.

Vijaymunni (2000): 'Housing and Amenities in Urban India: An interstate analysis', in Amitabh Kundu (edited) *Inequality, Mobility and Urbanisation*, Manak Publications New Delhi.

Wilderer, Martin Z. (2003): *Economic Growth, Environment and Development: The Significance of the Eco-Industrial Park Concept in India and Indonesia*, Manak Publications Ltd., New Delhi.

World Resource Institute (1997): *World Resources, A Guide to Urban Environment*, Oxford University Press, New York.

SECTION V

Urban Policies in India

19

Government Policies and Programmes for Urban India

A Critical Appraisal

Chandrani Dutta, Praveen Kumar Shukla and *Mala Mukherjee*

Introduction

It could be stated with a reasonable degree of certainty that the world in the twenty-first century is progressing towards an urbanised entity. Between 1950 and 1990, the cities grew more than twice as fast as villages. The last decade, 1990-2000, saw an increase of about 83 per cent in the world urban population, and the cities have added, on an average, about 81 million people annually. In 1950, the developing countries had about 39 per cent of the world's urban population. By 1990, this percentage had gone up to 63; today, it is estimated to be 70 (Jagmohan, 2005). In these countries, the number of mega-cities, without basic services, is rising. A recent report of the UN Centre for Human Settlement (2003) states: "At the beginning of the new century and millennium, the planet hosts 19 cities with 10 million or more people; 22 cities with five to 10 million people; 370 cities with one to five million people; and 433 cities with 0.5 to one million. Another 1.5 billion people live in urban areas of less than half a million people. The process of urbanisation will continue well into the twenty-first century and, by 2030, over 60 per cent of all people (4.9 billion out of 8.1 billion) will live in cities."

Moreover, the current world economic order and the pattern of economic development that is being followed by the developing countries bound to result in unhealthy and unsustainable super-urbansiation. One would witness not only mega-cities of about eight million or hyper-cities of 20 million or more, but also villages turning into semi-urban settlements and second-tier cities becoming larger ones with virtually no civic amenity (Jagmohan, 2005). This super-urbanisation would be accompanied by super-impoverishment of the urban poor who, according to researches conducted by the UN Urban Observatory, could by 2020 comprise as much as 50 per cent of the total population living in cities. New social classes of informal sector workers, whose living conditions are marked by low status, low wages, long hours, and insecure habitats, have emerged on the scene and are fast increasing. "As a result of liberalisation", stated in *The Challenge of Slums—Global Report on Human Settlements* (2003) "the cities of developing countries have become a dumping ground for a surplus population working in unskilled, unprotected and low-wage informal service industries and trade". The cities of the developing world are facing one of the most breathtaking tests in human history today.

Level of urbanisation on the other hand has been low in the developing countries with countries like India having only one-third of its total population living in urban areas. Urbanisation in developing countries has been brought about by the growth of population in the towns and cities, as seen in India where, out of a total population of 1028 million, 107.9 million live in the 35 metropolitan cities and account for 10.5 per cent of the country's population and 37.8 per cent of its urban population. 27.79 per cent of the total population in India is urban according to Census 2001, living in the 5161 towns (Premi, 2006). Urbanisation in developing countries has been more of a geographical process, with a growth of population taking place in the towns and cities, primarily through net rural to urban migration (Ramachandran, 1995). The basic difference between urbanisation in developed countries and developing countries has been the processes leading to it. While industrial revolution in the developed nations made the cities centres of industrial production and manufacturing activities, creating job opportunities, which led to the change in the structure of economy into industrial and non-primary in nature. Migration to these industrial centres was led by pull effects of these cities. On the other hand, urbanisation in developing countries has been mostly due to redistribution of rural population to the urban areas. The lack of development and poor living conditions in the rural areas have compelled huge numbers of people to migrate to urban areas in search of better livelihood. The pace of urban growth has been rapid in the developing countries with an overall rise in the total population mainly due to natural increase in these countries. Rate of urban growth had been 4.32 per cent during 1960 to 1970, which is double the rate in any European country. Thus urban growth has further accelerated due to the high natural increase of total population in both rural and urban areas (Bhattacharya, 2002).

Rapid urban growth in the developing countries has been taking place in the large urban centres. In India, the nature of urbanisation has thus been termed as 'top-heavy', where urban population has been concentrating in the largest cities having population more than hundred thousand. States like West Bengal has a total of 63 class one cities constituting 83.5 per cent of total urban population of the state (Premi, 2006).

India over the past decades has been experiencing concentrated urban growth in big cities that are getting bigger at the cost of the small towns. History of the growth of these urban centres has positive relationship with their current demographic profile. The cities have transformed from being mere market centres in ancient times to prosperous multi-functional units diversifying in a gamut of activities in the present century. But along with the growth of these big cities, India's rural population has also experienced simultaneous increase. The pressure of population on the rural agricultural land coupled with the development of private sector jobs along the peripheries of the large cities due to agglomeration have led people to migrate to these big cities making the metropolitan cities grow bigger in size (Bose, 1980). This has been termed as Metropolisation where the share of urban population has risen in the Class I cities from 26 per cent in 1901 to 68.67 per cent in 2001. The metropolitan growth has widened the gap in terms of medical facilities, education and employment between these cities and the small towns. The rapid growth in the metropolitan cities has also fostered intra-city differences creating zones of poor urban households within the cities (Ramachandran, 1995).

This unplanned urban growth has been accountable in creating inhospitable conditions within cities where there are people who are not entitled to healthy living conditions with availability of water, sanitation, electricity. The growth of slums in major cities is a characteristic of rapid urbanisation. Because rapid population growth cannot be satisfactorily accommodated, slums and shanty towns grow bigger and become more visible. This contributes to wide and increasing geographic divisions in well-being within urban areas (World Development Report, 2009). Thus the overcrowded settlements or slums are an aftermath of the burden of too much population on the strained city economy. The exodus of population to the cities from the rural areas and small towns every year has been responsible in increasing demands for basic services, liked piped water, sewerage, drainage and paved roads while they have been contributing nothing as taxes for the use of services. Hence, the problem of slums and other forms of illegal settlements in the big cities have necessitated the active role of the urban local bodies, in generating finances to cater to the needs of both the general as well as slum population of these cities.

Planning for development of cities has always been a priority among the city governments. The 1960s saw most of the states formulating master-plans for their respective cities. With the rising levels of slum and squatter population, city governments have geared themselves making provisions for the poor. Pro-poor policies like Basic Services for the Urban Poor have been implemented to reduce the disparities between the slum and non-slum population. The 74th Amendment Act has been a move towards decentralised urban governance giving maximum power to the local governments in the management of urban areas. There has been a growth of financial and credit institutions to provide funds for infrastructural development in the urban areas, examples being HUDCO in the late 1960s, and the National Commercial Banks. Policies and programmes for the provision of basic services have been implemented since the 1970s. Basic Services for the Urban Poor, Integrated Development of Small and Medium Towns, Low Cost Sanitation Programme have been few such policies. Poverty alleviation programmes by creating employment opportunities have also been implemented like the Nehru Rozgar Yojana and Prime Minister's Integrated Urban Poverty Eradication Programme. The fate of these policies and programmes have not met with much success as the devolution of funds have been mostly towards the large cities and the small and medium towns have been left out of the benefits (Kundu, 2006).[1] The neglect of the small and medium towns have further caused movement of huge population from these urban centres to the large cities thereby placing added pressure on the limited resources of the large cities. The most marked form of this disparity in the allocations of funds has been the growth of slum population in the big cities. Thus the growth of slum population has been both due to the lack of development in the rural areas as well as underdevelopment of the small and medium size towns in India. Thus a country's leading cities that are often diversified; both in terms of provision of goods and services and in cultural amenities have been witnessing a magnitude of problems with the swelling population of urban poor.

The Jawaharlal Nehru National Urban Renewal Mission thus has been launched with an aim of urban renewal of the metropolitan cities and the mega-cities along with few other important secondary cities in

India with special stress given to the conditions of urban poor and the provision of urban infrastructure.

Consequently, today, in every aspect of city life—density of population; availability of land; housing; slums and squatter settlements; municipal services; open spaces; the scale and character of migration; employment; traffic/transport; energy; communication; crime; health and environment, civic set-up and finance—the prevailing conditions present a deplorable picture. Considering, these problems encountered by the metropolitan cities of India, the present chapter will endeavour —

1. To appraise the different policies and programmes launched pertaining to the urbanisation and urban environment in recent and during the various five year plans of India.
2. To analyse the various aspects of urban environmental policy and programmes.
3. To study the programmes launched for providing housing amenities and urban development in India.
4. To analyse the plan-wise performance of housing and urban policy of India.

Database

To critically appraise and analyse the Government policies and programmes, data has been taken from various policy document of Government of India, Census of India, Reports of various Ministries, International Organisations, National Commission on Urban Affairs, NSSO Reports and other secondary data sources available.

Policy and Programmes Pertaining to the Urban Environment

Uncontrolled population concentration in the cities has resulted in considerable environmental degradation and has directly or indirectly resulted in the deteriorating environmental quality of life of the people living within these cities. Inadequate infrastructural and employment opportunities in the small towns and rural areas are leading people to migrate to big cities resulting in immense stress on the facilities and existing infrastructure. The skewed pattern of urbanisation and unbalanced development is leading to acute pressure on environment, quality of life and basic services. The main environment problem in urban India can be categorised into three types:

- **Firstly, changing pace of industrialisation and increasing vehicular traffic has taken a toll on the quality of ambient air in the cities,**
- **Secondly, population growth has posed a serious pressure on safe drinking water, solid waste disposable from residences and industries on land and water, and**
- **Lastly, the environment resource base of the cities is getting depleted at a fast rate due to uneven population growth.**

To overcome these environmental problems, Government of India has enacted several significant legislations, Acts and launched various policies and programmes during different Five Year Plans. These policies and programmes of Government are documented in the following section.

Institutional Mechanisms to Combat Environmental Degradation

(*a*) *Central Pollution Control Board (CPCB)*: The Central Pollution Control Board (CPCB), an autonomous body of the Ministry, was set-up in September 1974, under the provisions cf the Water (Prevention and Control of Pollution) Act, 1974. It coordinates the activities of the State Pollution Control Boards (SPCBs) and Pollution Control Committees (PCCs), and also advises the Central Government on all matters concerning the prevention and control of environmental pollution. CPCB also provides technical services to the Ministry for implementing the provisions of the Environment (Protection) Act, 1986.

(*b*) *Environmental Impact Assessment (EIA)*: This deals with the identification, prediction, evaluation of the possible economic, social and environmental impacts of any developmental activity as well the preparation of an action plan for remedy as a part of the overall Environment Management Plan. In 2006, additional activities like building/housing complexes have been included under the domain of environmentai clearance.

(*c*) *Environmental Audit:* This has been launched to promote the use of clean technologies in industrial production as well as to minimize generation of wastes, submission of Annual Environmental Statements by the industries which were deemed necessary to the CPCB or the SPCBs.

(*d*) *Eco-mark label:* An "Eco-mark" label has been introduced to label consumer products that are environment-friendly.

Various steps have been taken by many institutions to combat the different types of pollution in India. Such measures have been investigated with respect to urban areas of India taking recourse to documents from India: State of the Environment, 2001, State of Environment Report—India, 2009 and Report of the Working Group on Environment and Environmental Regulatory Mechanisms in Environment and Forests for the Eleventh Five Year Plan (2007-2012).

Combating Air Pollution

- The CPCB has identified 17 categories of industries (large, medium and small) as significantly polluting industries such as integrated iron and steel, thermal power plants, copper/zinc/alluminium smelters, cement, oil refineries, petrochemicals, pesticides and fertilizer units.
- According to the CPCB 2000, on 30 June 2000, 1324 out of the 1551 industries have been provided with the necessary pollution control facilities, 165 have been closed down and the remaining 62 industries have been labelled as defaulters.
- Vehicular emission is another source of air pollution. CPCB 1995 reveals that quantum of vehicular pollutants emitted is highest in Delhi, followed by Mumbai, Bangalore, Kolkata and Ahmedabad.
- To control vehicular pollution an Auto Fuel Policy has been brought to effect in 2002. As per the policy, in the urban scenario, Euro III equivalent emission norms for all new vehicles except 2-3 wheelers have been introduced in 11 major cities from 1st April, 2005.
- Among others, CNG vehicles were introduced in Mumbai and Delhi. All city buses in Delhi have been converted to CNG mode.
- CPCB has also come out with a programme of Nationwide Programme of Ambient Air Monitoring (NAMP), consisting of 342 monitoring stations covering 127 cities/towns in 26 states and 4 UTs. Respirable Suspended Particulate Matter (RSPM) has been identified by CPCB from 201 monitoring stations as main health concerns. On the basis of NAMP, CPCB has identified 16 cities: Hyderabad, Patna, Ahmedabad, Faridabad, Jharia, Bangalore, Pune, Mumbai, Sholapur, Chennai, Agra, Kanpur, Lucknow, Varanasi, and Kolkata as equal to or more polluted than Delhi.

- CPCB has formulated for the SPCBs action plans which emphasise on identification of sources of air pollution; assessment of pollution load and adoption of abatement measures for identified sources; setting up of an inter-departmental taskforce for implementing city specific action plans.

Air pollution from vehicular traffic is one of the main concerns and in order to curb this some measures have already been taken, but some stringent measures should be implemented.

Combating Water Pollution

India has formulated environmental legislation dealing with water pollution through the Indian Penal Code since 1860. It was not until the 1974 Water Prevention and Control of Pollution Act, that water quality was considered legally as an environmental issue. This Act, and the Environment Protection Act which followed in 1986, empowered the Central Pollution Board to lay down and maintain ambient water standards, to demand information regarding effluent emission, to shut down polluting activities, and to prevent new discharges of effluent and sewage. The high incidence of severe contamination adjacent to urban areas signifies the contribution of the industrial and domestic sectors. The following facts can be noted to this effect:

- In 1995, CPCB identified severely polluted stretches on 18 major rivers in India. Central and State Pollution Control Boards have identified 1532 severely polluted industries in India contributing to water pollution especially in urban areas, whereby it has also been found that none of these industries comply with the stipulated emission standards.
- Discharge of untreated domestic waste water is a major cause of water quality degradation. CPCB in 2006, has stated that 423 class I cities and 498 class II towns of the country with a population of 2001 Census generate about 3300 million litres per day of waste water.
- The Ministry of Environment and Forests (MoEF) has initiated programmes called the National River Conservation Plan to restore water quality in different rivers. Under the NRAP, in the first phase, the Ganga Action Plan, 29 towns were selected along the river Ganga.

- CPCB in collaboration with State Pollution Control boards established a nationwide network for water quality monitoring comprising 1019 stations in 27 states and 6 UTs.

Although these regulations give the national bodies and their state-level counterparts broad power to control the problem of water pollution, until recently, enforcement has been rather weak, and there is still ample room for improvement.

Management of Municipal Solid Waste

There has been a significant increase in the quantities of municipal solid waste and hazardous waste generated in India over the last few decades. The measures taken to overcome this problem can be appraised in following section:

There has been a significant increase in the generation of Municipal Solid Waste in India over the last few decades. While the population of Mumbai had increased to 8.2 million in 1981 to 12.3 million in 1991 (a growth of 49%), there was a corresponding rise of municipal solid waste generation from 3200 tonnes per day to 5355 tonnes per day (an increase of 67%).

- CPCB in association with NEERI has been engaged in a survey of the solid waste management in 59 cities of India, which includes 35 metropolitan cities and 24 state capitals.
- The institutional mechanisms which deal with the management of waste have been, namely the Hazardous Waste (Management and Handling) Rules, 1989, was introduced under Section 6, 8 and 25 of the Environment Protection Act of 1986. Implementation of these rules is done through the SPCBs and Pollution Control Committees in respective States and UTs. The MoEF, brought out the MSW Rules in the year 2000. These rules identify the CPCB as the agency which would be responsible in monitoring the implementation of these rules and the municipalities in concern would be required to submit the reports to CPCB.
- The Ministry of Urban Development under the Jawaharlal Nehru National Urban Renewal Mission (JNNURM), has introduced schemes which include low cost sanitation, SWM in selected cities and towns.

The strategy of ensuring scientific management of hazardous waste, which is expected to increase over the years due to growth in industry, should encompass all the aspects of waste management cycles starting from generation of waste to its handling, segregation, transportation, treatment, and disposal.

Managing Noise Pollution

Pollution from noise received serious attention only recently when in 2000, Ministry of Environment and Forests formulated the Noise level standard. It is necessary to think of some measures to curb noise pollution in the form of creating awareness among the masses about the resulting hazards and trauma to health due to noise and effective implementation of Noise Pollution Regulation and Control Rules.

International Cooperation

India has been party to three International Conventions, namely, the Basel Convention on the Control of Trans-boundary Movement of Hazardous Wastes and their Disposal, the Rotterdam Convention on the Prior Informed Consent (PIC) Procedure for Certain Hazardous Chemicals and Pesticides in International Trade and the Stockholm Convention on Persistent Organic Pollutants (POPs). As a signatory to the Basel Convention since 1992 the Ministry of Environment and Forests participated in the 7th Conference of Parties to the Basel Convention held in Geneva during October 2004. India signed the Stockholm Convention on POPs on 14 May, 2002. The convention seeks to eliminate products, use, import and export of 12 POPs wherever, techno-economically feasible and in the interim period, restrict the production and use of these chemicals.

The other international collaborations have been United Nations Conference on the Human Environment, Stockholm, 1972, Ramsar Convention 1971, 1975, United Nations Conference on Environment and Development (UNCED), 1992, 2002 (Agenda, 21, Rio Declaration, Millenium Development Goals), along with the Montreal Protocol on Ozone Depleting Substances (1992) and the Kyoto Protocol (1997).

Looking at the policy and programmes front for metropolitan India, it can be pointed out that despite the provision of various policies and programmes for environmental protection, there are serious deficiencies in effective implementation and efficient management.

Appraisal of Housing and Urban Policy of India through the Plan Periods

The Constitution of India has assigned the subjects pertaining to urban areas to the State Legislatures. In so far as the urban issues are concerned, the legislative powers of the Union are limited only to the following subject/areas, viz. Delhi and other Union Territories, Property of the Union, a subject of the State List which two or more State Legislatures authorize the Union Parliament to legislate and amend the Constitution of India. In exercise of these powers, the Parliament of India has enacted legislations, which are administrated by the Ministry of Urban Development and Poverty Alleviation.

The plan-wise appraisal of the housing and urban development policies and programmes initiated since the independence of the country are as:

- In the First Five Year Plan (1951-56), the emphasis was given to institution building and on construction of houses for Government employees and weaker sections. The Ministry of Works and Housing was constituted and the National Building Organisation and Town and Country Planning Organisation were set-up. A sizeable part of the plan outlay was spent for rehabilitation of the refugees from Pakistan and on building the new city of Chandigarh. An Industrial Housing Scheme was also initiated. The Central Government subsidised the Scheme to the extent of 50 per cent towards the cost of land and construction. The Low Income Group Housing Scheme in 1954 was one such important scheme which was initiated to provide long term easy loans.
- The scope of housing programme for the poor was expanded in the Second Plan (1956-61). Three new schemes were introduced, namely Rural Housing, Slum Clearance and Sweepers Housing. Town and Country Planning Legislations were enacted in many States and necessary organisations were also set-up for preparation of Master Plans for important towns. The Juggi-Jhompri Removals Scheme was launched in 1960 in Delhi and 44000 families were listed in the special Census to provide alternative housing, but only 22188 families got houses in the beginning of the year of 1968.
- The general directions for housing programmes in the Third Plan

(1961-66) were to co-ordinate the efforts of all agencies and to orient the programmes to the needs of the Low Income Groups. A Scheme was introduced in 1959 to give loans to State Governments for a period of 10 years for acquisition and development of land in order to make available building sites in sufficient numbers. Master Plans for major cities were prepared and the State Capitals of Gandhi Nagar and Bhubaneswar were developed. In this plan period setting up of the Central Housing Boards and the State Housing Boards were recommended. The Housing for the Dock Workers was set-up in Calcutta, Madras and Bombay. The government granted 80 per cent loans. The Middle Income Group Housing, The Rental Housing for State Government Employees (1959) was funded by the LIC (The Life Insurance Corporation).

- Balanced urban growth was accorded high priority in the Fourth Plan (1969-74). This was envisaged to be achieved by the creation of smaller towns and by planning the spatial location of economic activities. Housing and Urban Development Corporation (HUDCO) was established to fund the remunerative housing and urban development programmes, promising a quick turnover. A Scheme for Environmental Improvement of Urban Slums was undertaken in the Central Sector from 1972-73 with a view to provide a minimum level of services, like, water supply, sewerage, drainage, street pavements in 11 cities with a population of 8 lakh and above. The scheme was later extended to 9 more cities. Preparation of Master Plans were completed for the 52 Class I cities, 105 Class II towns and 49 tourist and pilgrimage centres. Co-operative Housing was developed in Gujarat, Maharashtra, Mysore and Odisha later extended to other states. In some states housing boards were set up with the help of HUDCO.
- The Fifth Plan (1974-79) reiterated the policies of the preceding plans to promote smaller towns and new urban centres, in order to ease the increasing pressure on urbanisation. This was to be supplemented by efforts to augment civic services in urban areas with particular emphasis on a comprehensive and regional approach to problems in metropolitan cities. A Task Force was set-up for development of small and medium towns. The Urban Land (Ceiling) Act was enacted to check concentration of land in the urban areas and to make available urban land for

construction of houses for the middle and low-income groups. In this plan the State Governments took up the Integrated Urban Development Programme in Calcutta, Bombay and Madras cities, Rs. 249.33 crore were allotted during 1974 to 1977. Now the main thrust was shifted towards the construction of the housing colonies for the landless labourers in the rural areas, but the equity participation increased in the HUDCO for working in the urban areas mainly. Basic civic amenities like the water supply, drainage, sewerage etc. got priority along with the public health sector.

- The thrust of the Sixth Plan (1980-85) was on integrated provision of services, mainly for the deprived sections. The Integrated Development of Small and Medium Towns (IDSMT) was launched in towns with population below one lakh for provision of roads, pavements, minor civic works, bus stands, markets, shopping complex etc. Positive facilities were proposed for setting up new industries and commercial and professional establishments in small, medium and intermediate towns. The Slum Improvement and Housing for the Economically Weaker Section (EWS) got priority and the HUDCO launched 718 schemes in 222 towns, and granted fresh loans. The Social Housing Scheme and the Police Housing Scheme were also launched.
- The Seventh Plan (1985-90) stressed on the need to entrust major responsibility of housing construction to the private sector. A three-fold role was assigned to the public sector, namely, mobilisation of resources for housing, provision for subsidised housing for the poor and acquisition and development of land. The National Housing Bank (NHB) was set-up to expand the base of housing finance. The NHB on the line of NABARD as a subsidiary of the RBI operated the Home Loan Account. The International Year of Shelter for the Homeless (IYSH) was observed in 1987. One such scheme was "Foot Path Dwellers' Night Shelter Scheme (1988-89)". NBO was reconstituted and a new organisation called Building Material Technology Promotion Council (BMTPC) was set-up for promoting commercial production of innovative building materials. A network of Building Centres was also set-up during this plan period. The Seventh Plan recognised the problems of the poor and an Urban Poverty Alleviation Scheme known as Urban Basic Services for the Poor (UBSP) was launched.

As a follow-up of the Global Shelter Strategy (GSS), National Housing Policy (NHP) was announced in 1988. The long-term goal of the National Housing Policy was to eradicate housing shortage, improve the living conditions of the improperly housed and provide civic services and amenities to all the sections of the population. The role of Government was determined, as a provider for the most poor and weaker sections and as a facilitator for other income groups and private sector by the removal of constraints and by raising supply of land and services.

- The Eighth Plan (1992-97) recognised the role and importance of urban sector for the economy. While growth rate of employment in the urban areas averaged around 3.8 per cent per annum, it dropped to about 1.6 per cent in the rural areas. Therefore, the urban areas have to be enabled to absorb larger increments of the labour force. In this plan period the following objectives were observed like expanding basic infrastructure, removal of legal constraints in increasing the supply of lands, role of private developers in the fringe areas, promotion of low cost buildings, materials and technology, self help housings, and setting up of the linkage between the formal and informal credit systems, environmental improvement of slums.
- The Ninth Plan (1997-2002) introduced a comprehensive Housing and Habitat Policy, 1998, that was formulated to address the issues of sustainable development, infrastructure and for strong public-private partnership (PPP) for shelter delivery. The Draft National Slum Policy was drawn up by the Department of Urban Employment and Poverty Alleviation in the Ministry of Urban Development in April 1999. The 'Two Million Housing Programme' was launched by the Government in the year 1998-99 with the objective of providing 'Housing for All' with emphasis on weaker sections and low income groups (LIG). The response of the Eighth Plan to urban scenario was the launching of Urban Poverty and Alleviation Programme of Nehru Rojgar Yojana (NRY). A centrally sponsored scheme called Valmiki Ambedkar Awas Yojana (VAMBAY) was launched for urban slum dwellers in 2001. The earlier scheme like AUSP, Environmental Improvement of Urban Slums (EIUS), and Urban Basic Services for the Poor (UBSP) and Integrated Development for SMTS (IDSMT) etc. also continued.

- The Tenth Plan (2002-07) emphasised on capacity building, public-private partnership (PPP), resource raising, expenditure control, proper financial management and transparency in functioning of Urban Local Bodies (ULBs) through Right to Information (RTI) Act, broad based urban sector reform, investment (FDI) and institutional efforts for integrated development of urban areas. The Housing and Urban Development Corporation (HUDCO) continued its efforts with motto of "Profitability with Social Justice" in the field of housing and urban infrastructure financing. It continued the programme of Model Villages (Adarsh Gram) and Model Improved Slums (Adarsh Basti) for providing integrated input for different purposes. Two Million Housing Programme continued with the objective of "Housing for All" as a priority area identified by the Government.
- The Eleventh Plan (2007-2012) has its focus on policies like Jawaharlal Nehru National Urban Renewal Mission (JNNURM) and the role of Urban Local Bodies (ULBs) in this era of globalisation. The plan reiterates that urban poverty alleviation, slum upgradation, basic services to urban poor should be handled through redistributive taxes at the Centre and the State Government promoting the Centre-State-ULB partnership to address emerging issues of urban development. Conducive atmosphere for the private sector in the field of urban infrastructure should be created and the public sector monopoly should be diffused along with the application of recent technology and innovations. Focusing on urban poverty alleviation, the Eleventh Plan proposes affordable shelter and decent living conditions, adequate provision of land for poor in the Master Plans, developing self-employment enterprises and job creation for wage employment earners and also protecting the economic interests and safety of women and other vulnerable sections of our society. (*5 Year Plans of India, Planning Commission of India, Ministry of Housing and Urban Poverty Alleviaton, and Urban Infratsructure, Housing, Basic Services, and Poverty Alleviation under the Eleventh Five Year Plan under the Planning Commission of India*).

The Planning Commission has been evaluating the on-going schemes and programmes under the various plan periods. Many schemes have become redundant over the plan periods, while many have been subsumed under big flagship programmes like the JNNURM. On the other hand, there have been many which have been newly introduced in the last plan period. There have been many programmes which have direct as well as indirect influence on poverty reduction like the Environment Improvement of Urban Slums, Integrated Development of Small and Medium Towns, Low Cost Sanitation Programme, Mega City Project and the like. All these programmes involved infrastructure development but the major share of the programmes has been devoted to the large cities. (Stuti Lall, 2002).

In the following section the status of these programmes in the current plan period have been discussed along with a brief discussion of the programmes and schemes introduced in the Eleventh Plan period (2007-12).

Integrated Development of Small and Medium Towns (IDSMT) was introduced during 1979-80 to improve the economic and physical infrastructure and to provide essential services in small and medium towns. The basic objective of this programme had been to promote dispersed urbanisation by slowing down migration from rural areas and smaller towns to large cities by the development of selected small and medium towns, those which are capable of generating economic growth and employment. Till 31st March, 2007, a total of 1854 towns out of 5092 small and medium towns were covered. Evaluation done on the scheme in the year 2002, revealed that capacity for implementation was strongly absent as well as the non-availability of matching states' share and also the non-availability of uncumbered land for the projects. This scheme has been subsumed under the JNNURM and has been renamed as the Urban Infrastructure Development Scheme for Small and Medium Towns (UIDSSMT).

Mega City Project has been a centrally sponsored scheme for the development of infrastructure in the megacities of India, namely, Delhi, Mumbai, Kolkata, Chennai, Hyderabad, Bengalore and Ahmedabad. This was launched in the year 1993-94 covering a wide range of development projects like water supply and sewerage, roads and bridges, city transport and solid waste management. During the Tenth Plan, the Central Share released had been Rs. 908.69 crores (anticipated expenditure) against an allocation of Rs. 1050 crore. This particular scheme has also been subsumed under the JNNURM.

Integrated Low Cost Sanitation Scheme was started during the year 1980-81 under the Ministry of Home Affairs and later through the Ministry of Social Justice and Empowerment. From 2003-04 this particular scheme got transferred to the Ministry of Urban Employment and Poverty Alleviation/Ministry of Housing and Urban Poverty Alleviation. This scheme was financed by a mix of subsidy from the Central Government and loan from the HUDCO initially and catered to 'whole town' basis and to all sections of the population (HIG, MIG, LIG, EWS). In the later years this scheme got revised and hence started getting funded by Central subsidy (75%), State subsidy (15%) and beneficiary share of 10 per cent. The scope of the scheme also got revised from whole town basis to only Economically Weaker Section (EWS) households only.

Programmes like VAMBAY and SJSRY have been introduced so as to provide adequate shelter for the poor and to generate employment opportunities in the urban areas.

The Government of India under the Valmiki Ambedkar Awas Yojana (VAMBAY) released a subsidy of Rs. 932.56 crores for the construction of 459728 dwelling units and 65580 toilet seats till 2005-06 since its inception. The NSDP also released funds of 3089.64 crores to different states and UTs which aimed to cover 436.28 lakh urban poor. The evidence of this scheme was found in the net addition of 19.52 million dwelling units during the period 1991-2001, having an annual average construction of 1.95 million houses.

On the other hand, the Swarna Jayanti Shahri Rozgar Yojana (SJSRY) which was launched in 1997 among the many employment guarantee schemes, aimed to provide gainful employment to the urban unemployed/ under-employed from the below poverty sections, through the creation of suitable community structures and delivery inputs through the ULBs. SJSRY encountered a lot of problems in providing effective employment opportunities and recently has been revised to give more importance to skill development with respect to public private participation, Self-Help Groups (SHGs), self-employment skills in addition to facilitation of credit for setting up of self-employment.

The new initiatives under the recent Eleventh Plan during the period (2007 to 2012) have been Pooled Finance Development Fund (PFDF), National Urban Infrastructure Fund, Development of Satellite Cities/ Counter Magnet Cities and lastly JNNURM.

The Pooled Finance Development Fund was launched on 29 September, 2006 to provide credit enhancement to the ULBs to access market borrowings based on their worthiness through State level Pooled Finance mechanisms. This scheme reinforces the need to make the ULBs in India more credible and accountable 100 crores have been siphoned by the Ministry of Urban Development for the period 2007 to 2008. For the entire Eleventh Plan period a provision of Rs. 2500 crore have been made.

In yet another way to enforce decentralisation and to secure the financial position of the ULBs, the National Urban Infrastructure Fund aims to create necessary comfort level amongst financial institutions with respect to repayment by direct exposure of commercial banks to the ULBs to lend for viable urban infrastructure projects.

The Development of Satellite Cities/Counter Magnet Cities is another programme which corresponds with the IDSMT, and aims to develop other settlements in the vicinity of the mother city as satellite/ counter magnets to reduce and redistribute the population and the population influx and to counter the unabated migration from these small towns to the big cities (Housing, Basic Services, and Poverty Alleviation under the Eleventh Five Year Plan under the Planning Commission of India).

Jawaharlal Nehru National Urban Renewal Mission (JNNURM)

On the eve of the launch of JNNURM in 2006, the Prime Minister of India, Dr. Manmohan Singh, made a speech regarding the growing urbanisation and its associated problems. According to him "Rapid Urbanisation has not only outpaced infrastructural development, but has also brought in its train a terrible downside—the downside of growing urban poverty and crime, of relentless march of pollution and ecological damage." "Our urban economy" according to the Prime Minister "has become an important driver of economic growth. It is also the bridge between the domestic economy and the global economy. It is a bridge we must strengthen. The latent creativity and vitality of our cities and the people who live in them must be tapped to facilitate higher economic growth." (Workshop on JNNURM, 2006). The address made by the Prime Minister has been very fundamental in drawing out the core issues requiring adoption in the charter of the document.

The seven point charter has taken into consideration security of tenure, water supply, affordable housing and sanitation along with health, education and social security. The thrust areas of JNNURM have been:

- Water Supply including desalination plants;
- Sewerage and Sanitation;
- Solid waste management including hospital waste management;
- Construction and improvement of drains and storm-water drainage system;
- Road network;

- Urban Transport;
- Construction and development of bus and truck terminals;
- Renewal and re-development of inner city areas;
- Development of heritage areas;
- Preservation of water bodies;
- Integrated development of slums; i.e. housing and development of infrastructure in slum settlements;
- Provision of basic services to the urban poor;
- Street lighting; and
- Conversion of health, education, and social security schemes for urban poor."

The inadmissible components or those components not directly under the intervention of the mission have been power, telecom, health, education, wage, employment and staff components, and creation of fresh employment opportunities. With these components, JNNURM has the objective to 'create economically productive, efficient, equitable and responsive cities.' The outcome predicted by JNNURM has been in the form of:

- Universal access to a minimum level of services;
- Establishment of city wide frameworks for planning and governance;
- Modern and transparent budgeting, accounting and financial management system at municipal levels;
- Financial sustainability for municipalities and other service delivery institutions;
- Introduction of e-governance in the core functions of municipal governments; and
- Transparency and accountability in urban basic delivery and management.

It has also been envisaged by the experts that JNNURM would be able to transform the local status of subservience of the local government to the state government to the status of local self-government enshrined in the Constitution. With the work of urban renewal the urban local bodies have less dependence on the Central Government which makes them more dependent on other public, private and civil organisations at the local level. The dependence further enhances the competition among the cities (Verhage, 2005).

Mandatory Reforms under JNNURM: The JNNURM under the guidance and supervision of National Steering Group at the Central level and State Level Steering Committees at the State level have proposed mandatory reforms at the state level in the form of:

1. Effective implementation of decentralisation initiatives as envisaged by the Constitution (Seventy-fourth) Amendment Act, 1992;
2. Repeal of Urban Land (Ceiling and Regulation) Act, 1976;
3. Reform of Rent Control laws, by balancing the interests of landlords and tenants;
4. Rationalisation of stamp duty to bring it down to no more than 5 per cent within 7 years;
5. Enactment of public disclosure law;
6. Enactment of a community participation law, so as to institutionalise citizens' participation in local decision-making; and
7. Association of elected city municipalities with the city planning function.

Two mandatory reforms, viz. Repeal of Urban Land (Ceiling and Regulation) Act, 1976 and Reform of Rent Control laws will be treated as optional with respect to schemes like Basic Services for Urban Poor and schemes for water supply and sanitation.

The mandatory reforms put forward by the JNNURM at the municipal corporation level have been:

1. Adoption of a modern, accrual based, double entry system of accounting;
2. Introduction of a system of e-governance using IT applications, GIS and MIS for various urban services;
3. Reform of property tax with GIS, and arrangements for its effective implementation so as to raise collection efficiency to 85 per cent;
4. Levy of reasonable user charges, with the objective that full cost of operation and maintenance is collected within seven years;
5. Internal earmarking of budgets for basic services to the urban poor; and
6. Provision of basic services to the urban poor, including security of tenure at affordable prices.

Among the optional reforms suggested by JNNURM, earmarking of at least 20 to 25 per cent developed land in housing projects for economically weaker sections and low income groups with a system of cross-subsidisation and encouraging public-private partnership have been important.

The reforms aim to ensure improvement in urban governance so that the urban local bodies and para-statal agencies become financially sound along with public-private participation models for provision of various services.

Thus the main objective of JNNURM is to have a decentralised structure of government which would inspire international donors to support numerous democratic local government programmes. Decentralisation as proposed by JNNURM means dispersion of power not only to rural and urban self-government institutions but also to self-help groups, local communities, and Non-Governmental Organisations (NGOs) (Kundu, 2006). Private-Public Partnership has also been envisaged by JNNURM to improve service delivery in cities, thereby reducing pressure on municipal budget. Important areas where public-private participation could be initiated are solid waste management, including collection, treatment and disposal of garbage, operation of water supply, maintenance of traffic islands, parks and street lights.

Decentralisation with the intention of providing autonomy to the Local Self-Government Institutions could be successful only by imparting financial, functional and administrative autonomy with the existence of active cooperation, coordination, complementation and integration. Introducing committee system in the local body administration ensures decentralisation. Thus formation of committees like Ward Committees, Standing Committees is beneficial ways of effective governance (George, 2006).

The Constitutional Amendment Act solicit every cities having population over three hundred thousand to have ward committees to increase empowerment of the local bodies. States like Kerala and West Bengal have reported to have established separate committees for each ward. In cities like Mumbai the ward committees have been empowered to give administrative approval to the plans and estimates up to Rs. 5 lakh for civic services undertaken in the respective wards. (Kundu, 2006). Along with the creation of ward committees, civil society organisations like Resident Welfare Organisations in the metropolitan cities have been seen to have immense importance by bringing people together and building local pressure on political parties. Thus JNNURM has given importance to all these organisations along with the Centre and the State to create opportunities and services for each and every section of the urban population especially for the urban poor. Even the introduction of Public-Private Partnership (PPP) would help in providing services in areas which were un-served, where it has been found in areas of past PPP there have been signs of improved services like street lighting, and environment where the private sector has taken the responsibility to convert solid waste into compost or energy.

Financing pattern of JNNURM: The allocation of finances to carry out the various reforms comprises funds coming from Centre, States/ULGs and financial institutions in the proportion of 35:15:50 for mega-cities with more than 4 million population. For cities having million plus population the proportion share of finance would be 50:20:30, while cities with less than one million population would have a proportion of 80:10:10. Table 19.1 gives the detailed design of the ways by which financial requirements would be met.

It is evident from the financing pattern of JNNURM that mega-cities have a higher monetary dependence on their local bodies and other organisations, to carry out the proposed reforms. While smaller cities, as seen from earlier studies would have the Central Government as the main beneficiary. Big cities would incorporate financial help from private and

Table 19.1: Financing Pattern of JNNURM

Categories	*Grant in %*		*Urban Local Bodies*
	Centre	*State*	*Share/Loan in % from financial institutions*
Cities/UAs with 4 million plus as per 2001 Census	35	15	50
Cities/UAs with million plus but less than 4 million population as per 2001 Census	50	20	30
Cities/Towns/UAs in NE states and Jammu and Kashmir	90	10	–
Cities/UAs other than those mentioned above	80	10	10
For Setting up desalination plants within 20 km from sea shore and other urban areas predominantly facing water scarcity due to brackish water and non-availability of surface source	80	10	10

Source: JNNURM Toolkit, Ministry of Urban Development, 2006.

other para-statal organisations to generate required finances. Private investment in the provision of services in the cities is highly coveted along with the functioning of the civil society organisations like the Resident Welfare Associations in the big cities. Apart from this, the Union Budget 2009 has endorsed JNNURM with a financial allocation of Rs. 12887 crore for Urban Renewal and Rs. 3973 crore to remove slums from the cities of India by the next 5 years. The Rajiv Gandhi Awas Yojana (RGAY) has been the newest development implemented to ensure housing and basic services to slum dwellers. A special allocation of Rs. 5000 crore has been made for this programme (*The Times of India*, 2009).

JNNURM: A Critical Appraisal

As on 20th March, 2008, City Development Plans for all the 63 cities have been submitted. 324 projects under various heads have been sanctioned with a total allocation of US$ 7.533 billion. It is very important to evaluate this mission in the light of its two main objectives; firstly, to provide urban infrastructure and secondly, to provide basic services for the urban poor. The other important component is the financial distribution across the various size-classes of cities. JNNURM has categorised cities on the basis of their population size. Urban poor in the cities have been growing in each of these cities due to different reasons. While rapid urbanisation in the big cities associated with rising migration have led to the growth of population who are forced to stay in unhygienic living conditions as they lack the sufficient resources to avail the basic amenities and security of tenure, the urban poor in the small cities is the resultant factor of negligence on the part of the city authorities and also the states. The transfer of finances from the centre to the state and then to the local bodies have been inadequate thus leading to a multitude of people in the cities without basic services. Hence what JNNURM aims to do is to provide the maximum financial requirement to these small cities from the centre, while the large cities as have happened before should attract private and other kind of investments to provide services.

Therefore, it is obvious that the cities have been categorised based on their population size to formulate a layout according to which funds would be disbursed from both the Centre and the State. Mega-cities have been a recipient of a huge amount of private investments and thus the financial transfers from centre to these states have been quite less compared to other parts of the country. There are states where, due to their economically developed status have been able to generate enough resources to provide services, such as Maharashtra, Gujarat and Punjab. While there have been cities like Kolkata, where despite being the third largest mega-city, has witnessed a resource crunch and has to depend for over 50 per cent of its municipal revenue on government grants.

On the other hand big cities have the maximum amount of slum population like, for example Mumbai with more than 50 per cent and Kolkata having more than 30 per cent of the urban population residing in slums. Private investments, if injected into the city economy would see selected areas of the cities getting developed as the private bodies would not work like the municipalities. Providing services to the urban poor is one important goal of this mission but inclusion of the private sector would only lead to the exclusion of the poor and the slum dwellers as they often are unable to pay the price for the private services delivered. Illegal use of water and electricity is borne by the municipalities in many situations, but it is not going to be entertained by the private authorities, as people have to pay as they consume and often these come at a very high price which the urban poor are unable to meet (Vira and Vira, 2005).

Another feature witnessed in the big cities is the presence of civil society organisations like Residential Welfare Associations (RWAs) and other schemes like Bhagidari Scheme in National Capital Territory, Janagraha in Bangalore and so on. It has been found that only the powerful RWAs are being able to voice their concerns and needs. The RWAs are often organised by the influential sections of the city to provide and maintain services. The urban poor are usually excluded because of their poor economic background. Even the Bhagidari Scheme has shown no involvement of slums and unauthorised colonies. These civil society organisations would further accentuate the disparity across the city (Kundu, 2006). Thus high income colonies of the cities have been constructing roads and organising cleaning drives while a huge section of slum population continues to live in a degraded environment. Even the formation of ward committees does not help in effective delivery, as in India, often due to bureaucratic problems; preferences are shown to residents of the particular ward belonging to the councillors of the party commanding power. (Vira and Vira, 2005). The pattern of investments laid by the mission hence do not show any help offered to the urban poor, while the rich and the middle class would eventually benefit. Shaw has observed that Indian middle class who had a played a crucial role has transformed into reactionary anti-poor, anti-state and a victim of consumerism (Vira and Vira, 2005).

Even provision of urban infrastructure like roads and highways as part of JNNURM would lead to further marginalisation of urban poor. Informal activities like road side vendors would be eliminated with the construction of rapid mass transit networks. This would further increase the level of poverty of these people. Thus the schemes prove to be contradictory. This could be taken care of by the mission by providing regular jobs to these people in areas of waste collection thereby utilising the informal labourers in a more organised way.

Lastly, it has been felt that the investment on infrastructure and basic services has not been sufficient to meet the requirements in India. Estimates of the cost of urban infrastructure and services by the Infrastructure Conference held in Delhi in 2006 had been $320 billion, while the current annual spending has been close to only $21 billion comprising 3.6 per cent of the Gross Domestic Product (GDP) out of which 2.8 per cent comes from Government and the rest 0.8 per cent from the private sector. Thus JNNURM has to meet a huge challenge of keeping up the level of investment and economic growth by a one-time grant of finances to support the demands of the 63 cities (Urban Development Series, 2009).

Thus the local government should channelise more funds to the community based organisations and local NGOs to look into the problems of urban environment and urban poor. Past experiences have shown NGOs hired by well-organised resident groups in cities like Delhi usually belonging to the middle class for the maintenance of the urban environment had worked satisfactorily (Vira and Vira, 2005). Hopefully JNNURM would be able to break the divide and there would be more NGO involved in the poorer areas of towns and cities. What JNNURM, as a Central Government sponsored scheme provides has been a design, but the ultimate work remains to be done by the state and the city authorities and efforts undertaken by every level of population in successfully implementing the policy. It would be also an efficient way to deal with the needs of each city if they had been categorised not according to their population size but based on their socio-demographic performance and given priority accordingly.

The above discussion on JNNURM throws light on many issues which have been newly introduced during the current Eleventh Plan period. A lot of urban reform measures have been promoted like Information Technology and E-Governance along with the 74th Constitutional Amendment Act. *(Housing, Basic Services, and Poverty Alleviation under the Eleventh Five Year Plan, Planning Commission of India).*

The other reforms which have been introduced have been:

- Involvement of Community and Elected Representatives in Decision making and Implementation.
- The 'bottom-up' approach in the programmes on urban development has been revamped with the creation of Ward Committees, Metropolitan Committees, District Planning Committees, rather from initially being 'top-down'.
- Emphasis has also been laid on the capacity building of the functionaries of the ULBs.
- Setting up independent regulatory institutions at the state level, to ensure ULBs working with autonomy but within the framework decided by the independent regulatory institution.

Rajiv Gandhi Awas Yojana (RGAY)

The Rajiv Gandhi Awas Yojana has been the newest development implemented to ensure housing and basic services to slum dwellers. A special allocation of Rs. 5000 crore has been made for this programme.

After a perusal of various socio-economic development programmes and appraisal of different Government policies pertaining the environment, housing and basic amenities and urban development, one finds a lack of proper and effective implementation of these policies and programmes that is responsible for the deteriorating quality of urban environment and stress exerted on various housing and basic amenities as well as on socio-economic infrastructure in urban India. So, to overcome these problems the following recommendations have been considered.

Recommendations

- The process of urbanisation and the protection of environment should not be treated separately, instead these two aspects should be viewed within a holistic manner.
- The acts, legislations, programmes, schemes catering to improvement of urban environment and infrastructure development in urban areas should be considered top priority areas in the field of urban management.
- Role of Urban Local Bodies (ULBs) and their revenue raising power should be given strong impetus by adopting municipal e-governance in every urban centre having municipal bodies.
- Decentralisation, according to the norms of Constitutional Amendment Act, should be strongly adhered to with all the cities'

adopting community participation law to create the lowest level of decision making in the form of Area Sabhas.

- The positive sides of public private participation should be investigated and adopted in the provisioning of urban infrastructure.

Conclusions

Contrary to popular concepts of a predominantly rural India, an increasingly larger percentage of Indian population lives in the urban areas. Today, India's urban population is second largest in the world after China. Over the last fifty years, while the country's population has grown by 2.5 times, in the urban areas it has grown by five times. It is estimated that in 1947, only 60 million people (15 per cent of the total population at that time) lived in urban areas, while it increased up to 285 million (27.78%) in 2001 and to 31.16 per cent in 2011 having the urban population about 377 million. In 2011, the number of metropolitan cities has jumped to 53 from 35 in 2011, which inhabit 160.73 million people, constituting 42.62 per cent of total urban population. The steep growth in number of people living is partly due to the skewed development that has led to proliferation of commercial activities and great job opportunities in towns and cities. This has resulted in environmental degradation and exerted a lot of pressure on the facilities like housing, sanitation, health, drinking water, education and on the infrastructure like roadways, telecommunication, airports, railways and ports. Although several policies and programmes of Government are going on to cater to this grim situation but due to lack of effective implementation they are unable to suffice to the needs of people in urban areas. The new vision must include comprehensive planning, a new urban land policy which treats land as a source for creating a social environment which can sustain itself in harmony; a new framework of urban institutions which can fulfil the emerging requirements of growing metropolises; a new cadre of urban administrators who have the training and motivation to meet new challenges geared towards the betterment of the society by devising a holistic approach.

REFERENCES

Abrams, Charles (1964): *Man's Struggle for Shelter in an Urbanizing World*, Cambridge MIT Press.

Agarwal, A. and S. Narain (1982): *Towards a Green World*, CSE, New Delhi.

Ahmed, S.S. (1996): "The Crisis of Municipal Services", in Seminar, 445, September, pp. 25-29.

Anon (1997): *Status and supply of waste water generation, collection, treatment and disposal in metro cities (1994-95)*, Control of Urban Pollution Series, 1997-98, Central Pollution Control Board (CPCB), New Delhi.

Bartone, Carl (1991): "Sustainable Responses to Growing Urban Environmental crisis", Paper presented at the IULA World Development Forum, Brussels, 4-6 April, 1990.

Benneh, George (1992): "Environmental Consequences of Different patterns of Urbanisation", in *Proceedings of the United Nations Expert Group Meeting* on 'Population, Environment and Development', January 1992, United Nations, New York, pp. 159-165.

Bhattacharya, P.C. (2002): "Urbanisation in Developing Countries", *Economic and Political Weekly,* October 12, 2002, Vol.XXXVII, No. 41, pp. 4419-4228.

Bose, A. (1980): *India's Urbanisation 1901-2001*, Tata McGraw Hill, New Delhi.

Bose, Ashish (1996), *India's Basic Demographic Statistics*, B.R. Publishing Corporation, Delhi, 110052.

Brockerhoff, Martin P. (2000): "An Urbanizing World", *Population Bulletin,* Population Reference Bureau, USA, Vol. 55, No. 3, September, pp. 1-42.

Census of India (1991): *"Emerging Trends of Urbanisation in India"*, Occasional paper No. 1 of 1993, Registrar General, New Delhi.

Census of India (1991): Series 1, India, *Provisional Population Totals: Rural Urban Distribution*, Paper 2 of 1991, Delhi: Controller of Publications 1991.

Census of India (2001): Series 1, India, *Primary Census Abstract*, Paper 1 of 2001, Delhi: Controller of Publications, 2001.

Census of India (2001): Series 1, India, *Provisional Population Totals*, Paper 1 of 2001, Delhi: Controller of Publications, 2001.

Census of India (2001): Series 1, India, *Provisional Population Totals*, Paper 2 of 2001, Delhi: Controller of Publications, 2001.

Census of India (2001): Series 8, Delhi, *Provisional Population Totals,* Paper 2 of 2001, Delhi: Controller of Publications, 2001.

Census of India 2011): Series 1, India, *Provisional Population Totals: Rural Urban Distribution*, Paper 2 of 2011, Delhi: Controller of Publications, 2011.

Central Pollution Control Board (CPCB) Reports (2001): "Assessment of Vehicular Pollution in Metropolitan Cities", Control of Urban Pollution Series, CPCB, New Delhi.

Chaudhary, M. (1995), "Global Population Growth, Economic Development and Environment Impact: Case Study of India, 1991-2100", *Economic and Political Weekly*, 30(49) (9 December 95): 3163-67.

Clarke, John I. and Leon Tabah (ed.),(1995): Population-Environment—

Development Interaction, CICRED, Comite *International de Cooperation dans les Recheches Nationales en Demograaphie,* Belgium.

Compendium of Environment Statistics, INDIA, 2002, Central Statistical Organisation (CSO), Ministry of Statistics and Programme Implementation, Government of India, New Delhi.

Delhi Development Authority: *Slums of Delhi: An Overview*, New Delhi, Socio-economic Survey Division, Slums and J.J. Department, Delhi Development Authority, 1985.

Delhi Master Plan, 2001.

Dutta, A. (1999): "Institutional Aspects of Urban Governance", in Mathur, O.P. (ed.) *India: the Challenge of Urban Governance*, National Institute of Public Finance and Policy, New Delhi.

Eighth Five Year Plan, 2007-2012, Planning Commission, Government of India, New Delhi.

Eleventh Five Year Plan, 2007-2012, Planning Commission, Government of India, New Delhi.

Fernandes (1999): "India's Cities in Crisis", *Spatio-Economic Development Record,* Vol. 6, No. 6, November-December, 1999, pp. 27-31.

Fifth Five Year Plan, 2007-2012, Planning Commission, Government of India, New Delhi.

First Five Year Plan, 2007-2012, Planning Commission, Government of India, New Delhi.

Fourth Five Year Plan, 2007-2012, Planning Commission, Government of India, New Delhi.

George (2006), 'Trends in Urbanisation and Urban Governance in Kerala' *Seminar on New Forms of Urban Governance in Indian Mega Cities: Under Indo-Dutch Programme on Alternatives in Development*, Jawaharlal Nehru University, New Delhi.

Ghosh, Archana (ed.) (2003): *Urban Environment Management: Local Government and Community Action*, New Delhi: Concept Publishing Company.

Gupta, R.C. (1999): "Environmental and Infrastructural Sustainability: Major Challenges facing Indian Metropolitan Cities", *Spatio-Economic Development Record,* Vol. 6, No. 1, January-February, pp. 43-49.

HABITAT II (1996): *"Second United Nations Conference on Human Settlement: India National Report"*, Government of India.

Hamza, Ahmed (1992): "Urban Settlement and Environment in Developing World: Trends and Challenges" in *Proceedings of United Nations Expert Group Meeting on 'Population, Environment and Development*, January, 1992, United Nations, New York, pp. 151-158.

Henderson, J. Vernon (1988), *Urban Development: Theory, Fact and Illusion*, Oxford University Press, Oxford.

Housing, Basic Services, and Poverty Alleviation under the Eleventh Five Year Plan, Planning Commission of India, http://planningcommission.nic.in/plans/planrel/fiveyr/11th/11_v3_ch77.pdf.

India (2003): *A Reference Annual,* Publication Division, Ministry of Information and Broadcasting (MoI&B), Government of India, New Delhi.

India: State of the Environment 2001, Ministry of Environment and Forests, Government of India.

Integrated Development of Small and Medium Towns (1995), Revised Guidelines, Ministry of Urban Affairs and Employment, Department of Urban Development, Government of India, New Delhi, August 1995, www.urbanindia.nic.in/writereaddata/GuidelinesofSchemes/90.pdf

Jacobi, Pedro (1992): "Urban Environmental Issues and Social Impacts" in *Proceedings of the United Nations Expert Group Meeting on 'Population, Environment and Development'*, January, 1992, United Nations, New York, pp. 166-172.

Jagmohan (2005): *Soul and Structure of Governance in India*, Allied Publishers, New Delhi, pp. 176-394.

Jagmohan (2008): *Shaping India's New Destiny*, Allied Publishers, New Delhi, pp. 125-126.

Jain, R.K. (2001): "Massive Urbanisation and Urban Governance: Some Issues", *Spatio-Economic Development Record,* Vol. 9, No. 2, March-April, pp. 25-27.

Kingsley Davis (1962): *Urbanisation in India—Past and Future*, in Turner, R. (ed.).

Kingsley Davis (1967): "The Origin and Growth of Urbanisation in the World", in H.H. Mayor and C.F. Cohn (ed.), *Readings in Urban Geography*, University of Chicago, Chicago.

Kundu (2006), 'Decentralisation Governance in Metro Cities—The Issues of Elite Capture with Special Reference to Delhi', Seminar on New Forms of Urban Governance in Indian Mega Cities: Under Indo-Dutch Programme on Alternatives in Development, Jawaharlal Nehru University, New Delhi.

Kundu (2006), 'Globalisation, Decentralisation and Crisis in Urban Governance: Providing Drinking Water and Sanitation facilities', *India Social Development Report*, Council for Social Development, Oxford University Press, New Delhi.

Kundu, A. (1993): *In the Name of the Urban Poor: Access to Basic Amenities*, Sage Publications, Delhi.

Kundu, A., Bagchi, S. and Kundu, D. (1999): "Regional Distribution of Infrastructure and Basic Amenities in Urban India—Issues Concerning Empowerment of Local Bodies", *Economic and Political Weekly*, 34(28), July 10.

Kundu, Amitabh (1999): "Empowerment of Urban local Bodies in India: A Search without Perspective", *Spatio-Economic Development Record,* Vol. 6, No. 6, November-December, 1999, pp. 15-20.

Lall, S. (2002), 'Integrated Urban Housing Development', Housing for the Poor and Urban Development, *The Indian Dynamics*, Working Paper 5, March 2002.

Lee, Yok-shiu F. (1991): *Myths of Urban Environmental Management and the Urban Poor*, East West Centre, Honolulu.

Maitra, A.K. (1999): "Urban Slums A Challenge for 21st Century Cities: Environmental Concerns", *Spatio-Economic Development Record,* Vol. 6, No. 6, November-December, pp. 41-46.

Meshram, D.S. (1994): "Making Municipalities More Effective", *Yojana*, September 30, 1994.

Millionaire Fund for Sleek, Slum-free India, *The Times of India*, New Delhi, Tuesday, July 7, 2009, p. 9.

Ministry of Environment & Forests (2002): *State of the Environment 2002*, Government of India, New Delhi.

Ministry of Finance (2001): *Economic Survey, 2000-2001*, Government of India, New Delhi.

Ministry of Housing and Urban Poverty Alleviation (2007): *National Urban Housing and Habitat Policy 2007*, Government of India, New Delhi, pp. 1-42.

Mohan, R. (1996): "Urbanisation in India: Patterns and Emerging Policy Issues", in Josef Gugler (ed.) *The Urban Transformation of the Developing World*, Oxford University Press, Oxford, pp. 93-131.

Nangia, Sudesh and Thorat, S. (2000): *Slum in Metropolis: The Living Environment*, Shipra Publications, Delhi.

National Commission on Urbanisation (1988): *Report of the National Commission on Urbanisation*, Vol. II, August, Ministry of Urban Affairs, Government of India.

National Institute of Urban Affairs (1983): "A study of Resources of Urban Local Bodies in India and the Level of Services Provided", New Delhi.

Navlakha, Gautam (2000): "Urban pollution: Driving Workers to Desperation", *Economic and Political Weekly,* December 16, Vol.XXXV, No. 51, pp. 4469-4471.

NEERI (1991): *Air Pollution Aspects of Three Indian Mega Cities*, Vol.-II, Bombay: National Environmental Engineering Research Institute, Nagpur.

Ninth Five Year Plan, 2007-2012, Planning Commission, Government of India, New Delhi.

Pacione, Michael (1990), *Urban Problem: An Applied Urban Analysis*, Routlede London and New York.

Perveen, Shama (2004), "Population Growth and Sustainable Development", *Economic and Political Weekly*, 29(7), 2004 (14-20 February): 629-33.

Population of India, Country Monograph, Series No. 10, Economic and Social Commission for Asia and the Pacific, United Nations, 1995.

Premi (2006): '*Population of India: In the New Millennium: Census 2001*, National Book Trust, New Delhi.

Premi, M.K. (1991): India's Urban Scene and its Future Implication, *Demography India*, Vol. 20, No. 1, pp. 41-52.

Preston, S.H. (1979): "Urban Growth in Developing Countries: A Demographic

Reappraisal", *Population and Development Review*, Vol. 5, No. 2, pp. 195-215.

Ramachandran, R. (1995): *Urbanisation and Urban Systems in India*, Oxford University Press, New Delhi.

Report of the Working Group on Environment and Environmental Regulatory Mechanisms in Environment & Forests for the Eleventh Five Year Plan (2007-2012), Planning Commission, Government of India, New Delhi, August 2007.

Riddell, Robert (2004), *Sustainable Urban Planning: Tipping the Balance*, Blackwell Publishing, Oxford.

Second Five Year Plan, 2007-2012, Planning Commission, Government of India, New Delhi.

Seventh Five Year Plan, 2007-2012, Planning Commission, Government of India, New Delhi.

Sharma, B.K. (1996): "Impact of Economic Development on Environment in Delhi", *Yojana*, June.

Shukla, Vibhooti and Kirit S. Parikh (1992): "The Environmental Consequences of Urban Growth", *Urban Geography*, Vol. 5.

Singh, Kulwant (2001): "Urban Governance in India: Trends and Issues in Decentralisation after Constitution (74th) Amendment Act, 1992", *Spatio-Economic Development Record*, Vol. 8, No. 5, September-October, pp. 13-20.

Sixth Five Year Plan, 2007-2012, Planning Commission, Government of India, New Delhi.

State of Environment Report India-2009, Environment Information System, Ministry of Environment and Forests, Government of India, http://www.moef.gov.in, http://envfor.nic.in

Stolnitz, George J. (1991): "Population and Environment: Patterns, Problems and some pathways to solutions," Working paper No. 92-98, Population Institute for Research and Training. March 1991.

Sudhakara Reddy, B. (2001): *The Urban Challenge*, Indira Gandhi Institute of Development and Research (IGIDR), Mumbai.

TEDDY (TERI Energy Data Directory and Yearbook), 1999-2000, Tata Energy Research Institute, New Delhi.

Tenth Five Year Plan, 2002-2007, Planning Commission, Government of India, New Delhi.

Third Five Year Plan, 2007-2012, Planning Commission, Government of India, New Delhi.

Thomas, A. (1993): *Metropolis-2000: Planning, Poverty and Politics*, Routledge, London, New York.

Tiwari, Piyush and Parikh, Jyoti (1998), "Affordability, Housing demand and housing policy in urban India", *Urban Studies*, 35(11), November, 2111-29.

Turner, R. (ed.) (1962): *India's Urban Future*, University of California Press, Berkeley.

UN Habitat (2003): *The Challenge of Slums: Global Report on Human Settlement*, 2003.

UNCHS (2001 & 2003), United Nation Centre for Human Settlements, Nairobi.

United Nations (2001): *World Urbanisation Prospects: 2001 Revision*, UN, New York.

"Urban Development: Experiences and Visions: India and the People's Republic of China", *Urban Development Series (ADB)*, http://www.adb.org/Documents/Reports/Urban-Visions/Urban-Visions.pdf, as viewed on Monday, July 20, 2009, pp. 1-71.

Verhage (2005): "Towards a Territorial Approach to Urban Renewal: A Comparison of Policies in France and Netherlands", *International Planning Studies*, Vol. 10, No. 2. pp. 129-143.

Vira and Vira (2005): "Governing India's Urban Environment: Problems, Policies and Politics", in Evelin Hurst and Mann (ed.), *Urbanisation and Governance in India*, Manohar Publishing and Distributors, New Delhi, p. 48.

Westfall, Mathews, S. and Victoria, A. de Villa (2001): "Urban Indicators for Managing Cities", *Asian Development Bank Report*.

Word Resource Institute (1997): *World Resources: A Guidelines to Urban Environment*, Oxford University Press, New York.

Workshop of JNNURM: Issues and Opportunities held on 22.09.2006 organised by SUSTAIN-PERT-UN-HABITAT-SICCI-CUPA-TUFIDCO, http://www.un_habitat.org/downloads/docs/4152_56990_WorkshopProceedings of JNNURM-Final Version R.S. Muralu_pdf, as viewed on Wednesday, September 10, 2008.

World Bank (2001): *World Development Report 2000/2001: Attacking Poverty* (Published for the World Bank), Oxford University Press, Oxford.

World Bank (2001): "Urban Environmental Priorities", Environment Strategy Background Papers, January, 2001, Washington D.C.: World Bank.

World Development Report, 2009, http://siteresources.worldbank.org/INTWDR2009/Resources/Outline.pdf, as viewed on 22nd March, 2009.

Worth, Louis (1938): "Urbanisation as way of Life", *American Journal of Sociology*, Vol. No. 44, pp. 11-13.

Index